ARMED GROUPS

STUDIES IN NATIONAL SECURITY, COUNTERTERRORISM, AND COUNTERINSURGENCY

JEFFREY H. NORWITZ, Editor

U.S. Naval War College
Newport, Rhode Island

The Naval War College expresses appreciation to the Naval War College Foundation, through the generous endowment of the John Nicholas Brown Chair of Counterterrorism.

The views expressed in *Armed Groups: Studies in National Security, Counterterrorism, and Counterinsurgency* are those of the authors and do not necessarily reflect the opinions of the Naval War College or the Department of the Navy.

Correspondence concerning this book may be addressed by mail to Jeffrey H. Norwitz, Naval War College, 686 Cushing Road, Newport, RI 02841; by telephone at 401.841.6410; or by e-mail at jeffrey.norwitz@nwc.navy.mil or jnorwitz@hotmail.com; or the editor may be contacted at www.jeffnorwitz.com.

ISBN 978-1-884733-52-9

Printed in the United States of America

Library of Congress Cataloging-in-Publication Data

Armed groups : studies in national security, counterterrorism, and counterinsurgency / Jeffrey H. Norwitz, editor.
    p. cm.
  Includes bibliographical references.
  ISBN 978-1-884733-52-9 (soft cover : alk. paper) 1. Terrorism—Case studies. 2. Terrorism—Prevention—Case studies. 3. Terrorists—Case studies. 4. Political violence—Case studies. 5. Guerrilla warfare—Case studies. I. Norwitz, Jeffrey H.
  HV6431.A757 2008
  355.02'18—dc22

                                                                2008016007

For sale by the Superintendent of Documents, U.S. Government Printing Office
Internet: bookstore.gpo.gov Phone: toll free (866) 512-1800; DC area (202) 512-1800
Fax: (202) 512-2104 Mail: Stop IDCC, Washington, DC 20402-0001

ISBN 978-1-884733-52-9

DEDICATION

This book is dedicated to all those Americans who, in the aftermath of 9/11, set aside earlier careers and dreams and, instead, found avenues to "contribute" toward America's defense. Patriotism was given new meaning for citizens of all ages, ethnicities, social statuses, and professional standings. Whether their choice was to join the armed forces or law enforcement, or dedicate their future to fighting conditions of human and political hopelessness, tens of thousands of individuals became determined to "make a difference" and selected new professional directions for themselves. For many, that choice will cost them their lives. For others, they will sacrifice affluence and fame for devotion to humankind and selfless service. And still others will enhance educational skills they need to resolve causes of conflict.

For those who wear the cloth of our nation, my dedication is particularly profound. Many military members entered the service at a time of peace. Yet they reaffirm the warrior spirit by remaining in today's armed forces despite unimaginable career and family pressure. Men and women who have led comrades in deadly combat. Who have been shot at in anger and who, themselves, have killed others. Who survived convoys blasted apart by roadside bombs. And who, the very next day, led another convoy on the same road. Who held dying comrades and smelled a battlefield. These are men and women who truly understand the nature of war, the power of war, and the limits of war.

To these heroes of American society, in and out of uniform, this book is respectfully dedicated.

ARMED GROUPS: STUDIES IN NATIONAL SECURITY, COUNTERTERRORISM, AND COUNTERINSURGENCY

TABLE OF CONTENTS

History and Armed Groups

Present Context and Environment

Religion as Inspiration

Thinking Differently about Armed Groups

The Shape of Things to Come

Appendix

FOREWORD

Stansfield Turner

It is gratifying to see the stimulus which the faculty of the Naval War College is continuing to provide to both the College and the Navy as a whole. In this instance, it is Professor Jeffrey Norwitz of that faculty who has prodded both institutions to think about how warfare has migrated from being between states to being between states and armed groups. Understanding how to deal with this growing dimension of warfare is critically important today. Jeffrey Norwitz has helped us to do that by bringing together a diverse, eclectic group of thinkers on contemporary war.

It is also gratifying to see the continuing support of the Naval War College Foundation for such projects. The Foundation has played, and does play, an important role in encouraging original thinking on naval matters. As President of the College some years ago, I found the Foundation's support invaluable for projects that were too exploratory to qualify readily for governmental funding. Yet exploring frontiers is essential in any profession.

Armed groups are challenging us on many fronts today. In dealing with them, though, we must not become so narrowly focused as to lose sight of our democratic principles and morals. We must not stoop to the tactics of opponents in combating them. For instance, it is tempting to invade the privacy of our citizens with surveillance in the name of detecting terrorists. If this is done other than under legal procedures and strict controls, we will lose our cherished right to individual privacy. We will have won only a Pyrrhic victory. This has to be a concern deserving the attention of both our civilian and military leaders.

Thinkers about naval matters must be able to step back from the pressures of day-to-day decision-making. They must place what the Navy should be doing now in the larger context of what the Navy must be able to do and sustain over the long run. That means not making compromises to meet deadlines or to please superiors at the expense of ethical principles.

Since at least Mahan's day, it has been one role of the Naval War College to make up for that by being on the cutting edge of naval strategy and tactics, free from more pressing, immediate concerns. Mahan's impact on our Navy was enormous. Jeffrey Norwitz's voice and the voices of his contributors deserve to be listened to carefully today.

Admiral Stansfield Turner, U.S. Navy (retired)
Director of Central Intelligence (1977–1981)

ACKNOWLEDGMENTS

A large edited collection is never the effort of a single editor. Rather, there are countless people that made it possible. A fascinating story of their patriotic passion and generosity deserves to be captured in these pages. It starts with Rear Admiral Joseph C. Strasser, USN ret, formerly the executive director of the Naval War College Foundation from 2000 to 2006 as well as Naval War College president from 1990 to 1995.[1]

Shortly after 9/11, the Naval War College Foundation aggressively launched a capital campaign to establish an endowed academic chair, named the John Nicholas Brown Chair of Counterterrorism in honor of the first foundation president and Rhode Island philanthropist, in order to focus faculty research, teaching, and publication on fighting terrorism. The campaign's patron was the Honorable George H. W. Bush, 41st president of the United States. The honorary cochairmen were the Honorable John McCain, United States senator, and Admiral Jay Johnson, USN ret, chief of naval operations, 1996–2000. For four years, Rear Admiral Strasser devoted his limitless energy and relentless marketing skills to fund the Brown Chair.

By 2006, the endowment had grown substantially owing to scores of individual generous donors. Only then did Rear Admiral Strasser announce the Chair's investiture and I was honored to be chosen the inaugural holder of the Brown Chair. Rear Admiral Strasser and I spoke on several occasions about doing something tangible so that current and potential future donors could actually see the fruits of their generosity. We quickly agreed to create a first-class academic publication. Likewise, the Naval War College provost, Dr. James F. Giblin, Jr., was first to suggest the book tackle the challenge of armed groups as an emerging phenomenon shaping strategic and military thought.

I learned that two academic pioneers had completed a concept paper looking at creating course material dealing with armed groups. Dr. Roy Godson (Georgetown University) and Dr. Richard Shultz (Tufts University) directed the Consortium for the Study of Intelligence, a project of the National Strategy Information Center (NSIC), based in Washington, DC. The 2006 Godson and Shultz concept paper identified a lack of high-quality teaching material and courses devoted to the study of armed groups. This superb study inspired me to seek world-class contributors for a graduate-level textbook to satisfy the paucity of thoughtful and comprehensive material on armed groups that Godson and Shultz recognized.

One after another, I began to attract accomplished authorities in varied disciplines. These included historians, political scientists, anthropologists, psychologists, diplomats, as well as intelligence operators and analysts. Many were already noted authors and

---

1. Information about the Naval War College Foundation is available at www.nwcfoundation.org/.

specialists who'd written extensively. Others were unpublished but had extraordinary practical experience that deserved print. All were excited about writing new material for the book.

Throughout the process, the Naval War College Foundation fully funded all activity associated with the forthcoming book. Toward that end, I am deeply indebted to the present foundation executive director, Rear Admiral Roger T. Nolan, USNR ret, and the wonderful foundation staff of Mr. Eric Archer, Ms. Melissa Cartee, Ms. Sharyl Jump, Ms. Deborah Marro, and Ms. Petrina Ross.

Meanwhile, because I'm a member of the Naval War College teaching faculty in the National Security Decision Making (NSDM) Department, my seniors gave me the flexibility to pursue this book. In particular, Dr. Joan Johnson-Freese, NSDM chair, allowed me the freedom to accomplish classroom commitments and perform the necessary editing duties for this book. I am particularly indebted to these War College colleagues who assumed extra work to make this book possible: Ms. Peggy Jones, Professor Kevin Kelley, Ms. Isabella Madarang, and Mr. Richard Menard. Nothing is done without skilled legal advice. Commander Jane Brill, staff judge advocate, USN, and Mr. James M. Kasischke, supervisory patent counsel with the Navy's Office of General Counsel, provided invaluable assistance.

An editor is only as good as the desktop publishing team that proofs the work and formats and typesets the manuscript. Mr. Robert H. Sampson, director of business operations, and Ms. Elizabeth Davis, head of the visual communications division, deserve my thanks for assigning War College resources to the project. Likewise, special gratitude goes to Intekras Desktop Publishing personnel Mr. Tom O'Rourke, Ms. Susan Meyer, Mr. Ken DeRouin, Ms. Shannon Cole, and Ms. Amanda Hazenfield for their dedicated professional work and advice in the layout and formatting of this publication. And special thanks to Mr. Albert F. Fassbender III, who is recognized for his remarkable proofreading and inspired suggestions, which improved the level of scholarship for the entire volume. I am indebted to Ms. Kerri Cole, who, with her artistic eye, designed the cover for this book using photos taken by my son, Sidney Norwitz. Yet I, alone, am responsible for any editorial errors, oversights, or omissions herein.

Of course, none of this would have been possible but for the Naval Criminal Investigative Service (NCIS), where I have worked since 1985. It was the vision of former NCIS director David Brant and current director Thomas Betro, who foresaw the value of assigning a federal special agent to the teaching faculty of the Naval War College. Not only did I bring a unique NCIS practitioner's perspective to the classroom, but NCIS was the beneficiary of my frequent visits to offices worldwide in order to share academia with field agents. Likewise, my own NCIS career is the basis by which I've achieved expertise in national security matters. Therefore, to NCIS I owe my professional credentials.

I also must acknowledge the encouragement of Dr. David Allen Rosenberg, distinguished historian, writer, and professor of maritime strategy, and these present and former War College colleagues for their mentoring, wisdom, and unconditional friendship in helping me navigate the waters of academia: Dr. Henry Charles "Chuck" Bartlett, Professor William Calhoun, Dr. Peter Liotta, Dr. Richmond Lloyd, Dr. William Martel,

Dr. James Miskel, Dr. Mackubin Owens, Jr., Professor Timothy Somes, and Dr. William Turcotte. I will always be your student.

There is a final acknowledgment necessary. As with all published works, the immeasurable time spent on such a project demands family sacrifice. I'm blessed with three understanding children, Sefra, Shale, and Sidney, as well as my wife of 30 years, Gezelle. This volume is my gift of a better world for them.

Thank you all.

Jeffrey II. Norwitz

INTRODUCTION

Jeffrey H. Norwitz, editor

What exactly is an armed group? The two words—*armed* and *group*—are clear enough and, when used together, conjure up any manner of mental images. Unshaven men in Western attire holding dirty rifles with straps of bullets hanging from their shoulders. Prohibition-era bank robbers standing on the running boards of a Ford Phaeton with Thompson machine guns tucked under their arms. Wild-eyed horsemen wearing furs charging across a Mongolian plateau. Somali teenagers hanging from the back of a speeding truck, hoisting AK-47 assault rifles. Heavily armed men in sunglasses escorting a political figure from an airplane.

For our purposes, this edited collection will consider armed groups to include classic insurgents, terrorists, guerrillas, militias, police agencies, criminal organizations,

Jeffrey H. Norwitz completed an undergraduate degree in criminal justice at Eastern Kentucky University in 1974. After graduation, he was commissioned a second lieutenant in the United States Army Military Police Corps and completed Airborne School before assignment to the 50th Ordnance Company, where his duties involved security of nuclear weapons. He concluded three years' active duty as the executive officer of the Fourth Military Police Company, Fort Carson, Colorado. Mr. Norwitz joined the El Paso County Sheriff's Office in Colorado Springs, Colorado, in 1978. As a patrol officer, he received awards for heroism, life saving, and superior performance. His specialty assignments included SWAT team sniper and firearms instructor, as well as commander of the bomb squad, responding to more than 500 incidents involving explosives. He was engaged in many prominent cases involving paramilitary groups and domestic terrorism. He joined the civilian ranks of the Naval Criminal Investigative Service (NCIS) in 1985 and served tours of duty stateside and overseas specializing in counterintelligence, counterespionage, and counterterrorism. This included an assignment at Camp Delta, Guantánamo, as part of the Criminal Investigative Task Force interviewing al-Qaeda and Taliban fighters (2003–04). His last assignment was as NCIS supervisory special agent responsible for counterintelligence throughout New England. In 2001, Mr. Norwitz earned an MA in national security and strategic studies from the Naval War College and joined the teaching faculty as the NCIS adviser. Mr. Norwitz holds the John Nicholas Brown Academic Chair of Counterterrorism at the U.S. Naval War College. His articles have been published in the *Naval War College Review*, *Military Review*, *Journal of Homeland Security*, and *Officer Review*. His scholarly work also appears in *Terrorism and Counterterrorism: Understanding the New Security Environment* (McGraw-Hill, 2003); *American Defense Policy*, 8th ed. (Johns Hopkins University Press, 2005); *Practical Bomb Scene Investigation* (CRC Press, 2006); and *Defending the Homeland: Historical Perspectives on Radicalism, Terrorism, and State Responses* (West Virginia University Press, 2007). His articles have been translated into Spanish and Portuguese for publication in South America. Mr. Norwitz lectures extensively across the country and for allied militaries on matters relating to terrorism, intelligence, and homeland security. In 1994, the Honorable John H. Dalton, secretary of the Navy, personally presented Special Agent Norwitz the Department of the Navy's Meritorious Civilian Service Medal for highly classified national security intelligence work. He received a second Meritorious Civilian Service Medal for his intelligence and counterterrorism accomplishments during the 1998 hostilities of Operation Desert Fox. In 2006, he was voted Eastern Kentucky University's College of Business and Technology's Distinguished Alumnus.

war-lords, privatized military organizations, mercenaries, pirates, drug cartels, apocalyptic religious extremists, orchestrated rioters and mobs, and tribal factions.

With this broad a definition we will need an equally broad set of disciplines with which to study armed groups. History, political science, anthropology, sociology, theology, and economics are traditional areas of research. But we will also delve into matters of ethics, technology, intelligence, education, the law, diplomacy, military science, and even mythology. The book is divided into five sections:

- History and armed groups,
- Present context and environment,
- Religion as inspiration,
- Thinking differently about armed groups, and
- The shape of things to come.

With one exception, each of these chapters was written exclusively for this volume. The contributors, all renowned in their fields and noted for their authorship and influential opinions, were individually invited to write for this edited collection. Some of the contributors are best-selling authors. Others are revered academics. Others are frequently on television and radio news programs. Still others spent decades doing highly classified work and consider notoriety an anathema. As a result, readers will find this anthology rich with academic rigor, practitioner experiences, endnotes, and citations for further research and study. The following is a brief narrative abstract of each chapter.

HISTORY AND ARMED GROUPS

Cicero, the Roman philosopher and political thinker, said, "Not to know what has been transacted in former times is to continue always a child." Therefore, this volume begins with a section on the history of armed groups. Case studies from the past offer a great deal when it comes to understanding the nature of armed groups. What are they? Who are the members? Why do they develop? And why do they disband?

In his chapter, entitled "Pirates, Vikings, and Teutonic Knights," Marine colonel and Naval War College professor **Peter T. Underwood** examines armed groups from a standpoint of evolutionary behavior. Underwood defines three basic categories falling along a spectrum from poorly organized, disjointed bands, to groups structured and motivated by greed, to highly organized groups led by ideologues. He cleverly demonstrates the characteristics of each category by looking at historic group attitudes exhibited first by pirates, who typify profit-driven criminal gangs. Next, Underwood examines Vikings, who blend a culture of conquest with marauding plunder, and, finally, Teutonic Knights, who added religious zeal to their otherwise armed might. He concludes that nation-states bear a measure of responsibility for armed groups, if only through mere tolerance, and that to remain unchecked, the group must remain beneath the level of serious annoyance.

Accomplished author and Naval War College professor Dr. **Paul J. Smith** offers a meticulous study of one of history's memorable armed groups in "The Italian Red Brigades (1969–1984): Political Revolution and Threats to the State." Smith takes a comprehensive look at the Red Brigades during their formative and most violent years. A classic example of structure, support, and tactics, the Red Brigades used murder, extortion, and kidnapping until such time that they caused the public to recoil at the level of violence. Smith then draws some insightful parallels between Italy's successful, albeit more-than-15-year, struggle against the Red Brigades and the global conflict with al-Qaeda.

Southeast Asia has its own unique history pertaining to armed groups. Eastern Kentucky University's Dr. **Carole Garrison,** chair of the Department of Criminal Justice and Police Studies, having been a supervisor with the United Nations Transitional Authority in Cambodia (UNTAC), writes about her experiences with the political process in the shadow of the Khmer Rouge's murderous violence. "Armed Conflict in Cambodia and the UN Response" looks at how one introduces UN standards for peacekeeping and fair elections when there is no history of it. What are some of the competing agendas when internationalists cannot agree on their own aspirations and values?

In close geographic proximity to Cambodia, Indonesia is the setting for the State Department's Ambassador **Gene Christy**'s chapter, "Armed Groups and Diplomacy: East Timor's FRETILIN Guerrillas." As a midlevel State Department foreign service officer, Christy was a pioneer in using the tools of diplomacy to deal with a violent armed group. Two decades later, Christy writes about how a guerrilla movement transitioned to be a legitimate voice of opposition, and then became the elected government. His firsthand account, which includes plunging helicopter rides and frighteningly close calls with ambushes, offers a window into the courageous work of foreign-service professionals who leverage diplomacy in the front lines with armed groups.

Another hallmark armed group is the subject of Naval War College professor Dr. **Timothy D. Hoyt**'s chapter, "Adapting to a Changing Environment—The Irish Republican Army as an Armed Group." Hoyt provides an illuminating look at the IRA from a standpoint of evidencing how changing factors on the ground hastened transformation within the organization. In particular, Hoyt argues that at different times, depending on shifting objectives, the IRA behaved as an armed-group chameleon becoming a guerrilla outfit, a classic insurgency, a terrorist organization, a militia, a police agency, a criminal organization, a mercenary organization, and finally orchestrated rioters and mobs. Hoyt warns that focusing exclusively on group methodology may confuse rather than clarify the situation—better to concentrate on the group objective instead of the form or function.

Retired Marine colonel and Naval War College professor **Theodore L. Gatchel** escorts us into the world of fighting insurgents in his chapter, "Pseudo Operations—A Double-Edged Sword of Counterinsurgency." A pseudo operation, Gatchel tells us, is where specially trained and equipped military forces use disguise and subterfuge to infiltrate into an armed group to capture or kill insurgent leaders and conduct psychological operations against them. Like ruses as tactics of war, pseudo operations have been very successful against armed groups. Gatchel offers three electrifying examples where these sorts of strategies tipped the scales in favor of the authorities who wrested control from armed groups in the Philippines, Kenya, and Rhodesia. Yet the use of such tactics may have negative consequences and this chapter explores all sides of the issue.

PRESENT CONTEXT AND ENVIRONMENT

The news is full of stories about armed violence. No nation is free from some level of armed brutality and bloodshed. This section is intended to clarify some of the driving factors that animate the challenges of armed groups today.

Perhaps one of the most respected researchers and authors on al-Qaeda and global terrorism is Dr. **Rohan Gunaratna,** head of the International Centre for Political Violence and Terrorism Research in Singapore. So widely accepted are his expert credentials that the U.S. Department of Justice sought his testimony in the successful 2007 prosecution of Jose Padilla and codefendants Adham Hassoun and Kifah Jayyousi, all convicted on charges of terrorist conspiracy. In his chapter entitled "The Threat to the Maritime Domain: How Real Is the Terrorist Threat?" Gunaratna explores the operational aspects of armed groups that operate on land and at sea. He concludes that maritime terrorist capabilities are actually an extension of land capabilities and, as such, maritime police and navies are limited in their responses to piracy. Instead, according to Gunaratna, preventing future maritime attacks can be done much more effectively by law enforcement and intelligence services operating on land. His three-part strategy calls for (1) creating land-based maritime conterterrorist commands, presumably with strong naval investigative and intelligence resources; (2) focusing on securing waters where terrorists and criminal groups are most active; and (3) protecting ships transporting strategic cargo such as oil and natural gas.

Attorney, legal scholar, and University of Washington professor, **Craig H. Allen** writes the quintessential legal chapter, appropriately entitled "Armed Groups and the Law." In it, Allen helps the reader wade through the myriad of conventions, treaties, customs, statutes, and principles that make up the essence of decisions we call international law. Allen reflectively says that strategies and policies to deal with armed groups have raced ahead of legal regime but we've reached a tipping point where the law will have to be given as much attention for solutions to emerge. Allen poses three legal issues that he thinks the reader should evaluate. First, to what extent should members of armed groups be killed by armed forces of a state without prior due process? Next, what are the standards applicable to their capture, interrogation, treatment and release? Finally, what is their criminal liability under the law of war or criminal laws typically applied in peacetime? His chapter provides a comprehensive foundation to find the answers.

Globalization touches every aspect of the twenty-first-century landscape and armed groups are no exception. National Defense University's Dr. **Querine H. Hanlon** investigates how globalization enables the transformation of armed groups and how this conversion will define future security. Her chapter, "Globalization and the Transformation of Armed Groups," first introduces four variants of globalization: economic, technological, cultural, and political. She then discerns how nonstate armed groups have been able to exploit each of these variants as enablers for transformation and, in so doing, emerge as global actors with the ability to threaten state sovereignty. Hanlon posits that globalization makes strong states stronger, while weakening lesser states. This enables armed groups to take advantage of governance made more vulnerable.

The cold war between the Soviet Union and the United States gave rise to theories such as mutually assured destruction, aptly abbreviated as MAD. Each side knew a nuclear exchange would lead to its own destruction and therefore was deterred from ever striking first. But retired Israeli brigadier general **Yosef Kuperwasser** asks us to consider the question posed by his chapter's title: "Is It Possible to Deter Armed Groups?" Given the changing political and operational landscapes, can armed groups be expected to behave the way the superpowers did? Kuperwasser challenges the concept of strategic deterrence in today's world of stateless actors, international terror organizations, and armed groups. In particular, he highlights the values held sacrosanct by liberal democracies as weaknesses when viewed by their enemies—such factors as the sanctity of life (citizens and soldiers); the importance of government truth, accountability, sovereignty, and transparency; the role of the media. These factors paralyze democracies when faced with unfettered terror organizations with no such moral or political limitations on how they behave. This, Kuperwasser argues, frames the dilemma of how to deter an adversary who operates with different factors than do liberal democracies. However, factors favorable to armed groups can be held at risk by democracies. Armed groups need credibility in the eyes of their constituencies, they need use of sanctuary, they need a way to avoid accountability, they need protection for leaders, they need patron support, and armed groups need sources of weapons and supplies. Successful deterrence will ultimately require democracies to aggressively attack armed groups where they are most vulnerable.

T. E. Lawrence (Lawrence of Arabia) described rebels as requiring "an unassailable base, something guarded not merely from attack but from the fear of it." Sanctuary is a term that refers to such a safe haven. Retired Marine colonel, esteemed author, and Naval War College professor Dr. **Mackubin Thomas Owens** provides a wonderful analysis and elaboration in his chapter, "Sanctuary: The Geopolitics of Terrorism and Insurgency." Starting with an exceptional explanation of classical geopolitics, Owens then treats the reader to a historic examination, citing strategic thinkers such as Halford Mackinder, Francis Fukuyama, Samuel Huntington, and Thomas Barnett. Owens's chapter is unique in that he deals with the concept of sanctuary on different scales of analysis. Using size as a determinant, Owens argues there are fundamental forces at work between the size of territorial sanctuary and the corresponding number of armed-group members. If true, this would allow for accurate predictions of group growth. The chapter concludes with two edifying case studies: one from the 1880's western United States and the other from 2004 Iraq.

What might it be like to be the senior American military officer in a multinational headquarters deployed to Afghanistan where your job is solving regional conflicts that date back hundreds of years? Army colonel and Marine Corps War College professor **Peter Curry** writes about his experiences dealing with Afghan tribal matters in his chapter, "Small Wars Are Local: Debunking Current Assumptions about Countering Small Armed Groups." Candid, informative, and matter-of-fact, Curry shares his experiences and analysis in a refreshing reevaluation of old assumptions about dealing with local warriors, and offers new ways of thinking. Curry concludes by observing that armed groups are living organisms that force one to change strategies and concepts over time. New assumptions create new mental models that will eventually lead to new strategies and operational approaches to counter armed groups.

Pirates have to be some of the most popularly studied armed groups in literature, film, and history. In a superb chapter entitled "Piracy and the Exploitation of Sanctuary," British researcher and prolific author **Martin N. Murphy** provides an intriguing comparison of pirates and maritime armed groups for which he offers seven factors of discrimination. One of his key points is that piracy is a land-based crime that is implemented at sea. Moreover, intelligence is the best tool against piracy. As a result, solutions must begin with coordinated enforcement against the terrestrial elements of planning, recruitment, logistics, and sanctuary.

Radical Islamic extremism and international armed groups seem to have overshadowed other forms of organized violence. Yet, at least in the United States, domestic terrorism and homegrown armed groups must also remain a focus of scrutiny for criminal and intelligence organizations trying to protect us. Dr. **Edward J. Valla** and **Gregory Comcowich,** both with the Federal Bureau of Investigation, coauthored a brilliant chapter entitled "Domestic Terrorism: Forgotten, But Not Gone." Long before Osama bin Laden was born, racist, antigovernment, Christian Identity, revolutionary armed groups were using improvised explosive devices to kill American judges and federal agents and bomb military recruiting stations. Throughout the 1960s and '70s, domestic terrorism was inflamed by antiwar activists. Today, antigovernment attacks, such as the Oklahoma City bombing in 1995, abortion clinic bombings, and environmentally driven acts of violence, remind us that domestic armed groups are still a potent enemy. The reader will be introduced to the latest threats inside America as well as some misperceptions about relative risk.

Those who study inner-city dynamics are keenly aware of gang violence. Graffiti on walls, buildings, vehicles, and billboards tells a story of turf battles and gang identity for those who know how to read the symbols. As explained by New York Institute of Technology professor Dr. **Edward J. Maggio** in his chapter, "The Threat of Armed Street Gangs in America," the current threats to our national security from armed street gangs are a real and frightening reality. Maggio offers us an inspired scholarly treatment of the origins of street gangs, with a heavy emphasis on social and psychological behavior patterns. He explores the concept of delinquency and group dynamics. What's more, Maggio explicates a seven-stage hate model from which he shows how street-gang activity escalates into organized armed groups. His chapter ends with discussion of the Mara Salvatrucha (MS-13) group, perhaps the most dangerous gang in America.

Steven Emerson is an internationally recognized expert on terrorism and national security and a best-selling author. Since 9/11, Emerson has testified before and briefed Congress dozens of times on terrorist financing and operational networks of al-Qaeda, Hamas, Hezbollah, Islamic Jihad, and the rest of the worldwide Islamic militant spectrum. In this chapter, Emerson takes us inside the courtroom of a notable trial involving an American-born imam of Iraqi descent and an American convert to Islam who had ties to terrorist groups overseas. "Prosecuting Homegrown Extremists: Case Study of the Virginia 'Paintball Jihad' Cell" is a comprehensive look at the influence that foreign terrorist organizations wield in the United States. Emerson pulls the curtains back on organizations such as the Council on American-Islamic Relations (CAIR) and other self-described Islamic civil rights and advocacy groups to reveal their direct associations with admitted American jihadists and those who wish to "wage war against the United States."

RELIGION AS INSPIRATION

It's difficult for Americans to contemplate that religion and armed-group violence have a causal relationship. It contradicts everything we believe about sanctity, theology, and spirituality. Nevertheless, history is replete with religious violence. This section will take a look at religious factors that define ancient as well as future forms of conflict.

Marine Corps Command and Staff College's Dr. **Pauletta Otis,** one of the most highly respected academics in the field of religiously fomented violence, provides a benchmark chapter by which readers can grasp the complexity of armed groups that are driven by spiritual ideology. "Armed with the Power of Religion: Not Just a War of Ideas" begins with the assumption that religion contributes to the lethality of armed groups for which sacred identity provides justification for their fights. Otis proposes that there are four sources of religious power. Resources such as buildings and congregation members are one source of power. Interpersonal power, which holds that religious leaders are often more believable than political leaders, is another. Communication is a source of power in that religious leaders communicate with the authority of God and the authority of man. Expertise is the fourth source of power, based on religious figures' having intimate knowledge of locale, history, medicine, education, and community dynamics. Within each of these sources of religious power are elements that leaders and communities can leverage to manipulate their environments with stunning effectiveness. The chapter then examines examples of this in Iraq, Afghanistan, Sudan, Uganda, Peru, and Rwanda. Otis concludes that understanding the source of religious power makes it possible to analyze the human-religious dimension of insurgency, counter the negative impact of religious factors, and support the positive aspects of religious power to compel peace.

How do religious beliefs in America turn into violent actions? U.S. Navy chaplain Commander **Timothy J. Demy** answers this question in an authoritative and analytical assessment of Christian extremists in the United States who have been responsible for murder, assault, destruction of property, and explosive- and firearms-related crimes. "Arming for Armageddon: Myths and Motivations of Violence in American Christian Apocalypticism" examines eschatology, the study of the end-of-times prophecies. Leveraging his remarkable academic and theological credentials, Demy gives the reader an astonishing glimpse into the minds of Christian zealots. Moreover, following four American case studies, Demy concludes with his "Ten Commandments for the cautiously concerned," which puts forward practicable solutions.

When one fights, for whatever purpose, the object of the struggle is to defeat the opponent. So when Dr. **Mehrdad Mozayyan,** Islamic intellectual and Naval War College professor, offers a counterintuitive title such as "Glory in Defeat and Other Islamist Ideologies," we are immediately captivated by his thesis. Mozayyan offers a well-documented and scholarly discussion of the elements of militant Islamic philosophy, which embrace the willingness to be martyred; to wage war on a larger enemy knowing full well what the earthly outcomes will be; and to be massacred while defending Muslim beliefs and, in doing so, ensure ultimate glory and salvation for oneself. The chapter discerns the schism between Sunni and Shiite foundations, with six main divisions, and also offers a geopolitical assessment of how the Islamic world perceives the West. Finally, the author argues that there is a cosmic war with infidel forces taking place and temporary setbacks for Islamic fanatics are not considered by them as harbingers of defeat.

THINKING DIFFERENTLY ABOUT ARMED GROUPS

So far, this edited collection has looked at armed groups in traditional ways. The chapters in this section purposely examine armed groups from different perspectives based on scholarly consideration of evidence as well as predictive analysis.

What might conflict look like without traditional norms of behavior, without respect for internationally accepted legal regimens, without regard for societal consequences? Dr. **Andrea J. Dew,** Naval War College professor and best-selling author, examines two key questions in her chapter, "The Erosion of Constraints in Armed-Group Warfare: Bloody Tactics and Vulnerable Targets." The first question deals with public support for future conflicts with armed groups when violence and exhaustion become too much to bear. How will we know when the public says, "Enough is enough?" The second question uses these indicators of public sentiment and looks for ways that policy makers and military strategists can plan for such conflicts. Dew then provides a five-part intellectual framework to analyze constraints and limitations that affect decision making. These are state cohesiveness, external and transnational actors, the role of ideology, the role of information technology, and duration of conflict. Dew concludes that the ability of states to wage warfare can be severely curtailed by lack of support at home for expenditure of blood and treasure. Moreover, one of the deliberate strategies of armed groups is to escalate the cost of the conflict by purposely prolonging its duration.

Dr. **James J. F. Forest,** prolific writer, author, and director of West Point's Combating Terrorism Center, looks at how armed groups pass on know-how and expertise to other like organizations. "Knowledge Transfer and Shared Learning among Armed Groups" is an in-depth study of the myriad ways collaboration between and among groups happens. Using historic examples and future predictions, Forest explains how armed groups utilize primitive training camps tucked into remote ravines, as well as Internet chat rooms, to share tradecraft. Forest then introduces a novel construction he calls a "trusted handshake" whereby associates verify bona fides of others. He concludes with eight well-considered implications for thinking differently about armed groups.

Anthropologist, attorney, Pentagon adviser, prolific author, and professor, **Montgomery McFate** presents an exceptional study into the roots of tribal behavior in her chapter, "The 'Memory of War': Tribes and the Legitimate Use of Force in Iraq." McFate begins with a discussion into what tribes are and how tribal systems demand different ways of thinking about them, not just as groups, but as political actors. McFate delves, based on her own time in the Iraqi theater, into how the history of the region shapes tribal behavior and attitudes. One of the most insightful portions is her discussion of what she calls the "algebra of honor," which ignores the numbers of casualties and, instead, is calculated on the basis of tribal honor and centuries of tradition. McFate concludes with an optimistic view that present doctrine, which stresses limited use of force, minimization of collateral damage, and cultural understanding, is very well suited to the social complexities of Iraq.

Dr. **Derek S. Reveron** of the Naval War College and Professor **Jeffrey Stevenson Murer** of the University of St. Andrews collaborate on their chapter, "Terrorist or Freedom Fighter? Tyrant or Guardian?" As the title suggests, the way we think about armed groups and sovereign states will define how we deal with them. This chapter is a solid discussion of political drivers. For example, the authors declare that terrorism is a tactic employed in a political context and that nation-states create policy connotations to their benefit by labeling political opponents as terrorists. Furthermore, while terrorism may threaten democracies, the response from the state may be the greater evil. The authors offer some historic examples of nation-states that purposely used the specter of national emergency to pursue political adversaries, thereby giving the government extraordinary power. They conclude with a warning about the dangers of using war as the context to look at armed groups.

Psychologist Dr. **Elena Mastors,** Naval War College professor and an accomplished author on matters of psychology and group behavior, teams with counterintelligence professional **Jeffrey H. Norwitz,** Naval War College professor and Naval Criminal Investigative Service (NCIS) special agent, in a fascinating chapter that blends theory and practical application. "Disrupting and Influencing Leaders of Armed Groups" proposes a four-step framework for examining the psychological underpinnings of leaders in which the authors focus on personal characteristics, operating environment, advisory system, and information environment—the combination of which informs strategies for influencing behavior and decision-making processes of armed-group leaders. Utilizing the unmatched ability of human intelligence practitioners to gain access to leaders and their advisers, often through clandestine and covert action, the authors lay out step-by-step strategies for manipulating leaders into self-destructive behaviors, thereby eliminating the group as a nemesis. The chapter is complete with a historic example of superb human intelligence work as well as a new case study on the personality of Ayman al-Zawahri.

The final chapter in this section considers anthropology as a discipline to study armed groups. Renowned anthropologist, author, and Naval War College professor Dr. **David W. Kriebel** views an armed group as a social unit existing within a larger society subject to the norms of one or more wider cultures. "Armed Groups through the Lens of Anthropology" is a captivating study of how culture, not biology, is the basis for human aggression. He presents three "lenses" of anthropology through which to analyze armed groups. The lens of "kinship" relates to familial dynamics. The lens of "cognitive" anthropology explores how ordinary people can act in extraordinarily violent inhuman ways. And the lens of "critical" anthropology eschews a neutral approach to its subject matter. Taken together, Kriebel states that the use of anthropological insight in studying armed groups and conflict is beneficial.

THE SHAPE OF THINGS TO COME

"I never think of the future—it comes soon enough." Albert Einstein's quintessential quote about the future is profound and perhaps suggests a measure of wait-and-see. Yet for the national security practitioner, the risk of inaction is too great. In the concluding section, we take a look at some of the harbingers of things to come relative to armed groups. If we fail to shape the future, we will be the beneficiaries of a future designed by others.

In a ground-breaking and frightening chapter based on his award-winning work and many published books and essays, Dr. **P. W. Singer,** senior fellow and director of the 21st Century Defense Initiative at the Brookings Institution, uncovers the ugly reality referenced in his chapter's title: "Children on the Battlefield: The Breakdown of Moral Norms." Dr. Singer is considered one of the world's leading experts on changes in twenty-first-century warfare. Written exclusively for this volume, this chapter captures a horrible dilemma for armed forces and police having to deal with armed groups that utilize child soldiers. Dr. Singer's most recent book, *Children at War* (Pantheon, 2005), was the first book to comprehensively explore the compelling and tragic rise of child-soldier groups and was recognized by the 2006 Robert F. Kennedy Memorial Book of the Year Award. His commentary on the issue was featured in a variety of venues ranging from NPR and Fox News to *Defense News* and *People* magazine. Dr. Singer has served as a consultant on the issue to the U.S. Marine Corps and Congress, and the recommendations in his book resulted in recent changes in the UN peacekeeping training program.

One of the worrisome specters of future conflict is where terrorism and organized crime intersect. "The 'New Silk Road' of Terrorism and Organized Crime: The Key to Countering the Terror-Crime Nexus" is a chapter authored by Brigadier General (retired) **Russell D. Howard,** director of the Jebsen Center for Counter-Terrorism Studies, and **Colleen M. Traughber,** a Jebsen graduate research assistant. Together, they offer the reader a geostrategic overview of the region from Afghanistan to western Europe that they call the new Silk Road. This chapter exposes activity across the expanse wherein terrorism, corruption, and organized crime have found a strategic partnership. Regional trafficking in drugs, weapons, and human cargo provides a fertile environment for terrorists to find sanctuary. The authors conclude with a four-step plan: counter the terror-crime nexus, establish interagency cooperation at the lowest levels, fight a network with a network, and indentify the level of collusion between terrorists and traffickers and respond accordingly.

Perhaps one of the most complex and vexing aspects of understanding armed groups is in the arena of financing. How do groups sustain themselves? What is the evidence to suggest state sponsorship? How do members move money for the benefit of individuals and the organization? What is the role of religion when it comes to money matters? Written by best-selling author and director of the American Center for Democracy, Dr. **Rachel Ehrenfeld,** and her assistant **Alyssa A. Lappen,** these questions and more are answered in the chapter entitled "Shari'a Financing and the Coming Ummah." The authors courageously uncover state and nonstate organizations, as well as business conspiracies, that keep armed groups and terror organizations funded and therefore operationally deadly. Dr. Ehrenfeld has an international reputation for exposing governments and nongovernmental organizations with clandestine economic ties to terror organizations. Her articles appear in print worldwide and she's given expert testimony on television, on radio news programs, and before U.S. courts and Congress. Ehrenfeld and Lappen craft an irrefutable argument, superbly researched and meticulously documented, that the West's reluctance to identify and understand the sharia financial complex is, by itself, a measure of the enemy's success.

The international scope of terrorism and armed groups is brilliantly captured in a paper presented by Stanford University's Dr. **Martha Crenshaw** to the Pontifical Catholic University of Rio de Janeiro's Conference on Terrorism and International Relations. In "Terrorism as an International Security Problem," Dr. Crenshaw answers five questions:

What is terrorism today? What are its causes? Why is terrorism a threat to international security? How has the international community responded? What does the future look like? Instructive, discerning, and visionary, Crenshaw's chapter is a splendid blend of astute answers to enduring questions.

Armed groups have clear objectives. They have identifiable goals. They exist for a specific purpose. Or do they? Perhaps they don't aspire to anything but mere anarchy and disorder? Dr. **P. H. Liotta,** executive director of the Pell Center for International Relations and Public Policy, takes his theory of chaos as strategy and expands it with his chapter, "Takin' It to the Streets: Hydra Networks, Chaos Strategies, and the 'New' Asymmetry." Referring to U.S. national security decision making as a rational process, Liotta suggests that there is an inherent vulnerability in this thinking that does not account for irrational (chaotic) choice by the adversary. He explains the implications for national security and force planning as well as ways to adapt to chaos where our adversary's essential aim is to achieve victory through avoiding defeat. Referring to the mythical, multiheaded Hydra, and using an adage from India, Liotta reminds us that one way to kill a tiger is to distract it from so many different sides that it tries to run in every direction at once. We must adapt to the new asymmetry or else face the fate of the tiger.

Tufts University's Dr. **Richard Shultz,** best-selling author and scholar on national security matters, writes a chapter entitled "Virtual Sanctuary Enables Global Insurgency." In it, he explores how the loss of physical sanctuary was a setback to al-Qaeda and the Taliban when, in 2001, the United States launched Operation Enduring Freedom in Afghanistan. Since then, according to Shultz, two strategic adaptations have occurred. One is the use of the Internet to establish a virtual sanctuary in cyberspace. The other, leveraging the first strategic adaptation, is to promote the global Salafi jihad movement. The chapter looks at seven categories of activities from which a global insurgency has replaced pre-2001 tactics, techniques, and procedures. They are propagating the Salafi ideology of jihad, inspiring and mobilizing the *ummah* to join the jihad, engaging in psychological warfare to demoralize the enemy, networking the global Salafi jihad insurgency, sharing manuals and handbooks, sharing training videos and courses, and collecting information for targeting.

The final chapter in the section is entitled "Armed Groups: Changing the Rules." Written by **T. X. Hammes,** best-selling author and retired Marine colonel, the chapter gives the reader an overview of a concept about which Hammes is a pioneer thinker: that of fourth-generation warfare. Hammes contends that armed groups fall into one of three categories of motivation: reactionary, opportunistic, or ideological. These categories are useful to understand how groups organize, grow, and operate. He includes a brief treatment of private military companies—for example, contractors who mirror small armies and are hired for protection and bodyguard duties. Hammes concludes by warning that political, economic, social, and technical trends are increasing the number, variety, and power of armed groups.

APPENDIX

The book is made more complete with the inclusion of *Guidelines on Humanitarian Negotiations with Armed Groups* as an appendix. Produced by the United Nations Office for the

Coordination of Humanitarian Affairs, these comprehensive guidelines summarize strategies and approaches for undertaking humanitarian negotiations with armed groups. As stated in the guidelines, the primary objectives of humanitarian negotiations are to ensure assistance and protection to vulnerable populations, preserve humanitarian space, and promote better respect for international law. According to the guidelines, a working definition of nonstate armed groups is

> Groups that: have the potential to employ arms in the use of force to achieve political, ideological or economic objectives; are not within the formal military structures of States, State-alliances or intergovernmental organizations; and are not under the control of the State(s) in which they operate.

The UN document explicates critical concepts that frame successful negotiation and reconciliation approaches. These include motivations for entering into negotiations, tips for knowing when to adopt a more cautious approach to negotiations, humanitarian partners in negotiations, international law relevant to humanitarian negotiations, possible negative implications of humanitarian negotiations, and suggestions for dealing with noncompliance. The guidelines conclude with a worksheet for mapping characteristics of armed groups. These guidelines have an 88-page partner UN publication, *Humanitarian Negotiations with Armed Groups: A Manual for Practitioners,* which is available online at www.reliefweb.int/rw/lib.nsf/db900sid/ruri-6lksa9.

Final thoughts

The future is full of uncertainty and the implications are grave for national security. As the editor of this comprehensive work, I encourage the reader to delve into these chapters and discover elements of wisdom for dealing with worldwide unrest. Globalization and interconnectedness will fuel discontent in some regions while dissuading disputes in others. Armed groups are merely one vestige of mankind's struggles in an increasingly smaller world.

The highest calling of selfless service is protecting those who will be victimized by conflict and violence. Prevention of hostilities or rapid resolution thereof demands new solutions. Consequently, we must start thinking about tomorrow's challenges today.

George Will, the Pulitzer Prize–winning author and political scientist, said, "The future has a way of arriving unannounced." The purpose of this volume is to prepare ourselves for when we discover, unexpectedly, that the future is here.

Jeffrey H. Norwitz
United States Naval War College

Part One

History and Armed Groups

1 Pirates, Vikings, and Teutonic Knights

Peter T. Underwood

Armed groups not directly springing from governmental authority, such as military and police forces, fall into three basic categories along a spectrum, ranging from poorly organized, disjointed, and motivated by greed, to highly organized, coordinated, and motivated by ideology. Recognizing where any particular group falls on this spectrum can help explain how and why the group behaves as it does. This in turn will aid in determining how to effectively deal with these groups.

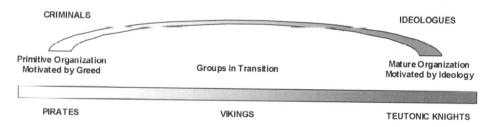

At one end of the spectrum are criminals, motivated by the simple prospect of plunder. At the other end are ideologues, driven by strong motives and seeking to change political and social conditions. Occupying the middle ground are groups in transition. Still motivated by greed, at some point they "mature" and want a bigger stake in the political, social, and economic order. The group seeks the trappings of authority more closely associated with traditional political power.

Identifying where a particular group is on the spectrum is important in determining how we deal with it. While these categories often overlap in their purposes and motivations, a common thread is their inevitable connection to an established political power. Whether from a modern nation-state, feudal kingdom, or colonial empire, some form of

Colonel Peter T. Underwood, U.S. Marine Corps, is presently the executive assistant for the Strategy and Policy Department, U.S. Naval War College. He holds a BA from the Virginia Military Institute, an MA in history from Duke University, and an MA in national security and strategic studies from the Naval War College. He is also a graduate of the Air Command and Staff College and the Armed Forces Staff College. His career has included multiple assignments in the Far East and Europe. Staff assignments have been at the battalion, regimental, air group, division, MARFOR, and unified command levels. He has served as a history instructor at the U.S. Naval Academy and holds the designations of joint service officer and Western European regional specialist. He commanded MEU Service Support Group-31, 31st MEU, and has most recently served as chief of staff, Marine Corps Logistics Command and commander, Multi-Commodity Maintenance Center, Albany, Georgia.

support from an existing government, tacit or overt, is present if any of these groups moves beyond the stage of routine criminal annoyance or fanatical fringe element.

THE PIRATES

The first group on the spectrum has a long history. Its members are organized criminals. Pirates are a classic example. Their goal is money. They don't want to change society or overthrow existing governments even though their actions may ultimately contribute to both. They simply want to prey on society and steal from others. In fact, their livelihood depends on the prosperity of the societies on which they prey. Since arguably their plunder comes from the wealth generated by productive societies, it is in their interest not to disrupt those societies to the point of decline or collapse. Pirates simply want to "skim the cream from the top."

As criminals driven by profit, pirates are usually found taking the path of least resistance. From the ancient world to today, the lucrative, easily taken merchant vessel is their target. They rarely challenge an authoritative presence in any region. They desire to exploit the trade routes, not control them.[1]

The struggle to control maritime trade is as old as seafaring itself. Yet the line between piracy and state-sponsored war was never clear in the ancient world until governments developed sufficient strength to actually police the seas. Until that point, piracy was not viewed as an illegal action but simply another form of armed conflict. Once governments developed sufficient power to build navies, or at least issue letters of marque, piracy could be, and was, declared an illegal activity. Pirates became lawbreakers, pure and simple.[2]

Piracy follows well-defined cycles. Initially small groups attack weak merchants. As small groups gain wealth and grow in size and power, they absorb or drive off other, smaller groups, a pattern readily recognizable in other organized criminal groups. When sufficient power is gained and pirates become a genuine threat to a state's stability, the sovereign will make a concerted effort to crush that threat. If the offensive is successful, piracy will return to a low level of annoyance. If not, pirates begin to be more than just criminal gangs.[3]

In the modern world, the percentage of trade affected by piracy is insignificant when compared to the total volume and the associated profits of worldwide shipping interests.[4] Most acts of piracy, if reported at all, suggest no pattern or logic other than random acts aimed at targets of opportunity. They are simply a criminal annoyance. However, in some regions, particularly Latin America, Africa, and Asia, there are signs of increased involvement by organized crime.[5] There is evidence of the systematic targeting and seizure of whole vessels and their cargoes, followed by quick, efficient disposal. This implies a level of sophistication beyond the capability of small-scale criminal activity driven by mere opportunity and convenience.[6] This pattern fits neatly with the previously identified cycle of piracy: small groups being absorbed by larger, more organized groups. Could such groups become regional threats?

In the past, pirate organizations have sometimes grown to such a scale that they in fact earned the privileges of governments, able to form alliances and treat with other governments. This process was invariably enabled by the support of existing political entities. In the ancient world, during periods of war and turmoil between existing states, opportunities for piracy grew as the warring factions turned a blind eye or even openly supported the predatory actions of pirates directed against their opponents. Starting a practice that endures today, city-states, kingdoms, and empires of the Mediterranean routinely supported piracy for their own political ends.[7]

The wars between Rome and Carthage, followed by nearly a century of Roman civil war, saw piracy on the greatest scale in all antiquity.[8] With no power able to adequately patrol the Mediterranean, pirates developed powerful strongholds. When King Mithradates of Pontus allied himself with pirates, acting as their protector and providing them with safe haven from the Romans, they became capable of advancing beyond random attacks against merchants and developed into naval organizations capable of coordinated action. They became so powerful that they threatened Rome, even raiding up the Tiber. In response, Rome undertook a campaign in 67 BCE, under Pompey the Great, to directly attack the pirate strongholds of Asia Minor. In addition to destroying the pirate lairs and absorbing Mithradates' kingdom into the empire, Pompey swept the pirate fleets from the sea, making commerce safe for centuries to come.[9] Nevertheless, Rome's power weakened eventually. With Rome gone, piracy once again emerged.[10]

The chaos of the Middle Ages proved profitable for pirates. By the thirteenth century, the cycle began to repeat itself. North Sea pirate bands grew so powerful that they decisively influenced events in the region for 200 years. The pirate Eustace the Monk, a mercenary willing to sell his services to the highest bidder, controlled a fleet so strong that it dominated the English Channel. From 1205–12, he sold his services to King John of England, plundering and raiding up the Seine. For this, the English monarch gave him letters of protection and royal gifts. With the king's blessing, Eustace even built a palatial residence in London. King John gave this largesse despite the fact that he simultaneously outlawed Eustace, who was plundering English vessels as well as French. When the time and price proved right, Eustace switched his services to the French king Philip and began massing a fleet large enough to invade England.[11]

Eustace and his pirate band suddenly became more than criminals. They were genuine threats to the safety and security of the existing order. The king and the merchants of the English Cinque Ports pooled their resources and crushed Eustace in 1217 once they realized that they could lose everything, and not just a percentage of their profits.[12]

The pirate threat was far from eliminated. Pirates continued to be powerful actors in the region, consistently with the support of existing states. From the thirteenth to the fifteenth century, the Hanseatic League, an association of merchant cities, was formed largely to protect their trade from pirates. Yet, in a fashion similar to the sparring French and English monarchs, the league encouraged pirates to prey on rivals and allied itself with pirates when warring with the Danish king.[13]

The European powers continued to foster piracy well into the early modern era. Muslim pirates, the Moors or Barbary pirates, became so powerful that in 1534, under the leadership of Khayr ad-Din Barbarossa, they seized Tunis and openly challenged Charles V. Though defeated by the Italian admiral Andrea Doria, Barbarossa's skills as a pirate remained useful to the regional powers. Appointed by the Ottoman sultan as governor of North Africa, he commanded the sultan's fleet sent to support Francis I, king of France. In support of Valois and Ottoman ambitions, Barbarossa plundered the Italian possessions of the Hapsburgs.[14] Ultimately, these pirates accrued such power and status within the Ottoman Empire that they became the relatively independent Barbary States, political entities that would continue as significant regional powers well into the eighteenth century.

These examples have a connecting thread. All three illustrate that when tolerated by existing governments and given tacit support, criminal activity, in this case piracy, can grow to the point that it becomes a genuine threat to regional stability. However, when not tolerated, such activity has difficulty in rising above the level of criminal annoyance. These examples also illustrate the gradual movement from poorly organized criminal activities motivated by the prospect of plunder to highly organized entities that gradually become regional power brokers or, as in the case of the Barbary pirates, regional powers with governmental authority.

THE VIKINGS

This evolution beyond the desire for mere plunder is also illustrated by the second group, the Vikings, who occupy the midrange on the scale, somewhere between simple criminals and their opposites, religious zealots. Usually characterized as fierce pirates focused on rapine and plunder, the Vikings were always more than that. With their own unique culture, sense of government, and commerce bolstered by a need to colonize, the Vikings were never representatives of society's criminal element nor were they religious proselytizers seeking to change the cultures they invaded. They eventually merged with the societies they were looting, became a part of them, adopted their religion, and accepted their customs while, at the same time, spreading their own unique traits and trademarks.[15]

While they were frequently bought off with tribute, when forcefully challenged, as they were in England by Alfred the Great, they continued to engage in piracy but were prevented from gaining sufficient power to displace or supplant the reigning government.[16] As their raids became annual events, they began marrying the locals and remaining behind. Forming their own communities, they eventually became parts of the local cultures, leaving their own mark to be sure, but absorbing religious, artistic, and administrative influences from their former victims.[17] Their incursions into the Frankish empire of Charlemagne would follow a different course when by 919 they acquiesced to the authority of the Frankish throne.[18]

In their role as marauding pirates, the Vikings were thoroughly professional. As with all pirates, they sought easy victims. The military power forged by the Holy Roman Emperor, Charlemagne, and bequeathed to his heirs, was formidable. The French coast proved a far more difficult military problem than had the English. The Vikings looked elsewhere for plunder. But the death of Charlemagne's son Louis brought an internal struggle for power that resulted in the empire's division by the Treaty of Verdun in 843. This internal struggle for power saw the coastal defenses of the newly divided and weakened kingdom ignored and fatally weakened. As a result, the Vikings returned.[19]

In 860 the Vikings began to systematically advance up the Seine valley during their annual campaigns. Similar to their practice in England, many of the Viking bands wintered over in France rather than return home at the end of the campaigning season. One such group, led by Weland, was particularly large and powerful. The increasingly hard-pressed French king, Charles the Bald, procured his services as a mercenary.[20] In return for payments from Charles, Weland began to eject other Viking bands and protect the region from all interlopers. In short order, Charles's payments took the form of danegeld, mandatory "protection" money. The Vikings were in France to stay.[21] Over the next 50 years, the thirst for land replaced the thirst for gold. The Viking camps became larger, more numerous, and more permanent. With the grudging acquiescence of the French kings, northern France became, in effect, an independent Viking colony.[22]

In the first decade of the tenth century, the Viking chieftain Rollo achieved such power in the Seine valley that the French king, Charles the Simple, could not challenge him as he looked covetously toward the Île de France. Recognizing the reality that the balance of power had irrevocably shifted, Charles the Simple simply gave Normandy to Rollo. At Saint-Clair-sur-Epte in 911, Rollo became the first duke of Normandy. The agreement gave Rollo the land he wanted in exchange for his allegiance to Charles. Charles got a buffer against further depredations as well as a vassal, subject to his will, at least in theory.[23]

Following the division of Charlemagne's empire, the French kings never had the power to completely repulse the Vikings. But once they began to use them to achieve their own political objectives, it only became a matter of time before the Vikings evolved from seasonal raiders to a military and political force that had to be recognized and treated as a legitimate power. Once again, the tolerance of an existing government, however grudgingly given, proved a key element in the Normans' rise to power. What had been a wide-ranging group of pirate raiders achieved political legitimacy and became a regional power influencing events for decades.

THE TEUTONIC KNIGHTS

Occupying the opposite end of the scale from ordinary criminal gangs are organizations that are motivated by ideology, are armed with significant military capability, and possess organizational infrastructures capable of implementing their ideological visions. Such armed groups are formidable. While the modern world seems to have no shortage of ideological zealots, even a cursory look at the past shows we have never suffered from such a shortage. One such group, bent on religious conversion through colonization and conquest, was the Teutonic Knights.

The Teutonic Knights of Saint Mary's Hospital of Jerusalem were crusaders. A military order founded in the Holy Land in 1198, they represented the religious spirit of their times.[24] Hardly limited to the Holy Land, the proselytizing zeal of crusaders propelled their banners throughout the Christian world from Spain to Russia. Nor were their efforts confined to Muslims. Pagans, heretics of every ilk, and, not surprisingly, Christians that were political opponents: all saw the shadow of the Knights' flags and felt the steel of their swords. Born of and nurtured by religious fervor, the Teutonic Knights made their greatest imprint in the Baltic.[25]

The crusading tradition ran deep in northern Europe as Christians expanded into heathen lands. As early as 1147, Saint Bernard proposed an expedition across the Elbe.[26]

The goal was colonization. This had great appeal to the Teutons' thirst for land. But professional priests always led the Baltic Crusades. Equally important as new land was the goal of gaining new converts for the church. This imparted a righteousness to their ventures. By converting new souls to their version of the "true religion," they justified their acts as acceptable to God. But their ventures also implied colonization. It thus had great appeal to the Teutons' thirst for land.[27] In this particular period of history, the expansion of Christian faith was often hard to separate from the increase in trade and economic power, which was in turn furthered by military power resulting in political power.

In practice, proselytizing monks brought merchants with them. Whether drawn by the word of God or superior trade goods, conversions seemed more plentiful when trading outposts grew and prospered. As always, wealthy merchants required protection from native chiefs whose power they threatened. Fortifications and the soldiers to man them grew in size and number to protect both the growing wealth and the growing number of converts. But castles cost money, and soldiers, no matter how religiously motivated, required pay. This hastened the need to rapidly spread the faith and convert more heathens, for, ironically, only Christians could be taxed.[28] Whether the monks gained more converts through the pulpit or by the sword can be disputed. But, in the end, bishops and archbishops controlled ever-larger territories in an expansion led by the Teutonic Knights that did not end until the Russians finally stopped them on the frozen waters of the river Neva in 1240.[29]

From the outset, the efforts of the Teutonic Knights were shaped by a complex political environment. In a familiar pattern, the authority of the governing bishops required military strength and administrative skill. Providing both, the Teutonic Knights clashed with their spiritual masters for temporal power.[30] Seen as useful agents by the Pope, the Holy Roman Emperor, and the German princes, the Knights held an enviable position. In 1229, the emperor bestowed the Knights with full sovereignty of the Baltic lands. The Pope, in turn, confirmed this sovereignty.[31]

The star of the Teutonic Knights seemed to wax full. Still, though increasingly powerful, they never achieved a truly independent status. Being useful to so many, they diffused their power, sending it in many directions. Pope, Holy Roman Emperor, French and English monarchs, and the endless number of German princes were all engaged in a constant series of power struggles, wars, and civil wars. Ultimately, the Teutonic Knights were but pawns in this larger struggle for power.[32]

The Knights' religious zeal, organizational abilities, and military skill were, in the end, tools employed by their more powerful patrons to serve their own ends. When their patrons' power declined or the Knights simply no longer provided useful leverage in the game of power politics, they simply faded and were absorbed by more skillful players. Whether their hunger for wealth and political power diffused their religious zeal, or religious zeal prevented them from consolidating their position in the practical world of politics, is difficult to say. In the end, it seems what made the Knights a powerful force was not their combination of ideological zeal and organization and military might but simply the support of numerous patrons, who, unfortunately, were at odds with each other. Once again, we see evidence that armed groups, irrespective of underlying aspirations, were often used as pawns by established powers. When the group serves some political, economic, or military purpose for an existing power, patrons turn a blind eye or provide support.

THE PAST AS PROLOGUE

Ultimately, the three groups examined here all came to desire and possess the economic, military, and political power needed to be treated as near-sovereign entities. While their original motivations differed, eventually each group gained sufficient power that it had to be dealt with as more than a criminal annoyance or transient threat.

While pirates and criminal groups will never go away, they are generally not an existential threat to the life of a state or society. They can be dealt with as criminals. However, if their power is allowed to grow unabated, at some point they will no longer be just criminals. New ways of dealing with them must be developed. Some will likely be distasteful, such as recognizing some degree of sovereignty, should they become powerful enough. If they gain enough power, as did the Barbary pirates and the Normans, governments will have to treat with them, as did the kings of France. The good news is that as they assume the trappings of states, they can be dealt with as states, which brings with it the potential for diplomatic action.

The last group, represented by the Teutonic Knights, is the most dangerous and difficult to deal with. Ideologically motivated, organized, and armed with the support of existing powers, these organizations pose immediate and genuine threats to society and existing states. While they are perhaps the most dependent on patrons, they are also the most difficult to destroy. They simply won't go away until the societies and states that succor them withdraw support.

While some may think it unlikely for criminal organizations to become statelike, with growing regional chaos, ungoverned territory, and budgetary pressures on the military and naval capabilities of established states, the cycle described is still plausible. If not challenged, at some point, such groups can begin to gain enough power to evolve into more than just criminal groups. Modern examples are narco-terrorists and drug cartels. This evolution readily conforms to the patterns already described, such as existing powers turning a blind eye, showing tolerance, and giving support, however tacitly, when it suits their needs.

Narco-terrorism is a problem that encompasses issues beyond simple criminal activity. In their quests for wealth, drug syndicates often use terrorist methods to confront a state's law enforcement agencies. But these same syndicates may in turn be "taxed" by politically motivated guerrillas, or the guerrillas may traffic in drugs themselves to finance their political agendas. States will also directly or indirectly sponsor drug crimes when it suits their needs.[33] Drugs can fuel many motives.

Just as weak governments in the Mediterranean and Europe gave openings for Vikings and Moors, unstable governments in Latin America provide opportunities for the drug trade to grow and prosper. Fueled by huge profits, drug syndicates, guerrilla insurgents, and paramilitary organizations wax as the indigenous governments wane.[34]

Emerging from the illegal-drug industry, narco-insurgent-paramilitary groups become increasingly organized and capable of exerting political influence that undermines the integrity and sovereignty of existing states. With their own executive-level leadership, systems of councils and courts, managers for local projects, and public affairs apparatuses, all fully funded and capable of using the most modern technology, these organizations are capable of exerting powerful political voices. Even though the source of their power can be tied to the trafficking of illegal drugs, they cannot be dismissed as simple law enforcement problems.[35]

The inability of indigenous governments to counter threats from armed groups furthers their growth. Whether insurgency or drug cartel, the vacuum left by weak government promotes the merger of these groups into ever-more-powerful paramilitary organizations that increasingly fill the political void. An excellent example is the Colombian paramilitary organization *Autodefensas Unidas de Colombia* (AUC). Profiting from the drug trade, this organization systematically expanded control of local governments in rural areas, even forming regional alliances. Though itself a narco-insurgency-paramilitary organization, as it consolidated its power, AUC began to drive out competing insurgents providing fundamental justice and security in the areas it controlled.[36] In September of 2001, the AUC announced the formation of the National Democratic Movement, a political organization to give it a legitimate political voice.[37]

Another Colombian example is the *Fuerzas Armadas Revolucionarias de Colombia* (FARC). The FARC is a significant narco-terror organization. Having connections with criminal organizations throughout the world, ranging from Mexico to Russia, it is a major actor on the international terror scene. Still, by 1999, its strength and influence had grown to the point where the Colombian government ceded to it 16,000 square miles of territory and opened a peace dialogue.[38] Similar scenarios unfolded in Peru and Mexico as insurgents, funded by criminal activity, gained control of territory and assumed the trappings of government, if only on the local level.[39]

While clearly criminal in many respects, these armed groups have also accepted some level of responsibility for the societies in which they exist. Whether provided by Viking Normans, or Colombian paramilitary drug traffickers, security and stable administration are basic functions of government. When effective, stable government and a secure environment have a strong appeal to society, and the organizations that provide it cannot long be ignored.

Similar to the cases of the Vikings and Mediterranean pirates, while modern criminal groups owe their success to weak indigenous governments, success is also dependent on the support or at least the tolerance of governments that see them as useful pawns in some larger geopolitical game. Narco-terrorism is often tolerated for political and economic reasons. For example, cultivation of drug-producing crops may be a signficant source of income for rural farmers, making the government reluctant to anger growers and risk losing political support. In Bolivia, President Evo Morales's rise to power began with his leadership of the coca growers union and his high-profile opposition to the U.S.-funded eradication of the coca crop. He helped to lead street demonstrations by Indian and union groups that toppled the country's last two presidents and elected him, in 2005, the country's first-ever indigenous president.[40] Even the United States turns a blind eye when it suited its higher geopolitical purposes.

The cold war and the struggle against communism often made unusual alliances. Beginning in the 1940s, the United States saw the need to tolerate corrupt forces linked to drug trafficking, provided they were anti-communists. This allowed the drug trade to prosper.[41] The political leverage gained by ignoring drug traffickers was deemed acceptable, provided the revenues benefited "allies." U.S. covert operations often formed "gray alliances" with organizations ranging from the Sicilian Mafia, French Corsican underworld, crime gangs of Southeast Asia's Golden Triangle, and Cuban exiles to Afghan opium smugglers. Yet these "alliances" greatly facilitated the flow of drugs to the world's markets.[42] This proved especially true when the Soviets established their own connections, particularly with their Cuban and Nicaraguan allies. Narco-terrorism became an increasingly useful weapon in the struggle between East and West.[43]

Perhaps it is no small coincidence that the U.S. invasion of Panama to depose its former ally turned drug suspect Manuel Noriega coincided so closely with the fall of the Berlin wall and the demise of communism. The game changed. Once-useful allies quickly became criminals, their activities were no longer tolerated, and their strongholds no longer protected. Methods and activities once surreptitiously deemed acceptable were suddenly publicly declaimed. No doubt Manuel Noriega, Eustace the Monk, and Khayr ad-Din Barbarossa could all compassionately empathize with each other.

We have seen examples of weak governments providing opportunities for armed groups originating from a desire for profit. Now we return to the example of strong governments providing opportunity for ideologically motivated zealots. The example of the Teutonic Knights, religiously motivated and bent on colonizing and proselytizing, has many similarities with modern armed groups, none more so than Hezbollah.

The Teutonic Knights were motivated by a complex mix of religious, economic, social, and political conditions. They grew in power as these conditions were exploited by a series of patrons seeking their own objectives. So too has Hezbollah.

Growing from a small politically motivated group with no distinct organization, Hezbollah has become a major actor in Lebanese politics. Created in 1982 as a break-away faction of the Islamic Amal Party, its roots are found in Iran's Shia religious academies and in its historical ties with Iran. While Islam does not recognize the Western concept of nationality, the cultural and religious links between Hezbollah and Iran stretch back to the days of the Persian Empire.[44] When the Iranian Revolution incited Islamic activism, Shia fundamentalism, and the creation of militant groups, Hezbollah emerged as a perfect pawn in the larger game being planned in Iran.[45] Its religious zeal is manipulated for purposes far beyond gaining converts.

Just as Palestine and the Baltic provided an outlet for the religious fervor of Christian crusaders a thousand years before, the unique conditions of Lebanon provide fertile ground for the "fire-brand clerics" providing the central foundation for Hezbollah.[46] Both Iran and Syria provide military training, administrative support, and funding to Hezbollah, rapidly transforming the organization into a military and political force in Lebanon.[47]

In a pattern not dissimilar to that of the Teutonic Knights, Hezbollah's success is derived from a complex set of conditions beyond simple military strength. Building on existing Shia organizations and religious institutions, Hezbollah increasingly brought administrative order as well as religious fervor, which, in combination, brought political power.[48]

Ideological indoctrination, sweetened with tangible material benefits, is a powerful force, particularly when the controlling administrative apparatus is culturally acceptable. With Iranian and Syrian funding, Hezbollah established schools, housing, hospitals, and social welfare facilities, all independent from the Lebanese government. Its return on investment has been duly elected membership in the Lebanese parliament and positions in the cabinet.[49]

How far the power of Hezbollah will grow remains to be seen. No doubt it will continue to receive Syrian and Iranian funding as long as it serves the purposes of those governments. The fact that it supports the concept of an integrated Islamic state over an independent Lebanon and rejects the renunciation of violence against both internal and external enemies makes it an ideal pawn in the hands of its more powerful Iranian and Syrian backers.[50]

Until Hezbollah no longer serves the ulterior motives of these states and the radical Islamist movement, or until the people of the region finally reject the use of violence as the primary means to solve their problems, Hezbollah will likely continue to grow in power. If Hezbollah, already a recognized part of the Lebanese political structure, continues to augment its position, it will increasingly become a force that has to be dealt with by established states.

Whether a pirate kingdom, religious order, or narco-terrorist cartel, and whether motivated by a desire for wealth, a desire for land, a desire for political power, a desire for converts, or a combination of all of these, armed groups as illustrated here share a common link. They only grow beyond the level of criminal annoyance when they remain unchallenged and have the support of existing governments.

The governments that tolerate the existence of these groups invariably do so not because they approve of them but because they find them useful for furthering their own ends. Even when they do approve of the basic motivations of the group in question, such as the religious motives of the Teutonic Knights, when it ceases to serve the goals of existing states, they will withdraw their support and, at worst, will actively attack, and destroy the group.

The dangerous exception is when an armed group, through the support of a patron government, is able to consolidate its power to the extent that it has the strength to openly challenge both its patron and other existing governments. Once this threshold is crossed, it can no longer be treated as a criminal annoyance. It must be dealt with as a co-equal entity. It can be eliminated through traditional methods of power politics as were the Teutonic Knights, openly attacked and destroyed as were the pirate kingdoms, or, as with the Norman Vikings, accepted as a coequal and integrated into the political order.

The last option is not particularly desirable. But then neither are the first two, which invariably prove costly in terms of blood, treasure, and political capital. At some point the piper must be paid. The question is when he will be paid, and what currency will be used.

NOTES

1. Mark C. Farley, *International and Regional Trends in Maritime Piracy, 1989–1993* (Monterey, CA: Naval Postgraduate School, 1993), 2.

2. Cyrus H. Karraker, *Piracy Was a Business* (Rindge, NH: Richard R. Smith Publisher, Inc., 1953), 15.

3. Philip Gosse, *The History of Piracy* (New York: Tudor Publishing Company, 1932), 1–2.

4. Michael Fabey, "Bad Times Spur Pirates," *Traffic World* 257, no. 8 (22 February 1999): 42–43.

5. Ibid.

6. Eric Ellen, *Shipping at Risk: The Rising Tide of Organized Crime* (Paris and Barking, UK: International Chamber of Commerce, 1997), 47.

7. Karraker, *Piracy Was a Business,* 16.

8. Gosse, *The History of Piracy,* 306.

9. Ibid., 307–308.

10. Karraker, *Piracy Was a Business,* 20.

11. Neville Williams, *Captains Outrageous: Seven Centuries of Piracy* (New York: MacMillan Company, 1962), 4–6.

12. Ibid.

13. Gosse, *The History of Piracy,* 91.

14 Karraker, *Piracy Was a Business,* 31–32.

15. Johannes Bronsted, *The Vikings* (Harmondsworth, Middlesex, England: Penguin Books, Ltd., 1960), 32–35

16. P. H. Sawyer, *The Age of the Vikings* (New York: St Martin's Press, 1971), 158.

17. Gosse, *The History of Piracy,* 89.

18. Ibid.

19. Bronsted, *The Vikings,* 45–48.

20. Ibid., 49–52.

21. Holger Arbman, *The Vikings* (New York: Praeger, 1961), 80–81.

22. Bronsted, *The Vikings,* 71.

23. Ibid.

24. Desmond Seward, *The Monks of War: The Military Religious Orders* (Hamden, CT: Archon Books, 1972), 91.

25. William Urban, *The Baltic Crusade* (DeKalb, IL: Northern Illinois University Press, 1975), xi

26. Seward, *The Monks of War,* 93–94.

27. Urban, *The Baltic Crusade,* xii.

28. Ibid., 25–33.

29. Seward, *The Monks of War,* 99.

30. Ibid., 94.

31. Ibid., 92–95.

32. Urban, *The Baltic Crusade,* 33–37.

33. Peter Dale Scott and Johnathan Marshall, *Cocaine Politics: Drugs, Armies and the CIA in Central America* (Berkeley: University of California Press, 1991), 23.

34. Max Manwaring, *Nonstate Actors in Colombia: Threat and Response* (Carlisle, PA: Strategic Studies Institute, May 2002), 2.

35. Ibid., 4–12.

36. Ibid., 6.

37. Dario Teicher, "The Colombian War and the Narco-Terrorist Threat," in *The Homeland Security Papers: Stemming the Tide of Terror,* ed. M. W. Ritz, R. G. Hensley, Jr., and J. C. Whitmire (Maxwell AFB, AL: USAF Counterproliferation Center, February 2004), 26–27.

38. Ibid., 28–29.

39. David Passage, *The United States and Colombia: Untying the Gordian Knot,* LeTort Papers 4 (Carlisle Barracks, PA: Strategic Studies Institute, March 2000), 3.

40. See "Evo Morales Sworn in as Bolivia's First Indigenous President, Hails Election as End of 'Colonial and Neo-Liberal Era,'" Democracy Now! www.democracynow.org/2006/1/23/evo_morales_sworn_in_as _bolivias.

41. Scott and Marshall, *Cocaine Politics,* 84–86.

42. Ibid., 4–5.

43. Ibid., 23–24.

44. Magnus Ranstorp, *Hizb'Allah in Lebanon* (New York, St Martin's Press, 1997), 25–26.

45. Simon Haddad, "The Origins of Popular Support for Lebanon's Hezbollah," *Studies in Conflict and Terrorism* 29 (2006): 24.

46. Ranstorp, *Hizb'Allah in Lebanon,* 38–39.

47. Ibid., 33–35.

48. Ibid., 36–37.

49. Haddad, "The Origins of Popular Support for Lebanon's Hezbollah," 23–24.

50. Ibid., 24–32.

2 The Italian Red Brigades (1969–1984): Political Revolution and Threats to the State

Paul J. Smith

INTRODUCTION

On 19 April 1974, Mario Sossi, an Italian district attorney known for his aggressive investigations of extremist groups in Italy, was kidnapped near his home in Genoa. Police later learned that Sossi's kidnappers belonged to the leftist militant group *Brigate Rosse* (BR), or Red Brigades. This was the same group that Sossi had once investigated in the late 1960s. Leaflets placed in a telephone booth informed police that Sossi's kidnappers were holding him in a "people's jail," until he could later be subjected to a trial conducted by a "revolutionary tribunal."[1]

As the "trial" proceeded, the BR released eight communiqués and two pictures of the "defendant." In exchange for Sossi's freedom, the BR demanded the release of eight convicted members of the October XXII Circle, a fellow leftist militant group. An Italian court agreed to the demands, although the ultimate release of the prisoners was blocked by Genoa's attorney general. Nevertheless, the BR released Sossi "in the apparent belief that the State's authority had been sufficiently undermined."[2]

Historically, the kidnapping of Mario Sossi is considered a major turning point in the evolution of BR ideology and tactics. The decision to kidnap Sossi was "the first concrete demonstration that the terrorist campaign of the BR was intended to strike beyond mere political adversaries or the capitalist system."[3] It was, instead, a direct challenge to the Italian state. The attack, moreover, would be a preview of the BR tactics and operations to come.

Today, discussions of terrorism in Italy evoke images of violent Islamist or *jihadi* networks operating out of major Italian cities and beyond. Recent intelligence reports and scholarly analyses support this view.[4] However, it could easily be argued that the fiercest

Paul J. Smith is an associate professor with the U.S. Naval War College in Newport, Rhode Island, where he specializes in transnational security issues related to East and Southeast Asia. He has contributed articles and essays on these and related subjects to such journals as *Fletcher Forum of World Affairs, Jane's Intelligence Review, Parameters, Orbis,* and *Survival.* He is editor of *Human Smuggling: Chinese Migrant Trafficking and the Challenge to America's Immigration Tradition* (Center for Strategic and International Studies, 1997), in addition to *Terrorism and Violence in Southeast Asia: Transnational Challenges to States and Regional Stability* (M.E. Sharpe, 2005). He has addressed academic and government audiences around the world on terrorism-related security issues. Smith studied in the People's Republic of China, Taiwan, and the United Kingdom and is conversant in Mandarin Chinese. He earned his BA from Washington and Lee University, his MA from the University of London, and his PhD from the University of Hawaii, Manoa.

and most savage terrorism experience in Italy occurred within the period from 1969 to 1984, when the Red Brigades were most active.

During this period, the Red Brigades, described by one scholar as "by far Europe's principal armed communist organization,"[5] spread a wide swath of human carnage and physical destruction. In fact, more than "twelve hundred people died or suffered grievous injury from this violence."[6] Key targets of Red Brigades terrorism included policemen, lawyers, judges, university professors, union leaders, industrialists, and an array of bystanders.[7] This may explain a 1984 national poll that listed terrorism as the top "historical development of the last fifty years to which future historians of Italy would devote the most attention."[8] No other issue—including the history of fascism, Italy's liberation in World War II, Italy's transformation into a modern industrial state, among others— came close to matching the significance of terrorism in the poll.[9]

ORIGINS OF THE RED BRIGADES (BR)

The origins of the Red Brigades can be traced back to the late 1960s at the University of Trento in northern Italy. The BR originally started as a small group of radical and communist students and workers who were commanded by a former student radical leader named Renato Curcio.[10] Curcio's spouse, Margherita "Mara" Cagol, also played a significant role in the BR's early history.[11] Although both Curcio and Cagol came from Catholic families and were married in a church, they found the prospect of living mundane lives (they had been trained in hotel management and bookkeeping) to be unappealing. Their "free floating idealism" drew them to the University of Trento, where they studied sociology and subsequently became enmeshed in the student movement.[12]

At the time, the University of Trento, located in a tranquil and socially conservative province in northern Italy, was a new university that specialized exclusively in social sciences. Trento was comparable to University of California–Berkeley in the United States or the Free University of Berlin in West Germany in that it was a hotbed for student activism, radicalism, and innovation.[13] With its flexible admissions policy, Trento attracted "socially concerned students" from throughout Italy.[14] The environment at Trento suited Curcio and Cagol; eventually, they would establish the "historical nucleus" of the BR.[15]

In 1969, Curcio and Cagol left the university and moved to Milan. They met another communist youth from the Italian region of Emilia-Romagna named Alberto Franceschini. The three of them founded the Metropolitan Political Collective, an organization that was intended "to coordinate and to radicalize the anticapitalist discontent of the students and workers."[16] When it became clear that the Italian Communist Party was unwilling to engage in revolution or work for the goals of the extreme Left, the Red Brigades emerged to play this role.[17]

Up until the late 1980s, the BR followed an ideology and doctrine that advocated "armed violence against the capitalist state."[18] A strong anticapitalist streak dominated the thinking of Curcio and his followers: "They saw multinational corporate capitalism as a monster preparing to devour the world."[19] Ideologically, the Red Brigades considered themselves to be true Marxists. They sought to create a true socialist state in Italy along the lines of Lenin's socialism from 1917 to 1924 and of Mao Zedong's Cultural Revolution.[20]

The Red Brigades were also influenced by the ideas and writings of Lin Biao, Che Guevara, Carlos Marighella, and Abraham Guillen. Marighella was the author of the *Mini-manual of Urban Guerrilla Warfare,* which described in detail how to conduct an urban campaign, which was the key strategy of the Red Brigades.[21] However, Marighella saw urban guerrilla warfare as an adjunct to the larger rural struggle, a point that the BR—which did not focus on rural areas—either missed or ignored.[22]

From a historical perspective, the Red Brigades emerged out of the milieu of the 1968 student protest movement and growing international antiwar sentiment generated by American involvement in the Vietnam War. Indeed, the year 1968 was particularly problematic for the U.S. Vietnam campaign because of the Tet Offensive, launched by the Vietcong and North Vietnamese regulars.[23] This offensive and the American response resulted in dramatic violence that was televised internationally. The attack "created stunning [television] images: American planes strafing villages, dropping napalm canisters that burst into rolling fireballs."[24] In addition to the Vietnam War experience, the year 1968 could also be characterized simply as a time of liberation, counterculture, and protest. Young people on both sides of the Atlantic were eager to challenge "the Establishment."[25]

However, the Red Brigades did not see themselves as merely a protest movement. As die-hard Marxists, they viewed their movement as the product of inevitable historical trends and forces, which brought about social and political changes that were natural, evolutionary, inevitable, and irreversible.[26] The BR believed it would eventually prevail against the Italian state. Its self-confidence was based on the belief that it was "correctly aligned with political, economic and social forces" that were—it believed—becoming dominant.

In the Italian context, the Red Brigades felt betrayed by the fact that the Italian Communist Party had turned on the "movement" and had reached a "historic compromise" with the Christian Democrats in an effort to share government power.[27] One of the key objectives of the Red Brigades was to disrupt cooperation between the Communist Party and the Christian Democrats, led by former prime minister Aldo Moro. The Red Brigades apparently targeted Aldo Moro—a former prime minister who would eventually be kidnapped and murdered in 1978—because he was considered "the architect of the arrangement between the parties, which according to the Red Brigades made him 'one of the persons who bears the greatest responsibility for the 30 years of dirty Christian Democratic rule.'"[28]

STRUCTURE, SUPPORT, AND TACTICS

The Red Brigades were organized vertically among at least six columns, which were in turn divided into brigades and then cells. Columns were located in Milan, Genoa, Turin, Rome, Naples, and the Veneto Region. The column concept was inherited from the structure of the Italian partisans who operated during World War II.[29] Certain columns, depending on their locations, had specific roles or tasks. The columns in the northern part of the country, for example, were active in areas of large concentrations of factory workers. The Rome column's strategic goal—not surprisingly—was to attack Italy's political leaders, and particularly those affiliated with the Christian Democratic Party.[30]

Areas that were not covered by columns would be managed by the regional revolutionary committees, which were seeds of future columns. Core members of the Red Brigades, estimated at 400 to 500 hard-core full-time members, received a salary of roughly 250,000 lire ($400 a month).[31] A second tier of members lived "above ground" and appeared to live a "seemingly normal existence as respected members of Italian society."[32]

At the apex of the Red Brigades' organizational structure was the Strategic Directorate (SD), which was responsible for forming the political-organizational program. The SD was considered the BR's "brain center" where "all members would merge and consolidate their experiences and knowledge."[33] The SD also solicited and gathered recommendations from all BR members. In addition, the SD published "resolutions," which were strategic texts that guided the organization.[34]

The Red Brigades recruited unemployed workers, students, and others who exhibited enthusiasm for revolutionary change. However, before entry into the organization, potential recruits would be tested to determine whether or not they could renounce a normal life, their family and friends, and sentimental liaisons.[35] Most important, the key criterion for membership was powerful idealism (not simply ideological conviction). The successful recruit would also need to be imbued with "an implacable desire to fight injustice to create a new society."[36]

Fund-raising for the Red Brigades was often accomplished from the proceeds of kidnappings or bank robberies. Ironically, the BR's reputation for violence sometimes helped to facilitate nonviolent bank robberies. In one case in 1978, a BR operative appeared at a bank in Genoa and, after identifying himself as a BR member, requested 80 million lire. The deputy manager stated that such a sum could not be paid without the manager's permission. When the manager appeared, the BR operative repeated the demand and made it clear that the Red Brigades organization knew everything about the manager's family. The bank subsequently paid the amount requested.[37]

Another important consideration related to support of the BR organization was the degree to which the organization was linked with—or received support from—other militant organizations located outside of Italy. The BR promoted the notion of a Third International, but it "never came to much."[38] Despite occasional contacts with fellow European "red" groups, the BR considered Italy to be the central focus of its revolutionary struggle. The organization that the BR had the most sympathy with was arguably the German Red Army Faction (RAF). As one former BR member stated, "we had a lot of respect for our RAF comrades. Personally, I thought it was very courageous of them to struggle on such difficult terrain as Germany."[39]

However, in some instances, police in countries outside Italy would capture BR members who were hiding in suspected terrorist hideouts. In April 1980, for instance, a massive French operation in Paris and Toulon led to the arrest of 22 suspected terrorists, including five Italians, one of which was Franco Pinna, who was considered a key figure in the Aldo Moro kidnapping and murder in 1978.[40] In addition, a BR operative, Antonio Savasta, admitted that the organization had contact with the Palestinian Liberation Organization (PLO), particularly after the murder of Aldo Moro, and that these meetings took place in France.[41] In addition, the PLO reportedly shipped a load of small arms to the Red Brigades in 1978.[42] Nevertheless, a U.S. intelligence report stated that links between the Red Brigades and other terrorist organizations seem to have been "of only modest importance."[43]

The tactical history of the Red Brigades can be divided up into four key periods. The first phase lasted from 1969 to 1972 and was centered primarily in Milan. In this phase, the BR primarily engaged in propaganda activities and attacks on private companies (primarily firebombings). The second phase, which ended in mid-1974, saw the BR expand to the industrial triangle of Milan, Turin, and Genoa. This period saw the BR turn to kidnapping activities, in which it learned how to "exploit the attendant media coverage."[44] The third phase—roughly 1974 to 1976—witnessed the ascent of the BR's second generation and a larger campaign to target the Italian state directly. The fourth phase (from 1977 to 1978) has been described as the BR's strategy of liquidation. "From 1977 on, terrorist attacks were carried out almost daily, usually in the form of 'campaigns' devoted to specific themes."[45]

THE STRATEGY OF LIQUIDATION AND THE MURDER OF ALDO MORO

The year 1978 seems to have been a particularly vigorous and violent year for Red Brigades ambush operations. Bankers and industrialists were common targets for BR attacks. In one typical attack, two youths on a motorcycle shot and wounded Giorgio Borhetti, a 53-year-old bank executive, only three blocks from the Vatican.[46] Following the attacks, anonymous callers who claimed to be BR members took credit for the attack. In April 1978, a Red Brigades ambush team shot and wounded Felice Schiavetti, president of the Genoa Industrialists Association, as he left home to head for his office.[47] Within 30 minutes of the ambush, a man called a Genoa newspaper and said, "This is the Red Brigades. An armed group has shot Felice Schiavetti, servant of the state."[48]

In May 1978, a particularly gruesome month, Red Brigades gunmen fired dozens of bullets into the legs of two industrialists in almost simultaneous attacks in separate cities. In Milan, Umberto degli Innocenti of Sit Siemens Telecommunications was attacked as he left his office.[49] Just moments later, Alfredo Lamberto of the Italsider metal plant in Genoa had his leg shattered by a Red Brigades gunman.[50] Approximately six days later in Milan, Marzio Astarita, who had just been named director of Chemical Bank's Milan operations, was departing his home for work.[51] As his wife waved goodbye to him from their balcony, a sedan pulled up alongside him with a masked man and woman who fired a gun at his left leg, wounding Astarita severely (although he later recovered).[52]

The year 1978 was also the year in which the BR accomplished its most ambitious operation to date with the abduction of former prime minister Aldo Moro.[53] The planning for the Moro kidnapping had been meticulous. On the day before the operation, the BR eliminated a vendor who normally sold flowers near the former prime minister's house so that he could not be a possible witness. On the day of the operation, approximately 12 BR operatives—11 men and one woman—conducted the kidnapping while wearing the uniform of Alitalia, the state airline.[54] As the 12 approached Moro and his party of bodyguards, they opened fire with automatic weapons, immediately killing four of Moro's bodyguards; the fifth died later in a hospital.[55]

The kidnapping shocked the Italian public and even elicited a personal plea from Pope Paul VI, who wrote (in a public statement): "Men of the Red Brigades, leave me . . .

the hope that in your souls there still is dwelling a victorious sentiment of humanity."[56] For its part, the Italian government launched a massive manhunt involving over 50,000 police and army troops. Feeling the intense pressure of government surveillance, Italian mobsters joined in on the search for Moro's abductors. Although crime bosses claimed they were motivated by patriotism, it was also obvious that they "were sick of watching their 'businesses' founder in the massive dragnet thrown over Italy."[57] Italian mobsters also threatened, via a communiqué, to have their "colleagues in prison . . . physically suppress all Red Brigades members within their jurisdictions."[58]

However, this combination of pleas and threats could not save Aldo Moro from his ultimate fate after a 55-day hostage standoff. On 9 May 1978, Italian police found the bullet-ridden body of former prime minister Aldo Moro, which was abandoned in the backseat of a burgundy red Renault R-4.[59] The discovery of the body capped a nearly two-month long, emotionally wrenching hostage crisis.

The kidnapping and the tense period afterward not only traumatized the Italian public but also catapulted the Red Brigades to world fame.[60] Only 11 days after the discovery of Moro's body, the BR issued a communiqué describing the kidnap-murder as an "act of legitimate revolutionary justice."[61] In addition, the BR eliminated all ambiguity about its true motives with regard to the Italian state. The murder of Aldo Moro, according to the BR, was "nothing other than the first act of a precise objective to destabilize, disarticulate and destroy the state."[62]

PUBLIC REVULSION AND THE STEADY DECLINE OF THE RED BRIGADES

Although the Red Brigades may have viewed the kidnapping and murder of Aldo Moro as a victory, many analysts and observers believe the incident actually signaled the steady decline of the BR in Italy. As indicated earlier, the incident shocked and galvanized the Italian public. But it also dramatically shifted public opinion strongly against the Red Brigades and their fellow leftists.[63] In addition, the Italian police launched major sweeps against BR members, which led to the arrest of Nadia Mantovani, the 28-year-old girlfriend of Renato Curcio, who had gone into hiding after violating parole. Also arrested were Lauro Azzolini, identified as one of the BR's original members (and who had been tied to the murders of several Italian officials), and Antonio Savino, who was arrested after firing a weapon at police.[64]

Although the Red Brigades, in the post–Aldo Moro era, were in steady decline, this fact did not temper the organization's violent tendencies. In addition to kidnapping and murdering Christian Democratic leader Aldo Moro, the Red Brigades continued their campaign against Christian Democratic leaders, including Fausto Cuocolo, a professor at the University of Genoa, who was shot by two young men who walked into his classroom and shut the door. Their first two shots missed, but as they moved closer to Mr. Cuocolo, they were able to pump at least two rounds into his body.[65] Fortunately, as news reports indicated, the bullets "had all lodged in flesh, damaging no bones or vital organs."[66] Within an hour of the attack, a call was made to the local newspaper and a person claiming to be part of the Red Brigades Genovese Column stated that "we lamed Fausto Cuocolo, one of the major representatives of the Genovese Christian Democratic Party."[67] Similar attacks against Christian Democrats during the period include the shooting of

Enrico Ghio, a candidate for the European Parliament, who was shot four times in the legs. In another case, a Christian Democratic city councilwoman was "tied up and had glue dumped all over her hair."[68]

In one brazen attack, Red Brigades guerrillas bombed a police barracks, "wounding 18 officers engaged in counterterrorist work."[69] After the attack, and according to usual custom, a Red Brigades spokesman telephoned several newspapers to announce that their "war against the state" was continuing.[70] Italian leaders initiated a new vigilance against the terrorist threat. "We are at war," Italian president Alessandro Pertini reportedly declared in 1980.[71]

THE GENERAL DOZIER DEBACLE

In 1981, the Red Brigades accomplished another prominent terrorist feat by kidnapping American General James Lee Dozier, who at the time was deputy chief of staff for logistics and administration at NATO's headquarters in southern Europe and also the highest-ranking American serving with that command. A graduate of West Point and recipient of the Silver Star from his duty in Vietnam, General Dozier was described by friends and colleagues as a "soldier's soldier" who was "low key and efficient."[72]

Dozier's kidnappers entered his home in Verona, Italy, dressed as plumbers. They hit Dozier on his head with a pistol butt and then tied his wife up and then sealed her eyes and mouth with adhesive tape.[73] After the kidnappers searched Dozier's apartment, they put Dozier into the trunk of a car.[74] Later they transported him to an apartment in the ground unit of a "drab modern building on the outskirts of Padua."[75] For more than a month, Dozier's right wrist and left ankle were chained to a steel cot, which was placed under a small tent. He was also forced to live under the "never-extinguished glare of an electric bulb."[76] Dozier's captors also required him to wear earphones and listen to loud music.[77]

During Dozier's captivity, the Red Brigades issued various communiqués to the government and the public generally, describing their demands or complaints. They issued the first communiqué only days after the kidnapping; it was striking for its lack of any ransom demand. Instead it dwelled on international matters of interest to the Red Brigades, including a tribute to the German Red Army Faction.[78] Subsequent communiqués also failed to mention ransom demands and even lacked any particular reference to Dozier.[79]

The fifth communiqué, retrieved from a trash can in downtown Rome, contained a number of anti-NATO and anti-American statements but did not make any specific demands for Dozier's release.[80] One of the consequences of the Dozier kidnapping was increased concern within the U.S. government that the kidnapping signaled that the Brigades had "decided to suspend operations against domestic Italian targets and move against U.S. and NATO targets."[81]

Shortly after the fifth communiqué was issued, however, the Italian government got its big break. A captured BR operative informed police of Dozier's location, and subsequently, the Italian authorities were able to mount a successful rescue of the NATO general. Dozier, who had been held for 42 days, would later report that as police stormed the apartment in which he was being held, a Red Brigades operative was "leveling a gun at his head."[82] After this rescue, the Red Brigades experienced further defections of its members, many of whom in turn acted as informants for the government.[83]

The rescue of General Dozier boosted the popularity and reputation of Prime Minister Giovanni Spadolini, who "had little sympathy for the [politically active, leftist] students and even less for the terrorists."[84] More important, it derailed what was later discovered to be a grand plot—of which the Dozier kidnapping was the initial stage—that featured a series of bold attacks across Italy, including the kidnapping of the managing director of Fiat and the "staging of commando-style raids to free jailed terrorists from prison."[85]

In the three months following the rescue of General Dozier, the Italian government launched a massive crackdown against the Red Brigades. More than 200 terrorists were arrested between December 1981 and March 1982.[86] Italian authorities also imposed harsh measures against Red Brigades members already in prison, such as revoking telephone privileges and disallowing receipt of outside packages.[87]

Among the by-products of the rescue of General Dozier was the capture of Antonio Savasta, described as one of the Red Brigades' "greatest betrayers."[88] Savasta quickly changed sides and offered up to police more than 100 names of fellow Red Brigades members (including locations of their hideouts).[89] The Savasta capture, combined with the various Italian enforcement measures against the Red Brigades, marked a period of steady subsequent decline for the organization. Although the group continued to conduct violent operations well into the 1980s, the number of attacks dropped off considerably.[90]

LESSONS FOR TODAY

On the surface, it would seem obvious that the Red Brigades, rooted in Marxist, anticapitalist ideology, should be regarded as being very different and distinct from Al Qaeda and its alignment movements, which are largely rooted in militant religious ideologies that feature or glorify, among other things, suicide bombings. Nevertheless, there are a number of interesting common features that apply to both movements.

First, and perhaps most significant, both movements reflect—and are reactions to—profound and disruptive changes and transformations that have occurred in the larger international system. The Red Brigades, as noted earlier in the chapter, reflected (and were arguably products of) the 1968 student protest movement as well as growing hostility toward U.S. military action in Vietnam, in addition to the overall tensions that emanated from the cold war. They also were part of a wave of "red" terrorist movements—such as the German Red Army Faction, the French *Action Directe,* American Weather Underground, and the Japanese Red Army—which saw themselves as "vanguards for the Third World Masses."[91]

Al Qaeda and aligned movements are similarly reflective of their international environment. The year 1979 was significant because of the Soviet invasion of Afghanistan, which generated the international mujahideen movement. The narrative resulting from the Soviet Union's withdrawal from Afghanistan—that a small group of determined mujahideen fighters could defeat a superpower—greatly emboldened the movement that would beget Al Qaeda. In addition, Al Qaeda is arguably a product of profound social, economic, and political forces of globalization that are manifest throughout the world. Audrey Kurth Cronin argues that the wave of international terrorism represented by Al Qaeda and similar groups is not only a reaction to globalization but is also facilitated by it.[92]

Second, both the Red Brigades and Al Qaeda exhibited or have exhibited a remarkable resilience and ability to survive in the face of massive military and political responses by states. In both cases, the resilience and viability of the organizations were or are sustained by "soft support" from their respective constituencies. Italian authorities, for example, were amazed at the BR's remarkable ability to sustain itself despite intense government enforcement measures. In the case of the Red Brigades, soft support was rooted in the fact that many people were sympathetic to the basic arguments of the Red Brigades, although they did not necessarily agree with their terrorist tactics. BR sympathizers were critical to the long-term success of the movement; they provided aid and shelter to BR operatives, which was particularly important when the latter were being actively pursued by police.[93] "The amazing destructiveness and staying power of the Red Brigades depended ultimately on their success in gaining the support of astonishingly large numbers of people who believed in revolution as something sacred."[94]

Similarly, Al Qaeda—and its aligned movements—has survived despite having borne the brunt of a "war on terrorism" implemented by the world's only superpower with global military reach. Soft support in the case of Al Qaeda largely has derived from the fact that many Muslims, while not directly supporting terrorism, nevertheless have been sympathetic to the larger "metanarrative" around which Al Qaeda has constructed its ideology. Central to this narrative is the notion that Muslims around the world are under assault and are mistreated by the dominant and powerful actors within the international system, a system that is ultimately led by the United States.

Anti-American sentiment has also helped fuel the narratives of both organizations. The Red Brigades benefited from—and promoted—a narrative that Italy's workers were being abused by corporate interests or were victims of an economic system dominated by the United States. In the case of Al Qaeda, anti-American sentiment has played a much more central role in the organization. After all, Osama bin Laden and his allies essentially declared war on the United States when, on 23 February 1998, they proclaimed the formation of the World Islamic Front, which declared a jihad against Jews and crusaders.[95] In addition, Al Qaeda thrives on the "political oxygen" generated by extremely unpopular U.S. policies in the Middle East.[96]

Buttressing this grievance narrative is the reality of poverty and despair in many of the constituent communities. At the leadership levels, the poverty link to terrorism is tenuous at best. Leaders within the Red Brigades or Al Qaeda have been, for the most part, relatively well educated and, presumably, economically prosperous (or at least they had access to the means to achieve prosperity). However, at the lower "worker" levels of the two organizations, poverty arguably has played a more significant role in fueling despair and thus facilitating recruitment.

In the case of Al Qaeda, it has been observed that although "bin Laden and many of his lieutenants and agents have not been victims of poverty or deprivation, tens of millions of people in the region have been."[97] Moreover, diaspora Muslims residing in Western Europe face much higher unemployment rates—typically double those of the native population—which provides a convenient pool of potential terrorist recruits.[98] In the case of the BR, many analysts speculated that the BR (and similar groups) and its ideology flourished within a breeding ground (in Italy during the 1970s) of 1.2 million unemployed young people between 18 and 29 years old.[99] Thus, poverty and unemployment may have played a role in fostering an enabling environment for both organizations.

A third important parallel between the two organizations is the fact that each sincerely has believed in its movement and perceived that historical circumstances had or are aligned in such a way that its vision could be fulfilled. In the case of Al Qaeda, many Al Qaeda members and their supporters "see their actions as pursuing a noble cause."[100] They see their efforts as a way to bring about a revolution followed by a new and religious-oriented international order. The BR similarly viewed its role as an actor in a larger struggle to bring about revolution in Italy. The Red Brigades sincerely believed that by creating an atmosphere of collapse and total anxiety, they would ultimately pave the way to total revolution.[101]

A fourth important parallel between the two organizations is the fact that both movements were constrained—although not completely disrupted—by aggressive state responses. In the case of the Red Brigades, the Italian government launched major counterterrorism operations periodically, but most significantly following the kidnapping and murder of Aldo Moro. Another major sweep was launched following the kidnapping and release of American General James Dozier in the early 1980s. In addition, the Italian authorities created a *pentiti* system that promised reduced punishment for those who helped the government in its investigation.

The *pentiti* system proved invaluable for turning key operatives—eager to save their own skins by betraying comrades—who gave authorities the critical information they needed to make arrests. "The special provisions governing the State's treatment of *pentiti* ultimately proved to be decisive in the defeat of the Red Brigades."[102] The confessions that came out of this system led to the discovery of hideouts and arms deposits and, ultimately, the neutralization (either by arrest or by death) of dozens of terrorists.[103] In one case, a confession obtained from a 27-year-old BR member led to the arrests of 45 additional individuals and to "new charges against already jailed suspects."[104]

In the case of Al Qaeda and aligned movements, the turning of lower-level operatives against the Al Qaeda organization has been critical to the unraveling of terrorist networks around the world. The arrests of leaders such as Riduan Isamuddin (a.k.a. Hambali), who was believed to be Al Qaeda's senior representative in Southeast Asia, have provided substantial intelligence about terrorist methodologies and future plans.[105] In addition, international cooperation in the realms of intelligence, law enforcement, and military deployments has severely confined Al Qaeda's functional space, evidenced by the lack of any major attack in the United States since September 11, 2001. Moreover, aggressive U.S. actions—including aggressive interrogation methods and rendition practices—illustrate the tension between the desire for effective security and the imperative to preserve those liberal and humanitarian-oriented values for which the United States has traditionally been highly regarded.

CONCLUSION

The Red Brigades were arguably one of the most serious threats to the Italian state in its recent history. The BR not only terrorized the Italian public but essentially struck at the heart of the Italian state. In this way, the Red Brigades defied the notion that terrorism, while dramatic and shocking, tends to have little political impact beyond its immediate consequences. As Walter Laqueur has stated, "[Terrorism] has been a tragedy for the victims, but seen in historical perspective it seldom has been more than a nuisance."[106] The Red Brigades' campaign against the Italian state for more than 15 years suggests the existence of a threat that rises above the level of mere "nuisance."

As noted above, perhaps the most fascinating feature of the BR's existence was its ability to sustain itself for more than 15 years despite intense law enforcement and intelligence activity directed against it. This can be attributed to the significant "soft support" that the organization enjoyed within the Italian public. This fact can also provide a lesson for the United States and allied states seeking to combat Al Qaeda and aligned movements. The BR was able to sustain itself via a narrative of injustice, inequality, and the need for revolution, just as Al Qaeda thrives on a narrative that it serves the needs of downtrodden Muslims who have been betrayed and abused by an international system that is dominated by the United States. Effectively countering the militant jihadi threat will require, among other measures, a sincere effort on the part of the United States to reduce the political oxygen that sustains contemporary terrorism.

NOTES

1. Vittorfranco S. Pisano, "The Red Brigades: A Challenge to Italian Democracy," in *Contemporary Terrorism*, ed. William Gutteridge (New York: Facts on File Publications, 1986), 177.

2. Ibid.

3. Ibid.

4. Tamara Makarenko, "Takfiri Presence Grows in Europe," *Jane's Intelligence Review*, 1 February 2005; Ed Blanche, "Ansar al-Islam Bolsters European Network," *Jane's Intelligence Review*, 1 October 2004; see also Alison Pargeter and Ahmed Al-Baddawy, "North Africa's Radical Diaspora in Europe Shift Focus to Iraq War," *Jane's Intelligence Review*, 1 April 2006.

5. Xavier Raufer, "The Red Brigades: Farewell to Arms," *Studies in Conflict and Terrorism*, 16:316.

6. Richard Drake, "Italy in the 1960s: A Legacy of Terrorism and Liberation," *South Central Review* 16, no. 4 (Winter/Spring 2000): 63.

7. Ibid.

8. Ibid., 62.

9. Ibid.

10. Ibid., 66.

11. Ibid.

12. Leonard Weinberg, "The Violent Life: An Analysis of Left- and Right-Wing Terrorism in Italy," in *Political Violence and Terror: Motifs and Motivations,* ed. Peter H. Merkl (Berkeley: University of California Press, 1986), 159.

13. Ibid., 153.

14. Ibid.

15. Ibid., 159.

16. Drake, "Italy in the 1960s," 66.

17. Ibid.

18. "Red Brigades Practice a Thesis of Armed Violence," *Christian Science Monitor,* 17 March 1978, 3.

19. Drake, "Italy in the 1960s," 65.

20. Raufer, "The Red Brigades," 319.

21. *Terrorist Scene in Italy Detailed* (Central Intelligence Agency, 8 April 1981), 2; now declassified and reproduced in *Declassified Documents Reference System* (Farmington Hills, MI: Gale Group, 2007).

22. Ibid.

23. Terry H. Anderson, "1968: The End and the Beginning in the United States and Western Europe," *South Central Review* 16, no. 4 (Winter/Spring 2000): 2.

24. Ibid.

25. Ibid., 14.

26. *Terrorist Scene in Italy Detailed,* 2.

27. Ibid., 1.

28. "Red Brigades: A Trail of Violence," *New York Times,* 10 May 1978, A16.

29. Raufer, "The Red Brigades," 320.

30. Ibid.

31. Henry Tanner, "Red Brigades Intimidates Italians but Fails in Effort to Start Civil War," *New York Times,* 17 May 1978, 25.

32. Ibid.

33. Raufer, "The Red Brigades," 322.

34. Ibid.

35. Ibid., 317–18.

36. Ibid.

37. Tanner, "Red Brigades Intimidates Italians but Fails in Effort to Start Civil War," 25.

38. *Terrorist Scene in Italy Detailed,* 13.

39. Raufer, "The Red Brigades," 323.

40. "New European Tactics on Terrorists Net 22 in France," *New York Times,* 2 April 1980, A3.

41. "Red Brigades and PLO," *Washington Post,* 17 March 1982, A26.

42. "Israelis Offered Red Brigades Arms, Study Says," *Globe and Mail* (Canada), 4 June 1983.

43. *Terrorist Scene in Italy Detailed,* 13.

44. Pisano, "The Red Brigades," 176.

45. Ely Karmon, *Coalitions between Terrorist Organizations: Revolutionaries, Nationalists and Islamists* (Leiden: Martinus Nijhoff Publishers, 2005), 102.

46. "Italian Banker Hurt in Leftist Attack," *Washington Post,* 24 February 1978, A18.

47. "Italian Industrialist Shot by Red Brigades," *Washington Post,* 8 April 1978, A16.

48. Ibid.

49. "Terrorists Wound Two Italian Industrialists," *Washington Post,* 5 May 1978, A21.

50. Ibid.

51. Ronald Koven and Sari Gilbert, "Italian Terrorists Wound Manager of U.S. Bank," *Washington Post,* 12 May 1978, A26.

52. Ibid.

53. R. W. Apple, Jr., "Kidnappers End Silence, Releasing a Photo of Moro and a Statement," *New York Times,* 19 March 1978, 3.

54. R. W. Apple, Jr., "Ex-Premier Moro Held by Group Demanding Radicals Be Freed," *New York Times,* 17 March 1978, NJ15.

55. Ibid.

56. "Text of Pope's Plea to Kidnappers," *New York Times,* 23 April 1978, 10.

57. "Crime Bosses in Italy Decide Red Brigades Are Bad for Business," *Washington Post,* 29 March 1978, A16.

58. Ibid.

59. "Moro Slain, Body Found in Rome: West's Leaders Assail Terror," *New York Times,* 10 May 1978, 21.

60. Drake, "Italy in the 1960s," 66.

61. "Red Brigades Vow to Destroy the Italian State," *Washington Post,* 21 May 1978, A23.

62. Ibid.

63. Gianni Statera, "Student Politics in Italy: From Utopia to Terrorism," *Higher Education* 8, no. 6 (November 1979): 660.

64. Ronald Koven, "7 Suspects Held in Italian Drive on Red Brigades," *Washington Post,* 3 October 1978, A13.

65. Ronald Koven, "Red Brigades Shoot Politician in Classroom," *Washington Post,* 1 June 1979, A15.

66. Ibid.

67. Ibid.

68. Ibid.

69. "Terrorist Bombing in Italy," *Washington Post,* 20 January 1980, A15.

70. Ibid.

71. Alexander MacLeod, "Terrorism Becomes Fact of Life for Europe's Democracies," *Christian Science Monitor,* 30 July 1980, 5.

72. George Wilson, "Kidnapped Officer Seen as a 'Soldier's Soldier,'" *Washington Post,* 18 December 1981, A52.

73. Sari Gilbert, "Red Brigades in Verona Seize U.S. General," *Washington Post,* 18 December 1981, A1.

74. Ibid.

75. David Fleming, "Italian Police Rescue Dozier after 42 Days," *Wall Street Journal,* 29 January 1982, 32.

76. Henry Kamm, "Dozier Tells of 42 Days in a Pup Tent," *New York Times,* 3 February 1982, A3.

77. Ibid.

78. Henry Tanner, "General's Captors Issue a Statement," *New York Times,* 20 December 1981, 1.

79. Sari Gilbert, "Red Brigades Release Message and Snapshot of Gen. Dozier," *Washington Post,* 26 January 1982, A1.

80. Ibid.

81. National Foreign Assessment Center, *General Dozier's Kidnapping: An Update,* memorandum (Central Intelligence Agency, 31 December 1981), 2; now declassified and reproduced in *Declassified Documents Reference System* (Farmington Hills, MI: Gale Group, 2007).

82. Sari Gilbert, "Raid in Padua Frees Gen. Dozier," *Washington Post,* 29 January 1982, A1.

83. Drake, "Italy in the 1960s," 67.

84. Wolfgang Achtner, "Obituary: Giovanni Spadolini," *The Independent* (London), 6 August 1994, 43.

85. James Buxton, "Red Brigades Admit Defeat," *Financial Times* (London), 29 March 1982, 4.

86. Carolyn Friday, "Why Italy Got Tough on Red Brigades Prisoners," *Christian Science Monitor,* 3 March 1982, 1.

87. Ibid.

88. Buxton, "Red Brigades Admit Defeat," 4.

89. Ibid.

90. Sari Gilbert, "Italy's Red Brigades Appear Split at Moro Assassination Trial," *Washington Post,* 5 December 1982, A1.

91. David C. Rapoport, "The Four Waves of Modern Terrorism," in *Attacking Terrorism: Elements of a Grand Strategy,* ed. Audrey Kurth Cronin and James M. Ludes (Washington, DC: Georgetown University Press, 2004), 56.

92. Audrey Kurth Cronin, "Behind the Curve: Globalization and International Terrorism," *International Security* 27, no. 3 (Winter 2002/2003): 30.

93. Raufer, "The Red Brigades," 318.

94. Drake, "Italy in the 1960s," 65.

95. Marc Sageman, *Understanding Terror Networks* (Philadelphia: University of Pennsylvania Press, 2004), 47.

96. Stephen M. Walt, "Beyond bin Laden: Reshaping U.S. Foreign Policy," *International Security* 26, no. 3 (Winter 2001/2002): 70.

97. Paul K. Davis, *Deterrence and Influence in Counterterrorism: A Component in the War on al Qaeda* (Santa Monica, CA: RAND, 2002), 17.

98. Timothy M. Savage, "Europe and Islam: Crescent Waxing, Cultures Clashing," *Washington Quarterly* 27, no. 3 (Summer 2004): 31.

99. Ronald Koven, "Italian Extremism Feeds on High Unemployment, Loss of Traditional Ties," *Washington Post,* 27 April 1978, A22.

100. Davis, *Deterrence and Influence in Counterterrorism,* 18.

101. Theodora Lurie, "Italian Terrorism: The Fanatics behind Moro Kidnapping," *Globe and Mail* (Canada), 17 March 1978.

102. Drake, "Italy in the 1960s," 67.

103. Ibid.

104. "New Leniency Laws Spur Italian Drive against Terrorism," *Washington Post,* 17 April 1980, A1.

105. Ed Blanche, "New Islamist Terrorist Leaders Replace Those Killed and Captured," *Jane's Intelligence Review,* 1 August 2004.

106. Walter Laqueur, *The New Terrorism: Fanaticism and the Arms of Mass Destruction* (Oxford University Press, 1999), 3.

3 Armed Conflict in Cambodia and the UN Response

Carole Garrison

BACKGROUND

While no two armed conflicts or their resolutions are exactly alike, they do share critical similarities that can assist in the prediction, management, and/or control of another. Some conflicts offer comprehensive lessons for crafting resolution strategies. The Cambodian civil war and genocide of the 1960s and '70s was such a conflict. Its origins were both internal and external, the result of ideology conflicting with the contemporary world and the regional political situation. There were deep historical political and social splits in Cambodian society exacerbated by the cold war, and more particularly the Vietnam War, destabilizing the government of King Sihanouk and unleashing 30 years of human violence and the destruction of social and economic infrastructure.[1]

The ultimate mechanism for resolution provided by the international community was UNTAC, the United Nations Transitional Authority in Cambodia. UNTAC was a peacekeeping operation mandated to organize national elections and establish a constitutional government in Cambodia.

The following descriptive account is from the author's experience as a district electoral supervisor with UNTAC and her continuous occupational, research and personal relationships through the present. Thus she was there during the peacekeeping mission and again during the 1997 coup. She has returned to Cambodia almost yearly since then.

Dr. Carole Garrison is chair and professor, Department of Criminal Justice and Police Studies, College of Justice and Safety, Eastern Kentucky University. Dr. Garrison teaches Ethics in Criminal Justice; her current research areas include comparative studies on policewomen and comparative research on police systems. Dr. Garrison earned her PhD in public administration with a concentration in criminal justice from the Ohio State University. Earlier, from 1972 to 1976 she served as a police officer with the Atlanta, Georgia, Bureau of Police Services, and in 1986 served as commander of a college–police academy that tested the State of Ohio's new Basic Peace Officer Curriculum. She received the police department's Award for Distinguished Service in 1975. In 1984 she was listed in "Who's Who of American Women" and was the 1985 Professional Woman of the Year of Summit County, Ohio. She received "Outstanding Faculty" recognition from the University of Akron's Board of Trustees in 1987, 1991, and 1992. In 1998 the governor inducted her into the Ohio Women's Hall of Fame for her work as a social activist. From May 1992 to May 1993 Dr. Garrison served as a district electoral supervisor in Cambodia as part of the UN peacekeeping mission, UNTAC, returning in 1996 to serve as the executive director of the Cooperation Committee for Cambodia, a coordinating network of all humanitarian and development NGOs in Cambodia. While there she adopted a six-year-old orphan, now her daughter and a U.S. citizen. She has 17 publications to her credit and has presented over 60 guest lectures, workshops, and conference papers since 1980.

CAMBODIAN TIME LINE:[2]

- 1954: France withdraws from Cambodia. Prince Sihanouk rules for 18 years. He tries unsuccessfully to keep the country out of the Vietnam War and away from both the communists and Western-bloc influences. He appoints Lon Nol as a puppet government.
- 1969–1973: The United States carpet bombs Cambodian countryside, further destabilizing the economic and political situations. The deepening political opposition to the bombing in Cambodia and the widening Watergate scandal lead to the House of Representatives' voting to cut off any funding for any form of U.S. combat anywhere in Indochina.[3]
- 1970: Sihanouk is ousted by pro-Western general Lon Nol.
- April 1975: The Khmer Rouge, led by Pol Pot, empties Cambodia's capital, Phnom Penh, and begins a Maoist-style reform resulting in close to 2 million Cambodian deaths over the next four years. Soon after the Khmer Rouge takes Phnom Penh, Saigon falls to the North Vietnamese.
- 1978: Vietnam invades Cambodia and removes Pol Pot from power in the capital; it establishes a government of predominantly Khmer Rouge defectors.
- 1979–1981: The Khmer Rouge, joined by two noncommunist factions, fights a guerrilla war against the Vietnamese-backed regime. The United States, European nations, and China support the various warring factions.
- 1988: Vietnam retreats from Cambodia.
- 1991: The UN Human Rights Sub-commission passes an amendment to prevent another Cambodian genocide, which is followed by a peace process beginning with the signing of the Paris Peace Accords and the initiation of the UN peacekeeping mission, UNTAC, and national elections.[4]
- 1993: UN national elections result in a victory for the royalists but Prince Sihanouk brokers a deal sharing power among the royalists, FUNCIPEC, and the CPP, the Vietnamese-backed party of Hun Sen. The government is unable to function.
- 1997: Hun Sen consolidates power in a week-long coup in the capital, Phnom Penh, and continues to control the government through 2007.

UN PEACEKEEPING: LESSONS LEARNED FROM CAMBODIA

While the author is a strong advocate of the Indian proverb "Sometimes you have to jump off the cliff and build your wings on the way down," it's not good advice for the United Nations. UN peacekeeping missions simply don't have the mechanisms to adapt rapidly. And yet peace missions, by their nature, are like deep chasms into which the UN pours people, money, and equipment endlessly over the abyss.

UNTAC, one of the largest and most ambitious peacekeeping missions, ended its operation and withdrew from Cambodia having conducted elections with a 93 percent voter turnout in May of 1993. The elections, which appeared at the surface to be a success for the UN's new peacekeeping agenda, were not the "free and fair" process envisioned by the 1991 Paris Peace Accords but, rather, "credible and survivable."

It was an exercise that, rather than producing a sophisticated democratic constituency, solidly rebuilt national infrastructure, and disarmed factions, resulted instead in the installation of Prince Sihanouk as king—something the Cambodian people were willing to do prior to any UN involvement.

The UNTAC mission suffered from lack of unity of command, poor planning, bureaucratic red tape, and a myriad of hidden agendas and vested interests. Direction and action from New York or Geneva were slow and often unrelated to the realities on the ground. The delay of the elections until the beginning of the rainy season created major logistical obstacles. The inability of UNTAC to abide by its own imperatives (cantonment and demobilization) undermined its authority and effectiveness. The provision of a neutral, free, and fair election was, on the face of it, unrealizable. The UN's response was a tautological ploy: that the UN would only hold such elections and, thus, if elections are held, they are, by definition, occurring in a neutral atmosphere.

Additionally, persons sent by member nations differed widely in abilities and commitments to the mission. Disparities in economic benefits created additional tensions among and within the various UNTAC units, and the UNTAC bureaucracy continuously violated the rights and dignity of the locally recruited personnel.

The lifestyle of UNTAC personnel and UNTAC itself were an anathema to the Cambodian culture and have produced serious consequences on the economy and on the health and safety of Cambodian people. Finally, rotation of key personnel at critical junctures seriously retarded progress in planning and implementing the electoral process.

In early spring, 1993, as the UN prepared to begin its operations in Somalia, a mission even larger than UNTAC, clear consequences for its activities in Cambodia emerged. UN personnel turned their attentions and reallocated their resources to the new undertaking. Top UNTAC officials admitted that the UN could not provide a neutral environment. The elections would proceed, but with little enthusiasm and without the full logistical support necessary to do anything but go through the exercise. The future of Cambodia was anyone's guess, but it appeared that peace and stability were not in its near future.

By May 1993, the Khmer Rouge had attacked Siem Riep, the location of the ancient Khmer empire, Angkor Wat, and the ideological center of the former Khmer Rouge regime. It had targeted and killed or robbed several UNTAC personnel, withdrawn its representatives from the capital, Phnom Penh, and massacred dozens of ethnic Vietnamese in floating villages on Cambodia's large interior lake, the Tonle Sap. Further, it had publicly pledged to violently disrupt the polling. The UN frantically gathered intelligence, fortified Phnom Penh, and tried to organize some kind of emergency evacuation plan! The UN secretary-general, Boutros Boutros-Ghali, and UNTAC's top echelon refused to cancel the elections but, instead, settled privately for "credible and survivable" elections and a 30 percent voter turnout, as opposed to the 70 percent mandate earlier required.

The UN would hold the elections and leave Cambodia as soon as possible. Most energies and resources were reallocated from supporting the elections to securing UN personnel and implementing the UN's withdrawal.

In the final weeks before the election, UNTAC was scrambling to gather intelligence on Khmer Rouge's positions, had "entrusted" the security of the polling stations to the Cambodian army and air force and was attempting to stretch remaining resources to support the elections while preparing for evacuation. It had to mollify UN civilians, especially the volunteer electoral workers who, following the assassination of a Japanese district electoral supervisor in the province of Kampong Thom, were threatening to boycott the entire process (over 60 returned to their countries prior to the elections). The terrible reality permeating both UNTAC employees and the Cambodian populace was that UNTAC was not in control and the UN would not, could not, protect or save them.

Despite a large percentage of polling stations having been eliminated or consolidated because of logistics or security, the Cambodian people voted in unprecedented numbers. By the third day of voting, 90 percent of registered voters had cast their ballots. They voted to return the "All-Father" Prince Sihanouk, they voted against the Vietnamese, and they voted in spite of their intense fear of the Khmer Rouge guerrillas and the very real threat of violence.

The elections were a success.

With the exception of a brief secessionist movement by the losing state of Cambodia's ruling party, Cambodia's new interim coalition government and constituent assembly seemed to be moving forward toward some form of national reconciliation. The Khmer Rouge, unable to retain any legitimacy given the size of the plebiscite, attempted to negotiate any place within the new government and at almost any cost.

It appears that none of the parties, including the United States and Japan, the two major players behind the scenes, got what they wanted, but perhaps they got what they deserved. Instead of a "winner," there was a fragile coalition government of pro- and anti-Vietnam factions, of royalists and communists. Without a solid foundation due to UNTAC's inability to achieve the rest of its mandate—demobilization and rehabilitation—these former enemies had an impossible task of maintaining a government, let alone rebuilding Cambodia's shattered infrastructure and society. The coalition government collapsed in a bloody coup July 1997. Hun Sen, the then second prime minister, took complete control of the government, his power affirmed in the second national elections held in 1998.

The UN's apparent success and failure in Cambodia demonstrates the intransigence of the problem, i.e., the reconciliation of disparate cultures in a global community that is, itself, not unified in its aspirations or values. If the UN is to ever realize its mandate, it must change significantly, both in its administrative structure and in its manner of operations, while its constituent bodies, including the United States, must internalize a unified commitment to world peace based on diversity and self-determination, not on vested interests and hidden global agendas. It cannot rely on being "lucky," as it has been in Cambodia. The UN's being there was critical to the election going forward, but, ironically, it was its failure to be effective in carrying out its mandate that finally forced even the most passive Khmer to go to the polls and vote!

EPILOGUE

Edwards's explanation for the civil war and genocide that overwhelmed Cambodia in the '60s and '70s was that it was the result of underlying latent tensions exacerbated by the Vietnam War. He goes on to conclude that the "political turmoil caused by the war formed a vacuum of authority that gave the Khmer Rouge an opportunity that otherwise might never have occurred."[5] In 2007 Cambodia is not yet a functioning democracy.

David Chandler, longtime Cambodian historian, describes modern Cambodia as an inward-looking, family-oriented conservative society, willing to be ruled, unwilling to join the scramble for development (allowing foreign investment to make the new money and siphon off its natural resources) and thus remaining a poor and underdeveloped nation relative to its Southeast Asian neighbors.[6]

The author spent three months in Cambodia in 2006, living mostly in Phnom Penh. HIV-AIDS, prostitution, gunrunning, gambling, human trafficking, and illegal logging seem to be the currency of the day. A few modern shopping centers and grocery stores struggle to service the small emerging middle class while the majority stays poor and undereducated. The government is autocratic and corrupt. Political opposition is stifled, sometimes ruthlessly. The genocide is over, the civil war is over, but whether or not Cambodia can become a twenty-first-century state is still uncertain.

On a more positive note, life is relatively peaceful and the middle class is evolving, albeit slowly. Young people are exploring nonviolence and democratic principles. Certainly the young men who were my translators in the 1992–1993 UNTAC mission argue well for the future; both now have MBAs, are married, and have good jobs in administration and banking. One is an entrepreneur who dreams of modernity and prosperity; the other reads the *Federalist Papers* and dreams of democracy. Unfortunately most of their neighbors are too busy eking out their survivals to dream of anything.

NOTES

1. M. Edwards, "The Rise of the Khmer Rouge in Cambodia: Internal or External Origins," *Asian Affairs* 35, no. 1 (2004): 59.

2. Primary source unless otherwise noted: D. Coday, "Young and Searching in Cambodia," *National Catholic Reporter,* 30 June 2000, 14–15.

3. Edwards, "The Rise of the Khmer Rouge in Cambodia," 64.

4. S. Williams, "Genocide: The Cambodian Experience," *International Criminal Law Review* 5 (2005): 452.

5. Edwards, "The Rise of the Khmer Rouge in Cambodia," 65.

6. D. Chandler, *A History of Cambodia,* 3rd ed. (Boulder, CO: Westview Press, 2000), 247.

4 Armed Groups and Diplomacy: East Timor's FRETILIN Guerrillas

Gene Christy

The Red Cross Bell helicopter flew low along the south coast. It was dry season. Only a few wispy clouds hovered over the nearby mountains. Visibility was great. Several hundred feet below, tin roofs gleamed from new villages strung along the coast road. A few Timorese looked up and waved. Most kept at their daily tasks. The scene made one wonder where FRETILIN guerrillas could hide.[1] Maybe they were just a few thieves and thugs as officials in Jakarta and Dili were saying in 1983.

Our stops in Ainaro and Viqueque had been uneventful. It was after lunch, but children greeted us with cries of *"selamat pagi"* (good morning). They were going to the new Indonesian schools. Warehouses were stocked with USAID corn and cooking oil.[2] A few shops had Pepsi and packaged ramen noodles. Not exactly a famine, we thought. There might still be problems, but food supplies and security in the south seemed much improved. The report to Washington would be positive.

Suddenly, the helicopter lurched upward. It turned out over the water. The pilot announced we could not stop in Los Palos. Something about an attack on soldiers at a weekly market, he said. Flying higher over the mountains than before, he set course north to Baucau.

The pilot set down in a military compound. He promised to return after refueling at a nearby airfield. The Indonesian commander welcomed his two unexpected guests. He offered cups of bitter local coffee. Much sooner than expected, we heard an incoming helicopter. Then the air was full of the thump, thump, thump of helicopters. The birds

A career member of the U.S. foreign service, Ambassador Christy is currently the State Department political adviser to the combatant commander, U.S. Pacific Command. Previously, he was the State Department adviser to the president of the Naval War College and a professor in the National Security Decision Making faculty. Prior to his arrival in Newport in September 2005, Ambassador Christy served as ambassador of the United States to the Southeast Asian nation of Brunei Darussalam from 2002 to 2005. In his 35-year career with the Department of State, Ambassador Christy served in Indonesia twice (both the U.S. consulate in Surabaya and the U.S. embassy in Jakarta), in Turkey two times (both at the U.S. embassy in Ankara), and at the U.S. embassy in Kuala Lumpur, Malaysia. Ambassador Christy was a pioneer in establishing the U.S. embassy in Ashgabat, Turkmenistan, after the fall of the Soviet Union (1992–94), and the ambassador served as political counselor at the U.S. embassy in Port-au-Prince, Haiti, both before and during the period of the U.S.-led intervention (1994–96). The ambassador has also served on several occasions in the State Department in Washington, DC. He was director for Asia at the National Security Council 2000–01. A member of the Senior Foreign Service, he has the rank of Minister Counselor.

landed one by one. Soldiers and medics ran to meet them. On some stretchers, wounded soldiers writhed. On others, nothing moved.

The commander squirmed in his chair. He muttered to himself in Indonesian. This was not part of the American diplomats' well-scripted program. They weren't even set to stop here. What would he tell Jakarta? Reality had trumped the best of military scheduling. On that fair day, FRETILIN was not a spent force. It was a deadly one.

ARMED GROUPS AND HUMAN RIGHTS REPORTING: INDONESIA AND EAST TIMOR[3]

My presence in Baucau with a foreign service colleague was not planned, but it was no accident. "Being there" was precisely the point of the trip. An armed group, FRETILIN (Revolutionary Front for an Independent East Timor), and U.S. diplomacy came together that day.

East Timor was an enigma. Most states accepted Indonesia's sovereign control of the territory. That extended to control of access. The Indonesian military managed the outward flow of people and information, but it did so incompletely. Stories of FRETILIN attacks and Indonesian counterattacks slipped out. There were claims of famine and health crises. The Indonesians countered that these were lies or exaggerations. The U.S. government required diplomats on the ground to make its own assessment. I was one of those diplomats.

The market attack happened on my second trip to Indonesian-controlled East Timor. The first took place in late November 1983. A few weeks before, during Defense Secretary Weinberger's stop in Bali, an Indonesian Navy captain interviewed me over dinner. Captain Sudibyo worked for military intelligence chief General Murdani. Sudibyo controlled access to Timor. He wanted to know if a year of study at Cornell's Southeast Asia Studies Program had prejudiced my views.[4] I passed muster.

In the embassy, I was responsible for human rights reporting. A midlevel foreign service officer, I had previous experience in Indonesia and as a political officer in Turkey. There, human rights was part of the job, too.

A graduate of State Department Indonesian-language training, I spoke the language with an East Java accent after serving from 1974 to 1976 in the U.S. consulate in Surabaya. That consulate covered all of southeastern Indonesia and Portuguese Timor. The principal officer was accredited to Lisbon. As junior officers, two of us visited the colony's capital briefly in 1974. The Portuguese were still in control. Dili had the look of a seaside Mediterranean town. There were no overt signs of the turmoil to come. That visit made a useful reference point for the visits I made between 1982 and 1985. It also proved to be an unexpected bookend to my Timor experiences when I returned 25 years later and met with the head of FRETILIN, who by that time was East Timor's acknowledged political leader as it prepared for independence.

In 1982, human rights held an important place in American diplomacy with Indonesia. Washington policy makers and analysts closely read embassy human rights reporting. The embassy prepared the first draft of the annual country human rights report, which was not just a compilation of facts. It was also a policy document, as both critics and supporters used it to back their cases for change or continuity in policy. U.S. assistance to Indonesia was at stake. A credible human rights report needed direct, documented information.

The Carter years had been complicated for the bilateral relationship. President Carter understood that Indonesia was important. He wanted to respond to Jakarta's requests for support. Development and military aid were at the top of the Indonesians' agenda. But Suharto's military-dominated "New Order" had a checkered history. It had brutally suppressed the Indonesian Communist Party. Members and sympathizers had been jailed for years. Many never had a trial. Giving economic development and stability highest priority, the New Order de-emphasized electoral politics and restricted freedoms of speech, assembly, and the press.

Also, the takeover of Timor in 1975 had been violent. The regime stood accused of violating bilateral agreements by using American arms. Members of Congress, already clamoring for the administration to win release of political detainees, pressed Carter to take action on East Timor. They talked of restricting U.S. military assistance.[5]

The pressure carried over into the new Reagan administration. Indonesian diplomacy had eroded support for a critical UN General Assembly resolution to the point that no country would sponsor a new one after 1982. Diplomats at the UN largely accepted Indonesia's argument that its incorporation of the former Portuguese colony was a success. Hearts and minds were being won. Indonesia's military was mopping up the last remnants of FRETILIN's fighting forces. So Indonesia and its international supporters argued.

A band of African and Portuguese diplomats and human rights advocates thought otherwise. FRETILIN also had diplomats. The best known was José Ramos-Horta, a key negotiator at the UN in New York who traveled on a diplomatic passport issued by Mozambique.[6] Their voices echoed in the halls of Congress, especially with Democratic Party members like Tony Hall (OH) and Steven Solarz (NY) and in the Senate with Paul Tsongas (MA).

The Reagan administration wanted to demonstrate renewed interest in Southeast Asia. Doing so called for stronger relations with Jakarta. The administration sought to increase security assistance levels. The Indonesians wanted to buy more American military equipment at favorable rates. U.S. officials worked to increase exchange opportunities under the International Military Education and Training program.[7] Congressional criticism of Indonesia's human rights record and threats to curtail military aid put these goals at risk.

One response was to set up regular on-the-ground embassy reporting from Timor. Credible reporting required frequent visits and, preferably, repeated ones. It called for talking to other diplomats, humanitarian relief and aid officials, and journalists. It demanded following up on allegations from human rights activists and FRETILIN supporters. And reconciling critics' allegations with Indonesian claims was never easy.

Diplomacy and FRETILIN came together in the human rights report. That was true of armed groups throughout the world.

ARMED GROUPS AND THE ANNUAL COUNTRY HUMAN RIGHTS REPORTS

The *Country Reports on Human Rights Practices* debuted in 1977.[8] They had their origin in struggles between Congress and the executive. In response to the allegedly amoral policies of President Nixon and Henry Kissinger, Congress sought to deny U.S. assistance or loans to governments that grossly violated human rights. Congress intended the reports to provide a public, objective basis to evaluate human rights practices.

Initially, Congress limited the reports to 82 recipients of U.S. economic and military assistance, including Indonesia. Later, coverage expanded to all UN members.[9] The reports produced significant tugs-of-war between Congress and the executive in the first years. Early disputes included which human rights criteria would be examined. Another source of contention was that "no one could agree on how to characterize a 'consistent pattern of gross violations.' There were no guidelines to what could be expected and no systematic way to compare human rights situations."[10]

Who would write the reports was also an issue. In 1978, the Library of Congress recommended that Congress find or set up an organization to prepare them. This reflected the experiences of the previous two years when reports seemed to align analysis with the policy preferences of the State Department's geographic bureaus. There were also tensions between State's reporting obligations, its mission to maintain diplomatic relations, and other foreign policy objectives.[11] Ultimately, responsibility for preparing the reports remained with State because it had presence in almost every country and because there was no consensus on an alternative.

After his inauguration in 1981, President Ronald Reagan set out to separate his approach to human rights from President Carter's. Realism would come before idealism. Reagan argued that the Carter approach was morally unsound, ineffective, and threatening to U.S. security interests. His policy team felt U.S. criticism seriously undermined regimes that might be authoritarian but at least were not totalitarian and communist.[12] The Reagan team wanted to focus on "quiet diplomacy" rather than punishing friends like Indonesia through restrictions on foreign assistance.

Governments' responses to armed groups, such as FRETILIN, often lead to allegations of human rights violations. Where rule of law is weak, military accountability is rare, and the state tightly controls access to information, violations are more likely to occur. By statute and practice, "the Country Reports on Human Rights Practices cover internationally recognized individual civil, political and workers rights, as set forth in the Universal Declaration of Human Rights. These rights include freedom from torture or other cruel, inhuman or degrading treatment or punishment, from prolonged detention without charges, from disappearances or clandestine detention, and from other flagrant violations of the right to life, liberty, and the security of the person."[13]

In response to rebellions or armed resistance, governments often restrict these rights. Because of a lack of transparency and accountability, authoritarian regimes are particularly subject to criticism for violations. These include torture; prolonged detention without trial; restrictions on freedoms of speech, association, and assembly; and forced displacement. Human rights report drafts I wrote while serving in both Indonesia and Turkey were laced with coverage of alleged government abuses of armed groups and their supporters.

In those early years of human rights reporting, guidelines were evolving. The State Department did not offer formal human rights training. Indeed, it was only in the mid-1980s that State started a training program for midcareer political officers. That course included political reporting skills, such as interviewing and visit preparation, but human rights reporting skills were not singled out for special emphasis.[14] Only in February 1990 did State's Foreign Service Institute open its first Human Rights in Diplomacy course.[15]

Few foreign service officers saw the absence of formal training about human rights and armed groups as a problem. We were bright. We were culturally aware. We usually had language skills. Our grasp of the policy environment was good. Where we followed an issue over a period of time or picked it up from a strong predecessor, we knew which questions were urgent. And State, driven by inquiries from Congress and the press, made sure embassy leaders knew what policy makers needed.

ARMED GROUPS: EAST TIMOR'S FRETILIN

For a human rights reporting officer in Indonesia, FRETILIN presented a challenge. Apart from a few diplomats at the UN in New York, U.S. officials did not knowingly engage with FRETILIN. Much of the information gathered about FRETILIN was inferential or secondhand.

FRETILIN was one of three political parties to emerge in Portuguese Timor. The others were the conservative UDT, Timorese Democratic Union, and APODETI, Timorese Popular Democratic Association, which initially called for integration with Indonesia. FRETILIN appeared a few weeks after the April 1974 Armed Forces Movement coup in Lisbon. It was the most ideological and left-leaning of the three parties. In those heady days, its founders declared the party to be based on "the universal doctrines of socialism and democracy."[16] FRETILIN found itself in control of the Portuguese territory in August 1975, after a brief civil conflict and withdrawal by Portuguese officials to the nearby island of Atauro.

Unwilling to accept the emergence of an independent and "communistic" ministate on its border, Indonesia responded. On 7 December Indonesian military forces launched an assault on the capital. Jakarta claimed its fighters were not soldiers but "volunteers" responding to a call from anti-FRETILIN Timorese. My wife and I watched on a number of mornings in this period as those Indonesian "volunteers" mounted military trucks lined up outside the marine base next to our house. They were headed to Surabaya's port and on to East Timor to fight.

In response to the Indonesian assault, FRETILIN's armed component, Falintil (Armed Forces for the National Liberation of East Timor), withdrew to the mountains and began a guerrilla campaign. At that time, it had about 20,000 men. Of these, 2,500 were a professional corps of regular troops. Another 7,000 had received military training under the Portuguese, while some 10,000 had been given short military courses. FRETILIN forces lacked formally trained leaders. But those it had, such as "Xanana" Gusmão, were shrewd and inspiring. FRETILIN also began its campaign with a substantial supply of modern NATO-type light weaponry, as the Portuguese had recently replenished their arsenal. Sympathetic Portuguese officers turned those arms over to Falintil.[17]

Over the next year, Indonesian forces took effective control of Dili, Baucau, and other significant towns. Once in control, the Indonesian government commenced a "hearts and minds" program. It included infrastructure building, agricultural development, and expanded educational and health services. More of Indonesia's development budget went to East Timor on a per capita basis than to any other province.

FRETILIN continued its guerrilla campaign. Numbers of fighters declined due to losses to Indonesian forces, disease and poor medical care, and exhaustion. However, a core of effective fighters remained six years after Indonesia's intervention.

FRETILIN AND EAST TIMOR: GROUND TRUTH

By 1982, Dili was stable and secure. Travel outside the capital was the only way to obtain a real sense of conditions. That presented problems. Roads were terrible. The few paved ones extended only a few kilometers beyond Dili and a handful of other towns. Most towns had no paved streets. Plus, security was an issue. Even Indonesian officials avoided road travel after dark because of concerns about FRETILIN or accidental Indonesian military assaults. Indonesian officials would not consider overnight stays for diplomats outside Dili. That policy ruled out extended road trips.

The combination of miserable roads and need to return to Dili each evening made travel by helicopter the only practical option. Initially, we hitched rides on a Bell helicopter leased by the International Committee of the Red Cross (ICRC). In theory, these flights were not for our benefit. We went where the Red Cross had programs or needed to follow up. Fortunately, our needs and those of the Red Cross often overlapped.

Flight plans required military approval. Itinerary changes were not allowed. Trip planners offered limited flexibility and close oversight. But the Red Cross aircraft had only four seats, meaning room for a pilot, two diplomats, and one more passenger. An ICRC or Catholic Relief Services (CRS) staffer often took the fourth seat. Rarely was there space for an official escort from Dili, although local officials met and accompanied visitors at each stop.

When there were two diplomats, we split up whenever possible at each stop. This increased chances of unscripted conversations and observations. Also, I always carried an Olympus OM-1 camera and took many photos. Usually dressed in their best outfits, senior local officials would tire of following the shutterbug down muddy paths, providing me unguarded moments to snap photos and talk to villagers.

Travel by helicopter was the only way to go, but it had its heart-stopping moments. The diversion of the flight to Baucau described earlier was one of those. Another coincided with my final visit in this period. The Red Cross helicopter was no longer available, so we boarded an Indonesian military helo in Dili. Just as it cleared the ground, there was a tremendous roar. The helicopter shook. Two Indonesian Air Force jets made a dangerously low pass a hundred feet over the airport. Had the helicopter lifted off a few seconds earlier . . . Better not to dwell on the risks of "friendly fire," we told ourselves at dinner that evening. Besides, a much greater concern during the flight was the steady drip of a reddish, oily fluid into the cabin. It was preferable not to think too much about the maintenance history of the aircraft until it touched down in Dili at the end of the day.

Fleshing out schedules for visits always tested our negotiating skills. Rarely did the requests we made in Jakarta for meetings or travel make it to Dili intact. Most trips began with a discussion of whom to see, where to go, and when. We always sought appointments with the governor and military commander. The former was generous with his time; the latter was frequently away or too busy. Meetings with Apostolic Administrator Monsignor Belo shortly after his investiture in 1983 were easy to arrange. As he became more outspoken and critical of Indonesian actions against FRETILIN, local hosts were less accommodating. Seeing Monsignor Belo became a kind of game.[18]

On one visit in 1984, State Department Indonesia desk officer Charles "Chuck" Morris came along. On arrival, we asked about our request for a meeting with the Timorese church leader. Trip organizers claimed he was unavailable. Exactly why was murky. Either he was out of Dili or he had too many official duties to fit us in.

At the end of the second day, the escorts dropped us at the hotel and confirmed the start time for the next day. A few minutes later, Chuck and I told hotel staff we were going for a walk . . . which we did, straight to Monsignor Belo's front gate. His staff said he was there and wanted to offer coffee. When we told him how lucky it was to find him at home and able to meet, the church leader was bemused. Neither travel plans nor pastoral duties prevented his giving up more than an hour to talk.

When our escorts said Monsignor Belo was not available, we had been skeptical. We thought they might be shaving the truth. It would be better to verify. Chuck had briefings for congressional staffers scheduled on his return to Washington. For him, meeting with the church leader was essential.

We also knew our hosts would learn of the meeting, since Belo's home was closely watched.[19] But up to the moment of our departure, neither they nor we said anything about the meeting.

ANY FRETILIN FIGHTERS AROUND HERE?

In all of the visits to East Timor during this time, I never knowingly saw a FRETILIN fighter. There was no doubt of their presence, however. Although allowing that FRETILIN continued to cause problems, Indonesian officials downplayed its numbers and threat. FRETILIN forces went from being described as "fighters" to "security disturbers," a catchall term also used on Java in 1984 to describe summarily executed criminals. Numbers were always vague, usually in the hundreds, and never more than 1,000 by official accounts.

Officials claimed local support for FRETILIN was dwindling. The Timorese no longer considered its members guerrillas but thieves and criminals. Farmers and herders did not want to leave the resettlement villages and return to their homes because moving back would make them vulnerable to FRETILIN pressure. Besides, they were now accustomed to the government-supplied goods and services, which would be harder to obtain in their upland villages. That was the official story. And in some places, such as the western section of the territory, it had a credible ring.[20]

When asked about the armed group, officials outside Dili usually claimed no problems. Perhaps there had been FRETILIN activity a year ago or perhaps over the mountain in another village, but not in their immediate areas recently. Even if there had been a problem, it was under control now.

Such was the story in Los Palos when two of us arrived in 1984. The local commander took the American diplomats to his headquarters briefing room. This kind of meeting was unusual. Local army commanders had a habit of being "away." Civilian diplomats frequently saw a subordinate who did not have much to share. Defense attachés had better luck. Their reception was warmer, if not necessarily more informative.

This instance was different. The commander ordered a soldier to open a curtain covering operational maps on the wall. No secrets here, he beamed. You are *orang kita* (one of us). While acknowledging there had been FRETILIN activity in the recent past (which is why we asked to visit Los Palos), he assured us FRETILIN was no longer a concern. The area was under control.

To prove the point, he set up travel east of town to the site of the last encounter with FRETILIN. We could see just how safe it was. As the open army vehicles plunged into a sea of tall reeds, the commander talked about the success of his local "hearts and minds" programs. More goods in the markets, more construction, more jobs, he said.

Suddenly, the sergeant in the following vehicle called the convoy to a stop. He was monitoring the radio. Soldiers jumped from the vehicles, set up a perimeter, and went into a defensive crouch. After a quick reconnaissance and consultation, the commander ordered a hasty exit. "Just being cautious," he explained. We appreciated the assurances. But the looks on the soldiers' faces told another story. And a brief exchange overheard on return to the local headquarters confirmed there had been reports of armed men moving through the reeds earlier that morning.

One of the hardest questions for a diplomat to address was the depth of local support for FRETILIN fighters. Sympathizers of FRETILIN outside Indonesia claimed it remained high. Indonesian officials argued it was in decline. There were no objective measures. Impressions were built on observation, official claims, often hasty bits of conversation, and rare, but treasured, candid exchanges with an official or individual Timorese.

In 1983, stories coming out of Timor said large numbers of villagers from Viqueque had been rounded up and abruptly deported to Atauro Island just north of Dili. Some said their relocations were a response to FRETILIN's breaking of a cease-fire. Later, the ICRC confirmed Indonesian officials were resettling villagers from temporary facilities on Atauro to a site in a river valley near Cailaco, west of Dili. CRS told USAID it had an emergency feeding program at Cailaco, which was near an existing CRS program site.

Human rights activists accused the Indonesian military of moving the villagers to punish their support for FRETILIN. Military officials claimed the villagers asked to move to avoid FRETILIN intimidation. Some of the villagers were still on Atauro when we flew there. Even the children were reluctant to talk. An ICRC nurse was mostly tight lipped. She said conditions for detainees had improved but were still not good. She expressed special concern about detainees' access to food and medical support at their destination.

At Cailaco, there were scores of freshly built plywood and tin-roofed houses. The settlement was remarkable for the very small number of men and boys, for the lack of private gardens, and for its sullen inhabitants. No one denied asking for resettlement, but the few who spoke said they hoped to return to their home area. This was a stop where the OM-1 camera was invaluable for a few unmonitored moments.

This particular visit began with conflicting claims from the Indonesians and their critics. We departed with a feeling that FRETILIN's appeal had not weakened, at least among these Timorese from Viqueque. Already resettled in their home area once, their loyalty was seen as so suspect that the government felt compelled to move them again without much preparation and apparently in response to a FRETILIN provocation. The challenge FRETILIN posed to Indonesia's control of the territory was significant enough to warrant a tactic that would become known and stir outsider criticism.

HUMAN RIGHTS REPORTS: REALISM BEFORE IDEALISM, BUT REALITY FIRST

The country reports on human rights practices for Indonesia during this period demonstrated the importance of monitoring FRETILIN and the value of access. The report for 1982, for instance, noted allegations of inhumane treatment and arbitrary arrest and imprisonment and said visitors had been unable to substantiate them.[21] Later reports offered more detail on these issues based on increased access through embassy visits and more productive exchanges with ICRC representatives, who themselves had wider and deeper access to detainees. The level of information about the number and whereabouts of detainees, for instance, expanded significantly between the 1982 and 1984 reports.[22]

By contrast, allegations of torture made by international human rights organizations, such as Amnesty International, were ongoing through the period. Conclusive evidence was virtually impossible to obtain. Individuals who might have been abused were, understandably, reluctant to come forward, as visitors' contacts were closely monitored and protection provided by rule of law was weak throughout Indonesia. Timorese officials were, at their most candid, circumspect. When asked in 1984 about the alleged existence of a "torture manual," for example, Governor Mario Carrascalão told two of us he was not aware of any such manual. The governor added that some unauthorized practices of the past, to include alleged physical abuse of detainees, had stopped. As a matter of policy, such treatment was unacceptable, he emphasized.

Because of the structure and public nature of the reports, such carefully constructed responses rarely found their ways into the published documents. Moreover, the topical structure of the reports (respect for the integrity of the persons, respect for civil rights, etc.) meant there was no single narrative with respect to East Timor or FRETILIN. The reports covered these issues within categories. And by 1985, other concerns, such as covert summary executions of criminals on Java and Sumatra and government responses to riots in Jakarta's port area, received at least as much coverage as East Timor.[23]

The reports were nevertheless important. There were very few other public sources of firsthand information about FRETILIN. Only a few journalists were able to visit East Timor. Amnesty International and advocates for the Timorese in Europe often had access to dated or indirect testimony. The U.S. human rights reports took account of a wide variety of sources, including information from the Indonesian government. They reflected direct access to the territory where FRETILIN operated. And they represented the official views of the U.S. government—which both gave them credibility and made them subject to criticism for being influenced by administration policy preferences.[24]

FRETILIN AND EAST TIMOR: EPILOGUE

A last chapter in my personal experience of FRETILIN happened in November 2000. By that time, the Timorese had voted for independence and were making the transition to independence under a UN mandate. As a director for Asia at the National Security Council, I was in Dili for an international conference on building Timor's national security forces. Resistance leader Xanana Gusmão had become provisional president of the emerging government. He opened our meetings, and I had a chance to speak to him briefly. Neither of us could recall a previous encounter.

FRETILIN's ascent to power began in late August 1999, when the people of East Timor voted overwhelmingly for separation from Indonesia. The preference for independence came as no surprise to most Timorese. The margin of support shocked Indonesians and many outside observers.

By that time, FRETILIN had been out of business as a fighting force for more than a decade. It had transformed from a guerrilla movement to become the leading member of a broad national resistance coalition. From the late 1980s on, the "troops" of that coalition were no longer Falintil fighters but mostly young students. Their weapons were no longer military arms but petitions and protests. Because FRETILIN had borne the brunt of the resistance effort in the early years, it maintained moral leadership among Timorese. After 1999, FRETILIN organized itself as a political party preparing to govern an independent East Timor.[25] And that was the setting for my meeting Xanana that morning in 2000.

NOTES

The views expressed in this article are those of the author, and do not necessarily reflect those of the U.S. Department of State or the U.S. Government.

1. Revolutionary Front for an Independent East Timor, or the *Frente Revolucionária de Timor-Leste Independente* (FRETILIN), was one of several parties that emerged in the wake of Lisbon's April 1974 "Carnation Revolution." It went on to lead the resistance movement and then reorganized as a political party after 1999. After East Timor gained its independence from Indonesia, FRETILIN became one of several parties competing for power in a multiparty system. See "Revolutionary Front for an Independent East Timor," Wikipedia, en.wikipedia.org/wiki/Revolutionary_Front_for_an_Independent_East_Timor.

2. United States Agency for International Development (USAID) is an independent federal government agency that receives overall foreign policy guidance from the secretary of state. See www.usaid.gov/.

3. Since restoration of independence on 20 May 2002, the official name of East Timor is Democratic Republic of Timor-Leste. During the period under consideration, 1982–1985, the U.S. government referred to the territory as East Timor and that name will be used in this paper.

4. Cornell had one of the top two Southeast Asia studies programs in the United States when I attended in 1980–1981 under State Department sponsorship. Many Suharto government officials considered the Cornell Modern Indonesia Project, headed by Professor George McT. Kahin, to be unfairly critical. Professor Kahin was my faculty adviser and mentor while at Cornell. He arranged for me to use office space in the CMIP building. Because of the quality of professors and researchers at Cornell, scholars and even Suharto government officials considered the CMIP and related Echols collection in the Cornell Library to be an academic mecca for Indonesia studies in the United States. Captain Sudibyo knew of my time at Cornell, and we discussed my course of study.

5. Bernard K. Gordon, "The United States and Asia in 1982: Year of Tenterhooks," *Asian Survey* 23, no. 1 (January 1983): 7; James Dunn, *Timor: A People Betrayed* (Milton, Queensland: Jacaranda Press, 1983), 350–55.

Gordon provides the broad context of U.S. policy in Asia during 1982, including events and key elements in U.S.-Indonesia policy. Dunn's critical assessment takes greater account of the U.S. government policy-making environment.

6. Dunn, *Timor,* 367. Support to FRETILIN from Mozambique and Angola was modest but important. In 1984, the embassy in Jakarta received a request from the U.S. embassy in Mozambique to comment on an application from Ramos-Horta for renewal of the diplomatic visa in his Mozambique passport. Notwithstanding U.S. acknowledgment of Indonesia's control of East Timor, Embassy Jakarta offered no objection, and Ramos-Horta received the new visa.

7. W. Scott Butcher, e-mail exchange with author, 4 April 2007. A retired foreign service officer, Scott was political counselor at the U.S. embassy in Jakarta 1981–1984; he traveled with a multinational diplomatic delegation to Timor in August 1981. Dunn, *Timor,* 354.

8. *International Security Assistance and Arms Export Control Act,* Public Law 94-329, *U.S. Statutes at Large* 90 (1976): 729, codified at *U.S. Code* 22, sec. 2151n.

9. Judith Innes de Neufville, "Human Rights Reporting as a Policy Tool: An Examination of the State Department *Country Reports,*" *Human Rights Quarterly* 8, no. 4 (November 1986): 683.

10. Ibid., 684.

11. Ibid., 685.

12. David Carleton and Michael Stohl, "The Foreign Policy of Human Rights: Rhetoric and Reality from Jimmy Carter to Ronald Reagan," *Human Rights Quarterly* 7, no. 2 (May 1985): 205.

13. Bureau of Democracy, Human Rights, and Labor, overview and acknowledgments of *Country Reports on Human Rights Practices,* 2006, available at www.state.gov/g/drl/rls/hrrpt/2006/78716.htm.

14. Barbara S. Harvey, e-mail exchange with author, 19 March 2007. A retired FSO, Barbara directed the Foreign Service Institute's political officer training program, including for midlevel officers, from 1987 to 1989.

15. Pat Coyne, Office of the Registrar, Foreign Service Institute, Department of State, Washington, DC, telephone conversation with author, 14 March 2007.

16. Dunn, *Timor,* 63.

17. Ibid., 291.

18. After being elevated to bishop of East Timor in 1988, Belo shared the Nobel Peace Prize with José Ramos-Horta in 1996 for his role as "the foremost leader of the people of East Timor."

19. Arnold S. Kohen, *From the Place of the Dead: The Epic Struggles of Bishop Belo of East Timor* (New York: St. Martin's Griffin, 1999), 138.

20. By the end of the 1980s, it became evident that FRETILIN's fighting days were ending. A combination of Indonesian civil and military programs, including offers of amnesty, separation from supporters in rural areas, and secret negotiations with Xanana Gusmão, ate away at FRETILIN's capabilities. This historic trend, however, was ambiguous in the first half of the 1980s.

21. Committee on Foreign Relations, U.S. Senate, and Committee on Foreign Affairs, U.S. House of Representatives, *Country Reports on Human Rights Practices for 1982,* report submitted by the Department of State in accordance with sections 116(d) and 502(b) of the Foreign Assistance Act of 1961, as amended, 98th Cong., 1st sess., 1983, Joint Committee Print; Committee on Foreign Affairs, U.S. House of Representatives, and Committee on Foreign Relations, U.S. Senate, *Country Reports on Human Rights Practices for 1983,* submitted by the Department of State in accordance with sections 116(d) and 502(b) of the Foreign Assistance Act of 1961, as amended, 98th Cong., 2nd sess., 1984, Joint Committee Print; Committee on Foreign Relations, U.S. Senate, and Committee on Foreign Affairs, U.S. House of Representatives, *Country Reports on Human Rights Practices for 1984,* submitted by the Department of State in accordance with sections 116(d) and 502(b) of the Foreign Assistance Act of 1961, as amended, 99th Cong., 1st sess., 1985, Joint Committee Print; Committee on Foreign Affairs, U.S. House of Representatives, and Committee on Foreign Relations, U.S. Senate, *Country Reports*

on Human Rights Practices for 1985, submitted by the Department of State in accordance with sections 116(d) and 502(b) of the Foreign Assistance Act of 1961, as amended, 99th Cong., 2nd sess., 1986, Joint Committee Print.

22. *Country Reports on Human Rights Practices for 1982,* 707–19; and *Country Reports on Human Rights Practices for 1984,* 771–83.

23. *Country Reports on Human Rights Practices for 1985,* 773–85.

24. The reports' importance to both the government of Indonesia and its critics was evident in their respective reactions. After issuance of the annual report each February, the Indonesian Department of Foreign Affairs registered Indonesia's objection to the U.S. presumption in assessing its human rights performance, as well as specifics of the report, in diplomatic exchanges with the embassy in Jakarta and/or at the State Department in Washington. Similarly, Amnesty International (AI), which had a long record of monitoring and criticizing Indonesian human rights practices, published its own annual human rights assessment that took issue with specifics in the State Department reports for Indonesia. Subsequent reports would then take account of AI's criticisms. As part of its information-gathering efforts, AI maintained contacts with FRETILIN representatives outside the territory, and it is my impression that FRETILIN viewed its association with AI, among other things, as a way to influence the content of the State Department reports. Beyond impressions gained from conversations with AI officials in this period and up to 1989 (I joined the Indonesia "desk" at State in 1985), the importance of AI to Timorese dissidents is evident in Kohen's biography of Bishop Belo (*From the Place of the Dead,* 169).

25. James Cotton, *East Timor, Australia and Regional Order: Intervention and Its Aftermath in Southeast Asia* (New York: RoutledgeCurzon, 2004), 152.

5 Adapting to a Changing Environment—The Irish Republican Army as an Armed Group

Timothy D. Hoyt

INTRODUCTION

For the purposes of this chapter, a working definition for armed groups includes but is not limited to classic insurgents, terrorists, guerrillas, militias, police agencies, criminal organizations, warlords, privatized military organizations, mercenaries, contracted security firms, pirates, drug cartels, apocalyptic religious extremists, orchestrated rioters and mobs, or tribal factions.

Each of the types of armed groups discussed here is an organization capable of perpetrating organized violence. They are distinguishable by their different forms and functions. Form refers here to their physical and organizational structures. Are they a small cell, for instance, or a large bureaucratic institution? How is authority conveyed and asserted? Function, on the other hand, refers to the role that they play in society and their operational and tactical methods. How do armed groups operate? How are they commanded? What types of violent acts do they commit, and at whose behest?

Some types of armed groups are usually associated with a central government and the maintenance of public order—police agencies and militias. Others are associated with the maintenance of local autonomy within an established political order—some militias, tribal factions, and warlords, for example, but also criminal organizations and drug cartels. Others are dedicated to opposing or overthrowing the existing political order—classic insurgents, terrorists, and guerrillas, and perhaps even orchestrated rioters and

Dr. Timothy D. Hoyt is a professor of strategy and policy at the U.S. Naval War College, where he has taught since 2002. He lectures on strategy, terrorism, counterinsurgency, totalitarian regimes, military transformation, and contemporary conflict, and also teaches an elective course on South Asian security. He received his undergraduate degrees from Swarthmore College, and his PhD in international relations and strategic studies from the Johns Hopkins University's Paul H. Nitze School of Advanced International Studies in 1997. Professor Hoyt taught graduate courses on security in the developing world, South Asian security, technology and international security, and military strategy at Georgetown University's School of Foreign Service from 1998 to 2002. In October 2003, he testified before two subcommittees of the House Committee on International Relations regarding terrorism in South and Southwest Asia. Dr. Hoyt is the author of *Military Industries and Regional Defense Policy* (Routledge, 2007), examining the role of military industry in the national security policies of India, Israel, and Iraq, and is beginning work on several book-length projects, including an analysis of American military strategy in the 21st century (London: Polity Press, forthcoming 2008–09) and a study of the strategy of the Irish Republican Army from 1913 to 2005. He is also the assistant editor of the *Journal of Strategic Studies*.

mobs. Finally, some exist primarily for profit—criminal organizations, privatized military organizations, mercenaries, contracted security firms, and pirates.

Some armed groups, particularly criminal groups, have no real higher aims. They are armed because violence is part of their occupation, and form and function are closely related for purely occupational reasons. Other armed groups defend society, communities, local elites, or a political class. In this case, their aims are relatively clear, and their forms and functions reflect the political systems or groups they are defending, the human and geographic terrains in which they operate, and traditional or professional standards inherited or acquired from similar groups and/or past experience.

This is not necessarily the case, however, with revolutionary political movements. These movements may find some or all of the different forms and functions of the various types of armed groups amenable to the pursuit of their broader political aims. Organizations taking one form—say, an insurgent or terrorist group—may still assume the functions of another (robbing banks, defending minority populations at risk). Revolutionary and political movements are using violence in the pursuit of political objectives—a type of war—and the various types of armed groups represent informal quasi-military structures or practice functions that can help achieve those aims. As a result, it is not surprising that they may demonstrate the characteristics of more than one type of armed group—sometimes sequentially, and sometimes simultaneously.

The year 2008 will be the 150th anniversary of the creation of the Irish Republican Brotherhood (IRB)—a transnational movement dedicated to the establishment of a united Irish republic through violence, and the antecedent of today's Irish Republican Army (IRA).[1] The Irish Republican Movement from its inception has been intensely political, deeply conspiratorial, and committed to the violent overthrow of British rule in Ireland. Its supporters, recruited by appeals to ideology, tradition, and even family links, co-opt and cooperate with a wide variety of social and political organizations, in addition to supporting violent activity in many forms. The overriding factor is the objective—the removal of official British presence in Ireland, and the unification of the island under local rule. The revolutionary movement the IRA represents has evolved and adapted itself to a wide range of forms and functions and has at various times looked and acted like many of the types of armed groups discussed in this volume. As a result, the IRA is a useful case study examining how and when armed groups shift their forms and/or their functions and how one kind of group can evolve into another.

This chapter is laid out in three sections. The first section is a (very) brief discussion of the history of the Irish Republican Movement and its evolution during the nineteenth and twentieth centuries. The second, and longest, section will look at the IRA's activities using the armed-groups methodology, highlighting the wide range of forms and functions the IRA has utilized during its long history. The final section will discuss the relevance of the IRA case to the future study of armed groups, emphasizing the importance of understanding underlying objectives. Revolutionary political movements may emerge and reemerge, exhibiting the characteristics of more than one type of armed group depending on their circumstances. In these cases, the armed-group methodology may confuse more than clarify, and the analyst must focus more on the objective than on the form or function of the organization.

IRELAND'S REPUBLICAN TRADITION

The Irish Republican Brotherhood was created as a secret, revolutionary movement to violently overthrow British rule in Ireland.[2] The president of the IRB, according to its by-laws, was the provisional leader of Ireland and all Irishmen until that day when a republic could be established.[3] IRB figures played key roles in Irish political and social life in the late nineteenth century, participating in legitimate politics (the Home Rule movement); clandestine and illegal violence (the Land League); and the flourishing of Irish culture, sports, and language in the late 1890s. In essence, the IRB attempted to secretly infiltrate and influence any activity that symbolically or actively opposed British rule. The one key unifying factor, however, was an understanding that legitimate politics could not and would not establish a republic. Revolutionary ideals were synonymous with violence, and the republic could not be established by the ballot box.[4]

The two organizations most closely associated with the Irish Republican Movement were formed, with considerable IRB participation, in the early 1900s. The Sinn Fein movement, later a political party, was intended to usurp British government authority through a policy of principled rejection of Britain's right to rule from Westminster. Sinn Fein later became an umbrella political movement for rejection of British rule from 1916 to 1921, and more recently has been the official political voice of the Irish Republican Army since 1948.[5] Today, Sinn Fein is the largest political party representing the nationalist (Catholic) community in Northern Ireland, and the only political party that runs in elections on both sides of the Irish/Northern Irish border.

The Irish Volunteers were organized as a nationalist militia in 1913, comprising over 180,000 members at the beginning of the First World War.[6] A small group of about 1,500 extremists, under the command of IRB leaders, seized central Dublin in 1916 (the "Easter Rising").[7] Survivors of the Rising provided the core of a larger organization that later called itself the Irish Republican Army (IRA). The IRA opposed British rule in the Anglo-Irish War of 1919–1921, relying on violent tactics, including assassination and insurgency, but also creating a shadow government acting as a police force and judiciary in many rural areas of Ireland. IRA and Sinn Fein leadership negotiated a cease-fire and later a treaty with the British government, establishing the Irish Free State (now the Irish Republic) and the province of Northern Ireland (which remains a part of the United Kingdom).[8] Extremists in the IRA rejected the treaty, fought and lost a civil war in1922–1923, and then became an underground movement still committed to the establishment of a 32-county Irish Republic.[9]

The IRA's rejection of partition and (until recently) the legitimacy of both the northern and southern political entities transformed the Irish Republican Movement. The IRA became, in the words of J. Bowyer Bell, "The Secret Army."[10] The dominating features of the organization were threefold. First, its commitment to violence as the only means of achieving the republic reversed, for all practical purposes, the traditional relationship of strategy subordinating itself to policy. The military leadership (embodied in the IRA General Executive and Army Council) effectively made all policy decisions, while the political leadership (Sinn Fein) docilely followed tradition and rejected participation at the national level on either side of the Irish border (a policy that changed in the 1960s in the case of the "Official" IRA and in the 1980s in the case of the "Provisional" IRA but that continues in effect with other splinter groups, including both the "Continuity" IRA and the "Real" IRA).[11] Second, the movement became quasi-clandestine and, because of its continuing efforts to procure arms and resources, frequently resorted to criminal activities. Third, because of the overtly discriminatory nature of the Protestant-dominated Northern Irish government, the IRA maintained legitimacy as both a defender of the Catholic minority and as a political symbol of national unity and resistance.[12] These features help explain the range of forms and functions that the IRA took from 1923–1969, and also shaped the IRA's revival and evolution in the Northern Irish Troubles (1969–1997).

TYPES OF ARMED GROUPS: THE IRA AS AN "ARMED-GROUP CHAMELEON"

Classic Insurgencies and Guerrilla Units

The IRA is often used as an archetype of a classic insurgent group, particularly when referencing the rural guerrilla operations of 1920–1921. The IRA in this period was organized on a territorial basis. Each county organized one or more "brigades," and each brigade was encouraged to organize a "flying column"—a small group of full-time guerrillas. To coordinate operations in multiple counties, provincial "divisions" were organized. None of these formations were of uniform strength, and their effectiveness varied widely based on local leadership and access to weapons—a constant problem for the IRA throughout its existence.[13]

During the Anglo-Irish War, the IRA benefited from broad political support and the availability of large numbers of part- and full-time volunteers, which made a territorial presence viable.[14] From 1923 to 1969, the IRA changed form several times, and during the 1956–1962 border campaign attempted to spark a *foco*-like rural insurgency in Northern Ireland.[15] "Flying columns" of volunteers based in the Irish Republic launched cross-border raids into the north. This campaign failed abysmally—not only did the Northern Irish population fail to rise (the IRA failed to appreciate both the coercive apparatus of the northern state and the determination of its Protestant majority) but security crackdowns in both the north and the south devastated the IRA's leadership and arms stores, and the campaign withered into incoherence. The IRA considered reviving the "flying column" in the mid-1980s, to take advantage of Libyan arms shipments, but rejected the idea as impractical.[16] The territorial structure of the IRA was maintained in the north, however, and was revitalized in the political crisis of 1969–1970.

Terrorist Cells

The IRA has pursued classic terrorist practices throughout its existence, including assassination, kidnapping, sectarian violence, and attacks on noncombatants—even while, in apparent contradiction, maintaining relatively strict discrimination in its targeting efforts.[17] As early as 1919, leaders of the IRA were demanding attacks on civilian crowds and British political targets, as well as considering the use of biological agents against British livestock.[18] The port of Liverpool was wrecked by firebombing in a 1920 attack.[19] Michael Collins's handpicked assassins devastated the intelligence capabilities of the Dublin Metropolitan Police and, to a lesser extent, British military intelligence.[20]

The IRA continued its traditional use of terrorist tactics after the civil war. Political assassination remained part of the Irish political scene throughout the late 1920s and early 1930s.[21] The IRA's 1939 campaign in England was based on urban terror, relying on small bombs in civilian areas to coerce Britain into withdrawing from Northern Ireland.[22] The 1956–1962 campaign made an effort to be more discriminating in both targets and tactics—the IRA's General Order Eight banned attacks on officials in the Irish Republic, and the campaign deliberately avoided urban and civilian targets.[23]

The IRA's reputation for terror, however, was demonstrated most dramatically during the Troubles. The IRA popularized the use of the car bomb in the early 1970s.[24] Under the crude justification of "economic targeting," bombing campaigns regularly devastated the downtown areas of major cities—Derry and Belfast, starting in 1972, and episodic campaigns attacking cities in the British mainland (the mid-1970s and early 1990s being particularly lethal). Bombs in crowded civic venues—Enniskillen in 1987 and the Real IRA's bombing of Omagh in 1998—had profoundly negative strategic and political effects. The IRA briefly resorted to "human bombing"—holding family members hostage and forcing an adult to drive a car bomb to its destination without providing the individual an opportunity to flee—in October 1990, which discredited it enormously and led to a significant loss of local support.[25]

The IRA also pursued deliberate policies of assassination and murder against a wide range of targets. Political leaders were frequent targets—the splinter group Irish National Liberation Army (INLA) killed member of Parliament Airey Neave in 1979, and the IRA attacks on Prime Minister Margaret Thatcher and 10 Downing Street failed in 1984 and 1991, respectively. Lord Mountbatten was killed by an IRA bomb in 1979 along with several innocents.[26] Members of the British Army and security forces were always targets—even when off duty, performing in noncombatant roles, or stationed overseas.[27] Members of the judiciary were selectively targeted.[28] On occasion, new targets were publicly identified (sometimes ex post facto) as "legitimate" due to their cooperation with the authorities—construction workers building police stations, for example.[29]

Organizationally, the IRA adopted a classic terrorist cell structure beginning in 1977.[30] This adaptation was part of the new "Long War" strategy, which intended to maintain significant resistance and political violence until attrition forced a British withdrawal.[31] Cell structures are less amenable to intelligence penetration—a significant weakness of the IRA's old territorial organization—and facilitated greater specialization and professionalism in the new "Active Service Units." The cell structure dramatically decreased the number of active fighters in the IRA organization—although the organization never suffered from an absence of potential recruits to replace operational losses. The cell system also allowed the gradual buildup of capacity to strike against British targets on foreign soil, including strikes in Germany and the Netherlands, and a spectacularly failed attack in Gibraltar in 1988.[32]

The IRA has benefited from transnational links. The American diaspora has always been a crucial supporter for Irish violence.[33] The IRA sought assistance from the Communist bloc in the 1970s (including Czech arms manufacturers), and formed fraternal alliances with other violent revolutionary movements, including Palestinian groups, the Basque ETA, and the Sandinistas.[34] The most important source of arms in the 1980s was

Libya, which provided roughly 150 tons of equipment between 1985 and 1987.[35] The IRA has also provided volunteers, advice, and expertise to other movements, including both sides in the Spanish civil war and, more recently, Colombia's FARC.[36]

Militias

The IRA acted as a community defense force of sorts in response to sectarian violence in the north—particularly in Belfast—in the 1930s.[37] The IRA reemerged as the defender of Catholic neighborhoods in 1969 and particularly in 1970.[38] The Northern Irish regime proved incapable of either managing political reform (including modest pressure from a nonviolent civil rights movement) or maintaining political order. Communal violence created significant urban destruction and mass population transfers, and the security vacuum was filled by the British Army and the IRA.[39]

Through 1977, the IRA remained organized on a territorial basis, the units of which functioned at times as an independent militia. The Belfast Brigade, for example, was organized in three battalions, each responsible for certain sectors of the city. The Belfast Brigade alone numbered 1,200 members in late 1971.[40] The IRA and local populations created "no-go zones" that briefly provided political autonomy and freedom from security force surveillance (until eliminated in "Operation Motorman"). Throughout the Troubles, the IRA staged operations intended to demonstrate its presence in both urban and rural areas, including the establishment of temporary checkpoints, roadblocks, and other methods of surveillance and traffic control. Although the IRA moved away from a territorial structure after 1977, it never completely abandoned its local roots. Some areas remained virtual "no-go" zones for the security forces until very late in the Troubles—particularly the remote and contested border region of South Armagh.[41]

Police Agencies

Because the IRA is an inherently political organization, it has attempted to set up shadow institutions that usurp legitimate functions in local communities. This is a useful means of not only demonstrating its political competence but also delegitimizing British rule. In the Anglo-Irish War, IRA supporters dominated town and county councils and guerrilla action gradually reduced police presence in the countryside. As a result, it was relatively easy for the IRA to take over local policing functions and even to set up competing judicial processes for handling routine legal matters.[42] In Northern Ireland, the Royal Ulster Constabulary was considered an illegitimate sectarian force by much of the minority Catholic population.[43] As a result, particularly in urban areas, the IRA took on local policing functions and often resolved local criminal complaints—a process including such punishments as beatings, deportation, "kneecapping," and execution.[44] At times, the IRA and its supporters dealt particularly harshly with drug dealers—a major political issue in Dublin during the 1980s and 1990s.[45]

Criminal Organizations and Drug Cartels

Underground revolutionary movements always need money and arms, and it is hardly surprising that the IRA has been heavily involved in a wide range of criminal activity during armed campaigns and in periods of peace. Arms raids were a regular event in the 1950s as the IRA geared up for the border campaign.[46] The IRA benefited from arms thefts and illegal transfers in the United States during the Troubles.[47] Money is always in short supply—robbing post offices in the Irish Republic has been an important source of funds for the IRA and its splinter groups. Major heists are more rare but still melodramatic and lucrative—the Great Train Robbery of 1976 or the Northern Bank raid of 2004 are prominent examples.[48]

The IRA and/or its followers have occasionally stooped to baser felonious behavior as well. Kidnapping has filled IRA coffers from time to time.[49] Although the Irish Republican Movement in general has been strongly antinarcotics, individual members have been engaged in drug trafficking, and cooperation with the FARC in 2001 did little to distance the IRA from claims of drug dealing.[50] Like the Mafia and other criminal organizations, the IRA is ruthless in pursuing informers. Unlike most criminal organizations, however, the IRA set up a dedicated counterintelligence organization known as the "Nutting Squad" that tortured and executed dozens of victims on both sides of the Irish border.[51]

Last but not least, the IRA became largely self-sustaining through a wide range of criminal and quasi-legitimate activities in Northern Ireland and on the border.[52] Smuggling goods, particularly fuel, was a lucrative means of taking advantage of subsidies and differences in currency exchange rates. The IRA owns many businesses and front companies in Belfast and elsewhere. Local drinking clubs add a small tax to the price of each drink, which helps fill IRA coffers.[53] The Falls Road Black Taxi service created employment for ex-prisoners and significant contributions for the IRA war effort. Insurance schemes, extortion, and coercion in the construction business also provided important income streams.[54]

Warlords

Ireland is too small for warlords of any significant scale, but the combination of difficult terrain and frequent political factionalism within the Irish Republican Movement has occasionally created unique autonomous actors. The splinter group Saor Uladh was an important faction in the 1950s, based in the border region and carrying out arms raids and attacks on the Northern Irish authorities.[55] Various IRA splinter groups have carved out small territorial niches for themselves—the INLA was very active in the Divis Flats multistory housing project in West Belfast, for instance.[56]

Perhaps the most pronounced autonomous region, however, was the operations area of the IRA's South Armagh brigade, headed by Thomas "Slab" Murphy.[57] This section of the Irish border is known as "Bandit Country," and the Murphy farm straddles the border (allowing de facto sanctuary by simply fleeing across the house or farm complex and crossing the border). The Murphy farm complex was the base for a massive smuggling effort that operated for over 20 years. This smuggling effort made the South Armagh brigade functionally self-sustaining, and politically irreplaceable—it not only funded its own operations and weapons research and development, but its resources were vital to IRA HQ and operations throughout the province.[58]

The South Armagh brigade also benefited from a benign operating environment. The local population was either actively supportive or relatively passive. Security forces received little assistance and few tips from the local population. Unusual activity of any kind was quickly reported to the local IRA. The core of the brigade leadership, and its active service units, were locals who had lived in the area most of their lives and were completely loyal. Unlike other IRA commands, which had relatively high turnover rates due to death and capture, and which were increasingly penetrated through electronic surveillance and informers, the South Armagh brigade remained a stable and secure organization. As a result, it was increasingly given more latitude for independent operations and greater responsibility.[59] Slab Murphy—one of the quintessential IRA "hard men"—was brought into the IRA Army Council and eventually reportedly was made the chief of staff of the IRA.[60] The brigade was given responsibility for running the bombing campaign in England in the 1990s, bypassing existing organizations that would normally have been in charge of creating the bombs and the "sleeper cells" in England.[61] By 1996–1997, when the IRA briefly renewed the conflict, the South Armagh brigade was the only element of the IRA still capable of sustained and effective operations.[62] In 2006, a combined operation by Irish and Northern Irish security forces finally simultaneously raided the Murphy compound on both sides of the border, seizing vast amounts of cash, computer and paper records, and other valuable intelligence materials. Since that time, British investigations have shut down a number of other front companies and investments reportedly owned by the Murphy family.[63]

Mercenaries

Although the mercenary IRA man is now a mythic figure in airport fiction, thanks to the writings of Jack Higgins and Tom Clancy, actual mercenary involvement by the IRA has been rare. As mentioned above, IRA volunteers served with both sides in the Spanish civil war. More recently, Colombian authorities arrested three members of the IRA in 2001—two longtime experts from South Armagh and a Sinn Fein spokesman representing the party's interests in Cuba. They were reportedly engaged in training FARC in the creation of mortars and other advanced munitions.[64]

Orchestrated Rioters and Mobs

At various times, when the IRA has been particularly weak or in the midst of a dormant period, IRA activists have emerged as the core of organized rioters or mobsters. The IRA was active in opposing the neofascist Blueshirt movement (headed by a former IRA chief of staff) in the 1930s.[65] It played a leading role in the civil rights protests of the 1960s in Northern Ireland (where it provided both active membership and security during marches and demonstrations—many of which unfortunately degenerated into communal violence).[66] The IRA was active in organizing riots and mobs during the Troubles, often using them as cover for other activities.

CONCLUSION

Armed-groups methodology is a valuable analytical contribution to the study of nonstate violence, particularly at the intersection between law enforcement and military activities. Using a narrow definition that focuses on form and function, this methodology is particularly good at making distinctions between groups with different, but not necessarily political, motives.

Groups that do have political motives, and particularly revolutionary ones, may actually take on a wide range of the functions associated with armed groups. FARC, for example, has demonstrated criminal behavior, including an intimate association with the narcotics trade. At the same time, however, it takes the form of a terrorist group and, in "liberated areas," both a militia and a classic insurgency.

The IRA is perhaps the best example of a multifunction armed group that also, occasionally, changes form. This is at least partly the result of its history of successes and failures, which contribute to its multigenerational nature and deep political roots. The IRA actually "won" the Anglo-Irish War, but a substantial minority felt that a more complete and total success was not only possible but that accepting any compromise was actually an act of treason. This provided the base for continued campaigns, some obvious failures (1939–1945, 1956–1962) and others more protracted and complicated in nature and outcome (1969–1997).

Throughout its existence, the IRA has engaged in certain functions associated with more narrowly defined groups—criminal activity (bank robbing, kidnapping, gun smuggling), terrorism (assassination), and militia-type behavior (defense of the minority community in Northern Ireland). Other activities have been adapted as the organization's strength and influence increased—police activity, for example, is only possible with substantial community support and the relative absence or weakness of local security forces. In short, trying to assess the capacity or threat of an armed group purely by its function can be misleading, unless the analyst takes a broad view to see if the same group is engaged—simultaneously or episodically—in multiple functions. A group carrying out multiple functions may be fundamentally more robust, more dangerous, and possess far greater capacity than a single-function group.

Overfocusing on form holds an even greater opportunity for misunderstanding. The IRA has changed form at various times during its existence, generally mirroring its relative strength and popular support. This has not meant, however, that the IRA was not pursuing greater ambitions. Any perfunctory analysis of the IRA in 1945 or in the mid-1960s would have dismissed it as a defunct organization, gradually deteriorating into either a debating society or a drinking club, with only a minor ability to carry out mischievous criminal or demonstrative acts. In each case, however, the IRA reshaped itself, taking on different forms and functions as it gained power, authority, and legitimacy. The IRA of the 1940s became a tightly organized criminal group focusing on arms raids, and gradually built itself into a more formidable (but ultimately unsuccessful) guerrilla structure. The IRA in the late 1960s reemerged in response to civic violence and took advantage of political unrest and British intervention to re-create itself both as one of the most successful terrorist networks in history and, more recently, as a powerful and influential political movement.[67]

Change in form can also reflect weakness, of course. The IRA's activities today consist primarily of local coercion and intimidation (for economic or political purposes) and the occasional spectacular bank robbery. It has, in essence, taken the form once again of a criminal enterprise—albeit a powerful and politically connected one. Splinter groups—the Real IRA and the Continuity IRA—continue occasional acts of terrorism, but lack the capacity and multiplicity of functions that the IRA demonstrated for almost 30 years. Still, if the history of the Irish Republican Movement demonstrates anything, it is that a small group with only modest functional capacity still possesses the possibility to rise, in the Provisional IRA's metaphor, "like a phoenix from the ashes"—drawing on the legitimacy and historical tradition of the republican ideal to once again become a more significant problem, if the proper circumstances arise. For this reason, if for no other, we should hope that Sinn Fein's reemergence as a political party can redirect the republican ideal into more peaceful, democratic pursuits.

NOTES

1. For the purposes of this chapter, the term *Irish Republican Army (IRA)* will be used to refer to the organization of that name up through 1969, and specifically to refer to the Provisional IRA from 1970 onwards. The Northern Irish conflict has sparked many divisions and splinter groups—when necessary, they will be referred to by their own names (Official IRA, Real IRA, Continuity IRA), while the generic form will be reserved for the most powerful and influential faction (the Provisionals).

2. A recent, comprehensive examination of the Irish Republican Brotherhood is Owen McGee, *The IRB: The Irish Republican Brotherhood from the Land League to Sinn Fein* (Dublin: Four Courts Press, 2005).

3. Dorothy Macardle, *The Irish Republic* (New York: Farrar, Straus and Giroux, 1965).

4. Charles Townshend, *Easter 1916: The Irish Rebellion* (London: Penguin, 2005), 3–6.

5. Brian Feeney, *Sinn Fein: A Hundred Turbulent Years* (Madison, WI: University of Wisconsin Press, 2003), 186–95.

6. David Fitzpatrick, "Militarism in Ireland" in *A Military History of Ireland*, ed. Thomas Bartlett and Keith Jeffery (Cambridge: Cambridge University Press, 1996), gives a figure of 191,000 (386); Robert Kee, *The Green Flag: A History of Irish Nationalism* (London: Penguin, 1972), gives a figure of 188,000 (520).

7. Townshend, *Easter 1916*; Tim Pat Coogan, *1916: The Easter Rising* (London: Phoenix, 2001); and Max Caulfield, *The Easter Rebellion: Dublin 1916* (Boulder, CO: Roberts Rinehart Publishers, 1995).

8. Michael Hopkinson, *The Irish War of Independence* (Montreal and Kingston: MacGill-Queen's Press, 2002); Francis Costello, *The Irish Revolution and Its Aftermath, 1916–1923: Years of Revolt* (Dublin: Irish Academic Press, 2003); Michael Laffan, *The Resurrection of Ireland: The Sinn Féin Party, 1916–1923* (Cambridge: Cambridge University Press, 1999); Peter Hart, *The I.R.A. at War, 1916–1923* (Oxford: Oxford University Press, 2003).

9. Michael Hopkinson, *Green against Green: The Irish Civil War* (Dublin: Gill and MacMillan, 1988); Calton Younger, *Ireland's Civil War* (Glasgow: William Collins Sons & Co., 1982).

10. The classic works on the IRA, begun in the 1960s and updated regularly, are J. Bowyer Bell, *The Secret Army: The IRA*, 3rd ed. (New Brunswick: Transaction Publishers, 1997); and Tim Pat Coogan, *The IRA*, rev. ed. (New York: Palgrave, 2002).

11. Recent works on the IRA that discuss the strategy of the Irish Republican Movement include M. L. R. Smith, *Fighting for Ireland? The Militant Strategy of the Irish Republican Movement* (London: Routledge, 1995); Richard English, *Armed Struggle: The History of the IRA* (Oxford: Oxford University Press, 2003); and Ed Moloney, *A Secret History of the IRA* (New York: W.W. Norton, 2002). The Clausewitzian interpretation is my own.

12. For IRA actions and preparedness early in the Troubles in Northern Ireland, see Bell, *The Secret Army*, 357, 365–66; Coogan, *The IRA*, 334–35. For an inflammatory but informative description of the evolution of Northern Ireland's political crisis, see Michael O'Farrell, *Northern Ireland: The Orange State* (London: Pluto Press, 1976). Other works on the origins of the Troubles include Richard Rose, *Governing without Consensus: An Irish Perspective* (Boston: Beacon Press, 1971); Eamonn McCann, *War and an Irish Town* (London: Pluto Press, 1980); Tim Pat Coogan, *The Troubles: Ireland's Ordeal and the Search for Peace* (New York: Palgrave, 1996); and J. Bowyer Bell, *The Irish Troubles: A Generation of Violence, 1967–1992* (New York: St. Martin's, 1993).

13. A romantic depiction by the commandant of West Cork's flying column is Tom Barry, *Guerilla Days in Ireland* (Dublin: Irish Press, 1949). A more scholarly analysis of the IRA volunteers in this period is Joost Augusteijn, *From Public Defiance to Guerrilla Warfare* (London: Irish Academic Press, 1996).

14. Feeney, *Sinn Fein*; Bell, *The Secret Army*, 16–28; Macardle, *The Irish Republic*. A detailed examination of the evolution of the IRA in county Cork, the most militant of Ireland's rural provinces, is Peter Hart, *The I.R.A. & Its Enemies* (Oxford: Oxford University Press, 1998).

15. For a history of the border campaign, see Coogan, *The IRA*, 297–329; Bell, *The Secret Army*, 255–336; Smith, *Fighting for Ireland?* 66–72; English, *Armed Struggle*, 71–78. An IRA tactical handbook from the period has been republished as General Headquarters, Irish Republican Army, *Handbook for Volunteers of the Irish Republican Army: Notes on Guerrilla Warfare* (Boulder, CO: Paladin Press, 1985).

16. Moloney, *A Secret History of the IRA*, 312–13, 333–34.

17. Smith, *Fighting for Ireland?* 31–35.

18. Michael T. Foy, *Michael Collins's Intelligence War: The Struggle between the British and the IRA, 1919–1921* (Gloucestershire, UK: Sutton Publishing, 2006), 127–28. Plans drawn up by IRA chief of staff Richard Mulcahy examined the possibility of infecting British troops with typhoid and British horses with glanders.

19. For a detailed analysis of IRA operations in Britain in 1920–1921, see Hart, *The I.R.A. at War, 1916–1923*, 141–77.

20. See Foy, *Michael Collins's Intelligence War*; T. Ryle Dwyer, *The Squad and the Intelligence Operations of Michael Collins* (Cork: Mercier Press, 2005); and James Gleeson, *Bloody Sunday* (London: Peter Davies, 1962).

21. Conor Foley, *Legion of the Rearguard: The IRA and the Modern Irish State* (London: Pluto Press, 1992), is an excellent history of the IRA in this period.

22. On IRA efforts from 1939–1945, see Coogan, *The IRA*, 113–217; Bell, *The Secret Army*, 145–236.

23. See Brendan O'Brien, *The Long War: The IRA and Sinn Fein, 1985 to Today* (Syracuse: Syracuse University Press, 1995), 355–57 (Appendix 2: IRA General Army Orders [As Amended by the Army Council] October 1973); Feeney, *Sinn Fein*, 187.

24. Sean MacStiofain, *Revolutionary in Ireland* (Edinburgh: R&R Clark, 1975), 243–44.

25. Moloney, *A Secret History of the IRA*, 347–49.

26. According to at least one informer account, an attack was also planned against Prince Charles and Princess Diana in the early 1980s. See Sean O'Callaghan, *The Informer* (London: Bantam Press, 1998), 144, 151, 156. On the Mountbatten assassination, see Patrick Bishop and Eamonn Mallie, *The Provisional IRA* (London: Heinemann, 1987), 248–49; and Toby Harnden, *"Bandit Country": The IRA & South Armagh* (London: Hodder & Stoughton, 1999), 201–205. On IRA targets more generally, see J. Bowyer Bell, *IRA Tactics and Targets: An Analysis of Tactical Aspects of the Armed Struggle 1969–1989* (Dublin: Poolbeg Press, 1990).

27. Bell, *IRA Tactics and Targets*, 30, 41–44.

28. Lord Justice Sir Maurice Gibson was specifically targeted because of his hard anti-IRA stance, dying with his wife in an ambush in 1987. An attempt to kill Justice Ian Higgins in the same region failed shortly thereafter. Harnden, *"Bandit Country,"* 224–28.

29. Bell, *IRA Tactics and Targets*, 31.

30. Smith, *Fighting for Ireland?* 153, 160, 188; Moloney, *A Secret History of the IRA*, 148–62, 332–34. The cell structure was, in fact, unevenly applied. An excellent analysis of IRA organization in the Troubles is J. Bowyer Bell, *The IRA, 1968–2000: Analysis of a Secret Army* (London: Frank Cass, 2000), 126–47.

31. Peter Taylor, *Behind the Mask: The IRA and Sinn Fein* (New York: TV Books, 1999), 245–64; Smith, *Fighting for Ireland?* 143–68.

32. Bell, *The IRA, 1968–2000*, 35; English, *Armed Struggle*, 256.

33. On the U.S. connection in more recent years, see Jack Holland, *The American Connection: U.S. Guns, Money & Influence in Northern Ireland* (New York: Viking Penguin, 1988); and James Adams, *The Financing of Terror* (New York: Simon & Schuster, 1986), 131–55. The importance of U.S. financing and weapons faded over time, due in no small part to the committed efforts of U.S. law-enforcement and intelligence communities.

34. See Feeney, *Sinn Fein*, 359. On the Czech arms fiasco, see Maria McGuire, *To Take Arms: A Year in the Provisional IRA* (London: MacMillan, 1973). The prisons acted as centers of leftist thought and philosophy, which influenced both IRA and Sinn Fein leadership. See English, *Armed Struggle*, 233–37; and Laurence McKeown, *Out of Time: Irish Republican Prisoners; Long Kesh, 1972–2000* (Belfast: BTP Publications, 2001).

35. Moloney, *A Secret History of the IRA*, 8–33; O'Brien, *The Long War*, 131–53. Another 150-ton shipment from Libya was intercepted.

36. On the Spanish civil war, see Foley, *Legion of the Rearguard*, 164–72; Bell, *The Secret Army*, 130–35. On the FARC connection, see Moloney, *A Secret History of the IRA,* 489–91; Feeney, *Sinn Fein,* 424.

37. Coogan, *The IRA*, 160–65.

38. English, *Armed Struggle*, 120–37; Smith, *Fighting for Ireland?* 91–95; Feeney, *Sinn Fein*, 253–67.

39. Bell, *The Secret Army*, 373–79; McCann, *War and an Irish Town*.

40. Moloney, *A Secret History of the IRA*, 103. This was impressive growth, as the IRA could only muster 50 fighters in Belfast in 1969.

41. Harnden, *"Bandit Country,"* is an excellent description of the British government's ongoing difficulties in this region.

42. Arthur Mitchell, "Alternative Government: 'Exit Britannia'—The Formation of the Irish National State 1918–21," in *The Irish Revolution, 1913–1923,* ed. Joost Augusteijn (New York: Palgrave, 2002), 70–86; Macardle, *The Irish Republic,* 347–53.

43. Reflections on the RUC can be found in a wide literature, including Raymond Murray, *State Violence: Northern Ireland, 1969–1997* (Dublin: Mercier Press, 1998), 33–36; Kevin Kelley, *The Longest War: Northern Ireland and the IRA* (London: Zed Press, 1982); McCann, *War and an Irish Town*; and O'Farrell, *Northern Ireland.*

44. Bishop and Mallie, *The Provisional IRA,* 318–23; Moloney, *A Secret History of the IRA*, 153.

45. Antinarcotics activity carried out under a false name (Direct Action against Drugs) is discussed in Moloney, *A Secret History of the IRA*, 437, 400.

46. Bell, *The Secret Army*, 255–71.

47. Holland, *The American Connection.*

48. On the Great Train Robbery, see Bell, *IRA Tactics and Targets*, 92–98. A bank robbery in Newry, on 10 November 1994, netted 131,000 pounds sterling (and resulted in the death of a postal worker), even though the IRA was technically in a cease-fire at the time. Bell, *The Secret Army*, 655. The Northern Bank raid netted over 25 million pounds sterling. BBC News, "Police Say IRA behind Bank Raid," January 2005, news.bbc.co.uk/1/hi/northern_ireland/4154657.stm (accessed 11 October 2007).

49. See, for example, Coogan, *The IRA*, 521–24; Bishop and Mallie, *The Provisional IRA*, 349.

50. On the FARC connection, see English, *Armed Struggle,* 331–32.

51. Moloney, *A Secret History of the IRA*, 154–55. According to recent reports, the "Nutting Squad" was penetrated at the highest levels by British agents. See Martin Ingram and Greg Harkin, *Stakeknife: Britain's Secret Agents in Ireland* (Madison: University of Wisconsin Press, 2005).

52. Adams, *The Financing of Terror*, 156–84; Harnden, *"Bandit Country,"* 11–47.

53. Bishop and Mallie, *The Provisional IRA*, 312.

54. Adams, *The Financing of Terror*, 156–84; Bishop and Mallie, *The Provisional IRA*, 312–13; Moloney, *A Secret History of the IRA,* 459–61.

55. Coogan, *The IRA*, 283–89; Bell, *The Secret Army,* 255, 275–80, 316–18.

56. Bell, *The Secret Army,* 413–14, 421–22, 443–44; Coogan, *The IRA*, 534–43; O'Brien, *The Long War*, 333–35.

57. Murphy is a key figure in Moloney's *A Secret History of the IRA*, as well as in Harnden's *"Bandit Country."* One of the first major mentions of him by name is in Adams, *The Financing of Terror*.

58. Moloney, *A Secret History of the IRA*, 459–60; Adams, *The Financing of Terror*, 156–60; Harnden, *"Bandit Country,"* 5–47, 348–51.

59. See Harnden, *"Bandit Country"*; and Moloney, *A Secret History of the IRA,* 160–61, 262, 459.

60. Moloney, *A Secret History of the IRA*, 478–79, 513.

61. Ibid., 441–43.

62. Harnden, *"Bandit Country."*

63. A brief synopsis of Murphy's recent career, including reports of a major cross border raid staged by both Irish and Northern Irish security services, can be found at en.wikipedia.org/wiki/Thomas_Murphy_(Irish_republican) (accessed on 11 October 2007).

64. Martin Hodgson, Henry McDonald, and Peter Beaumont, "IRA Blunder in the Jungle Sparks US Rage," *Observer,* 19 August 2001, available at observer.guardian.co.uk/print/0,,4241717-110236,00.html (accessed 12 October 2007); Rosie Cowan, "IRA 'Approved Weapons Tests in Colombia,'" *Guardian,* 14 June 2002, available at www.guardian.co.uk/colombia/story/0,11502,737240,00.html (accessed 12 October 2007).

65. Bell, *The Secret Army,* 105–17.

66. Tony Geraghty, *The Irish War: The Hidden Conflict between the IRA and British Intelligence* (Baltimore: Johns Hopkins University Press, 2000), 3–28.

67. A useful short study of British errors early in the Northern Ireland Troubles is Rod Thornton, "Getting It Wrong: The Crucial Mistakes Made in the Early Stages of the British Army's Deployment to Northern Ireland (August 1969 to March 1972)," *Journal of Strategic Studies* 30, no. 1 (February 2007): 73–107.

6 Pseudo Operations—A Double-Edged Sword of Counterinsurgency

Theodore L. Gatchel

In 1948, the government of the newly independent Republic of the Philippines was facing an insurgency led by communist holdovers from the *Hukbo ng Bayan Laban sa Hapon,* or "Anti-Japanese Army," that was formed in 1942 by the merger of the Communist Party of the Philippines and various socialist organizations. Capitalizing on the dissatisfaction of many Filipinos with the policies of the government they elected after the war, the organization changed its name to the *Hukbong Magapalaya ng Bayan,* or "People's Liberation Army," and set out to overthrow the government. During the ensuing conflict, the organization was commonly referred to by the shortened form of its original name, *Hukbalahap,* and its members were called simply "Huks."[1]

Geographically, the insurgency centered on a region in central Luzon near Mount Arayat that became known as "Huklandia." Other more or less independent groups operated in southern Luzon, and one of those groups decided to join forces with the Huks in central Luzon after the death of its leader. In April 1948, the central group received reports of a skirmish between the southern Huk group and a company of the Philippine Constabulary that had caused casualties on both sides.

Several days later, the remnants of the southern Huk force arrived in Huklandia carrying with them two members suffering from gunshot wounds. Having no way of verifying the authenticity of the southern group, the northern command subjected the newly arrived insurgents to a detailed interrogation until they were certain that the group was what it claimed to be. For several days, the two groups fraternized and exchanged information. The northern group fed their new reinforcements and cared for their wounded.

Four days after their arrival, the members of the southern group detected a change in attitude among their northern comrades. Outnumbered three to one and afraid of what the larger group might be planning, the southern group suddenly opened fire on the northern Huks, killing 82 of them, including three commanders. What appeared to be an unfortunate friendly-fire incident was nothing of the kind. The southern Huk group was, in fact, a specially trained counterguerrilla organization from the Philippine Constabulary known as Force X. The Huks had fallen prey to a carefully executed pseudo operation.[2]

Theodore L. Gatchel is a professor of joint military operations at the Naval War College and a retired U.S. Marine Corps colonel who commanded infantry units from the platoon to the battalion and served two combat tours in Vietnam during his 30-year career. He is the author of a book on amphibious warfare; numerous monographs, book chapters, and articles; and a monthy newspaper column on military affairs.

BACKGROUND

For purposes of this essay, pseudo operations are defined as actions in which specially trained and equipped counterinsurgency forces disguise themselves as insurgent bands in order to gain intelligence, carry out attacks against insurgent forces or facilities, capture or kill insurgent leaders, and conduct psychological operations against the insurgents.[3]

A pseudo operation is a ruse of war, a tactic that has been used throughout military history, and has been recognized as legitimate as long as certain constraints have been observed. Ruses are recognized by the Geneva Conventions as "acts which are intended to mislead an adversary or to induce him to act recklessly but which infringe no rule of international law applicable in armed combat and which are not perfidious because they do not invite the confidence of an adversary with respect to protection under that law."[4] The discussion of pseudo operations in this essay is limited strictly to their employment as a counterinsurgency tactic.

THE PHILIPPINES, KENYA, AND RHODESIA

Although a number of cases exist in which counterinsurgency forces have used or attempted to use pseudo operations, three stand out because of the systematic nature of their executions and because their principal architects have provided first-hand accounts of the operations.[5] The cases are

- Operations by the Philippine government against the Huk insurrection from the initial encounter between the Huks and the Philippine Military in May 1946 to the surrender of Huk leader Luis Taruc in May 1954, which effectively ended the insurrection
- Operations by the British against the Mau Mau uprising in Kenya from the declaration of a state of emergency in October 1952 to Kenyan independence in December 1963
- Operations by the Rhodesians against several black-nationalist insurgent groups from the Unilateral Declaration of Independence (UDI) of Rhodesia from Great Britain by a white-ruled government in November 1965 to the reestablishment of British sovereignty in December 1979.

THE PHILIPPINES

The background of the Huk insurrection and an example of one successful use of pseudo operations against the Huks were described earlier. The use of Force X had been initiated by Colonel Napoleon Valeriano, commander of a special Philippine Constabulary unit at the time, but after its initial successful use, pseudo operations gradually gave way to more conventional counterinsurgency tactics. Under the direction of Philippine secretary of national defense Ramon Magsaysay, a veteran of guerrilla operations against the Japanese in World War II, the concept of pseudo operations was revitalized in 1951.[6]

Initially the Philippine Army employed companies posing as Huk squadrons in operations that were called "large unit infiltrations." As those operations gained success, however, the Huks became increasingly wary of large units. In response, the army began using smaller teams in their pseudo operations. The smaller sizes of these units required better training, which, in turn, required increased reliance on captured Huks to provide the information needed to keep the pseudo units current with respect to Huk operating procedures. By the time the insurrection was winding down in 1954, pseudo operations were employed routinely by a specially trained unit called A-H for à la Huk.[7]

KENYA

In 1948, about the same time that the Huk insurrection was beginning to take hold in the Philippines, British officials in the east African colony of Kenya began receiving reports of a shadowy organization that the British called the Mau Mau.[8] A militant movement that advocated terrorism to achieve its anticolonial goals, the Mau Mau parlayed a relatively minor land dispute between the Kikuyu, Kenya's largest ethnic group, and the government into a grievance by all black Kenyans against the white colonial authorities.[9] Formed into small groups that the British referred to as gangs, the Mau Mau conducted small-scale attacks on British farms, killing the farmers, their families, and their black employees in the most vicious ways imaginable in an effort to create terror.

The British initially treated the matter as a law enforcement problem and tried to deal with it by using the Kenya Police, the Kenya Police Reserve, and, later, a locally recruited Kikuyu Guard. As these police efforts proved inadequate, the British turned to military methods, including the dispatch of a British Army battalion to Kenya in October 1952. Initially the army tended to rely on conventional tactics such as cordon and search operations to isolate the gangs and massive sweeps to hunt them down.

In March 1954, Frank Kitson, a young British officer serving as a field intelligence assistant (FIA), stumbled on the idea of using pseudo operations against the Mau Mau. The inspiration for Kitson's concept was an incident in which a Mau Mau member whom he had captured agreed to lead him to the rest of his gang.[10] Kitson accepted the offer, which eventually resulted in the capture or killing of the remaining members of the turned insurgent's gang. This small success set in motion a chain of events in which Kitson established a training center for pseudo operations and formed "countergangs" composed of loyal Kikuyu and former Mau Mau insurgents that were led by selected white police and military personnel.

RHODESIA

As with the previous two cases, pseudo operations started in Rhodesia in a more or less ad hoc way. In January 1973, the special branch of the police in Salisbury, the capital of Rhodesia, formed an all-African pseudo unit to impersonate insurgents from the Zimbabwe African National Liberation Army (ZANLA).[11] This unit never engaged ZANLA forces in combat, but did collect some useful information. Encouraged by the results, the Rhodesian Army assigned Major Ron Reid Daly in 1973 the task of creating the Selous Scouts, an organization designed specifically to conduct pseudo operations.[12] Named for Frederick Courteney Selous, a famous big game hunter who was killed during World War I, the Selous Scouts were officered by white Rhodesians but manned by a mix of white and black soldiers that included a large percentage of turned insurgents. After initially giving priority to locating insurgents, who would then be attacked by "fire forces" from units such as the Rhodesian Light Infantry, the Scouts became increasingly involved with mobile, flying columns used to attack insurgent training camps and supporting infrastructure in neighboring countries. In addition to typical pseudo operations, they also provided trackers, long-range reconnaissance, and even spies.

CONSIDERATIONS FOR EMPLOYING PSEUDO OPERATIONS

Four broad issues run through all three of the cases described that must be considered when planning pseudo operations. These involve the organization, training, and control of forces used to conduct pseudo operations and what types of missions they should be assigned. Two additional issues of importance are the overall evaluation of the effectiveness of pseudo operations and the legal implications of conducting them.

In all three cases, the pseudo forces employed a mix of individuals loyal to the government and former insurgents who agreed to change sides after being captured. In Kenya and Rhodesia, the situation was further complicated by the inclusion of white personnel in units designed to impersonate insurgent forces that were exclusively black. This seemingly impossible feat was accomplished, in part, by effective use of camouflage and disguise and by operating at night whenever possible. A more important factor in the success of these units was the employment of former insurgents.

Given the nature of the Huks, the Mau Mau, and the various nationalist insurgent groups in Rhodesia, the probability of significant numbers of captured personnel agreeing to fight against their former comrades would seem unlikely. Former insurgents nevertheless became an invaluable part of pseudo operations in all three cases. Individuals charged with creating the pseudo forces understandably had concerns about the ultimate loyalty of turned insurgents, but their concerns proved to be largely unwarranted. With only a minor number of exceptions, the former insurgents proved their loyalties in combat, and many gave their lives in the services of their newly adopted causes.

Methods for converting captured insurgents varied somewhat. As a result of his experience in a number of counterinsurgency efforts, Kitson came to the conclusion that there is a more or less universal formula for success.

> Briefly it is that three separate factors have to be brought into play in order to make a man change his allegiance. First, he must be given an incentive that is strong enough to make him want to do so. This is the carrot. Then he must be made to realize that failure will result in something very unpleasant happening to him. This is the stick. Third, he must be given a reasonable opportunity of proving both to himself and to his friends that there is nothing fundamentally dishonorable about his action.[13]

Accounts about the Philippine case are largely silent on the subject. In Kenya the British used a three-stage approach, initially treating a captured insurgent "harshly" and then gradually relaxing the pressure.[14] The Rhodesians generally used a more subtle approach from the start, particularly with respect to wounded insurgents, who were given a high priority for medical evacuation and treatment.[15] In Daly's words, "The turning itself comprised no magic formula . . . no one was ever beaten up by his Special Branch interrogators . . . in fact, quite the reverse was the interrogational technique, as it was vital a trusting relationship be quickly established between the prisoner and the questioner."[16] In both cases, emphasis was placed on convincing the turned insurgents that they were completely trusted members of their new teams. In the case of Kenya, Kitson explains:

> From the beginning of stage three it was essential that the man should feel that he was trusted. Once he had joined us there were no reservations. He could sleep with the others, carry arms, do sentry duty or go out by himself. Frequently on one of his first patrols Eric

or I would give him our pistol and carry only a simi [a Kenyan knife] to make him realize that he was absolutely one of the team.[17]

For use in turning captured insurgents, counterinsurgency forces in both Kenya and Rhodesia had a similar "stick" in the form of emergency laws that imposed severe penalties for such violations as possessing firearms and belonging to subversive organizations. Captured insurgents who refused to cooperate would be turned over to the police, where they faced the possibility of long prison sentences or even hanging.

As incredible as the idea of insurgents swapping sides might seem, the pattern fits Eric Hoffer's evaluation of the psychology of individuals who become members of mass movements. In his view, membership in a revolutionary or nationalistic movement fills a certain need, and members of one movement have frequently converted to a diametrically opposed one, apparently without reservations. Hoffer points out, for example, that Ernst Röhm, leader of the Nazi SA, the infamous brownshirt storm troopers, boasted that he could convert the most die hard communist into a Nazi in four weeks.[18] Regarding candidates for conversion, Kitson expressed a somewhat different view. With the systematic approach that typified his view of counterinsurgency, Kitson classified captured Mau Mau members into three categories with respect to the likelihood of being able to turn them into pseudo insurgents. The least likely converts were individuals who joined the Mau Mau because of a fanatic devotion to the cause. A larger group that was easier to convert consisted of men who had joined because their friends had done so. The easiest individuals to convert were those who joined primarily out of a spirit of adventure.[19]

In addition to serving with other members of the counterinsurgency forces in pseudo units, former insurgents play a vital role in training. The success of a pseudo operation and the safety of the individuals conducting it depend on their being able to pass themselves off as genuine insurgents. In all three cases, the insurgents became exceptionally suspicious of alleged insurgent units and subjected them to intensive interrogation before accepting them. A wrong phrase or lack of knowledge about the camp where they had received training or even the latest insurgent songs could lead to sudden death. The members of the Philippine Force X learned after their initial operation that the Huks had become suspicious of them because they had too much bright new ammunition for a genuine insurgent unit.[20] Only a former insurgent could provide the information needed to prevent such missteps, and newly captured insurgents were essential to keep the necessary information up to date.[21]

Because pseudo forces tended to develop in an ad hoc way, so did formal training. Force X in the Philippines underwent its month-long training in a field site that was created for that specific purpose. When the use of pseudo operations was restarted by the 7th Battalion Combat Team (BCT) under the command of Colonel Valeriano, the unit created a secret training base in the Sierra Madre and instituted a rigorous eight-week course to prepare its men to operate as Huks.[22] In Kenya, Kitson was forced to use his own resources and captured Mau Mau to build a training center for his countergangs. The Rhodesians were the most advanced in this respect, eventually building a base where the Selous Scouts could train in secrecy and where members could bring their families to live in comparative comfort and safety.

The first issue regarding command and control of pseudo operations that needs to be resolved involves determining what part of a nation's security apparatus will control them. Most experts agree that a successful counterinsurgency requires close cooperation among a nation's police, military, and intelligence agencies. The leaders of those communities usually agree on that principle, but they frequently disagree as to which group should have overall control. In all three cases, the insurgency was initially treated as a law enforcement problem to be handled by the police. Only after police methods proved inadequate did military forces become involved.

In the Philippines, the Philippine Constabulary was initially responsible for counterinsurgency, including the first use of pseudo operations. When Ramon Magsaysay became secretary of national defense in 1950, he orchestrated a reorganization under which the constabulary was placed under military control for the duration of the campaign against the Huks.[23] As was the case in the Philippines, the authorities in Kenya initially tried to handle the Mau Mau problem as a law enforcement issue and resisted advice that the military should be involved. In 1953, as the situation continued to deteriorate, General Sir George Erskine was ordered to Kenya as commander in chief with command of military forces and operational control over the police and its auxiliaries. When he was appointed, General Erskine asked for overall command of both military and civilian authorities, along the lines that had been used in Malaya during the emergency there. That request was denied, but he was given the authority to declare martial law should that become necessary.[24] Below the national level, provincial and district commissioners chaired emergency committees that had army and police representatives. These committees controlled the activities of the security forces, including pseudo gangs, in their areas. This system remained in force until 1955 when the responsibility for pseudo operations was centralized in a special forces command.[25] In Rhodesia, command and control of pseudo operations was particularly complicated because of the wide range of missions assigned to the Selous Scouts and their responsibility for operations both inside and outside of Rhodesia. Initially the Scouts received instructions from a variety of military, police, and intelligence organizations.[26] To reduce the inevitable problems caused by a split command system, a Combined Operations Headquarters was created in 1977 to direct the war, including control of the Selous Scouts.[27]

Another command and control issue involves the measures needed to prevent blue-on-blue or fratricide incidents resulting from counterinsurgency forces' mistaking pseudo insurgents for real ones. All three cases provide examples of such incidents. The principal method used by the Selous Scouts to reduce the possibility of such incidents was to declare an area in which one of their units was operating as "frozen." Once frozen, no other security force units were allowed to operate in that area. In spite of that precaution, mistakes were inevitable. In June 1978, for example, a Selous Scouts operations officer failed to correctly designate a frozen area, which resulted in a police anti-terrorist unit engaging, and killing four Selous Scouts acting as insurgents. Because of the secrecy of their operations, the Selous Scouts could not even inform the police of the mistake.[28]

The three cases also illustrate different approaches regarding the types of missions that should be assigned to pseudo forces. Regarding the Philippine case, for example,

Valeriano and Bohannan expressed their view that the top three missions in order of importance are

- Killing enemy leaders or "outstanding fanatics"
- Destroying enemy elite units
- Penetrating and destroying effective enemy support units.[29]

Although Kitson does not delineate missions for his countergangs in the same way, a rough idea can be drawn from the examples he provides. In general, the countergangs operated in very small groups in an effort to make contact with real insurgents. When contact occurred, the reaction depended on the situation. When possible, the countergang tried to withdraw and notify police or military units that were staged nearby to kill or capture the insurgents. Unlike Valeriano and Bohannan, Kitson placed priority on capturing insurgents whenever possible.[30] Kitson also discusses the trade-off between using pseudo forces for offensive operations and for intelligence collection. In his words, "Despite the strong temptation to use the information for offensive purposes at once, we decided that we would not do so unless there was some exceptional prize to be gained, such as the elimination of an important gangster."[31]

When they were created, the overall purpose of the Selous Scouts was "the clandestine elimination of terrorism and terrorists both within and outside the country."[32] After operating in a manner not unlike that of the Philippine Army's Force X, Ron Daly, commander of the Selous Scouts, decided that a change in tactics was warranted. In his words, the new role of the Scouts would be "to infiltrate the tribal population and the terrorist networks, pinpoint the terrorist camps and bases and then direct conventional forces in to carry out the actual attacks."[33]

In all three cases, pseudo operations proved to be successful at the tactical level. In the case of Rhodesia, for example, 68 percent of the insurgents killed died as a result of direct or indirect action by the Selous Scouts.[34]

In spite of the physical damage done to insurgents by pseudo operations, the more important effect is probably psychological. The very nature of insurgency tends to cause its practitioners to become extremely security conscious, if not outright paranoid. Knowing that pseudo forces are operating in a region reinforces that feeling of paranoia. The resulting suspicion of any armed groups increases the chances of insurgents inadvertently engaging other insurgents. One ZANLA insurgent captured in Rhodesia told his interrogator that he had been involved in 10 firefights since infiltrating into Rhodesia. On checking the records, the interrogator determined that only 2 of the firefights had been with Rhodesian security forces. The remaining 8 had been with other ZANLA forces.[35]

Insurgents in Rhodesia were especially vulnerable to pseudo operations because of the natures of the two insurgent groups that were competing for control of the insurgency, and ultimately of an independent Zimbabwe. The two groups, the Zimbabwe African National Liberation Army (ZANLA) and the Zimbabwe People's Revolutionary Army (ZIPRA), represented political groups that reflected different revolutionary ideologies, were supported by different parts of the communist world, operated from bases in different foreign countries, and recruited their members largely from different ethnic groups.[36] These differences were exploited by the Selous Scouts, who impersonated forces from one group while operating in areas controlled by the other, thereby precipitating engagements that caused the insurgents to believe they had been attacked by their rivals.

Although perhaps not as spectacular, similar results in Kenya caused Kitson to note, "There can be little doubt that the most effective means of getting information and killing Mau Mau gangsters was the pseudo gang technique."[37] Equivalent assessments have been made regarding the use of pseudo operations against the Huks in the Philippines. In a study of insurgencies in the Philippines from 1899 to 1955, for example, the Special Operations Research Office of the American University listed as one of its essential lessons learned, "Operations in which friendly forces were disguised as the enemy were often most productive."[38]

Any consideration of pseudo operations must also take into account the applicable laws of armed conflict. Unfortunately the relevant issues are complicated ones that are largely beyond the scope of this essay. Several points need to be made nevertheless. As was pointed out earlier, ruses are acceptable under the laws of armed conflict as long as certain conditions are met. One of those conditions involves the use of enemy uniforms and symbols.

Historically, the general view regarding the use of enemy uniforms in land warfare was that such use constituted a lawful ruse as long as the enemy uniforms were discarded before actual combat took place. The 1907 Hague Convention IV on land warfare prohibits the "improper" use of an enemy's national flag, military insignia, or uniform, but fails to define improper use.[39] By the time the Additional Protocols to the 1949 Geneva Conventions were being drafted in the 1970s, a body of opinion had developed that the use of enemy uniforms was unlawful at any time. Although proposals were made in the relevant committees to make such restrictions explicit, the final results were left deliberately vague. In the words of Article 39 of Additional Protocol I, "It is prohibited to make use of the flags or military emblems, insignia or uniforms of adverse Parties while engaging in attacks or in order to shield, favour, protect or impede military operations."[40] It is also worth noting that the Rome Statute of the International Criminal Court classifies the "improper" use of an enemy's flag, military insignia, or uniform as a serious violation of the "laws and customs applicable in international armed conflict."[41]

Additional Protocol I further complicated the issue by applying its provisions not just to international armed conflicts but to "conflicts in which peoples are fighting against colonial domination and alien occupation and against racist régimes in the exercise of their right of self-determination."[42] Because pseudo insurgents often operate in civilian clothes to disguise themselves as actual insurgents, justifying that practice under international law requires answering what one source calls the "problematic question" of "how to distinguish permitted cases of operating in civilian clothes (guerrilla fighters in occupied territories and in wars of national liberation) from cases of legally forbidden perfidy."[43]

The argument that a nation's armed forces, including special forces that would presumably include pseudo units, are never permitted to operate in civilian clothes runs along the following general lines:

- Armed forces on both sides have an absolute obligation to distinguish themselves from civilians.

- Because of the conditions under which they are forced to fight the rules regarding distinction are relaxed for insurgents fighting against colonial domination and racist regimes.
- The use of civilian clothes in combat is therefore lawful on the part of the insurgents but perfidious on the part of pseudo forces trying to disguise themselves as insurgents.

This line of reasoning represents only one side of this contentious issue, but any nation planning to conduct pseudo operations should expect to have their legality challenged and must be prepared to justify them in terms of international law.[44]

Some of these questions may be more academic than practical ones, however, because of the nature of enemies against whom pseudo operations are most useful. In the three cases described in this essay, the insurgent forces displayed little regard for the niceties of international law except in those circumstances in which they were able to use them against the counterinsurgency forces for propaganda purposes. That use of propaganda is precisely what makes pseudo operations a double-edged sword of counterinsurgency.

THE DOUBLE-EDGED SWORD

In the three cases discussed here, the insurgents waged a particularly vicious form of warfare. In the cases of Kenya and Rhodesia, the insurgents deliberately murdered civilians in savage ways in hopes of inspiring terror. Given that form of combat, it would be naive not to expect the security forces to exact revenge on occasion. In the two African cases, the likelihood of abuses was increased by the racist attitudes of many of the white citizens, both civilian and military. In his book, *Mau Mau: An African Crucible,* Robert Edgerton devotes a chapter to various forms of brutality perpetrated by the British in Kenya involving the police, the military, the Kikuyu Guard, and white settlers.[45] None of the abuses described are attributed to British pseudo gangs. That is not the case with Rhodesia, however, where the Selous Scouts were routinely accused of crimes ranging from murdering prisoners to poisoning wells and waging biological warfare with anthrax.[46]

The problem is to sort out the real cases of abuse from the false accusations and punish the wrongdoers appropriately. The inherent nature of pseudo operations complicates this task because pseudo forces are nearly perfect targets for insurgent propaganda and disinformation campaigns. Any abuse on the part of insurgents can readily be blamed on their impersonators. The victims themselves may not even know who their tormentors were, but, in Kenya and Rhodesia, revulsion over colonial and racist policies on the part of the governments caused many people with no firsthand knowledge of the situation to believe any accusations made against the security forces.

The insurgents were quick to exploit such sympathies. Kitson captures the situation succinctly:

> When, however, certain sections of the press expressed indignation at one or two apparent lapses on the part of authority, the Mau Mau, advised by their legal friends, were quick to realize that they had a powerful weapon within their grasp. By cashing in on the atmosphere which the newspapers had built up they could spread completely false stories about certain people who were particularly effective at frustrating their plans. Thus, if the officer in charge of a certain police station was exceptionally efficient, you could be sure that he would soon find himself the subject of an investigation: he would learn how he had brutally murdered some harmless African whom he claimed to have killed in a fair fight. If the

F.I.A. [field intelligence assistant] was learning too much about the Mau Mau organization in his area, you could be sure he would soon be charged with ill-treating a prisoner whom he had once interrogated. No one was immune from this highly organized form of attack.[47]

This "highly organized form of attack" has been used so extensively in Iraq and Afghanistan today that it has been given a name: lawfare.

CONCLUSIONS

In the final analysis, the pseudo operation has proved to be a valuable technique when used wisely and selectively by military and police forces to counter insurgency. It is only one of many useful techniques, however, and it must be used in coordination with others to be truly effective. Furthermore, no military or police technique will be decisive if it is not used in support of a larger political strategy designed to deal with the causes of the insurgency. In spite of the inherent liabilities associated with pseudo operations, they should be an integral part of any counterinsurgency force's repertoire from the start and not something that comes about inadvertently as has been the case too often in the past.

NOTES

1. For an account of the background of the Huk movement, see Lawrence M. Greenberg, *The Hukbalahap Insurrection: A Case Study of a Successful Anti-insurgency Operation in the Philippines, 1946–1955* (Washington, DC: U.S. Army Center of Military History, 1987) 1–56.

2. The description of this operation was taken from Napoleon D. Valeriano and T. R. Bohannan, *Counter-guerrilla Operations: The Philippine Experience* (New York: Frederick A. Praeger, 1962) 145–46; and Napoleon D. Valeriano, "Military Operations," in *Counter-guerrilla Operations in the Philippines, 1946–1953: A Seminar on the Huk Campaign Held at Ft. Bragg, N.C., 15 June 1961*, 33–38.

3. For a slightly different definition see the seminal monograph by Lawrence E. Cline, *Pseudo Operations and Counterinsurgency: Lessons from Other Countries* (Carlisle, PA: Strategic Studies Institute, U.S. Army War College, 2005), 1. This monograph is an excellent starting point for research on pseudo operations.

4. "Protocol Additional to the Geneva Conventions of 12 August 1949, and Relating to the Protection of Victims of International Armed Conflicts" [Additional Protocol I], art. 37(2), available at www.icrc.org/IHL.nsf.

5. Although no single individual was entirely responsible for pseudo operations in the selected cases, the three principal sources referred to are Valeriano and Bohannan, *Counter-guerrilla Operations* for the Philippines; Frank Kitson, *Gangs and Counter-gangs* (London: Barrie and Rockliff, 1960) for Kenya; and Ron Reid Daly and Peter Stiff, *Selous Scouts: Top Secret War* (London: Galago, 1982) for Rhodesia.

6. For background regarding pseudo operations against the Huks, see Greenberg, *The Hukbalahap Insurrection*, 71–74, 117–28; Valeriano and Bohannan, *Counter-guerrilla Operations*, 142–56; and Paul Melshen, "The JUSMAG in the Philippines, 1947–55: Lessons Learned from a Successful Counterinsurgency Campaign," *Low Intensity Conflict & Law Enforcement* 6 (Summer 1997), 77–89.

7. Melshen, "The JUSMAG in the Philippines, 1947–55," 82–83.

8. The insurgents did not refer to themselves as Mau Mau. For an explanation of the possible origins of the term, see Donald L. Barnett and Karari Njama, *Mau Mau from Within: Autobiography and Analysis of Kenya's Peasant Revolt* (New York: Monthly Review Press, 1966), 51–55. For a different explanation of the term, see Josiah Mwangi Kariuki, *'Mau Mau' Detainee: The Account by a Kenya African of His Experiences in Detention Camps 1953–1960* (London: Oxford University Press, 1963), 23–24.

9. For a concise account of the origins of Mau Mau and its operations against the British, see Robert B. Asprey, *War in the Shadows: The Guerrilla in History*, vol. 2 (Garden City, NY: Doubleday and Co., 1975), 862–86.

10. Frank Kitson, "Counterinsurrection in Kenya," in *Guerrilla Strategies: An Historical Anthology from the Long March to Afghanistan*, ed. Gérard Chaliand (Berkeley, CA: University of California Press, 1982), 163–65.

11. ZANLA, the military wing of the Zimbabwe African National Union (ZANU), was one of two major insurgent groups that competed for control of the insurgency, and ultimately for control of an independent Zimbabwe. The other group was the Zimbabwe People's Revolutionary Army (ZIPRA), the military wing of the Zimbabwe African People's Union (ZAPU).

12. For background on the formation of the Selous Scouts, see Daly and Stiff, *Selous Scouts,* 44–83.

13. Kitson, "Counterinsurrection in Kenya," 171–72.

14. Kitson, *Gangs and Counter-gangs,* 126.

15. Daly and Stiff, *Selous Scouts,* 103–104.

16. Ibid., 104.

17. Kitson, *Gangs and Counter-gangs,* 127.

18. Eric Hoffer, *The True Believer: Thoughts on the Nature of Mass Movements* (New York: Perennial Classics, 2002), 17.

19. Kitson, *Gangs and Counter-gangs,* 126.

20. Valeriano, "Military Operations," 39.

21. Valeriano and Bohannan, *Counter-guerrilla Operations,* 147–48.

22. Charles Bohannan, "Unconventional Operations," in *Counter-guerrilla Operations in the Philippines, 1946–1953: A Seminar on the Huk Campaign Held at Ft. Bragg, N.C., 15 June 1961,* 65–66.

23. Greenberg, *The Hukbalahap Insurrection,* 88–89.

24. For details of the command arrangements, see Anthony Clayton, *Counter-insurgency in Kenya: A Study of Military Operations against the Mau Mau* (Manhattan, KS: Sunflower University Press, 1984), 3–12.

25. Kitson, *Gangs and Counter-gangs*, 11–12, 185–88.

26. Daly and Stiff, *Selous Scouts,* 47.

27. Ibid., 264.

28. Ibid., 308.

29. Valeriano and Bohannan, *Counter-guerrilla Operations,* 147.

30. Kitson, *Gangs and Counter-gangs,* 95.

31. Ibid., 76–77.

32. Daly and Stiff, *Selous Scouts,* 47.

33. Ibid., 76.

34. Ibid., 330.

35. Ibid., 125.

36. ZANLA was the military wing of the Zimbabwe African National Union (ZANU) that was eventually led by Robert Mugabe. The majority of its combatants were Shona. It espoused a Mao-like form of rural insurgency and was supported by the People's Republic of China. Its main bases were in Mozambique. ZIPRA was the military wing of the Zimbabwe African People's Union (ZAPU) that was led by Mugabe's rival Joshua Nkomo. Its combatants were largely Ndebele who were recruited in Botswana and trained in Zambia and Angola by advisers from the Soviet Union. Unlike ZANLA, whose forces operated as guerrillas, ZIPRA also trained its members to be conventional forces. ZIPRA appears to have held some of its forces in reserve for an anticipated battle with ZANLA after the defeat of Rhodesia. For details, see Steven C. Rubert and R. Kent Rasmussen, *Historical Dictionary of Zimbabwe*, 3rd ed. (Lanham, MD: Scarecrow Press, 2001), 357–70.

37. Kitson, *Gangs and Counter-gangs,* 170.

38. Andrew D. Sens, comp., *A Summary of the U.S. Role in Insurgency Situations in the Philippine Islands 1899–1955* (Washington, DC: Special Operations Research Office, The American University, 1964), 24.

39. "Convention Respecting the Laws and Customs of War on Land" [Hague Convention IV], 1907, "Annex to the Convention: Regulations Respecting the Laws and Customs of War on Land," art. 23(f), available at www.icrc.org/IHL.nsf.

40. Additional Protocol I, art. 39(2). For some of the efforts to clarify the language, see Howard S. Levie, *Protection of War Victims: Protocol 1 to the 1949 Geneva Conventions*, vol. 2 (Dobbs Ferry, NY: Oceana Publications, 1980), 319–28.

41. "Rome Statute of the International Criminal Court," 1998, art. 8(b)(vii), available at www.un.org/law/icc/statute/romefra.htm.

42. Additional Protocol I, art. 1(4).

43. Dieter Fleck, ed., *The Handbook of Humanitarian Law in Armed Conflicts* (Oxford: Oxford University Press, 1995), 201.

44. For a detailed discussion of this issue and an extensive list of operations in which military forces wore civilian clothes or enemy uniforms, see Hays Parks, "Special Forces' Wear of Non-standard Uniforms," *Chicago Journal of International Law* 4 (Fall 2003).

45. Robert B. Edgerton, *Mau Mau: An African Crucible* (New York: Free Press, 1989), 142–72.

46. See, for example, Ian Martinez, "Rhodesian Anthrax: The Use of Bacteriological & Chemical Agents during the Liberation War of 1965–80," *Indiana International & Comparative Law Review* 13 (2003). Available online through LexisNexis Academic.

47. Kitson, *Gangs and Counter-gangs,* 46.

Part Two

Present Context and Environment

7 The Threat to the Maritime Domain: How Real Is the Terrorist Threat?

Rohan Gunaratna

INTRODUCTION

Armed groups seek to attack aviation, maritime, and land transportation targets. In the class of threats, the terrorists' intentions and capabilities to strike transportation infrastructure have grown dramatically since September 11, 2001. Although land transportation remains more vulnerable to attack, aviation remains the preferred target of multiple threat groups. Since Al Qaeda used commercial aircraft to attack America's iconic targets, multiple attempts to target aviation have been detected and disrupted by security, intelligence, and law enforcement. The United Kingdom authorities disrupted an elaborate plot in August 2006 to attack a dozen aircraft from London bound for the United States. The threat has been sustained.[1] Similarly, the successful attacks on land transportation targets in Madrid on 11 March 2004, in London on 7 July 2006, and in Mumbai (formerly Bombay) on 11 July 2006 demonstrate both the dispersed and the enduring nature of the threat. The failed attack in London on 21 July 2006, and several attempts in continental Europe and elsewhere, demonstrate that the threat is recurrent.

To assess the current and emerging threat, it is necessary to understand how armed groups exploit the maritime domain. The lack of understanding of the guerrilla and terrorist interface with the maritime environment has led to a hyping of the threat. This has led the commercial and naval communities to invest billions of dollars in protecting and securing maritime assets. What is the real threat to onshore and offshore maritime infrastructure from sea, land, and air? This chapter will examine the development of maritime

Rohan Gunaratna is head, International Centre for Political Violence and Terrorism Research, Institute of Defence and Strategic Studies in Singapore. He is also a senior fellow, Fletcher School of Law and Diplomacy's Jebsen Center for Counter-terrorism Studies, Boston; a senior fellow, National Memorial Institute for the Prevention of Terrorism, Oklahoma; an honorary fellow and member of the Advisory Council, International Policy Institute for Counter-terrorism, Israel; and a member, Steering Committee, George Washington University's Homeland Security Policy Institute. He holds a master's degree in international peace studies from Notre Dame, United States, where he was a Hesburgh Scholar, and a doctorate in international relations from St. Andrews, where he was a British Chevening Scholar. Dr. Gunaratna has over 20 years of academic, policy, and operational experience in counterterrorism. He led the specialist team that designed and built the UN database on the mobility, weapons, and finance of al-Qaeda, the Taliban, and their entities. He is the author of 12 books, including *Inside Al Qaeda: Global Network of Terror,* published by Columbia University Press, an international best seller. He serves on the editorial boards of *Studies in Conflict and Terrorism* and *Terrorism and Political Violence,* the leading counterterrorism academic journals.

terrorist and guerrilla capabilities and how guerrilla and terrorist groups have penetrated the maritime domain both to support their operations and to mount attacks.

UNDERSTANDING THE MARITIME DOMAIN

A study of maritime-capable groups worldwide demonstrates that only a few armed groups have developed the capabilities to mount attacks on maritime targets. Most groups exploit the maritime environment to transport goods and personnel.[2] The attacks in the aviation domain are not restricted to aircraft. Armed groups seek to attack not only aircraft, ships, and land transportation but also airports, ports, and land transportation hubs. Attacking an airport could have the same effect as attacking an aircraft. Similarly, an attack on a railway station could have the same effect as attacking a train. Likewise, an attack on a port will have the same effect as—or a greater effect than—an attack on a ship. Unlike the aviation and land transportation domains, the maritime domain does not naturally constitute an attractive domain to attack. The terrorist preference is to attack a high-profile national symbol. In a globalized world, an attack on an aircraft in any part of the highly visible aviation arena will have global implications. In contrast to damaging a ship on the sea surface, bombing an airliner in the skies or an international airport will draw extensive publicity and generate fear. As such, the threat to aviation and airports is very high compared to the threat to the maritime and land domains.

It has been argued that hardening aviation and airport targets has shifted the threat to maritime targets. Certainly threat displacement has taken place, but still, due to the potential for high publicity, the terrorist preference is to attack hardened targets. After 9/11, more than a dozen plots to attack airliners, both in the sky and on the ground, have been foiled or aborted. This demonstrates that contemporary terrorists are keen to identify the gaps and loopholes in security and penetrate the aviation domain rather than strike the maritime domain.

In most cases, guerrilla and terrorist groups will attack a maritime target only if it is attractive or profitable. Attacking a ship on the high seas is like a tree falling in the forest. Guerrilla and terrorist groups seek to mount low-cost, high-impact attacks. As armed groups seek publicity, their preference is to attack a target near the waterfront or in port. Furthermore, most groups do not have access to large boats or ships that can operate outside territorial waters. Except to steal cargo or kidnap personnel and passengers, the guerrillas and terrorists prefer to attack targets not far away from shore. As such, guerrilla and terrorist target choices reduce the threat to maritime infrastructure. By nature, most guerrillas and terrorists are landlubbers.

UNDERSTANDING THE MARITIME THREAT

Maritime guerrilla and terrorist capabilities are extensions of their land capabilities. However, maritime intentions are different from maritime capabilities. Translating intentions into capabilities requires significant human expertise (experience and training) and resources. If a guerrilla and terrorist group can develop its understanding and knowledge of the maritime environment, it will begin to exploit that domain. In the early phases, most groups use the maritime environment to support land operations and, second, to mount attacks.

At this point in time, only a few groups have the domain expertise. Even fewer groups have developed the capacities to operate out at sea. If they are to operate in a sustained manner, they must possess or have access to a fleet of craft, usually fishing craft, and seafarers. The overall terrorist and guerrilla know-how and understanding of operating in the maritime domain are limited. The body of knowledge and understanding is growing by direct transfer and by emulation. More armed groups are likely to mount guerrilla and terrorist tactics in the maritime domain in the future.

Among the contemporary terrorist and guerrilla groups, only half-a-dozen groups have developed maritime attack capabilities. The most prominent among them are the Palestinian Hamas, the Lebanese Hezbollah, the Abu Sayyaf Group (ASG), the Free Aceh Movement, the Moro Islamic Liberation Front, Al Qaeda, and the Liberation Tigers of Tamil Eelam (LTTE). We consider two case studies here: Al Qaeda and the LTTE. Of these two groups, the LTTE has built a state-of-the-art blue-, brown-, and green-water capability, both for support and for attack operations. To penetrate the maritime domain, the LTTE operations serve as a model for other terrorist and guerrilla groups.

THE LTTE MARITIME STRUCTURE

The LTTE maritime organizational structure provides insight into the future capabilities of terrorist and guerrilla groups seeking to operate in the maritime environment.

1. Sea battle regiments
2. Underwater demolition teams
3. Sea Tiger strike groups
4. Marine engineering and boat-building unit
5. Radar and telecom unit
6. Marine weapons armory and dump group
7. Maritime school and academy
8. Recruiting section
9. Political, financial, and propaganda section
10. Exclusive economic zone–marine logistics support team
11. Reconnaissance team and intelligence section
12. Welfare and registry.

The LTTE was able to build a robust maritime infrastructure because of the initial assistance it received from India's foreign intelligence service, Research and Analysis Wing (RAW). In 1986–1987, RAW trained LTTE members in Vishakhapatnam, a seaport in Andhra Pradesh, and facilitated the LTTE's construction of a blue-water fleet. After the LTTE declared war on the government of India in 1987, the LTTE maritime capabilities suffered extensively. After the LTTE support structures moved out of India's sphere of influence, the LTTE built up a state-of-the-art shipping and procurement network in Europe to procure and ship dual-user technologies and weapons. For instance, the LTTE procured 60 tonnes of high explosives from the Ukraine and transported it onboard MV *Baris* (previously MV *Illiyana,* and thereafter MV *Tara 1* and MV *Venus*) during the peace talks in 1994. After the shipping network in Europe was disrupted under Indian pressure, the LTTE strengthened its existing financial, procurement, and shipping network in Southeast Asia. The LTTE used its commercial presence in Southeast Asia to build operational bases, primarily using Myanmar's island of Twante and, thereafter, Thailand's Pukhet. The LTTE boatyard in Pukhet was building a minisubmarine.

After the Thai authorities shut down the boatyard, the LTTE moved its boat-building activities to New Zealand. Boat designs procured in Australia and built in New Zealand were used in maritime suicide attacks in Sri Lanka.

As the LTTE is not an Islamist group, it is not perceived as a threat by most foreign governments. Thus, the LTTE continues to operate both in Sri Lanka and globally through front, cover, and sympathetic organizations. They include trading and commercial firms, especially fertilizer and shipping companies.

AL QAEDA'S MARITIME STRUCTURE

In contrast to the LTTE, Al Qaeda does not possess a permanent and robust infrastructure dedicated to maritime operations. Unlike the LTTE, Al Qaeda has neither a blue- nor a brown-water fleet. Although two dozen ships linked with Al Qaeda members, supporters, and families have been identified by the intelligence community, to date no ship has been intercepted transporting weapons. However, Al Qaeda mounted a number of terrorist attacks, successfully and unsuccessfully. Al Qaeda leadership tasked its operations leader in the Arabian Peninsula[3]—Abd al Rahim al Nashiri, alias Abu Bilal, alias Mullah Bilal, alias the Prince of the Sea, a specialist in explosives—to mount maritime attacks in 1999. Osama bin Laden specifically instructed al Nashiri to attack oil supertankers. A Saudi of Yemeni roots, al Nashiri operated largely out of Yemen, both with Al Qaeda and with other Islamist groups. He had links with individuals and groups in the Arabian Peninsula and North Africa.

As there was no dedicated maritime component in Al Qaeda, the rest of the organization assisted al Nashiri. For instance, Tawfiq bin Attash alias Khallad, deputy of Khalid Sheikh Mohamed (9/11 mastermind), visited with al Nashiri and his associates to support his operations both in the Middle East and in Southeast Asia. Al Qaeda studied LTTE maritime attacks recorded from international television.[4] This enabled Al Qaeda to copy LTTE maritime tactics as well as develop its own repertoire of techniques. They included blowing up explosives-laden vessels near naval, merchant, and cruise ships; blowing up explosives-laden vessels at seaports; using big ships, including tankers, to crash into smaller vessels; diving aircraft into ships, including into an aircraft carrier; using underwater demolition teams to destroy ships; and sinking ships in narrow channels. Responsible for attacking the USS *Cole* and MV *Limburg*, al Nashiri succeeded in blowing up explosives-laden boats near naval and merchant ships.

Even in the conduct of maritime operations, Al Qaeda had no problem with working with like-minded individuals and other groups. As a result, Al Qaeda traces were found in maritime operations mounted by other groups. Al Qaeda trained in Iraq and funded an operational cell in Turkey that was planning and preparing to strike an Israeli cruise ship. Other leaders and members of Al Qaeda and its associated groups attempted a number of other maritime attacks. In Singapore, working with Al Qaeda, Jemaah Islamiyah (JI) members mounted surveillance on U.S. warships. Video footage of U.S. ships was recovered both in the residence of a JI member in Singapore and in the bombed residence of Abu Hafs in Afghanistan. In Malaysia, Al Qaeda associate group Kumpulan Militan

Malaysia (KMM) planned to kill U.S. sailors but, fearing retaliation, aborted the operation. Tawfiq bin Attash flew to Malaysia and planned to attack U.S. vessels in Port Klang in Malaysia. Al Qaeda's senior representative in Southeast Asia, Omar al Farouq, an Iraqi-Kuwaiti, and Ghalib, a Somali, planned a suicide attack on U.S. vessels exercising off Surabaya, Indonesia.

AL QAEDA'S MARITIME OPERATION

Al Qaeda developed its road to maritime attacks the same way most other threat groups graduate from support to attack operations. Al Qaeda used trawlers and other vessels to transport arms, ammunition, and explosives from Yemen to neighboring countries. In fishing vessels, Al Qaeda also transported explosives into Kenya for the east Africa attack in August 1998. An Al Qaeda cell in Yemen began planning to hit USS *The Sullivans* in the spring of 1999 and made preparations in the summer of 1999. Al Qaeda began recruiting Saudis of Yemeni background and Yemeni residents, including those who wished to be suicide operatives. Al Qaeda preparations included leasing a safe house for six months, installing a gate, procuring a truck, and procuring and modifying a boat to accommodate more explosives. On 3 January 2000, when USS *The Sullivans* arrived in port, the explosives-laden suicide boat was launched from a nearby beach. From its weight, the boat sank almost immediately. USS *The Sullivans* departed unaware of the attempt. The boat and explosives were recovered the next day for use in the USS *Cole* attack. As Al Qaeda in Yemen needed financing to execute the next attack, its members decided to meet with Tawfiq bin Attash in Singapore. As there were visa requirements for Singapore, they shifted the venue of the meeting to Thailand. Two Al Qaeda members, Nibras and Quso, departed for Bangkok, where they met with Khallad, who gave them the money. After returning to Yemen, they made preparations in the spring and summer of 2000 to attack the USS *Cole*.

In preparation for the USS *Cole* attack, Al Qaeda built a much more extensive land infrastructure. A metal fence was built around the house it rented in an Aden suburb to keep its activities hidden from neighbors. In addition to renting a new safe house and adding a higher fence, Al Qaeda rented another apartment with a harbor view. This safe house functioned as the perfect observation post. Al Qaeda modified the boat, painted it, laid a red carpet, and refitted the insulation. Although the neighbors reported the noise of construction and power outages, the authorities failed to investigate. Compared to the USS *The Sullivans* attack, the investment Al Qaeda made to ensure the success of the attack on USS *Cole* was significant. Learning from the USS *The Sullivans* failure, Al Qaeda rehearsed the operation. To ensure that the boat had the right quantity of explosives, Al Qaeda conducted a dry run. Al Qaeda even tested the explosives. One month before the attack, in keeping with the standard operating procedure for Al Qaeda leaders, al Nashiri departed for Afghanistan.

The USS *Cole*, a guided-missile destroyer (DDG), had a crew of 346. The 154-meter-long and 21-meter-wide ship had a displacement of 8,422 tons. The ship had a maximum speed of 33 knots. Its armaments included antiaircraft missiles, antiship missiles, torpedoes, a five-inch gun, and Phalanx close-in weapon system. The sequence of events was:

- 0849 local—USS *Cole* moors for refueling in Aden Harbor.
- 1115 local—Ship is approached by small boat; two adult males are aboard.

- 1122 local—Boat comes along port side of USS *Cole*.
- Detonation occurs immediately afterward.

The execution phase of the attack was less than 30 minutes; the attack phase was seven minutes. The sneak attack killed 17 and injured 42, most sailors gathering at the galley area for lunch. The repairing of the ship cost $250 million. The $1 billion ship was out of commission for two years. The U.S. government did not retaliate against Al Qaeda. In the eyes of the jihadists, USS *Cole* was America's state-of-the-art warship. In retaliation for the attacks on the U.S. embassies in east Africa in August 1998, USS *Cole* had fired cruise missiles at the Al Qaeda camps in Afghanistan. As such, the attack against USS *Cole* was considered a huge victory. Al Qaeda wanted to exploit the publicity to recruit and generate support. Using a secret pager code, Al Qaeda leadership had instructed Quso to videotape the attack, but he overslept on the day of the attack. Osama bin Laden was keen to screen the USS *Cole* attack video at his son's wedding in early 2001. Osama authorized $5,000 to buy the camera equipment and videotape the attack. Thus, Quso did not endear himself to Osama. Although the failure to videotape the attack was a disappointment personally for Osama, the attack itself was a significant victory for Al Qaeda.

Two years after the attack on USS *Cole*, Al Qaeda reconstituted its personnel and resources to mount a second attack in Yemen. The next visiting U.S. warship was to be the next target. But when the naval ship failed to turn up, Al Qaeda attacked MV *Limburg*, a target of opportunity. A very large crude carrier (VLCC), the 25-crew MV *Limburg* was Belgian owned and French flagged. The 332-meter-long and 58-meter-wide ship has a displacement of 300,000 tons. MV *Limburg* has a capacity for 2.16 million barrels, but the cargo at the time of the attack was 397,000 barrels. Early in the morning on 6 October 2002, when *Limburg* was within visual range of shore (approximately three nautical miles), an attack boat rammed the starboard (seaward) side. The oil tanker was moving slowly toward the terminal, and a pilot boat was coming along the port side. While one crew member was killed, 90,000 barrels of oil spilled. As in the USS *Cole* attack, a safe house was used with a walled courtyard, and the boat was transported to a launch site just before the attack. Directed by al Nashiri, two suicide bombers in an explosives-laden boat attacked the near-stationary vessel. Unlike in the case of the USS *Cole*, Al Qaeda targeted an oil tanker instead of a warship. Furthermore, Al Qaeda leveraged an existing indigenous extremist network. It consisted of former members and supporters of the Islamic Army of the Abyan, a group that was dismantled by the Yemeni authorities two years earlier. The Al Qaeda plan was for the attack on MV *Limburg* to coincide with a simultaneous land-based attack. Although the Al Qaeda leadership had mentioned economic targets, the attack shocked the maritime community. The Yemeni authorities briefly held the ship owner, thinking that an accident on board the *Limburg* had caused the oil to spill.

Within a month of the attack on MV *Limburg*, al Nashiri was tracked down and captured. Al Nashiri was escaping from Yemen to Malaysia at the time. He was planning and preparing several maritime operations. When al Nashiri was arrested in November 2002, a 180-page dossier of targets was recovered from his laptop. An operation al Nashiri was planning against U.S. and UK ships in the Strait of Gibraltar, off the northern coast of

Morocco, was disrupted in June 2002. Three Saudi Al Qaeda members with Moroccan wives pretending to be businessmen constituted the attack team. They had received $5,000 and direction from al Nashiri to mount reconnaissance on both land and maritime targets. When the Al Qaeda reconnaissance cell was disrupted in June 2002, no explosives were found. NATO maritime forces responded by boarding high-risk and suspicious ships, and German naval ships escorted tankers through the Strait of Gibraltar.

MARITIME ATTACK CAPABILITIES

Most terrorist and guerrilla groups can build maritime support capabilities by chartering ships or leasing boats. But to mount sustained attacks, they must build their own fleet and personnel. Unlike the LTTE, Al Qaeda failed to harness its existing expertise to operate in the maritime domain. Al Qaeda failed to build a dedicated maritime infrastructure of personnel and resources to attack maritime assets. Although Al Qaeda had experts who understood the maritime domain and operational infrastructure, it failed to grow its expertise. This was largely because the group's capabilities were scattered and had no permanent safe haven near the sea.

After the attack on USS *The Sullivans* failed, Al Qaeda explosives expert Abdul Rahman al Mohajir al Masri designed a shaped charge. A trainer at al Farook in Mes Aynak, southeast of Kabul (before the camp moved in 2000 to Kandahar), Abdul Rahman al Mohajir served under Abu Mohamed al Masri and later Hamza al Rabbiyah, the successive heads of training.[5] His reputation as the successful designer of the USS *Cole* attack was such that the leader of Al Qaeda in Iraq, Abu Musab al Zarqawi, requested the then-head of Al Qaeda's external operations, Faraj al Libi, to dispatch Abdul Rahman al Mohajir to Iraq.[6] Instead, the Al Qaeda leadership on the Pakistan-Afghanistan border offered Hamza al Rabbiyah, but Zarqawi preferred Abdul Rahman al Mohajir. Zarqawi, who had mounted one maritime attack, was keen to use his expertise to mount more maritime attacks. Zarqawi also funded an attack on an Israeli cruise ship in the Turkish Mediterranean port of Antalya. However, Zarqawi, too, failed to develop a permanent operational infrastructure—both personnel and resources—dedicated to attacking maritime targets.

Immediately after Operation Enduring Freedom began in Afghanistan, Al Qaeda also considered hijacking an aircraft and crashing it onto a U.S. aircraft carrier in the Indian Ocean. The U.S. government released a NOTEM (note to mariners) of the impending threat. Until Al Qaeda operational leaders with the competence to operate in the maritime domain were captured or killed, Al Qaeda's maritime capabilities focused on mounting surface operations. Nonetheless, Al Qaeda was planning to build an underwater-diving capability. Recoveries from the residence of Abu Hafs al Masri, alias Mohammed Atef—the Al Qaeda military commander killed in November 2001—included a diving manual. The Al Qaeda documents indicated that the group had recruited a specialist who understood diving, diving medicine, and closed-circuit and semi-closed-circuit gear. As the group needed operational cover, Al Qaeda intended to enlist the support of commercial and recreational divers to build an underwater-diving capability. Furthermore, Al Qaeda had plans to establish its own diving schools. When Al Qaeda's infrastructure in Afghanistan was dismantled and its plans disrupted, its associated groups invested in building diving capabilities in Europe and in Asia. Although the Al Qaeda attempt to penetrate a diving school in Holland was detected, its training activities continued uninterrupted in Southeast Asia. With the assistance of Arab diving instructors, the ASG in the Philippines has trained at least 40 of its members in Jolo in the Sulu Archipelago and Mindanao since 2001.

With the diffusion of Al Qaeda's ideology of global jihad focusing on killing Westerners in large numbers, several of its associated groups are behaving like Al Qaeda. On 27 February 2004, ASG mounted an operation using a member of the Rajah Solaiman Revolutionary Movement. Redento Cain Dellosa, trained by JI, planted an explosives-laden television set in the tourist compartment of *SuperFerry 14*, plying between Manila and the southern Philippines. Next to the television improvised explosive device, the bomber left a plate of hot food to indicate that he was a passenger who had briefly stepped out of his cabin. The explosion and the subsequent fire killed 118 passengers; it was the worst maritime terrorist attack in history. Several other attempts to bomb ferries, before and after the sinking of *SuperFerry 14*, were frustrated by the Philippine authorities. However, the threat of terrorist groups planting bombs on ferries is very real, both in Southeast Asia and beyond. Thus, future maritime threats to ships will not only be from surface and underwater attacks but also from bombs carried on board the ships.

LESSONS IDENTIFIED

Most guerrilla and terrorist groups learn incrementally. Most groups are not innovative but imitative. Contrary to the prevalent view, they learn both by emulation and technology transfer. More than benefiting from the direct transfer of technologies, they copy technologies, tactics, and techniques. For instance, Al Qaeda's attack on USS *Cole* was a copycat of the LTTE's attack on *Abheetha,* a Sri Lankan navy supply ship. On 4 May 1991, *Abheetha* was anchored six miles north of Point Pedro, northern Sri Lanka, when an explosives-laden suicide boat rammed it. The attack caused extensive damage to the ship, and killed six and injured 18 naval personnel. The LTTE maritime suicide wing (Black Sea Tigers) members Captain Sithambaram and Captain Jeyanthan were also killed.

Similarly, it is very likely that one attack inspires another. After the alarm and publicity generated after Al Qaeda's attack on the USS *Cole* on 12 October 2000, many terrorist and guerrilla groups became interested in mounting attacks in the maritime domain. Within a month of the USS *Cole* suicide bombing on 12 October, the terrorist "copycat effect" was demonstrated. LTTE suicide stealth boats breached the defenses of Trincomalee, the most protected Sri Lankan naval port, and destroyed a fast personnel carrier on 23 October; and a Palestinian Hamas suicide boat attacked an Israeli naval craft on 7 November 2000. As the bomber detonated prematurely, only the skin of the Israeli craft was damaged.

Since 9/11, Al Qaeda has become operationally weak but it has provided its associated groups both the inspiration and the knowledge to conduct maritime terrorist attacks. Although Al Qaeda itself is capable of mounting maritime attacks, the greater threat to maritime security stems from Al Qaeda's associated groups in Asia, Africa, the Middle East, and the West. In Pakistan's Federally Administered Tribal Areas (FATA) and in Iraq, Al Qaeda has suffered the death or incarceration of its specialist bomb makers, but there are others who understand how to plan, prepare, and execute maritime operations. Nevertheless, Al Qaeda continues to inspire both its associated groups and homegrown cells—especially those trained by Al Qaeda in FATA and elsewhere—to mount maritime attacks. Similarly, using its multimedia arm Al Sahab, Al Qaeda inspires the wider global jihad movement to operate on land, sea, and air. As a matter of fact, the first of over 100 videos produced by Al Sahab was on the USS *Cole*. In it, celebrating the *Cole* attack at his son Mohamed's Kandahar wedding in February 2001, Osama bin Laden is shown reciting a poem stating, "And in Aden, they charged and destroyed a destroyer that fearsome people fear, one that evokes horror when it docks and when it sails." Although the poem does not name the warship, the film flaunts an image of a fiery explosion with superimposed Arabic words, "the destruction of the American Destroyer Cole."[7]

To attack maritime targets, terrorist groups build their support and operational infrastructures on land, not at sea. Thus, the logical starting point in preventing future maritime attacks is to disrupt and degrade the terrorist infrastructure on land. The USS *The Sullivans,* USS *Cole,* MV *Limburg,* and several other case studies demonstrate that both maritime terrorism and piracy should be fought on land. As the terrorist and criminal infrastructure and personnel are based on land, they can be identified and targeted much more effectively by law enforcement and intelligence services operating on land. The failure to detect the planning and preparations of a maritime terrorist or piratical attack on land will lead the terrorist group or the criminal group to successfully launch the maritime attack. In a maritime terrorist or piratical attack, the time the terrorists and pirates spend out at sea is a few minutes. Unless the method, the place, and the exact time of the attack is known, it is not possible to interdict a maritime terrorist or piratical attack out at sea. As such, the maritime police units·and navies have a very limited opportunity to successfully respond to maritime terrorism and piracy.

CONCLUSION

Most threat groups exploit the maritime domain for support, not offensive operations. More groups are interested in developing and expanding their range of maritime capabilities. Over time, most threat groups with access to water move from conducting support operations to guiding surface and underwater attack capabilities. Traditionally maritime terrorist technologies originated in the Middle East, but now they can be seen increasingly in Asia. In the coming years, the Asian threat groups are likely to innovate certain technologies and tactics that Middle Eastern groups are likely to copy.

Compared to the threat to aviation and land transportation, the threat from terrorism to naval ships and commercial shipping is medium to low. While the maritime assets are vulnerable to terrorist attack, the actual threat to maritime assets is medium to low for two reasons. First, very few terrorist groups have the capabilities to attack maritime targets. Second, very few attractive maritime targets could be attacked without expending many resources. Although naval vessels can be protected by enhanced perimeter security, it is neither feasible nor cost effective to protect every merchant vessel. An effective strategy for consideration by law enforcement and intelligence services should include (a) creating dedicated maritime counterterrorist commands to target terrorist groups with land-based maritime assets; (b) securing waterways used by ships operating in areas where terrorist and criminal groups are active; and (c) protecting cruise liners, oil tankers, liquefied natural gas and liquefied propane gas carriers, and other vessels transporting strategic cargo operating in areas where terrorist and criminal groups are known to be active.

The threat of a maritime attack is of low probability. Depending on the target attacked, the consequences can be medium or high. As 95 percent of the world's trade moves by sea, even if ten vessels are attacked in a single day, shipping will continue. Certainly the rising insurance premiums and investment in security will increase the cost of transportation and goods. However, the dependence of nations on the maritime component of trade and commerce is of such paramount consideration that governments and the private sector will not seek alternative modes of transport. If the number of maritime attacks increases, governments and the private sector will invest excessively in securing the maritime domain. As of today, most of the investment to secure the maritime domain is driven by fear, not by an understanding of the threat. At the dawn of the twenty-first century, with the emergence of Al Qaeda, a trendsetter, the global maritime threat landscape has been changed forever.

NOTES

This chapter is a revision of a paper originally presented at a workshop on economics and maritime strategy sponsored by the William B. Ruger Chair of National Security Economics in Newport, Rhode Island, in November 2006.

1. On 22 December 2001, Richard Reid, wearing a triacetone triperoxide–laden operational shoe bomb, boarded a Paris-to-Miami American Airline flight. In Operation Snagged, an identical shoe bomb was recovered from 44 St. James Street, Gloucester, UK, on 27 November 2003. In Operation Dover Port, Andrew Rowe was arrested at a port in France on 26 October 2003. He was planning to attack Heathrow. On 15 September 2004, a fully operational shoe bomb mailed from Thailand to California was detected at the Carson mail facility in California. In 2005, an Algerian terrorist prosecuted in Northern Ireland had a manual advising the bomber to detonate his shoe bomb in the aircraft toilet. International Center for Political Violence and Terrorism Research Global PathFinder Database, www.icpvtrdatabase.org (accessed 11 November 2006).

2. It is very much like the terrorist and the extremist use of the Internet. Instead of mounting attacks on information infrastructure, terrorist and guerrilla groups use the Internet to disseminate propaganda, raise funds, train, rehearse, and coordinate operations. Likewise, the maritime domain is primarily a medium to support operations and not to mount attacks.

3. Al Nashiri, the first head of the Al Qaeda organization in the Arabian Peninsula, was succeeded by Yousef al Aiyyeri. After al Aiyyeri was killed by Saudi security forces in May 2003, Abu Hazim al Shair al Yemeni, a former bodyguard of Osama and a poet, was appointed. Abu Hazim al Shair recruited pilots to attack Heathrow. Abu Hazim al Shair was succeeded by Abdu Aziz al Mukrin. After al Mukrin was killed, he was succeeded by Salih Sufi. There has been a very high attrition rate of the Al Qaeda leadership in the Arabian Peninsula. As the bulk of the recruits and finance for Al Qaeda originated in the Arabian Peninsula, Osama handpicked the leaders of the Arabian Peninsula. While most of them were former bodyguards of Osama bin Laden, they had long-standing contact with Khalid Sheikh Mohamed and Tawfiq bin Attash, also a former bodyguard of the Al Qaeda leader.

4. CNN's Nic Robertson recovered about 200 tapes from the Al Qaeda registry in Afghanistan. These included several clips of LTTE maritime attacks. Nic Robertson, "Tapes Shed New Light on bin Laden's Network," *CNN.com,* 19 August 2002, archives.cnn.com/2002/US/08/18/terror.tape.main/index.html.

5. After Al Qaeda was dislodged from Afghanistan, Abdul Rahman al Mohajir accompanied Hamza al Rabbiyah to South Waziristan and thereafter to North Waziristan. Under pressure from the Pakistani military, Al Qaeda

dismantled its camps in South Waziristan and moved to North Waziristan to establish camps. Only the Chechens, Uighurs, and central Asian jihadists of the Islamic Movement of Uzbekistan remained in the south. When Abdul Rahman al Mohajir was killed by Pakistani forces in April 2006, he was head of training in Waziristan.

6. Zarqawi's driver was captured and Zarqawi's computer seized by the United States in February 2005. Correspondence recovered from the computer showed that instead of Abdul Rahman al Mohajir, Faraj al Libi offered Hamza al Rabiyyah. Later Faraj al Libi told CIA interrogators that Zarqawi did not have the skills of Hamza al Rabbiyah and that is why Zarqawi insisted on Abdul Rahman al Mohajir.

7. "A Claim for the Cole: Bin Laden Recruitment Tape Boasts the Bombing of the USS Cole," CBS News, 20 June 2001, www.cbsnews.com/stories/2001/06/20/world/main297600.shtml.

8 Armed Groups and the Law

Craig H. Allen

INTRODUCTION

In the tumultuous opening decade of the twenty-first century, the debate over which legal regime should be applied to armed groups leaped from its historical position in the pages of military manuals and academic journals to the front pages of leading newspapers and cable news services. As the violence by armed groups metastasizes and takes on new and ever-more-virulent forms, the legal system and its practitioners have struggled to keep up. There is every reason to believe that the United States is approaching a tipping point on the matter, and will soon be compelled to give the legal regime as much attention as has been given to strategies and policies for responding to the threats.

National security and defense strategists have long referred to the "spectrum of conflict," which stretches from low-level crime or civil disturbances in an otherwise "peaceful" situation at one end to unrestricted war between states at the other. Bookstores and leading journals are increasingly filled with dark and disturbing assessments documenting the emergence of a "new generation" of warfare operating in the middle of the spectrum—one characterized by strategies and tactics that blur the distinction between combatants and civilians, and that are often deployed in densely populated urban centers where avoiding collateral injury or damage to civilians and civilian objects is particularly difficult, and one that has now spread throughout what has been labeled the "arc of instability," with deadly forays into New York, Bali, Madrid, and London. The proponents and perpetrators of this new generation of warfare, which some believe now represents the dominant warfare paradigm, and which might soon be utterly transformed by the addition of weapons of mass destruction, pose a daunting challenge to our existing legal regime.

We find ourselves with a legal regime for large-scale violence that is seen by some as binary and yet, ironically, complete. On the one hand, we have a "warfare" paradigm for formal belligerencies and insurgencies, while on the other we rely on a law enforcement paradigm for violence at the low-level end of the spectrum of conflict. The choice has

Craig H. Allen joined the University of Washington law school faculty in 1996, following his retirement from the U.S. Coast Guard. Professor Allen is on the board of editors of *Ocean Development and International Law* and authored *Farwell's Rules of the Nautical Road* (Naval Institute Press, 2004). His most recent book is *Maritime Counterproliferation Operations and the Rule of Law* (Praeger, 2007). In 2003 he was named a Washington Law Foundation Scholar, and in 2005 he was appointed the Judson Falknor Professor of Law. During the 2006–07 academic year he served as the Charles H. Stockton Chair in International Law at the U.S. Naval War College in Newport, Rhode Island.

important consequences for issues regarding the use of force against members of armed groups, as well as their capture, detention, interrogation, and punishment. The warfare paradigm is principally grounded in the Hague Rules,[1] the Four Geneva Conventions,[2] and a body of customary international law, while the law enforcement paradigm is set out in a complex web of international conventions, bilateral treaties, and national laws. The warfare paradigm distinguishes between combatants and civilians; prescribes penalties for "war crimes," while otherwise immunizing lawful combatants for killing the enemy; and includes provisions for detention of enemy combatants and even civilians. The law enforcement paradigm consists of a broad set of criminal proscriptions, together with a body of international and national laws governing the extraterritorial application of national law, extradition, the rights of the accused, trial procedures, and, more recently, the relationship between national and international courts.

This chapter seeks to provide the reader with an introduction to the legal principles applicable to armed groups, with the more specific aim of providing the reader with the necessary background to evaluate three issues. The first is the extent to which members of armed groups may be targeted—that is, whether they can be killed by members of the armed forces of a state without benefit of prior due process of law. The second issue concerns the long-term detention of members of armed groups and the legal standards applicable to their capture, classification, interrogation, treatment, and release. The final issue focuses on the criminal liability of members of armed groups, either under the law of war or the ordinary international and national criminal laws typically applied in peacetime.

I. THE NATURE OF ARMED GROUPS AND THE THREATS THEY POSE

The terms coined to describe the various forms of "irregular" forces are numerous and oftentimes confusing.[3] Over the years, the term has been applied to armed bands, armed groups, armed opposition groups, guerrillas, insurgents, militias, organized resistance movements, rebels, transnational armed groups, volunteer corps, and the *levée en masse*. More specific labels, such as pirates, terrorist organizations, and criminal syndicates, and value-laden terms like "freedom fighters" and "liberation movements" are also common.

As the section below on the armed-conflict approach will discuss more fully, the term "armed group" can refer to "organized" armed groups that operate under a responsible commander and are linked to a state party to an armed conflict, to similarly organized groups that are not affiliated with any state, or to groups that fail to meet the test for an "organized" armed group. Armed groups might be assisting the state in its defense against another state, an occupying force (a "resistance" movement) or another armed group; or they may be attempting to overthrow the existing government of the state ("opposition" groups) or to secede from the state and form a new state (perhaps invoking some version of the right of self-determination). Until recently, armed groups generally operated within a single state or engaged in only occasional cross-border raids in an adjacent state.[4] Al Qaeda is the clear exception, with its demonstrated capability and intent to project power transnationally and to inflict strategic impacts and consequences.

This chapter will focus on armed groups engaged in organized violent acts that rise to the level of active hostilities. It will not address gangs, criminal organizations, or other groups that for the most part present lesser levels of violence. The analysis will also distinguish between armed groups associated with a state and nonstate armed groups. The analysis will draw on a variety of international legal authorities, including treaties, customary international law,[5] and decisions of United Nations bodies (particularly the Security Council and the International Court of Justice), as well as U.S. sources, including the Constitution and federal statutes and judicial decisions. The reader is cautioned that the legal effect of international law in U.S. courts is governed by rules and canons that are complex, confounding, and sometimes conflicting, and that this chapter can only provide an introduction to the subject.

II. ARMED GROUPS AND THE INSTRUMENTS OF NATIONAL POWER

States draw on their instruments of national power to promote and achieve their security interests. Traditionally, those instruments included diplomatic, information, military, and economic powers (collectively captured in the "DIME" acronym). "Hard power" approaches, like the use of armed force, while by no means obsolete or unnecessary, are increasingly supplemented by "strategic communications," information operations, and "soft power" methods, which are designed to extend the nation's influence and "win hearts and minds." At the same time, a variety of other instruments, including law enforcement and financial tools, export controls, and restrictions on access to militarily useful technology or information are brought to bear against nonstate actors, particularly those who might be seeking to acquire weapons of mass destruction. Within the United States, the president oversees the actual deployment of most of the instruments of national power, either as the commander in chief of the armed forces or as the chief executive. In doing so, however, the president must operate within existing constitutional and statutory authorities and is subject to judicial review.

Having a broad range of instruments of national power provides flexibility, but it also requires the national leadership to choose the instruments that will best achieve the national goals. As the introduction suggests, the debate over the "best" approach to large-scale violence by armed groups is often framed as a choice between two paradigms. However, a nation that capitalizes on the full range of its instruments of national power will not see its options in such narrow, dichotomous terms but rather will call for the selection of the optimal mix of all of the instruments available. That mix will be determined by the respective state agencies' legal authorities, capabilities, and capacities to act, as well as their abilities to attract partners to assist them in achieving the ends sought.

III. THE LAW ENFORCEMENT APPROACH

For some, the threat posed by transnational armed groups like Al Qaeda falls squarely within the ambit of the criminal justice approach to law enforcement. For example, in sentencing Richard Reid to life imprisonment for attempting to blow up a commercial airliner with a bomb implanted in his shoe, and after Reid made comments pledging his allegiance to Osama bin Laden, federal district judge William Young explained his status this way:

We are not afraid of any of your terrorist co-conspirators, Mr. Reid. We are Americans. We have been through the fire before. There is all too much war talk here. . . . You are not an enemy combatant. You are a terrorist. You are not a soldier in any way. You are a terrorist. To give you that reference, to call you a soldier, gives you far too much stature. . . . And we do not negotiate with terrorists. . . . We hunt them down, one by one, and we bring them to justice. So war talk is way out of line in this court. You're a big fellow. But you're not that big. You are no warrior. I know warriors. You are a terrorist. A species of criminal, guilty of multiple attempted murders.[6]

Armed Groups and the Criminal Law

The path to bring terrorists like Richard Reid and other armed-group members to justice is typically long and complex and criminal convictions are by no means assured. It is therefore not surprising that not everyone shares Judge Young's somewhat simplistic view of the issues. A criminal justice system requires that laws be prescribed, enforced, and adjudicated. The applicable law may be that of the state where the crime was committed, the state of nationality of the accused or the victim, a third state exercising universal jurisdiction, or an international tribunal. U.S. statutes potentially applicable to conduct by armed groups include, among others, those prohibiting murder and assault (both are generally limited to such offenses in the "special maritime and territorial jurisdiction of the United States"), weapons offenses, certain terrorist activities, war crimes, genocide, racketeering, torture, and treason. Interestingly, several of those criminal prohibitions include jurisdictional limits on their application. For example, Congress limited the war crimes statute to cases in which either the alleged perpetrator or the victim is a U.S. national. Until it was amended in 2007 the genocide statute was limited to acts within the United States or against a U.S. national. By contrast, the torture statute applies only to acts occurring outside the United States.

The territorial reach of national laws is also limited by international law. International law recognizes five bases for a state to prescribe laws. The two most widely accepted principles are territoriality (jurisdiction over conduct occurring or having an effect in the state's territory) and nationality (jurisdiction over conduct by nationals of the state or that was committed on vessels and aircraft registered in the state). The final three bases of jurisdiction, protective, passive personality, and universality, are less clearly established or accepted. Protective jurisdiction permits a state to prescribe laws to protect its vital national interests, such as the security of its currency against counterfeiting. Passive personality jurisdiction refers to the principle that a state may prescribe laws governing conduct that injures one of its nationals. The U.S. genocide statute cited above is an example. Universal jurisdiction applies to those acts, such as piracy, that are universally condemned and that all states have jurisdiction to proscribe, regardless of where the crime was committed or of the nationalities of the actors.

Even where a state might have jurisdiction as a matter of international law to proscribe certain conduct, or to take action to enforce those laws, it might not choose to do so in a given case (as Congress did in the examples cited above). Courts in the United States have, in fact, adopted a presumption that U.S. statutes do not apply extraterritorially, absent a clearly expressed intent by Congress, at least for statutes other than criminal laws that do not logically depend on their locality for the government's jurisdiction. In addition, some federal courts require, as a matter of due process, a nexus between the conduct of the accused and the United States, thus further limiting their extraterritorial applications.

International Criminal Tribunals

In the years since World War II, a number of ad hoc international criminal tribunals were constituted to adjudicate cases involving violations of international law during wars. Several of those ad hoc tribunals, including the international criminal tribunals for the Former Yugoslavia and for Rwanda, are still active. In 2002, the International Criminal Court (ICC) at The Hague became the first standing international criminal tribunal. The convention establishing the ICC, known as the Rome Statute,[7] in reference to the city where the treaty negotiations took place, now constitutes an important source of international criminal law. The statute defines, for example, war crimes, crimes against humanity, and the crime of genocide. In the near future a definition of the crime of aggression will likely be added by the states party to the Rome Statute.

Issues in the Law Enforcement Approach

The criminal justice system is carried out by government personnel charged with conducting investigations, prosecutions, adjudications, and incarcerations. The means and methods drawn upon to enforce laws vary from one nation-state to another. Within the United States, the criminal justice system functions within an elaborate system of checks and balances. Congress enacts the laws (all federal criminal laws are based on statutes), the executive branch investigates and initiates prosecutions when warranted, and the judicial branch adjudicates individual cases, while also exercising the power of judicial review over the other two branches to ensure they conform to the Constitution.

Any evaluation of the merits of the law enforcement approach to armed groups must acknowledge the obvious, but often-overlooked, requirement that a person may only be convicted of a crime where an applicable law prohibited the conduct at the time it was committed. This principle, known in the United States as the prohibition on *ex post facto* laws,[8] and internationally by the somewhat broader rule of *nullum crimen, nulla poena sine* (no crime can be committed and no punishment can be imposed without having been prescribed by a previous penal law), is a core tenet of the rule of law. Mature criminal justice systems also recognize a number of basic "due process" principles, including a presumption of innocence, the right to a speedy trial before an impartial judge and fact finder, conviction only upon proof of guilt beyond a reasonable doubt, and a right to appeal in cases of error at trial. Most such systems also include a right to be present during the trial, the right to confront witnesses in court, and the right to have the assistance of counsel throughout the proceedings.

Use of force against armed groups

The section on the armed-conflict approach that follows will describe the *jus ad bellum* restrictions on the use of armed force. For this section, however, it is important to bear in mind that not every use of force by a member of the armed forces constitutes an application of "armed force" under the UN Charter and the law of armed conflict. The focus of this section is on "police" force directed against private individuals who might be members of an armed group, but not agents of a government. The section that follows addresses the use of armed force by members of a state's armed forces.

Enforcement actions within the United States, or involving U.S. nationals beyond the U.S. border, are constrained by the U.S. Constitution. The Supreme Court has made it clear that any use of force by the government to effect a seizure (including a seizure of a person) must be "reasonable" under the Fourth Amendment.[9] As a result, the reasonableness test is the standard by which a claim of excessive force in any seizure will be measured.[10] In defining the contours of the reasonableness test the Supreme Court recognized that "police officers are often forced to make split-second judgments—in circumstances that are tense, uncertain, and rapidly evolving—about the amount of force that is necessary in a particular situation."[11] Accordingly, the Court held, the reasonableness of the officer's belief as to the appropriate level of force should be judged by that on-scene perspective.

The Court has articulated a three-part balancing test for the use of force that turns on the severity of the crime at issue, whether the suspect posed an immediate threat to others, and whether the suspect was actively resisting arrest or attempting to evade arrest by flight. If an officer reasonably, but mistakenly, believes that a suspect is likely to fight back, the officer is justified in using more force than might in fact be needed.[12] Law enforcement agents may also use force, including deadly force,[13] in self-defense. However, only that force reasonably necessary under the circumstances may be used. Force may not be used where assigned duties can be discharged without the use of force. However, there is no duty to retreat to avoid law enforcement situations justifying the use of force, including deadly force.

Like the application of national laws, the exercise of law enforcement authority outside the territorial limits of the state may be governed in part by international law. Under international law, the use of force in actions not amounting to armed conflict may be authorized or limited by treaty, customary international law, and general principles of law. For example, the Basic Principles on the Use of Force and Firearms by Law Enforcement Officials adopted by the United Nations[14] provide nonbinding guidance on the use of force in enforcement operations. Drawing on Article 3 of the UN Code of Conduct for Law Enforcement Officials,[15] the Basic Principles state that "law enforcement officials may use force only when strictly necessary and to the extent required for the performance of their duty." It generally argues against the use of firearms and asserts:

> Governments and law enforcement agencies should develop a range of means as broad as possible and equip law enforcement officials with various types of weapons and ammunition that would allow for a differentiated use of force and firearms. These would include the development of non-lethal incapacitating weapons for use in appropriate situations, with a view to increasingly restraining the application of means capable of causing death or injury to persons. For the same purpose, it should also be possible for law enforcement officials to be equipped with self-defensive equipment such as shields, helmets, bullet-proof vests and bullet-proof means of transportation, in order to decrease the need to use weapons of any kind.[16]

The commentary accompanying the Code of Conduct "emphasizes that the use of force by law enforcement officials should be exceptional." Whether such an approach is reasonable in situations involving members of armed groups is questionable.

Gathering intelligence and evidence on armed groups

The U.S. Constitution provides a number of important safeguards for persons suspected of or charged with a crime. Those rights include, for example, the rights to be free from unreasonable searches and seizures, to be provided "*Miranda* warnings" before being subjected to a custodial interrogation, and to have the assistance of legal counsel at certain critical stages in the criminal justice process. Typically, those safeguards are enforced by the exclusionary rule, which provides (with important exceptions) that evidence obtained in violation of the Constitution is not admissible against the defendant at trial.

The Supreme Court has held that the reasonableness requirement for searches under the Fourth Amendment does not apply to actions by U.S. law enforcement personnel acting outside U.S. territory when the action is taken against a nonnational of the United States.[17] Moreover, the reasonableness of foreign searches involving U.S. nationals is judged by reference to the law of the place where they were conducted.[18] At the same time, however, extraterritorial conduct by law enforcement officers amounting to "deliberate and unnecessary lawlessness" has on at least one occasion led the Court to dismiss the charges against the defendant.[19] Alternatively, such conduct may be analyzed under the applicable international human rights laws, which may provide additional or different protections.

Detention or expulsion of armed-group members

Responses to threats posed by armed groups may include expulsion or detention of aliens who have been determined to present a security risk to the nation. The Constitution of the United States and the International Covenant on Civil and Political Rights limit the state's power to detain an individual.[20] To be sure, there are well recognized exceptions. For example, in the United States persons may be detained for a reasonable period of time while awaiting trial or to serve as a material witness in a criminal case. The USA PATRIOT Act added or amended provisions authorizing the detention of aliens awaiting exclusion or deportation, and of suspected alien terrorists.[21] Nevertheless, such detentions are subject to a variety of substantive and procedural protections and are strictly limited in time.

Prosecution of armed-group members

There is nothing particularly remarkable about the practice of prosecuting members of armed groups under the ordinary criminal laws, so long as the prosecuting state has probable cause to believe that the persons charged committed a crime under laws applicable to their conduct and evidence sufficient to support a conviction. Prosecution might be carried out by the state where the conduct occurred, the state of nationality of the accused or the victim, a third state claiming treaty-based or universal jurisdiction over the offense, or an international criminal tribunal, such as the ICC. The choice of forum turns on questions of jurisdiction, the location of the accused, availability of witnesses and evidence, international comity, and the policies and predilections of the relevant states and their judges and prosecutors. It should be noted that membership in an armed group is almost never a defense to conduct proscribed by an applicable law. The notable exception is for conduct falling within the phrase "combatant immunity" discussed below in the section on the armed-conflict approach.

Evaluation of the Law Enforcement Approach

The criminal justice system is premised on the belief that criminal activity can be prevented or controlled through deterrence. Deterrence takes two forms. Specific deterrence refers to the practice, usually through imprisonment, of disabling a particular actor from committing future crimes. Richard Reid will be specifically deterred from committing future acts of airborne terror while imprisoned. General deterrence refers to the "public example" effect of such punishment in deterring others from committing crimes. General deterrence presumes a rational actor will refrain from criminal behavior if the potential cost, as discounted by the probability of apprehension and conviction, is too high. To the extent that a general-deterrence approach to criminal justice relies on the "choice theory" of criminal behavior,[22] which views the decision to engage in criminal activity as a rational choice based on the perceived consequences of engaging or not engaging in such conduct, the deterrence approach tends to break down with respect to terrorists (particularly those who engage in suicidal attacks) or those who plot their crimes in locations beyond the criminal jurisdictions of states able and willing to take action. It can also be seen that the law enforcement approach is by nature reactive. In contrast to the futuristic vision depicted in the film *Minority Report*, in which those who would otherwise commit a crime in the future are arrested *ex ante*, today's criminal justice professionals generally seek to identify persons who have already committed crimes and to then gather the evidence necessary for their indictment, prosecution, and conviction.

The prosecutions that followed the 1993 World Trade Center attack and the 1994 Pacific airliner bombing plot demonstrated that it is certainly feasible to prosecute members of terrorist groups (if they live through the attack),[23] and even the number of persons being detained at the Guantánamo Bay facility would not present an insurmountable challenge to the federal criminal justice system. However, the challenges to doing so would be far greater than many are willing to admit. A law enforcement approach implicates issues regarding application of the Posse Comitatus Act,[24] which places restrictions on Department of Defense support of civilian law-enforcement activities. Gathering the evidence necessary for a conviction from overseas locations can be carried out only with the consent and cooperation of the host state. Not all states will be willing to cooperate, and some (the failed and failing states) may be unable to offer any assistance. Asserting jurisdiction over members of armed groups and securing their presences through extradition can be thwarted by the absence of an extradition treaty, invocation of a "political offense" exception in an extradition treaty, or a refusal to extradite any person to a state where the death penalty might be awarded if the person is convicted. The security measures required for judges, jurors, prosecutors, and witnesses in trials of terrorists in New York and Washington, DC, provided a preview of the personal and financial costs of such prosecutions. In many cases some evidence against the accused will be classified or will require subpoenaing witnesses from overseas and calling members of the U.S. armed forces away from duties to testify at trial. The chilling prospect of being compelled to provide classified information to Al Qaeda members for their use at trial brings the national security implications of the criminal justice approach into sharp focus.

IV. THE ARMED-CONFLICT (WAR) APPROACH

If the law enforcement approach is characterized as one that seeks to prevent criminal conduct through specific and general deterrence, the armed-conflict approach can be seen as one that seeks to provide for the "common defense" of the nation and its people by employing the armed forces and related intelligence assets of the nation to combat states or armed groups that pose a security threat to the nation or its allies. As the Supreme Court recognized, it is "obvious and inarguable" that no governmental interest is more compelling than the security of the nation.[25] Accordingly, threats to the nation call for the employment of all of the relevant instruments of national power. In the terrorism context, the armed-conflict approach is woven into the four-prong strategy set out in the 2003 *National Strategy for Combating Terrorism*, which calls for defeating terrorists and their organizations; denying sponsorship, support, and sanctuary to terrorists; diminishing the underlying conditions that terrorists seek to exploit; and defending U.S. citizens and interests at home and abroad. The "defeat terrorist" prong in turn calls for expanding law enforcement efforts while at the same time focusing "decisive military power and specialized intelligence resources to defeat terrorist networks globally."[26]

Armed Groups and the *Jus ad Bellum*

The body of international law governing the use of armed force—commonly referred to as the *jus ad bellum*—comprises articles of the UN Charter, customary international law, and resolutions of the UN Security Council. Article 2(4) of the UN Charter forbids the use or threat of use of armed force against the territorial integrity or political independence of any state, or in any other manner inconsistent with the purposes of the UN. At the same time, Article 51 of the charter recognizes each state's inherent right of self-defense in cases of armed attack. The use of force in self-defense is subject to the customary-law limits of necessity, proportionality, and immediacy. Beyond the use of force in self-defense under Article 51, military measures are also lawful when authorized by the UN Security Council acting under its Chapter VII power to take action necessary to maintain or restore international peace and security.

Until recently there was some question whether the state's right of self-defense applied to armed attacks by members of a nonstate armed group. Importantly, nothing in Article 51 suggests that only armed attacks by nation-states (as opposed to armed groups) fall within the inherent right of self-defense. Indeed, the leading case on the law of anticipatory self-defense, which arose out of the destruction of the vessel *Caroline*, involved an 1837 British military expedition against nonstate actors in the United States.[27] More important, following the September 11, 2001, attacks by Al Qaeda, nearly all of the relevant international and national authorities agreed that the right of individual and collective self-defense applied.[28] Armed groups and their leaders have also been the subjects of Chapter VII measures imposed by the Security Council on several occasions. Resolution 1267, issued in 1999, identified a nonstate actor, Osama bin Laden, as a threat to international peace and security. Similarly, resolutions 1373 and 1540 deal with threats by nonstate actors and international measures to address those threats. Surprisingly, however, a majority of the judges on the International Court of Justice still suggest that the right of self-defense does not apply to attacks by armed groups.[29] The court offered no reasoning for its conclusion and did not attempt to reconcile its conclusion with the text of Article 51, historical cases like the *Caroline*, or resolutions issued by the UN Security Council in the wake of the September 11, 2001, attacks.

Armed Groups and the Law of Armed Conflict

The law of armed conflict ("LOAC"), sometimes called the *jus in bello*, "law of war"[30] or "international humanitarian law," refers to the body of law that regulates the actual conduct of armed conflict. It is important to bear in mind that the LOAC applies regardless of whether the conflict itself is "legal" under the *jus ad bellum*. The LOAC sets out standards of humane conduct that apply to all parties engaged in an armed conflict. In this usage the term "armed conflict" is broader than "war," in that it includes not just wars in the traditional sense but also lesser levels of armed conflict. However, the term does not include "internal disturbances and tensions, such as riots, isolated and sporadic acts of violence, or other acts of a similar nature."[31] Assuming a conflict rises to the level of an armed conflict under the LOAC, such conflicts are divided into international armed conflicts and armed conflicts not of an international character.

An armed conflict cannot exist without two or more parties, either states or armed groups. All parties engaged in an armed conflict, including armed groups, are required to comply with the law of armed conflict.[32] A person who commits a serious violation of the LOAC may be subject to prosecution under international criminal law. At the same time, under the law of some states, including the United States,[33] violations of such laws may give rise to civil liability and a suit for compensation.

It is well established that whenever armed force is used the choice of means and methods is not unlimited. This rule is reflected in a number of LOAC instruments.[34] Any use of force is also governed by well-established principles, including the rules regarding distinction, humanity, and proportionality.[35] More specifically, under the LOAC, acts or threats of violence intended primarily to spread terror among civilians are forbidden, even if carried out for military purposes.[36]

Common Article 2 in the four Geneva Conventions (so named because it is "common" to all four conventions) defines an international armed conflict as "all cases of declared war or of any other armed conflict which may arise between two or more of the High Contracting Parties, even if the state of war is not recognized by one of them." In an international armed conflict between states that are parties to the Geneva Conventions, all four conventions apply. In addition, Additional Protocol I to those conventions applies among states that are party to the protocol, as well as any applicable customary international law.[37] Additional Protocol I to the Geneva Conventions expands the definition of international armed conflict[38] and the potential application of all four conventions.[39] However, the United States is not a party to Additional Protocol I, and it has rejected its more expansive definition of international armed conflicts.[40]

"Noninternational armed conflicts" refer to armed conflicts occurring within the territory of a single state. The term is limited to conflicts between a state and an armed group or between two armed groups within the state.[41] Because states sometimes direct, control, sponsor, or support armed groups, the law of state responsibility must be considered in determining whether an armed conflict involving an armed group is an international armed conflict.[42] In most circumstances, the four Geneva Conventions do not apply to noninternational armed conflicts. However, to assure a minimal level of humane treatment, Common Article 3 of those conventions provides that[43]

> In the case of armed conflict not of an international character occurring in the territory of one of the High Contracting Parties, each party to the conflict shall be bound to apply, as a minimum, the following provisions:
>
> > 1. Persons taking no active part in the hostilities, including members of armed forces who have laid down their arms and those placed hors de combat by sickness, wounds, detention, or any other cause, shall in all circumstances be treated humanely, without any adverse distinction founded on race, colour, religion or faith, sex, birth or wealth, or any other similar criteria.
> >
> > > To this end the following acts are and shall remain prohibited at any time and in any place whatsoever with respect to the above-mentioned persons:
> > >
> > > > (a) Violence to life and person, in particular murder of all kinds, mutilation, cruel treatment and torture;
> > > >
> > > > (b) Taking of hostages;
> > > >
> > > > (c) Outrages upon personal dignity, in particular, humiliating and degrading treatment;
> > > >
> > > > (d) The passing of sentences and the carrying out of executions without previous judgment pronounced by a regularly constituted court affording all the judicial guarantees which are recognized as indispensable by civilized peoples.
> >
> > 2. The wounded and sick shall be collected and cared for.

For those states that are party to Additional Protocol II to the Geneva Conventions, that protocol supplements the Common Article 3 protections applicable to noninternational armed conflicts.

Issues in the Armed-Conflict Approach

Like the law enforcement approach, the armed-conflict approach to combating violence by armed groups presents a number of legal and practical issues. The most contentious issues concern targeting, detention, interrogation, and prosecution. Each of those issues is in turn affected by the person's status as a combatant (lawful or unlawful) or civilian.

Classification of members of armed groups

In general, the LOAC distinguishes between combatants and civilians. Civilians are those who are not combatants.[44] The starting point for the definition of "combatant" is Article 1 of Hague Regulations IV[45] and Article 4 of the Third Geneva Convention (which addresses treatment of prisoners of war). Article 1 of Hague Regulations IV uses the classification to assign application of "laws, rights, and duty of war." Article 4 of the Third

Geneva Convention is more limited, in that it provides a definition of those persons who are entitled to prisoner-of-war status. Those persons include, inter alia,

1. Members of the armed forces of a Party to the conflict as well as members of militias or volunteer corps forming part of such armed forces.

2. Members of other militias and members of other volunteer corps, including those of organized resistance movements, belonging to a Party to the conflict and operating in or outside their own territory, even if this territory is occupied, provided that such militias or volunteer corps, including such organized resistance movements, fulfill the following conditions:

(a) That of being commanded by a person responsible for his subordinates;

(b) That of having a fixed distinctive sign recognizable at a distance;

(c) That of carrying arms openly;

(d) That of conducting their operations in accordance with the laws and customs of war.

3. Members of regular armed forces who profess allegiance to a government or an authority not recognized by the Detaining Power.

4. Persons who accompany the armed forces without actually being members thereof, such as civilian members of military aircraft crews, war correspondents, supply contractors, members of labor units or of services responsible for the welfare of the armed forces, provided that they have received authorization from the armed forces which they accompany, who shall provide them for that purpose with an identity card similar to the annexed model. . . .

6. Inhabitants of a non-occupied territory, who on the approach of the enemy spontaneously take up arms to resist the invading forces, without having had time to form themselves into regular armed units, provided they carry arms openly and respect the laws and customs of war.[46]

Additional Protocol I has muddied the definition of a combatant. For example, Article 43 of the protocol provides an alternative definition of "armed forces/combatants" that varies from Article 4 of the Third Geneva Convention. Article 43 provides that

1. The armed forces of a Party to a conflict consist of all organized armed forces, groups and units which are under a command responsible to that Party for the conduct of its subordinates, even if that Party is represented by a government or an authority not recognized by an adverse Party. Such armed forces shall be subject to an internal disciplinary system which, inter alia, shall enforce compliance with the rules of international law applicable in armed conflict.

2. Members of the armed forces of a Party to a conflict (other than medical personnel and chaplains covered by Article 33 of the Third Convention) are combatants, that is to say, they have the right to participate directly in hostilities.

3. Whenever a Party to a conflict incorporates a paramilitary or armed law enforcement agency into its armed forces it shall so notify the other Parties to the conflict.

Article 44 of the protocol further departs from the Geneva Convention approach, particularly in its controversial provisions that permit combatants to blend into the civilian population.[47] Article 44 also conflicts with Article 37, which prohibits "perfidy" by feigning civilian, noncombatant status.[48] Article 45 of the protocol creates a presumption that any person who takes part in hostilities, falls into the hands of an adverse party, and claims status as a prisoner of war is entitled to the prisoner-of-war protections under the Geneva Convention. If the claim is refuted, the person is nevertheless entitled to the protections set out in Article 75 of the protocol.

Use of force against armed groups

Assuming that the use of armed force is justified under the *jus ad bellum*, combatants and military objectives may be directly targeted.[49] Accordingly, members of armed groups and other persons meeting the legal test for "combatant" status are lawful targets for the duration of their memberships in the groups,[50] subject to the limits imposed by the applicable rules of engagement (ROE).[51] As one author puts it:

> Combatants may be targeted wherever found, armed or unarmed, awake or asleep, on a front line or a mile or a hundred miles behind the lines, "whether in the zone of hostilities, occupied territory, or elsewhere." Combatants can withdraw from hostilities only by retiring and becoming civilians, by becoming hors de combat, or by laying down their arms.[52]

What about members of armed groups and other persons who do not meet the combatant status test?[53] It will be recalled that under the LOAC civilians may not ordinarily be targeted. However, civilians lose their protection from attack if they take an active or direct part in hostilities.[54] Such persons have been variously classified as "unlawful combatants," "unprivileged belligerents," or simply civilians. For states-parties to Additional Protocol I or II, the loss of protection for civilians exists only for such time as the civilian takes a direct part in hostilities;[55] however, that qualification is not a customary-law rule and is therefore not binding on states that are not party to the protocols.

Assuming that force may be used against members of an armed group, such use of force is limited by the LOAC principles of necessity and proportionality, just as it is with lawful combatants.[56] Independently of the use of force under the *jus ad bellum*, the section on the law enforcement approach above demonstrates that the law generally recognizes a right of self-defense, to include deadly force when necessary, against any person who poses an imminent threat of death or serious bodily injury.

Use of force by armed groups

Members of armed groups and other persons who meet the test for lawful-combatant status have the right to participate directly in hostilities[57] and to target enemy combatants and military objectives, subject to the limits imposed by the law of armed conflict.[58] This so-called combatant immunity does not extend to members of armed groups and others who do not meet the legal test for combatant status.[59] Such persons may therefore be punished for crimes, such as killing an enemy combatant or destroying a military object, under circumstances where a lawful combatant would enjoy immunity (if carried out in compliance with the LOAC).[60]

Gathering intelligence on armed groups

In the post-9/11 environment, terrorism has been deemed to be the national and homeland security communities' most important mission, and intelligence has been touted as the nation's first line of defense. Without timely, effective intelligence the layered defense that facilitates preventive action is virtually impossible. The most important source of intelligence in such cases is generally the members of the armed group, and that intelligence will in nearly all cases come from human and signals intelligence methods. Both methods present a host of legal and practical problems.

Historically, intelligence goals and processes differed in several important respects between the law enforcement and armed-force approaches. The intelligence community gathers information, analyzes it, and reports its findings and assessments to those empowered to take action to prevent harm to the nation. By contrast, law enforcement agents gather evidence ex post facto to convict criminals. Both information-gathering systems are constrained by law, but the limits on intelligence gathering for national security are less onerous. For example, under U.S. law, persons associated with foreign powers and terrorist organizations are subject to more intrusive intelligence collection measures.[61] At the same time, however, it is important to bear in mind that, for a variety of reasons, information gathered through intelligence methods or by the armed forces might not be admissible in an ordinary criminal trial in the United States, thus complicating the usability of information transferred between the two domains. Although some of the impediments were addressed by the 2001 USA PATRIOT Act and 2004 Intelligence Reform and Terrorism Prevention Act,[62] others remain embedded in the constitutional and statutory protections and procedures applicable to criminal trials.

Detention and interrogation of armed-group members

The discussion of detention of armed-group members begins with the Supreme Court's conclusion that the lesser power to detain combatants falls within the authority to use force against them.[63] In fact, detention is the humanitarian alternative to the days when no quarter was given to enemy combatants. Restrictions on detaining members of an armed group turn in part on their status under the Third and Fourth Geneva Conventions when those conventions apply. In international armed conflicts, the Third Geneva Convention permits detention of enemy prisoners of war until the cessation of active hostilities.[64] Such persons are, however, entitled to the protections accorded to prisoners of war.[65] The Fourth Geneva Convention, which provides for the protection of civilians during armed conflicts and periods of occupation, provides for two forms of detention. First, persons protected under the convention may be detained for offenses committed ("criminal detainees").[66] Second, the occupying power may detain other persons for imperative reasons of security ("security detainees").[67] Regardless of the reasons for detention, civilians under the control of a party to an armed conflict must be treated humanely. This obligation includes, for example, the duty to take care of the wounded and sick and prohibitions on murder; torture and humiliating and degrading treatment; rape; extrajudicial executions; discrimination on grounds such as race, sex, or religion; and hostage taking.[68]

In international armed conflicts, restrictions on interrogation of members of an armed group also turn in part on their possible status under the Third and Fourth

Geneva Conventions. The Third Geneva Convention prohibits interrogation of enemy prisoners of war.[69] The Fourth Geneva Convention, applicable to civilians, does not foreclose questioning such persons, but it forbids the use of physical or moral coercion, in particular to obtain information from them or from third parties.[70]

Parties to a noninternational armed conflict are subject to many of the same requirements applicable in international conflicts. They are required by Common Article 3 to treat persons not taking an active part in the hostilities "humanely, without any adverse distinction founded on race, color, religion or faith, sex, birth or wealth, or any other similar criteria." Common Article 3 also expressly prohibits certain acts, including, inter alia, cruel treatment, torture, outrages upon personal dignity, and, in particular, humiliating and degrading treatment.

After quoting the text of Common Article 3, including the final sentence declaring that nothing in Article 3 affects the legal status of the parties to the conflict, the Department of the Army's *Counterinsurgency* (COIN) field manual explains the status and treatment of insurgents:

> The final sentence of Common Article 3 makes clear that insurgents have no special status under international law. They are not, when captured, prisoners of war. Insurgents may be prosecuted legally as criminals for bearing arms against the government and for other offenses, so long as they are accorded the minimum protections described in Common Article 3. U.S. forces conducting COIN should remember that the insurgents are, as a legal matter, criminal suspects within the legal system of the host nation. Counterinsurgents must carefully preserve weapons, witness statements, photographs, and other evidence collected at the scene. This evidence will be used to process the insurgents into the legal system and thus hold them accountable for their crimes while still promoting the rule of law.[71]

Turning to U.S. law, a plurality of the Supreme Court in *Hamdi v. Rumsfeld* upheld the government's right to detain enemy combatants who were part of, or supporting, forces hostile to the United States or its coalition partners,[72] but the Court also held that the authorized use of military force did not authorize indefinite detention only for purposes of interrogation.[73] To guard against unjustified detentions, in 2004 the Department of Defense (DoD) implemented provisions for a Combatant Status Review Tribunal and an Administrative Review Board,[74] to determine whether each detainee is an "enemy combatant." DoD Directive 2310.01E now defines the terms "enemy combatant," "lawful enemy combatant," and "unlawful enemy combatant."[75]

Within the United States, treatment of detainees is addressed by the Detainee Treatment Act (DTA),[76] DoD directives,[77] and Army field manuals.[78] All DoD and Army directives are, of course, subject to any requirements imposed by the Constitution or applicable federal statutes, including the Detainee Treatment Act (a table adapted from the *Counterinsurgency* manual summarizing the effect of the DTA is included in the appendix to this chapter). Similarly, interrogation procedures are now governed by the DTA,[79] DoD directives,[80] and Army field manuals.[81] The Detainee Treatment Act established Army Field Manual 2-22.3 as the legal standard for interrogations.[82] No techniques other than those prescribed by the field manual are authorized by DoD personnel.

Under the new Army field manual, regardless of the precise legal statuses of those persons captured, detained, or otherwise held in custody by U.S. forces, they must receive humane treatment until properly released. Specially trained, organized, and equipped military police units in adequately designed and resourced facilities should administer any prolonged detention. The military police personnel operating such facilities shall not be used to assist in or "set the conditions for" interrogation (as they allegedly did at the Abu Ghraib prison). There are also certain conditions under which U.S. forces may not transfer the custody of detainees to the host nation or any other foreign government. For example, U.S. forces will retain custody if they have substantial grounds to believe that the detainees would be in danger in the custody of others. Such dangers might include the risk of being subjected to torture or inhumane treatment.[83]

Prosecution of armed-group members and leaders

International criminal law refers to crimes defined as such by treaty, such as the Geneva Conventions or the Rome Statute, or customary international law. Lawful combatants are subject to prosecution under the international criminal law and the laws of their states for a variety of war-related offenses, including war crimes, crimes against humanity, and genocide. Moreover, nothing in the law of armed conflict precludes a state from prosecuting a member of the armed forces or an armed group for other crimes not arising under the law of armed conflict.[84] When it applies, the Third Geneva Convention provides that enemy prisoners of war may be prosecuted "only if the sentence has been pronounced by the same courts according to the same procedure as in the case of members of the armed forces of the Detaining Power."[85] Similarly, the Fourth Geneva Convention provides important safeguards applicable in any trial of a person protected under that convention.[86] In noninternational armed conflicts, Common Article 3 provides that no person may be convicted of a crime related to the hostilities except by a "regularly constituted court, affording all the judicial guarantees which are recognized as indispensable."

In an international armed conflict, where the four Geneva Conventions apply, grave breaches of those conventions constitute "war crimes."[87] States that are party to the Geneva Conventions are required to search for persons suspected of grave breaches of the conventions and to bring them before the states' own courts, extradite them to another state willing to prosecute them, or surrender them to an international criminal court with jurisdiction. A similar duty exists under the UN Convention against Torture with respect to torture committed during peacetime or armed conflict. An offense not constituting a "grave breach" of one of the Geneva Conventions may be punished under other international criminal laws, such as those prohibiting genocide, crimes against humanity, and war crimes not constituting grave breaches. For example, the Rome Statute of the International Criminal Court lists 26 war crimes applicable in international armed conflicts and 12 for noninternational armed conflicts.[88]

Under customary international law, war crimes can also be committed during noninternational armed conflicts. Such criminal prohibitions extend to willful killing, torture or inhuman treatment, the taking of hostages, the intentional direction of attacks against a civilian population, and indiscriminate attacks that fail to distinguish between civilians and civilian objects and members of armed forces and military objectives. Killing or wounding another "treacherously" by, for example, approaching enemy soldiers pretending to be a civilian, to attack them by surprise, is also a war crime.[89] Finally, it should be noted that the principle of command and superior responsibility, which, under specified circumstances, imposes individual criminal responsibility on commanders or superiors for acts of people under their effective command and control, is also applicable to leaders of armed groups. For crimes such as war crimes, genocide, crimes against humanity, and other crimes under international law, the question of whether the alleged offender belonged to a formal armed force or an armed group is largely irrelevant.

Within the United States, the choice of forum for trials of armed-group members has been highly controversial. Options include federal courts established under Article III of the Constitution, courts-martial, or military commissions.[90] One key Civil War–era case limited the use of military commissions to cases where ordinary law enforcement has broken down and civilian courts are not functioning.[91] In a later case involving German saboteurs captured during World War II, the Supreme Court upheld their trial by military commission, even though the civil courts were open and functioning.[92] In 2001, shortly after the United States responded to the September 11 attacks, the president issued a military order directing the detention and trial of persons responsible for those attacks.[93] Under the order, enemy combatants were to be subject to trial and punishment by military commission;[94] however, the presidentially created commissions did not survive legal challenges.[95] As a result, Congress enacted the Military Commission Act of 2006 to remedy the earlier defects.[96] The legality of the new congressionally created commissions has not yet been authoritatively determined.

Evaluation of the Armed-Conflict Approach

Where and when states have lost their monopoly on the large-scale use of violence within their borders, either because of the size of the group or the weapons and other capabilities it possesses, law enforcement measures will continue to be a necessary "endgame," but they may not be sufficient to ensure the desired level of security. Under circumstances where the threat posed by armed groups is too great to rely on a reactive law enforcement approach, law enforcement efforts will likely continue to be supplemented by military forces and intelligence assets. Additionally, where the armed group posing such a threat operates beyond the borders and jurisdiction of a nation's law enforcement authorities, and law enforcement and other control measures by the host state are absent or ineffective, the nation under threat will have to look beyond enforcement to protect itself.

At the same time, we must be mindful of Alexander Hamilton's suggestion in the *Federalist Papers* that overreliance on military power can enervate civil institutions, as the people become increasingly dependent on the armed forces for their security.[97] Relying too heavily on the U.S. armed forces may also degrade their readiness for major combat operations, undermine morale, and lead to disciplinary problems as service members increasingly experience mission ambiguity, frustration, the inevitable erosion of public support,[98] and abandonment by coalition partners and the United Nations. Finally, such a choice does nothing to lessen apprehensions of U.S. hegemony abroad.

Accordingly, the "warfare" approach should be limited to those conflicts where the regularity, intensity, and scale combine to pose a threat that exceeds the authority, competency, and capability of law enforcement agencies to provide the needed level of security. These will include situations where law enforcement forces lack jurisdiction and international cooperation options, or those where the threat to the homeland exceeds the capabilities of law enforcement forces. Military measures should be applied only to those actively participating in hostilities and must conform to the applicable *jus ad bellum* and LOAC. The fact that military measures are used against members of an armed group does not preclude those members from later being prosecuted; however, the circumstances that led to their captures may not be conducive to producing the evidence necessary for convictions.

To admit the need for the military forces to combat the threats posed by armed groups should not blind us to deficiencies in the accompanying legal regime. Most modern armed conflicts are not international, rendering many of the protections of the Geneva Conventions irrelevant except as customary law. The battle space has increasingly moved to urban centers where combatants mingle with civilians, and often wear civilian attire, rendering distinction nearly impossible. Although Common Article 3 sets a reasonable floor for humane treatment, the LOAC otherwise fails to provide adequate standards for the means and methods of conducting noninternational armed conflict. Moreover, outside states assisting a host state in operations against opposition armed groups are severely constrained in their authority to detain individuals in such noninternational armed conflicts (where the "imperative security" detainee rule in the Fourth Geneva Convention does not apply).

The conceptual, practical, and diplomatic problems with a stubborn reliance on a law-of-war approach were perceptively summarized by Benjamin Wittes:

> For all the administration's commitment to the war analogy, its ill fit has become glaring, particularly in the area of detentions. It starts with the fact that the laws of war generally presume there exists little or no doubt that a captured enemy fighter is, indeed, a captured enemy fighter. Detentions in the current conflict, by contrast, are rife with factual ambiguity and uncertainty. . . . Most fundamentally, the laws of war presuppose detentions to be a temporary incapacitation of the fighters until the warring parties make peace and arrange their repatriation. No such presumption makes any sense here. This conflict seems like a permanent state of affairs and, if it someday does end, it will end only because all members of al Qaeda are caught or killed. Releasing them then would only reignite the conflict. The administration can kid itself that it is merely applying the laws of war. But something else is going on too: the adjudication of the justice of incarcerations based on contested facts. And that is a subject that judges know something about.[99]

If the use of armed force to combat violence by armed groups is necessary but not sufficient, and the accompanying legal regime is so problematic, perhaps it is time to search for a third way.

A THIRD WAY?

The threats posed by armed groups plainly challenge our traditional paradigms for preventing and controlling large-scale violence. Conflicts with armed groups such as Al Qaeda—whose members are not found on the battlefield, who "hide in plain sight" among civilians, and who flout the principles of distinction and humanity that are so central to the law of armed conflict—do not fit nicely into the "war" construct, and yet the magnitude of the risk posed by those groups does not fit within our traditional understanding of "crime." In short, the threat is too lethal to be treated as a mere crime and too private to be called a war.

In trying to force transnational armed groups into the existing legal regimes for armed conflict or criminal justice we run the danger of debasing both and compromising their utility for the purposes for which they were designed. The rule sets for detention and interrogation of combatants or criminal suspects are particularly susceptible to being twisted out of shape to fit the new threat.

Perhaps it is time to reject the binary thinking that fuels the present destructive debate and acknowledge that the existing regimes do not, individually or collectively, adequately address the present needs for an ordered approach to the myriad forms of contemporary large-scale violence by armed groups. Such a declaration is, perhaps, the indispensable first step in formulating a new and more flexible regime that will allow us to harness law as an ordering force in what has become an increasingly disordered world. Some reform proposals in the United States advocate that Congress establish a new hybrid federal court that would aim for the Aristotelian "golden mean" between the armed-force and criminal justice approaches.[100] Under some proposals, the government would still have the power to detain individuals who pose a significant threat to the security of the nation, as determined by a legal framework prescribed by Congress, but such detentions would be subject to review by the new federal court, thus preserving separation of powers. That same court—one established under Article III of the Constitution and presided over by judges nominated by the president, confirmed by the Senate, and enjoying the independence that comes with life tenure—would have jurisdiction over criminal trials of persons charged with the national security offenses prescribed by Congress, following trial procedures that provide due process protections for the accused yet are also consistent with the government's security concerns and the nature and location of the evidence available, along with its classification levels and sources.

But many are reluctant to take seriously any reform proposals, whether at the international or national level. They argue that there is not sufficient international will or cohesion to develop and ratify a new international regime. Perhaps they also fear that an admission that the existing regime does not cover the present situation would be an invitation to an unprincipled nation or its executive to exploit the gap, while arguing that the law does not constrain it. On the national level, the fierce and debilitating partisan divide and the dizzying sine curve of public opinion cast serious doubt on the prospects for any reform, particularly one that would establish a basis for preventive detentions and provide for criminal trials with fewer protections than those afforded to ordinary criminal defendants.

In the final analysis, program analysts and policy makers must determine which approach best provides the optimal level of security, liberty, and protections for the accused. More than a half century ago Abraham Maslow reminded us that in the hierarchy of human needs none is more fundamental than security. If security is defined as the freedom from violent acts, an effective security regime must do more than merely respond to attacks; it must also prevent them when possible—particularly those that might include unleashing a weapon of mass destruction.

NOTES

1. The "Hague Rules" refer to the conventions and regulations respecting the laws and customs of warfare adopted at peace conferences held at The Hague in 1899 and 1907.

2. "Geneva Convention for the Amelioration of the Condition of the Wounded and Sick in Armed Forces in the Field," 12 August 1949, *United States Treaties and Other International Agreements* 6:3114, United Nations *Treaty Series* 75:31 [hereinafter "Geneva Convention I"]; "Geneva Convention for the Amelioration of the Condition of the Wounded, Sick and Shipwrecked Members of Armed Forces at Sea," 12 August 1949, *United States Treaties and Other International Agreements* 6:3217, *Treaties and Other International Acts Series* 3363, United Nations *Treaty Series* 75:85 [hereinafter "Geneva Convention II"]; "Geneva Convention Relative to the Treatment of Prisoners of War," 12 August 1949, *United States Treaties and Other International Agreements* 6:3316, United Nations *Treaty Series* 75:135 [hereinafter "Geneva Convention III"]; "Geneva Convention Relative to the Protection of Civilian Persons in Time of War," 12 August 1949, *United States Treaties and Other International Agreements* 6:3516, United Nations *Treaty Series* 75:287 [hereinafter "Geneva Convention IV"].

3. See Richard H. Shultz et al., "Taxonomy of Armed Groups," in *Armed Groups: A Tier-One Security Threat*, INSS Occasional Paper 57 (USAF Institute for National Security Studies, September 2004), 14–31.

4. The scale of the threat is demonstrated by armed groups like Hezbollah, which is armed with sophisticated antiship missiles and unmanned aerial vehicles and capable of launching thousands of rockets and missiles into cities in northern Israel.

5. "Customary international law" refers to international rules derived from a general and consistent practice of states followed out of a sense of legal right or obligation.

6. "Reid: 'I Am at War with Your Country,'" *CNN.com*, 31 January 2003, www.cnn.com/2003/LAW/01/31/reid.transcript/.

7. "Rome Statute of the International Criminal Court," 17 July 1998, UN Doc. A/CONF.183/9, *International Legal Materials* 37 (1998): 999 [hereinafter "Rome Statute"]. The statute entered into force on 1 July 2002. The United States is not a party.

8. U.S. Constitution, art. 1, secs. 9 and 10. The Constitution also prohibits punishment by a "bill of attainder"—that is, an act of the legislature declaring a person or group of persons guilty of some crime and punishing the individual or group without benefit of a trial. Ibid.

9. *Tennessee v. Garner,* 471 U.S. 1, 7–12 (1985) (holding that the use of deadly force to stop a fleeing suspect is only reasonable if the officer has probable cause to believe that the suspect poses a significant threat of death or physical injury to the officer or others). See also *Scott v. Harris,* 127 S. Ct. 1769 (2007) (explaining that *Garner* did not establish a magical on/off switch that triggers rigid preconditions whenever an officer's actions constitute "deadly force." The Court there simply applied the Fourth Amendment's "reasonableness" test to the use of a particular type of force in a particular situation.).

10. *Graham v. Connor,* 490 U.S. 386, 388 (1989).

11. Ibid., 397.

12. *Saucier v. Katz,* 533 U.S. 194, 205 (2001).

13. Deadly force is defined as any force that is likely to cause death or serious physical injury. See *Model Penal Code* (American Law Institute, 1985), sec. 3.11(2). The Model Penal Code (MPC) serves as a template for defining the elements of crimes and defenses for many jurisdictions and sets out several defenses to what would otherwise be crimes involving the use of force. The MPC is not legally binding.

14. *Basic Principles on the Use of Force and Firearms by Law Enforcement Officials*, UN Doc. E/CN.15/1996/16/Add.2 [hereinafter Basic Principles].

15. *UN Code of Conduct for Law Enforcement Officials,* adopted by the UN General Assembly Resolution 34/169, 17 December 1997, UN Doc. A/RES/34/169 (1997).

16. *Basic Principles,* para. 2. The European Court of Human Rights held that Turkey was responsible under human rights law for failing to equip its security forces with nonlethal-force equipment when they responded to a large internal civil disturbance, leaving the forces no alternative to the use of deadly force. *Güleç v. Turkey,* 1998 Eur. Ct. H.R. 21593/93, paras. 71, 73, 83.

17. *United States v. Verdugo-Urquidez,* 494 U.S. 259, 274–75 (1990). See also *Zadvydas v. Davis,* 533 U.S. 678, 693 (2001) (confirming it is "well established that certain constitutional protections available to persons inside the United States are unavailable to aliens outside of our geographic borders").

18. *United States v. Peterson,* 812 F.2d 486, 491 (9th Cir. 1987) (holding that a foreign search is reasonable if it conforms to the requirements of foreign law). But see *United States v. Bin Laden,* 132 F. Supp.2d 168, 186–87 (S.D.N.Y. 2001) (holding that Fifth Amendment protections relating to self-incrimination apply to the use, in a U.S. court, of statement obtained in a foreign custodial interrogation by U.S. government agents because the Fifth Amendment "violation" occurs when the statement is used at trial, not when it was obtained).

19. *United States v. Toscanino,* 500 F.2d 267, 274–75 (2d Cir. 1974). In *Ker v. Illinois,* 119 U.S. 436 (1886), however, the Court held that a defendant who was forcibly abducted in Peru for trial in the United States was not entitled to have the charges dismissed on grounds that his right to due process was violated.

20. "International Covenant on Civil and Political Rights," 23 March 1976, United Nations *Treaty Series* 999:171, *International Legal Materials* 6 (1992): 368. Whether the ICCPR applies in time of armed conflict or outside the territory of the state-party is not settled.

21. *USA PATRIOT Act,* Public Law 107-56, *United States Statutes at Large* 115 (26 October 2001): 272–403, sec. 412(a).

22. James Q. Wilson and Richard J. Herrnstein, *Crime and Human Nature,* chaps. 2 and 19 (New York: Simon and Schuster, 1986).

23. See, e.g., *United States v. Yousef,* 327 F.3d 56 (2d Cir. 2003); *United States v. Bin Laden,* 186–87; *United States v. Rahman,* 189 F.3d 88 (2d Cir. 1999); *United States v. Yunis,* 924 F.2d 1086, 1092 (D.C. Cir. 1991).

24. *Posse Comitatus Act, U.S. Code* 18, sec. 1385. See also *U.S. Code* 10, sec. 375, Department of Defense, *DoD Cooperation with Civilian Law Enforcement Officials,* DoD Directive 5525.5 (15 January 1986).

25. *Haig v. Agee,* 453 U.S. 280, 307 (1981) (citations omitted).

26. *National Strategy for Combating Terrorism* (Washington, DC: Executive Office of the President, February 2003), 17, available at www.whitehouse.gov/news/releases/2003/02/counter_terrorism/counter_terrorism_strategy.pdf. A new version was released in 2006.

27. The *Caroline* (exchange of diplomatic notes between Great Britain and the United States, 1842), in *A Digest of International Law,* by John Bassett Moore, vol. 2 (Washington, DC: Government Printing Office, 1906), 409.

28. See, e.g., UN Security Council resolutions 1368 and 1373. Member states of the NATO and OAS alliances also invoked the relevant articles in those collective self-defense treaties. Similarly, in its widely publicized decision on targeted killings of terrorists, the Israeli Supreme Court ruled that "the law that applies to the armed conflict between Israel and the terrorist organizations in the area is the international law dealing with armed conflicts." Public Committee against Torture in *Israel v. Government of Israel,* Supreme Court Sitting as the High Court of Justice, 11 December 2005, para. 21 [hereinafter "Committee against Torture"].

29. See Legal Consequences of the Construction of a Wall in the Occupied Palestinian Territory, International Court of Justice, Advisory Opinion, 2004 I.C.J. Rep. 136, para. 139 (9 July) [hereinafter "Israeli Security Barrier opinion"] (concluding that the UN Charter provisions on self-defense had "no relevance" to Israel's construction of a security barrier because Israel did "not claim that the attacks against it are imputable to a foreign State").

30. The U.S. Department of Defense defines the "law of war" as

> That part of international law that regulates the conduct of armed hostilities. It is often called the "law of armed conflict." The law of war encompasses all international law for the conduct of hostilities binding

on the United States or its individual citizens, including treaties and international agreements to which the United States is a party, and applicable customary international law.

Department of Defense, *The Law of War Program,* DoD Directive 2311.01E (9 May 2006).

31. See "Protocol Additional to the Geneva Conventions of 12 August 1949, Relating to the Protection of Victims of Non-International Armed Conflicts (Protocol II)," 8 June 1977, United Nations *Treaty Series* 1125: 609, *International Legal Materials* 16 (1977): 1442 [hereinafter "Additional Protocol II"], art. 1.2. It is the policy of the United States to apply the LOAC "during all armed conflicts, however such conflicts are characterized, and in all other military operations." DoD Directive 2311.01E, para. 4.1.

32. See Marco Sassòli, *Transnational Armed Groups and International Humanitarian Law*, Program on Humanitarian Policy and Conflict Research Occasional Paper Series 6 (Harvard University, Winter 2006).

33. See *Alien Tort Statute, U.S. Code* 28, sec. 1350; *Torture Victim Protection Act, United States Code Annotated* 28, sec. 1350n.

34. See, e.g., "Convention IV Respecting the Laws and Customs of War on Land, with Annex of Regulations," 18 October 1907, *United States Statutes at Large* 36:2277, *Treaty Series* 539 [hereinafter "Hague Regulations IV"], art. 22; and "Protocol Additional to the Geneva Conventions of 12 August 1949, Relating to the Protection of Victims of International Armed Conflicts (Protocol I)," 8 June 1977, United Nations *Treaty Series* 1125:3, *International Legal Materials* 16 (1977): 1391 [hereinafter "Additional Protocol I"], art. 35.1.

35. Although there are no explicit provisions for proportionality directly applicable to noninternational armed conflicts, the obligation is considered to be inherent in the principle of humanity that is applicable to these conflicts. See Jean-Marie Henckaerts and Louise Doswald-Beck, *Customary International Humanitarian Law* (Cambridge: Cambridge University Press, 2005), 1:48–49.

36. See Additional Protocol II, art. 13.2, which is generally accepted as reflective of customary international law applicable in a noninternational armed conflict. See also ibid., art. 4.2(d), which prohibits acts of terrorism "at any time and in any place whatsoever" against "persons who do not take a direct part or have ceased to take a direct part in hostilities."

37. Additional Protocol I. Because some parts of Additional Protocol I represent customary international law, those parts are binding even on states not party to the protocol, except where a state has persistently objected to the rule. See Henckaerts and Doswald-Beck, *Customary International Humanitarian Law*.

38. See Additional Protocol I, art. 1.4, which extends beyond Common Article 2 to include

> armed conflicts in which peoples are fighting against colonial domination and alien occupation and against racist regimes in the exercise of their right of self-determination, as enshrined in the Charter of the United Nations and the Declaration on Principles of International Law concerning Friendly Relations and Co-operation among States in accordance with the Charter of the United Nations.

39. See ibid, art. 3(a), which would extend application of the four Geneva Conventions to conflicts falling outside of Common Article 2, but within Article 1(4) of the protocol.

40. See Michael J. Matheson, "The United States Position on the Relation of Customary International Law to the 1977 Protocols Additional to the 1949 Geneva Convention," *American University Journal of International Law and Policy* 2 (1987): 424–27. Editorials in the *New York Times* and *Washington Post* strongly condemned Additional Protocol I and its provisions on "national liberation movements" as a "shield for terrorists." See "Denied: A Shield for Terrorists," *New York Times*, 17 February 1987, A22; "Hijacking the Geneva Conventions," *Washington Post,* 18 February 1987, A18.

41. Noninternational armed conflicts do not include conflicts in which two or more states are engaged against each other. Nor do they encompass conflicts extending to the territories of two or more states. When a foreign state extends its military support to the government of a state within which a noninternational armed conflict is taking place (as the NATO members are presently doing in Afghanistan), the conflict remains noninternational in character. Conversely, should a foreign state extend military support to an armed group acting against the government, the conflict will become international in character. See Yoram Dinstein et al.,

eds., *The Manual on the Law of Non-international Armed Conflict* (International Institute of Humanitarian Law, March 2006).

42. If the conduct of the armed group is attributable to the state, the conflict may be deemed an international armed conflict. For example, if the conduct of Hezbollah during the 2006 conflict with Israel is attributable to the state of Lebanon, that conflict would be deemed international. The Israeli Supreme Court's decision in the Committee against Torture case suggests that the Hezbollah conflict was an international one even if not attributable to the state of Lebanon.

43. The International Court of Justice has opined that Common Article 3 represents customary international law in both international and noninternational armed conflict. Military and Paramilitary Activities in and against Nicaragua *(Nicaragua v. United States)*, Merits, 1986 I.C.J. Rep. 4 (June 27), paras. 118–20.

44. See Geneva Convention IV, art. 4. See also Geneva Conventions I and II, art. 13; Additional Protocol I, art. 50. Under the protocol definition, if there is any doubt whether a person is a civilian (for purposes of applying protected-person status) the person will be considered to be a civilian.

45. Hague Regulations IV, annex 1, art. 1.

46. See Geneva Convention III, art. 4. Article 5 then goes on to say:

> The present Convention shall apply to the persons referred to in Article 4 from the time they fall into the power of the enemy and until their final release and repatriation.
>
> Should any doubt arise as to whether persons, having committed a belligerent act and having fallen into the hands of the enemy, belong to any of the categories enumerated in Article 4, such persons shall enjoy the protection of the present Convention until such time as their status has been determined by a competent tribunal.

47. See Additional Protocol I, art. 44.3. Some criticize Article 44 for blurring the distinction between combatants and civilians, diminishing legal protections for the latter.

48. Ibid., art. 37.1(c).

49. The law of armed conflict, broadly defined, may limit the means used. For example, there may be restrictions on the use of nonlethal weapons and riot control agents.

50. See Additional Protocol I, art. 43.2; Additional Protocol II, arts. 1, 13.

51. See Chairman, Joint Chiefs of Staff, *Standing Rules of Engagement/Standing Rules for the Use of Force for US Armed Forces,* Chairman, Joint Chiefs of Staff Instruction 3121.01B (13 June 2005).

52. Gary Solis, "Targeted Killings and the Law of Armed Conflict," *Naval War College Review* 60, no. 127 (Spring 2007): 130 (quoting Army Field Manual 27-10, para. 31). It should be added that this is true only while the armed conflict is ongoing.

53. Kenneth Watkin, "Humans in the Cross-Hairs: Targeting and Assassination in Contemporary Armed Conflict," in *New Wars, New Laws? Applying the Laws of War in 21st Century Conflicts,* ed. David Wippman and Matthew Evangelista (Ardsley, NY: Transnational, 2005).

54. See Geneva Convention IV, arts. 3, 5; Additional Protocol I, art. 51.3; Additional Protocol II, art. 13(3). The phrases "active participation" and "direct participation" in hostilities are often used interchangeably. Common Article 3 uses the word "active," while Article 13.3 of Additional Protocol II uses the word "direct." There is no substantive distinction between the two terms. Each requires "a sufficient causal relationship between the active participation and its immediate consequences." See Yves Sandoz, Christophe Swinarski, Bruno Zimmermann, eds., *Commentary on the Additional Protocols of 8 June 1977* (Geneva: Martinus Nijhoff, 1987), para. 4787.

55. Additional Protocol I, art. 51.3; Additional Protocol II, art. 13.3.

56. See Committee against Torture, para. 60 (holding that the proportionality standard applies to "targeted killing" of civilian terrorists taking a direct part in hostilities).

57. See Additional Protocol I, art. 43.2.

58. UK Ministry of Defence, *The Manual of the Law of Armed Conflict* (Oxford: Oxford University Press, 2004), para. 4.1 ("Combatants have the right to attack and to resist the enemy by all the methods not forbidden by the law of armed conflict.").

59. Combatant immunity is derived from articles 87 and 99 of the Third Geneva Convention.

60. See International Committee of the Red Cross, *Model Manual on the Law of Armed Conflict for Armed Forces* (1999), 34, para. 610. The Israeli Supreme Court put it this way:

> That is the law regarding unlawful combatants. As long as he preserves his status as a civilian—that is, as long as he does not become part of the army—but takes part in combat, he ceases to enjoy the protection granted to the civilian, and is subject to the risks of attack just like a combatant, without enjoying the rights of a combatant as a prisoner of war. Indeed, terrorists who take part in hostilities are not entitled to the protection granted to civilians. True, terrorists participating in hostilities do not cease to be civilians, but by their acts they deny themselves the aspect of their civilian status which grants them protection from military attack. Nor do they enjoy the rights of combatants, e.g. the status of prisoners of war.

Committee against Torture, para. 31.

61. See, e.g., *Foreign Intelligence Surveillance Act, U.S. Code* 50, secs. 1801–1802 (establishing electronic surveillance authority for "foreign powers" and agents of foreign powers). FISA was amended by the 2001 USA PATRIOT Act. See also Executive Order no. 12,333, *Code of Federal Regulations* title 3 (1981), 200 (reprinted in *United States Code Annotated* 50, sec. 401n), paras. 2.3 and 3.4(i) (restricting intelligence collection activities involving "United States persons").

62. *Intelligence Reform and Terrorism Prevention Act of 2004,* sec. 1016, Public Law 108-458, *United States Statutes at Large* 118 (2004): 3638, codified at *U.S. Code* 6, sec. 485.

63. *Ex parte Quirin,* 317 U.S. 1, 28 (1942).

64. Geneva Convention III, art. 118. See also *Hamdi v. Rumsfeld,* 542 U.S. 507 (2004) (holding that persons legitimately determined to be Taliban combatants could be detained so long as active hostilities continue). But see *Al Marri v. Wright,* 487 F.3d 160 (4th Cir. 2007) (holding that because Al Qaeda is not a state, Al Qaeda members like al-Marri must be treated as civilians, subject to prosecution, but not as enemy combatants, subject to detention until cessation of active hostilities. The circuit court reasoned that the Supreme Court concluded that the conflict in Afghanistan is an internal armed conflict, and the International Committee of the Red Cross has concluded that the legal classification of "enemy combatant" does not apply in such conflicts). The circuit court's holding plainly steers the United States away from the armed-conflict approach and toward the law enforcement approach. See generally Peter Berkowitz, ed., *Terrorism, the Laws of War, and the Constitution: Debating the Enemy Combatant Cases* (Stanford, CA: Hoover Institute Press, 2005).

65. See Geneva Convention III, art. 4. See also Additional Protocol I, art. 44.1; Hague Regulations IV, annex 1, arts. 4–20.

66. Geneva Convention IV, art. 76. Article 77 makes it clear that such persons must be turned over at the close of occupation to authorities of the liberated state.

67. Ibid., art. 78.

68. Additional Protocol II, art. 5. Common Article 3 to the Geneva Conventions also requires the humane treatment of those who are detained, although it does not set forth specific requirements. See also *Hamdan v. Rumsfeld,* 548 U.S.__, 126 S. Ct. 2479 (2006).

69. Geneva Convention III, art. 17.

70. Geneva Convention IV, art. 31.

71. U.S. Department of the Army, *Counterinsurgency,* Field Manual 3-24/U.S. Marine Corps Warfighting Publication 3-33.5 (December 2006) [hereinafter "Counterinsurgency Manual"], D-4.

72. *Hamdi v. Rumsfeld,* 518.

73. Ibid., 521. The Court left open the question whether detention was authorized to prevent the detainee from returning to the battlefield.

74. The CSRT procedures have been criticized on the grounds that they do not provide the same kind of protections that would be accorded to a person suspected of a crime, but nearly all agree that they meet or exceed the requirements established by Article 5 of the Third Geneva Convention.

75. Department of Defense, *The Department of Defense Detainee Program,* DoD Directive 2310.01E (5 September 2006). The Military Commissions Act of 2006 provides statutory definitions of each term.

76. *Detainee Treatment Act,* Public Law 109-148, *United States Statutes at Large* 119 (2005): 2739–40, codified at *U.S. Code* chap. 10, 47A. Section 1003 of the act prohibits cruel, inhuman, or degrading treatment or punishment (as defined in the act) of detainees.

77. DoD Directive 2310.01E.

78. Counterinsurgency Manual, D-4 to D-6; U.S. Department of the Army, *The Law of Land Warfare,* Field Manual 27-10 (1956); U.S. Department of the Army, *Internment and Resettlement Operations,* FM 3-19.40 (1 August 2001); U.S. Department of the Army, *Police Intelligence Operations,* FM 3-19.50 (21 July 2006).

79. *Detainee Treatment Act,* secs. 1002–1003.

80. U.S. Department of Defense, *DoD Intelligence Interrogations, Detainee Debriefings, and Tactical Questioning,* DoD Directive 3115.09 (3 November 2005).

81. U.S. Department of the Army, *Human Intelligence Collector Operations,* Field Manual 2-22.3 [formerly FM 34-52] (September 2006).

82. *Detainee Treatment Act,* sec. 1002.

83. See also DoD Directive 2310.01E.

84. See, e.g., *United States v. Noriega,* 808 F. Supp. 791 (S.D. Fl. 1992).

85. Geneva Convention III, arts. 99–108.

86. Geneva Convention IV, art. 71.

87. "Grave breaches" are defined in Geneva Convention I, art. 50; Geneva Convention II, art. 51; Geneva Convention III, art. 130; Geneva Convention IV, art. 147.

88. Rome Statute, art. 8. The classification of the armed conflict is critical. Note, for example, that intentionally launching a disproportionate attack is only a war crime in an international armed conflict. Note also that the war crimes provision of the Rome Statute for noninternational armed conflicts only applies to "protracted" armed conflicts. Ibid., art. 8(2)(f).

89. Ibid., art. 8(2)(e)(ix).

90. See Louis Fisher, *Military Tribunals and Presidential Power* (Lawrence, KS: University Press of Kansas, 2005). Although military commissions were widely used following World War II, some allies, including the United Kingdom, now consider them politically unacceptable.

91. *Ex parte Milligan,* 71 U.S. (4 Wall.) 2 (1866).

92. *Ex parte Quirin.*

93. President, Military Order, "Detention, Treatment, and Trial of Certain Non-citizens in the War against Terrorism," *Federal Register* 66 (13 November 2001): 57,833. Section 3 of the order addressed detentions and Section 4 addressed trials by military commission. See also *Code of Federal Regulations,* title 32, pts. 9–11; *Ex parte Quirin* (upholding the trial of Nazi saboteurs by military commission and distinguishing *Ex parte Milligan*).

94. *Military Commissions Act of 2006 (MCA),* Public Law 109-366, *United States Statutes at Large* 120 (17 October 2006): 2600, enacted to provide the legislative authority for military commissions the Supreme Court found lacking in *Hamdan v. Rumsfeld* (2006).

95. See *Hamdan v. Rumsfeld* (2006).

96. On 13 December 2006, Salim Ahmed Hamdan challenged the MCA's denial of habeas corpus to "alien un-lawful enemy combatants" in the U.S. District Court for the District of Columbia. Judge James Robertson, who ruled in favor of Hamdan in the *Hamdan v. Rumsfeld* 2004 case, ruled against him in this case, writing: "The Constitution does not provide alien enemy combatants detained at Guantanamo Bay with the constitutional right to file a petition for habeas corpus in our civilian courts, and thus Congress may regulate those combatants' access to the courts." But see *Al Marri v. Wright* (holding that, in applying the authorized use of military force, mere affiliation with Al Qaeda does not make a person an "enemy combatant" who can be detained indefinitely).

97. Alexander Hamilton, "The Consequences of Hostilities between the States" [Federalist 8], *New York Packet,* 20 November 1787, available at www.constitution.org/fed/feder08.htm. A contrary argument can be made that the balance between liberty and security is easier to preserve with a military approach to violent armed groups. By relying on the armed forces to prevent and contain the violence, adjustments to the law enforcement system are obviated, reducing the risk of a runaway police state or an erosion of rights for the ordinary criminal defendant.

98. Throughout U.S. history, the "remarkable trinity" described by Clausewitz as the military, government, and public, has suffered from any long-term reliance on the military, as the media and other antiwar influences highlight failures and obscure successes.

99. Benjamin Wittes, "Terrorism, the Military and the Courts: What Kind of Process is Due Detainees?" *Policy Review,* June/July 2007.

100. See, e.g., Jack L. Goldsmith and Neal Katyal, "The Terrorists' Court," *New York Times,* 11 July 2007.

Appendix: Summary of the Detainee Treatment Act of 2005

Section 1002: Uniform Standards for the Interrogation of Persons Under the Detention of the Department of Defense

(a) In General.—No person in the custody or under the effective control of the Department of Defense or under detention in a Department of Defense facility shall be subject to any treatment or technique of interrogation not authorized by and listed in the United States Army Field Manual on Intelligence Interrogation [U.S. Army Field Manual 2-22.3].

(b) Applicability.—Subsection (a) shall not apply with respect to any person in the custody or under the effective control of the Department of Defense pursuant to a criminal law or immigration law of the United States.

(c) Construction.—Nothing in this section shall be construed to affect the rights under the United States Constitution of any person in the custody or under the physical jurisdiction of the United States.

Section 1003: Prohibition on Cruel, Inhuman, or Degrading Treatment or Punishment of Persons Under Custody or Control of the United States Government

(a) In General.—No individual in the custody or under the physical control of the United States Government, regardless of nationality or physical location, shall be subject to cruel, inhuman, or degrading treatment or punishment.

(b) Construction.—Nothing in this section shall be construed to impose any geographical limitation on the applicability of the prohibition against cruel, inhuman, or degrading treatment or punishment under this section.

(c) Limitation on Supersedure.—The provisions of this section shall not be superseded, except by a provision of law enacted after the date of the enactment of this Act which specifically repeals, modifies, or supersedes the provisions of this section.

(d) Cruel, Inhuman, or Degrading Treatment or Punishment Defined.—In this section, the term "cruel, inhuman, or degrading treatment or punishment" means the cruel, unusual, and inhumane treatment or punishment prohibited by the Fifth, Eighth, and Fourteenth Amendments to the Constitution of the United States, as defined in the United States Reservations, Declarations and Understandings to the United Nations Convention Against Torture and Other Forms of Cruel, Inhuman, or Degrading Treatment or Punishment done at New York, December 10, 1984.

9 Globalization and the Transformation of Armed Groups

Querine H. Hanlon

Globalization has enabled the transformation of armed groups, broadly defined to include terrorists, insurgents, militias, and criminal organizations, from regional challenges to a major, strategic security threat. Globalization has heightened their organizational effectiveness, their lethality, and their ability to operate on a truly worldwide scale. Although armed groups are not a new phenomenon, what is new is their ability to exploit the opportunities inherent in a globalized world. The twenty-first-century armed group is no longer relegated to the far reaches of the earth, but operates in the major urban centers of the very Western powers that are said to command globalization.

The transformation of armed groups is a key aspect of a newly emerging security paradigm for the twenty-first century. Armed groups exploit the opportunities inherent in a globalized world in ways that states, particularly weak states, cannot. Connected by the instantaneous and virtually untraceable communications technologies of the modern age, armed groups find refuge in the weak and ungoverned spaces between states, while directing operations at the heart of the globalized world. The integrated world economy provides the markets and the means to move goods from previously isolated zones of conflict, vastly increasing the financial strength of armed groups. The networks that move drugs now move people too—not just human traffickers and their wretched cargo, but well-trained operatives who exploit the anonymity of globalization to conduct operations and raise funds. Globalization has also created strange bedfellows. Criminal organizations in Asia and Latin America are linked to Marxist insurgencies, right-wing militias, and terrorist groups that find themselves increasingly motivated by the profit such trade brings. This network vastly increases the organizational reach and the resource base of armed groups. It also expands the nature of the threat to individual states, regions, and the broader international system.

Querine H. Hanlon is assistant professor of international security studies at National Defense University, School for National Security Executive Education, in Washington, DC. She is also a fellow at the National Strategy Information Center, where she is working on a project on armed groups. Previously she was adjunct professor of strategy and policy at the U.S. Naval War College, College of Distance Education. She earned her PhD from the Fletcher School of Law and Diplomacy in 1999 and has a bachelor's degree from Georgetown University's School of Foreign Service. Dr. Hanlon is the author of *The Three Images of Ethnic War* (forthcoming Praeger, 2008). She is currently working on *Old Groups and New Wars: Ethnic and Sectarian Violence in a Globalized World* (forthcoming Praeger, 2009).

The purpose of this chapter is twofold. First, it will explore how globalization enables the transformation of armed groups by examining the direct ways in which they exploit the economic, technological, and cultural variants of globalization and the indirect ways in which armed groups have exploited the impact of globalization on the state. The second purpose of this chapter is to consider how the transformation of armed groups has emerged as a key component of a new security paradigm for the twenty-first century. This transformation is intimately tied to the nature of weak and failed states. I will argue that demise of the state is *not* a key component of this new paradigm, despite arguments to the contrary from the globalization school. Instead, two key aspects of this new paradigm are the *uneven* erosion of state sovereignty and the emergence of the armed group as a significant global actor and a major strategic threat.

FOUR VARIANTS OF GLOBALIZATION

Conceptually, *globalization* is an imprecise term. The literature varies widely, and there is little agreement on what globalization is beyond a vague theme of "interconnectedness," a linkage between the global and the local, and an equally vague sense about change. Globalization can be defined simply as a "sum of techniques"[1]—containerized shipping, satellite communications, and networked connectivity—or more broadly as a process, a transformation, even a revolution. The effects of globalization have not been uniformly felt. It brings greater interdependence and propels isolated peoples and regions into modernity with all its attendant benefits. Yet the dark side of globalization is its power to obliterate traditional cultures, weaken sovereignty, and further isolate the "haves" from the "have-nots."

It is useful to distinguish four variants of globalization. *Economic* globalization is the most widely acknowledged and accepted version of globalization. It encompasses large and rapid change in terms of the flow of trade, investment, finance, capital, and labor, all of which have created a truly global integrated economy.[2] In macroeconomic theory, greater integration is a positive-sum game—everyone benefits from greater efficiency in resource allocation, rising income, and improved distribution of world income.[3] Yet the greater interpenetration of global economic markets has not resulted in a uniform spread of the costs and benefits. Whereas strong states have seen their economies grow and their global market share increase, weaker states invariably have not. The result is a widening gap between rich and poor states, a disparity that further undermines the sovereignty, security, and legitimacy of those states on the fringes of the globalized world.

The second variant is *technological* globalization. It arises from the fundamental changes in communications wrought by the technologies that brought us the Internet, open and free access to knowledge and information, and instant communications. Armed groups exploit these technologies to broadcast their messages across the globe, to recruit, to mobilize, and to conduct and control operations. The technologies of globalization have transformed the armed group into a formidable foe, one whose activities are hard to trace and even harder to combat.

The third variant is *cultural* globalization, often viewed as synonymous with "Americanization," the source of a new unbridled imperialism that will destroy traditional societies. The more extreme version of this argument characterizes globalization as a cultural invasion aimed at global homogenization.[4] A more nuanced view acknowledges that globalization fosters conflict and resentment.[5] Through "individually accessible, ordinary networked communications such as personal computers, DVDs, videotapes, and cell phones,"[6] as well as movies, radio, and television, cultural globalization encompasses the transmission of other cultures. These media glorify the "branded products" and "branded lifestyles" associated with a mostly Western culture.[7] For populations living subsistence lifestyles, these images starkly contrast the lives of those in the West who benefit the most from globalization with those on the fringes of the globalized world. Cultural globalization has made these populations profoundly aware of just how badly they live. Societies excluded from the benefits of globalization increasingly challenge the legitimacy of the governments that rule them. Powerless and dislocated, these populations are ripe for exploitation. Armed groups use these images of disparity, exclusion, and cultural onslaught to mobilize and recruit.

Political globalization broadly defines the impact of the other three variants on the state. This variant of globalization suffers the most from a lack of definitional clarity. At one extreme, political globalization is seen as a force that will ultimately destroy the state.[8] Yet the economic and technological forces of globalization have also strengthened the state's ability to monitor its citizens and their movements, collect revenue, and combat the rising challenge of armed groups. Herein lies the paradox of globalization. Strong states are made stronger by globalization and weak states are further weakened by it. As Wolf notes, globalization is a choice.[9] To participate in an integrated world economy, states choose to loosen restrictions on capital flows, goods and services, and people.[10] Loosening controls to participate in international trade creates opportunities armed groups can exploit. For weak states, the decision to participate fully in the integrated global economy is thus fraught with peril.

These four variants of globalization have each contributed to the transformation of armed groups. As we attempt to identify how these broad changes have enabled armed groups in more specific terms, it is important to note that these categories, while conceptually distinct, are interrelated in practice. Armed groups have directly exploited the economic, technological, and cultural variants of globalization while benefiting indirectly from the impact of globalization on the state.

THE DIRECT EXPLOITATION OF GLOBALIZATION

The sheer volume, speed, and geographic spread of globalization confer a degree of anonymity on those who participate. Armed groups have effectively exploited this anonymity in three distinct ways. First, the sheer size of the global economy enables armed groups to mask their trade of legal and illegal goods, to move people, and to evade detection. Second, the ability to communicate and operate anonymously over vast distances enables armed groups to create linkages with other groups having disparate ideologies, objectives, memberships, and operational structures. Third, the heightened connectivity of the globalized world has enabled armed groups to transmit information and recruit on an international scale while masking their authorship and intentions amid the noise of legitimate global interaction.

Therefore, globalization has compressed time and space. The technology of global transport now links the vast reaches in record time. Tracing the transit of illegal goods requires highly sophisticated means of detection and highly reliable anticipatory intelligence, both of which are frequently beyond the capacities of weak states in which many armed groups operate. The magnitude and speed of worldwide transit further compound the detection and intelligence tasks. When the time to off-load is measured in hours in many of the world's busiest ports, such cargo easily disappears amid the sheer number of containers transiting a port in any given day.[11] Similar issues of speed and size affect air, rail, and truck transport. Detecting illicit cargo remains a challenge for the wealthiest and most technologically advanced states. For states that barely manage to provide basic services, such technologies are simply beyond their capacities to employ. The vast quantity of goods being moved and the speed with which they transit ports of entry are highly exploitable given the severely constrained capabilities of most states in which, and through which, armed groups operate.

Armed groups exploit the sheer volume of trade and the compression of time and space to evade detection. Criminal organizations benefit from the anonymity of the global market to move drugs and other illegal cargo. Insurgents and militia can procure the necessary arms, including large weapons, and export their illicit goods, masking their shipments amid the vast trade in legal goods.

Armed groups have also exploited the anonymity of globalization to move people, masking the movements of advance teams and operatives among those of the large numbers of legitimate businessmen, students, and vacation travelers as well as the large movements of populations escaping zones of conflict. The sheer number of people who travel for legitimate purposes allows armed groups to penetrate states, particularly where state regulation of movement is compromised. In the West, where the technologies to track people and the intelligence to anticipate such movements are robust, this ability of armed groups has been constrained. They have thus adapted. Al-Qaeda now targets Muslim converts in the West, exploiting their Western passports and identities to move operatives and mount operations within the West.

The anonymity of globalization has created "marriages of convenience" among groups with vastly different ideological and political goals. The result has been a shift away from "stand-alone groups" to "transnationally internetted groups,"[12] or what others have termed "mixed groups."[13] Hezbollah forged alliances with criminal organizations to move drugs and provide transshipment protection in return for financial gain.[14] The Revolutionary Armed Forces of Colombia (FARC) and the National Liberation Army (ELN) have forged partnerships with major drug organizations, protecting the coca cultivation, processing, and shipment in areas they control. These are only a few examples of a growing network of connected armed groups that coordinate activities and forge profitable relationships to procure goods and resources, such as arms, and vastly expand their global reaches. Such linkages among disparate groups further cloak the origins and purposes of their activities and multiply exponentially the task of those who seek to monitor and track them.

Finally, armed groups exploit the anonymity inherent in global connectivity to transmit information. Globalization has fueled an "expansion of chaotic connectivity" with "few institutional frameworks or standards [to] provide structure in cyberspace."[15] The Internet has opened new "highways of evasion."[16] Worldwide, more than a billion users are now connected to the Internet, and achieving the ability to control the flow of information, to restrict access to the Internet, and to identify suspect Web sites and chat rooms is a nearly impossible task even for the most technologically advanced states in the West.

The anonymity of the Internet means that the authority of information and sources can rapidly become meaningless. Cronin characterizes this flow of information as the "dark side of freedom of speech."[17] Do the details and pictures of violence against Muslims depict real events or have the images been doctored to promote a group's ideology? Who posts the information and under what authority? The challenge is not only to identify the source of information on the Web but also to verify the veracity of images that can be altered with increasingly sophisticated technologies that are becoming widely accessible. Such media are powerful tools to mobilize populations, and the image-based nature of the information resonates even among target populations where literacy is low or nonexistent.[18]

In regions of the world where landline telephones are absent or unreliable or where high-speed Internet is not available, cell phones are an inexpensive and readily accessible alternate conduit for downloading images and videos. Tracking the flow of information and images via the use of individual cell phones requires highly sophisticated technologies beyond the capacities of many of the states whose populations are targeted by armed groups. Absent the cell phone and the Internet, slick productions on DVDs can be passed from person to person, replacing oral messages on cassette tape.

Another direct enabler of armed groups is the information and communication technologies that have transformed how armed groups are organized and how they operate. This transformation is apparent in three significant changes. First, globalization has fostered new network organizational structures that ensure the survivability and redundancy of armed-group leaderships and allow the organization to shift operations swiftly from one geographic region to another. Second, decentralized organizational structures shift the initiative to the local level and heighten the group's lethality and its operational effectiveness. Finally, information and communication technologies ensure that armed groups can maintain direction over cells and subgroups dispersed across the globe and coordinate operations over vast distances.

Information and communications technologies have fostered new network forms of organization that are flatter and less hierarchical in structure.[19] These new organizational structures have transformed how armed groups operate. Armed groups that adopt a network structure have little or no hierarchical structure and multiple leaders. The networked armed group thus has an organizational measure of redundancy and hence of survivability. If a prominent leader is killed, the organization survives. Network forms of organization also enable the dispersal of subgroups or cells across regions and around the world. This dispersed structure ensures that when groups have to relocate operations swiftly, there are other established cells or subgroups that can continue the group's mission and ensure its survival.[20]

Network organizations enable decentralized operations and decision making, allowing for local initiative and autonomy. Given that armed groups are increasingly dispersed over vast distances, an organizational structure that facilitates local initiative and decision making reduces the likelihood of communications being intercepted and operations being compromised. It also increases the capacity of the group to seize opportunities created by local conditions. The flatter organizational design of a network ensures that "members do not have to resort to a hierarchy—they know what they have to do."[21] Local initiative and decentralization transform the armed group into a more efficient and potentially more lethal organization. The increasing reliance on converts by al-Qaeda in Europe adds another dimension to the benefits of local initiative. Given that local converts have far greater knowledge of the physical and political terrains, an armed group that is organized to encourage local initiative will be able to operate with far greater effectiveness and lethality.

Finally, information and communication technologies ensure that the armed group can maintain direction over cells and substructures dispersed internationally. Although globalization has eased the movement of people, a key constraint on such wide dispersal is the need to maintain control and direction.[22] Globalization has enabled armed groups to overcome this constraining variable. Through the use of the World Wide Web, e-mail, and electronic bulletin boards and through cell phones, fax machines, and computer conferencing, the armed group can share operational information and coordinate attacks over vast distances. Chat rooms allow dispersed groups such as Hamas to conduct and coordinate the planning of operations and the movement of people. The cell phone can be used to pinpoint the timing of explosions or to facilitate coordination among linked armed groups.[23] These same technologies link criminal organizations as they coordinate the movement of goods across broad regions.

Yet another direct enabler of armed groups is the integrated global economy, which has transformed the capacities of armed groups to profit from the trade of both legal and illegal goods and resources and to circumvent the penetration of their financial networks by the state. Since the 1990s, many armed groups have lost their state sponsors, and thus their main sources of arms and financial resources. Some armed groups have seized control of the production of key resources in the regions they control, plying these goods on the global market to fund expanded operations and further weakening the capacities of the states in which these groups operate. Others have forged highly profitable alliances with other armed groups, particularly criminal organizations, trading protection and transport for a share in the vast profits. These "marriages of convenience" have further expanded the networks of armed groups, many of which operate on a global scale.

As the efforts to trace the assets of armed groups have become increasingly sophisticated, groups like al-Qaeda have turned to commodities not only as a source of profit but also as a way to protect and move funds. In the case of al-Qaeda, the decision was made to shift its financial resources from the formal banking system, trading it for commodities such as diamonds and tanzanite, which hold their value over time, are difficult to trace, have a high value-to-bulk ratio, and can be easily sold in small quantities on the world market.[24] Estimates suggest that al-Qaeda transferred some $30 to $300 million into commodities through a lucrative connection with the Revolutionary United Front (RUF) in Sierra Leone.[25] The significance of this network illustrates how globalization has enabled armed groups to expand their financial resources despite the loss of state sponsors by exploiting nontraditional financial methods made possible by a globalized economy. These methods have the added benefit of shielding the group's activities and its resources from international efforts to monitor them and seize their assets.

The global economy has also expanded access to the means necessary to conduct operations. Although the needs of an insurgency or militia may differ greatly from those of a terrorist group or a criminal organization, all armed groups need some basic weapons and basic survival goods.[26] Some armed groups can manufacture their own explosive devices.[27] Others rely on unsophisticated weapons and explosives obtainable locally, usually by theft or "trade" with local militaries. But most must rely on the global arms trade to procure the necessary weapons. Globalization has made the supply of goods, particularly arms, easily available in even the most remote parts of the world.[28] Globalization has vastly expanded the market, facilitating linkages among buyers and suppliers and easing the transit of arms and other supplies. Most significant for global security, globalization removed the armed group's dependence on the state for arms and other key resources. The result has been to further weaken state sovereignty while expanding the lethality and operational effectiveness of the armed group.

Armed groups have thus exploited globalization in direct ways to mask their activities and intentions, to evade detection, to adopt new organizational structures, and to foster highly lethal and profitable networks. They have exploited the integrated global economy to reduce their dependence on the state and to conduct increasingly lethal operations. By directly exploiting the benefits and opportunities inherent in an increasingly globalized world, armed groups have been transformed into a truly worldwide threat that directly challenges the sovereignty of the state.

THE INDIRECT EXPLOITATION OF GLOBALIZATION

Armed groups have also indirectly exploited globalization through its impact on the state. Globalization has not led to the demise of the state, but it has served to further undermine weak states, creating crises of governability and legitimacy. Armed groups need the state, albeit weakened, to function and survive. Weak states can be categorized as "bad government states" and "fractured society states."[29] Both categories are characterized by fundamental legitimacy deficits.

Holsti suggests that there are two dimensions to legitimacy: the vertical and the horizontal.[30] The vertical dimension involves the "right to rule." It is measured by the degree to which populations accept the authority of the state, consent to its rule, and offer their loyalties to the state and its institutions. The horizontal dimension of legitimacy involves the definition of the community that is to be ruled. States that define citizenship irrespective of ethnic or sectarian affiliation are states that enjoy a high degree of horizontal legitimacy. States that restrict the definition of citizenship to only one ethnic or sectarian group are states that suffer from a horizontal legitimacy deficit. The nature of the legitimacy deficit translates into two categories of weak states: the bad government state and the fractured society state.

The bad government state is a category of weak state defined in terms of *state capacity*. In bad government states, the social contract collapses and the government is deemed illegitimate because it fails to provide key political goods to its inhabitants.[31] Rotberg identifies a hierarchy of political goods, the most important of which is security, especially human security. The state's prime responsibility—its part of the social contract—is to prevent cross-border infiltrations, eliminate domestic threats, prevent crime, and enable citizens to resolve their differences without recourse to violence.[32]

Security is the gateway for the provision of other political goods, including key social services such as education; public health policies and medical care; public infrastructures, including basic utilities, communications systems, and transportation networks, as well as a money and banking system, a reliable infrastructure for fiscal extraction, and an effective judicial system. None of these public goods can be provided with uniformity if a basic level of state security cannot be maintained.

The bad government state is one that fails to provide some or all of these political goods. Given that many of these states are also on the margins of the globalized world, their capacities to respond to the challenge of armed groups is severely constrained. In much of Africa, we find states that exhibit an almost complete inability to provide basic services to their populations. Human security is nonexistent, and large parts of their territories are left unadministered. This fundamental weakness creates both political and geographic vacuums that armed groups exploit.

The fractured society state is a category of weak state defined not by its failure to deliver security and other essential political goods (although it frequently fails to provide these goods to all of its citizens) but by a fundamental lack of *legitimacy*.[33] Fractured society states are deeply divided states.[34] Populations are fractured along ethnic and sectarian cleavages, and political power resides with only one ethnic or sectarian group. In fractured society states, some or all of the population rejects the government's right to rule, and the rights of citizenship are restricted to one population group, often a group that shares the same ethnic identity with those who rule. Fractured society states thus suffer from both a horizontal and a vertical legitimacy deficit.

Many fractured society states were created during the period of decolonization after 1945. Many of these states are what Jackson terms "quasi-states": states that are granted external sovereignty without any meaningful internal sovereignty.[35] Many contain "captured populations"—groups encapsulated in states with little historic or ethnic affiliation to the states in which they find themselves or to the ruling parties. As a result, fractured society states are states whose territorial confines include populations that may be merely disenfranchised but are more likely to suffer from some form of discrimination if not violence. These states frequently exist on the margins of the globalized economy, not because of a lack of capacity, as is the case with bad government states, but because they are shunned by the international community for their exclusionary policies, as was the case with Serbia during the 1990s, or because they suffer from severe communal conflict. Although the number of violent communal conflicts has declined since the 1990s, many of the underlying issues remain unresolved.[36] These conflicts leave a legacy of wounded societies that are ripe for exploitation. These legacies are also difficult to overcome given that portions of the population view the fractured society state as illegitimate.

Bad government and fractured society states are both exploited by armed groups in different ways. Armed groups fill the vacuums created by the incapacity of bad government states to occupy and control regions where government rule is absent. These vacuums become the safe havens and sanctuaries armed groups exploit to evade detection, plan operations, train forces, and stockpile supplies. These safe havens can also be exploited to produce key resources, such as drugs, and to provide key corridors through which these drugs and operatives can move between regions and across the globe. In some cases the bad government state is an unwitting ally. Its sovereignty is exploited to shield the armed group, and the state is frequently too weak to take steps to counter the armed group's influence. In other instances, the state forms an alliance with the armed group, "taxing" the group's profits in exchange for protection and key political goods such as diplomatic passports. Both vastly increase the capacity of the armed group and the challenge it presents to international security.

Armed groups exploit fractured society states in different ways. In these states, armed groups exploit the state's legitimacy deficit, targeting excluded populations, particularly if they are ethnic kindred. They step into the vacuum created by the legitimacy deficit to offer alternate governments—ones that provide security, employment, and even basic social services, as Hezbollah has done in Lebanon. These armed groups fundamentally challenge the fractured society state because they can claim legitimacy in ways the state cannot.

In fractured society states, armed groups can function as states within the state. They tax populations, engage in international diplomacy, provide political goods and services, and field forces capable of challenging the security forces of the state. Armed groups thus offer alternate governance. Given the profits armed groups can earn by exploiting globalization, these groups frequently have budgets that exceed those of the states they challenge.

The armed group is a powerful enemy. It may enjoy a greater degree of legitimacy than the sovereign government. It may also have resources that dwarf those of the sovereign state. As these weak states attempt to counter armed groups using the meager resources they control, their ability to provide services to still-loyal populations is further constrained. Such states face a vicious cycle compounded by ever-increasing demands on their constrained resources against an enemy that can exploit globalization in ways the weak states cannot.

ARMED GROUPS AND THE 21ST-CENTURY SECURITY PARADIGM

The transformation of armed groups has far-reaching implications for how we define the security landscape of the twenty-first century. This chapter has addressed two interrelated aspects of the new security landscape, namely, the uneven erosion of state sovereignty and the rise of the armed group as a strategic threat.

Globalization has been a key factor in both the transformation of armed groups and the declining ability of weak states to counter them. Globalization has heightened the operational effectiveness of armed groups and it has undermined both state capacity and state legitimacy. Bad government states and fractured society states are caught in the paradox of globalization. Efforts to loosen restrictions on the movement of goods, people, and ideas in order to expand state capacity also expand the capacity of armed groups. The disturbing conclusion is that armed groups are uniquely positioned to exploit the benefits of globalization in ways the state, particularly the weak state, cannot. Globalization has created a far more capable and lethal enemy. The transformed armed group operates on an international scale, exploiting globalization to heighten its organizational effectiveness and lethality. The ability of weak states to counter this growing threat has been severely constrained by the erosion of state governability and legitimacy.

It is clear that the transformation of armed groups and the erosion of state sovereignty are two significant changes that will shape how we define a new security paradigm for the twenty-first century. The point here is not to suggest that the state is on the verge of disappearance but rather to argue that sovereignty is being undermined and eroded where states are already weak. I do not suggest that the armed group is the sole cause of this erosion of sovereignty. Rather, the armed group exploits already-weakened states to heighten its operational effectiveness and its global reach. In this way, weak states are further undermined. Coupled with their marginalization in the global economy, weak states are increasingly disempowered by globalization while the armed group is empowered by it.

The transformation of armed groups has far-reaching implications. Although states remain the predominant actors in the international system, by exploiting the forces of globalization, the nonstate armed group has emerged as a qualitatively and quantitatively new global actor.

NOTES

1. See Stanley Hoffman, "Clash of Globalizations," *Foreign Affairs* 81 (July/August 2002).

2. Keith Griffin, "Economic Globalization and Institutions of Global Governance," *Development and Change* 34, no. 5 (November 2004): 790.

3. Ibid., 789.

4. Fauzi Najjar, "The Arabs, Islam and Globalization," *Middle East Policy* 12 (Fall 2005): 92.

5. Hoffman, "Clash of Globalizations," 113.

6. Audrey Kurth Cronin, "Cyber-Mobilization: The New *Levée en Masse*," *Parameters* 36, no. 2 (Summer 2006): 77.

7. John Mackinlay, *Globalisation and Insurgency*, Adelphi Paper 352 (London: International Institute for Strategic Studies, 2002), 24.

8. For a discussion of this debate, see Jan Aart Scholte, "Global Capitalism and the State," *International Affairs* 73, no. 3 (July 1997): 427–29.

9. Martin Wolf, "Will the Nation-State Survive Globalization?" *Foreign Affairs,* January/February 2001, 182.

10. Ibid., 184.

11. Mackinlay, *Globalisation and Insurgency,* 19.

12. John Arquilla, David Ronfeldt, and Michele Zanini, "Networks, Netwar, and Information-Age Terrorism," in *Terrorism and Counterterrorism: Understanding the New Security Environment; Readings and Interpretations,* ed. Russell Howard and Reid Sawyer (New York: McGraw Hill, 2006), 41.

13. See Thomas X. Hammes, *Transnational and Non-state Actors and the New Landscape of War* (Cambridge: Radcliff Institute for Advanced Study, 9–10 March 2007), 6.

14. Richard H. Shultz, Jr., "The Era of Armed Groups," 23, in *The Future of American Intelligence,* ed. Peter Berkowitz (Hoover Press, 2005), available at media.hoover.org/documents/0817946624_1.pdf (accessed 23 September 2007).

15. Cronin, "Cyber-Mobilization," 82.

16. Mackinlay, *Globalisation and Insurgency,* 22.

17. Cronin, "Cyber-Mobilization," 84.

18. Ibid., 83.

19. Arquilla, Ronfeldt, and Zanini, "Networks, Netwar, and Information-Age Terrorism," 39.

20. Ibid., 63.

21. Louis Beam, quoted in ibid., 51.

22. Anthony Vinci, "The 'Problems of Mobilization' and the Analysis of Armed Groups," *Parameters* 36, no. 1 (Spring 2006): 52.

23. James Briggs, "Guide to the Armed Groups Operating in the Niger Delta, Part 2," *Terrorism Monitor* 5 (26 April 2007): 8, available at www.jamestown.org/terrorism/news/uploads/TM_005_008.pdf (accessed 23 September 2007).

24. Douglas Farah, "The Role of Conflict Diamonds in Al Qaeda's Financial Structure," Social Science Research Council, programs.ssrc.org/gsc/gsc_activities/farah/ (accessed 15 September 2007).

25. Ibid.

26. Vinci, "The 'Problems of Mobilization' and the Analysis of Armed Groups," 51.

27. Ibid., 55.

28. David Capie, "Armed Groups, Weapons Availability and Misuse: An Overview of the Issues and Options for Action" (background paper, meeting organized by the Centre for Humanitarian Dialogue in advance of the Sixth Meeting of the Human Security Network, Bamako, Mali, 25 May 2004), www.smallarmssurvey.org/files/portal/issueareas/perpetrators/armgroup.html (accessed 6 September 2007).

29. Dorff suggests two different categories of weak states—the bad government state and the ungovernable state. I have chosen to use the term "fractured society state" in place of "ungovernable state" to highlight the absence of horizontal *and* vertical legitimacy in multiethnic states. See Robert H. Dorff, "Failed States after 9/11: What Did We Know and What Have We Learned?" *International Studies Perspectives* 6, no. 1 (February 2005): 22–24.

30. Kalevi J. Holsti, *The State, War, and the State of War* (Cambridge: Cambridge University Press, 1996), 97.

31. Dorff, "Failed States after 9/11," 22.

32. Robert I. Rotberg, "The Failure and Collapse of Nation-States: Breakdown, Prevention, and Repair," in *When States Fail: Causes and Consequences*, ed. Robert I. Rotberg (Princeton: Princeton University Press, 2004), 3.

33. Holsti, *The State, War, and the State of War,* 84.

34. Donald L. Horowitz, *Ethnic Groups in Conflict* (Berkeley: University of California Press, 1985), 291.

35. Robert H. Jackson, *Quasi-states: Sovereignty, International Relations and the Third World* (Cambridge: Cambridge University Press, 1990), 21.

36. Monty G. Marshall and Ted Robert Gurr, *Peace and Conflict 2005: A Global Survey of Armed Conflicts, Self-Determination Movements, and Democracy* (College Park, MD: Center for International Development & Conflict Management, May 2005), 1.

10 Is It Possible to Deter Armed Groups?

Yosef Kuperwasser

The notion of "strategic deterrence" as one of the key pillars of a nation's military strategy has been weakened as concepts of warfare have shifted from traditional or regular to what the American administration calls "irregular" warfare. Traditional warfare between nation-states had a predictable chilling effect that sometimes prevented war or, at least, limited the way force was used. Each side's perception about how the adversary would react to a specific strategy, or the intent to attack certain targets, had a restraining effect on the way wars were fought.

The threat of mutual destruction, for example, had a profound impact on the way America and the Soviet Union treated their military capabilities during the later part of the cold war. In the end, the Soviets feared they could not maintain their counterstrike capability due to the "Star Wars" program, which changed the entire strategic perception of the cold war and contributed significantly to its termination with what everybody perceived as a decisive victory, without the use of any weapons.[1]

The logic of deterrence is based on the idea that if a state wishes to affect its adversary's strategy it has, first of all, to balance the cost and benefit for the adoption of a certain strategy, such as developing a nuclear weapon or deploying strategic missiles. Then it has to analyze the way the adversary develops its assessment about what the deterring state is going to do in various circumstances. Using this knowledge, the deterring state has to convince potential enemies that it has the capability and the determination to exact a price enemies are not willing to pay.

Brigadier General Yosef Kuperwasser is vice president of Global Comprehensive Security Transformation, a security consulting company. He was the head of the Analysis and Production Division of the Israeli Defense Forces (IDF) Directorate of Military Intelligence (Aman) for five years until June 2006. In this capacity he was responsible for preparing Israel's national intelligence assessments and for early warning. General Kuperwasser served as assistant defense attaché for intelligence at the Israeli embassy in Washington, DC (1992–94), and as the intelligence officer of the IDF Central Command (1998–2001). During his military service he had been involved in shaping the way Israel has coped with the threat of terror and understood regional developments and in sharing those understandings with U.S. and other foreign officials. Between October 2006 and January 2007, General Kuperwasser was the Andrea and Charles Bronfman Visiting Fellow in the Saban Center for Middle East Policy at the Brookings Institution. General Kuperwasser has a BA in Arabic language and literature from Haifa University and an MA in economics from Tel Aviv University.

SHAPING THE ARGUMENT

The emergence of armed groups was to some extent an outcome of the problems some states and organizations had in facing the growing strategic deterrence that liberal democracies like the United States and Israel managed to develop. The tactic used by armed groups, and especially terror organizations, is to change the way traditional wars are fought and, in doing so, change the deterrence equation. Under the new paradigm, terror groups can deter democratic states and societies committed to the values of liberalism from adopting certain policies and at the same time deprive democracies of the ability to deter armed groups and their state sponsors. This idea is based on the assumption that certain sets of liberal values may be used against democracies in the context of deterrence. In other words, liberal democracies honor the value of *life* higher than any other intrinsic concept. This means that almost nothing is worth risking your life for and that the manner in which force is used should minimize casualties. The value of life is the fundamental element in the relationship between the state and its citizens. A state protects the lives of its citizens and, in turn, citizens grant power of authority to the state to govern and levy taxes.

This was always the case, but nowadays a new expectation has been added. It's not only the protection of the lives of the citizens that should be considered before using force but the protection of the lives of the soldiers too. Protecting the life of the soldier was of course always an important issue, because it was needed for preserving the force and achieving the desired victory. But today it stems not only from military considerations but from existential philosophical origins too. Moreover, since the sanctity of life is a general value, it applies to the population that supports the enemy as well. That is why democracies hesitate to take steps that would endanger the lives of citizens of states who support armed groups. This makes it possible for armed groups to practice a sort of de facto strategic deterrence vis-à-vis liberal democracies in many cases.

The bombing of the Marines' barracks in Beirut in 1982 and the attack against the U.S. military compound in Riyadh had dramatic impacts on the American presence in Lebanon and Saudi Arabia, for example. In many cases the wars against armed groups have turned into a count of the number of the dead soldiers the liberal democracies had, and of the so-called innocent civilians on the other hand, and both have become a burden that liberal democratic societies could not sustain, though in the past, they could have in a traditional war.

This problem is exacerbated since democracies tend to adopt a wider meaning to the value of life as well as the quality of life. It's not only about existence; it's about welfare. It's about enabling people to pursue their happiness. Anything that interferes with that, namely, anything that contradicts what Western democracies term as human rights, is unacceptable, regardless of if it refers to the citizens of these democracies or to anybody else. When there is a contradiction between the security needs and the commitment to human rights, it's not clear which the superior value is. This is a perceived weakness of liberal democratic societies from the viewpoint of armed groups. There are others too.

The next one is the commitment to the idea of accountability and the guilt complex that is attached to it. Democratic regimes are going to be held accountable for any breach of the "safety and security" arrangement between the state and its citizens and for any harm done to the well-being of civilians. The perception is that the government is at fault when harm befalls its population. This notion has of course a paralyzing effect on democratic leaders who try to avoid the blame and guilt that will follow any military move against terror groups if it puts the lives of civilians on both sides or of their own soldiers in danger. Moreover the democratic leaders are bound to be blamed for being unable to achieve a decisive victory in their war against terror groups, since they and their constituency were never prepared for this kind of war and were led to believe that it is an asymmetric war in which they are supposed to have the upper hand quite easily.

Another characteristic of liberal democracies that plays into the hands of armed groups is the role of the media. The media, not the government, has assumed the leading role of shaping public opinion, the political agenda, and the way people differentiate between right and wrong. The Western mainstream media, for a variety of reasons that will not be elaborated here, amplifies the problems mentioned above. It considers sowing distrust toward the regime as its main mission and is ready to serve as a loudspeaker of terror groups' propaganda—too often without employing basic criticism to judge its accuracy.

Finally there is the issue of sovereignty, which is another perceived weakness of democracies. Western democracies are committed to the concept of sovereignty as the basic idea according to which control and the responsibility for the use of force and the rule of law in the world is shared. Therefore they always look for the sovereign entity, usually a state, to exercise its sovereignty over what happens in the territory it controls. This serves as an impediment and deterrence to the use of force in areas that are supposed to be under the dominion of another entity even in the cases where this logic is clearly baseless or worse—dangerous. This is also a contentious point that undermines United Nations unity to act against some of the world's worst atrocities. The matter of "sovereignty rights" at the UN is sometimes used to halt well-intentioned democracies from intervening into the matters of despotic and dictatorial regimes. The irony is inescapable.

On the other hand, armed groups and terror organizations are committed to an exactly opposite set of values, and therefore are able to claim that they cannot be deterred. First of all they adopt a totally different approach to the value of life. Life is just a tool to gain more important values (a revolution in the situation of their communities or entrance to paradise). The readiness to sacrifice and to suffer replaces the sanctity of life and the commitment to provide public welfare (hence Hamas's willingness to let Gaza citizens suffer). The pursuit of cultural/religious respect, and of their version of justice (often revenge), is their alternative to life's sacredness and pursuit of happiness. They have managed to build a theory that justifies the use of force against civilians and that puts the entire responsibility for all their problems and suffering on the shoulders of the West. Relying on this worldview, armed groups and terror organizations manage to avoid any accountability or responsibility. They then leverage the commitment of the democracies to the notion of sovereignty in order to find refuge in nongoverned areas and to develop more areas of this kind. They have absolute control of their media and a good capability to manipulate the Western mainstream media. Thanks to that advantage, armed groups and terror organizations are able to shape the political agenda and the political vocabulary within their constituencies and elsewhere.

THE CONSEQUENCES

So far, this chapter may seem to suggest that armed groups and terror organizations are without vulnerabilities. Since those who search for martyrdom cannot be threatened by death, since those who fight a mighty demon cannot fear being blamed for failure, since those who are not sovereign entities are not afraid of losing the control over a certain piece of land or being held accountable, they therefore have created, from their point of view, a win-win situation. Suffering means success and failure proves the authenticity of their interpretation of the world order and why it should be changed. At the same time success in escaping total annihilation or in causing suffering to the enemy without abiding by norms of warfare are of course steps toward the inevitable victory.

How then can the terror groups be deterred and deprived of the ability to deter the democracies they fight? In some respects, discussion of strategic deterrence may seem inapplicable to armed groups. After all, the context of strategic deterrence emerged from wars between states, not from conflict with nonstate actors. But as a matter of fact, the notion of deterrence is relevant to armed groups as well, though the elements with which armed groups can be deterred are different from those used against states. Just like in the case of developing an ability to deter states, one has to look first at those things that terror organizations most fear losing. Surprisingly, these are all well known to the liberal democracies.

VULNERABILITIES

The most precious asset terror organizations have is their credibility in the eyes of their own constituencies and the support they expect to get based on that credibility. They have to prove again and again that they behave like they preach. They must glorify their readiness to sacrifice and proclaim their own achievements against a seemingly hollow and cumbersome enemy. At the same time terror organizations have to make sure that their supporters don't lose hope that this sort of war will get them closer to the set of goals the terror groups set forth, the most immediate of which is to humiliate the enemy. The terrorists' greatest fear is that supporters of the movements begin to question the groups' own commitments to the causes, or have second thoughts about the goals and the feasibility of the terrorists' aims.

The second-most-valuable asset they fear losing is their ability to use ungoverned territories, or areas that are governed by state supporters, as a way to enjoy plausible deniability. If an armed group or terrorist organization brings trouble for its own constituency, it may lose the geographic freedom it benefits from. For example, the cases of groups like Hezbollah and Hamas, which in fact control certain areas and are supposed to be answerable, are very telling of how important nonaccountability is. Hezbollah prefers to point at the Lebanese government as the power responsible, and Hamas, which came to power recently in the Gaza Strip, still maintains the policy of deniability regarding attacks from that area toward Israel.[2] Hamas blames the Palestinian Authority and the rest of the world for any difficulty it encounters. One may argue that the cases of these terrorist organizations are a bit different from those of other armed groups, but actually, they all fear being held accountable and try to avoid responsibility as part of their survival strategy.

Next on the list of importance for armed groups are the lives of the activists and their freedoms of action. Contrary to their philosophical approach to the value of life, and unlike the people on the end of the terror chain who are really ready and sometimes even eager to kill themselves upon killing the enemy (even if the enemy is helpless civilians), the terror organizations' activists and leaders value their own lives highly. They try very hard to protect themselves, and when they feel that the danger is real, they spend much more time in attempts to save themselves than in contemplating martyrdom. This is especially true for the supreme leadership. Therefore, leaders of armed groups are not unlike leaders of liberal democracies; neither really wants to die.

Another very important asset to a terror organization is the support of the patron, who is usually a state. The groups have to make sure that their patrons continue to look at them more as assets than as liabilities. If they do not deliver the political and operational goods; or if the patrons begin to have doubts about their loyalties and common sense; or if the political, military, and financial burdens the groups constitute for the patrons grow too much, the armed groups might risk losing their vital state support. It's a bit strange, but since the terror group's supporters may be affected by the way other nations regard the group, it is very important from the supporters' point of view to be acceptable by the international community.

Finally, the terror groups have to make sure that their sources of arms supply, new recruits, and financial resources remain safe and sound. The fear of steps taken against them by the international community is relevant in this respect too. The terror group Hezbollah has voiced several regrets following its precipitous actions that led to hostilities with Israel in the summer of 2006. Speaking of having killed three Israeli soldiers and kidnapping two others, Hassan Nasrallah, the secretary general of Hezbollah, said, "We did not think, even one percent, that the capture would lead to a war at this time and of this magnitude. You ask me, if I had known on July 11 . . . that the operation would lead to such a war, would I do it? I say no, absolutely not."[3] Moreover, Hezbollah's actions placed the group in a precarious position with its patrons and certainly the international community.

Therefore, there are vulnerabilities that armed groups and terror organizations have. The challenge is to hold these vulnerabilities at risk. Threaten armed groups where it hurts. Find what they care about, and go after it.

CHALLENGES OF DETERRENCE

On the surface it seems that liberal democracies have done their homework, studied the vulnerabilities of armed groups, and developed strategies for fighting them. In general, democratic nations are trying to fight a war of ideas in the media, threaten the lives of the key group leaders, take action against states that support terror groups, and intimidate those who give arms and money to the terror groups. Yet a deeper analysis will discover that the problem is not with understanding what should be done but with building a posture of deterrence: having the political courage to act and ensuring armed groups and terror organizations believe it—specifically, understanding the way terror groups make their decisions and convincing them that liberal democracies are able and determined to charge them with a heavy price if they continue to try to carry out terror attacks. The reasons why this is not done properly are a combination of many problems that liberal democracies have in changing their way of learning about the situation they are entangled in and about the threat and the enemy they face.

First of all, it's pretty difficult to turn away from the paradigm of regular warfare and fully comprehend the characteristics of the new paradigm—that of irregular warfare. One of the key errors is to focus on the physical components of irregular warfare, neglecting the more abstract parts of it—in other words, thinking that if this is war, then the armed forces should be the main element fighting it. Using brute force without developing a strategy that is relevant to specifics of the new war is counterproductive since it serves as proof for the terror groups' claims that liberal democracies are ruthless and hideous and, at the same time, unable to beat them. The lessons of recent wars against terror groups have shown that the armed groups are indeed worried about the possibility that liberal democracies would try to use their military might in order to try to root them out of ungoverned areas. But at the same time they exemplified how poor the results can be if the democracies don't prepare well, especially mentally, for the long war that follows the major regular warfare stage. In this way the ability to deter the terror groups is significantly eroded.

But an even greater challenge to deterrence is the lack of coherence between what the democracies say while they fight the war of ideas and what they do. It's extremely hard to shake the credibility of the terror groups if your own credibility is questionable. If you say that you are going to take harsh measures against terror groups and their supporters, and immediately thereafter adopt a relatively soft attitude toward them, avoid calling them by name, and behave as if subconsciously you have empathy or even sympathy to their way of action, then your efforts to deter these groups are doomed. If the way liberal democracies behave sends the message that they are hesitant to pay a price in order to win the war—be it in casualties or in showing readiness to reexamine their commitment to the idea of sovereignty, in order to cope with the threats emanating from ungoverned areas—there is no chance that they will convince terror groups that they should worry about the reaction to their activities. In other words, by inconsistent words and actions, liberal democracies undermine their own credibility and, at the same time, their own ability to deter armed groups.

To some extent it is also an intelligence problem. The intelligence services of the liberal democracies find it hard to understand the decision-making processes of the terror groups because their rationales are based on a different logic. The armed groups attribute much more importance to the issue of respect than to happiness, they recognize no standard of international morality when it comes to using force, and they can easily believe the conspiracy theories they themselves invented for the consumption of their constituencies. They think in a deductive way—namely, they have an assumption about the nature of the liberal democracies and their mind-set allows them to accept only those impressions that fit with this perception. This means that any gesture the democracies make is either a part of the conspiracy or a manifestation of their weakness or both.

It is also a problem of culture. The transparency of the liberal democracies and their open debates expose the disagreements within their societies regarding the proper way to cope with the threats posed by the terror groups. This in turn undermines the credibility of their threats and serves as a proof for the ineffectiveness of any deterrence capability. Moreover the liberal culture of accountability, guilt, and speaking the truth makes it extremely difficult for these societies to participate as a real competitor in the battle waged in the media. At the same time, liberal democracies often evidence a feeling of superiority over other societies, making it very difficult for them to actually reach the minds of the people in these other cultures and have an impact on the way the terrorists and their supporters think. The main reason liberal democracies, and especially the United States, are subject to such world hatred is that they are perceived as arrogant. If this could be changed, it would significantly threaten the ability of terror groups to mobilize the masses.

In order to be able to deter the terrorists and eventually win the war against them, liberal democracies have to find ways to overcome these inherent challenges without compromising their values. The fundamental difficulty for liberal democracies is that real life is very complicated for those who don't believe in absolute values. Yet liberal democracies have to decide what is worth putting their soldiers' lives at jeopardy for. The most effective way for liberal democracies to overcome this tension is to openly show how proud they are of their system of government, demonstrate through actions that they live by their beliefs, showcase a standard of living and quality of life that come from democratic ideals—without demeaning those who have other principles.

NOTES

1. "The Strategic Defense Initiative (commonly referred to as Star Wars) was a proposal by U.S. President Ronald Reagan on March 23, 1983 to use ground-based and space-based systems to protect the United States from attack by strategic nuclear ballistic missiles. The initiative focused on strategic defense rather than the prior strategic offense doctrine of mutual assured destruction (MAD)." "Strategic Defense Initiative," Wikipedia, en.wikipedia.org/wiki/Strategic_Defense_Initiative.

2. According to the Israeli Ministry of Foreign Affairs, 428 missiles and 590 mortar bombs were fired at Israeli cities between mid-June 2007, when Hamas took over the Gaza Strip, and the end of that year. See "The Hamas Terror War against Israel," Israel Ministry of Foreign Affairs, www.mfa.gov.il/MFA/Terrorism-%2BObstacle%2Bto%2BPeace/Palestinian%2Bterror%2Bsince%2B2000/Missile%2Bfire%2Bfrom%2BGaza%2Bon%2BIsraeli%2Bcivilian%2Btargets%2BAug%2B2007.htm.

3. Herb Keinon, "Nasrallah: I Would Not Have Kidnapped Troops Had I Known the Outcome," *Jerusalem Post,* 28 August 2006, available at www.jpost.com/servlet/Satellite?cid=1154525950456&pagename=JPost%2FJPArticle%2FShowFull.

11 Sanctuary: The Geopolitics of Terrorism and Insurgency

Mackubin Thomas Owens

For the fourteenth edition of the *Encyclopaedia Britannica* (1929), the editor commissioned T. E. Lawrence (Lawrence of Arabia) to write a piece on guerrilla warfare. Lawrence's article is a remarkable achievement—a concise but comprehensive treatment of a complex subject viewed through the lens of his own experience during the Arab revolt against the Turks in 1916–1918. In a short essay brimming with insights about the nature of guerrilla warfare, his discussion of the importance of sanctuary stands out.

Quoting Sir Francis Bacon, Lawrence compares guerrilla warfare in the desert to naval warfare. The key component of both is mobility. In both modes of warfare, a force must be able to move and strike.

> In character these operations were like naval warfare, in their mobility, their ubiquity, their independence of bases and communications, in their ignoring of ground features, of strategic areas, of fixed directions, of fixed points. "He who commands the sea is at great liberty, and may take as much or as little of the war as he will": he who commands the desert is equally fortunate. Camel raiding-parties, self-contained like ships, could cruise securely along the enemy's land-frontier, just out of sight of his posts along the edge of cultivation, and tap or raid into his lines where it seemed fittest or easiest or most profitable. . . .

Dr. Mackubin Thomas Owens is associate dean of academics for electives and directed research and professor of national security affairs at the U.S. Naval War College in Newport, Rhode Island. He specializes in the planning of U.S. strategy and forces, especially naval and power projection forces; the political economy of national security; national security organization; strategic geography; and American civil-military relations. From 1990 to 1997, Dr. Owens was editor in chief of the quarterly defense journal *Strategic Review* and adjunct professor of international relations at Boston University. Dr. Owens is a contributing editor to *National Review Online,* writing primarily on security affairs and the character of American republican government, and a senior fellow of the Foreign Policy Research Institute in Philadelphia. His articles on national security issues have appeared in such publications as *International Security, Orbis, Armed Forces Journal, Joint Force Quarterly,* the *Public Interest,* the *Weekly Standard, Defence Analysis,* U.S. Naval Institute *Proceedings, Marine Corps Gazette, Comparative Strategy, National Review, New York Times, Los Angeles Times, Jerusalem Post, St. Louis Lawyer, Washington Times,* and *Wall Street Journal.* He is coeditor of the textbook *Strategy and Force Planning,* now in its fourth edition, for which he also wrote the chapters titled "The Political Economy of National Security" and "Thinking About Strategy." He currently is working on a book for the University Press of Kentucky tentatively titled *Sword of Republican Empire: A History of U.S. Civil-Military Relation.* Dr. Owens earned his PhD in politics from the University of Dallas, an MA in economics from Oklahoma University, and his BA from the University of California at Santa Barbara.

But mobility is only part of the equation. The striking force must also have a safe haven, enabling it, in Lawrence's case, to always keep a means of "sure retreat . . . into an element which the [enemy cannot] enter." In other words, as important as striking power is for guerrillas, they also require a secure base.[1] Lawrence summarizes his "thesis" at the end of his article:

> Rebellion must have an unassailable base, something guarded not merely from attack, but from the fear of it: such a base as the Arab revolt had in the Red Sea ports, the desert, or in the minds of men converted to its creed. It must have a sophisticated alien enemy, in the form of a disciplined army of occupation too small to fulfil the doctrine of acreage: too few to adjust number to space, in order to dominate the whole area effectively from fortified posts. It must have a friendly population, not actively friendly, but sympathetic to the point of not betraying rebel movements to the enemy. Rebellions can be made by 2% active in a striking force, and 98% passively sympathetic. The few active rebels must have the qualities of speed and endurance, ubiquity and independence of arteries of supply. They must have the technical equipment to destroy or paralyze the enemy's organized communications, for irregular war is fairly Willisen's definition of strategy, "the study of communication," in its extreme degree, of attack where the enemy is not. In 50 words: Granted mobility, security (in the form of denying targets to the enemy), time, and doctrine (the idea to convert every subject to friendliness), victory will rest with the insurgents, for the algebraical factors are in the end decisive, and against them perfections of means and spirit struggle quite in vain.[2]

Thus in order to have any hope of success, a guerrilla force must be able to operate from a secure base. That base may be geographical but it may also be conceptual—lying within the minds of a friendly or sympathetic population.

Although Lawrence was concerned in this article with the operational level of war, the principle applies to all levels—the strategic as well as the operational. Understanding this fact permits us to recognize the importance of "sanctuary" as the cornerstone of the geopolitics of insurgency and terrorism and the reason that insurgents, terrorists, and other armed groups must rely on the likes of Waziristan, the Sierra Maestre, or Shaanxi.

CLASSICAL GEOPOLITICS

Classical geopolitics recognized the important influence of geography—the physical setting of human activity, whether political, economic, or strategic—on the formulation of strategy.[3] As Nicholas Spykman observed, "geography is the most fundamental factor in foreign policy because it is the most permanent."[4] The geographic setting imposes distinctive constraints on a nation's foreign policy and strategy while at the same time providing distinctive opportunities. As Colin Gray has remarked, geography at a minimum defines the players in international relations, the stakes for which the players contend, and the terms by which they measure their security relative to others.[5]

Geopolitics—"the relation of international political power to the geographical setting"[6]—is concerned with the study of the political and strategic relevance of geography in the pursuit of international power. As such, it is most closely related to strategic geography, which is concerned with the control of, or access to, spatial areas that have an impact on the security and prosperity of nations.

Adherents of geopolitics contend that the study of the international scene from a spatial viewpoint, by which one better understands the whole, has strategic implications. The main directions of proper strategy may be deduced from an understanding of the overarching spatial relationships among political actors: by discerning broad geographical patterns, it is possible to develop better strategic options for ensuring states their places in the world.

The geopolitical perspective in international relations has given rise to spatial "pivotal binaries," categories that shape how we look at the world and suggest strategic steps to enhance state power, the most enduring of which include East and West, "sea power" and "land power," "maritime" and "continental," "heartland" and "rimland," and "core areas" and peripheral "shatterbelts." These are, of course, mental constructs, but strategy is directly connected to perceptions about the geographic attributes that configure the global space in which conflict occurs. We might call these "mental maps."[7]

Mental maps reflect another important aspect of geopolitics: "strategic culture." It is undeniable that different countries manifest different approaches to international politics. For instance, sea powers envision their security differently than land powers. As Gray observes, "Distinctive political culture, which substantially determines national style in foreign and military affairs, is the product of a distinctive national historical experience—and that distinctive historical experience reflects no less distinctive a blend of national geographical conditions."[8]

Since geopolitics describes the nexus of geographic factors; relative power, including economic power; and militarily significant technology, these geopolitical categories tend to be dynamic, not static. This point is often lost on critics of geopolitics. Thus Halford Mackinder revised his concept of the heartland three times and Saul Cohen modified his idea of which regions constituted the world's shatterbelts several times. Such changes reflect modified circumstances arising from changes in relative power among states, including economic development, or advances in technology.

This is a critically important point to remember: technology and economics are not extraneous to geopolitical analysis. They are integral to geopolitics. The shift from sail to coal to oil to nuclear ship propulsion significantly changed the geopolitical landscape, as did the railroad and the development of air power. Some analysts suggested that nuclear weapons spelled the end of geopolitics. Some make that claim now on behalf of information technology and cyberspace. But while technological advances can alter, they do not negate the importance of the geographic determinants of policy and strategy. The same is true of economic development. The infusion of capital may modify but not negate the importance of a particular geographic space.

Real strategy must take account of such factors as technology, the availability of resources, and geopolitical realities. This last factor is critical, although in a globalized world we sometimes forget that strategy is developed and implemented in real time and space. A state must consciously adapt its strategy to geopolitical realities. The strategy of a state is not self-correcting. If conditions change, policy makers must be able to discern these changes and modify the strategy and strategic goals accordingly.[9]

From World War I up to the collapse of the Soviet Union, U.S. strategy was based on the 1904 heartland theory of Sir Halford John Mackinder, modified by Nicholas

Spykman's rimland concept.[10] However, 9/11 and the rise of China have shown the shortcomings of such a theory.[11] But while U.S. policy makers have paid lip service to the idea that U.S. strategic focus must change as a result of the collapse of the Soviet empire, there is much evidence to indicate that America's focus has not changed.

THE EMERGING GEOPOLITICS OF TERRORISM AND INSURGENCY

When strategy makers, operators, and force planners do not adapt to changing conditions, serious problems can result. Jakub Grygiel shows how a failure to adapt strategy to geopolitical change led to the decline of Venice (1000–1600), the Ottoman Empire (1300–1699), and Ming China (1364–1644).[12] Each actor faced changing circumstances but made wrong strategic choices. These cases are cautionary for the United States, since it now is facing geopolitical changes of the same magnitude.

During the 1990s, serious thinking about security and strategy took a holiday. The end of the cold war led some to suggest optimistic alternatives to the bipolar structure of the world that had arisen from the struggle between the United States and the Soviet Union.

By far the most optimistic and ambitious alternative appeared in a watershed article by Francis Fukuyama for the Summer 1989 issue of the *National Interest*. In "The End of History?" Fukuyama suggested that the end of the cold war meant that liberalism had defeated its one remaining ideological competitor to become the dominant force in the world. Fascism had been destroyed with the Allied victory in World War II. Now communism had joined it on the ash heap of history.[13]

Fukuyama was answered almost immediately by Samuel Huntington, who argued that the end of ideological war did not mean that major fault lines had disappeared in the world. In place of ideological conflict, he postulated a "clash of civilizations."[14] Robert Kaplan also joined the fray, arguing that in many parts of the world, "history" was very much still in evidence.[15] As one wag said of the Balkans: "too much history; too little space."

Fukuyama followed up his original article in the *National Interest* with a book in which he addressed his critics, acknowledging that, despite the progress of "a universal and directional history" leading to the end state of liberal democracy, there were many parts of the world in which liberal democracy had not yet triumphed. Nonetheless, he argued, there was an increasing acceptance of the idea that "liberal democracy in reality constitutes the best possible solution to the human problem."[16]

The corollary to the universal triumph of liberal democracy was "globalization," the dynamic, worldwide process of capitalistic economic integration and the irresistible expansion of global capitalist markets. Advocates of globalization concluded that interdependence and cooperation had replaced competition in international affairs and that the result would be more or less spontaneous peace and prosperity. Political scientists and economists alike agreed that this was the most important characteristic of our epoch, against which other forces didn't stand a chance. "Global interdependence" advanced the idea that the pursuit of power in its geographic setting had been supplanted by liberal economic cooperation. For many, the process of globalization was autonomous and self-regulating.

Of course, 9/11 called into question the assumption that globalization was an unambiguously beneficial phenomenon. We now began to discern what some commentators called the "dark underbelly" of globalization, represented by such enemies of Western liberalism as Osama bin Laden.

While a number of analysts tried to shoehorn 9/11 into previous paradigms, Thomas Barnett, a former research professor at the Naval War College, offered an innovative explanation of the link between globalization and terrorism in a controversial article for the March 2003 issue of *Esquire* entitled "The Pentagon's New Map." According to Barnett, 9/11 revealed the emerging geopolitical reality that the world's most important "fault line" was not between the rich and the poor but between those who accept modernity and those who reject it. The former part of the globe Barnett called the "Functioning Core"; the latter, the "Non-Integrating Gap."[17]

The Core, where "globalization is thick with network connectivity, financial transactions, liberal media flows, and collective security," is characterized by "stable governments, rising standards of living, and more deaths by suicide than murder." The Gap, where "globalization is thinning or just plain absent," is "plagued by politically repressive regimes, widespread poverty and disease, routine mass murder, and—most important—the chronic conflicts that incubate the next generation of global terrorists."[18]

Barnett, like Fukuyama, Huntington, and Kaplan before him, expanded his article into a book: *The Pentagon's New Map: War and Peace in the Twenty-first Century,*[19] which offers a persuasive analysis of the post-9/11 world as well as policy prescriptions flowing from that analysis. It supports the idea that the necessary (but not sufficient) cause of prosperity is security—in other words, that the expansion of a liberal world order (globalization) is not automatic—it must be underwritten by a power or powers willing to provide the public good of security. Just as the theories of such geopolitical writers as Sir Halford Mackinder and Nicholas Spykman provided the intellectual underpinnings of U.S. grand strategy during the cold war, Barnett offers the outline of a geopolitics rationale for a grand strategy to counter the new terrorism.

Barnett's Core is composed of North America, Europe, Japan, Russia, India, China, Brazil, Chile, and Argentina. The Gap includes South America (minus Brazil, Argentina, and Chile), most of Africa, the Middle East, and central Asia. This part of the world contains most of the "failed states" that epitomize the perceived failures of globalization. Before 9/11, U.S. policy makers acted in accordance with a "rule set" that focused on interstate conflict within the Core and consigned security concerns within the Gap to the status of "lesser included cases."

Policy makers in both the Clinton and Bush administrations failed to anticipate the events of 9/11 not primarily because of intelligence failures, important as they may have been, but because their attention was focused elsewhere. The former saw globalization as a panacea for the world's ills and ignored its failures in the Gap. The latter were focused on preventing the emergence of a competing great power—e.g., China—in the Core. The dominant rule set during the 1990s was a continuation of the cold war rule set, stressing arms control, deterrence, and the management of globalization. The dream was to create a Kantian world of "perpetual peace" among democratic states.

But this rule set left much of the Gap—the "disconnected" regions of the world—in a Hobbesian "state of nature," wherein the life of man is "solitary, poor, nasty, brutish, and short." Led by educated elites such as Osama bin Laden who desired to keep their regions disconnected from the grasp of globalization and American "empire," the Gap struck directly at the Core. In Barnett's view, 9/11 was the revenge of the "lesser includeds."

For Barnett, the key to future global security and prosperity is the requirement of the Core to "shrink" the Gap. Managing the Gap—a policy of containment—is not enough: such an approach further reduces what little connectivity the Gap has with the Core and renders it more dangerous to the Core over the long haul. The Core must export security into the Gap, providing the stability necessary for the regions within to achieve "connectivity" with the rest of the world and thereby position themselves to benefit from globalization. Otherwise, the Gap will continue to export terrorism to the Core, as it has been doing over the last decade.

Barnett argues that "bin Laden and Al Qaeda are pure products of the Gap—in effect, its most violent feedback to the Core." The attacks of 9/11 represented an attempt by bin Laden to create a "systems perturbation" in the Core so that he would be able to take the Islamic world "off-line" from globalization and return it to some seventh-century definition of the good life. For Barnett, the proper strategic response to 9/11 is to create a countervailing systems perturbation in the Gap—which is exactly what the Bush administration did by striking Afghanistan and Iraq.

The point here is that Barnett's "Gap" is critical to understanding the new geopolitics of terrorism. The Gap is sanctuary writ large. It provides the "ungoverned space" that terrorists, guerrillas, and armed groups can exploit to provide the "unassailable base" that Lawrence believed to be so important to the success of irregular fighters. As Lawrence observed, such a base may be not only physical but also psychological, existing "in the minds of men" who accept the creed of the guerrilla or who are intimidated into acquiescence. Whether it is located in South Waziristan, Pankisi Gorge, the Bekaa Valley, Fallujah, or the *banlieues* of Paris, terrorism needs some physical, geographical, or psychological locus in order to exert a material force.

ARMED GROUPS AND SANCTUARY

Sanctuary takes several forms. The most obvious example of sanctuary is the use of foreign territory as a base. The likelihood that an insurgency will succeed increases significantly if it can gain sanctuary in neighboring states and can obtain assistance from state and nonstate actors. Indeed, a territorial base outside of the state in which the insurgency is operating is positively correlated with the insurgency's success.[20]

But armed groups can also find sanctuary in remote areas within a state, e.g., a backwoods or highland area, illustrated by such cases as the Chinese communists in Shaanxi, the Cuban revolutionaries in the Sierra Maestre, and anti-Musharraf insurgents in Waziristan.[21]

Many of these areas had long histories as in-state sanctuaries. For instance, in the case of the Chinese Revolution, the base areas for the communists were located in the peripheries of agricultural macroregions that had served the same function for nine-teenth-century revolts against imperial China.[22]

Armed groups may also find sanctuary within an ethnic diaspora, either within the insurgency state or without. Diasporas often provide a source of recruits, training, finance, arms, logistics, diplomatic backing, etc., for the insurgency. In the case of Islamic terrorism and insurgency, this form of sanctuary has been boosted by the emergence of a transnational *jihadi* network, which creates synergy between local and global groups.

Finally, terrorist organizations have been able to find sanctuary in cyberspace. Cybersanctuary is similar in nature to sanctuary provided by an ethnic diaspora. In the case of al Qaeda, *jihadis* are able to use the Internet to spread its ideology, to raise money, to gain recruits, and to signal operatives.

> Osama bin Laden's al Qaeda is not a hierarchical organization, but a network of like-minded Muslim fundamentalists with jihadi "spear carriers." Its expansion no longer depends on bin Laden and his deputy, the Egyptian doctor Ayman al-Zawahri (whose group assassinated Egyptian President Anwar Sadat in 1981). The Internet, with more than 1 billion people on line, and reckoned to double to 2 billion by 2010, does that job for them automatically.[23]

The former commander of U.S. Central Command, General John Abizaid, recently observed that "Al Qaeda's organizing ability in cyberspace is unprecedented." Al Qaeda operates in cyberspace with impunity, using 6,000-plus Web sites to recruit, proselytize, and plan, exploiting the virtual reality of Islam's global *ummah*.

Sanctuary is subject to different scales of analysis.[24] The physical size of a sanctuary is a critical determinant of whether a terrorist group can transform itself into a full-blown insurgency. John Robb explains the relationship between sanctuary and the size of an armed group.[25]

He argues that terrorist networks are distributed and dynamic and cannot scale like hierarchical networks, because the same network design that makes them resilient when attacked also establishes absolute limits on their size.

He begins his analysis by citing the extensive data on the limits to group size within peaceful online communities. One theoretical limit is the so-called Dunbar Number. R. I. M. Dunbar is an anthropologist at the University College of London, who has hypothesized that

> there is a cognitive limit to the number of individuals with whom any one person can maintain stable relationships, that this limit is a direct function of relative neocortex size, and that this in turn limits group size. . . . [T]he limit imposed by neocortical processing capacity is simply on the number of individuals with whom a stable inter-personal relationship can be maintained.[26]

Dunbar predicts that 147.8 is the "mean group size" for humans, which matches census data on various village and tribe sizes in many cultures. The Dunbar Number seems to be applicable here because terrorist networks are essentially geographically dispersed online communities.

But Robb cites research by Christopher Allen[27] demonstrating that the optimal size of a terrorist group is far less than the Dunbar Number of 150. According to Allen, there is a gradual falloff in the effectiveness of a terrorist network at 80 members, with an absolute falloff at 150 members. "The initial fall-off occurs . . . due to an increasing amount of effort spent on 'grooming' the group to maintain cohesion. The absolute fall-off at 150 members occurs when grooming fails to stem dissatisfaction and dissension, which causes the group to cleave apart into smaller subgroups (that may remain affiliated)."

According to Robb and Allen, there are two optimal sizes for terrorist networks: small and medium. Small groups (or cells), the minimum size capable of carrying out the tasks assigned, are optimized at seven to eight members. The lower boundary is five members because such a small group lacks sufficient resources to be effective. The upper boundary is nine for reasons of span of control.

> Medium sized groups are optimal at 45–50 members, with a lower limit of 25 and an upper limit of 80. Between these levels is a chasm that must be surmounted with significant peril to the group. This is due to the need for groups above 9–10 members to have some level of specialization by function. This specialization requires too much management oversight to be effective given the limited number of participants in each function. At 25 members, the group gains positive returns on specialization given the management effort applied (a break-even point).

> This chasm (between 9–25 members) nicely matches the problem period in the development of terrorist and guerrilla networks that studies of guerrilla groups refer to. The amount of damage a small (7–8 member) group can do is limited to narrow geographies and therefore does not represent a major threat. Once a network grows to 45–50 members, they can mount large attacks across multiple geographies. They are also very difficult to eliminate due to geographically [*sic*] dispersion of cells. However, during the transition to a larger group they are vulnerable to disruption. This vulnerability necessitates fast counter-terrorist action (this gives credibility to the military strategists who claim we didn't have enough troops in Iraq immediately after the war, nor were we quick enough to establish martial law) during that short period of time a network is transitioning in size.[28]

Of course, limits on organizational size do not mean that armed groups are not able to expand their ranks on a temporary basis. This is because of the availability of "contract" employees and the potential for intergroup cooperation.[29]

However, when a terrorist network possesses a sanctuary, it can grow larger than suggested by Allen's research because physical security and proximity permit it to operate as a hierarchy along military lines, complete with middle management. Before the United States responded to 9/11, al Qaeda operated in this mode in Afghanistan, while maintaining distributed networks outside of Afghanistan. Once the Taliban and al Qaeda were driven from Afghanistan, they tended to fragment into smaller, less effective groups.

The implication here is that without a sanctuary, terrorist networks are limited to cells of about 100 in order to maintain security. Since security is achieved at the expense of performance and flexibility, large cells cannot remain operationally secure without a sanctuary. This means that possession of a sanctuary allows terrorists to expand their networks to a larger and more potent size. Without a sanctuary, terrorists and other armed groups are transformed into small, clandestine hunted bands.[30] Thus dismantling terrorist enclaves is a critical component of antiterrorism and counterinsurgency.

This was the lesson of Afghanistan in 2002 and Fallujah in 2004. It also explains why al Qaeda has been able to reconstitute itself in Waziristan and why this sanctuary cannot be tolerated.

DENYING SANCTUARY: TWO CASE STUDIES

Geronimo[31]

In 1881, a series of unfortunate events exacerbated by corruption and incompetence on the part of U.S. Indian Affairs officials led to an Apache uprising in the American Southwest. Several bands left their reservation at San Carlos, taking refuge in the Sierra Madre, a massive, towering mountain range that dominates the western Mexican state of Sonora. Depredations against reservation officials and settlers in Arizona in January of 1882 spurred the U.S. Army into action. For the most part, the response was ineffectual. The superior mobility of the Apache bands and their knowledge of the terrain gave them a decided advantage over their pursuers.

Displeased with the Army's progress against the Apache rejectionists, general in chief of the Army William Tecumseh Sherman appointed General George Crook to command the Arizona Department. Crook identified three objectives: to bring the reservation Indians under control, to protect the lives and property of citizens, and to subjugate the hostiles operating from the Sierra Madre.[32] The second depended on the other two and the first ultimately depended on the third.

Crook improved the lot of the reservation Indians, removing a major source of discontent. He then prepared to campaign in Mexico, if necessary. His ability to do so was helped by a reciprocal crossing agreement signed by the Díaz government in July of 1882.

Crook was something of an eccentric character who sported a beard braided in two long tails. But he gained the affection of his troops, who appreciated his reticence and lack of pretentiousness. More importantly he was also an innovator who understood the special conditions and requirements of Indian warfare. "The adult Apache is the embodiment of physical endurance—lean, well proportioned, medium sized, with sinews like steel, insensible to hunger, fatigue, or physical pains." Crook understood that the only way to defeat such warriors was with other Apaches. As such he employed Apache scouts as his main tactical arm and pack trains in lieu of wagons for logistical support.

In March of 1883, an Apache raiding party under the Apache leaders Chato and Benito struck into Arizona near Fort Huachuca, plundering and killing for nearly a week before slipping back into Mexico. Sherman ordered Crook to pursue and destroy the Apaches without regard to department or national boundaries.[33]

Crook responded with alacrity and energy. Deploying the Third and Sixth cavalries to guard strategic points on the border, Crook himself led a compact and carefully balanced column in pursuit of the raiders into their stronghold of the Sierra Madre, which Crook described as "a natural fortress." Crook's column was composed of 193 Apache scouts and a small detachment of the Sixth Cavalry, supported by pack mules carrying ammunition and rations for 60 days. On 15 May, Crook's Apache scouts attacked the camps of Chato and Benito, killing a number of warriors and routing the rest. Crook's success in the very heart of the Apache stronghold led the leaders, including Geronimo, to negotiate a return to the San Carlos reservation.

Geronimo tarried in Mexico for some time but, from late 1883 until March 1884, the Apaches filtered back to the United States and were returned to San Carlos. But discontent reemerged and, in 1885, Apaches again fled the reservation. Crook repeated his operational approach during the exhausting and less successful Sierra Madre campaign of 1885. Not only were the fugitives able to avoid Crook's columns this time, but, in November, an Apache band launched a raid that dwarfed most that had gone before.

Crook's column eventually located the main Apache camp on 19 January 1886. The pending attack was given away by a braying mule and the hostiles hastily vacated the position, but their shattered sense of security led the Apaches to open negotiations with Captain Emmett Crawford, the commander of Crook's Apache scouts. The Apaches agreed to surrender, but in late March, as they were being escorted back to the United States, Geronimo and a group of followers scattered into the mountains.

Crook's methods had been questioned by his superiors, especially General Phil Sheridan. Geronimo's escape led Sheridan to question the reliability of Crook's Apache scouts and to call for a defensive cordon against Apache depredations. Crook knew that this was a vain approach and asked to be relieved. Sheridan obliged, replacing him as commander of the Department of Arizona with Brigadier General Nelson Miles.

Despite Sheridan's charge to Miles to mount a vigorous campaign against the Apache rejectionists "making active and prominent use of the Regular troops of your command" rather than Apache scouts, Miles's approach actually mirrored that of Crook. He relied on mobile striking forces to wear down and root out the hostiles. Although composed mainly of regulars, they still relied on Apache scouts. Defensively, he established a system of heliographs designed to alert the mobile columns to any band of Indians sighted.[34]

To pursue Geronimo into Mexico, Miles organized a force of hand-picked regular troops and Apache scouts, and a small pack train under the command of Captain Henry Lawton. This column pursued its quarry for four months over a track of 2,000 miles of difficult terrain. Simultaneously, Miles also pursued a peace initiative to bring about Geronimo's surrender, which was effected on 4 September 1886.

In one respect, Lawton's offensive failed. Geronimo did not surrender to him but to Miles's peace envoy. Nonetheless, "Lawton's persistent campaigning almost certainly helped put Geronimo in a frame of mind conducive to peace talks."[35] It was the *offensive* and the lack of sanctuary that wore down Geronimo, inducing him to give up. His surrender ended the Apache threat to Arizona, New Mexico, and Mexico.

Fallujah and the Tigris-Euphrates "Ratlines"

The central goal of the U.S. strategy in Iraq in 2004 was to destroy the insurgency by depriving it of its base in the Sunni Triangle and its "ratlines"—the infiltration routes that run from the Syrian border into the heart of Iraq. One ratline follows the Euphrates River corridor—running from Syria to Husayba on the Syrian border and then through Qaim, Rawa, Hadithah, Asad, Hit, and Fallujah to Baghdad. The other follows the course of the Tigris—from the north through Mosul–Tel Afar to Tikrit and on to Baghdad. These two "river corridors" constitute the main spatial elements of a campaign to implement U.S. strategy.

Actual strategy, as opposed to strategy in theory, occurs in time and geographic space. These corridors constituted the main spatial elements of a campaign that began in November 2004 with the takedown of Fallujah. A campaign is a series of coordinated events—movements, battles, and supporting operations—designed to achieve strategic or operational objectives within a military theater. The key to a successful campaign is the proper sequencing of events designed to bring about the desired end. That sequencing depends on the circumstances.[36]

Wresting Fallujah from the rebels was critically important: Control of the town had given them the infrastructure—human and physical—necessary to maintain a high tempo of attacks against the Iraqi government and coalition forces. In and of itself, the loss of Fallujah didn't cause the insurgency to collapse, but it did deprive the rebels of an indispensable sanctuary. Absent such a sanctuary, large terrorist networks cannot easily survive, being reduced to small, hunted bands.

With Fallujah captured, the coalition continued a high tempo of offensive operations. After losing the city, the al Qaeda leader in Iraq, Abu Musab al-Zarqawi, apparently tried to reconstitute the insurgency in Mosul, but was unable to do so because of continued U.S. pressure. In Mosul as in Fallujah, coalition forces killed and captured insurgents—forcing Zarqawi to move west into Anbar province. In March 2005, an Iraqi special operations unit captured an insurgent camp near Lake Tharthar on the border of Anbar and Salaheddin provinces. Such operations forced Zarqawi back to positions along the Syrian border.

Next came the "Rivers Campaign," designed to destroy the insurgent infrastructure west and northwest of Fallujah and shut down those "ratlines." The so-called surge beginning in early 2007 and the "Anbar Awakening," which saw many Sunni sheikhs turn against their erstwhile ally, al Qaeda, combined to deprive the latter of a very important sanctuary.[37]

The results of these actions validated Lawrence's observations on the importance of a base to provide them a "safe haven," enabling them to always keep a means of "sure retreat . . . into an element which the [enemy cannot] enter," which in turn was necessary to support the guerrillas' "ubiquity" and "mobility." When Fallujah was taken, Zarqawi's group was dispersed, reduced to the small hunted bands described by Allen and Robb. The "Rivers Campaign" and the subsequent surge denied Zarqawi and his adherents other safe havens in Anbar, and they began to suffer from the lack of logistical, moral, and command support that only coalescence in a physical place can provide. The outcome in Iraq still remains in question, but the campaign that began with the seizure of Fallujah in November 2004 illustrates what must be done if a counterinsurgency has any hope at all of succeeding.

CONCLUSION

Sanctuary is indispensable to the success of guerrillas, terrorists, or other armed groups. At the strategic level, the need to deny sanctuary to such groups supports Tom Barnett's argument that the "Gap" cannot be merely managed, but must be shrunk. Otherwise, as noted above, the Gap will continue to export terrorism to the Core, as it has for the last decade. This was the justification for undertaking very difficult and demanding operations to deny al Qaeda sanctuary in Afghanistan and to prevent it from turning Iraq into a safe haven.

At the operational level, the two cases above illustrate that when armed groups are deprived of sanctuary, their effectiveness drops off considerably. As Fallujah indicates, denying the enemy sanctuary can be a difficult and bloody undertaking but it is necessary if armed groups are to be defeated. This is true of sanctuary in both geographic space as well as cyberspace.

NOTES

1. Reprinted under the title of "Science of Guerrilla Warfare" in *T.E. Lawrence in War and Peace*, ed. Malcolm Brown (London: Greenhill Books, 2005), 281.

2. Ibid., 284.

3. For an overview of classical geopolitics, see Mackubin Thomas Owens, "In Defense of Classical Geopolitics," *Naval War College Review* 52, no. 4 (Autumn 1999); and Colin Gray and Geoffrey Sloan, eds., *Geopolitics: Geography and Strategy* (London: Frank Cass, 1999).

4. Nicholas J. Spykman, *The Geography of the Peace* (New York: Harcourt, Brace, 1944), 41.

5. Colin S. Gray, "The Continued Primacy of Geography," *Orbis*, Spring 1996, 248–49.

6. Saul B. Cohen, *Geography and Politics in a World Divided,* 2nd ed. (New York: Oxford University Press, 1973), 29.

7. Patrick O'Sullivan, *Geopolitics* (New York: St. Martin's Press, 1986), 2–6, 23–38.

8. Colin Gray, *The Geopolitics of the Nuclear Era: Heartland, Rimlands, and the Technological Revolution* (New York: Crane, Russak & Company, 1977), 33.

9. Jakub J. Grygiel, *Great Powers and Geopolitical Change* (Baltimore: Johns Hopkins University Press, 2006).

10. Mackinder believed that changes in technology, especially the revolution in land transportation associated with the railroad, had altered the balance of power between sea power and land power, bringing the "Columbian Age" of dominant sea power to a close. In the new, closed international global system, land power would hold the advantage. The center of emerging land power was the Eurasian core area Mackinder first called the "geographical pivot of history" and later the *heartland.* This core area was inaccessible to sea power and therefore capable of sheltering a land power able to dominate the Eurasian "World-Island" from its central continental fortress: "The oversetting of the balance of power in favor of the pivot state, resulting in its expansion over the marginal lands of Euro-Asia, would permit the vast continental resources for fleet-building, and the empire of the world would then be in sight." For Mackinder, Eastern Europe was the gateway to the heartland. Mackinder's geopolitical thesis, which influenced the victors at Versailles after World War I, was whispered by an "airy cherub" to the statesmen of the world: "Who rules East Europe commands the Heartland; Who rules the Heartland commands the World-Island; Who rules the World-Island commands the world."

Surrounding the heartland were two crescents: a wholly maritime outer crescent consisting of the Americas, the British Isles, Australia, and sub-Saharan Africa; and a partly continental and partly maritime inner crescent, extending along the Eurasian littoral from Iberia to Siberia and including most of continental Europe west of Russia, the Maghreb, the Middle East, and continental South, Southeast, and East Asia. This "marginal region" contained the vast majority of the world's population and was the origin of most of the world's great civilizations, religions, and empires. Because of its location, Mackinder believed, the inner crescent would forever be a zone of conflict.

Spykman contended that Mackinder had overemphasized the power potential of the heartland, having overestimated the impact of the revolution in land transportation and underestimated the power of the inner and outer crescents. Spykman argued that the critical geopolitical area of the globe was Mackinder's inner crescent, which he renamed the "rimland."

Spykman's approach greatly influenced the U.S. cold war policy of containment. Indeed, if George Kennan is the "father of containment," Spykman is its godfather. Kennan wrote that vis-à-vis the Soviet Union, the United States should follow a "policy of containment, designed to confront the Russians with unalterable counter-force at every point where they show signs of encroaching upon the interests of a peaceful and stable world." Thus containment is a particular manifestation of Spykman's dictum that the United States had a universal interest in "the prevention of hegemony, a power position which would permit the domination of all within [a hegemon's] reach."

Mackinder's seminal articles on geopolitics are "The Scope and Methods of Geography," *Proceedings of the Royal Geographical Society and Monthly Record of Geography* 9 (1887): 141–60; "The Geographical Pivot of History," *Geographical Journal* 23 (1904): 421–37; *Democratic Ideals and Reality* (1919); and "The Round World and the Winning of the Peace," *Foreign Affairs* 21, no. 4 (July 1943). All are reprinted in Halford J. Mackinder, *Democratic Ideals and Reality* (New York: Norton, 1962). Cf. also W. H. Parker, *Mackinder: Geography as an Aid to Statecraft* (Oxford: Clarendon Press, 1982). Spykman's major geopolitical works are *The Geography of the Peace* and *America's Strategy in World Politics* (New York: Harcourt, Brace, 1942). See also Owens, "In Defense of Classical Geopolitics," esp. 65.

11. But see C. Dale Watson, *Geopolitics and the Great Powers in the 21st Century: Multipolarity and the Revolution in Strategic Perspective* (London: Routledge, 2007).

12. Grygiel, *Great Powers and Geopolitical Change*, 51–161.

13. Francis Fukuyama, "The End of History?" *National Interest*, Summer 1989.

14. Samuel Huntington, "The Clash of Civilizations?" *Foreign Affairs*, Summer 1993; Samuel Huntington, *The Clash of Civilizations and the Remaking of the World Order* (New York: Simon and Schuster, 1996)

15. Robert Kaplan, "The Coming Anarchy," *Atlantic Monthly*, February 1994. Kaplan has recently become one of several writers arguing that the United States has shifted too far in the direction of irregular warfare, thus ignoring the possibility of traditional large-scale interstate warfare. See Robert Kaplan, "America's Elegant Decline," *Atlantic Monthly*, October 2007; Colin Gray, *Another Bloody Century: Future Warfare* (London: Weidenfeld & Nicolson, 2005). Cf. Colin Gray, "Future Warfare, or The Triumph of History," *RUSI Journal*, October 2005.

16. Francis Fukuyama, *The End of History and the Last Man* (New York: The Free Press, 1992).

17. Thomas Barnett, "The Pentagon's New Map," *Esquire*, March 2003.

18. In addition to Barnett, see John Robb, *Brave New War: The Next Stage of Terrorism and the End of Globalization* (Hoboken: John Wiley and Sons, 2007).

19. Thomas Barnett, *The Pentagon's New Map: War and Peace in the Twenty-first Century* (New York: Putnam, 2004).

20. James D. Feron and David D. Laitin, "Ethnicity, Insurgency, and Civil War," *American Political Science Review* 97, no. 1 (February 2003): 75–90.

21. Gonzalo Aguirre Beltran, *Regions of Refuge* (Washington, DC: Society for Applied Anthropology, 1979).

22. Robert McColl, "The Rise of Territorial Communism in China, 1921–34: The Geography behind Politics" (PhD diss., Department of Geography, University of Washington, Seattle, 1957).

23. Arnaud de Borchgrave, "Al Qaeda on the Ropes?" *Washington Times*, 28 September 2007.

24. For the discussion that follows, I am particularly indebted to the Weblog "The Belmont Club," which discussed some of the concepts developed on the Web sites cited below. "The Belmont Club" site can be accessed at fallbackbelmont.blogspot.com/.

25. John Robb, "The Optimal Size of a Terrorist Network," Global Guerrillas, posted 24 March 2004, globalguerrillas.typepad.com/globalguerrillas/2004/03/what_is_the_opt.html.

26. R. I. M. Dunbar, "Coevolution of Neocortical Size, Group Size and Language in Humans," *Behavioral and Brain Sciences* 16, no. 4 (Fall 1993), available at www.bbsonline.org/documents/a/00/00/05/65/bbs00000565-00/bbs.dunbar.html.

27. Christopher Allen's Weblog is "Life with Alacrity." For his discussion of the Dunbar Number, see "The Dunbar Number as a Limit to Group Size," Life with Alacrity, posted 10 March 2004, www.lifewithalacrity .com/2004/03/the_dunbar_numb.html.

28. Robb, "The Optimal Size of a Terrorist Network."

29. On the social mapping of terrorist networks, see Vladis E. Krebs, "Uncloaking Terrorist Networks," *First Monday,* www.firstmonday.dk/issues/issue7_4/krebs/. Social network mapping was used to take down Saddam Hussein. See Vernon Loeb, "Clan, Family Ties Called Key to Army's Capture of Hussein: 'Link Diagrams' Showed Everyone Related by Blood or Tribe," *Washington Post,* 16 December 2003, A23, available at www.washingtonpost.com/ac2/wp-dyn/A3075-2003Dec15?language=printer.

30. "Dark Networks," The Belmont Club, posted 24 September 2004, belmontclub.blogspot.com/2004/09/ dark-networks-vladis-krebs-has-case.html.

31. The account here relies heavily on Robert M. Utley's indispensable study of the Indian wars, "Geronimo, 1881–1886," chap. 19 in *Frontier Regulars: The United States Army and the Indian, 1866–1890* (New York: Macmillan, 1973).

32. Ibid., 377.

33. Ibid., 379.

34. See "The Heliograph," Douglas Self Site, www.dself.dsl.pipex.com/MUSEUM/COMMS/heliograph/ heliograph.htm. "The Heliograph was a simple but highly effective instrument for instantaneous optical communication over 50 miles or more in the 19th century. Its major uses were for military and survey work. The heliograph sent its signals by reflecting sunlight towards the intended recipient with a mirror or mirrors, the beam being keyed on and off with a shutter or a tilting mirror, allowing Morse code to be sent."

35. Utley, *Frontier Regulars,* 391.

36. On the takedown of Fallujah, see Bing West, *No True Glory: A Frontline Account of the Battle for Fallujah* (New York: Bantam, 2005).

37. On the campaign against the "ratlines subsequent to the battle of Fallujah," see Mackubin Thomas Owens, "Rollin' on the Rivers," *New York Post,* 23 June 2005, available at www.ashbrook.org/publicat/oped/owens/ 05/rivers.html; and Mackubin T. Owens, "Behind the Casualties," *New York Post,* 24 August 2005, available at www.ashbrook.org/publicat/oped/owens/05/casualties.html.

12 Small Wars Are Local: Debunking Current Assumptions about Countering Small Armed Groups

Peter Curry

In 2005, I was chief of operations in a multinational headquarters that deployed to Kabul, Afghanistan. The headquarters had no American generals and only a small American contingent—a unique experience in my 25-year experience as a soldier. As the person who managed day-to-day operations, I witnessed many approaches to the challenges of dealing with various armed groups. Upon returning to the United States and being assigned to the academic environs of Brookings and Marine Corps University, I have had time to reflect on those experiences and discuss them with other combat leaders who had served on other battlefields. The result of that reflection is that there is an evolving set of new assumptions about countering armed groups in the developing world. Contrary to academic opinion that Americans do not have a methodology for dealing with small armed groups, I contend there is a common mental model being used by most Western nations and that model has several faulty assumptions that are exposed on the battlefields of today.

What follows are one learned soldier's considered observations on this Western model and is not intended to be a classic work of political science. Evident in this chapter

---

Colonel Peter Curry was commissioned in 1983 as an armor officer from Frostburg State College, Maryland, ROTC. His first assignment was as a section leader and operations officer assigned to the 82nd Airborne Division. Colonel Curry also served as the cavalry liaison officer for the 505th Parachute Infantry Regiment. After attending the Aviation Advanced Course, Colonel Curry served in the Second Armored Cavalry Regiment from 1988 to 1991. Upon the demise of the Soviet bloc, he led this unit in Operation Desert Storm as part of the covering force for the VII U.S. Corps. Following Iraq, Colonel Curry served as a senior tactics instructor at Fort Sill, Oklahoma. Subsequent assignments include the 10th Mountain Division and again with the 82nd Airborne Division as commander of First Battalion, 82nd Aviation (Attack). While attending the National War College from 2001 to 2002, Colonel Curry was a major contributor to the Student Combating Terrorism Task Force. The efforts of this task force contributed significantly to formulation of the U.S. strategy on the global war on terrorism. Upon graduation, Colonel Curry served as national security instructor at the Naval War College. In 2004, Colonel Curry became director of operations (G3) of the NATO Rapid Deployable Corps–Turkey at Istanbul. In 2005, he was also the chief of operations (CJ3) of the 36-nation International Security Assistance Force in Kabul, Afghanistan. Colonel Curry returned to the United States, serving as the Army's federal executive fellow at the Brookings Institution in Washington, DC. Colonel Curry teaches national security and joint warfare at the Marine Corps War College and concurrently holds the Chairman, Joint Chiefs of Staff, Army's Chair. Colonel Curry's awards include the Bronze Star, the Defense Meritorious Service Medal, the Air Medal with "V" (Valor) device, and the Valorous Unit Award. He has earned the Air Assault, the Master Parachutist, and the Master Aviator badges.

is a clear American-centric, operational bias modified by observing the actions and exchanging concepts with many other Western officers. Though my experience and lessons may be unique now, it is likely that many American officers in the future will find themselves deployed in similar situations. This chapter is about new or relearned assumptions. First, old assumptions are identified. Next, updated and consciously contrarian assumptions are offered to replace the old assumptions, not with the clarity of empirical data, but with the intuition of those who have served at war's pointy end. Hopefully, with these new assumptions offered, new strategies will be developed to handle the complex issue of countering armed groups. At the very least, gaining a deeper understanding of ourselves and our capabilities, limitations, and deeply implicit beliefs can help in future battlefields.

DIVERGENCE BETWEEN BOOK AND BATTLEFIELD

The gulf between current literature and the battlefield has much to do with our current doctrinal understanding. Current doctrine is a useful starting point, for the strategist or operator, but the battlefield's rapid pace of change is causing significant divergence between the battlefield and the literature. Doctrine will never keep pace with the constantly evolving situation, so soldiers and academics must make assumptions to fill in the gaps of our knowledge and those in the conflict must be able to use their education and training to be effective.

At the risk of oversimplification, our general concept of small wars is too anchored in the revolutionary, Maoist or "*foco*" models of the 1950s and '60s. Today's armed groups may employ elements of vanguardism or tactically "swim among the fishes," but to assume that modern armed groups have strategic aims and motivations similar to Mao or Guevara is incorrect. If we accept the revolutionary model, then we subscribe to the revolutionary model's main weakness that reduces the conflict to three basic sides: (1) the antigovernment insurgent, (2) the government (the counterinsurgent), and (3) the bulk of the population. In this model the first two sides compete for the allegiance of the third in order to gain power and control the nation-state.[1] My experience suggests that this is a limiting and counterproductive mental model. The battlefield environment is more complex than the three-sided model and clinging to this mental blueprint limits our effectiveness.

We need a more up-to-date and realistic approach to the armed-group problem than what is currently available.[2] The study of history provides context to this "wicked problem,"[3] but understanding how to counter small groups from a historical context is very different from current operational application. The historical record on armed groups is a necessary starting point, but the battlefield has evolved well beyond the classic Western model. There is nothing wrong with learning from the classic small-war literature, but when this ternary framework of insurgent versus counterinsurgent versus neutral locals becomes normative, it anchors a mind-set, creates a set of faulty assumptions, and ultimately causes weak and faulty operational implementation. Valuable time is lost "unlearning" some past lessons. I offer new assumptions that should be tested and retested, but I think they get us closer to the current state of fighting small groups in small wars.

RETHINKING ASSUMPTIONS

Old Assumption: *The government and the antigovernment elements are vying for the allegiance of the locals.*

New Assumption: *Small wars are local.*

A major assumption of the Western small-wars model treats the insurgents as a relatively homogeneous group with largely convergent political ends and assumes that the counterinsurgent government group also has convergent political goals. The model equates the remainder of the local population's neutrality with helplessness or passivity, whereby the indifference of the people can be manipulated or "won" by either side. In communist-inspired revolutions or anticolonial situations, this model had some arguable utility. Today, this model is limited. Diverse factions are the rule today, with a "balkanization" of former nation-states occurring. The clan is the fundamental element in today's developing countries and many armed groups are an amalgam of different clans with divergent internal factions and goals. Any goal convergence is largely temporal and expedient; there are coalitions of convenience that tend to fracture once the urgent threat is gone. Goals among groups range from the existential to more ideological, cultural, religious, economic, or political ends. Armed groups are difficult to categorize, especially into the two broad camps of insurgents and counterinsurgents.

Some military officers noticing the change in war's character have called fighting armed groups and insurgencies more akin to "armed politics."[4] There is a diffusion of conflict. Small groups of people fight for political power and social justice at the local level. Armed groups fight a collection of "microwars," where local agendas are paramount and goals are attained through violent and nonviolent means. Rupert Smith correctly posits that wars today are truly "amongst the people."[5] If all politics are local, then it follows that (sm)all wars are local as well.

As a result, the natures of armed groups parallel societal trends. Modern groups are becoming less hierarchical and more interconnected and find niches or nodes in the business of combat. Each node can have tremendous capability, hence influence, especially at the local level. Groups no longer take instruction from upper-echelon groups; both insurgent and counterinsurgent (if those terms even still apply) operate with increasing autonomy. Few groups take orders from headquarters as they once did; they pursue different ends because they can gather their own means. They are flattening their structures, outsourcing support tasks, and contracting other groups to meet operational goals. Armed-groups methodologies have evolved, so Western approaches will have to be updated as well.

Today's small wars are a "fur ball" of enabled groups vying for influence. Below is just a sampling of group types that may compete with each other:
- The local population,
- The local informal governing groups (tribes, clans, families),
- The local formal governing groups,
- The "national" governing groups,
- The antigovernmental groups,
- International governments and governmental organizations (IGOs),

- Nongovernmental organizations (NGOs),
- Private entities,
- Possible outside intervention or assistance forces, and
- Local and international media.

Within each of these categories, there are several subgroups, each with proprietary agendas and interests. Each subgroup has different capabilities and influences based on local conditions. Additionally, different agendas influence local, regional, and global media. Each with its own point of view. Each with its own biases. And each with its own incomplete understanding of the situation.

So dealing with armed groups is more than complex; it is "complexity squared"—each group taking action, which causes a subsequent, possibly unpredictable reaction, creating a violently dynamic environment with infinite permutations. Armed groups make modern wars kaleidoscopic; the issues are narrow and as the political viewpoint changes or the conditions change ever so slightly, the security picture changes as well.[6] Solutions to perceived problems that work in one area under one set of conditions could be disastrous under another set of conditions or in a different location.

Old Assumption: *Power is an absolute. The side with the most power will eventually win.*

New Assumption: *Power is a relationship, not an absolute.*[7]
One cannot equate capability with power. When fighting armed groups, we believe the side with the most combat power, resources, and political clout will probably "win" the fight. However, power is a relationship, not an absolute. In any situation, one group will have a power advantage relative to another group, and under different circumstances that relationship could be reversed. Each group possesses some power and will use that leverage wherever and whenever it can. Effective groups, not surprisingly, understand their relative strengths and weaknesses and, perhaps most important, know how to wield power and fashion weakness into political strength. Not understanding the reciprocal nature of power can be fatal to any plan.

Local power reigns supreme. In places such as failed states or the outer provinces of weak states that have no governmental checks and balances, no judicial system, and no Western-model structured social justice, power must be gained and maintained in order to survive. In lawless places, people use power in an existential, zero-sum game. Power is not shared; it is gained through any means available, including theft, intimidation, or coercion. The loss of power is equivalent to public humiliation and fear of humiliation is one of the most powerful human motivators. A group must maintain whatever power it has at all costs. This need leads to coalitions of convenience.

Old Assumption: *War and peace are mutually exclusive, and these wars can be won.*

New Assumption: *Conflict is constant. States of war and peace are temporary.*
Most wars, including small ones, rarely have defined conclusions. The corollary to Clausewitz's dictum—war is politics by other means—might be that politics is conflict by other means. Peace, as defined as a cessation of hostilities, rarely ends the political conflict. Politically, we must accept that chaos and progress coexist when fighting armed groups. War and peace are temporary arrangements. Political conflict continues until one

side of the struggle becomes incapable of armed struggle, is unwilling to continue, or loses credibility. Complete annihilation of a group will certainly end the conflict but annihilation is usually not politically feasible (especially if a group is good at using the power of weakness) and militarily impossible. Any good small-war strategy aims to change attitudes, to force the opponent into the political process while eliminating the recalcitrant elements. The tenet of political primacy guarantees that violence and negotiation will exist as a natural course of events.

The idea of a desired military and political "end state" must be adjusted to a goal of an acceptable steady state. The military, regardless of its conventional or unconventional methods, can rarely "win" these wars; it can only set conditions that allow some acceptable outcome. The military is a means to an end, not the end itself. Strategically, "victory" in small wars will have elements of *peace* and *war* merging to reach "par," a set of acceptable conditions. Peace, as understood in the West, will have an acceptable level of political agitation that occasionally turns violent. The military can only secure peace as the political actors define it.

Old Assumption: *Neutrality is possible and preferable.*

New Assumption: *Neutrality is not possible and many times is not even preferable.*
When outside or allied troops enter a local situation, regardless of intention, a sort of "observer effect" phenomenon occurs.[8] The very presence of "outside" troops inevitably alters the situation, people's perception of the situation, and the local balance of power. Military power is to be respected, feared, or tested. Without question, outside troop actions are measured and evaluated by all groups resident in the immediate area. Alternative opposing strategies will develop. Any outside force, regardless of whether it is made of foreigners or native groups, will be viewed as a competing group. Troops become a factor in any power equation resident in the local mix.

An outside force's attempt at neutrality creates confusion among all groups, including the force claiming neutrality. Neutrality cannot be claimed; it is a status given to an outside force by the indigenous groups. An outside force must earn "neutrality" by its actions. Also, by assuming its own claimed "neutrality," the military force weakens its credibility with competing groups. Competing groups view any neutral status as a sham ripe for exploitation. For the outside force, earning local respect is the critical element. In order to achieve that respect, the aim of any outside force should be transparency, not neutrality. Transparency involves telling the locals what you are going to do, and then following through to completion. Stopping short of stated outcomes is weakness. Military forces must demonstrate transparency with restraint until action is required, but when it is employed, muscular force must be swift, accurate, and clear in its purpose. Convincing small groups that the outcome is not in doubt sets the proper conditions to end local violence—a critical condition for progress. Failure to use the appropriate level of force within the laws of armed conflict and appropriate social norms creates a lack of trust within the population. Trust is a luxury that most villagers caught in a "small" war can ill afford. At the local level, action strips away any ambiguity. Neutrality creates ambiguity and ambiguity is seen as the tactic of the weak and disrespected.

Old Assumption: *The truth is absolute and objective.*

New Assumption: *There is no truth; there is only the perception of truth.*[9]
Western-based societies rely on reason to reveal the truth; the facts speak for themselves. Of course this assumes facts are attainable and agreed upon. In many tribal and honor-based societies what really matters are not facts but honor and position. The facts do not speak for themselves and, often, reality is suspended to "save face." When one loses honor, community standing and power are also lost. Retaining honor through deception is expected; therefore every word and deed will be viewed with a large dose of skepticism. Revealing "the truth" makes one vulnerable and vulnerability in a lawless world can be a death sentence. Often, this asymmetry of perceptions leads Westerners into the "correlation is causation" trap. However, outside observers cannot always believe what they see or hear.

Information flow is nearly impossible to manage in tribal societies. Information operations should be based on the facts, but the messages must also be sensitive to the rumor mill. Local rumors easily outpace any Western-force public affairs operation. Any slight can be strategically significant, because a sense of injustice or humiliation is quick to surface. Messages, no matter how well intentioned or well crafted from our point of view, rarely take root in the sanitary soil of truth. Messages root themselves in the compost of a decaying Hobbesian situation, where every slight can be magnified and any cause can be exploited to gain power. Cultural sensitivity will help us understand this challenge, but Westerners in general must understand that our deeply ingrained desire for truth and rule of law is one of the most difficult needs to fill.

Old Assumption: *"Winning Hearts and Minds" is paramount.*

New Assumption: *You cannot "win" their hearts and minds.*
The "Win Hearts and Minds" cliché is simply not useful. Hearts-and-minds approaches assume the neutrality of the locals, a very flawed assumption that drives Western perception. The local population has power and interests. People affiliate with groups for several reasons, but most reasons are highly pragmatic. The central question of the population is "What's in it for me?" They perceive that the group they have aligned themselves with will help achieve their ends. Rarely do locals form strong political affiliations with armed groups or the government. People avoid risk, hedge their bets, and throw their support behind the group that will get them what they want.

Because of the highly political nature of fighting armed groups, what the people think and feel is still the center of gravity. In the current models, however, the "neutrals" are usually portrayed as a group that is just waiting to be "won" with hearts-and-minds campaigns. It has been my experience that people cannot be "won" in the sense that once we have "won" them, they are forever on our side. People's aspirations change, and the more successful you are at helping people attain their goals, the higher their expectations become. No one is really neutral; everyone has personal agendas and desires and is waiting for some group to demonstrate its ability to help achieve those desires. Our strategies should not be aimed at becoming popular—that is an impossibility—we won't "win" that game because expectations continually change. Our goal should be to gain and maintain respect, a respect for our restrained but potential power (if required) and our ability to keep the promises that we do make.

Old Assumption: *Better governance and administration are the key to victory.*

New Assumption: *Being governed is not always welcome.*

Westerners expect a responsive, benevolent government. Combine that expectation with the belief that the locals can be manipulated, and the conditions are set for a high probability of failure. In an area where governments have been weak, the locals view government agents and agencies as tax-levying parasites or gangsters who extract resources and return little benefit—often an accurate description of some government officials. Resident antipathy resists any government-sponsored program. Ungoverned people believe that no government is preferable to bad government, and in their experience any government is bad.

While a negative view of the government does not equate to active resistance, almost all government programs are met with significant skepticism. A typical scenario goes something like this. First, the existing local power structure will view any outside program as a challenge to its authority, especially if executed without prior consultation. Second, the project is likely to be financed and conceived elsewhere, oblivious to the desires or needs of the locals. The locals perceive the government and its proxies as an arrogant, paternalistic group of outsiders with an exploitive agenda. Consequently, the warlord views such actions as a challenge to be confronted, and the local believes the project is a colossal waste of money from an ineffective government. In short order the project is destroyed by a local power broker or neglected by the local people because few have an interest to sustain it.

At best, reconstruction and development projects become prohibitively expensive because of the faulty assumptions that villagers will see the goodness of the projects. At worst, the situation can become catastrophic through mutual misunderstanding. The government misreads local intentions and sees active resistance to the government when there is none. Soon the village is classified as opposing the government. It is not long before the government is either eradicating the "opposition," which of course drives the locals toward the opposition, or shunting aid to places more responsive to government largess. There are times when the government is better off leaving the village alone until a more inclusive and comprehensive program can be set up. While they won't love the government, the locals probably will not actively support the opposition either. Again, the populace is not neutral. They do have hearts and minds and they will use them more than we sometimes give them credit for.

Old Assumption: *Security first, then build the society.*

New Assumption: *The nature of the conflict dictates what comes first.*

What makes countering armed groups seem different and more intractable is the dual nature of two monumental tasks: (1) building a nation and (2) countering the armed threat. Armed groups exist because the government was perceived as so unresponsive that the group decided it was in its best interests to adopt violence as a political act. Developing strategies to counter groups becomes a "chicken or egg" problem. Ultimately the goal is to build a nation. However, if groups have an alternative end state, what comes first, building the nation or fighting the groups?

Of course, the academic answer is to create comprehensive government programs that emphasize a multidimensional response to armed groups requiring (1) a balance of security, (2) economic development, (3) social justice, and (4) political reform. The difficulty in orchestrating the need for harmonious action of all four elements guarantees that in every situation a paradox confronts the government. If economic development occurs without security, then government improvement projects become "insurgent magnets" that armed groups must destroy in order to gain group credibility. If security is gained without responsive economic development, armed groups will recruit and pay the unemployed to fight the government. If security occurs without a rudimentary judicial system, then there is no ability to challenge authority peacefully. People perceive the incarceration of most able-bodied men as unjust. Without real political reform, a power status quo will remain with the warlords retaining power. Attempts at bringing those warlords into the government fold can be problematic if promises of reform have been made, since that is a threat to their power. A coordinated multidimensional response is obvious, but attaining success is easier said than done.

There is a relationship between how long the "nation-state" has not functioned and an inability to build a new government. The relationship deteriorates exponentially the deeper into chaos a state sinks. The longer the downward spiral, the more acute the "brain drain" of professionals, and over time the state lacks managers to perform even the most basic of administrative tasks. Every facet of modern life becomes a challenge, from adequate education to adequate infrastructure to an adequate business environment. A failing state eventually becomes an illiterate nation incapable of building institutions. Little trust exists in the few existing institutions. Self-preservation is paramount. Jeffersonian-inspired democracy is not even a dream; it is simply not fathomable to most people caught in these situations.

A societal "hourglass" paradox develops. At the bottom of the hourglass are the large numbers of people who need assistance within the failed state. At the top is the relatively large amount of assistance that is available from the international community. In the narrow middle is the dearth of trained managers to get the massive assistance into the hands of the many needy people. Aid trickles in. If expedient measures are taken and

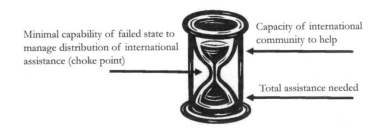

Minimal capability of failed state to manage distribution of international assistance (choke point)

Capacity of international community to help

Total assistance needed

Societal "Hourglass" Paradox

management expands too quickly, corruption and a dependence on outside sources develop. If expansion is slow, then developmental programs slow, international donors lose interest, and the system collapses. There must be a balance between foreign assistance and developing indigenous capabilities to handle all forms of governance. Too often there is an imbalance; nations do not provide assistance for years. Then once a situation becomes an "international crisis," both governments and nongovernmental organizations easily overmatch the paltry indigenous capacity. This hourglass phenomenon is a large reason why countering armed groups and insurgencies takes sometimes decades. One cannot win the war while gutting the society.

Old Assumption: *Multilateralism is always better than going it alone . . . as long as there is unity of effort.*

New Assumption: *The goal of unity of effort is elusive; unity of goals is about as good as it will get.*

If our bias is that more government is better, then we also have a bias that more governments and organizations are better still. Multilateralism is still a positive term in the international community, but "multilateralism is always good" is the last of our faulty assumptions. The assumption is that governments and nongovernmental organizations in the area will work toward the same goals. In reality, this is not only untrue but also unrealistic. Just as the enemy and the locals are multifaceted, so are friends and allies. Our partners have their own interests and must honor their constituencies and benefactors. Organizational policy tends to drive action; and to the members of those organizations, nothing matters more than pursuing the charters and guidelines envisioned in the organizations' creations. Whether friend or foe, independent groups compound war's complexity with additional layers.

The first layer is the multinational military force. Troops and security forces from different countries have different mandates—usually expressed in caveats. Caveats are a nice term for restrictions, or "what our forces cannot or will not do." Often these restrictions are minor obstacles, but are subject to interpretation by senior leaders on the ground. At times, the political exigencies at home dictate the most cautious interpretation possible and will likely be contrary to the stated purpose of the deployment. Nations may be operating under rules of a charter or alliance, but the senior alliance commander has little or no leverage to employ forces under his "command."

The next layer of complexity is the nongovernmental organizations and international governmental organizations that are instrumental to the success and stability of a region. They bring a wealth of expertise in most non-security-related fields and fiercely guard their independence. These organizations will likely operate independently of the security aims of the local military commander. Communication and cooperation is a function of organizational charters. Too often, these groups operate under the notion of neutrality and feel that coordination with military forces violates that neutrality. NGOs and IGOs are free agents in the field with agendas that may compromise or "suboptimize" security goals (as the military defines them) in pursuit of their own agendas.

To effectively operate in an area, military leaders must accept the complexity of the competing interests that are on "your side." It is naive to assume that all of the organizations, with their national mandates and organizational agendas, will operate in concert with one another. Allied groups are independent operators on the battlefield. With scant leverage to coerce any allied group, the military professional must build consensus to reach an acceptable set of conditions that will achieve the end state. Trying to get all organizations to follow one leader is a high-cost, low-payoff strategy. Coalescing around convergent goals is a worthwhile endeavor, but the military should lower its expectations of control within any given area. From a military standpoint, the upside is that success can be measured by the increasing amount of consensus building required. Increased security brings more independent groups into an area. As much as military professionals disdain a lack of unity in command, the military has to accept a "command by committee" approach in many situations.

CONCLUSION

It is time to dispense with the old assumptions of countering armed groups and insurgencies. Armed groups are enabled as never before. They are not beholden to any masters from a larger organization. Strategically, armed groups may be loosely driven by broad ideologies, but tactically they generally fight for pragmatic reasons. Operationally, the grass roots political issues increase battlefield complexity—countering armed groups is more a series of microwars than a broad, three-sided struggle. A new Western model must embrace complexity as it exists on the battlefield.

What armed groups lack in military firepower, they make up with the politics of power. Successful groups turn battlefield weakness into strategic political strength. Masters at understanding the reciprocal nature of power, armed groups focus less on "the truth" of physical capability and more on the perceptions of honor and reputation. Countering armed groups begins with changing the perceptions of reputations, not by completely eliminating the armed group, but by negating its message and reducing its physical influence.

Changing perceptions is not "winning hearts and minds" to win popular support. Popularity is short lived, as perceptions change rapidly. Any new model must change from winning hearts and minds to earning respect for the authority of your power in all its forms: moral, ethical, and physical. Transparency, not neutrality, earns that respect in the Hobbesian world where significant numbers of armed groups exist. Neutrality is in the eyes of the beholder; therefore it is impossible to build a meaningful, political-military strategy around it. The strategy must have local support where strategic goals and local agendas converge, while accounting for local deviations. Those local deviations will occur with allies as well.

Armed groups are living organisms, not mechanistic organizational structures. Groups change, morph, and recombine in infinite permutations that force strategies and concepts to change over time. The contrast between book (theory) and battlefield (application) is caused by reliance on old mental models of revolutionary war. Classic literature is still useful in understanding the character and nature of countering armed groups, but the model needs updating. It is time to question the old assumptions and replace them with new ones. Moreover, the new assumptions of today will have to be tested and undoubtedly replaced by even newer ones. When considering long-term strategic goals to counter armed groups, it is wise to remember that when implementing strategy, small wars are local.

NOTES

1. This model is most explicit in the classic work of Sir Robert Thompson's, *Defeating Communist Insurgency* (New York: Praeger, 1966). Thompson's work is still valid and some of the concepts for this paper's new or re-learned assumptions can be traced back to Thompson and other authors. The issue is not the work of Thompson's era but the templating of their model in the twenty-first century.

2. David Kilcullen is one author who is recognizing the changes and has written extensively on the subject. His "Counterinsurgency Redux," *Survival* 48 (Winter 2006–2007), is an excellent review of the Western model as well as his emerging thoughts on counterinsurgency. This paper shares many of Kilcullen's views, but its focus is on armed groups in a broader context than counterinsurgency.

3. The idea of wicked problems in design was originally proposed by H. J. Rittel and M. M. Webber (1984). In solving a wicked problem, the solution of one aspect of the problem may reveal another, more complex problem. Discrepancies in representing a wicked problem can be explained in numerous ways. The choice of explanation determines the nature of the problem's resolution. Hence how you model the problem largely governs the solution set. Reference: www.cs.utexas.edu/users/almstrum/classes/cs373/fa99/cs373fa99-e1.html.

4. "Politics" in this sense is of the "polity" or the people's interests instead of a narrow sense of politics.

5. Rupert Smith, *The Utility of Force: The Art of War in the Modern World* (London: Penguin Group, 2005), 17.

6. For complex issues, sometimes a metaphor is most useful in trying to describe something that is difficult to describe. A senior Special Forces officer with recent combat tours offered the kaleidoscope metaphor as a way of describing how quickly events on the ground can change perception.

7. Conversations with a retired senior officer from a NATO member nation.

8. The "observer effect" refers to how the act of observing changes what is being observed. Both security forces and local groups alter their behaviors when they know they are being observed, especially in politically motivated conflicts. A certain observer bias is at work as well. Observers tend to give credence to their expected outcomes and discount unexpected ones. Simply put, people believe what they want to believe.

9. Officers from many different countries that have been deployed to many different geographic areas where honor-based societies exist have repeatedly emphasized this point. Their experiences were so global that I consider it a universal assumption of Western militaries.

13 Piracy and the Exploitation of Sanctuary

Martin N. Murphy

Piracy is a land-based crime that takes place at sea. Intensive maritime patrolling can deter piracy in narrow waters, providing that is its sole purpose. When piracy suppression is incidental, the effect of patrolling can be limited. Patrolling against piracy on the open ocean is often a hit-or miss affair given the huge spaces involved. Consequently, it is fair to say that piracy is only effectively controlled when maritime patrols act in concert with land-based policing, and is only suppressed when piracy becomes politically and economically unattractive. What this demonstrates is that maritime crime and violence can only be perpetrated, and certainly can only be sustained, from the sanctuary of secure bases on land.

THE FAVORABLE FACTORS

There are seven factors that enable piracy to occur. As it pertains to armed groups operating at sea, there are eight similar and largely common factors. In both cases, these factors interact one with another and, although circumstances determine which predominate, all are usually present to some degree. Differences between the two, where they exist, are often ones of nuance.[1]

All of these factors, with the exception of charismatic and effective leadership, are elements in the notion of sanctuary.[2] This chapter discusses these factors and how they apply to maritime armed groups.

Geography

Pirates used to be called "rovers," but they never roved aimlessly. Piracy has only ever been sustainable in places that offer a combination of rewarding hunting grounds, acceptable levels of risk, and proximate safe havens, and this combination remains the case today.[3] Ships that are anchored in ports or awaiting berths are more at risk than ships under way, but if ships are attacked when moving then this generally occurs in narrow waters such as straits and around archipelagoes.[4] The Straits of Malacca and Singapore, and the waters around Indonesia, famously offer these conditions.

Dr. Martin N. Murphy is a research fellow at the Corbett Centre for Maritime Policy Studies, King's College London. He is the author of *Contemporary Piracy and Maritime Terrorism* (Routledge, 2007) and a longer study, *Small Boats, Weak States, Dirty Money* (Columbia University Press, Fall 2008). In addition, he has published widely on irregular warfare, naval special forces, littoral warfare, maritime security, and marine insurance.

Piracy	Maritime Armed Groups
Favorable geography	Geographic necessity
Cultural acceptability	Maritime tradition
Conflict and disorder	
Reward	Reward
	Secure base areas
	Charismatic and effective leadership
Underfunded law enforcement	Inadequate security
Permissive political environment	State support
Legal and jurisdictional opportunities	Legal and jurisdictional opportunities

Factors favoring piracy and maritime armed groups

In most cases, but not always, geography determines whether armed groups need to go to sea or not. It shapes the why and the how of what they do on the water. The Nicaraguan "contras" did not have to use the sea, nor did al Qaeda, whereas the LTTE insurgency on the island of Sri Lanka could not survive without access to sanctuaries overseas, and secure communications between these bases and its operational areas on Sri Lanka itself. The secure base areas were located originally in the Indian state of Tamil Nadu; when the Indian government no longer welcomed their presence, the bases were moved to islands off the southern coast of Burma, where they operated with the permission of the ruling junta between 1987 and 1995, before moving again to the area around Phuket in Thailand, where they existed more covertly, and now, apparently, to Indonesia. The Tamil Tigers invested in a fleet of ocean-going freighters to bring supplies from these secure areas to Sri Lanka, and a protonaval capability to guard their vital cargoes during the final stage of their journey to the Sri Lankan coast, where they were, until Sri Lanka gained access to long-range maritime surveillance information, most vulnerable to interdiction by the Sri Lanka Navy.

Cultural Acceptability/Maritime Tradition

Piracy can only take root in areas with a maritime tradition and the skills that go with it. Trading patterns are one factor that helps to determine this acceptability: it is possible that piracy has deeper roots in Southeast Asia than in west Africa because important trading routes have bisected Southeast Asian archipelagoes for centuries, making piracy there a way of life often on a clan or family basis.[5] This tradition can provide armed groups with a platform upon which to build. For example, the Tauseg communities of the Sulu Archipelago, which stretches between the southern Philippines and Borneo, have sustained the Abu Sayyaf Group (ASG), while the Tamil maritime trading tradition based on the port of Velvettiturai is the foundation for the LTTE's maritime expertise.

Conflict and Disorder

Piracy—and criminality at sea generally—can thrive when coastal regions are troubled by war or civil disturbance, or their aftermath. The piracy that plagued the Gulf of Thailand between 1975 and the early 1990s fed on the refugees fleeing Vietnam. Lebanon during the civil war from 1975 to 1990 became a haven for criminal activity; "unofficial" ports sprang up along the coast to handle stolen cargo and refit stolen ships.[6] Similarly the sundering of Somalia into warring fiefdoms following the collapse of General Mohamed Siad Barre's dictatorial regime in January 1991 appears to have triggered the country's piracy problem.

Reward

Maritime sanctuaries, however, are only of use if they offer ready access to targets. No opportunity, however great, would be exploited without the promise of reward, and piracy can be "a highly lucrative venture," as the Organisation for Economic Co-operation and Development (OECD) points out.[7] Real rewards, however, are only earned when entire ships are hijacked and the cargo sold or the crew is kidnapped and held to ransom. Both types of crime have been a feature of Southeast Asian piracy. Ships hijacked in the region have usually been boarded in international waters by pirate crews drawn from many states, all of whom move internationally using false or stolen documents, and are able to melt back into the sanctuary of their local communities, whose members generally know what they do but have little incentive to report them. Somali pirates have largely eschewed cargo theft in preference for crew kidnap and ransom because, despite the bleak and unfavorable geography of Somalia's Indian Ocean coast, they are able to keep their hostages captive on their own ships (which are often readily observable on satellite photographs) due to the lawlessness that prevails on land and the reluctance of the foreign navies patrolling offshore to enter Somali territorial waters.

Armed groups, like pirates, would also not put to sea without the promise of reward. Terrorists are most successful when their actions attract publicity. It is the "information" side of their operations that has primacy, while physical destruction and death are merely the means to achieve a propaganda result.[8] Attracting publicity can be difficult away from land. Consequently, the armed groups that have used the sea most successfully have generally been those with long-term goals at the insurgent end of the spectrum, which have recognized that the contribution (or "reward") that the maritime component can make to their efforts overall will come from its support for the campaigns on land, either by moving cadres and supplies, or by linking various campaigns in different theaters.[9]

Underfunded Law Enforcement/Inadequate Security

Many states find it impossible to sustain adequate levels of security in their coastal waters.[10] Inadequate state funding and training for enforcement organizations, whether these are the judiciary, police, coast guard, or navy, allow pirates the freedom to operate. Many states simply cannot afford the personnel, equipment, and degree of organization that is required or, like Indonesia, believe what resources they do have should be expended on other priorities. There are, moreover, huge sea areas to be covered, and if search and interdiction is to be carried out effectively, surface ships need air support for surveillance and reconnaissance.

Inadequate security is a given for any insurgency to succeed. The Sea Tigers have fought the Sri Lanka Navy to a virtual stalemate for long periods. Neither has been able to overcome the other. In Southeast Asia, the ASG and the Moro Islamic Liberation Front (MILF) in the Philippines, Gerakan Aceh Merdeka (GAM) in Aceh, and groups such as Jemaah Islamiyah (JI) that needed to move personnel and supplies by sea benefited from underinvestment in maritime security by Indonesia and the Philippines and poor international security cooperation between all the states in the region.

Permissive Political Environment/State Support

To flourish, piracy requires not only weak law but also lax law enforcement. This laxity is almost always the consequence of state weakness. In the absence of a maritime hegemonic power this has been the normal condition on the high seas throughout most of human history. When and where permissive environments exist within states and their territorial waters, they generally come about either because the political environment is corrupt locally or nationally and allows illegal activity to take place for its benefit, or because law enforcement is underfunded and therefore lacks the resources to deal with it. Often, of course, both conditions apply simultaneously. Whatever the reason, a supportive, criminal infrastructure can develop. The likelihood is that corrupt law enforcement officials are a feature of all areas affected by piracy.

State support for armed groups with a significant maritime operational arm has taken several forms. The state government of Sabah in Malaysia reportedly gave the Moro National Liberation Front (MNLF) logistical support and turned a blind eye to its operations on its territory. The LTTE was supported first by the Indian government and the Tamil Nadu state government and then by the Burmese junta. Anti-Israel groups such as Fatah and PFLP-GC, which were unlikely to have been able to operate at sea without the practical and financial support they received from the former Soviet Union and Arab states, depended on a string of bases and workshops in Lebanon from which to mount their maritime penetration and supply operations against the Israeli coast. When these bases were moved to Libya and even as far away as Algeria in 1982 following the Israeli invasion of Lebanon, their operations were hampered severely. It is evident that since then Hizbollah has established bases in the southern suburbs of Beirut to support its maritime operations, one of which had (or played host to) an antiship-missile launch capability.

Legal and Jurisdictional Opportunities

Sanctuary, however, is not always a quality of place. It can also be found in the more "virtual" world of international law.

Ships on the high seas do not sail in a legal vacuum.[11] Each one comes under the jurisdiction of its flag state, which is responsible for ensuring that it observes national and international law. However, if a flag state fails to exercise its jurisdiction effectively, other states have few grounds upon which to take action while the ship remains on the high seas. States have traditionally been reluctant to conduct search and seizure operations that could undermine the principle of free navigation. Even though piracy is regarded as a "universal" crime, and pirate ships can theoretically be boarded by the government vessels of any state, in practice, state action has always been circumscribed by operational and political considerations, customary international law, and, latterly, by the relevant codified forms of international law of which the most important is the UN Convention on the Law of the Sea (UNCLOS, which is sometimes referred to in the United States as the Law of the Sea Treaty or LOST). This has several weaknesses when it comes to piracy. These date from the first attempts to codify the law in the 1920s, which were based upon the long-established distinction between piracy and privateering.[12] As the codification process proceeded it was influenced at every stage by the prevailing view that piracy was a problem of the past—a view that was still held when the convention was initialed in 1982.[13] Although territorial waters were recognized long before UNCLOS, the convention contributed to the growth of sanctuaries by enlarging them fourfold. Therefore, in the waters of those states that are unable to discharge their security responsibilities (such as Somalia) or do so only with reluctance (such as Indonesia)—and where opportunities for piracy exist—refuges have effectively been created that have been used by pirates and are also open for exploitation by armed groups.[14]

However, armed groups are more likely to use ships and boats to transport weapons and operatives. Most legal attention has, understandably, been given to the proliferation of nuclear arms and components, and while the legal basis of the U.S.-inspired Proliferation Security Initiative has not been clarified fully, it has possibly "protected most of the world's shipping from [involvement in] proliferation."[15] But it is conventional arms that will be transported most frequently. Libya shipped arms to the IRA by sea and Iran has sent supplies to the Palestinians the same way. Al Qaeda reputedly delivered the explosives in the 1998 east African embassy bombings by sea. The LTTE depends on sea transport. JI and the Philippine "Moro" armed groups such as Abu Sayyaf have generally been free to move without hindrance throughout what is now described as the "tri-border region" between the Malaysian state of Sabah and the Philippine island of Mindanao. Criminal groups, some of them, such as the Arakanese smugglers in the Bay of Bengal, with known connections to armed groups, and others, such as the human smugglers who transport migrants across the Mediterranean or the Gulf of Aden, that might transport fighters and terrorists wittingly or unwittingly, exploit free movement at sea.[16] Reaching general agreement on restricting the movement of conventional arms and other supplies for armed groups, or even for particular action, will, unlike restrictions on nuclear proliferation, continue to present significant practical and legal difficulties. These will arise despite the fact that freedom of navigation is not an absolute right and even though the Security Council has issued an unconditional condemnation of terrorism (but not armed-group activity more generally) under Chapter VII of the UN Charter, which places all states under a duty to suppress terrorism, including those states that lack the resources to do so, because they are under an implied obligation to give their consents to such suppression by others.[17]

Because piracy is a "universal" crime it has been suggested that the international law against it could be extended to terrorists.[18] The omens for such a move are not good. Every attempt to extend piracy law to cover other forms of violence at sea has failed.[19] International agreements designed to suppress specific forms of maritime violence have been signed instead. One example is the Suppression of Unlawful Acts (SUA) Convention.[20] However, many states are not signatories and its powers are extremely limited (it does not, for example, authorize preventative or precautionary action), which has meant that, apart from one minor case in U.S. waters, it has never been invoked.[21]

In 2005, protocols were added to SUA that were intended to prevent armed groups using ships to transport WMD materials or as "floating bombs." However, the effectiveness of these changes was limited: the authority to board ships to search for these materials was more restricted than the powers granted to board fishing vessels suspected of contravening the "Straddling Fish Stocks Agreement."[22] Sanctuary at sea, therefore, is under some pressure, but in most cases and most places it is not under immediate threat.

PIRACY IS A LAND-BASED CRIME THAT IS IMPLEMENTED AT SEA

Men, however, live upon the land and, however useful sanctuary at sea might be, sanctuary on land, as piracy demonstrates, is more important. In Southeast Asia, pirates appear to be known regardless of whether they live on islands such as Batam in Indonesia, where all forms of crime are rife, or in coastal villages. They are sheltered by a combination of official indifference, intimidation, and cultural acceptability. The French researcher Eric Frécon noted that on Batam the police were "not only tolerant of the criminal activities of pirates but [they were] also accomplices and act as bodyguards."[23] In the Malaysian town of Semporna, on the other hand, residents who were subject to regular attacks talked about recognizing some of their attackers and that they came from a poor village with a violent reputation.[24]

In Bangladesh, piracy is concentrated either in the port of Chittagong in the southeast, where much of the activity appears to take place with the connivance of the corrupt port authorities; or along the coast between Chittagong and Cox's Bazaar, where coastal villagers welcome smugglers and "provide the perpetrators with shelter and no social sanctions are in place for the traditional maritime bandits";[25] or in the southwestern delta region, where the pirates can find shelter in the Sunderbans mangrove forest, which is cut through with an intricate network of interconnected water channels.[26] Similarly in Nigeria, piracy during the 1970s and 1980s was concentrated around the port of Lagos in the west but in the first decade of the twenty-first century became as prevalent in the Niger Delta in the southeast. There the Movement for the Emancipation of the Niger Delta (MEND) and others, whose political or criminal provenances can be hard to discern but which all appear to enjoy widespread local support, are able to exploit the cover of mangroves and the myriad water channels to escape detection.[27]

The situation in Somalia is similarly complex: in much of the southern part of the country piracy emerged out of, and has sometimes been confused with, local fishermen protecting their livelihoods from the depredations of foreign fleets.[28] In the north, piracy appears to be an opportunistic sideline for the gangs that smuggle migrants north to Yemen and guns south to Somalia with the knowledge and support of at least some senior figures in the breakaway state of Puntland.[29] The pirates who operate from the main piracy center of Xarardheere, located near the Horn of Africa, have been shielded from international intervention by the reluctance of the foreign navies patrolling offshore to enter Somali territorial waters, and from internal suppression by the continuing interclan rivalry that is making the country virtually ungovernable.

MARITIME ARMED GROUPS AND THE IMPERATIVE OF SECURE BASES

Sanctuary can exist informally. Terrestrial armed groups have shown they can hide in anonymous urban environments. Pirates have demonstrated that it is possible to hide in coastal communities using boats and equipment that are common to fishermen and other seafarers. Maritime armed groups, however, can rarely share such craft, except perhaps on a contract basis, and need to undertake more elaborate activities, including boat modification and attack training, that generally require discretion. Sanctuary and secure bases are not therefore synonymous, but armed groups that want or need to mount sustained campaigns in the maritime domain require both. While all insurgent groups need secure base areas for planning, rest, logistical support, and training, the fact that people cannot live permanently at sea and depend upon reliable boats in order to survive when they venture upon it makes those groups that operate at sea arguably more dependent on bases than their land-based counterparts.

This does not mean that groups lacking such facilities, such as al Qaeda, have not mounted successful maritime operations. On the contrary, they most obviously have. Rohan Gunaratna has pointed out the lengths to which the al Qaeda cell in Aden went to mount its attacks, first (unsuccessfully) against the USS *The Sullivans* and then on the USS *Cole,* and the elaborate (and in hindsight rather obvious) precautions it took to disguise what it was doing. However, as Gunaratna also observes, perhaps the principal reason why al Qaeda, in contrast to the LTTE, GAM, and others, failed to sustain its initial success was because it was unable to establish secure base areas close to its desired targets.[30]

WHAT OF THE FUTURE?

The ocean space is shrinking. The demand for resources and for living space on land is spurring a "migration to the sea," or what one astute observer describes more graphically as a "scramble for the sea"—a scramble that might be exacerbated by the effects of climate change.[31]

Coastal states may, in addition, seek to assert and protect proprietary rights, driven in many cases by concern for the "environment," farther and farther from their own shores. In the case of failed or even weak states this phenomenon, which has already been labeled "creeping jurisdiction," could have the possible effect of extending the sanctuary that is available to pirates and armed groups. As pressure for the sea's resources mounts, a shifting mix of asserted regulation and, in too many cases, unasserted sovereignty will be tested possibly to the point of conflict.

Other challenges will come from criminals and armed groups that are able to take advantage of the complex physical, human, and informational environment of coastal waters and the contiguous littorals.[32] Some armed groups will be able to fight with statelike intensity in what U.S. Marine Corps lieutenant general James Mattis has called "hybrid war."[33] Other conflicts will involve hybrid opponents where state and nonstate actors combine together or states work through nonstate proxies.

Areas with the potential to become sanctuaries are usually identifiable some years in advance. Whether they will develop into sanctuaries or not obviously depends on a number of topical factors, some of which are amenable to external influence. Reacting to an already-established sanctuary using expeditionary forces could affect a temporary solution but this is unlikely to become permanent unless the intervention is succeeded by effective state-building. Anticipating the formation of sanctuaries and preventing armed groups from gaining access to them demands, if possible, the establishment of a persistent presence wherever they are likely to occur.

Four regions are noticeable for the combination of geography, maritime expertise, jurisdictional disputes and uncertainty, inadequate security and law enforcement, and either existing conflict or the potential for conflict in the future that suggests that sanctuaries for maritime armed groups might develop:

Southeast Asia

The most significant activity has taken place in the maritime "tri-border region" between the Philippines, Indonesia, and Malaysia, which borders the Sulu and Celebes seas. It is bisected by the Sulu Archipelago, which is the home of the ASG. Although it has been the subject of intense counterinsurgency activity by the Philippine armed forces, with U.S. and Australian support, the region's ethnic and religious makeup, lack of economic development, and the fact that it has been the haunt of pirates and smugglers for centuries suggest that the potential for sanctuary continues to exist.

West Africa

The instability that has affected the Niger Delta is particular to that region, and while the stimulus of oil has not so far afflicted other parts of the Gulf of Guinea, it is fringed by weak states that are, like Sierra Leone and Liberia, vulnerable to corruption and internal conflict and others, such as Guinea-Bissau and Ivory Coast, where these weaknesses are compounded by intricate maritime geography so well suited to smuggling that they have already become targets for drug cartels.

Yemen and the Horn of Africa

Somalia and Yemen border the Bab el Mandeb Strait, through which shipping has to pass to reach the Suez Canal. The primary allegiance of the peoples that inhabit both areas is to their clans, and while the political situation in Yemen is currently more stable than that in Somalia, which has been torn apart by clan conflict, this is not guaranteed to continue. Islamism is an element in both, although its influence can be exaggerated as was demonstrated in 2006 when its ability to unite the clans of southern Somalia proved short lived. Nonetheless, the lack of recognized and effective authority that has allowed pirate and smuggling groups to operate largely without constraint (and possibly with official connivance) in what, because of the paucity of roads, is an essentially maritime theater, coupled with the continuing potential for conflict among Ethiopia, Eritrea, and Somalia, means that the opportunity for the creation of sanctuaries remains a real threat.

Lebanon and Gaza

Parts of Lebanon and much of Gaza are effectively sanctuaries for armed groups.[34] Hizbollah and Hamas predominate but other armed groups and criminal gangs have their territories. Although ship hijacking occurred off Lebanon during the 1970s, piracy is no longer practiced. It is, however, a maritime theater where smuggling is a way of life and one that remains of interest to armed groups keen to exploit Israel's seaward flank.

Denying armed groups and criminals the opportunity to exploit areas of weak governance cannot be a strictly naval task or even one for a more broadly based armed force. It is one where such forces need to support the political, economic, and informational elements of national power. Countering the influence of armed groups at sea, and preventing the formation of sanctuaries they need, will demand that the U.S. and other navies develop a counter-irregular-warfare element that takes account of the lessons learned from the past 50 years of counterinsurgency on land:

- The need to understand and respect the adversary
- The need for sustained presence to build the necessary understanding, demonstrate commitment, and foster host-nation capacity
- The need to work with local people and understand their interests
- The need to recognize that the use of force has political consequences
- The need to deliver a unified response by integrating naval action with other military and civilian agencies, the host nation, and allies under clearly defined, political leadership.

The patient accumulation of intelligence coupled with experience of the likely theaters will be the key to success. Insurgent and criminal activity is multifaceted. More than one insurgent player, and usually more than one organized crime group, is usually active at any one time within any one theater. Some armed groups will have state sponsors; others will not. Some will certainly have criminal connections, while others will confront criminal activity. Whatever stance an individual group might take, the wider problem of poorly regulated maritime space can give license to larger threats.

NOTES

1. Martin N. Murphy, *Contemporary Piracy and Maritime Terrorism*, Adelphi Paper 388 (Abingdon and New York: Routledge, 2007), 9 and 47.

2. The section that follows is based on the discussion in Murphy, *Contemporary Piracy and Maritime Terrorism*, 13–18 and 47–50.

3. See Jack A. Gottschalk and Brian P. Flanagan, *Jolly Roger with an Uzi: The Rise and Threat of Modern Piracy* (Annapolis: Naval Institute Press, 2000), 3.

4. For a definition of "narrow seas," particularly in the naval sense, and the related terms of "coastal waters," "shallow waters," and "confined waters" see Milan N. Vego, *Naval Strategy and Operations on Narrow Seas* (London and Portland: Frank Cass, 1999), 5–7.

5. See Samuel Pyeatt Menefee, *Trends in Maritime Violence* (Coulsdon: Jane's Information Group, 1996), 132, on the existence of "pirate societies" in Southeast Asia, the Red Sea, and—arguably—the Caribbean; the societal acceptability of piracy in Southeast Asia has been noted by several writers including Jon Vagg, "Rough Seas? Contemporary Piracy in South East Asia," *British Journal of Criminology* 35, no. 1 (1995): 67–68; I. R. Hyslop, "Contemporary Piracy," in *Piracy at Sea,* ed. Eric Ellen (Paris: ICC Publishing, 1989), 12 and 28. Stefan Eklöf, on the other hand, argues that the roots of Riau piracy lie in recent, rapid social and economic change driven by the expansion of global capitalism. Stefan Eklöf, *Pirates in Paradise* (Copenhagen: NIAS Press, 2006), 58.

6. Barbara Conway, *The Piracy Business* (London: Hamlyn Paperbacks, 1981), 15.

7. Maritime Transport Committee, "Security in Mar[i]time Transport: Risk Factors and Economic Impact," Organisation for Economic Co-operation and Development, 14, www.oecd.org/dataoecd/63/13/4375896.pdf.

8. David Kilcullen, "New Paradigms for 21st Century Conflict," *E-Journal USA,* May 2007, usinfo.state.gov/journals/itps/0507/ijpc/kilcullen.htm.

9. The relationship between maritime strategy and terrorist "strategy" is tenuous at best. Nonetheless, Julian Corbett's famous observation that, however profound the influence of the maritime dimension might be, all conflicts ("except in the rarest cases") have been decided on land loses none of its force even when one or both protagonists adopt "irregular" methods. Julian S. Corbett, *Some Principles of Maritime Strategy* (1911; repr. Annapolis, MD: Naval Institute Press, 1988), 16.

10. Thomas B. Hunter, "The Growing Threat of Modern Piracy," U.S. Naval Institute *Proceedings* 125, no. 7 (July 1999): 75.

11. Rüdiger Wolfrum, "Fighting Terrorism at Sea: Options and Limitations under International Law"(twenty-eighth Doherty Lecture, organized by the Center for Oceans Law and Policy of the University of Virginia School of Law, Washington, DC, 13 April 2006), 23, available at www.virginia.edu/colp/pdf/Wolfrum -Doherty-Lecture-Terrorism-at-Sea.pdf.

12. For a review of these weaknesses see ibid., 4–8; also Martin N. Murphy, "Piracy and UNCLOS: Does International Law Help Regional States Combat Piracy?" in *Violence at Sea: Piracy in the Age of Terrorism,* ed. Peter Lehr (New York: Routledge, 2007): 159–72.

13. For a brief history of this evolution see Murphy, "Piracy and UNCLOS," 155–59. For the definitive history refer to Alfred P. Rubin, *The Law of Piracy,* 2nd ed. (Irvington-on-Hudson, NY: Transnational Publishers, 1998).

14. Murphy, "Piracy and UNCLOS," 165; Wolfrum, "Fighting Terrorism at Sea," 6–8.

15. Wolfrum, "Fighting Terrorism at Sea," 16; J. Ashley Roach, "PSI and SUA: An Update" (paper, 31st University of Virginia Law of the Sea Conference, Max Planck Institute, Heidelberg, Germany, 24–26 May 2007).

16. Murphy, *Contemporary Piracy and Maritime Terrorism,* 63 and 77.

17. Wolfrum, "Fighting Terrorism at Sea," 24.

18. See, for example, Douglas R. Burgess, Jr., "The Dread Pirate Bin Laden: How Thinking about Terrorists as Pirates Can Help Win the War on Terror," *Legal Affairs,* July/August 2005, available at www.legalaffairs.org/ issues/July-August-2005/feature_burgess_julaug05.msp.

19. Wolfrum, "Fighting Terrorism at Sea," 3.

20. "Convention for the Suppression of Unlawful Acts against the Safety of Maritime Navigation, 1988" and the companion "Protocol for the Suppression of Unlawful Acts against the Safety of Fixed Platforms Located on the Continental Shelf, 1988," available at www.imo.org/Conventions/mainframe.asp?topic_id=259&doc _id=686.

21. Murphy, "Piracy and UNCLOS," 165; Wolfrum, "Fighting Terrorism at Sea," 13.

22. "The United Nations Agreement for the Implementation of the United Nations Convention on the Law of the Sea of 10 December 1982 Relating to the Conservation and Management of Straddling Fish Stocks and Highly Migratory Fish Stocks," available at www.un.org/Depts/los/convention_agreements/convention _overview_fish_stocks.htm; Wolfrum, "Fighting Terrorism at Sea," 14.

23. Richel Langit-Dursin, "Indonesia Key to End Piracy in Malacca Straits," *Jakarta Post,* 6 August 2006.

24. Chong Chee Kin, "Attack Is No Surprise for Semporna Folk," e-mail message, 29 April 2000, available at www.malaysia.net/lists/sangkancil/2000-04/msg01132.html.

25. Commodore Md. Khurshed Alan [*sic*], Bangladesh Navy, "Curbing Maritime Piracy in Bangladesh," *Daily Star,* 20 January 2006, available at www.thedailystar.net/strategic/2006/01/02/strategic.htm.

26. It is perhaps worth also noting that the area from Chittagong south through Cox's Bazaar to the Burmese border is also the home of the country's most prominent fundamentalist Islamic party, Jamaat-e-Islami, and other extreme groups. Bertil Lintner, "A Cocoon of Terror," *Far Eastern Economic Review*, 4 April 2002.

27. "Rivers of Blood: Guns, Oil and Power in Nigeria's Rivers State; Human Rights Watch Briefing Paper, February 2005," Human Rights Watch, hrw.org/backgrounder/africa/nigeria0205/index.htm.

28. Scott Coffen-Smout, "Pirates, Warlords and Rogue Fishing Vessels in Somalia's Unruly Seas," Chebucto Community Net, www.chebucto.ns.ca/~ar120/somalia.html.

29. Mohamed Adow, "Somalia's Trafficking Boom Town," BBC News, 28 April 2004; "The Path to Ruin," *The Economist,* 10 August 2006.

30. Rohan Gunaratna, "The Threat to the Maritime Domain: How Real Is the Terrorist Threat?" in *Economics and Maritime Strategy: Implications for the 21st Century,* ed. Richmond M. Lloyd (Newport, RI: Naval War College, 2006) 86–87.

31. Rear Admiral Chris Parry, Royal Navy, "The Future Maritime Strategic Context" (lecture, RUSI Future Maritime Operations Conference, London, 22–23 November 2006).

32. "Complex Irregular Warfare: The Face of Contemporary Conflict," *The Military Balance, 2005–2006* (London: Routledge, 2005), 414; Frank G. Hoffman, "Complex Irregular Warfare: The Next Revolution in Military Affairs," *Orbis* 50, no. 3 (Summer 2006): 398–99 and 411, available at www.fpri.org/orbis/5003/hoffman .complexirregularwarfare.pdf.

33. James N. Mattis and Frank Hoffman, "Future Warfare: The Rise of Hybrid Wars," U.S. Naval Institute *Proceedings* 131, no. 11 (November 2005): 19; Frank Hoffman, "How the Marines Are Preparing for Hybrid Wars," *Armed Forces Journal,* March 2006, available at www.armedforcesjournal.com/2006/03/1813952/.

34. On Gaza, see Yaakov Amidror and David Keyes, "Will Gaza 'Hamas-stan' Become a Future Al-Qaeda Sanctuary?" Intelligence and Terrorism Information Center at the Center for Special Studies, www.intelligence.org .il/eng/sib/11_04/images/nov14_04.pdf; and Matthew Levitt, "PolicyWatch #1255: Gaza: The Next Terrorist Safe Haven?" The Washington Institute for Near East Policy, 29 June 2007, www.washingtoninstitute .org/templateC05.php?CID=2631. For an analysis of the clan groups that could oppose Hamas and Islamist influence see International Crisis Group, "Inside Gaza: The Challenge of Clans and Families," Middle East Report 71 (20 December 2007), available at www.crisisgroup.org/library/documents/middle_east___north _africa/arab_israeli_conflict/71_inside_gaza___the_challenge_of_clans_and_families.pdf.

14 Domestic Terrorism: Forgotten, But Not Gone

Edward J. Valla and Gregory Comcowich

The six years following the terrorist attacks against the United States on 11 September 2001 (9/11) witnessed exponential growth of an industry of security professionals, academics, and policy makers who sought to understand, prevent, deter, and disrupt future terrorist acts undertaken by international terrorist groups.[1] The overwhelming majority of those who flocked to counterterrorism after 9/11 believe those horrific attacks to be a defining moment in the history of terrorism. Shaped in part by the international dimension of those attacks, the conventional wisdom among many policy makers, academics, security professionals, and some members of the Intelligence Community holds that the primary terrorist threat to the United States comes from al-Qa'ida, Sunni terrorist groups allied with it, and other international terrorist groups motivated by a vehement hatred of the United States.[2]

We acknowledge that al-Qa'ida, its allies, and other international terrorist groups pose a significant threat to U.S. national security and will, in all likelihood, continue to remain a threat well into the future.[3] We argue here, however, that the nearly one-dimensional focus on international terrorism by policy makers, academics, the intelligence services, and, to a much lesser extent, local, state, and federal law-enforcement agencies provides an incomplete picture of the terrorist threat. It also does little to advance our overall understanding of the very real threat that domestic terrorists pose and the special challenges that such individuals and groups present for the intelligence and law enforcement communities. In simple terms, we believe that domestic terrorism has become the proverbial stepchild in counterterrorism preparedness even though a number of domestic terrorist groups continue to operate in the United States[4] and, historically, have conducted lethal attacks against a wide variety of targets. U.S. citizens having no connection or affiliation with international terrorist groups or their agendas have demonstrated that they are as capable and willing to carry out terrorist attacks in the United States on a scale equivalent to attacks that could be conducted by international

Edward J. Valla holds a PhD in political science from the University of Connecticut. He has been a counterterrorism analyst and analyst supervisor for the FBI's Boston Field Office for over 10 years. Dr. Valla also served as a military intelligence officer in the U.S. Army Reserve for 20 years, retiring at the rank of major. He has taught at the National Defense Intelligence College and is currently a visiting associate professor at Bridgewater State College.

Gregory J. Comcowich holds a BA in political science and an MA in public administration. He is a special agent in the FBI.

terrorists. In the balance of this chapter, we use historical examples to illustrate the fact that domestic terrorists have been and can be just as deadly as international terrorists. We also suggest that the perception of international terrorists being more nefarious has resulted in a dearth of academic literature on domestic terrorism. Finally, we advance the idea that the goal of new antiterrorism federal legislation post-9/11, such as the Patriot Act, was squarely focused on the international threat.

Many contend that the 9/11 attacks are a defining moment in the history of terrorism in the United States. The attacks gave rise to a notion that a new era of terrorism had been unleashed, chiefly characterized by mass civilian casualties, and directed against symbolic and economic targets. Hand in hand with the desire to inflict mass casualties, the attacks raised the specter that international terrorists would obtain and use a weapon of mass destruction. However, scrutiny of past incidents committed by domestic terrorists, who are characterized as U.S. citizens acting against U.S. interests within the United States, indicates that with the exception of the high number of casualties, the 2001 attacks are no different than prior terrorist activity by U.S. citizens. What may come as a surprise to some readers is the fact that well prior to 2001, domestic terrorists had already successfully attacked strikingly similar targets to those that were attacked on 9/11.

Eighty-one years earlier, on 16 September 1920 a group calling itself the American Anarchist Fighters placed a bomb in a horse cart and left it on Wall Street in New York City. When the bomb detonated it indiscriminately killed 30 and injured 300. Ten others later died of their injuries.[5] The American Anarchist Fighters undoubtedly chose to target Wall Street for the same reasons as did al-Qa'ida. To the anarchists, Wall Street was a symbol of the financial, economic, and imperialist power of the United States and was a symbol known worldwide. In 1954, extremists associated with the Puerto Rican Nationalist Party, considered then to be domestic terrorists by the FBI, opened fire in the gallery of the United States House of Representatives, wounding five members of Congress. This attack occurred 47 years before United Airlines Flight 93 crashed into a Pennsylvania field before it could destroy the apparent target—the U.S. Capitol. The Puerto Rican separatists' ultimate goal then, as it remains to this day, was independence from what they perceived as the U.S. imperialist governance of the island. The United States Senate has not been spared terrorist attacks, having been bombed twice by left-wing domestic terrorists. In 1971 and 1983 separate left-wing groups placed bombs in the Senate that caused damage but no injuries or deaths.[6] Three decades before the terrorist hijackers aboard American Airlines Flight 77 set their sights on the Pentagon, the Weather Underground,[7] a particularly violent left-wing group believed to have been responsible for over 30 bombings, placed a bomb in a Pentagon bathroom to protest military action in Vietnam and to pressure the United States to withdraw its troops from that country. Fundamentally, the Weather Underground viewed the Pentagon as the enforcer of the country's unjust foreign policy. While both domestic terrorists and al-Qa'ida's ultimate overall political objectives were different in these instances, they selected targets for the same reasons. Each sought to strike at the symbols of America's financial, military, and political might.

THE MISPERCEPTION THAT DOMESTIC TERRORISTS ARE LESS LETHAL

There is a perception that international terrorists are more diabolical than domestic terrorists. That perception appears to be driven by three main presumptions. First, many contend that international terrorists, particularly those associated with radical Islam, are inherently dangerous due to their religious zealotry. Second, many believe that international terrorists pose a greater danger to U.S. national security because some groups seek to obtain and use chemical, biological, radiological, and nuclear (CBRN) weapons. Finally, and perhaps most significantly, international groups are viewed as more dangerous because they seek to cause indiscriminate mass casualties, often by focusing their attacks against relatively unprotected critical infrastructure. There is little doubt that all of these contentions ring true for some international terrorists, particularly al-Qa'ida and similarly motivated groups. However, a review of terrorism that has taken place in the United States over the past century shows that domestic terrorists have already beaten international groups to the punch on each of these counts.[8]

Terrorist groups are generally categorized as politically motivated, religiously motivated, or single interest, i.e., those driven by one particular goal. While achieving a political or social goal is a fundamental motivator of all three groups, those driven by a religious imperative are often viewed as the most unpredictable. To members of such groups, religious "ends" almost exclusively justify their means to achieve them. Radical Islamic groups have been held up as the prime examples of religiously motivated terrorism and many contend that they pose the greatest danger to the United States. Yet the United States has a host of domestically based religiously motivated terrorist groups, all of whom essentially believe that the world is on the verge of a final apocalyptic race war between God's chosen people and Satan's allies, which include the U.S. government.[9] Like radical Islamists, many adherents of these racist religions, which hold both white-supremacist and black-supremacist views, believe that they have been chosen by God to alter society in a manner consistent with their theological beliefs and, just like many jihadists, believe that in order to get to their versions of heaven, they must die in a battle against their oppressors. For example, some adherents of the white-supremacist Christian Identity ideology refer to themselves as Phineas Priests. They interpret the biblical example of Phinehas to justify killing in defense of their interpretation of God's laws, which condemns race mixing, homosexuality, the banking system, and abortion. There are multiple examples of terrorist activity based on these beliefs. Joseph Paul Franklin, a Phineas Priest, killed at least 11 individuals who were in mixed-race relationships.[10] He also attempted to murder civil rights leader Vernon Jordan and Larry Flynt, the publisher of *Hustler* magazine.[11] In 1996, a group of Phineas Priests, dubbed the Spokane Bank Robbers, placed bombs at an abortion clinic and the offices of a newspaper in separate incidents in Spokane, Washington. After each bombing they robbed a bank.[12] Eric Rudolph, who placed a bomb at the 1996 Olympics, and later at two abortion clinics and a homosexual nightclub, killing a total of two people, is noteworthy. He spent time at a Christian Identity compound during his formative years. But, at the time of his bombings, he appears to have become aligned with the Army of God, whose chief goal is to end abortion, not to achieve a state of white supremacy. Almost uniformly those associated with the Army of God are not white supremacists; rather they are influenced by their unique interpretation of Christianity. Although he claimed the Olympic Park bombings on behalf of the Army of God, not in the name of Christian Identity, the locations of the bombings and the letter he wrote taking claim for them reflects the religiously based targets associated with both Christian Identity and the Army of God.

Like some radical Islamists, a few adherents to the Odinist religion contend that salvation and immortality can only be obtained by dying in a race war. In the early 1980s, Odinist Bob Mathews led the Order, which engaged in bank robberies, murder, and bombings with the goal of creating a "whites only" homeland in the northwestern United States. After evading FBI agents in a gun battle, he wrote, "I have been a good soldier, a fearless warrior. I will die with honor and join my brothers in [heaven]."[13] Matthews's martyrdom ideology led to his death in 1984, when he died during a standoff with federal agents. Another Odinist, John William King, killed James Byrd, Jr., an African American, by dragging Byrd behind King's car. King was content with the belief that he might be sentenced to death for his actions.[14]

Perhaps the worst imaginable terrorism incident involves the use of chemical, biological, radiological, or nuclear (CBRN) weaponry. There is little doubt that Usama bin Laden and al-Qa'ida seek to obtain such weaponry.[15] Significantly, the desire is just as strong for some domestic groups. Individuals with ties to domestic terrorist groups have already demonstrated a capability to produce and employ CBRN weapons. For example, in June 2004, Michael Crooker, an antigovernment extremist living in rural Massachusetts, was arrested on charges relating to his illegal transportation of a firearm. During the search of his apartment, items found indicated that Crooker was successfully manufacturing ricin, a highly lethal biological weapon made from castor beans.[16] Ricin is one of the most toxic and easily produced plant toxins. When inhaled as a respiratory aerosol, ricin causes severe tissue damage of the airways and may result in death.[17] Crooker's manufacture and intended use of ricin is hardly a new or isolated incident involving a domestic individual with extremist views. In November 1999, the FBI arrested James Kenneth Gluck for threatening to kill judges in Jefferson County, Colorado, through the use of biological weapons. A search of Gluck's residence discovered a makeshift laboratory, the necessary ingredients to make ricin, and a copy of the *Anarchist's Cookbook*.[18] In March 1998, three members of the North American Militia in Michigan were arrested on weapons and conspiracy charges. In searching the homes of these men, federal authorities discovered an arsenal of weapons and a videotape that gave detailed instructions on the method for extracting ricin from castor beans. Ricin was also part of a plot by four men from Minnesota who were part of the tax-protesting militia known as the Minnesota Patriot's Council, whose goal was to overthrow the government. In 1991, the group had planned to use ricin to kill a deputy U.S. marshal and a sheriff who had served court orders on members of the group. The amount of ricin the group had manufactured could have killed 100 people if it had been deployed effectively.[19] The four men were the first to be tried, and, in 1995, convicted, under the 1989 Biological Weapons Anti-terrorism Act for possessing ricin.

While ricin has been the choice for some domestic extremists, it hasn't been the only one. Demetrius "Van" Crocker was sentenced to 30 years in prison in November 2006 after having been convicted of attempting to obtain chemical weapons, in this case deadly sarin gas,[20] and for possession of stolen explosives. A former member of the right-wing National Socialist Movement, Crocker's objective was to build a dirty bomb and use it to destroy a state or federal court house.[21] A white supremacist, William Krar, was arrested by the FBI in 2003. At the time of his arrest, Krar had approximately two pounds of sodium cyanide, which, when mixed with acids or other substances, creates hydrogen cyanide, a gas that is lethal in small amounts.[22] He also had 65 pipe bombs, several remote-controlled briefcase bombs, and over 500,000 rounds of ammunition.[23] In 2000, animal rights extremists placed a similar cyanide-based chemical in a McDonald's restaurant in Minneapolis, Minnesota, in conjunction with protests at an animal genetics convention.[24] Three militia members were arrested in December 1999 before they could carry out a plan to destroy a 24-million-gallon propane facility in Elk Grove, California, near Sacramento. At the time of their arrest, the subjects were in possession of bomb-making equipment, including detonation cord and blasting caps. In this regard, it is instructive to note that the U.S. Department of Energy's Lawrence Livermore Laboratory found that had this attack taken place as planned, it "would likely [have] result[ed] in a firestorm that could [have] reach[ed] as far out as fourteen kilometers from the site and could [have] cause[d] a fatality rate as high as fifty percent up to five miles away."[25] A similar plot occurred in 1997 when four members of the True Knights of the Ku Klux Klan from Wise County, Texas, were arrested for planning an elaborate scheme to rob an armored car. Part of their plan involved a diversionary bombing at the Mitchell Energy and Development Corporation's natural gas processing and storage facility. The plotters believed that the resulting explosions could have caused so many deaths that it would take law enforcement authorities "three or four days" to remove the casualties.[26]

Congruent with some domestic terrorists' desire to employ chemical, biological or radiological devices, the examples cited above also illustrate the fact that, as with most international terrorist groups, domestic terrorists exhibit the same propensity to direct their attacks against "soft" civilian targets. The plot against the Mitchell Energy and Development Corporation facility exemplifies the same disregard many domestic terrorists have for those who are killed or injured by their activity as do international groups. One of the plotters, Catherine Dee Adams, was caught on an FBI videotape discussing the possibility that children near the facility might die as a result of their actions. She is heard saying, "There's a few kids right there, but hopefully they'll be in school. I hate to say this, but if it has to be, it has to be."[27] Adams's husband commented on the mass casualties he expected by saying that law enforcement and firefighting personnel would be kept busy for days.[28] Timothy McVeigh, the convicted Oklahoma City bomber, expressed similar disregard for children when he was asked about the 19 children among the 168 who died in his attack on the Alfred P. Murrah Federal Building. He described their deaths as "collateral damage."[29] The attack on the Murrah Federal Building is among the largest terrorist attacks ever perpetrated. It is both the second-deadliest attack on U.S. soil and the third-deadliest attack against a U.S. civilian target. In terms of U.S. civilian deaths it only trails behind the 9/11 attacks and the 1988 Pam Am bombing over Lockerbie, Scotland, which killed 217.[30]

The 9/11 attacks, the bombings of the subways in London and Madrid, and continued warning that al-Qa'ida remains interested in targeting critical infrastructure in order to inflict large numbers of casualties resulted in a tremendous allocation of resources aimed at protecting our critical infrastructure. Transportation links, water supply systems, and electrical grid and telecommunications networks remain critical nodes, and because they are largely unprotected, they remain vulnerable to terrorist attack.[31] However, international terrorists are not the first to set their sights on infrastructure. Animal rights and environmental extremists who believe that many types of infrastructure are harmful to animals and the environment have targeted infrastructure repeatedly and with some success. For example, in 1989 four members of a domestic environmental extremist group, the Evan Mecham Eco-Terrorist International Conspiracy (EMETIC), were charged in relation to a plot to destroy power lines which comprised part of the infrastructure of four nuclear facilities in three states. The group targeted lines leading to the Central Arizona Project and Palo Verde Nuclear Generating Stations located in Arizona, the Diablo Canyon facility in California, and Colorado's Rocky Flats facility. A fifth person was subsequently indicted on charges of destruction of a nuclear facility.[32]

Those convictions notwithstanding, power lines and other infrastructure remain viable targets for animal rights and environmental extremists. Recent examples demonstrate this predilection. On 25 January 2006, three environmental extremists, Eric McDavid, Zachary Jenson, and Lauren Weiner, were indicted by the U.S. Department of Justice for conspiracy to damage and destroy property by fire and an explosive. Specifically, the individuals had targeted cellular telephone towers, electrical power stations, a dam, a fish hatchery, and a government building. The group had conducted preoperational surveillance on the targets, purchased the ingredients necessary for the explosive device, and begun to manufacture the chemicals to be used for the explosive.[33] Similarly, in January 2006, 11 defendants were charged with acts of domestic terrorism undertaken on behalf of the Earth Liberation Front and Animal Liberation Front that caused a total of $80 million in damage.[34] The indictment charges that these individuals conducted a multitude of crimes from 1996 to 2001, including the destruction of a high-tension power line near Bend, Oregon, that serves the Bonneville Power Administration energy facility.

Environmental and animal rights extremists are not alone among domestic extremists in targeting infrastructure. In 2000, Leo Felton, a member of a gang called Aryan Unit One, discussed bombing the New England Holocaust Memorial in Boston and the Leonard P. Zakim Bridge, which connects Boston to Cambridge, Massachusetts. Subsequent to his arrest, a search of his apartment found bomb-making materials and 28 kilograms of ammonium nitrate, a precursor used to make explosives.[35] Earlier, in 1995, an Amtrak train derailed in rural Hyder, Arizona, killing one passenger and injuring others. Though unsolved, the FBI describes this act as a suspected terrorism incident.[36] An analysis of the note claiming credit for the derailment, which was signed by the "Sons of Gestapo," indicates that the perpetrators were associated with a domestic right-wing ideology.

POSSIBLE EXPLANATIONS FOR THE MISPERCEPTION

As evidenced from the domestic terrorist activity highlighted above, it is a mistake to think that domestic terrorists are any less capable or violent than international groups. Despite domestic terrorists' demonstrated history of attacking the same and similar targets as international terrorists, with the same force and disregard for human life, it appears that their actions do not attract the same concern as international terrorism. While it is difficult to quantify perceptions about the differences in dangerousness between domestic and international terrorists, several factors can be used to illustrate that there appears to be a distinct presumption that international terrorists are more nefarious than domestic ones. Evidence from public policy and scholarly research supports this contention.

The perception that domestic terrorism is less lethal is likely perpetuated, in part, due to the bureaucratic composition of the agencies assigned to combat terrorism. The Defense Department, Central Intelligence Agency, and National Security Agency receive the lion's share of intelligence funding, personnel, and other antiterrorism resources, which strongly influences how the terrorist threat is perceived. Because those agencies are precluded by statute, with minor exceptions, from investigating domestic terrorists, they do not have the proverbial dog in the domestic terrorism fight. Thus, investigating domestic terrorism is left largely to the FBI and to state and local law enforcement[37] even when domestic terrorists target Pentagon assets in the United States.[38]

In turn, because the bulk of those assigned to a counterterrorism role within the government are mainly concerned with international terrorism, it is logical that, given the interplay between academics and government policy, a majority of the research on terrorism focuses attention on international groups and their actions. It is not surprising then that since 2001, the main thrust of academic research and publishing on terrorism has focused almost exclusively on the phenomenon's international aspects. One only has to conduct a cursory examination of the literature to find that the scholarly community has responded, like moths to a flame, by publishing a host of journal articles and monographs that describe international terrorist groups and Islamic extremism and seek to quantify the strategic threat posed by al-Qa'ida.[39] Significant attention has also been given to the terrorist recruitment process,[40] suicide terrorism,[41] terrorist motivation,[42] the evolution of international Islamic jihad,[43] and recommendations as to how the global war on terror should be waged.[44]

Two journals, *Studies in Conflict* and *Terrorism and Political Violence*, are widely recognized as the main publishing venues for scholarly articles on the topic of politically motivated violence. A review of articles published in these two journals since 2001 reveals few articles that examine or address an aspect of domestic terrorism. From January 2001 through January 2007, *Studies in Conflict and Terrorism* contained over 187 articles on an eclectic range of themes. Yet only three of these had as their focus domestic terrorist groups or U.S. extremism.[45] Similarly, *Terrorism and Political Violence* published 189 articles, the overwhelming majority of which centered upon terrorism's international aspects. Six explored recent activity by U.S. domestic groups.[46] We note that, despite the publication of excellent works by noted terrorism experts, few monographs or doctoral dissertations exploring domestic terrorism have been published since 2001.[47] Even in the aftermath of the Oklahoma City bombing, which at the time was by far the largest attack against the United States and one of the largest worldwide, scholars showed little interest in domestic terrorism.[48] Finally, many of the Internet Web sites that provide background on terrorist groups, biographies of key leaders, terrorist incidents, and terrorist modi operandi focus almost exclusively on international terrorism.[49]

Mirroring the academic focus on international terrorism, the post-9/11 wide-ranging public debate focused exclusively on methods to prevent, deter, and disrupt international terrorist groups. Domestic terrorism prevention has been almost uniformly left out of this debate. Even though terrorism is a focal point of the nation's overall National Security Strategy, the global war on terror does not seem to include domestic groups. In fact, *The National Security Strategy of the United States of America* and *The National Intelligence Strategy of the United States of America* make no mention of domestic groups and are focused exclusively on external threats.[50]

Domestic terrorism's exclusion from these strategies is most certainly deliberate and not born out of ignorance. Undoubtedly, Congress and others involved in the legislative process are keenly aware of the threat posed by domestic terrorism. The FBI, the federal agency that is statutorily empowered to investigate both domestic and international terrorism within the United States and international terrorism outside of it, is consistent in its frequent testimony before Congress that domestic terrorists and international terrorists are of equal concern to the FBI.[51] In particular, FBI testimony appears to take pains to highlight the past use of WMD by domestic terrorists and note that their lethal intentions are effectively no different than international terrorists'. Nonetheless, the United States Congress, the United States Department of Justice, and other policy makers have purposefully made only minor changes to the policies that govern domestic antiterrorism efforts. Only insignificant changes were made post-9/11, chiefly because the largely unchanged policies that were implemented in the 1970s have demonstrated that they strike the appropriate balance between liberty and security. While there is an overwhelming consensus in Congress and within the Department of Justice that the current policies are appropriate and reflective of a measured balance between liberty and security, it is possible that the apparent effect of U.S. laws and policies that make distinctions between international and domestic terrorism reinforces the perception that domestic terrorists are less threatening.

THE PERCEPTION'S IMPACT

Regardless of how the perception came to be that domestic terrorists are less evil minded, the perception matters greatly. Particularly significant is the likelihood that government policies affect how federal, state, and local individuals involved in the counterterrorism effort perceive domestic terrorism. Federal law enforcement agencies rely heavily on state and local law enforcement for spotting suspicious people and activity and assisting with investigations. Should these countless eyes and ears on the street believe that domestic terrorists are not worthy of concern, they, and the large number of those involved in private security, may dismiss the danger. Importantly, domestic terrorists have a consistent history of engaging in fatal acts against law enforcement during routine law-enforcement activity, such as traffic stops. Thus, the perception of domestic terrorism not only affects the gathering of information against domestic terrorist groups, the cornerstone of prevention; it also could result in deadly consequences for local and state law-enforcement officials who are in constant contact with extremists in their daily activities.

Ultimately, the perception of domestic terrorists as less motivated, capable, and lethal, combined with the nearly one-dimensional focus on foreign threats after 9/11, is creating an imbalance in further understanding the particular characteristics of domestic extremists, as well as possible trajectories as groups evolve, mature, or adjust their raisons d'être to new social and political realities. This imbalance may lead to missed opportunities in identifying strategies, laws, and innovative policing methods aimed at more effectively thwarting domestic extremism. By generally ignoring domestic terrorism as an area worthy of continued academic scholarship, we reduce our chances of developing a comprehensive understanding of what causes individuals and groups to terrorize, what factors may indicate future violence, what factors escalate or de-escalate terrorism, and which punitive or nonpunitive measures are effective in stopping terrorism. All these areas would likely be of keen interest to the federal, state, and local law-enforcement communities as well as to policy makers. Increasing our understanding of domestic terrorism provides the potential for sound and accurate analysis, and may enhance policy makers' ability to craft more efficient, effective, and innovative policies to deter domestic terrorism.

DOMESTIC TERRORISM: NOT NECESSARILY BOMBS

Domestic terrorism is different from international terrorism because some of the most active groups operating in the United States today do not limit themselves to the blunt instruments of international terrorism. Most international terrorist incidents boil down to killing or injuring people using explosives. Moreover, "martyrdom" as an objective often underpins their motives and planning. Alternatively, domestic terrorists generally want to live to fight another day. They employ a plethora of criminal activity that they believe will enable them to achieve their goals.

In fact, it appears that when domestic terrorist groups use all the tools available to them, from constitutionally protected activity through lethal attacks, their efforts are more effective than the deadly violence associated with international terrorists. Consider that one of al-Qa'ida's chief objectives in striking the United States was to coerce the United States to remove its military forces and overall influence from the Middle East and the broader Muslim world. Instead, U.S. presence has increased dramatically in Iraq and Afghanistan. Likewise, McVeigh's and Nichol's onetime-spectacular attack did nothing to achieve their goal of engineering a revolution. In contrast, the domestic terrorist groups, especially single-issue ones, that use the full gamut of activity available to them appear to be able to greatly influence the behavior of those they target.

The extreme antiabortion movement, specifically defined as those who employ criminal activity of a terrorist nature, is a prime example of a single-issue group that has effectively utilized a full range of criminal activity in an effort to achieve its goal of stopping abortion. While the movement appears to be declining, and has yet to achieve its ultimate goal, there is strong evidence that its use of constitutionally protected activity, in combination with constant low levels of criminal activity and infrequent lethal violence, is extremely effective in intimidating those who provide abortion-related services. After the Supreme Court's 1973 landmark decision that abortion was a constitutional right, a social and political movement formed with the goal of overturning the ruling. By the late 1980s and 1990s, there were large antiabortion demonstrations throughout the country during which individuals simply exercised their First Amendment rights. Then, like other domestic terrorist groups before them, such as the left-wing violence that arose out of the anti–Vietnam War era, a tiny fraction of the broader movement became frustrated at the perceived lack of goal attainment. For a handful of extremists, legitimate political activity would not suffice in stopping abortion. By the early 1990s, after years of escalating criminal activity, violence aimed at preventing individuals from exercising what the Supreme Court considers a constitutional right reached a fever pitch. Moving away from the movement's fundamental belief that all human life is sacred, extremists contended that killing was justified to save the lives of unborn children. Doctors and their staffs became murder targets. The first murder occurred in 1993 during an antiabortion demonstration outside of a Pensacola, Florida, clinic when an antiabortion extremist murdered Dr. David Gunn. Dr. Gunn, who had been subjected to years of harassment, threats, and civil disobedience, was the first of seven individuals murdered by extremists. Additionally, there have been 17 attempted murders against clinic personnel.[52] By 1993, a loose coalition of individuals popularized the moniker Army of God to take credit for lethal criminal activity. Some of the most notorious acts the Army of God claimed to have conducted were the bombings by Eric Rudolph at the 1996 Olympics in Atlanta, Georgia, and the subsequent bombings against two abortion clinics that resulted in two deaths. According to one watchdog group, from 1977 through 2004 there were at least 41 bombings, 171 arsons, and 82 attempted bombings and arsons.[53] Additionally, clinic doctors and their employees have been subject to a wide variety of activity, such as the posting of their photos and personal information on the Internet, placing of noxious chemicals in facilities, surveillance of employees, and sending of hoax WMD letters, among a multitude of other similar activities.

Ultimately, single-issue terrorism appears to have met with a measurable degree of success in this case. While the violent activities were relatively sporadic, the clinic personnel targeted via consistent low-level harassment, threats, and vandalism were the de facto targets of the violent acts due to the notoriety of the violence conducted by extremists. Since the height of terrorist activity against clinics, which took place throughout the 1990s, the number of doctors who perform abortions and the number of places that offer abortion services have declined. While there are many possible reasons for this decline, including changing social views, more restrictive laws governing abortion, and higher medical insurance, among others, those who work at clinics cite fear as one of the factors why fewer doctors and medical support personnel are willing to participate in the delivery of this constitutionally protected medical procedure. Exemplifying this fear, one physician closed his facility in Washington, DC, citing the strain caused by antiabortion extremism. In explaining his decision, he wrote to his patients that "Sadly, the ongoing threat to my life and my concern for the safety of my loved ones has extracted a heavy toll on me, making it necessary that I discontinue practicing OB-GYN."[54]

Like the antiabortion movement, the extreme animal rights and environmental movements utilize a multitude of tactics aimed at achieving their goal of preventing perceived abuses of animals or causing harm to the environment. The movements, which are often indiscernible from each other, have coalesced with the burgeoning anarchist movement, and are currently active throughout the nation. Their illegal activity is a prominent focus of FBI attention. Considered single-issue movements, they also have achieved an extraordinary degree of success by using the entire spectrum of activity available to domestic terrorists. Individuals associated with these movements often utilize the names Animal Liberation Front and the Earth Liberation Front when conducting activity aimed at preventing the abuse of animals and harm to the environment. Since 1996, the FBI estimates that ELF, ALF, and related extremist groups engaged in approximately 1,100 criminal acts causing over $100 million in damage.[55]

One of the most formalized animal rights groups operating today is Stop Huntingdon Animal Cruelty (SHAC). Its goal is to force Huntingdon Life Sciences (HLS), a company that conducts drug and product testing, out of business. While the SHAC campaign frequently utilizes constitutionally protected activity to accomplish its objective, it also uses a host of illegal methods. The most egregious illegal activities associated with SHAC were the bombings of two of its targets. In 2003, the Chiron Corporation and Shaklee Corporation, both located in California, were targeted because of their associations with HLS. A group calling itself the Revolutionary Cells of the Animal Liberation Brigade claimed responsibility for the attack, and in a prepared statement claimed, "We gave all of the customers the chance, the choice, to withdraw their business from HLS. Now you will reap what you have sown. All customers and their families are considered legitimate targets. . . . [N]o more will all the killing be done by the oppressors, now the oppressed will strike back."[56] A federal arrest warrant was issued for the alleged perpetrator, Daniel Andreas San Diego. San Diego, currently a fugitive, was active in the animal rights movement.

The more nuanced terrorist activity done on behalf of SHAC comes in the form of criminal harassment, stalking, and other crimes intended to intimidate and coerce employees and companies associated with animal testing or other individuals associated with HLS and associated targets. For example, in 2006, after a long FBI investigation the group and six of its members were convicted of violating the Animal Enterprise Protection Act and interstate stalking.[57] Four of its members were charged with telephone harassment. One employee of an insurance company associated with HLS testified that personal information about her and her family was posted on SHAC's Web site, including, among other information, her name, the name of her seven-year-old son, and the fact that her son sang in a boys choir.[58] The woman testified that she received an e-mail threatening to fill her son with poison and slice her son, "the way Huntingdon does with animals." Another person testified that SHAC broke all of the windows of his home and overturned his wife's car.[59]

The SHAC campaign has undoubtedly been successful. The insurance company that employed the woman threatened by SHAC chose to cut its business dealings with HLS. Likewise, more than 100 companies targeted by SHAC because of their associations with HLS have stopped conducting business with the company, including Aetna Insurance, Citibank, Deloitte and Touche, Johnson and Johnson, and Merck.[60] SHAC's success comes from its use of the wide range of activity it employs. To reiterate, it is apparent that even nonlethal or low-level criminal activity has the effect of creating a coercive environment. Those targeted by SHAC are well aware that the group has utilized bombings and other tactics to instill fear. The movement also does not hide the fact that one of the movement's well-known leaders contends that killing individuals associated with animal research is a legitimate tactic. Dr. Jerry Vlasak, an emergency room doctor, testified before the Senate in 2005 in a hearing on SHAC that he stood by an earlier statement advocating the murder of animal researchers in which he said, "I don't think you'd have to kill too many. I think five lives, ten lives, fifteen human lives, we could save a million, two million or ten million nonhuman lives."[61] Clearly the extremist animal rights movement is evolving in a pattern similar to that of the antiabortion movement. Some members perceive that they are having difficulty achieving their social and political goals via the democratic process. Consequently, they become frustrated. In turn, they modify their original ideological stances and become willing to use criminal activity to achieve their goals. The animal rights movement initially contended that all living beings, both humans and animals, must be protected. Now, it appears that the ideology of some in the movement has evolved to the point where they embrace the view of Dr. Vlasak.

DOMESTIC TERRORISM—NOT DOWN, NOT OUT

As we have illustrated above, domestic terrorists have not faded into the twilight. Domestic terrorists have been as motivated and are as capable of conducting attacks and engaging in other criminal activity as international terrorists. Simply because domestic terrorists have not conducted a single mass-casualty attack on the scale of 9/11 is no reason to ignore them or view their actions as having minimal impact on American civil society. The political and social issues that have motivated diverse groups of extremists have not been resolved to their satisfactions. Globalization, abortion, animal rights, deeply held concerns about the environment, racism, immigration policies, and fear of an overly powerful government are some of the issues that continue to spawn small cadres of people who willingly engage in violent activity in order to achieve their political or social objectives. The nation should not be lulled into a false sense of complacency regarding domestic terrorist groups, nor should we be surprised at continued criminal and violent activity undertaken by such groups.

NOTES

The views and opinions expressed in this chapter are those of the authors and do not necessarily reflect the official policy or position of the Federal Bureau of Investigation, the Department of Justice, or the U.S. government.

1. Terrorism has many definitions. For this chapter we use the FBI's, which defines domestic terrorism as activities that involve acts dangerous to human life that are a violation of the criminal laws of the United States or of any state; appear to be intended to intimidate or coerce a civilian population and to influence the policy of a government by mass destruction, assassination, or kidnapping; and occur primarily within the territorial jurisdiction of the United States. Domestic terrorist groups have no support from or connections to foreign governments or organizations. International terrorism involves the territory or citizens of more than one country. The term "homegrown terrorism" is being used increasingly to describe groups or individuals who are inspired by al-Qa'ida and other radical Islamist ideologues. Single-issue terrorism may be defined as extremist militancy on the part of groups or individuals protesting a perceived grievance or wrong usually attributed to government action or inaction. Three issues generally fall under the definition: animal rights,

environmentalism, and abortion. For complete definitions see Federal Bureau of Investigation, U.S. Department of Justice, *Terrorism 2000/2001* (Government Printing Office), available at www.fbi.gov/publications/terror/terror2000_2001.htm; and the *Federal Criminal Code and Rules*, 2007 ed. (Thomson West), title 18, sec. 2331(5). For a detailed discussion of how the meaning of the term "terrorism" has evolved, see Bruce Hoffman, "Defining Terrorism," in *Inside Terrorism,* rev. ed. (New York: Columbia University Press, 2006), 1–41.

2. The heavily weighted focus on international terrorism is understandable given that al-Qa'ida's senior leaders, Usama bin Laden and Ayman Al-Zawahiri, survived the U.S. military campaign to capture or kill them. Though their ability to plan and direct terrorist attacks has been severely degraded, they remain powerful symbols for those Islamic radicals who oppose U.S. policies and who seek to kill Americans. There is extensive debate about whether these groups "hate us" because of "who we are" versus "what we do." For an excellent overview of the various schools of thought regarding al-Qa'ida's motivations, see Max Abrams, "Al Qaeda's Scorecard: A Progress Report on Al Qaeda's Objectives," *Studies in Conflict and Terrorism* 29, no. 5 (July/August 2006): 509–29.

3. Al-Qa'ida has evolved into a global movement comprised of Islamic radicals. Despite the loss of senior operatives and the favorable training environment in Afghanistan, al-Qa'ida continues to recruit and inspire an undetermined number of new operatives, who have in turn mounted successful attacks in Western Europe, in Southeast Asia, and in the Middle East. Perhaps the most ominous, in terms of illustrating al-Qa'ida's continued interest in conducting mass-casualty attacks, was the attempt in August 2006 to destroy multiple aircraft in flight over the Atlantic Ocean. This plot was adroitly thwarted by the British law-enforcement and intelligence services. There are, of course, a series of well-known post-9/11 attacks that have been conducted by al-Qa'ida or its affiliates. The Indonesia-based Jemaah Islamiya detonated a suicide car bomb at a Bali nightclub on 12 October 2002, killing over 200 people. On 16 May 2003 five bombs exploded at various targets in Casablanca, killing 45 people. Spanish authorities identified the Moroccan Combatant Group, an al-Qa'ida ally, as being a prime suspect for the attack. The Abu Hafs Al-Masri Brigade and Secret Organization of Al-Qa'ida in Europe claimed credit for attacking the Madrid train station on 11 March 2004 and London subway system on 7 July 2005. In Madrid, nearly 200 people were killed and over 1,200 injured. The suicide bombings in London killed 56 people and wounded 700 more.

4. The FBI's Office of Public Affairs reported that domestic terrorism cases nearly doubled from almost 3,500 in 1999 to over 6,000 in 2003, from "Preventing Terrorist Attacks on U.S. Soil," news release, 9 April 2004, available at www.fbi.gov/page2/April04/040904Krar.htm.

5. Nathan Ward, "The Fire Last Time: When Terrorists First Struck New York's Financial District," *American Heritage*, November/December 2001, available at www.americanheritage.com/articles/magazine/ah/2001/8/2001_8_46.shtml.

6. Partly because the Senate had adjourned earlier than normal for the day on 7 November 1983, no one was injured. Additional details are available at www.senate.gov/artandhistory/minute/bomb_explodes_in_capitol.htm.

7. Regarding the history, personalities, and activities of the Weather Underground see Ron Jacobs, *The Way the Wind Blew: A History of the Weather Underground* (London: Verso Press, 1997); and Dan Berger, *Outlaws of America: The Weather Underground and the Politics of Solidarity* (Oakland: AK Press, 2006).

8. In this brief chapter we do not attempt an exhaustive survey of activity by domestic terrorists. Instead, we provide some representative actions undertaken by a diverse array of groups and individuals.

9. See the FBI's "Project Megiddo," reproduced in its entirety in *Terrorism and Political Violence* 14, no. 1 (Spring 2002): 27–52.

10. See Danny W. Harris, "Al-Qaeda and the Phineas Priesthood: Terrorist Groups with a Common Enemy and Similar Justifications for Terror Tactics" (PhD diss., Texas A&M University, 2003).

11. Michael Rutledge, "Need for Notoriety Drove Franklin," *Cincinnati Post*, 16 April 1997.

12. Counterterrorism Threat Assessment and Warning Unit, National Security Division, Federal Bureau of Investigation, U.S. Department of Justice, *Terrorism in the United States,* 1996, 15.

13. FBI, "Project Megiddo," 31.

14. Scott Baldauf, "Messages from a Stern Verdict," *Christian Science Monitor*, 25 February 1999.

15. Noted terrorism expert Rohan Gunaratna writes that al-Qa'ida will not hesitate to use chemical, biological, radiological, or nuclear weapons against population centers. Rohan Gunaratna, *Inside Al Qaeda: Global Network of Terror* (New York: Columbia University Press, 2002), 11.

16. U.S. Department of Justice, *Counterterrorism White Paper* (June 2006), 65, available at nefafoundation.org/miscellaneous/FeaturedDocs/DOJ_CTWhitePaper.pdf.

17. U.S. Department of the Army, *Textbook of Military Medicine: Medical Aspects of Chemical and Biological Warfare* (Office of the Surgeon General, 1989), 631–42.

18. "Alleged Author of Threat Letter Held without Bond in Florida," *Colorado Springs Gazette*, 9 November 1999; and "Man Arrested for Alleged Poisoning Threats," *Colorado Springs Gazette*, 7 November 1999.

19. Terrorist Research and Analytical Center, National Security Division, Federal Bureau of Investigation, U.S. Department of Justice, *Terrorism in the United States,* 1995, 6.

20. Sarin came to prominence after the Japanese terrorist group Aum Shinrikyo used it in the Tokyo subway in 1995.

21. Anti-defamation League, "Tennessee White Supremacist Sentenced to 30 Years on Chemical Weapons Charges," www.adl.org/learn/extremism_in_the_news/White Supremacists.

22. U.S. Department of Health and Human Services, *Pocket Guide to Chemical Hazards* (Washington, DC: Government Printing Office, June 1997).

23. Michael Reynolds, "Homegrown Terror," *Bulletin of Atomic Scientists*, November/December 2004, 48–57.

24. "Police: Animal Genetics Protesters Left Traces of Poison Behind," *CNN.com,* 25 July 2000, available at archives.cnn.com/2000/nature/07/25/animal.protest.ap.

25. Jennifer Kerr, "Affidavit Tells of Bomb Plot," Associated Press, 6 December 1999.

26. Scott Parks, "3 Suspected in KKK Plot Ordered Held without Bond," *Dallas Morning News*, 29 April 1997.

27. Laura Vozzella, "Couple Talk on Video about Bombing Gas Plant," *Fort Worth Star Telegram*, 29 April 1997.

28. Parks, "3 Suspected in KKK Plot Ordered Held without Bond."

29. "Book: A Remorseless McVeigh Calls Dead Children 'Collateral Damage,'" CourtTVNews, www.courttv.com/archive/news/2001/0328/mcveigh_ap.html.

30. We consider the 23 October 1983 attack in Lebanon that killed 241 U.S. Marines an attack against a military, versus civilian, target.

31. Michael Poulin, a self-described anarchist, sabotaged electrical transmission towers in Klamath Falls, Oregon, and Anderson, California. Interestingly, Poulin claimed to have been attempting to demonstrate the grid's lack of security.

32. Terrorist Research and Analytical Center, Counterterrorism Section, Intelligence Division, Federal Bureau of Investigation, U.S. Department of Justice, *Terrorism in the United States*, 1991, 4–5.

33. U.S. Department of Justice, "Eco-terrorists Indicted: Trio Foiled in Their Plot to Attack Government and Private Property," news release, 25 January 2006, available at sacramento.fbi.gov/dojpressrel/pressrel06/sc01252006.htm.

34. U.S. Department of Justice, "Eco-terror Indictments: Operation Backfire Nets 11," news release, 20 January 2006.

35. Bob Moser, "From the Belly of the Beast," *Intelligence Report* (Winter 2002). The indictment for Leo Felton and his girlfriend, Erica Chase, is available on the Memorial Institute for the Prevention of Terrorism (MIPT) Web site, www.tkb.org.

36. Counterterrorism Threat Assessment and Warning Unit, Counterrorism Division, Federal Bureau of Investigation, U.S. Department of Justice, *Terrorism in the United States,* 1999, 3.

37. The authors of this chapter have been directly involved with providing antiterrorism training to state and local law-enforcement agencies under the SLATT (state and local antiterrorism training) program. During training sessions, we emphasize that the threat of domestic terrorism has not disappeared. With the establishment of fusion centers in each state, there is an opportunity for additional resources—both investigative and analytical—to be devoted to addressing domestic extremist activity.

38. Research establishes that domestic terror organizations see the military as a source of training, weapons, and explosives. Investigations demonstrate that terrorist and antigovernment movements welcome members with military experience. Additionally, extremist group members have entered the armed forces explicitly to obtain training and access to explosives. As a result, the military criminal investigative organizations (Naval Criminal Investigative Service, Air Force Office of Special Investigations, Army Criminal Investigative Division) aggressively work jointly with the FBI to uncover, neutralize, and prosecute these cases.

39. *Imperial Hubris: Why the West Is Losing the War on Terror* (Washington, DC: Brassey's Inc., 2004); and Gunaratna, *Inside Al Qaeda.*

40. Marc Sageman, *Understanding Terror Networks* (Philadelphia: University of Pennsylvania Press, 2004).

41. Robert A. Pape, *Dying to Win: The Strategic Logic of Suicide Terrorism* (New York: Random House, 2005).

42. David J. Whittaker, *Terrorists and Terrorism in the Contemporary World* (London: Routledge Press, 2004).

43. Fawaz A. Gerges, *The Far Enemy: Why Jihad Went Global* (New York: Cambridge University Press, 2005); and Gilles Kepel, *Jihad: The Trail of Political Islam* (Cambridge: Harvard University Press, 2002).

44. Daniel Benjamin and Steven Simon, *The Next Attack: The Failure of the War on Terror and a Strategy for Getting It Right* (New York: Times Books, 2005).

45. Kathleen M. Blee, "Women and Organized Racial Terrorism in the United States," *Studies in Conflict and Terrorism* 28, no. 5 (September/October 2005). 421–33; Randy Borum and Chuck Tilby, "Anarchist Direct Actions: A Challenge for Law Enforcement," *Studies in Conflict and Terrorism* 28, no. 3 (May/June 2005): 201–23; Brad Whitsel, "Ideological Mutation and Millennial Belief in the American Neo-Nazi Movement," *Studies in Conflict and Terrorism* 24, no. 2 (April 2001): 89–106.

46. George Michael, "RAHOWA! A History of the World Church of the Creator," *Terrorism and Political Violence* 18, no. 4 (Winter 2006): 561–83; R. Jensen, "The United States, International Policing and the War against Anarchist Terrorism, 1900–1914," *Terrorism and Political Violence* 13, no. 1 (Spring 2001): 15–46; FBI, "Project Megiddo"; "The American Far Right and 9/11," *Terrorism and Political Violence* 15, no. 2 (Summer 2003): 96–111; Stefan H. Leader and Peter Probst, "The Earth Liberation Front and Environmental Terrorism," *Terrorism and Political Violence* 15, no. 4 (Winter 2003): 37–58; George Michael, "The Revolutionary Model of Dr. William L. Pierce," *Terrorism and Political Violence* 15, no. 3 (Autumn 2003): 62–80.

47. Exceptions include Daniel Levitas, *The Terrorist Next Door* (New York: Thomas Dunne Books, 2002); and Walter Laquer, "The Far Right," in *No End to War: Terrorism in the 21st Century* (New York: Continuum Publishers, 2003). For an excellent pre-9/11 treatment of domestic terrorism, see Brent L. Smith, *Terrorism in America: Pipe Bombs and Pipe Dreams* (New York: SUNY Press, 1994). A search of doctoral dissertation abstracts on the keyword "terrorism" from 2001–2006 identified 179 dissertations. Only six had domestic groups as their focus: John M. Cotter, "Societal Insecurity and the Reaction of Extremist Groups in Northern Ireland, Great Britain and the United States of America" (PhD diss., University of Kentucky, 2002); Kevin J. Cummings, "Terrorism, Democracy, and the Public Sphere: An Analysis of the Argumentation Surrounding the Oklahoma City Bombing" (PhD diss., University of Denver, 2004); Danny W. Davis, "Al-Qaeda and the Phineas Priesthood" (PhD diss., Texas A&M University, 2003); Eugenia K. Guilmartin, "An Empirical

Analysis of Right Wing Domestic Terrorism in the United States (1995–2001)" (PhD diss., Stanford University, 2002); David C. Lobb, "An Ivory Tower of Fear: Academics of the Racist Right" (PhD diss., Syracuse University, 2001); and George J. Michael, "The United States Response to Domestic Right Wing Terrorism and Extremism: A Government and NGO Partnership" (PhD diss., George Mason University, 2001). Interestingly, none centered upon left-wing or single-issue groups despite FBI congressional testimony since 2001 stating that some of these groups continue to operate in the United States and engage in a wide range of criminal activity.

48. Several works published shortly after the Oklahoma City bombing that explored the intricacies of the militia movement in the United States include Michael Barkun, *Religion and the Racist Right: The Origins of the Christian Identity Movement* (North Carolina: University of North Carolina Press, 1997); Robert L. Snow, *Terrorists among US: The Militia Threat* (Cambridge: Perseus Publishers, 1999); and Kenneth S. Stern, *A Force upon the Plain: The American Militia Movement and the Politics of Hate* (Oklahoma: University of Oklahoma Press, 1997).

49. There are myriad Web sites focused upon the terrorist phenomenon. Two that we consider useful for researchers and students are the National Memorial Institute for the Prevention of Terrorism, www.tkb.org, and the Terrorism Research Center, www.terrorism.com.

50. In the *National Military Strategic Plan for the War on Terror*, the enemy is described as a transnational movement of extremist organizations, networks, and individuals—and their state and nonstate supporters—that have in common that they exploit Islam and use terrorism for ideological ends. The al-Qa'ida Associated Movement (AQAM), comprised of al-Qa'ida and affiliated extremists, is the most dangerous present manifestation of such extremism.

51. See, for example, Section Chief James F. Jarboe, "The Threat of Eco-terrorism," testimony to the House Resources Committee, Subcommittee on Forests and Forest Health, 107th Cong., 2nd sess., 12 February 2002, available at www.fbi.gov/congress/congress02.htm; Deputy Assistant Director John E. Lewis, "Animal Rights Extremism and Eco-terrorism," statement to the Senate Judiciary Committee, 108th Cong., 2nd sess., 18 May 2004, available at www.fbi.gov/congress/congress04.htm; Deputy Assistant Director John E. Lewis, "Addressing the Threat of Animal Rights Extremism and Eco-Terrorism," statement to the Senate Committee on Environment and Public Works, 109th Cong., 1st sess., 18 May 2005, available at www.fbi.gov/congress/congress05.htm; and, finally, Deputy Assistant Director John E. Lewis, "Investigating and Preventing Animal Rights Extremism," statement to the Senate Committee on Environment and Public Works, 109th Cong. 1st sess., 26 October 2005, available at www.fbi.gov/congress/congress05.htm.

52. NARAL Pro-Choice America Foundation, "Clinic Violence and Intimidation," www.prochoiceamerica.org.

53. Ibid.

54. Avram Goldstein, "Doctor Quits, Cites Antiabortion Threats," *Washington Post*, 4 November 1999.

55. U.S. Department of Justice, "Eco-terror Indictments."

56. Lewis, "Investigating and Preventing Animal Rights Extremism."

57. Associated Press, "Animal Rights Group Guilty of Inciting Terror," 2 March 2006.

58. Jeffrey Gold "Group Concerned with Animal Suffering Blamed for Abuse of People," Associated Press, 2 March 2006.

59. Ibid.

60. Lewis, "Investigating and Preventing Animal Rights Extremism."

61. Edward Epstein, "Feinstein Pushes Tough Penalties for Animal Rights Violence," *San Francisco Chronicle,* 9 September 2006.

15 The Threat of Armed Street Gangs in America

Edward J. Maggio

INTRODUCTION

The current threats to our national security from armed street gangs are a real and a frightening reality. Gang organizations can develop from low-level criminal groups to become highly organized in structure with developed ideological views. What begins as a group of impressionable and alienated young adults forming gangs has the potential to evolve into widespread armed criminal organizations across numerous jurisdictions. To control and prevent the threats posed by armed street gangs, the common social development and psychology of such organizations must be fully explored. In particular, criminal organizations such as MS 13 and neo-Nazi-based/skinhead gangs must be understood, based on their activities, as evolving and moving toward the status of the hyperorganized armed groups with structures and belief systems. As street-gang membership in the United States has reached numbers estimated around 700,000, the threat to our communities cannot be ignored.[1] With key factors present, the movement from armed street gangs to organizations that create domestic threats to U.S. national security is quite possible.

ORIGINS

Throughout American history and the development of organized communities, there have been groups with different interests and activities outside the established mainstream society.[2] Often led by negatively controlling and charismatic leaders with different interests, they begin a process of claiming territory, while encouraging members of a

Professor Edward J. Maggio, Esq., is the professor of criminal justice at the New York Institute of Technology (NYIT) in Old Westbury, New York. Currently he lectures in courses covering numerous topics within the criminal justice, security, and criminology field. He is the youngest professor to ever be appointed to such a professorship within the Department of Behavioral Sciences. Professor Maggio has also served as an adjunct professor at Dowling College in Oakdale, New York, for the Department of Sociology. He has also lectured on narcotics and terrorism at Oxford University. Professor Maggio graduated Phi Beta Kappa and magna cum laude from Virginia Polytechnic Institute, where he earned a bachelor's degree in history focused on Middle Eastern/military studies and a bachelor's degree in political science. He completed his doctoral degree in law at the New York Law School. Maggio was invited to attend the law school at Oxford University in the United Kingdom, where he became one of the few Americans to graduate with a master of science degree in criminology and criminal justice after completing research at the Oxford University Centre for Criminology. Professor Maggio is frequently invited to speak about criminal justice/security topics on college campuses, at business events, and in different communities around the world along with working on publications to raise awareness of developments in the criminal justice/counterterrorism field.

social group to engage in deviant acts.[3] It has been difficult, if not impossible, in the twenty-first century, as it has been in the past, to develop an all-encompassing definition of such social organizations that ultimately emerge as gangs within American society. When individuals with a negative purpose begin to assemble on a regular basis, they are first seen as a distinct cluster by the members of a given community.[4] Once assembled, the newly formed members begin to engage in activities that result in a negative response from the authorities and community at large. A labeling process and a new negative identity then become adopted by the assembled group as it moves toward learning new forms of criminal behavior.[5]

All assemblies of young people in the United States go through this process whether they are Caucasian or part of a minority population, such as African Americans or Hispanics. Regardless of race, gangs thrive when certain conditions in a community are present. Young people existing in a working- and lower-class population, whether rural or urban, are potential gang members of the future.[6] An area of the nation with continuous poverty, low education rates, and decreased social opportunities also can raise the potential for street gangs to emerge.[7] The neighborhoods from which individual members of gangs originate have a strong psychological impact on the lives of young people. Impoverished neighborhoods where young people dwell can create an atmosphere in which they feel opportunities for advancement and respect are nonexistent, especially if they are young people who are first-generation Americans.[8] A "left behind" culture develops among potential and current gang members as others find ways to move up the economic and social ladders. Having little option or support from family, schools, or other social influences, the remaining young people are pulled together in a social vacuum struggling to find some identity among themselves.[9] The quality of home life and a sense of group identity are crucial factors in youth development.

Juvenile gang delinquency and criminal behavior are a result of poor socialization and an inability to accept the rules of society. The child is exposed to cultural and societal expectations by agents of socialization—parents and family, the schools, peers, the media, religion—that should influence a young person to act in accordance with the law and ethical societal norms. The socialization that takes place at an early stage in a child's life is known as primary socialization. The primary influence on young people is parents and the immediate family.[10] The key here is that primary socialization is not always successful, as many families fail to properly socialize their children.[11] When the parenting of a child is inadequate, a child's maturation process may potentially be damaged and the end result is antisocial or criminal behavior by the young person.[12] Over time many young people develop voids in their social developments that are ultimately filled by negative or socially undesirable beliefs and behaviors. If a young adult is devoid of opportunities for advancement and the possibility to earn respect and develop an identity/purpose in his or her life, in addition to missing positive social influences the young adult is left vulnerable to filling these voids through socially undesirable outlets. Gang culture is one realm in which these voids may be filled in a relatively immediate manner for these young adults. It gives them a sense of belonging, identity, and a purpose.[13] It creates an earlier social purpose of being part of a society of "us versus them" struggling to exist in an unfriendly and unforgiving environment.

It is also possible to describe the situation in terms of social disabilities. Social disabilities are manifested behaviors that are socially disabling and unacceptable. This is a key notion in what fosters gang behavior since in normal society, social disabilities effectively lower a person's self-esteem and make one view society negatively.[14] It can lead to a decreased participation in healthy social environments, such as school and community functions, thus resulting in outward rebellion against parents, teachers, police officers, and all those with authority. This also leads to an increased dependence on the acceptance of the gang and fuels any activity that might help the individual's status within the gang.[15]

A gang is any group of individuals who gather for an illicit purpose.[16] However, when rules, leadership, customs, and punishments become established and practiced within a gang organization, such a gang can now develop into what can be classified as an ethnic street power organization that terrorizes a local community, or "thug-life street gang," such as the Bloods, Crips, Latin Kings, or MS-13. The word "thug," from the Hindustani word for deception, came from the original "Thugee" Indian thief terror gang. It is interesting to note that the Thugee gang provides us with an early example of an organized domestic terror gang whose psychological makeup was no different from that of current "thug-life street gangs."[17] A gang that doesn't reach the heights of becoming a major street power organization may develop and organize into a powerful street-based racial hate gang such as the current neo-Nazi/skinhead organizations.

A group of delinquents who evolve their organization from a small group of juvenile delinquents into a budding thug-life street gang or a racial hate gang actually change the makeup of the gang in order to grow. Like an onion, most thug-life street gangs or racial hate gangs develop into layers. At the center is the leader(s) of a gang who determines at what level of criminal activity the gang will function and what strategic criminal objectives need to be accomplished in a given area. Characteristics of the leader(s) are reflected in the day-to-day criminal activities of the gang. The leader is all-powerful. The next layer is the hard-core gang members. They are usually the older gang members, the individuals who are culturally and criminally enmeshed in the gang and are at risk of being so for life. Most violent gang activity and crime, as well as the majority of recruiting of young people, emanate from this portion of the gang organization. Hard core gang members usually make up about 10–15 percent of the total gang membership.[18] This is followed by the associate gang members, who have usually made a personal commitment to the gang culture and are dedicated to achieving the level of recognition needed to attain hard-core status. The next level is the fringe level of gang participation. The fringe gang member is still able to function outside of the gang structure and has not made a total commitment to a life in the criminal gang culture. This type of member drifts in and out of the gang and seems to lack direction. The final level of gang membership is entry-level, or "wannabe," caste. It is important to understand that "wannabe" personnel are not actually gang members. They are youth who view the gang as an exciting place to be, a place where they could become "somebody" on the street. They are viewed as the future members of the gangs.[19] Wannabes may emulate gang dress, graffiti, hand signs, and other gang cultural symbols, and they may associate with known gang members, but they have not yet been accepted fully into the gang. Therefore they may in engage in violent acts like the hard-core members in order to prove themselves.

Each layer of a developed street gang has been found in general to have differences in measured intelligence, impulse control, school performance, and group dependence. It is interesting to note the organizational parallel between a street gang and the military. Rank, structure, and clothing indicators are important in understanding the power structure and allegiance to a group within both military units and street gangs.[20]

With such a structure in place, rules and customs set by the leader(s) allow the gang to develop its culture and propaganda, which serve as an alluring attractive force for a young person looking to fill the voids in his or her life. As the culture and image of the gang develop, the gang is able to recruit in an organized fashion through the efforts of the hard-core members through seduction. For a long time gangs have used this technique to recruit new members. They create glorified fraternal myths about the gang that are very attractive to young recruits, and very often these myths become the foundation for young recruits.[21] For a group such as MS-13 or the neo-Nazi street gang, an easily communicated "us versus them" emotional appeal is a powerful recruiting and selling point on the merits of such organizations. Many armed gangs take the "obligation approach" by teaching young people that joining the gang helps the community.[22] The most powerful of these trappings, however, are the promises of money, sex, and glamour. The symbols of the gang (the graffiti, hand signs, colors, tattoos, clothing, etc.) can create a visual attraction for young people. Young people realize that with these symbols they are part of something organized and powerful. Parties are also very useful ways for recruiters to seduce young people into the gang. At the party they have fun, come under the influence of alcohol and drugs, and believe the rhetoric they are bombarded with by other gang members. In other cases, street gangs may use a coercive approach to recruitment through intimidation.[23] Coercion and intimidation tactics may also include both physical and psychological tactics.[24]

For hate-based street gangs, we must make a major differentiation from other street gangs. All major established gangs have similar recruiting, structure, and psychological differences depending on the membership status of the individual in the group. However, hate-based groups have a focus on extreme hatred of a particular group in society and a greater social belief system in the "us versus them" attitude. This is notable in terms of the development of the belief structure of this type of group, which goes beyond a need to fill voids; instead it pushes them toward adopting and adhering to reactionary, racist, or anti-Semitic ideology.[25]

FROM STREET GANG TO ORGANIZED ARMED GROUP

The tougher stage of development from a local street gang to an organized armed group can be explored with an understanding that a thug-life street gang or hate-based gang can move toward a much more violent and dangerous extremist organization. The terms "extremist" and "radical" are often used to label those who advocate for or use violence against the will of the larger social body, but they are also used by some to describe those who advocate for or use violence to enforce their wills on the social body, such as a government or majority constituency.[26] It is important to note that street gangs are not usually considered extremist organizations since the common perception is that they do not take a position in the realm of politics, while they place their focus on profit from illegal criminal enterprises or local power struggles on the street. In reality, upon reaching a high point in its development, a developing street gang does reach a political stage in terms of influencing the culture in a neighborhood and can challenge legitimate democratic institutions for the purpose of protecting the values of the gang organization and its ability to engage in illegal activities. Street gangs also began as youths who were the outsiders in the community and soon realized that the armed muscle of their organization could demonstrate power on many scales. Once a group has reached significant power through acquiring money, weapons, and a large number of members, it can now fully influence the political and cultural environments of its location for its own benefit. For example, the thug-life street gang the "Crips" was a rebirth of a gang previously called "The Cribs," founded in Los Angeles, California, in 1969 by 15-year-old Raymond Washington and Stanley "Tookie" Wilson. Washington initially called the gang the "Baby Avenues" or "Cribs" in an attempt to emulate older gangs and activities carried out by the politically active Black Panthers organization.[27] While the origins of the name "Crips" is not clearly known, it has been suggested by many that the gang's name change from "Cribs" to "Crips" was made to reflect the new abbreviated motto and status of the gang when it reached a point of power as a "Community Revolution in Progress."[28]

When a group goes from a street gang to an armed organization with extremist characteristics, it is also clear that the research within the walls of such a group is extremely limited. While a totally all-encompassing theory is impossible to build, the Federal Bureau of Investigation (FBI) bulletin for law enforcement has described the seven stages of hate that help show the evolution from a small gang to a fully developed armed and organized criminal group. These seven stages, while developed to understand extremist groups, are easily applicable in understanding the development from a formation point early in the history of the gang to the execution of its goals as a major armed street organization.

Stage 1

Hate is an emotional fire that often goes cold over time. To maintain a constant state of hatred requires a constant rekindling of hate that is accomplished much more easily in a group surrounding. Irrational haters seldom hate alone. They feel compelled, almost driven, to entreat others to hate as they do. Groups, besides rekindling hate, also provide peer validation, which bolsters a sense of self-worth while at the same time preventing introspection that reveals personal insecurities. Frustrated and angry, individuals that are otherwise ineffective as threats to others now become empowered when they join groups that also provide anonymity and diminished accountability for criminal hatred-driven actions.[29] The hatred against police, the community, and rival gangs can be constantly maintained by key members in a gang in order to keep personnel motivated and loyal to the gang.

Stage 2

A gang can form identities through symbols, rituals, and mythologies that enhance the members' status as having power while degrading the people who are a source of their hate. For example, skinhead groups may adopt the swastika, the Iron Cross, the

Confederate flag, and other supremacist symbols. Thug-life street gangs such as the Bloods or Crips use hand signals and specific graffiti symbols. Group-specific symbols or clothing often differentiate hate groups from original street gangs looking for money and respect.[30] Group rituals, such as secret hand signals and secret greetings, further fortify members as members of an almost mystical and religious organization.[31] Gangs then incorporate some form of self-sacrifice to their codes, which allows members to willingly jeopardize their well-beings for the greater good of the causes. Giving one's life to a cause provides the ultimate sense of value and worth to life to an individual that has fallen for ideology. Skinheads and neo-Nazi organizations often see themselves as soldiers in a race war and potential martyrs for the cause of a pure white race. Likewise Hispanic street gangs such as MS-13 or the Latin Kings foster the belief that they must strive against a white America that is denying them true liberty and opportunities.

Stage 3

Hate is the sustenance that emotionally and psychologically binds haters to one another and to a common cause. By constantly verbally debasing the object of their hate, haters enhance their self-images as powerful, as well as their groups' status as legitimate. Graffiti, for example, on buildings done by thug-life street gangs is demonstrative of this point. In fact, researchers have found that the more often a person thinks about aggression, the greater the chance for aggressive behavior to occur in a given society.[32] Thus, after constant verbal denigration of members of the community or rival gangs, the gang members in an organization progress to the next stage of development.

Stage 4

Hate, by its nature, changes incrementally. Time cools the emotionally charged fire of hate, thus forcing the hater to look inward toward him- or herself. To avoid introspection, leaders of a gang or the hard-core gang members may use ever-increasing degrees of rhetoric and violence to maintain high levels of agitation and anger. Taunts and offensive gestures serve this purpose. In this stage, again using skinheads as an example, they typically shout racial slurs from moving cars or from afar. The hand signals and graffiti by thug-life street gangs or hate-based groups that use Nazi salutes often accompany comments toward the targets of hate. Most gangs claim control of turf proximate to the neighborhoods in which they dwell. One study indicated that a majority of gang-related crimes occur when a gang member of a target group travels through the group's perceived turf.[33]

Stage 5

This stage is critical because it differentiates vocally abusive gang members from physically abusive ones. In this stage, the group becomes more aggressive, prowling its area seeking vulnerable targets. Violence unites a gang and further isolates it from mainstream society. Gangs, almost without exception, attack in groups and target single victims where opportunity for success is likely. Research has shown that physical violence and the element of thrill seeking are rampant in young delinquents. Researchers have found that 60 percent of hate offenders were "thrill seekers."[34] The adrenaline "high" intoxicates the attackers. The initial adrenaline surge lasts for several minutes; however, the effects of adrenaline keep the body in a state of heightened alert for up to several days. Each successive anger-provoking thought or action builds on residual adrenaline and triggers a more violent response than the one that originally initiated the sequence of attack. Anger builds on more anger. The adrenaline high combined with hate becomes a deadly combination when directed at a target. Hard-core members of gangs often keep themselves at a level where the slightest provocation triggers aggression toward others.[35]

Stage 6

Several studies confirm that a large number of attacks involve weapons. Some attackers use firearms to commit crimes, but some attackers prefer weapons, such as broken bottles, baseball bats, blunt objects, screwdrivers, and belt buckles, that increase the level of injuries on victims. These types of weapons require the attacker to be in close proximity to the victim, which further demonstrates the depth of personal anger, as opposed to discharging firearms at a distance, thus avoiding personal contact. Close-in onslaughts require the assailants to see their victims eye-to-eye and to become bloodied during the assault. Hands-on violence allows groups to express their hate toward the intended targets in a way a gun cannot. Personal contact empowers and fulfills a deep-seated need to have dominance over a target.

Stage 7

The ultimate goal of people with hatred in a gang is to destroy the object of their hate. Mastery over life and death imbues the hater with feelings of omnipotence and power. With this power comes a great sense of self-worth and value. These are the very qualities that group members lack and have desired from the beginning when they first associated with a local gang. However, in reality, hate physically and psychologically destroys both the hater and the target.[36] As more and more members of a gang go through these stages, the more the organization gets dedicated members that will help the organization grow and engage in more daring criminal acts as well as recruit new members for the future.

A LOOK AT ARMED SKINHEAD AND NEO-NAZI GANGS

Extremism in any organization serves as an emotional outlet for severe feelings being experienced by a person. In examining Nazi-doctrine-based gangs such as the skinheads or neo-Nazi organizations, we can see a clearer development of organizations that are becoming more sophisticated and closer toward dangerous groups capable of organized attacks and security breaches in American society.

Skinheads and neo-Nazi organizations began as gangs based primarily on hate and may in fact not necessarily have particular neighborhoods or turfs that they feel a need to defend.[37] In terms of contemporary American history, early skinhead and Nazi-based gangs focused on hatred toward African American and Jewish citizens. However, in the early 1970s such groups did not per se believe in Nazism and Nazi doctrine.[38] Skinhead groups in the 1970s in the United States were a developed offshoot from skinhead punk rock groups in Britain and were considered just local nuisances by law enforcement groups. In the later twentieth century, skinheads were at one point the visible foot soldiers for more organized neo-Nazi groups that did adopt Nazi doctrine as valid. Many of these politically focused Nazi-doctrine groups, such as the White Aryan Resistance

Group, the National Alliance, the Church of the Creator, and the New Order, have imploded and collapsed with the arrest of their leaders by the end of 2004.[39] This has left many skinheads on their own to form local gangs. It is likely at this time that skinhead and neo-Nazi gangs that are growing in vast numbers are in a free-for-all phase with new and unaffiliated street gangs proliferating rapidly.[40] Groups such as the Hammerskin Nation and the Vinlanders are consolidating skinhead and neo-Nazi gang members across the country, establishing a uniform code of appearances and conduct to avoid detection as more young people are engaging in gang activity in smaller groups.[41] Today's skinhead and neo-Nazi gang members are more violent and more technically savvy, using the Internet to organize and grow. While an established gang is dangerous, newly emerging skinhead and neo-Nazi gangs and wannabes that wish to join them are unknown to local law enforcement and the federal government. Such young adults are looking to prove their worth and are likely to engage in more violent acts than seen previously. Additionally adult members of such organizations now indoctrinate young people toward the worship of "Holy Father Hitler" and include a religious component of their organization that is impressed strongly upon young adults. Adult members teach the younger members that their violence and views toward minorities and Jews is the first step toward the revolutionary creation of a fascist political state, or "Fourth Reich," in America. Such a movement in America would strip all nonwhite citizens of constitutional protections and deport immigrants and foreign nationals. Each of these young adults is a virtual "human hand grenade" waiting to go off in a neighborhood or toward law enforcement personnel as more hate-based gangs emerge and grow both in size and in the nature of their criminal activities. Hate-based gangs in particular have now found a way to have an edge over thug-life street gangs, which jeopardizes our national security.

THE HIDDEN DANGER WITHIN THE RANKS

With the pressing need to meet recruiting goals for the U.S. armed services, the current rush to get new recruits has allowed neo-Nazi street gangs a new opportunity. Neo-Nazi groups dream of a race war, counterrevolution, and violence among the U.S. population. Serving in the U.S. military offers the members of these groups a new opportunity to learn new fighting skills to enhance their hate-based street organizations. Adult leaders of hate-based street gangs encourage younger members to enlist in the U.S. military. The possibility of receiving advanced training and having access to weapons is guaranteed according to a 1998 study commissioned by the Department of Defense.[42]

Soldiers are trained to be skilled and proficient with military weapons and intense combat tactics and to understand organized violence on the battlefield. The reality is that military recruiters and base commanders around the world are looking the other way at suspected hate-based-street-gang members in the ranks. Although there is a need to bend to pressure to keep the ranks filled, once hate-based street gangs have made it inside a unit, they begin to use the Internet and other methods of communication to link up with fellow members.[43] Military investigators have uncovered an online network of 57 skinhead/neo-Nazi gang members who are also active-duty military personnel notably at Fort Lewis, Fort Hood, Fort Bragg, Fort Stewart, and Camp Pendleton.[44] Department of Defense gang detective Scott Barfield noted in *Intelligence Report* the rise of hate-based-gang graffiti in Baghdad, noting that when it comes to such activity that is blatantly out in the open, "That's a problem."[45] When hate-based-street-gang members return to the United States or from a local base, they are now fit and trained and possess established contacts of colleagues that are all over the country. Such gang members by themselves hurt military readiness, unit cohesion, and morale by being in the ranks. It is not surprising that other street gangs such as the Crips, Bloods, and Latin Kings are now following suit and have their members joining the ranks of our military to balance the power on the streets of America. The potential time bomb of gang violence in the future is staggering to even imagine. However, while hate-based groups may be posing a threat in American communities and within U.S. military units, there is one thug-life street gang that has reached a point of development that can only be described using one word—epidemic.

MS-13—THE MOST DANGEROUS GANG IN AMERICA

Of all the thug-life street and ethnic-based street gangs operating within America, there is no question that MS-13 is a major leader. With violent killings and criminal activity committed by this Los Angeles–based street gang at an all-time high, MS-13 has gone from obscurity to infamous notoriety.[46] It is considered the fastest-growing, most violent, and least understood of the nation's armed street gangs. With the focus on the war on terrorism by federal law enforcement, the past few years have allowed this unique gang to reach an estimated size of 8,000 to 10,000 members in 33 states, and tens of thousands in Central America.[47] Membership worldwide is believed to exceed 100,000 members.[48]

Origins of MS-13

Composed mostly of Salvadorans and other Central Americans, MS-13 began in the 1980s by children fleeing the civil war in El Salvador.[49] Once arriving in the United States from the violent turmoil of El Salvador, they quickly faced new violence from Mexican gangs in the inner-city Los Angeles neighborhoods. El Salvadorans soon responded by banding together as groups of young people in a "*mara*," or small gang unit, composed of *salvatruchas*, or street-hardened El Salvadorans.[50] The number 13 was added as a number signifying southern California to officially mark the emergence of the "wild El Salavadorans" of southern California. As El Salvadoran, and later Central American, youth found more opposition from Mexican gangs and economic opportunities to advance in their hometowns, MS-13 began to seek out former El Salvadoran paramilitaries that had received military training.[51] It is important to note that many of the paramilitaries were possibly trained or received their weapons from U.S. personnel during the 1980s.[52] This recruitment of paramilitaries is key because it changed the organization from a low-level street gang to an organization that was disciplined enough to engage in extortion and drug trafficking across different borders.[53]

As MS-13 began to grow and begin operating in the New York City, Los Angeles, and Washington, DC, areas, the initial response by the federal government was to employ the FBI and Immigration Customs Enforcement (ICE) officers in using immigration laws as an antigang measure. The FBI and ICE worked together to deport hundreds of the gang members since most hard-core gang members were undocumented aliens. Members returning to El Salvador or their nations of origin responded by reorganizing themselves abroad and created outposts for MS-13 in El Salvador, Honduras, and Guatemala.[54] To the surprise of federal law enforcement, deported members returned to the United States together with new recruits to spread through the United States in different locations. In addition MS-13 has allowed different races to join the gang organization in an effort to overpower other existing thug-life street gangs or local street-gang organizations. The organization has leaders in a given area, but one MS-13 clique in a city doesn't have complete authority over other MS-13 groups operating in distant locations. Local MS-13 units, or "*clicas*" have local leaders and treasurers who answer to the leaders of MS-13, but otherwise the local MS-13 groups operate independently.[55] With no clear hierarchy or structure to the entire organization, it is difficult to contain the organization, since making an arrest of one leader doesn't put a command/control dent in the organization as a whole as it does in the case of organized crime groups such as the Italian Mafia. Taking out the heart of the leadership is very hard when combating MS-13 if there is no definitive leadership for the organization as a whole.[56] According to the *Washington Times*, MS-13 "is thought to have established a major smuggling center" in Mexico that has helped the rise of cocaine distribution in the country at this time.[57] There are also numerous reports that MS-13 members have been sent to Arizona to target border guards and Minuteman Project volunteers.[58] Today MS-13 criminal activities at last count include international drug smuggling and sales, black-market gun sales, human trafficking, assassinations for hire, theft, and assaults on law enforcement officials. With the rapid increase of money and power, MS-13 may now in fact be moving toward a national command structure for all MS-13 cliques in the United States. According to a 2004 report by the National Drug Intelligence Center, MS-13 "may be increasing its coordination with MS-13 chapters in Los Angeles, Washington, D.C./Northern Virginia, and New York City, possibly signaling an attempt to build a national command structure."[59] On New York's Long Island, in 2003, an MS-13 leader arrived from the West Coast to try to organize these various cliques or sets into a more formal structure.[60] In northern Virginia, U.S. attorney Paul McNulty observed that "in some of the violent crimes occurring in the area, there seems to be a kind of approval process in some kind of hierarchy beyond the clique."[61] If MS-13 is indeed moving toward a national command structure for the gang, it is likely to be emulating its model in El Salvador. The El Salvador clique is highly organized and disciplined, with a vertical command structure. As a result, its criminal operations are more efficient and profitable.[62] MS-13 stands on the verge of merging into one of the most formidable organizations local law enforcement and federal authorities are likely to ever combat as the gang grows in the coming years.

CONCLUSION

Armed street gangs are no longer a growing social problem faced by only local law enforcement agencies and community leaders. Such armed groups will continue to pose a security threat for our nation as they grow, evolve, and engage in more unthinkable criminal practices. By infiltrating the armed forces of the United States and engaging in organized transnational criminal activities, the future of violence within American communities will be shaped by armed street gangs.

NOTES

1. Tim Delaney, *American Street Gangs* (Upper Saddle River, NJ: Prentice Hall, 2006).

2. Ibid.

3. Herbert Ashbury, "The Gangs of New York," in *Gangs*, ed. Sean Donohue (Knopf, 1927; New York: Thunder's Mouth Press, 2002).

4. Albert Cohen, *Delinquent Boys: The Culture of the Gang* (New York: Free Press, 1955).

5. Frank Williams and Marilyn McShane, *Criminological Theory* (Englewood Cliffs, NJ: Prentice Hall, 1994).

6. Randall Shelden, Sharon Tracy, and William Brown, *Youth Gangs in American Society* (Belmont, CA: Wadsworth, 2001).

7. Peter Kratcoski and Lucille Dunn Kratcoski, *Juvenile Delinquency,* 4th ed. (Upper Saddle River, NJ: Prentice Hall, 1996).

8. Lori Duffy, "Experts Say Gangs Offer Acceptance," *Syracuse Post-Standard*, 7 November 1996, A16.

9. Delaney, *American Street Gangs.*

10. Tim Delaney, *Community, Sport, and Leisure* (Auburn, NY: Legend Books, 2001).

11. Felix Padilla, *The Gang as an American Enterprise* (New Brunswick, NJ: Rutgers University Press, 1992).

12. Ibid.

13. James Vigil, "Learning from Gangs: The Mexican American Experience," *Eric Digest,* 1997, available at www.cd.gov/databases/ERIC_Digests.

14. Larry Siegel, Brandon C. Welsh, and Joseph J. Senna, *Juvenile Delinquency,* 8th ed. (Belmont, CA: Wadsworth, 2003).

15. William Thorton and Lydia Voight, *Delinquency and Justice,* 3rd ed. (New York: McGraw-Hill, 1992).

16. Delaney, *American Street Gangs.*

17. Lou Savelli, "Introduction to East Coast Gangs," National Alliance of Gang Investigators' Associations, www.nagia.org/Gang%20Articles/East%20Coast%20Gangs.htm.

18. I. Reiner, *Gangs, Crime, and Violence in Los Angeles: Findings and Proposals from the District Attorney's Office* (Arlington, VA: National Youth Gang Information Center, 1992).

19. Ibid.

20. Eric Schneider, *Vampire, Dragons, and Egyptian Kings: Youth Gangs in Postwar New York* (Princeton, NJ: Princeton University Press, 1999).

21. Delaney, *American Street Gangs.*

22. Martin Sanchez Jankowski, *Islands in the Streets: Gangs and American Urban Society* (Berkeley: University of California Press, 1991).

23. Ibid.

24. Shelden, Tracy, and Brown, *Youth Gangs in American Society.*

25. Delaney, *American Street Gangs.*

26. John George and Laird Wilcox, *Nazis, Communists, Klansmen, and Others on the Fringe: Political Extremism in America* (Prometheus Books, 1992).

27. *Street Gangs: A Secret History,* DVD (A&E Home Video, 2001).

28. Ibid.

29. John R. Schafer and Joe Navarro, "The Seven-Stage Hate Model: The Psychopathology of Hate Groups," *FBI Law Enforcement Bulletin,* March 2003.

30. Delaney, *American Street Gangs.*

31. Schafer and Navarro, "The Seven-Stage Hate Model."

32. Ibid.

33. Ibid.

34. Ibid.

35. Ibid.

36. Ibid.

37. Delaney, *American Street Gangs.*

38. Jack Moore, *Skinheads Shaved for Battle* (Bowling Green, OH: Bowling Green State University Press, 1993).

39. Mark Anderson and Mark Jenkins, *Dance of the Days* (New York: Soft Skull Press, 2001).

40. "Center Report Details Dangerous Shifts in Racist Skinhead Movement," *SPLC Report* 36, no. 4 (December 2006).

41. Ibid.

42. Mark Falacks and Martin Wiskoff, *Gangs, Extremists Groups, and the Military: Screening for Service,* A155953 (Monterey, CA: Security Research Center, 1998).

43. David Holthouse, "A Few Bad Men," Southern Poverty Law Center, available at www.splcenter.org/intel/news/item.jsp?aid=66.

44. "Center Report Exposes Racist Extremists Active in Military," *SPLC Report* 36, no. 3 (September 2006).

45. Ibid.

46. Dan Rather, "The Fight against MS-13," *60 Minutes,* CBS, 4 December 2005, available at www.cbs.com.

47. Arian Campo-Flores, "The Most Dangerous Gang in America," *Newsweek,* 28 March 2006.

48. Mandalit del Barco, "The International Reach of the Mara Salvatrucha," *All Things Considered,* National Public Radio, 17 March 2005.

49. Tom Hayden, *Street Wars: Gangs and the Future of Violence* (New York: New Press, 2004).

50. See Campo-Flores, "The Most Dangerous Gang in America."

51. Ibid.

52. Hayden, *Street Wars.*

53. Ibid.

54. Campo-Flores, "The Most Dangerous Gang in America."

55. Delaney, *American Street Gangs.*

56. Hayden, *Street Wars.*

57. Jerry Seper, "100 Members of Street Gang Arrested in U.S. Sweep," *Washington Times,* 15 March 2005.

58. Jerry Seper, "Gang Will Target Minuteman Vigil on Mexico Border," *Washington Times,* 28 March 2005.

59. Hayden, *Street Wars.*

60. Ibid.

61. Ibid.

62. Ibid.

16 Prosecuting Homegrown Extremists: Case Study of the Virginia "Paintball Jihad" Cell

Steven Emerson

INTRODUCTION

The United States is a country with a population that is deeply diverse religiously and ethnically. All nationalities and religious groups have a presence here, many maintaining distinct ties to communities and countries abroad. Normally, this situation is not only harmless but often beneficial to the American fabric. However, since Osama bin Laden's notorious February 1998 *fatwa*[1]—an Islamic religious proclamation—declaring war on the United States, certain elements within American society have awoken, as Bin Laden's call to jihad—and other similar fatwas from a variety of radical sources—have been heard by individuals and cells, and even, sometimes, answered.

In 1993, foreign Islamic extremists attacked the World Trade Center, killing six people and injuring more than a thousand.[2] And in 2001, another cell of Middle Eastern born Islamic terrorists finished the job, destroying the Twin Towers and severely damaging the Pentagon, in the worst terrorist attack in American history, killing nearly 3,000 people. But while the most "successful" attacks against American interests have been perpetrated by foreign jihadists, more than a handful of American citizens have sought to take up arms against their own country, or to go off to battle foreign allies, in the name of divinely ordained holy war.

While the phenomenon of an American-born and -bred Islamic suicide bomber has thankfully yet to occur, various American Muslims have in fact taken up arms against their own country, or trained to do just that, while still others have joined their *mujahideen*

Steven Emerson is an internationally recognized expert on terrorism and national security and considered one of the leading world authorities on Islamic extremist networks, financing, and operations. He now serves as the executive director of the Investigative Project on Terrorism, one of the world's largest archival data and intelligence institutes on Islamic and Middle Eastern terrorist groups. Mr. Emerson has testified and briefed Congress dozens of times on terrorist financing and operational networks of al-Qaeda, Hamas, Hezbollah, Islamic Jihad, and the rest of the worldwide Islamic militant spectrum. He and his organization have been quoted or profiled in hundreds of newspaper and television stories since 9/11. Mr. Emerson is recognized as having been the first and only terrorist expert to have testified and warned about the threat of Islamic militant networks operating in the United States and their connections worldwide. Mr. Emerson has authored or coauthored six books: *Jihad Incorporated* (Prometheus, 2006), *American Jihad: The Terrorists Living among Us* (Free Press, 2002), *Terrorist: The Inside Story of the Highest-Ranking Iraqi Terrorist Ever to Defect to the West* (Villard/Random House, 1991), *The Fall of Pan Am 103: Inside the Lockerbie Investigation* (Putnam, 1990), *Secret Warriors: Inside the Covert Military Operations of the Reagan Era* (Putnam, 1988), and *The American House of Saud: The Secret Petrodollar Connection* (Franklin Watts, 1985).

—or Islamic holy warriors—comrades overseas in fighting that does not involve the United States at all.

The best-known case of an American *mujahid* is that of John Walker Lindh, the so-called American Taliban, the District of Columbia–born student who went to Afghanistan on a spiritual journey and ended up joining the military forces of the Taliban regime to fight the U.S. military after its post-9/11 invasion of Afghanistan.

The phenomenon of American-based jihadists (whether born and bred, converts, or immigrants) has created new challenges for our legal system, as prosecutors and legislators wrestle with issues stemming from investigating, detaining, and prosecuting Islamist terrorists and fighters before they act on their violent, and criminal, desires.

As a corollary to such legal challenges, another battle is being waged—in the court of public opinion. Almost every instance in which authorities arrest or investigate individuals and organizations on charges related to Islamist terrorism, a cadre of America's own Muslim Brotherhood front organizations, presenting themselves as "civil rights" and "advocacy" groups, enter the fray, proclaiming the innocence of the government's target, often writing press releases and holding press conferences to that effect, denouncing investigations and arrests as "Islamophobic" or "anti-Muslim witch hunts."

As strategies mature and develop for investigating and prosecuting terrorists, approaches to combat the disinformation campaigns and pressure tactics applied by domestic Islamist groups on behalf of defendants need to evolve as well.

PRIMARY LEGAL ISSUES AND STRATEGIES

Lindh was captured on the battlefield and brought back to the United States, specifically to the Eastern District of Virginia, and brought to trial. Intuitively, one would surmise that Lindh was an ideal candidate to be charged with treason, having taken up arms against his own countrymen. Article III of the Constitution defines the crime thus: "Treason against the United States, shall consist only in levying War against them, or in adhering to their Enemies, giving them Aid and Comfort."[3]

However, actual treason cases are notoriously hard to prove and are rarely brought by the federal government as the second part of the treason clause states, "No Person shall be convicted of Treason unless on the Testimony of two Witnesses to the same overt Act, or on Confession in open Court."[4] Because of the difficulties of prosecuting a treason charge, Congress has devised numerous statutes to apply specifically to terrorism, notably the "material support" statute housed in Title 18, Section 2339 of the U.S. Criminal Code.

The government has also resorted to tried-and-true strategies, similar to those used against organized crime, going after known terrorists and accomplices on charges of perjury and obstruction of justice, and has also employed novel—and arguably controversial—strategies, including trying one notable defendant on charges of "soliciting others to wage war against the United States" and "counseling others to engage in a conspiracy to levy War against the United States," both of which will be outlined below.

Specifically, in lay terms, although Lindh clearly had engaged in "levying War against" the United States, as well as in adhering, and giving aid and comfort, to our enemies, he was not charged as such. Instead, federal prosecutors charged Lindh with providing material support and resources, and conspiracy to provide material support and resources, to al Qaeda and the Taliban, as well as other non-terrorism-related, yet serious, charges such as conspiracy to commit murder, and using and carrying firearms and destructive devices during crimes of violence.[5]

Lindh ended up pleading guilty to the counts involving assisting the Taliban and the weapons charges, and was sentenced to 20 years in prison.[6] Lindh stipulated to the following pertinent facts:

> In or about late May or June 2001, the defendant reported to the Dar ul-Anan Headquarters of the Mujahideen in Kabul, Afghanistan, which was used as a Taliban recruiting center. The defendant told personnel at that facility that he was an American and that he wanted to go to the front lines to fight.

> In or about late May or June 2001, the defendant agreed to attend a training camp for additional and extensive military training. In or about June 2001, the defendant traveled to the al-Farooq training camp, a facility associated with Usama Bin Laden, located several hours west of Kandahar, in Afghanistan. In or about June and July 2001, the defendant remained at the al-Farooq camp and participated fully in its training activities, including courses in weapons, orienteering, navigation, explosives and battlefield combat.

> Having sworn allegiance to jihad, in or about July or August 2001, after completing his training, the defendant traveled to Kabul, Afghanistan to assist the Taliban. In or about July or August 2001, the defendant carried an AKM rifle issued by the Taliban while he traveled, together with approximately 150 non-Afghani fighters, from Kabul to the front line in Takhar, in northeastern Afghanistan. Between about September and November, 2001, the defendant's fighting group was divided into smaller groups, and rotated in one to two week shifts in the Takhar trenches, opposing Northern Alliance troops.

> In or about July 2001 to November 2001, during the commission of a felony which may be prosecuted in a court of the United States, namely, Supplying Services to the Taliban as charged in Count Nine of the Indictment, the defendant knowingly carried with him an AKM rifle and two grenades.

> The defendant's supplying services to the Taliban, by fighting in support of the Taliban, constituted a felony that involved, or was intended to promote, a federal crime of terrorism within the meaning of U.S.S.G. § 3A1.4, in that the Taliban's control of Afghanistan, and the activities of those individuals fighting in support of the Taliban, provided protection and sanctuary to al Qaeda, a designated foreign terrorist organization.[7]

And while the case of the American Taliban might seem shocking, he is hardly alone. Other individuals and cells from other communities, of varying ethnic and religious backgrounds, have taken up arms—or trained to—against U.S. forces in foreign theaters, or joined various mujahideen in other holy wars, and, for the most part, federal prosecutors have handled such cases in a similar manner.

In the Pacific Northwest, the "Portland Seven" cell members, a mix of natural-born Muslims and converts, were convicted on similar charges to Lindh's—attempting to fight American forces on behalf of the Taliban—although they were never able to reach their goal of joining the front line of the jihad.[8] The court sentenced members of the cell to prison terms of up to 18 years.

Similarly, in upstate New York, the so-called Lackawanna Six, American citizens of Yemeni descent, received sentences of seven to 10 years in prison for providing material support to al Qaeda by training at the same Al Farooq camp attended by John Walker Lindh.[9]

More recently, in July 2007 Texas native Daniel Joseph Maldonado, a.k.a. Daniel Aljughaifi, was sentenced to 10 years in prison for receiving military training from a foreign terrorist organization. Maldonado's story is interesting, and his transformation into a radical Islamic jihadist came years ago:

> [Maldonado] traveled from Houston to Africa in November 2005 and then on to Somalia in December 2006 to join the Islamic Courts Union (ICU) and elements of Al Qaeda to fight "jihad" against the Transitional Federal Government to establish an independent Islamic State in Somalia.

> While in Somalia, Maldonado was provided an AK-47, equipped with military combat uniforms and boots in Mogadishu, and participated in training camps in Kismaayo and Jilib, Somalia. The camps included physical fitness, firearms and explosives training, all in preparation to go to the front to fight for the ICU. Al Qaeda members were present at the training camps. ICU and al Qaeda, a recognized foreign terrorist organization, worked together to train fighters in the camps to fight jihad to establish an independent Islamic state in Somalia.

> Maldonado was captured by Kenyan military forces on January 21, 2007 as he fled to avoid Ethiopian and Somalian forces. Expelled by Kenyan officials, Maldonado was turned over to American authorities and flown to Houston accompanied by Special Agents of the Federal Bureau of Investigation.[10]

Although Maldonado's call to jihad was not directly against U.S. forces, it was certainly against U.S. interests. And the law presumes that anyone training with al Qaeda is a current and future threat to the United States, based on the words and deeds of al Qaeda leaders such as Bin Laden and his number two, Ayman al-Zawahiri, as well as of the numerous al Qaeda operatives who have left a wake of devastation and destruction in their paths.

American-based jihadists have one thing in common: a desire to strike at America and American interests and do as much damage as possible. Some American-born terrorists have made it overseas to undertake their jihad, while others are ferreted out by the government during the planning stages. This chapter will examine one such case, interrupted by the FBI before the jihad was carried out, and successfully prosecuted by the Department of Justice.

THE VIRGINIA "PAINTBALL JIHAD" CELL

Another example of homegrown extremists, led by an American-born imam of Iraqi descent and an American convert from Missouri, was the now-notorious Virginia "paintball jihad" cell, whose members, as the name suggests, trained for their jihad using paintball guns on American soil. Like most Islamic terrorists, whether foreign born or domestic, the cell had ties to a specific terrorist group overseas. For the paintballers, their allegiance was to a Pakistani-based terrorist group chiefly, but not solely, fighting for the "liberation" of Kashmir from India, *Lashkar e Taiba* (LeT), or Army of the Righteous.

FROM VIRGINIA TO *LASHKAR E TAIBA* (LET)

LeT was designated a foreign terrorist organization by the State Department on 26 December 2001.[11] LeT is a Pakistani-based affiliate of al Qaeda and, according to the federal government, "claims to have trained thousands of *mujahideen* to fight in areas including Afghanistan, Kashmir, Bosnia, Chechnya, Kosovo, and the Philippines."[12]

But the theater of concern for LeT rhetoric, if not actions, is much wider, concerning the waging of violent jihad against the United States, Britain, Russia, and Israel,[13] and the group has sworn to "plant Islamic flags in Delhi, Tel Aviv, and Washington."[14]

Originally founded in the mid-1980s to assist with the Afghanistan jihad against the Soviet Union, LeT started as an offshoot of an organization called *Markaz Dawa Wa'al Irshad,* loosely meaning "Center for Invitation (to Islam) and Instructions," which expanded to include a military wing.[15]

After the Russian defeat at the hands of the mujahideen, LeT shifted its focus toward fighting the Indian government and "liberating" Kashmir.[16]

Beginning in the early 1990s, LeT has undertaken numerous terrorist and military operations targeting Indian troops and civilian targets in Kashmir and India proper. According to the U.S. government, LeT is believed to have killed nearly 100 people—mostly Indian Hindus—in eight separate terrorist attacks in August 2001 alone.[17]

THE INDICTMENT OF ISMAIL "RANDALL" ROYER AND THE PAINTBALL JIHADIS

This case gained notoriety when Randall Todd, a.k.a. "Ismail," Royer, at the time an employee of the Council on American-Islamic Relations (CAIR)— a self-described Islamic civil rights and advocacy organization—was arrested and charged for his role in a northern Virginia–based cell of Islamic radicals training to fight Americans overseas.

On 22 September 2001, police pulled Royer over for a traffic violation. Royer had in his possession an AK-47-style rifle and 219 rounds of ammunition.[18] According to court documents, Royer spent a portion of the previous year at LeT training camps in Pakistan, even firing a machine gun at "enemy positions."[19] Royer told the members of his cell that he could get them into LeT terrorist camps to train to join the Taliban to fight the U.S. military.

In summary, Ismail Royer admitted that he was engaged in unlawful activities on behalf of a designated terrorist group and that he attempted to recruit jihadists for LeT with the intention of joining the Taliban to fight U.S. forces in Afghanistan.

Initially indicted in June 2003 with charges ranging from participation in a criminal conspiracy to the use of a firearm in a crime of violence,[20] Royer had additional charges, including conspiracy to levy war against the United States and providing material support to al Qaeda and the Taliban, added against him in September 2003.[21] In January 2004, Royer pled to "aiding and abetting the use and discharge of a firearm during and in relation to a crime of violence, and with aiding and abetting the carrying of an explosive during the commission of a felony"[22] in a deal that included his cooperation to testify against various cell members. Royer has admitted that both charges are related to his activities on behalf of a terrorist group. According to the Department of Justice,

> Royer also admitted to helping co-defendant Ibrahim Ahmed Al-Hamdi gain entry to the Lashkar-e-Taiba camp, where Al-Hamdi received training in the use of a rocket-propelled grenade in furtherance of a conspiracy to conduct military operations against India. Royer acknowledged that he committed his offenses to help other jihadists gain entry to the Lashkar-e-Taiba training camp following a meeting on Sept. 16, 2001, at which an un-indicted conspirator said that the terrorist attacks on Sept. 11, 2001, would be used as an excuse to trigger a global war against Islam, and that the time had come for them to go abroad and, if possible, join the mujahideen.[23]

COUNSELING OTHERS TO LEVY WAR AGAINST THE UNITED STATES

The unindicted coconspirator referenced in the sentencing press release for Royer is Ali al-Timimi, an American-born imam of Iraqi descent, and spiritual leader to Royer and his cohorts. In April 2005, al-Timimi was himself convicted on charges of "soliciting others to wage war against the United States; counseling others to engage in a conspiracy to levy war against the United States; attempting to aid the Taliban, counseling others to attempt to aid the Taliban; counseling others to violate the Neutrality Act, and counseling others to use firearms and explosives in furtherance of crimes of violence."[24]

Al-Timimi, the "primary lecturer" at the Dar al Arqam Islamic Center in northern Virginia,[25] had convened private "prayer" and "study" sessions in the homes of some of the cell members that were much more than spiritual or academic meetings. According to the government, "in the Taiba Bulletin that Timimi subscribed to, the leader of LET, his friend, Hafiz Saeed, said the real jihad is to kill the Jews in their own homes, the right path. This is what he's telling young Muslim men, converts in Northern Virginia."[26]

In October 2001, al-Timimi implored members of the paintball jihad cell to join the jihad in Afghanistan. According to the indictment statements, al-Timimi "provided . . . historical examples from Islamic history justifying attacks on civilians," telling the cell members that the "muhajideen killed while fighting Americans in Afghanistan would die as martyrs," and recommended that they "obtain jihad training from Lashkar e Taiba because its belief system was good and it focused on combat."[27]

Al-Timimi was convicted in April 2005 and, in July 2005, sentenced to life in prison.[28] Yet despite overwhelming evidence of criminality and ill intent, al-Timimi had his defenders.

During the course of his trial and his sentencing, the Muslim American Society (MAS) tried to portray al-Timimi as an innocent victim of an overzealous federal government, only targeting Muslims to curtail their free speech rights.[29]

Mahdi Bray, executive director of the MAS "Freedom Foundation," wrote the following letter to the *Washington Post* after al-Timimi's conviction:

> The verdict in Dr. Al-Timimi's case is a sad day for American Muslims and the U.S. Constitution. It bodes ill for the Bill of Rights, and especially the First Amendment (Freedom of Speech). I agreed with many of America's lawyers and constitutional scholars that Dr. Al-Timimi's speech is constitutionally protected, even if others find it repugnant and inflammatory.

Since free speech is supposed to be guaranteed in this country, the issue of speech is always juxtaposed against the right to harm others. You have free speech, but you can't shout 'fire' in a crowed theater. I don't believe that was Dr. Al-Timimi's intent, or that his words were intended to have people go and take his words and translate them into killing other human beings, particularly Americans. However, it appears that the jury didn't understand that, and thought that Dr. Al-Timimi shouted 'fire'.

It's rather ironic that a speech similar to Dr. Al-Timimi's was not viewed by our government as criminal during the period when the Russians occupied Afghanistan. Clearly, the bar for free speech has been raised since the tragic events of 9/11, and this backlash is adversely affecting American Muslims.

However, we expect vindications of Dr. Al-Timimi upon appeal. Additionally, American Muslims must not let this and other similar decisions make them afraid to speak out or resist injustice. We must resist any and all efforts to relegate out status in this country to second-class citizenship.

Free speech is not just a constitutional right; it is a God-given right.

Sincerely,

Mahdi Bray

Executive Director

MAS Freedom Foundation[30]

Bray apparently believes that organizing and encouraging American Muslims to fight against U.S. troops should be viewed in the same way as fighting the Soviet Union. Yet these sentiments should surprise no one, as Randall Royer himself was once the communications director of MAS,[31] and this illustrates both the dangers of certain so-called civil rights groups and the lengths they will go to conflate the legitimate targeting of radical Islamists who are purveyors of violence against the United States and others with the targeting of Muslims in general.

Their goal is to create a climate of fear among their own constituents, an indoctrination process that results in radicalization and further adherence to fundamentalism, meant to isolate and separate them from society at large. Clearly, average citizens not soliciting and counseling others to levy war against the United States—the vast majority of all Americans, including Muslim Americans—have nothing to fear from the precedent set by the al-Timimi conviction, and are only made safer by such a ruling. MAS—an American branch of the Muslim Brotherhood[32]—however, unsurprisingly espouses the belief that soliciting individuals to fight against U.S. forces should not be considered a criminal act.

PERJURY AND OBSTRUCTION OF JUSTICE

The government sometimes uses seemingly more minor charges to prosecute cell members, and the paintball jihad case also provides such an example.

The last member of the paintball jihad cell to be convicted was Sabri Benkahla. Initially acquitted of terrorism charges after the judge granted a motion to sever his trial from the other cell members',[33] prosecutors then called Benkahla as a witness in the grand jury investigation against Ali al-Timimi.

Benkahla proceeded to lie under oath about his activities and travels and was "convicted of making materially false statements both in his grand jury appearances in 2004, as well as to the FBI in 2004."[34] The jury concluded that Benkahla lied about his attendance at a terrorist training camp and also lied about various contacts with specially designated global terrorists, including Omar Ahmed Abu Ali, convicted of planning to assassinate President Bush as well as providing material support to al Qaeda.[35] Interestingly enough, Abu Ali's case was also championed by the MAS Freedom Foundation.[36]

U.S. attorney Chuck Rosenberg described the reasoning behind his office's legal approach to the Benkahla case, stating of the conviction, "Truthful and complete information is a cornerstone of our war on terror. We need and expect the truth; when we do not get it, as Mr. Benkahla now knows, we prosecute perjury and obstruction of justice aggressively."[37]

CHALLENGES IN THE PUBLIC SPHERE: PRETENSE OF "MUSLIM ADVOCACY"

As noted above with MAS's defenses of Ali al-Timimi and Omar Ahmed Abu Ali, various Muslim organizations that purport to safeguard the civil rights of Muslims act as advocates on behalf of accused terrorists, often acting in complete disregard to the severity of the charge or the nature of the evidence. Oftentimes, as seen with the al-Timimi and Abu Ali cases, defendants are embraced by Muslim "civil rights" groups.

In the case of the Virginia "paintball jihad" cell, and Ismail Royer specifically— an employee at one time or another with two of the larger American Islamic advocacy groups—CAIR employed a different tactic: simultaneously attempting to diminish the nature and scope of Royer's charges, his role in the global jihad, *and* his ties to CAIR.

Interestingly, CAIR itself has recently been dragged from the court of public opinion to the courtroom itself. Federal prosecutors in Dallas officially named CAIR as an unindicted coconspirator and member of the "Palestine Committee" of the Muslim Brotherhood in the 2007 trial against the Holy Land Foundation for Relief and Development (HLF), the largest terrorist fund-raising trial in U.S. history.[38] HLF allegedly funneled over $12 million to Hamas-linked organizations,[39] CAIR's ties to the HLF were extensive, and its own leadership has multiple ties to Hamas and Hamas-front groups in the United States.[40]

With such a dubious background, it is not surprising the lengths CAIR has gone to hide its agenda and obscure the facts. For example, in January 2007, CAIR released an open letter, ironically titled "De-mystifying 'Urban Legends' about CAIR,"[41] in which the organization engages in its patented brand of mythmaking, once again downplaying its well-known ties to terrorists and, as expected, demonizing and defaming its critics. CAIR's word games cannot change the actual facts: that its employee conspired to engage in a holy war against an ally of the United States and, as Royer has also admitted, against the United States itself. Those are the facts, admitted by Royer, and well known to

CAIR. But that does not stop it from sending out a disingenuous press release, "demystifying" so-called "urban legends" by dissembling in the worst way.

Why is it relevant to examine the words and statements of an Islamic "civil rights" group? There are two reasons. First is simply because of the fact that one large component of this battle, working in tandem with our justice system, is the court of public opinion. CAIR, and groups like it, has the ability to poison jury pools and to pull the wool over the eyes of some lazy members of the media, giving the impression that there is some kind of focused effort by law enforcement authorities to target innocent Muslims, rather than an effort to safeguard American citizens against actual and legitimate threats from Islamic radicals.

Secondly, such efforts on the part of CAIR actually serve to radicalize the domestic Muslim population. CAIR and similar groups repeatedly claim that such prosecutions amount to the federal government's engaging in what CAIR calls a "war on Islam." As recently as July 2007, CAIR chairman Parvez Ahmed did just that, writing in the *Dallas Morning News* that "[t]his irrational fear, or Islamophobia, leads to discrimination against Muslims, the exclusion of Muslims from the sociopolitical process, guilt by association and even hate crimes" and concluding that "[t]here now seems to be a perception that the U.S. has entered into a war against Islam itself."[42]

In a federal court filing from December 2007, federal prosecutors described CAIR as "having conspired with other affiliates of the Muslim Brotherhood to support terrorists," in *United States v. Sari Benkahla,* a trial related to the "paintball jihad" case. The government also stated that "proof that the conspirators used deception to conceal from the American public their connections to terrorists was introduced" in the Dallas Holy Land Foundation trial last year. The government also stated that another organization, the Muslim American Society, was "founded as the overt arm of the Muslim Brotherhood in the United States." This appears to be the first time the U.S. government has officially described the true origins and ulterior agenda of the Muslim American Society.[43]

Yet a study conducted by the Canadian Security Intelligence Service (CSIS), published in 2007, concluded that the repeated refrain that Western governments are engaged in a "war on Islam," rather than in the fighting of terrorists, is a direct cause of the radicalization of so-called homegrown jihadists.[44] And, thus, CAIR and other Muslim Brotherhood–linked organizations are actually making the job of U.S. law enforcement agencies doubly difficult.

CONCLUSION

Since September 11, 2001, when al Qaeda terrorists brought their war to American soil, the war on terror has been fought and prosecuted on several fronts, both militarily and in our criminal courts. The Department of Justice has had many victories prosecuting the war on terror from a legal standpoint, yet it has faced various setbacks as well. While those seeking to take up arms against American interests and U.S. forces overseas have routinely been convicted and sentenced to relatively stiff punishments, prosecuting terrorist financiers has proved much more difficult.

While the United States has been a cash cow for assorted Islamic "charities" who have raised money here for the mujahideen overseas, much of the evidence has either been stale—as official U.S. designations of terrorist groups often occurred well after American-based organizations decided to fund their holy warriors of choice (the "charities" often became much more careful about public statements and record keeping after official U.S. government terrorist designations), or documentary evidence found overseas, not subject to Fourth Amendment limitations, has been an easy target for defense lawyers and often considered less than compelling by American juries. Regardless, the Department of Justice deserves much credit for taking on these difficult and complex cases, because other organizations predisposed to funding mujahideen overseas are on notice that the government is watching.

The main charge of "providing material support" to terrorist groups has, overall, been a successful tool in the prosecution of violent terrorists and homegrown armed insurgents, whether lone wolves or larger cells. This particular instrument, along with more traditional prosecutorial tools such as obstruction of justice, and novel means such as "solicitation" and "counseling" charges, were used in combination to wrap up a jihadist cell of Washington, DC, suburbanites, prepping to kill American soldiers in Afghanistan.

The prosecution of the Virginia "paintball jihad" cell indicates, more than anything else, that the war on terror is not limited to battlegrounds in the Middle East, despite the protests of the Muslim Brotherhood front groups that there is no domestic threat from radical Islamists. As the ambitions of the global mujahideen show no signs of slowing, and as more and more Americans hear and obey the call to jihad, whether emanating from an overseas fatwa from Osama bin Laden or Ayman al-Zawahiri or from a U.S.-based imam such as Ali al-Timimi, American law enforcement will, unfortunately, have more and more opportunities to test in a court of law the approaches described above.

NOTES

1. "Al Qaeda's Fatwa, " Online NewsHour, www.pbs.org/newshour/terrorism/international/fatwa_1998.html.

2. Larry Neumeister, "1st Trade Center Attack: 10 Years Ago," CBS News, 26 February 2003, www.cbsnews .com/stories/2003/02/12/attack/main540376.shtml.

3. U.S. Constitution, art. 3, sec. 3, available at caselaw.lp.findlaw.com/data/constitution/article03/.

4. Ibid.

5. *United States v. John Phillip Walker Lindh,* 02-CR-37, Indictment, EDVA, 5 February 2002.

6. Office of Public Affairs, Department of Justice, "Department of Justice Examples of Terrorism Convictions since Sept. 11, 2001," news release, 23 June 2006, www.usdoj.gov/opa/pr/2006/June/06_crm_389.html.

7. *United States v. John Phillip Walker Lindh,* 02-CR-37, Statement of Facts, EDVA, 15 July 2002.

8. "War on Terror: 'Portland Seven' Terrorism Investigation," OregonLive.com, www.oregonlive.com/special/ terror/index.ssf?/special/terror/pdx_archive.html.

9. Roya Aziz and Monica Lam, "Profiles: The Lackawanna Cell" Frontline, www.pbs.org/wgbh/pages/ frontline/shows/sleeper/inside/profiles.html.

10. Southern District of Texas U.S. Attorney's Office, Department of Justice, "US Citizen Sentenced to Prison for Receiving Military Training from a Terrorist Organization," news release, 20 July 2007, houston.fbi.gov/ dojpressrel/pressrel07/houston072007.htm.

11. U.S. Department of State, "Powell Names Two Groups as Terrorist Organizations," news release, 26 December 2001.

12. *United States v. Royer et al.,* 03-CR-296, Indictment, EDVA, 25 June 2003.

13. U.S. Department of Justice, "Defendants Convicted in Northern Virginia Jihad Trial," news release, 4 March 2004.

14. David E. Kaplan et al., "Hundreds of Americans Have Followed the Path to Jihad," *U.S. News & World Report,* 10 June 2002.

15. *United States v. Royer et al.,* Indictment.

16. Ibid., 3.

17. Department of Homeland Security, "Day 100 of the War on Terrorism: More Steps to Shut Down Terrorist Support Networks," news release, 20 December 2001.

18. *United States v. Royer et al.,* 03-CR-296, Superceding indictment, EDVA, 23 September 2003.

19. *United States v. Royer et al.,* 03-CR-296, Statement of Facts, EDVA, 28 January 2004.

20. *United States v. Royer et al.,* Indictment.

21. *United States v. Royer et al.,* Superseding Indictment.

22. Department of Justice, "Randall Todd Royer and Ibrahim Ahmed Al-Hamdi Sentenced for Participation in Virginia Jihad Network," news release, 9 April 2004, www.usdoj.gov/opa/pr/2004/April/04_crm_225.htm.

23. Ibid.

24. Eastern District of Virginia United States Attorney, Department of Justice, news release, 26 April 2005, www.usdoj.gov/usao/vae/Pressreleases/04-AprilPDFArchive/05/42605TimimiPR.pdf.

25. *United States v. Al-Timimi,* 04-CR-385, Indictment, EDVA, 23 September 2004.

26. *United States v. Al-Timimi,* 04-CR-385, Opening Statement, Transcript of Jury Trial before the Honorable Leonie M. Brinkemam, United States District Judge, EDVA, 4 April 2005.

27. *United States v. Al Timimi,* Indictment.

28. Office of Public Affairs, "Department of Justice Examples of Terrorism Convictions since Sept. 11, 2001."

29. Mahdi Bray, "MAS Freedom Executive Director's Open Letter on Dr. Ali Al-Timimi Verdict in the Washington Post," Muslim American Society, www.masnet.org/takeaction.asp?id=2380.

30. Ibid.

31. Ismail Royer, "America Must Revise Stance towards Islamic World," Muslim American Society, www.masnet.org/articlesandpapers.asp?id=33.

32. "A Rare Look at Secretive Brotherhood in America," *Chicago Tribune,* 19 September 2004, available at www.chicagotribune.com/chi-0409190261sep19,0,693751.story?page=6&coll=chi-site-nav.

33. Eastern District of Virginia United States Attorney's Office, "'Virginia Jihad' Member Convicted of Perjury, Obstruction," news release, 5 February 2007, www.usdoj.gov/usao/vae/Pressreleases/02-FebruaryPDFArchive/07/20070205benkahlanr.pdf.

34. Ibid.

35. *United States v. Abu Ali,* 05-CR-53, Judgment, EDVA, 17 April 2006.

36. "Why We Support the Abu Ali Case," Muslim American Society, www.masnet.org/takeaction.asp?id=2412.

37. Eastern District of Virginia United States Attorney's Office, "'Virginia Jihad' Member Convicted of Perjury, Obstruction."

38. *United States v. Holy Land Foundation et al.*, 04-CR-240, Attachment A: List of Unindicted Co-conspirators and/or Joint Venturers, NDTX, 29 May 2007, available at www.investigativeproject.org/documents/case_docs/423.pdf.

39. *United States v. Holy Land Foundation et al.*, 04-CR-240, Indictment, NDTX, 26 July 2004, fl1.findlaw.com/news.findlaw.com/cnn/docs/hlf/ushlf72604ind.pdf.

40. See Steven Emerson, "HLF and CAIR, A Supplement to Mainstream Reporting," Counterterrorism Blog, entry posted 25 August 2007, counterterrorismblog.org/2007/08/hlf_and_cair_a_supplement_to_m.php.

41. Council on American-Islamic Relations, "De-mystifying 'Urban Legends' about CAIR," www.cairphilly.org/files/Demystifying_Urban_Legends_About_CAIR.pdf.

42. "Parvez Ahmed: U.S. Can Ill Afford the Perception That We Are at War with Islam," *Dallas Morning News*, 5 July 2007, quoting the congressional testimony of Steven Kull, editor of WorldPublicOpinion.org, www.dallasnews.com/sharedcontent/dws/dn/opinion/viewpoints/stories/DN-ahmed_05edi.ART.State.Edition1.4319f5f.html.

43. "For the Record: Government Reminds Court of CAIR/MAS Ties to Terrorists," The Investigative Project on Terrorism (IPT News), www.investigativeproject.org/article/597 (accessed 15 February 2008).

44. Stewart Bell, "Jihadization of Youth a 'Rapid Process'; CSIS: Study of Extremism," *National Post,* 26 January 2007, available at www.canada.com/nationalpost/news/story.html?id=25e76872-b309-47a7-841b-938bdd9ffd71.

Part Three

Religion as Inspiration

17 Armed with the Power of Religion: Not Just a War of Ideas

Pauletta Otis

It is clear that religion, especially as it impacts violence, is no longer simply the purview of theologians and misguided adherents. Anyone remotely aware of current political and military issues in the Middle East, Africa, Europe, China, South Asia, or even the United States, knows that religion cannot be ignored. The U.S. military is fully cognizant of the role of religion in Afghanistan and Iraq. However, and this is important, anyone studying the current proliferation of armed groups in the global arena cannot help but notice that although religion always plays a role of some kind, it is never a single-factor explanation.

This chapter is based on the assumption that religion contributes to the lethality of armed groups. It is assumed that each member of an armed group has religion in a personal life-and-death way and that each group uses religious power to achieve its goals. Religious identity helps frame the "us" and "them," provides justification for the "cause," and contributes specific power currencies to the struggle. This is different from the "religion as ideology" framework—that in explaining everything, explains nothing.

The "religious factor" for armed groups can be overestimated or underestimated. Religion is overestimated when it is assumed to have predictive capability—"religion explains everything." It is underestimated when it is either ignored or misunderstood. The importance of "getting it right"—information, analysis, understanding, and knowledge—is undoubtedly one of the most important intellectual challenges of this century. It is undoubtedly the single most problematic, complicated, sensitive, volatile, and debated subject in the current strategic environment.

Dr. Otis is professor of strategic studies at the United States Marine Corps Command and Staff College, Quantico, Virginia. Previously she was the academic coordinator for the Marine Corps Center for Advanced Operational Cultural Learning. As professor of strategic studies at the Joint Military Intelligence College, Department of Defense, she had major teaching responsibilities in the studies of intelligence, contemporary conflict, and regional analysis. She was senior researcher for religion and international affairs at Pew Forum, 2005. Prior to that time, she was a tenured professor of political science and international studies and chairman of the Political Science Department at Colorado State University at Pueblo (1989–2004). She holds MA degrees in anthropology and political science and a PhD in international studies from the University of Denver. She has also worked in the military security community as a subject matter expert in the areas of terrorism, counterterrorism, and religious violence. Dr. Otis combines theoretical discipline and operational experience and has conducted field research in conflict situations around the globe, publishing on the topics of human rights, genocide, refugees, diasporas, religious violence, indication and warning systems, conflict management, peace operations, and asymmetric and urban warfare.

Efforts to deal with religion—Islam, in particular—have often been inaccurate, inconsistent, and inadequate. This indictment has been leveled at the Defense Department, State Department, and even the American public. Some go so far as to say that "U.S. efforts are seen as naïve, lacking understanding of the Muslim world and [being] off target at best and dangerous at worst."[1] Prior to the events of September 11, 2001, religion was talked about in rather hushed, apologetic tones in the Department of State, the Department of Defense, and the Intelligence Community almost as if it were an embarrassment. There were no academic courses at any of the command and staff colleges that addressed the subject of religion and warfare; academics working for the Pentagon were not focused on religion; and even the best strategic analysis and intelligence professionals were not prepared to take on the topic. The fear was that individuals could not and would not be objective but would bring personal beliefs into the analyses inappropriately.

In the current strategic environment, religion is the topic du jour and has been elevated from playing a role to being a single-factor explanation of all violence. In fact, there seems to be a growing belief that in some way religion is responsible for the current strategic imbroglio around the world.[2] There is an uncomfortable trend to explain the motivation and intent of all armed groups in light of Al Qaeda or Islamic radicalism. A closer examination reveals the palpable falsity of this position. Armed groups, insurgencies, revolutions, and conflict certainly predate Al Qaeda. They are found in all religious traditions, in all parts of the globe, and "use" and "abuse" religion in different ways.

OVERESTIMATING THE POWER OF THEOLOGY

Religion is overestimated when the ideas incumbent in the theology are assumed to have predictive power. This is similar to the perspective held during the cold war that the ideologies of communism, socialism, totalitarianism, and anarchism determined the fate of societies and, as such, had to be fought either by a better idea (democracy) or by defeating the source of the idea—in the 1950s assumed to be the Soviet Union or the People's Republic of China.

Religion, when viewed as ideology with a "God factor," is assumed to be the single most important determining factor in international conflict. In the current strategic environment, the so-called war of ideas pits the Western (Christian) way against the Islamic world and the Muslim way. There are assumed to be two paths to fight this religious ideology—either by a "better idea" or by defeating the source of the idea—in this case assumed to be centered somewhere in the Middle East.

Within the war of ideas, there is an implicit assumption that reason, persuasion, influence, perspective, and ultimately truth will persuade the peoples of the Middle East to abandon their atavistic lifestyle, give up their religious ideologies, and join the modern world. Islam, as theology, is often cynically described as backward, traditional, repressive, and prone to violence, and although the people of the Middle East might be OK, the theology of Islam holds them back or, worse, propels them to violence. In this scenario, so-called moderates are encouraged to help others understand the error of their ways. Alternatively, there is a suggestion that Islam go through a reformation, like Christianity, to "get with the program."

On closer examination, few scholars believe that theology can predict individual be-havior, and although religion contributes to the welfare of individuals and groups, as a single-factor explanation, it seldom provides more than general guidance for understand-ing individual/group behaviors. In the most obvious case, many people do not know the tenets of their religions, and if they do, are seldom the perfect adherents.[3]

In the counterinsurgency literature, religion is seldom mentioned as a contributing factor, in spite of the fact that the terrorist literature sui generis is replete with religious causality. In fact, the "religious terrorism" literature is virtually a growth industry. Most of that literature overemphasizes the religious factor by assuming that religious ideology or theology is the single motivating factor in armed violence—particularly in the Middle East. How religious factors as identifiable beliefs and behaviors contribute is seldom ad-dressed. In-depth analysis requires a closer look at the specific indicators found in local religious beliefs and behaviors as found in armed groups themselves and in their "sup-porting populations."

FRAMING THE ISSUE OF RELIGIOUS FACTORS IN VIOLENCE

Religious factors in violence are underestimated when the power of religious beliefs and behaviors at the local level are not assessed as a type of sociocultural power. Religion is more than a set of ideas. It is a way of life complete with beliefs and behaviors integrated into the complex cultural patterns of peoples' daily lives. Instead of addressing religion as divorced from the reality of daily life, it is helpful to see religion as part of a complex cultural system.

Most people acknowledge that religion is a two-edged sword. Religion supports the most beautiful and idealistic of worldviews, yet is often associated with the most tragic situations of maximum human suffering. The principles of faith, hope, and love can be denigrated to cynicism, despair, and hate. That which should support life can support death; that which supports peace can be used to perpetuate war. It is suggested that reli-gion plays a role in all aspects of warfare. It is invariably linked to support for violence and support for peace. This is true not only of the principles and theological perspectives but of the religious power on the ground, the religious personages, and the religious insti-tutions that come into play in both lethal circumstances and mobilizations for peace.

Where beliefs or the strengths of beliefs are hard to measure and the effects of belief systems are inconsistent over time, the institutions, behaviors, and patterned ways of integrating religion into cultural systems are rather predictable. Beliefs and behaviors can be abstracted and understood by looking at the complex whole of the power of religion in the lives of individuals, groups, nations, and states. In this context, religious ideas pro-vide the framework for group adaptation to the social environment, and religious behav-iors are seen as related to all other aspects of group survival—identity, territory, language, economics, and authority (politics). These are individual and group behaviors that are knowable. In other words, they can be subjected to examination using historical-pattern analysis, variable analysis, and tests of reliability and validity. It brings religion down from the transcendent and gives it a human face.

The following diagram illustrates how religion translates into behaviors. Theology provides the mind-set and defines good versus evil. Codes for living identify rewards and sanctions. Local beliefs result in observable behaviors that can be examined using a *power analysis*.

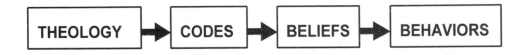

THE POWER OF RELIGION

When examining contemporary armed groups, a power analysis can provide insight, information, and guidance in regard to political and military activities. Religious factors are "power resources" in the sense that religious institutions and leaders control resources, define interpersonal relationships, establish and maintain group communication, and provide expertise. The resources include control over goods and services; organizational capabilities; social networks that are community based but may also be global in scope; and various types of support for political personages, agendas, and programs. The resources of religious personages and institutions are direct results of their numbers, reputations, coherence, and willingness to mobilize for political or religious purposes.

Religion is an important power broker in human relationships. Religion helps define the attributes of a good and trustable person; prescribe rules concerning how individuals transact social, political, and economic business; and identify "friend" and "enemy" according to a set of traditional and legitimate factors. When states fail, or particular political personages are delegitimized, religious personages often help define who a new political leader will be and when and under what conditions this leader will emerge. Most important, religious authorities are also assumed to be in touch with the power of a Supreme Being and therefore have special insight concerning social relations among God's children.

Religion provides for common language and means of communication among members of a group. Religious leaders communicate with authority; generally have written and spoken expertise; have access to media; and know significant music, poetry, and art forms of nonverbal, symbolic communication. Historical languages often provide a sense of continuity and may be used for motivation or in symbolic communication. Religious personages and institutions are often deeply involved in the education of children and the training of future generations. Parents rely on religious educational and medical institutions when the state fails to provide those resources. Religious leaders are often accustomed to keeping confidences or secrets and are trusted for their discretion. Most important, religious leaders are often more *believable* in local areas than political leaders from the central government and therefore have power above and beyond the sheer strength of numbers or observable resources.

Religious leaders, as force multipliers, have significant sociocultural power and are able to affect war and peace more than is commonly recognized. Religious authorities have expertise in many areas above and beyond that of the general population. They generally have an in-depth knowledge of people, places, and communities. They know the sensitivities of the community. They know the personal history of leaders and their families. They move easily in a community and have access to areas off-limits to others. Quite literally, they know where the bodies are buried. In a very real sense, religious personages and communities know more about food, water, and health than others in the community. They are the individuals that people "go to" when all else fails. The following are four common sources of religious power:[4]

1.   Resources: Most religious communities and institutions have the following resources:

- Churches, mosques, synagogues, temples, and other places of worship that own land, control money and banking, provide a center for social services, provide medicine and health services
- Control of membership in the group by providing burial space for individuals and families, control of inheritance through marriage and family law, provision of sanctuary for travelers
- Communications technology
- Historical repositories of information about individuals and the community
- Individuals who can be human resources deployed for any number of tasks
- Income
- Organization
- Law and religious tradition with rules or sanctions for appropriate social behavior
- Institutions that are both community based and have global reach.

Two examples may suffice: The *vakif* system in northern Cyprus is grounded in religious tradition and authority; it influences or controls inheritance, ownership of property, social services, marriage, and burial, and impacts the social and economic development of northern Cyprus. The Greek Orthodox Church does the same, albeit in a different pattern, for the Republic of Cyprus. Both impact the population in very real ways—ways not at all reflective of theology—only of the practical power of religion in a sociocultural context.

In another example, one of the first signals of impending violence in the Croatia-Serbia conflict was the ethnic cleansing of cemeteries by church authorities. The use of the symbol of the Ustache cross in Croatia, a Christian symbol but also the symbol of the Nazi Party in Croatia, is an example of the power of religious symbols quite divorced from theological principles.

2.   Interpersonal power: Religious leaders are often more *believable* in failed or fragile states than political leaders and therefore have power above and beyond the sheer strength of numbers or observable resources. Regardless of which side they are on, religious leaders are expected to engage the topic of peace and use their inherent power to move toward a more peaceful world in order to be constructive. Most religions have the following interpersonal power:

- Shared history—communication shortcuts
- Shared identity—knowledge of "trustable"
- Shared rules
- Shared behaviors
- Shared learning
- Patterned interaction and exchange mechanisms
- Music, art, literature, enculturation, gestures, education, respect, assumptions and expectations.

To use a specific, nonattributable example: A missionary in one of the western African countries was compelled by his conscience to talk to the cruel, powerful dictator who was clearly abusing his power. The missionary used as his entrée into the conversation the fact that he had known the dictator's mother, and that she would clearly be disappointed in her son's activities and descent into violence and cruelty. It was reported that the ruler acquiesced—releasing prisoners that had been tortured and detained.

In another instance, Archbishop Makarios in Cyprus was clearly the leader not only of a religious community but of the Greek Cypriots. His activities and influence on the island had enormous consequences for both the Greek and Turkish Cypriots.

In 2007, the events in Myanmar pitted monks against the government. Their silence, vows of nonviolence, and public demonstrations were evidence of the power of religion to elicit regime change. In this case, Buddhist theology, which has ingrained principles of *just war,* was not invoked—only the principle and practice of nonviolence.

3.   Communication: Religious leaders communicate with the authority of "God" and the authority of "man." Most religions have the following power of communication:

- Vertical and horizontal communication
- Written and spoken expertise
- Access to media
- Symbolism—music, poetry, art forms
- Nonverbal communication—gestures and gutturals
- Use of symbols—written, linguistic, pictograph, literary.

In an example of communication, the religious poetry of Islam was used to communicate place and time during Desert Storm, 2001. As American troops advanced, the Iraqi indigenous population used a form of ancient poetry to indicate when and where the resistance would take place. In a different example, the guitar has been known as a religious revolutionary instrument since the early 1300s.

4.   Expertise: Most religions have individuals or groups with the following types of expertise:

- Knowledge of place
- Knowledge of problem individuals and families
- Knowledge of historical languages
- Medical knowledge
- Education (formal and informal)
- Knowledge of criminal elements and prison networks
- Knowledge of cults and radical individuals or groups
- Knowledge of cemeteries.

Graveyard ethnic cleansing was known in Croatia and Serbia. Although the graves were in church cemeteries, on some occasions the bodies were dug up and dumped in the appropriate "ethnic" enclaves. This particularly gruesome form of ethnic cleansing is not unique in human history.

It is often said that when militaries invade a town, the first people that come out to meet them are police, firefighters, and clerics. If the local government is removed, religious leaders will appear as if by magic and assume responsibility for speaking for the people and with the "invaders."

THE CHANGE DYNAMIC

In addition to this "flat" analytical framework, it is important to follow through with the questions of how religious factors change and develop in response to

1. technical change and development,
2. climate and environmental changes—especially disaster areas,
3. internal or civil warfare, and
4. intervention by international forces in conventional or unconventional warfare.

Another way to analyze religious factors in conflict is to go directly to the form of violence used by an armed group and identify the specific religious content over the stages and phases of a particular conflict situation. In the preparation for war, religion contributes to the identities of friend and foe. In the heat of battle, religion contributes all of the power resources available plus solace and sanctuary, and, near the end of conflict, religious personages and ideas contribute to both theologically based peacemaking strategies and information and insight in very practical community matters. Over the course of an insurgency, religion will play different parts given the needs of the cultural foundations of the armed group.

CASES: HOW ARMED RELIGION CONTRIBUTES TO THE POWER OF ARMED GROUPS

Every situation that concerns the composition and activities of a contemporary armed group can be assessed with regard to religious factors, or lack thereof. Some of the more well-known situations include Iraq, Afghanistan, Sudan, Uganda, Peru, and Rwanda.

In Iraq, between 2001 and 2007, the religious factor was misrepresented and misunderstood. Religion was assumed to be a prime, single-factor explanation for violence and this turned out to be blatantly untrue. In 2001, the people of Iraq were reported to be no more theologically sophisticated than other people in other countries. It is entirely possible that most people knew the Seven Pillars of Islam.[5] It is also entirely possible that few could talk in depth about the nature of Allah, the history of the three holy cities, the reasons why some food items are "halal," or how Allah will judge children who die from war-related injury.[6] The Baathist regime was socialist although its members were identified as religiously Muslim. There was a separation between "church and state" even though the population was nominally Muslim.

After 9/11, however, it was assumed that since Iraqis were "Muslim" they were bound by the theology and religious practices in extremis. American military forces were given cultural indoctrination and teaching that invariably emphasized the Islamic "way of life." In other words, behaviors were assumed to have linear causality from the tenets of the Koran.[7] It was also assumed that all Muslims, therefore all Iraqis, were primarily motivated by their religion and "if you understood Islam, you would understand Iraq." This was misleading, faulty, and dangerously simplistic thinking.

According to a recently returned Marine, religion played almost no part in the Marine Corps' dealings with people in Anbar province. It was also thought that Muqtada al-Sadr became an important religious leader because a clerical position could be unquestioningly inherited from a father. Working on this faulty assumption, the coalition leadership assumed al-Sadr had power and influence that he did not have. Sadly, it was something of a self-fulfilling prophecy when he assumed the influential role that the coalition assigned to him and became spokesman without the traditional authority and legitimacy. The fact that Iraq was a Muslim country seemed to derail traditional predictive analysis vis-à-vis everyday behavior let alone conflict and violence.

Many soldiers, Marines, and airmen were astonished to find out that religion did not define Iraq—it was merely part of the picture, but not the only part and not always the most important. There were any number of things which couldn't be explained on the basis of Islam or Islamic theology. For instance, it was impossible to find out whether road-side bombs were supported or not supported by the religious teachers or even religious leaders in Iraq. It was equally hard to assess the level of criminality and corruption on the basis of Koranic teachings. Genocide is not respected in Islam. Torture is not religiously justified. Foreign fighters who may have been fellow believers were generally not accepted by the sectarian tribal leaders on the ground. There were genuine disagreements about the authority of the tribe in relationship to the authority of clerics. And finally, if the *umma* is a theologically based principle, why are there such strong disagreements among the Kurds, Shia, and Sunnis?

In trying to analyze the "religious factor" in violence in Iraq, it is therefore necessary to see religion as theology, codes, beliefs, and behaviors in localized cultural areas. Religion does play a role in the violence in Iraq and it is important to be able to leverage that power in a positive sense, but also an understanding of how religious identity helps define Iraqi identity contributes to the understanding of foreign fighters that go to Iraq under the misguided assumption that fellow believers will welcome a "jihadi" and that they will be welcomed as brothers. A more realistic assessment based on cultural and religious analysis would indicate that even fellow believers, if they are of another ethnic, religious, class, or outsider group, would not be welcomed into a war zone where everyone is suspicious of everyone else and draws lines around the kin or tribal group.

In Afghanistan, religion plays a role but theology does not determine the behavior of individuals, tribal groups, or the country. The Taliban may have taken a strong religious stance, but that reflected the Pashtun culture, which had been interpreted and reinterpreted by theologians and practitioners, and changed as the Taliban leadership became more mature. The form and lethality of violence was that of a tribal armed group, motivated by a variety of factor, including the expulsion of English, Russians, and Americans as well as protection from the dominance of other Afghan tribal groups. Theology did guide the Taliban, but it was only part of the story. The rest of the profile includes the religious beliefs and behaviors of the Pashtun people.

Their relationship with Al Qaeda is instructive. When Bin Laden and his group were resident in Afghanistan, the Taliban claimed to be "religiously motivated." Restoring justice by jihad was the mantra. If Al Qaeda and the Taliban were both driven by similar Islamic theology, and if religion shapes armed-group behavior, then such analysis is seriously lacking in predictive power. Al Qaeda is an international jihadist group that uses violence for specific international objectives. The Taliban were a tribal group that used Islam for the purpose of tribal dominance in the region.

African armed groups are variously identified with their respective religions but it is doubtful that theology alone can explain their relationships with their respective governments, other sociocultural groups in the area, or even the goals of their insurgencies. Clearly, religion is invoked by public speakers and political managers, but religion is not the only factor in motivation and intent. Religion plays a role. Religious actors use resources, interpersonal skills, communication assets, and expertise but these are only a part of the total complex array of social and cultural mechanisms.

In Sudan, there are two major disputes. The southern tribal groups have fought the central government in Khartoum for decades; the Darfur area is teeming with the violence of the *Janjaweed*.[8] The central government wants to control the borders—particularly in the south for several reasons. The south has natural resources, including petroleum, and there is an internationally recognized principle of "sovereignty" that upholds the government's right to control the landmass. However, the southerners are imputed to be Christian-animist and are "African" rather than Arab—so the cultural configurations of the dispute take on the elements of racism and prejudice. The southern Sudan People's Liberation Army (SPLA), or splinter groups thereof, fights with the government forces for autonomy, independence, freedom—and rights to the economic resources of the south. Religion plays a role specifically insofar as foreign aid is mobilized through the NGO (nongovernmental organization) community—particularly the Christians of the United States, England, and Canada. The message is that the government of Sudan enslaves the southerners as "part of Islam versus Christianity." That southern tribal groups have had various forms of slavery for centuries seems to elude the messengers. Religion is mobilized in the international context more than the internal context in this situation.

In Darfur, the *Janjaweed* may claim Islamic jihad but the claim rings empty: the economic destruction, exploitation, and basic brutality bears no relationship to a religious framework. All of this said, the religious community in Khartoum is extremely concerned and is trying actively to bring a halt to the violence. Although each of the religious communities denies its involvement in the brutality, and decries the other for its brutality, each seems appalled by the scope and level of the violence and, when clearer heads prevail, will contribute to the peace-making process. None of the religious leaders claim that the violence is demanded or sanctioned by religious authority. In the case of Sudan, in both the south and Darfur regions, the role of religion is and will be to help restore peoples' lives, as they have been impacted by starvation, disease, and the basic destruction of their society. The refugee camps are supported by international organizations, both religious and nonreligious.

It is reported that Africa has some 15,000 "new" religions. Religion is a factor in the armed violence in Nigeria, Sierra Leone, and Chad. Other explanations, such as economics, politics, colonialism, and corruption, are also valid. Again, a religious power analysis contributes to the explanation but cannot explain all. In Nigeria, for example, it is easy to cite the Muslim north and the Christian south as the cause for conflict. In reality, the factors of tribal identity, corruption, the aftermath of the Biafran war, and sharing petroleum resources contribute to the explanation of violence.

Europe has its own set of problems. The armed groups in the news often claim religious motivation. Closer inspection reveals that terrorist acts have often included individuals or groups with serious complaints against the central government, lack of inclusion in economic and social life, and even the cry of racism. Sweden, the Netherlands, Spain, France, and the United Kingdom have dissident groups that may mobilize around a religious identity but clearly have other complaints based on economic, political, and social exclusion.

The central government of China is concerned about the rise of Islamic fundamentalism in Xinjiang Uyghur Autonomous Region. A closer inspection reveals that the plight and position of the Uighur population is based on its relationship with China, not the rise of a new compelling ideology from the Arab Middle East.

CONCLUSION

Religion is an integral part of the daily life of most individuals and groups. It contributes explanations of life and death, purpose for living, and ideas about right and wrong. As ideology or theology, it is compelling and important and helps us explain the natural and supernatural. When it comes to armed violence, the theologies take on real life in beliefs and behaviors found on the ground. A *power analysis,* which looks at how religious beliefs and behaviors lead to violence, contributes to a more complete understanding of the operational environment. With this understanding, it should be possible to (a) understand and analyze the human-religious dimension of counterinsurgency, (b) use appropriate measures to counter the negative impact of religious factors, and (c) support the positive aspects of religious power to compel peace.

NOTES

1. Critics cited in "From Uncle Ben's to Uncle Sam," *Economist,* 23 February, 2002, 70.

2. There have been so many reports on Islam and Islamic violence that one observer wondered whether the Department of Defense was becoming the Department of Comparative Theology.

3. This is evidenced by the religious wars between 1400 and 1800 that engulfed all of Europe.

4. These are neither comprehensive nor exclusive lists—only ideas concerning the most obvious or known factors. Each armed group's religion can be assessed differently knowing that the group will choose that which resonates most clearly with respective group supporters.

5. The Shia Seven Pillars of Islam have three doctrines that are not included in the Sunni Five Pillars of Islam. "Seven Pillars of Islam (Ismaili)," Answers.com, www.answers.com/topic/seven-pillars-of-islam.

6. According to some reports, less than 20 percent of the Iraqis prior to 2001 attended Friday mosque services with any regularity.

7. Some of the teaching materials disseminated by the Defense Department were entitled "Arab and Muslim Culture." Although "Arab" may be an ethnic group with an identifiable culture, certainly Islam is a religion.

8. According to Human Rights Watch, "The term 'Janjaweed' has become the source of increasing controversy, with different actors using the term in very different ways. Literally, the term is reported to be an amalgamation of three Arabic words for ghost, gun, and horse that historically referred to criminals, bandits or outlaws. In the wake of the conflict in Darfur, many 'African' victims of attacks have used the term to refer to the government-backed militias attacking their villages, many of whom are drawn from nomadic groups of Arab ethnic origin." "Darfur Documents Confirm Government Policy of Militia Support: A Human Rights Watch Briefing Paper, July 20, 2004, " Human Rights Watch, hrw.org/english/docs/2004/07/19/darfur9096.htm#3.

18   Arming for Armageddon: Myths and Motivations of Violence in American Christian Apocalypticism

Timothy J. Demy

How do religious beliefs about the end of the world turn into violent actions? This essay provides an overview of belief about the end times within American Protestantism, evangelicalism, the so-called religious Right, and the radical extremists, the latter often drawing upon and reinterpreting broader Christian doctrines to justify violence and hate. The presentation will hopefully correct misconceptions about the religious beliefs of a large segment of American society, yet also show why some political and religious groups believe their faith requires militant preparation for and participation in apocalyptic events.

No religion is monolithic. There is diversity in every faith tradition and each has a fanatical fringe element that departs from what the majority within the tradition consider normative and orthodox. For a variety of reasons—cultural, social, political, historical, and theological—militancy and violence also may, at times, be part of the dynamics of the radical faithful. Sometimes the violence is a derivative of doctrine, sometimes it arises due to persecution, and, in yet other instances, violent acts arise from political beliefs that are subsequently infused with religious imagery and language.

Christianity has no immunity to such violence and, in recent years, American Christianity has experienced it several times. Attacks on abortion clinics and staff, destructive acts by militia groups, a catastrophic conflict at a schismatic religious compound, and a terrorist act on a federal office building all had religious connections. Thus, a decade ago, Mark Juergensmeyer noted:

> What is significant about the recent forms of Christian violence is not so much the violence as the ideology that lies behind it: the perception that the secular social and political

Commander Timothy Demy is chaplain and electives professor at the U.S. Naval War College, Newport, Rhode Island. He is a career Navy officer with more than 27 years of reserve and active service and he has held assignments afloat and ashore with the Navy, Marine Corps, and Coast Guard. He received undergraduate training at Texas Christian University, where he earned the BA degree in history. He then completed seminary and theological training at Dallas Theological Seminary, earning the ThM and ThD degrees in historical theology. Additionally, he has earned master's degrees in European history (The University of Texas at Arlington), national security and strategic studies (U.S. Naval War College), and human development (Salve Regina University). He also earned the PhD degree at Salve Regina University and completed the MSt degree in international relations at the University of Cambridge. He is the author and editor of numerous articles and books on a variety of historical, ethical, and theological subjects.

order of America is caught up in satanic conspiracies of spiritual and personal control. These perceived plots provide Christian activists with reasons for using violent means.[1]

Little has changed since these words were penned, and international events, including a rise in religiously motivated terrorism, have intensified religious convictions for many militants. For some, there is also a strong apocalyptic element that provides theological motivation, meaning, and justification for violence. Apocalypticism as used in this essay is "a belief that at some divinely appointed time in the future, the world as we know it will end through a cataclysmic confrontation between the forces of good and evil, out of which will emerge the righteous kingdom of God."[2]

Although there are similarities among the participants in violent acts of armed apocalypticism, there are also differences, and an understanding and appreciation of the religious perspectives can aid those who seek to uphold justice, security, and constitutional rights for American citizens in the present and future. Not all militia groups in the United States have religious ties, but some do. Similarly, not all religious minority groups and sects support violence and rebellion against the state. However, there is enough of each, along with confusion about apocalyptic theology, to merit further study.

CHRISTIANITY AND THE END TIMES

"He will come to judge the living and the dead." These words from the Apostles' Creed and similar words from other Christian affirmations of faith have been voiced for centuries as public declarations of belief in the yet-future return of Jesus Christ to earth. Likewise have been the words "Thy kingdom come. Thy will be done, on earth as it is in heaven." Countless times every day for almost 2,000 years, Christians around the globe have voiced this prayer modeling one Jesus gave to his disciples (as recorded in the New Testament, Matthew 6:9–13 and Luke 11:2–4). Why do many Christians understand these statements to be fulfillment of prophecy and part of contemporary and future world events? More specifically, what do Christians believe to be their function in preparation for these events? For the majority of Christians, it is anticipation; for a minority, it is violence.

PROPHETS OF DOOM

Most people have seen cartoons of individuals wearing or holding placards that proclaim, "The end is near!" Occasionally, such prophets of doom can be seen on busy American street corners or in city parks preaching a message of imminent global destruction. Their expressions and sentiments reflect belief in and fascination with apocalypticism and its relationship to current events. Apocalyptic violence is not new in Christian history. Two examples from the past are the populist millennial revolt led by Thomas Müntzer during the 1525 Peasants' War in Germany and the Anabaptist revolt in Münster during 1533–35. In recent U.S. history, the April 1993 tragedy in Waco, Texas, at the Branch Davidian compound under the religious leadership of Vernon Howell, a.k.a. David Koresh, is a vivid example of apocalyptic faith coupled with armed violence.[3] Such incidents have occurred for centuries.

Some apocalyptic groups (Christian or other) may initiate violence because of stressors within the group or may experience leadership dynamics that instigate violence. This is what happened with the Peoples Temple in Jonestown, Guyana, on 18 November 1978 and with the non-Christian group Aum Shinrikyo in Tokyo on 20 March 1995. Other groups initiate violence in response to external pressures such as confrontation with law enforcement agencies. For example, as a backdrop to the 1992 confrontation at Ruby Ridge between federal agents and the Weaver family was the apocalyptic theology that was part of the Weavers' belief system. Finally, some groups may initiate violence based on their apocalyptic theologies. This was the case with the Branch Davidians from February to April 1993 and also in the 81-day confrontation with the Montana Freemen in 1996.[4] Apocalyptic beliefs were part of each scenario, but were functionally different in each instance. Beliefs may either be a catalyst for violence that is viewed as part of the prophetic plan of history, or condone violence that is not specifically understood as apocalyptic but still part of a larger theological plan.

PROPHETIC PERSPECTIVES ON THE END TIMES

In American culture, belief in Bible prophecy has a long and varied history.[5] Within Christian theology eschatology is the study of last things. Eschatology is a detailed field of theological inquiry with many terms and concepts. Failure to understand the definitions and distinctions within it can lead to confusion for the prophecy student and catastrophe for law enforcement agencies when faced with the possibility or reality of armed apocalyptic individuals or groups.[6]

All Christians believe that Jesus Christ will return to earth in an event known as the Second Coming or Second Advent. They also believe in something known as the millennium. According to Revelation 20:1–7, there is a period of 1,000 years during which Jesus Christ will establish a kingdom and reign and rule over the world. However, there is disagreement on the nature and timing of that kingdom in relation to the Second Advent. Some view the millennium as a literal physical kingdom lasting 1,000 years, while others view it as a spiritual kingdom. In answer to the question "What is the relationship of the millennium to the Second Coming?" there are three possibilities: amillennialism, postmillennialism, and premillennialism.

Amillennialism teaches that there will be no literal, future 1,000-year reign of Jesus Christ on earth. Rather, there is a present spiritual form of that kingdom. Amillennialists (Protestant, Roman Catholic, and Eastern Orthodox) believe that from the ascension of Jesus Christ in the first century (Acts 1:6–11) until the Second Coming, both good and evil will increase in the world as Jesus Christ reigns spiritually in the lives of Christians. When Jesus Christ returns, the end of the world will occur with a general resurrection of the dead and a judgment of all people. Amillennialism has been the most widely held view throughout the church's history. *Apocalyptic violence is not usually associated with this perspective.*

Postmillennialism teaches that Christ's kingdom is currently being extended spiritually and physically throughout the world through the proclamation of the gospel of Jesus Christ. Its advocates believe that, at some point, a majority of the world's inhabitants will be converted to Christianity, resulting in a Christianization of society and culture. Postmillennialism teaches that the current age is the millennium, but it is not necessarily a literal 1,000-year period. Postmillennialists believe that there will be progressive growth of righteousness, prosperity, and development in every sphere of life as a growing majority of Christians eventually culturally subdue the world for Christ. Then, after Christianity has dominated the world for a long time, Christ will return. Postmillennialism was the dominant view of American Protestantism during much of the late eighteenth and nineteenth centuries but waned during the first half of the twentieth century. In the latter part of the twentieth century there was a resurgence of it through the Christian Reconstruction Movement, also known as dominion theology.

Apocalyptic violence is not found with the majority of postmillennial advocates, although it does exist in some militia groups and in isolated instances. Most postmillennialists reject such violence, believing it to be inconsistent with postmillennial tenets. For example, in published correspondence with Paul J. Hill, the Presbyterian minister convicted and executed for the murder of a Florida abortionist, prominent Christian Reconstructionist Gary North wrote, "you have moved away from biblical law into open revolution."[7] North rejects Hill's actions (and the similar actions of others) as "vigilante theology" and instead favors nonviolence and nonviolent resistance.[8] Most postmillennialists are within mainstream American Christianity, but others, such as Christian militia advocates, are outside the mainstream of Christian orthodoxy, distrusting traditional Christian faith communities.

Premillennialism, the third and final millennial view, teaches that the Second Coming of Jesus Christ occurs before the 1000-year reign of Christ in a literal and physical kingdom that will be established on earth. Within premillennialism there is also debate over the concept of an event known as the rapture, in which Jesus Christ appears in the heavens and calls Christians to heaven and then later returns with them in the Second Coming. Depending upon one's view, the rapture occurs either before, during, or after a seven-year period of intense trial and trauma on earth known as the tribulation, as recorded in Revelation 6–19. It is during this time of tribulation that events occur that correspond to such terminology as "bowl judgments," "seal judgments," "trumpet judgments," and "Armageddon." Thus one hears of eschatological schemes such as pretribulationism, midtribulationism, and posttribulationism—all within a premillennial framework and referring to the timing of the rapture in relation to the tribulation that occurs before the millennium.

Within premillennialism that is midtribulational or posttribulational there is also a view regarding the timing of the prophetic events of the tribulation known as historicism. Historicists believe that the events of the tribulation can be equated with events and periods of history that either have occurred since the first century or are currently happening. Within Protestantism, historicism was common from the Reformation era until about 100 years ago. Most historicist schemes focus on European history, equating personalities such as various popes or political leaders such as Napoleon or Hitler with the prophetic figure of the Antichrist (Daniel 9:26–27; 2 Thessalonians 2:3).[9] However, some historicists (such as David Koresh and the Branch Davidians) have replaced Europe with the United States. *Violent apocalyptic Christians in the United States have usually been associated with historicism because they see past or current events as equating with the events of the tribulation period that culminates in a final conflict known as Armageddon.*

The violence that they initiate or in which they participate is understood to be part of the fulfillment of biblical prophecy.

The majority of premillennialists (including most American evangelicals) are known as dispensationalists. They hold that there will be a future, literal and physical 1,000-year reign of Jesus Christ on earth following the events of the rapture, tribulation, and Second Coming. Unlike historicists, dispensationalists are pretribulationists and futurists, believing that all prophetic events will not occur in the present age. Rather, the events will transpire during the yet-future tribulation, Second Coming, and millennium. Since the 1970s, dispensationalism has been popularized through the writings of authors such as Hal Lindsey (*The Late Great Planet Earth*) and Tim LaHaye and Jerry Jenkins (Left Behind series). *Although they have a strong apocalyptic theology, dispensationalists have no history of or propensity for apocalyptic violence.* This is because they believe that prophecy will be fulfilled in the future in God's timing and without human assistance.

Each of the above views has received extensive theological consideration and propagation by respective proponents in attempts to accurately interpret biblical passages. The views are deeply held and ultimately also affect other Christian doctrines. Although the views may be confusing or bewildering to those unfamiliar with them, they are an integral part of Christian theology. *No millennial view necessitates instigating or participating in armed violence.*

Eschatology is part of every Christian theological framework. Apocalyptic beliefs are not an aberration of theology, but pursuing violence as a consequence of apocalyptic belief *is* contrary to orthodox Christianity. A clear understanding of the end-times framework of individuals and groups participating in apocalyptic violence can greatly assist those trying to combat it.

ESCHATOLOGY AND VIOLENCE: FOUR AMERICAN CASES

For the armed apocalypticist, prophecy matters, and individual acts of violence can even be attempts at "hot-wiring" the apocalypse. An overview of four examples of violence that had apocalyptic connotations helps to show some of the significance, distinctions, and outworking of violent apocalyptic theology.

1. *Militia advocates* with strong religious overtones (and not all groups have these) are usually postmillennial, but they are not motivated primarily by eschatology. They often draw from Christian Reconstructionism's ideology and postmillennial eschatology but move beyond its normal parameters. Some militia advocates are premillennial and view their actions as part of the eschatological era of the tribulation.

The patriot/militia movement in America is a loosely knit network of individuals and organizations with religious and nonreligious convictions. Some claim a Christian orientation and some do not. Both religious and nonreligious patriot/militia advocates share common perspectives that often include an obsessive suspicion of the government, belief in antigovernment conspiracy theories, a deep-seated hatred of government officials, and a belief that the United States Constitution has been discarded by government officials and political leaders.[10]

Blending with these political ideas, there is among the religious advocates a combination of conservative Protestant Christianity, white-supremacist views, and pseudo-Christian thought. It is a unique political subculture supported by doctrinal distortion, anti-Semitism, and misappropriated apocalyptic beliefs. The result is a complex system of religious and political belief that may have apocalyptic views as its catalyst for violence. Richard Abanes observes:

> To complicate matters, large segments of the patriot/militia movement are being driven by religious beliefs and/or racism, two powerful forces that historically have often led to episodes of violence. This raises another disturbing issue: the unholy alliance that has formed between racists and anti-Semites on the one hand, and some conservative Christians on the other. The common ground between these two groups is apocalypticism.[11]

The blending of these ideologies and the distortion of and preoccupation with eschatological themes creates a worldview in which an Armageddon-like racial confrontation is viewed as imminent and desirable. Aberrant social, political, and theological values create a vicious cycle of hatred and violence.

The origins of the contemporary Christian militia movement are found in a genealogy of hatred and anti-Semitism dating to nineteenth-century England and a concept known as British Israelism. This idea, promulgated through a book by John Wilson entitled *Lectures on Our Israelitish Origin* (1840), contends that Jesus was not Semitic but Aryan and that the migrating Israelite tribes of the northern Kingdom of Israel were Aryans whose descendants eventually migrated to the British Isles and were the then-present-day Englishmen.[12] Through the teachings of Gerald L. K. Smith and the writings of William J. Cameron, editor of the *Dearborn Independent* (1919–27), British Israelism came to the United States and from it eventually came the Christian Identity Movement.

The Christian Identity Movement founders were Bertram Comparet and Wesley Swift, the latter a Ku Klux Klan member who, in 1946, founded the Church of Jesus Christ–Christian. This church was the basis for the Christian Defense League founded in the 1960s by Bill Gale and from which came later the Posse Comitatus and the Aryan Nation.[13] Common to all of these groups is the belief that there must be Anglo-Saxon domination and purity in the United States if the nation is to maintain its national and international viability. Such teachings are far from orthodox Christian doctrine and mainstream American Christianity, and, with regard to the genealogy and humanity of Jesus, the views of these groups are heretical. However, this vitriolic political and theological perspective produces a mind-set that accepts violence as necessary and normative.

The postmillennial tenets of the Christian Identity Movement include the belief that there is an impending collapse of worldly institutions and that the apocalypse will include a great racial battle. Coupled with a conspiratorial view of government, these beliefs have fueled intense anti-Semitism, racism, and survivalism. For Identity advocates, part of the postmillennial vision of the present and future entails a coming period of tribulation, conflict, and purging of the races in which white supremacy will prevail.

There are also strands of historicist premillennialism among some within the militia movement, especially those for whom the Branch Davidian episode in Waco is a rallying point seen as part of the tribulation. Philip Jenkins notes:

Some interpretations [of the Waco event] even proposed that the final catastrophe was a massacre deliberately undertaken by federal authorities, who purposely set the fires and machine-gunned survivors. It was this version of affairs that led to Waco becoming an apocalyptic symbol for the extreme right wing. The conflict provided a potent battlecry for white supremacist groups deeply imbued with premillenarian theology, often in Christian Identity guise. Remembering Waco became a basic creed for the militias, survivalists, and paramilitary groups dedicated to resistance against the Beast and One-Worldism. The massive bombing of the federal office building in Oklahoma City occurred precisely two years after the Waco inferno as an act of direct vengeance.[14]

When premillennial, these apocalyptic advocates are posttribulationists, believing that Christians will go through an intense period of cultural collapse and global tribulation. Unlike dispensationalists and other pretribulational premillennialists, who believe that Christians will be saved from the tribulation era because of the rapture, these posttribulationists believe the world is in or very near the tribulation and therefore their acts of violence have eschatological significance.[15]

2. *The Oklahoma City bombing* was committed and supported by individuals with a postmillennial perspective, but it was not motivated primarily by that eschatology. Instead, the eschatology blended with and supported racial and political ideas along with some militia influence. Timothy McVeigh was not the lone terrorist, as some believe. Rather, he had ties to the Christian Identity Movement.[16] Acting in revenge against the U.S. government, frequently called the Zionist Occupied Government (ZOG), and inspired by the fictional work *The Turner Diaries,* by William Pierce, McVeigh killed 168 people when he bombed the Alfred P. Murrah Federal Building on 19 April 1995. Although he was raised as a Roman Catholic, many of his ideas coincided with Christian Identity theology and politics.[17] Common with other acts of violence stemming from the militia movement were his anti-Semitism and a conspiratorial view of government.

3. *The Branch Davidians* in Waco, Texas, were historicist premillennialists and motivated primarily by eschatology. The explosive ending of the 51-day standoff between David Koresh and federal agents and the tragic fire in Waco that killed 79 people was the culmination of a theological perspective wherein Koresh believed he was, and was accepted by others as being, "the Lamb" of Revelation, a title understood in Christianity as referring to Jesus Christ.[18]

Under the leadership of Koresh, the Branch Davidians were an eschatologically confident community that had long expected that the American government, whom they identified as the Beast of Revelation (mentioned over 30 times in the book), would one day arrive seeking to destroy them—God's righteous remnant people. Fire also played a major part in the eschatology and teachings of Koresh.[19]

Revelation 6:1–8:6 refers to seven seal judgments that are the first of a series of three divine judgments (seals, trumpets, bowls) consisting of seven parts each that occur during the tribulation. Believing himself to be the Lamb of God, Koresh declared that he was opening the sixth seal and the one that is most severe (Revelation 6:12–17).[20] The end result, the fire, must be seen in this context. The armed violence of the Branch Davidians throughout the siege was historicist premillennial in its eschatology and motivated primarily by that eschatology.

4.   *Attacks on abortion clinics and staff by Christian militia advocates and others* have frequently come from those who are postmillennial in eschatology. Although their actions have been supported by their eschatology, they are motivated primarily by the desire to save the unborn. They view their violent actions as defensive actions that are necessary and more effective than the nonviolent protests of other antiabortion activists.[21] One of the most prominent of these attacks was that by Paul Hill, a former Presbyterian pastor who shot and killed Dr. John Bayard Britton and his security escort in Pensacola, Florida, on 29 July 1994. Hill, a Christian Reconstructionist, argued that he was not using violence, only force, and that he was justified in killing the doctor because it was the doctor who was perpetuating violence by performing abortions.[22] Postmillennial in eschatology, Hill declared, "Christ's kingdom and principles will ultimately prevail. God is in control—and he will bring about victory—we must obey him. Sooner or later America will become a Christian nation. Only Christians will be elected to public office. No false worship allowed."[23]

Some violence from abortion opponents and militia and Christian Identity advocates comes from a concept known as the Phinehas Priesthood, articulated by Richard Kelly Hoskins in his book *Vigilantes of Christendom* (1990). These individuals take their name from the Old Testament personality who killed an Israelite and his Midianite wife (Numbers 25:1–18). These Old Testament deaths are interpreted as occurring because of racial mixing (rather than idolatry as stated in the biblical text) and used as justification for violent acts against others, including abortionists. Though not necessarily postmillennialists, the actions of the Phinehas Priesthood share with Christian Reconstructionists an emphasis on Old Testament events and teachings.

HEAVENLY WARFARE ON EARTHLY BATTLEFIELDS

Acts of apocalyptic violence are committed because its perpetrators believe the violence is morally acceptable, divinely sanctioned, and fulfilling a divine prophetic plan. They believe that the world and society are in chaos and disorder and that their actions are key moments in which they are bringing sacred order and structure on secular society. For them, a spiritual battle is taking place on earth with violent physical manifestations as human history draws to a close. There is a dualistic view of the world, not dissimilar to Manichaeism and Gnosticism, in which there is an oversimplification of good and evil.

Those who participate in apocalyptic violence identify personally with the spiritual struggle that they believe is occurring in the world. Their actions are integral to the cosmic conflict as spiritual warfare becomes physical warfare. Because the struggle in which they are engaged is seen as primarily spiritual in nature, their acts of violence have spiritual as well as temporal effects. What may be literally earth-shattering ramifications are believed to receive applause and approval from God.

POLITICS WITH PROPHECY OR PROPHECY WITH POLITICS?

Every circumstance is different but some questions to consider regarding violence and armed groups include

- What is the primary ideological force—politics or prophecy?

- Are the rhetoric and actions of the group grounded in political ideology fused with theology or is the foundation theological commitments fused with politics?
- What is the eschatological framework of the individual or group?
- What prophetic terminology and symbols are being used?
- What is the history of the group?
- What other organizations or ideas are affiliated with the group?
- What books or writings are used for ideological or theological support?

Understanding the actions and motivations of individuals and groups supporting apocalyptic violence can be elusive. Mixed motivations, eclectic theology, acceptance of conspiracy theories, anti-Semitism, racism, and a variety of other political and theological aberrations may be woven together to create a tapestry of terror and violence. Yet to claim the actions as irrational can also be detrimental. What is needed, in part, is an understanding of the apocalyptic actors' worldviews and theologies.

TEN COMMANDMENTS FOR THE CAUTIOUSLY CONCERNED

What can be done? There is no single solution, but there are common errors that can lead to oversimplification, stereotyping, and misidentification of apocalyptic advocates and, thus, exacerbate specific incidents of violence.

1. *Don't underestimate religious fervor.* People will kill and die for their faiths. The power of religion to promote peace and violence is enormous and should never be ignored. In a democratic society and culture where the separation and compartmentalization of the sacred and the secular are prized, it is easy to forget that there is no unanimity of worldviews. For some, separation and compartmentalization are a threat.

2. *Don't confuse political violence and religious violence.* Although the two types of violence often overlap, understanding the core motivation for each type is essential to combating it. The religious militant and religious terrorist act first and foremost in response to a perceived divine mandate. They are acting for an audience of one—God.

3. *Don't confuse doctrines.* Understand the theological terminology used in Christian eschatology. Words matter. An appreciation of the historical and doctrinal distinctions within Christianity can be a great asset in understanding rhetoric and beliefs. Words such as *Armageddon, Beast, millennium, seal judgments, bowl judgments, trumpet judgments, premillennialism, postmillennialism, historicism,* and others, have specific and different meanings depending upon the theological traditions of those who are using them.

4. *Don't mistake the part for the whole.* The vast majority of Protestant conservatives, including evangelicals and the "religious Right," vociferously reject religious violence as immoral, illegal, and unbiblical.

5. *Don't dehumanize people who practice different or unusual religious values.*[24]

6. *Don't promote actions toward, and communication with, apocalyptic militants that can be perceived as persecution.* Persecution will confirm apocalyptic beliefs and strengthen religious resolve and resistance. Although that is impossible to completely control, every effort must be made to minimize and alleviate religious language and ideology in law enforcement actions and media presentations.

7. *Don't equate apocalypticism with armed violence.* Apocalyptic beliefs do not imply support of apocalyptic violence.[25]

8. *Don't confuse individuals and groups, assuming similarities or distinctions that do not exist.*

9. *Don't assume everyone in a group or organization will act the same way.* Even if a group supports apocalyptic violence or violence for other reasons, its members may or may not act in unison. "Individual operatives can have their own reasons for turning to terrorist violence unrelated to the group's purported goals."[26]

10. *Don't assume millennial expectations and the potential for violence is limited to Protestant Christianity.* Roman Catholicism as well as non-Christian religions can also uphold apocalyptic perspectives (such as the concept of the Mahdi in Islamic eschatology). Aum Shinrikyo devotees involved in the 1995 Tokyo subway sarin gas attack blended tenets of Hinduism, Buddhism, Christianity, and New Age spirituality, and believed that the world would be destroyed in an Armageddon scenario after which their leader, Shoko Asahara, would reign in a millennial kingdom.[27]

CONCLUSION

For the apocalyptic militant, Chicken Little was right—the sky is falling. Civilization and the world as we know it is on the verge of collapse and catastrophe, and it is the duty of the faithful to prepare for that end, or, depending on the theology, initiate it as part of the divine plan of history and in response to a divine mandate. Every field of study has foundational principles and specialized vocabulary. Theology is no different. An understanding of the concepts, distinctions, and terminology of Christian apocalypticism can aid scholars, journalists, law enforcement agents, and other interested parties in dealing constructively with the dynamics of millennial groups. In so doing, it may also help to minimize or alleviate apocalyptic armed violence.

NOTES

1. Mark Juergensmeyer, "Christian Violence in America," *Annals of the American Academy of Political and Social Science* 558 (July 1998): 89.

2. Richard Abanes, *American Militias: Rebellion, Racism, and Religion* (Downers Grove, IL: InterVarsity Press, 1996), 3.

3. For a summary history of the movement, see Kenneth G. C. Newport, "The Davidian Seventh-day Adventists and Millennial Expectations, 1959–2004," in *Expecting the End: Millennialism in Social and Historical Context,* ed. Kenneth G. C. Newport and Crawford Gribben (Waco, TX: Baylor University Press, 2006), 131–46.

4. Catherine Wessinger, "When the Millennium Comes Violently: A Comparison of Jonestown, Aum Shinrikyo, the Branch Davidians, and the Montana Freemen" (Yamauchi Lecture in Religion, Loyola University, New Orleans, 2 March 1997), 7–14. See also her book, *How the Millennium Comes Violently: From Jonestown to Heaven's Gate* (New York: Seven Bridges Press, 2000), 12–29. While Wessinger sees the Waco event as violence initiated due to confrontation with authorities and thus places it in the second group, I understand it as more theological and therefore in the final category. Either way, this shows how the theology and violence blend.

5. For an overview history, see Paul Boyer, *When Time Shall Be No More: Prophecy Belief in American Culture* (Cambridge, MA: Belknap/Harvard University Press), 1992.

6. For a simple guide to Bible prophecy, see the author's work coauthored with Thomas Ice, *Fast Facts on Bible Prophecy from A to Z* (Eugene, OR: Harvest House Publishers), 1997.

7. Gary North, *Lone Gunners for Jesus: Letters to Paul J. Hill* (Tyler, TX: Institute for Christian Economics, 1994), 11.

8. Ibid., 25.

9. Ice and Demy, *Fast Facts on Bible Prophecy from A to Z,* 83–84, 98–100.

10. Abanes, *American Militias*, 2.

11. Ibid., 3.

12. Michael Barkun, *Religion and the Racist Right: The Origins of the Christian Identity Movement* (Chapel Hill: University of North Carolina Press, 1994), 7.

13. Juergensmeyer, "Christian Violence in America," 97.

14. Philip Jenkins, *Mystics and Messiahs: Cults and New Religions in American History* (New York: Oxford University Press, 2000), 218.

15. Jessica Stern, *Terror in the Name of God: Why Religious Militants Kill* (New York: HarperCollins, 2003), 17–19.

16. Mike German, "Behind the Lone Terrorist, a Pack Mentality," *Washington Post,* 5 June 2005, B01, available at www.washingtonpost.com/wp-dyn/content/article/2005/06/04AR2005060400147_pf.html (accessed 5 November 2007).

17. Stern, *Terror in the Name of God,* 27–29.

18. Kenneth Samples et al., *Prophets of the Apocalypse: David Koresh & Other American Messiahs* (Grand Rapids, MI: Baker Books, 1994), 68–69.

19. See ibid., 78–88, and Abanes, 55–58, for specific teachings of Koresh pertaining to fire and eschatology.

20. Samples et al., *Prophets of the Apocalypse,* 79–80.

21. Stern, *Terror in the Name of God,* 152–53.

22. Ibid., 169.

23. Paul J. Hill, interview by Jessica Stern, 27 April 1999, cited in ibid.

24. Wessinger, "When the Millennium Comes Violently," 3.

25. For example, after more than 30 years of studying Christian eschatology, the author knows of no acts of religious violence stemming from dispensationalism, the eschatological perspective popularized in the writings of Hal Lindsey and the best-selling Left Behind religious novels of Tim LaHaye and Jerry Jenkins.

26. Stern, *Terror in the Name of God,* 164.

27. See Manabu Watanabe, "Religion and Violence in Japan Today: A Chronological and Doctrinal Analysis of Aum Shinrikyo," *Terrorism and Political Violence* 10, no. 4 (Winter 1998): 80–100.

19 Glory in Defeat and Other Islamist Ideologies

Mehrdad Mozayyan

HISTORICAL BACKGROUND[1]

Other than a number of rapidly developing city-states in the Persian Gulf, today's Islamic countries of the Middle East are barely a shadow of what they once were. As the fruits of the Renaissance and Reformation ripened, the Christian West began outdistancing the Moslem East. The Industrial Revolution, leading to scientific advancements and financial strength, gave greater impetus to opening the world to Western exploration and also exploitation. The colonial age had now begun and the retreat of the Moslems became the inevitable sign of the latter's reversal of fortune. One side had failed to keep pace with change; the other was now dictating that change.

In the Far East, the disparity was no less stark. However, a number of countries there made a planned and directed effort to compensate for their lag, eventually breaking through their underdevelopment. By the early twentieth century, Japan, a small island country, emerged as a great power, vanquishing colossal Russia in the 1905 Russo-Japanese War. The road to success had been charted, and Japan's neighbors would take on the challenge of emulating its efforts. Thus, despite the experiences of a colonial heritage or war, states like Taiwan, Singapore, and South Korea overcame major obstacles to become Asia's leading industrial states. Similarly, energy-dependent and highly populated China and India, with recent and long histories of harsh colonial rules, continued to push ahead as though driven by their ancient legacies of great civilizations.

By the turn of the twenty-first century, after monumental sacrifices in human life and liberty, China became a world economic power. India, somewhat less successful on the economic front, claimed the title of world's largest democracy, with equally consequential sociopolitical reforms and scientific achievements. In comparison to the above newly developed countries, however, the Middle East has not fared well, despite benefiting from relatively small populations and abundant natural resources.[2]

But this inability to modernize and establish functioning civil societies was not due to a less impressive historical past; nor had they always lagged behind the Far East. For example, up until the mid-nineteenth century, Egypt was not far behind the now highly

Dr. Mozayyan completed his undergraduate and graduate degrees at the University of Pennsylvania, receiving a BA in economics, an MA in international relations (with honors), an MBA (from the Wharton School), and a PhD in political science. His academic fields of concentration were international relations theory and comparative politics. He has taught in Europe and at the Naval War College as associate professor, and has written a number of articles on the Middle East and Iran, in English and Farsi.

advanced Japan. Paradoxically, of all the major countries in the Middle East, only oil-less Turkey, with a younger history than many of its neighbors, is making solid strides toward full democracy and overcoming underdevelopment. What it lacks in oil and gas is compensated for by a nationalistic state that has, since the early 1920s, consistently and, when needed, by authoritarian measures, pursued secular law and modernization.[3]

In much of the Islamic world, rather than study the above countries' success stories as blueprints for advancement, introversion has taken place. The 1979 revolution in Iran ushered a widespread rejectionist philosophy changing the Moslems' views of themselves and their position in the world, as well as their approaches to daily life and politics. In modern times, anti-Western feelings in the Middle East have been traceable to the effects of European colonization and the colonizers' heavy-handed approaches toward their colonies. More recently, the seeds of public dissent were sown and the grounds for rejecting Western ways were plowed by an American regional presence, which the masses viewed as benefiting only Washington and its conservative local allies, Israel in particular. Those who saw their solution in changing the status quo by staging mass uprisings, revolution, and a return to sharia law now felt increasingly victimized and discriminated against.

Local frustration and disillusionment also had a domestic component that focused on corrupt and ineffective political leaders who espoused Western ideologies but could neither improve their people's well-being nor succeed in defeating the much smaller state of Israel. However, it was the Islamists' gaining and holding power in Iran, ironically a country that was showing signs of progress, that produced a wake-up call throughout the Moslem world and led to widespread Islamic resurgence. The event provided a blueprint for oppositional and militant action against Westward-leaning regimes, demonstrating the tenacity and effectiveness of Islamist groups. Further, it was testimony to the fact that through unity, determination, blind faith, and readiness to sacrifice lives, powerful and deeply entrenched regimes could be overthrown, and dominant world powers put on the defensive.

Prior to 1979 one would be hard pressed to find terrorists for whom acts of suicide were a common methodology for voicing dissent. Nor were incidents of hostage taking a prevalent approach to intimidation and retribution. The taking of 52 American hostages, sanctioned by Ayatollah Khomeini; his bestowing the title of *Shaheedparvar* (those who breed martyrs or suicide warriors) on his followers; and his demanding that they cause "torrents of blood" to flow changed the nature of conflict and the political discourse that had been dominant among dissident Moslems.[4]

New standards were now set, and a new discourse gained currency that targeted the "enemies of Islam" through revolutionary, militant, and martyr-oriented strategies. Life became readily expendable, especially if it hindered the advancement of Islamist agendas. Islam thus became a means and an end for the frustrated masses, giving rise to leaders who spoke in terms of Islamic communities (*ummat*), and pushed the need to restore Islam to its former position of power by removing the corrupting Western influences that hindered the promotion of their own millenarian beliefs.

Previously, the angry masses and their nonstate leaders did not know how to channel their frustrations or where to direct their grievances. In the post-1979 period, rather than directing their explosive energies at laying the groundwork for creating institutions through which national grievances and shortcomings could be addressed, or building peaceful and constructive channels of communication, an opposite approach was adopted that promoted conflict and extremism. Thus, the ideas that emanated from Iran encouraged the Moslem masses toward action, while alarming their political leaders. Time would gradually alter most people's initially positive perception of the 1979 Revolution, but the train that carried extremism and Islamic fundamentalism had now received sufficient jolt to leave the station.

Other than by effectively eliminating their opponents in Iran, the clerics gained considerable credibility in the Islamic world by maintaining a self-righteous stance that resorted to intimidation tactics and belittled the West, all with considerable impunity. The lessons learned were that such tactics are most rewarding because they allow the leadership of smaller states to solidify their rules and broaden their popular support, despite poor performance on other fronts. The key was to appeal, by attacking the United States and its close allies, to people's low self-esteems, their perpetual sense of being wronged, and their desires for recognition. Many grievances against the West were legitimate, but what the new approach entailed was to make it the sole scapegoat for all existing problems.

As proved by leaders like Nasser, Gadhafi, and Castro, words and actions that degraded the West worked wonders for failing regimes. Now, regardless of how hollow, self-damaging, or misguided such policies were, their promotion made sense because they provided people a psychological boost, a sense of being avenged, and a source on which all their own failures could be blamed. The instructive lesson for the newly emerged Islamist leaders was to keep the stakes high and never retreat from one's goals, except temporarily, and then, only when absolutely necessary. Indeed, if Saddam had played by these rules, he may well have survived.

Iraq and Afghanistan (where the United States has failed to establish order) have only served to strengthen the perception that the only weapon against which the West is vulnerable is true Islam. Thus, Ayatollah Khomeini's repeated declaration that "America cannot do a damned thing" continues to ring true, despite the allied invasion of Iraq, which resulted in the unintended outcome of strengthening the Islamists. At the very least, Iran's clerics demonstrated that, with a degree of shrewdness, the red line that might trigger a severe U.S. response was much further into the horizon than previously believed. Playing the game of intimidation, softened by occasional words of conciliation, and supplemented by cleverly breathing discord among the great powers, has worked wonders in keeping their enemies confused and off balance.

Finally, Islamists have been emboldened by the retreat of the American armada from Lebanon after the annihilation of the Marines' barrack in Beirut by suicide bombers (1983), the 1989 victory of the primitively armed Afghani mujahideen against the former Soviet Union, Palestinian successes against the Israelis during their intifada uprisings from 1987 to 1993 and again in 2000–2006, Hezbollah's ability to emerge unscathed after a strong 2006 Israeli military campaign to uproot it from southern Lebanon, the stunning 2006 victory in the first Palestinian parliamentary elections by Islamic resistance movement Hamas, and the West's continued inability to prevent Tehran from pushing forward with its nuclear objective. These developments have provided fuel for resurgent Islam and convinced the Islamists that fighting rather than compromising better serves their cause.

REDEFINING ONE'S EARTHLY PROBLEMS

Due to the noteworthy successes that anti-Western and Islamist groups have scored in the past decades, and the continued hardship and disillusionment of the masses in the Middle East, key questions that focus on why Islamic states have failed to keep pace, or why their modern armies repeatedly lost to Israel, have been replaced by questions that project blame on others, particularly on the West. By asking such increasingly popular but rhetorical questions as, How can Moslems stand tall and overcome their problems as long as they resort to Western ideologies and rely on their methodologies? people have effectively rejected socialism, modernism, secularism, and nationalism, which were supposed to have improved their conditions.[5] Since the West is viewed as selfishly pursuing its old colonial or imperialistic agendas, it stands to reason that its ideologies cannot serve others. Needless to say, the U.S. military involvement in Iraq has had a devastating effect on this already-negative perception. Importantly, for the Moslems, what gives immense credibility to rejectionist views of the West is that these views can also be supported by old text. Islamists have made effective use of established religious writings where Christians and Jews were treated as "the West," and "Westernization" as "an insidious scheme to undermine Islam."[6]

Adding complexity to an already complex and negative view of the world are the powerful conspiratorial beliefs that maintain that nothing of substance happens unless supported by Washington, London, and the oil cartels, or backed by powerful lobbies and kingmakers in the West. These perspectives have become increasingly dominant among Moslems today. Consequently, the religion has sidestepped any self-reflection of core values and behaviors to find shortcomings. Under rare incidents when fundamentalists do internalize blame, it is at the politically nonpartisan oppressed masses that they direct it, for their failure to rise up, and "for their weakness in following the oppressor."[7] Ayatollah Khomeini often admonished his followers that blame goes to those who do nothing to uproot injustice by opposing the oppressor (*mostakbar*). But if neither Western ideology nor methodology has answers to the Moslems' laggard position in the world, what alternatives might they pursue?

Resurgent Islam, which proposes to remedy this situation, has forced not only pro-Western but also anti-American and secular regimes of the Middle East to modify their behaviors. The increased need to adopt Islamic characteristics or promote an Islamic facade is best exemplified by the Baathist Saddam Hussein's modification of the Iraqi flag during the Iran-Iraq war by decorating it with the words *Allah o akbar* (God is great).[8] Similarly, to improve his legitimacy, the secular Baathist Hafiz al-Assad of Syria asked Iranian clerics to confirm the Islamic (Shiite) nature of his Alawi regime. Further, Egypt's secular regime has allowed the Muslim Brotherhood to participate in politics again.[9]

The answers and conclusions that are propagated in the Middle East mostly support the notion that the difficulties Islamic states face cannot be resolved outside of an Islamic framework. In other words, the problems have stemmed from the fact that political lead-ers in the Middle East have abandoned Islam, and that it is time to adopt "The Islamic Solution" (*Hal al-Islami*).[10] Given that Islam encompasses all aspects of life (religious as well as sociopolitical and economic), it has not been difficult to see it as providing an-swers to all mankind's problems. Not surprisingly, this has meant looking to the distant past to find solutions for the present. However, this past, which is focused on Islam's days of glory or great piety, seems less interested in a future that guarantees independent thought, social liberty, modernity, and economic remuneration in this world. Rather, it primarily assures the true believer of spiritual salvation and an eternally joyful existence in the world beyond. Any steps that may contradict Islamic law (sharia) may not be pur-sued, even if it benefits the country—and, by that definition, those who live in it.

Consequently, where other developing countries advanced by overcoming such stan-dard problems as lack of resources, deplorable economic and industrial infrastructure, untrained labor, poor medical care, illiteracy, corruption, nepotism, foreign intervention, and a colonial legacy, the Middle East staggers. Having returned to religious dogma, so-cioeconomic development and ecological goals have lost their urgency. As Ayatollah Khomeini reminded Iranians, "Economics is for donkeys [idiots]"[11] and "Revolution was not about the price of watermelons."[12] Moreover, citizenry (*mellat*) is subjugated to the Islamic community (*ummat*), and notions of a cultural or national identity that refer-ence a pre-Islamic past are opposed and systematically erased, unless the regime is secular.

Not only have issues relating to national identity and socioeconomic problems been redefined but so have concepts of war and peace. Fundamentalists maintain that peace will come when the enemies of Islam have been routed, and conflict will not cease until this goal is achieved. However, the notion of war within a religious context (jihad) differs from regular warfare. The former is more nuanced and is not limited to the battlefield; nor does it have to be fought by standard rules, methods, or arms.

Given the disparity of power between East and West, martyrdom, propaganda, de-ception, and imagery have become key components in Islamists' arsenals; and there is substantial and detailed literature going back to Islam's early period that elaborates the use of such tactics. Presently, the war is cast in religious terms, where David and Goliath are evoked, and true believers are directed into action by being reminded of the unex-pected outcome of that confrontation. David had contributed his faith, devotion, cour-age, and selflessness, just as Moslems are called to do; God did, and will do, the rest. In such instances, it is critical that God be seen "as a personal participant in the fighting pro-cess." It is God that grants victory so that "truth" may "nullify falsehood." Similarly, when Moslems won in the Battle of Badr,[13] the Qur'an states, "It was not you who slew them, but Allah. . . ."[14]

Many of the references to jihad in the Qur'an were aimed at encouraging those who were reluctant to fight, reminding them that God is fighting along their side, and of the "fantastic rewards" to be given to those who fight. There is a considerable body of litera-ture dealing with the rewards and the high status reserved for martyrs.[15] But in the end, the choice is not for the Moslems to make. To have submitted to God means trusting

Him, or facing devastating consequences. Islamic holy texts allocate considerable space to punishment and the need to fear God. As the Qur'an reminds Moslems,

> Fighting is prescribed for you, and ye dislike it. But it is possible that ye dislike a thing which is good for you. And that ye love a thing which is bad for you. But God knoweth, and ye know not.[16]

SECTARIAN IDEOLOGIES AND CALLS TO ACTION

Sunni and Shiite views and perspectives about the problems Moslems face, and the ideologies Sunnis and Shiites resort to for resolving them, are often dissimilar. They may cooperate for convenience, but beyond subduing common enemies, their goals and aspirations are not the same. Nor does each sect enjoy full harmony with all its subgroups. Hence, in their lineup to confront their problems, Sunnis generally reach out to Sunnis, and Shiites to Shiites.[17] Six main divisions are readily distinguishable in the Middle East:

1.   The Sunni populations of the region. By and large, they oppose the United States, are unsupportive of their own Westward-leaning regimes, and harbor deep resentment toward Israel and the Shiites, and most support the ideas of resurgent Sunni Islam.[18]

2.   The non-Iranian Shiites. Except for those in Iraq and Bahrain, they live under Sunni rule and resent their more numerous coreligionists. They are favorable toward Iran's clerical regime, harbor negative sentiments toward the United States and its allies,[19] and aim to strengthen their positions by bridging the territorial gaps that separate them. Many Sunnis feel threatened by them, especially where much of their oil fields are in Shiite lands.

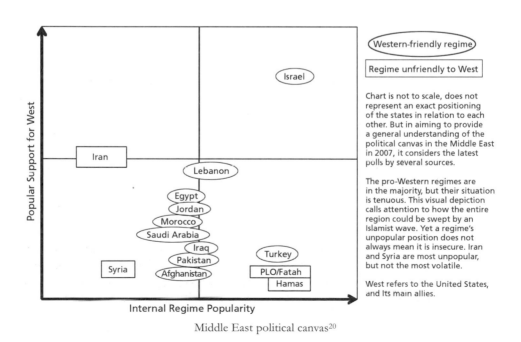

Middle East political canvas[20]

3.   The non-Arab Shiite Iranians. Most treat religion from a practical perspective. The Arab-Israeli conflict is not of primary concern to them; most do not harbor deep anti-American sentiments but oppose their own regime.[21]

4.   Pro-Western Sunni regimes. They mostly adhere to sharia law, but remain threatened by Islamic extremists who oppose the West, and any entity that befriends it. They oppose Israel without openly confronting it, and harbor much animosity toward Shiites.[22]

5.   Iran's Islamic Republic. This is a revolutionary and fundamentalist Shiite state that sees the United States, Israel, and Western culture as its primary foes. It supports Syria and promotes any extremist group that opposes U.S. regional presence and its allies.

6.   The Baathist regime of Syria. This Alawi (a Shiite offshoot) regime rules over a Sunni majority, opposes America, and is a major opponent of Israel. It supports Iran, but is itself a secular regime that fears its own Sunni population. Therefore, it is supportive of the Shiites in Lebanon, while feeling threatened by Islamists who shun secular government and demand a return to strict sharia law.[23]

THE GOLDEN AGE OF ISLAM

In recent times, political reference to a vague and idealized period known as "the Golden Age of Islam" has become frequent. This utopian perception is a highly idealized rendition of a period that some equate with the Abbasid caliphate (750–1258),[24] when the Islamic empire reached its peak, covering territories that stretched over three continents. Some Islamists showcase this bygone era and make its reestablishment an objective. But they maintain that succeeding in this goal requires an Islamic revival, the rejection of Western ways and influences, and the ejection of the West and its allies from Islamic lands.[25] In essence, meeting these prerequisites has become the Islamists' main focus.

However, the importance of Islam's "Golden Age" is primarily for the Sunnis and more so for Sunni Arabs, because it symbolizes the height of Islam's grandeur when they brought vast territories under their rule. By drawing from and combining the ancient knowledge of Greece, Persia, and India, they promoted the spread of sciences and general learning.[26] Thus, this revered period provides a sense of identity, unity, and achievement, while assuring them a place in the world. Indeed, most people and cultures have some type of a golden age that for them remains highly idealized and unassailable.[27]

There are others who associate Islam's "Golden Age" with its first 40 years of history (621–661), which includes the leadership of its first four caliphs, known as the "Rightly Guided." It was during this period that Islam established itself as a major religion, made large conquests, and is believed to have remained in its purest form, largely untouched by alien thoughts or widespread dissent. Those who stress this period maintain that the problems Moslems now face are due to their divergence from Islam's true path and their internal disagreements over progress. If only Moslems resumed their original ways, became pious again, and rejected corrupting foreign thoughts, the doors that have been shut to them would reopen, and their desired conditions be reestablished.

Finally, the idea of a golden age has also been equated with notable individuals, groups, or events. This type of focus is more descriptive of the Shiites, who, unlike the Sunnis, were not often in dominant positions, and lack the historical memory of a large empire,[28] centrally ruled by a caliph. Consequently, they looked to other sources of identity, legitimacy, and inspiration to anchor themselves. Since the grandeur of the Islamic empire had come at the cost of other cultures and empires, not all people in the Middle East have identified with the same period or harbored identical feelings toward it. Indeed, nowhere is the concept of Islam's "Golden Age" in greater conflict than among Iranians, possessing their own pre-Islamic identity and geopolitical references.

This old conflict stems from two opposing views: one looking to Iran (Persia) with its ancient, pre-Islamic days of imperial glory and civilization, the other cherishing the country's post-Islamic period with its own periods of conquest and achievement, albeit at a fraction of what it once was. In 1501, particularly, the Safavid dynasty succeeded in reunifying Iran under Shiism, where it had remained fragmented since its fall to Moslem armies after 642. The present disconnect between Iranian state and society, or the old conflict between Iranian nationalists and clergy, stems from these opposing points of reference. While the latter have worked hard to erase all historical memory of a distinctly Iranian entity nourished by its ancient past, the former have tried to preserve it.[29] Thus, for centuries, proponents of Shiism like Ali Shariati (an Iranian Marxist-Islamist theoretician), have argued,

> Islamic civilization has worked like scissors and has cut us off completely from our pre-Islamic past. . . . Our people remember nothing from this distant past and do not care to learn about the pre-Islamic civilizations. . . . Consequently, for us a return to our roots means not a rediscovery of pre-Islamic Iran, but a return to our Islamic, especially Shiah roots.[30]

SUNNI AND SHIITE FOUNDATIONS

The difference between the Sunni and Shiite fundamentalist positions is also of interest. The Sunnis are galvanizing around the idea of reclaiming their lost power and prestige, the Shiites around the notion of reestablishing just and legitimate rule, usurped by the Sunnis. Justice will be served when the reins of power are turned over to leading Shiites, awaiting the return of Mohammad al-Mahdi, the Hidden Twelfth Imam (also known as the Mahdi), who is said to have gone into occultation in the year 874.[31]

Except for Iranian Shiites, who have not been the religious underdogs for over five centuries, and the Shiites living in Lebanon, who view Israel as their primary enemy, other Shiites have traditionally viewed the Sunnis as their main foe. Since the Iranian Revolution, however, the United States and Israel are viewed with at least as much disdain among Shiites as are the Sunnis. This anti-Western sentiment and desire to undo the region's pro-Western regimes are two broad objectives over which the Islamists, disillusioned Moslems, and Tehran find common ground. In this endeavor, jihadist ideology and martyrdom, supported by a strong psychological component, disseminated through different channels of communication, have become the Islamists' weapons of choice.

Sunni Islamists are primarily informed by *Wahhabi*[32] and *Salafi*[33] ideologies with jihadi overtones. *Jihad* originally referred to defensive wars, allowing the newly Moslem converts to resist their more powerful internal enemies. But as Islam grew in strength, "the doctrine came to mean the existence of one single Islamic state, ruling the entire umma."[34] However, through the centuries, Sunnis (and Shiites to a much smaller degree) have used the term as both defensive and offensive to thwart their adversaries. Indeed, the interpretation has often been a matter of convenience. For example, a popular argument now maintains that evicting the enemies of Islam from Moslem lands is a defensive act.

Irrespective of this debate, jihadist ideology has been the ready-made vehicle with which to oppose the West. Both Sunni and Shiite sects resort to it, but other than differing goals and perceptions, there is also a technical difference that distinguishes them. This pertains to the fact that for Shiites, jihad may only be waged under the leadership of a rightful imam.[35] That a large majority of terrorist acts outside of the Middle East have been conducted by Sunnis may be partially explained by this.

For the Shiites, what best captures their soul and unifies them for action is a historical event known as the "Battle of Karbala'," fought in the year 680. It is there that their third imam (Hussein ibn Ali) and his clan of 71 are believed to have been brutally massacred by Yazid's much larger forces.[36] The conflict arose after Ali (the cousin and son-in-law of the Prophet, the fourth and last of the "Rightly Guided" caliphs, and the first Shiite imam) died of a stab wound in 661. His partisans (the Shiites) had always maintained that he, rather than the other three caliphs, should have ruled after Muhammad's death. After Ali, his older son, Hassan, conceded the leadership of the Islamic community to Yazid, but Hassan's younger brother Hussein did not. This conflict eventually played itself out on the plains of Karbala', resulting in Hussein's death, which created such an unbridgeable chasm between the Shiites and Sunnis that not even the passage of 13 centuries has been able to bridge it.

The importance of this episode for militant Shiites and jihadists is the ideological foundation it provides for opposing what Shiite leaders identify as illegal or unjust. It serves as a call to action, and gives strong encouragement to those who lack sufficient hope or courage to fight more powerful enemies. Hussein's martyrdom at Karbala' was made into an epic story to mentally prepare the Shiites for war and help them view their defeats as only temporary setbacks. To Shiite clerics and their true believers who resort to their own sources of legitimacy and moments of historical pride, hereditary rule and leadership over the Islamic community must remain with the Prophet's household, i.e., Ali and his male descents, all of whom are considered to be immaculate and divine.

According to Shiites, Muhammad had told Ali that he was next in line as the chosen one to lead the Moslems. To confirm this, Ali and his descendents are often quoted as stating that the Prophet entrusted Islam's leadership to them. For example, according to Ja'far as-Sadiq (the sixth imam), Ali had recounted the following story about the time when God ordered the Prophet to appoint a successor. The Apostle of God asked: "Who? O Lord." And He replied: "Appoint your cousin [Ali]. . . . " Similarly, the eighth imam (Reza) is quoted as saying the Prophet had personally told Ali: "You and the Imam from among your descendents, O Ali, are the Proof of God to his creation after me. . . . For you are of me, you are created of my substance, and I am of you."[37]

Given the Shiites' belief that the leadership positions of Ali's descendents had been usurped by Sunni caliphs, the classical Shiite approach to politics became one that focused on reestablishing "just" and "legitimate" rule by reinstituting the Prophets' household. After the disappearance of the Twelfth Imam, the issue became maintaining a robust Shiite community with its saints and leading clerics, many of whom also claimed descent from the Prophet.

To achieve this goal during a period of Sunni supremacy, a variety of religiously sanctioned techniques were perfected that were based on the notion that ends justify the means. The more important and effective of these were *khod'eh,* known as denial and misrepresentation; *tanfieh,* best described as pretense; and *taqiyah,* or dissimulation that translates into concealing the truth.[38] These techniques, which had their roots in early Islam, were practiced as weapons of the weak against the strong. They proved so successful as to slowly enter mainstream politics. On rare occasions, the option of resorting to acts of martyrdom, rather than accepting what religious leaders identified as illegitimate rule, was also exercised.

It was mostly the uncompromising and militant approach among these options that Khomeini emphasized in order to bring the clerics to power. However, it is important to note that this view differs from classical Sunni doctrine, which maintains that life under tyranny and hardship is still preferential to haphazard rule and chaos. In other words, the Shiites' view was more revolutionary and demanding of change, while the Sunnis' was more conformist and accepting of the status quo.

The Shiites' traditional understanding of and approach to the Battle of Karbala' was one that viewed Imam Hussein and his clan as the disinherited (*mazloom*). The image associated with this depiction conjured immense sympathy among the masses, and great empathy from those who felt they too had been wronged in life. From this angle, Hussein was projected as a passive saint who was massacred while defending his beliefs and his clan. Thus, his passive actions of neither renouncing his claim to leadership nor taking flight are what ultimately led to his martyrdom. For centuries, in an effort to relive Karbala' and remind people what occurred there, play acts known as *Ta'zieh* have been staged during the two holy days of *Tassua* and *Ashura*, in the month of Muharram. Large crowds gather on open street corners to watch the entire battle scene, culminating in the beheading of Imam Hussein by his Sunni enemies, all played out by armature actors.

Although Hussein's forces were too few to have presented a viable resistance against Yazid, the battle he waged at Karbala was never depicted as being in vain. The imam had been defeated, but the ultimate glory was his. Through his intransigence and martyrdom, Hussein showed his followers the way to salvation. He also proved to his enemies that the Shiites would not give in to unjust and illegitimate rule. However, this traditional depiction did not introduce Hussein as a proactive leader, or a warrior who actively sought war with his enemies in order to ensure justice was established.

Although the political nature of Shiism has made it into a powerful tool for stirring up emotions and provoking militant action, Hussein's generally reactive image proved lacking to Iran's revolutionary Islamists who needed a more potent force to galvanize the masses against the Shah. Through delicate manipulation, they redefined Hussein's true personality and objectives, thereby extracting important additional benefits from the events in Karbala'.

This was achieved by reintroducing Hussein, but not as a passive leader who was victimized, or whose martyrdom should evoke a sense of defeat and deep grief. Nor was his massacre to be viewed as a tragedy that was forced upon him. On the contrary, the glory of the war he waged, and his willingness to be martyred were to be emphasized and idealized as a moment of glory in Shiite history. Karbala' was depicted as Hussein's conscious decision to wage war on his larger enemy, knowing full well what the earthly outcome would be. Indeed, it was not the immediate earthly outcome that mattered most.

GLORY IN DEFEAT

This newly modified approach to militant Islamic philosophy was first successfully used to overthrow the Shah, who was depicted as Yazid, and Ayatollah Khomeini as the embodiment of Imam Hussein, or, some argued, the Mahdi himself. Much the same approach was used in the Iran-Iraq war to delegitimize Saddam Hussein and his Baathist regime. Similarly to the Shah, Saddam was cast as an "infidel," and his rule as "unjust." Equally bold and imaginative was the way in which the Iraq war was equated with Karbala', and the dead Iranian soldiers with its martyrs. In recruiting and ensuring ongoing public support for the war, people were told to marvel at Imam Hussein's accomplishment and imitate his way with great joy and pride.

Families that had lost their sons to war were told to rejoice, because their fallen soldiers of Islam had now entered heaven. Many families of martyrs were congratulated by officials from the regime, given pastries and sweets, and told to celebrate. Imam Hussein had shown the way to salvation and, by his death, promoted the cult of saints and martyrdom among Shiites. By following his example, this imaginative ideology argued, truth would prevail over falsehood, and justice would be reestablished under true Islam.[39]

The Shiite theory of "just war" is nuanced and dynamic, and goes beyond Sunni interpretations. The idea of a golden age as a sought-after period that once existed under the Abbasids is absent here, but it is matched by the idea of a golden age that awaits mankind after the return of the Hidden Imam. This will happen when the world is filled with corruption and injustice, a situation that his arrival is to remedy. Until then, the Islamic community must reject illegitimate rulers and unjust conditions, as prescribed by its leading ayatollahs.[40] Today, the views of Shiite and Sunni masses are mostly aligned in equating falsehood, injustice, and illegitimate rule with the presence and influence of the United States, its allies, and surrogate regimes. Be it in the Middle East, or on the global scene, or at the UN, they are perceived as a primary source of evil that must be defeated, or forced to retreat.

Shiism is the more politicized of Islam's two main sects, since its ayatollahs possess considerable influence over their followers. Their ability to legally interpret the holy texts, provide their own explanations for different circumstances, and call their followers to action gives them an important edge over their Sunni counterparts. This local and regional power they presently enjoy is the result of the Iranian Revolution, which caused a watershed in Islam's history of leadership. "Throughout all periods of Islamic history the 'ulama [leading theologians and clerics] were politically and economically subservient to political rulers."[41] The events in Iran would change all that, giving them unparalleled access to wealth and power.

The grand ayatollahs may now assume the title of regents to the Hidden Imam, act as a source of emulation, and pass judgment on all earthly matters. The pillars of the Islamic republic rest on a concept known as *velayat-e faghih* (or the leadership of the jurisprudence), first successfully articulated and implemented by Ayatollah Khomeini. It holds that pending the return of the Twelfth Imam (on Judgment Day), the custodianship of the state and the Islamic community rests with the leading grand ayatollah. In relation to this, some Shiites believe that the Hidden Imam's return must be hastened, while others are of the opinion that it should be left to follow its own preordained course. Clearly, the former position, which Iran's current president Mahmoud Ahmadinejad supports, entails an apocalyptic view of the world, with all the requirements and implications that accompany its realization.

A question arises here as to how Shiite clerics were able to convince the masses of the accuracy of their bold religious interpretation. It helps to remember that almost all senior ayatollahs claim descent from the Prophet, a unique status that gives their claim to leadership a degree of legitimacy. Moreover, in the eyes of Moslems, Muhammad "was not only the transmitter of the Qur'an to mankind at large but also its primary recipient: certain aspects of its meaning were reserved for him alone."[42] According to the Sunnis, Allah did not grant this privilege to anyone else. But to the Twelver Shiites, this unique power was passed on to Ali by the Prophet,[43] and Ali passed it down to his infallible sons, until the line ended with the Mahdi. But since the Mahdi is in occultation, the clerics have argued, only the most devout and learned of the faithful can discover or unveil (*kashf*) the deeper meanings embedded in the Qur'an. This is a domain in which the Sunni clergy have not dared tread. This may provide an explanation as to why non-clerical figures like Bin Laden can spearhead a jihadist movement among the Sunnis, but the Shiites are prone to look to the likes of Ayatollah Khomeini before rising up.

SUMMARY

The ideologies that propel jihadist movements are different. Yet some of the core beliefs among Islamists are similar, although they are not easily harmonized. A key element in all this is the notion of a cosmic war that should not be seen as lost due to "temporary setbacks." Therefore:

1. It is the Moslems' duty to fight "infidels" and all foreign intrusion. Although war should not take place among Muhammad's followers, the term "infidel" has been applied to Moslems as well. The issue here is one of designation and promotion by a figure of authority.

2. Moslems should propagate Islam and expand its influence. Although both the Sunnis and Shiites pursue this objective, their end goals are different. Hence, other than cooperating to eliminate common enemies, they do not combine forces.

3. Moslems should be ready to give their lives in the way of Allah. Thus, Islamists aim to convince their followers of the great benefits in achieving martyrdom. These benefits, depicted as both spiritual and physical, take up considerable space in

Islamic literature, as does the topic of jihad. Both sects promote martyrdom, but the Shiites' perspective is more political and better developed.

In the final analysis, the most prudent approach to facing Islamic extremism is to understand what it means and entails, followed by actions that demonstrate to its leaders and proponents that their "setbacks" are not temporary. Equally important is establishing lines of communications with Moslems, making them aware of the harmful effects and self-defeating policies of their militant or revolutionary leaders.

NOTES

1. The focus of this paper is on Islamists or (militant) fundamentalists who espouse extremist views and promote violence. This article, which is written with nonspecialists in mind, does not suggest that all Moslems are extremists, but it does contend that the fundamentalist strain in Islam has been penetrating mainstream Moslem societies at an accelerated rate, particularly since the Iranian Revolution and the current conflict in Iraq. Where the words "fundamentalist" or "revivalist" appear, the reference is to extremist and militant Islam. Otherwise, both terms can be used without the same negative connotations. While most of the literature dealing with Islam and terrorism is focused on the Sunnis, this article allocates equal attention to the Shiites.

2. For an overview and general discussion on how and why some states have broken through underdevelopment but not others, see Lawrence E. Harrison and Samuel P. Huntington, *Culture Matters: How Values Shape Human Progress* (New York: Basic Books, 2000), xiii–xvi and 2–13.

3. A comparison between Turkey and Iran is instructive. Turkey's revenue from tourism alone is now about one-third of Iran's from oil. And with comparable populations, but despite great increase in Iran's revenues due to higher oil prices, Turkey's 2006 gross domestic product and gross domestic product per capita were about twice those of Iran. Only three decades earlier, the reverse of this situation was true.

4. Iran's extensive use of children in its war with Iraq was also a new development, where boys 12 and younger died by marching over Iraqi minefields. Similar tactics were later applied in the Palestinian Intifada, where suicide bombers included youngsters.

5. Bassam Tibi, "The Renewed Role of Islam in the Political and Social Development of the Middle East," *The Middle East Journal* 37, no. 1 (1983): 4–9.

6. Yazbeck Yvonne Haddad, "The Qur'anic Justification for an Islamic Revolution: The View of Sayyid Qutb," *The Middle East Journal* 37, no. 1 (Winter 1983): 24.

7. Ibid., 22–23.

8. Some believe Saddam altered the flag during the U.S. Gulf War, but this occurred before. See BBC News, "Iraqis Unimpressed by Flag Design," 27 April 2004, news.bbc.co.uk/1/hi/world/middle_east/3663387.stm; also see SourceWatch, "New Iraqi Flag," www.sourcewatch.org/index.php?title=New_Iraqi_flag.

9. The current anti-Western approach is not solely the product of the clerics' negative promotions. Since the early 1950s, Middle Eastern leaders of all stripes have promoted and benefited from a paranoid perception that equates strong leadership and legitimacy with the degree to which those in high public office firmly and fearlessly stand up to the West and challenge it. That this often confrontational approach may also prove very harmful to their countries' interests has been treated as unimportant or irrelevant.

10. Tibi, "The Renewed Role of Islam in the Political and Social Development of the Middle East," 5.

11. Amir Taheri, "Preparing for War and Heading towards an Economic Crisis," *Asharq Alawsat,* 11 May 2007, www.aawsat.com/english/news.asp?section=2&id=8916.

12. Daniel Byman, Shahram Chubin, Anoushiravan Ehteshami, and Jerrold Green, *Iran's Security Policy in the Post-revolutionary Era* (National Defense Research Institute, Rand, 2001), 16.

13. The Battle of Badr (624) was Muhammad's first military victory. The defeat of his Meccan enemies strengthened the prestige and position of the Moslems in Medina, and made them into a viable force in Arabia.

14. David Cook, *Martyrdom in Islam* (Cambridge: Cambridge University Press, 2007), 18.

15. Ibid.

16. Qur'an, 2:216 (Sura of the Cow).

17. The following groups focus on Islam as a way to advance their causes, but not with equal militancy: *al-Qaeda* (the Base) and *al-Haraka al-Islahiya al-Islamiya* (Islamic Reform Movement) of Saudi Arabia; *Jamaat al-Tawhid wa al-Jihad* (Society of Unity of God and Jihad) of Jordan, Iraq, and Afghanistan; *Hizbe-e Wahdat* (Party of Unity) of Afghanistan; *Jamaat-e Islami* (Islamic Party) and *Tahrik-e Jafaria* (Shia Movement) of Pakistan; *al-Da'wa* (the Islamic Call) of Iraq; *al-Wifaq* (the Accord) of Bahrain; the *Amal* (Hope) created by Lebanese clerics of Iranian origin and *Hezbollah* (Party of God) of Lebanon but supported by Iran; *Hamas* of Palestine (also supported by Iran); the *Badr Brigade* (now *Corp*) of Iraq, which was created and is supported by Iran; the *Mahdi Army* of Iraq (headed by Muqtada al-Sadr); the *Ikhwan al-Muslimin* (Muslim Brotherhood) of Egypt; and the *Supreme Council for the Islamic Revolution in Iraq* (SCIRI) supported by Iran. In Iran, the main groups with external influence include *Hezbollah* (Party of God), the *Pasdaran* (Revolutionary Guards), the *Basijees* (a large militant vigilante group supported and promoted by the regime), and the *Entehari* (the Suicide Army). There are also smaller groups in Iran that focus on internal issues, namely, the *Haqqani Circle* (an ultraconservative group that rejects individuals' rights and popular sovereignty) and *Ansar-e Islam* (made up of reactionary vigilantes whose mission is to enforce Islamic social codes). These groups ensure the regime's survival.

18. The history of the Middle East, covering the colonial period; the Arab-Israeli wars; the direct U.S. involvement in Lebanon, Iraq, and Afghanistan; and U.S. support for Israel, and mostly unpopular pro-Western leaders, are the main reasons for this negative sentiment.

19. Anti-American demonstrations by Shiites are common throughout the Middle East. In Pakistan, large demonstrations took place in March 2000, reported in the March 24 edition of PBS's *The NewsHour with Jim Lehrer*. In 2006, 4,000 Shiites from the port city of Karachi carried portraits of Ayatollah Khomeini, President Ahmadinejad, and Hassan Nasrallah, to mark al-Quds Day. See "6,000 Pakistani Muslims Hold Anti-Israel Rallies," *Jerusalem Post,* www.jpost.com, 20 October 2006. In April 2006, similar demonstrations occurred among Bahraini Shiites, many of whom display pictures of Ayatollah Khomeini in their homes. See Hassan M. Fattah, "An Island Kingdom Feels the Ripples from Iraq and Iran," *New York Times,* 16 April 2006. In Iraq and Lebanon, the anti-U.S. sentiments propagated by the Mahdi Army and Hezbollah are well known. In Lebanon, only 7 percent of the Shiites are favorable toward the United States compared to 52 percent of the Sunnis. See WorldPublicOpinion.org. In support of Hezbollah, Shiites have demonstrated in Westernized Istanbul. Due to their history and cultural affinities with the West, Iranians are more U.S. friendly and less resentful.

20. For data on the Middle East diagram, see "Global Unease with Major World Powers," The Pew Global Attitude Project, 27 June 2007, www.pewglobal.org; WorldPublicOpinion.org, "Iranians and Americans Believe Islam and the West Can Find Common Ground." Different polls do not fully support each other. Still, in having a favorable view of Americans, Iran received the highest marks after Israel and the Christian Lebanese. Turkey, the Palestinian territories, Pakistan, and Morocco received the lowest marks in terms of having a positive view of the United States and Americans. Polls taken in 2006–2007 showed the following levels of positive views toward the United States: Egypt (21 percent), Iran (22 percent), Israel (78 percent), Jordan (20 percent), Lebanon (47 percent), Morocco (15 percent), Pakistan (15 percent), Palestine (13 percent), Turkey (9 percent). The following had a favorable view of Americans: Egypt (31 percent), Iran (45 percent), Jordan (36 percent), Lebanon (69 percent), Morocco (25 percent), Pakistan (19 percent), Palestine (21 percent), and Turkey (13 percent). Most reports suggest a more favorable view of Americans by Iranians.

21. There are numerous reports of positive American encounters with Iranians inside Iran. For example, see Nicholas D. Kristof, "Those Friendly Iranians," *New York Times,* 5 May 2004; also see Ali G. Scotten,

"Iranians' Love Affair with America," *Christian Science Monitor,* 19 January 2007. Christian Amanpoor of CNN has also indicated that in her experience, Iranians' feelings toward Americans have been positive (reported on 24 September 2007, in relation to Ahamadinejad's visit to Columbia University). However, recent polls indicate a less favorable Iranian perspective. See "Iranians and Americans Believe Islam and the West Can Find Common Ground," published by WorldPublicOpinion.org, 30 January 2007, www.worldpublicopinion.org/ pipa/articles/home_page/312.php?nid=&id=&pnt=312&lb=hmpg2. Although events in Iraq have caused a growing disillusionment among Iranians, official polling in Iran is complex and not fully representative.

22. For Saudi Arabia, the following information is noteworthy: a poll showed that while "only 4.9% supported a bin Laden Presidency, 48.7% had a positive opinion of his rhetoric." See Nawaf Obaid, "An Unprecedented Poll of Saudi Opinion: Yes to Bin Laden; No to Al Qaeda Violence," *International Herald Tribune,* 28 June 2004. Also, 24 percent of Saudis (most probably the Shiites) express a positive view of Iran. "Global Poll: Iran Seen Playing Negative Role," Globe Scan, www.globescan.com/news_archives/bbc06-3/index.html.

23. Since 2002, polls show substantial decline among those who had a positive view of the United States and Americans. The current conflict in Iraq has been the main reason for this. Although similar negative trends apply to Iran, there are also reports that contradict the negative polls by suggesting Iranians remain mostly U.S. friendly, especially among the young who are Westward looking and oppose the Islamic system their regime has imposed. During Khatami's presidency, when the negative sentiments toward the regime were well below the present-day level, "the results of a questionnaire completed by 75,000 14 to 29-year-olds" indicated that 54 percent "[did] not approve of the plans and performance of the government." Also, young people who are in the majority had "limited esteem for the performance of parliament, the judiciary and the police." "Iranian Youth Disappointed with Khatami Government," IranMania.com, 29 April 2003, www.iranmania .com/News/ArticleView/Default.asp?NewsCode=15313&NewsKind=Current%20Affairs.

24. The Abbasid caliphate is typically divided into three periods: the early Abbasids (750–929), the middle Abbasids (930–1099), and the late Abbasids (1100–1258). They held different territories during these times, with varying degrees of influence.

25. It is mostly over these three aims that the Sunnis and Shiites are in agreement. Each sect promotes its own ideal state and ideologies as a replacement for Western values and system of government. It is in achieving this goal that they may selectively cooperate.

26. Justin Wintle, *The Timeline History of Islam* (New York: Barnes & Noble, 2005), 146.

27. See Stephen Humphreys, "Modern Arab Historians and the Challenge of the Islamic Past," in *Middle Eastern Lectures,* ed. Martin Kramer, Middle Eastern Lectures 1 (Tel Aviv: The Moshe Dayan Center for Middle Eastern and African Studies at the Tel Aviv University, 1995), 120–21.

28. Except for notable Shiite dynasties like the Fatimids (910–1171), with their capital city in Cairo, and the Iranian Shiite dynasties of the Buyids (932–1045), Safavids (1501–1736), and Qajars (1795–1925), with capital cities in Shiraz, Esfahan, and Tehran, respectively.

29. Those residing in Iran cannot voice their opinions in too critical a manner. Even if government officials may be openly questioned, criticizing the theocratic system itself is far riskier. As most of those who have the opportunity to leave Iran do so, and repression allows for no meaningful dissension, at least one poll indicates the regime as gaining ground on the traditional nationalists who identify with Iran before identifying with Islam. See WorldPublicOpinion.org, "Poll of the Iranian Public," with Search for Common Ground and the U.S. Institute of Peace Program on International Policy Attitudes (PIPA) (16 January 2007).

30. Ali Shariati, *Bazgasht* [Return] (n.p., 1978), 11–30.

31. The Hidden Imam is a central figure for the Shiite Twelvers, who dominate Iran. After Muhammad, Ali, and Hussein, no other figure is equally dominant; and, in some ways, he is no less important than others. The entire Shiite ideology, empowering the clerics to lead the Islamic community, is predicated on the idea that the senior ulema are his representatives. Thus, they are empowered by him and by God to lead until his return. Yet information about the Hidden Imam is sketchy. Some claimed he was killed at a young age; others negated his very existence—among them, the man who would be his uncle stated that his brother had no sons.

Various dates have been provided for his age and his occultations. Depending on which of his two disappearances one views as the more important one (since he was never seen again after the first disappearance), dates can vary by several years. His first disappearance, known as the lesser occultation, is said to have occurred when his father died in 874. He is said to have been seven, but others state he was five, depending on which text one uses. His second disappearance, known as the greater occultation, is said to have occurred in 939, but there is no definitive agreement on this date either. See Moojan Momen, *An Introduction to Shi'i Islam* (New Haven: Yale University Press, 1985), 161–65.

32. Wahhabism is a movement whose followers trace themselves to Abdul Wahab, born in the early 1700s. He opposed medieval Islamic superstition and the cult of saints, which is closely associated with Shiism. The focus was the early teachings of the Qur'an and the Hadith. The leader was a supporter of the Saud family that came to power in 1745. The movement's followers were strict practitioners of Islamic law and forbade music, dancing, and other such displays.

33. The *Salafiya* Movement was influenced by Afghani, a nineteenth-century militant Shiite Iranian theologian. The movement's adherents' ideology revolved around revering their ancient ancestors who followed closely along the Prophet's path. They are mostly a clandestine group that has been active in Kuwait since the mid-1970s and in Saudi Arabia since the late 1970s. They believe that since the "Rightly Guided" caliphs who followed Muhammad were all elected, hereditary regimes are not legitimized by Islam. This explains their animosity toward the Shiites. They were among those who attacked Mecca in 1979, but now hold parliamentary seats in Kuwait.

34. Andrew G. Bostom, ed., *The Legacy of Jihad: Islamic Holy War and the Fate of Non-Muslims* (Amherst, NY: Prometheus Books), 322.

35. Ibid.

36. Yazid was the son of Mu'awiyah. The latter was the founder of the Umayyad dynasty (661–750). Yazid succeeded his father as the second caliph of this first Islamic dynasty. The Umayyads eventually lost power to the Abbasids, at which time Islam's capital city was moved from Damascus to Baghdad, bringing the Abbasids under considerable Persian influence.

37. For greater elaboration see Momen, *An Introduction to Shi'i Islam,* 157–59.

38. Marvin Zonis, *The Majestic Failure* (Chicago: University of Chicago Press, 1991), 269–70. Also see Baqer Moin, *Khomeini: Life of the Ayatollah* (New York: St. Martin's Press, 1999), 56.

39. For a detailed discussion of how Imam Hussein's traditional image was recast by the revolutionary Islamists in Iran, see Hamid Enayat, *Modern Islamic Political Thought* (University of Texas Press, 1982). This is a thorough analysis of Shiite and Sunni responses to the challenges of the twentieth century. The Islamist idea of presenting a more revolutionary image of Imam Hussein was first examined by Salehi Najafabadi's work, entitled *Shaid-e javid* (The eternal martyr), published in Tehran.

40. Since illegitimacy is often in the eyes of the beholder, and Shiites are not the underdogs they once were—at least not in Iran, Iraq, or Lebanon—and power is mostly held by their extremist elements, it is not surprising that the interpretations of such terms have taken unique turns. Thus, Sunni leaders are doubly illegitimate today: first for being Sunnis who rule by decree; second, because they are Western friendly and do not unite to undo Israel.

41. Tibi, "The Renewed Role of Islam in the Political and Social Development of the Middle East," 4. It should be noted, however, that in Iran, since the early Safavid period, the clergy began enjoying a degree of economic independence, due to their custodianship of Shiite shrines, holy sites, and the lands that had been allocated to these. By the Qajar period, the leading clerics had access to considerable independent wealth and were influential enough to be considered a state within a state. However, actual political power still remained in the hands of the ruling monarchs—a situation that the clerics tolerated, but often viewed with contempt.

42. Ruhollah Khomeini, *Islam and Revolution: Writings and Declarations of Imam Khomeini,* trans. Hamid Algar (Berkeley: Mizan Press, 1981), 430.

43. Ibid., 394.

Part Four

Thinking Differently about Armed Groups

20 The Erosion of Constraints in Armed-Group Warfare: Bloody Tactics and Vulnerable Targets

Andrea J. Dew

Since Alexander the Great's time, states and their militaries have been grappling with the threat to national security posed by armed groups. And, as other chapters in this volume discuss, history is replete with examples of armed groups— insurgents, terrorists, militias, and criminal groups—that have fought against each other, fought against states, and fought with states against other armed groups.

However, three trends since the end of the cold war—the proliferation of failed and failing states, globalized travel and trade networks, and advances in information technology—have increasingly made the threat from armed groups a high-level national security issue for many states.[1] Recall, for example, that it was an armed group—al Qaeda—that planned and executed the 9/11 attacks on the United States; armed groups in Iraq continue to wreak havoc on attempts to establish lasting peace and security; armed groups— the mujahideen—forced a superpower out of Afghanistan; and armed groups, including the resurgent Taliban, continue to plague NATO efforts to rebuild roads, schools, and infrastructure in that country.

The problem for states and their militaries in dealing with the threat from armed groups is not that these groups have overwhelming firepower or even overwhelming numbers. Rather, the problem is one of how states can maintain public support—domestic or international—for continuing the conflict when the targets and tactics selected by armed groups become increasingly bloody and horrific and when constraints and limitations on warfare by armed groups have been swept away.[2]

Given this context, the questions that animate this chapter are twofold. First, if future conflicts involving armed groups have the potential to become increasingly bloody

Andrea J. Dew is currently an assistant professor for strategy and policy at the Naval War College, Newport, Rhode Island, and a senior research fellow for counter-terrorism studies at the Jebsen Counter-terrorism Center at the Fletcher School. She holds a BA in history from Southampton University, UK, and an MALD and PhD in international relations from the Fletcher School of Law and Diplomacy, Boston, Massachusetts. Before joining the faculty of the Naval War College, she served as a research fellow at the Belfer Center for Science in International Affairs at Harvard University and a research associate for the International Security Studies Program at the Fletcher School. Recent publications include "Irregular Warfare, Armed Groups, and the Long War: A New Analytical Framework," in *Economics and Maritime Security: Implications for the 21st Century* (Naval War College, 2006); (coauthored with Richard Shultz) *Insurgents, Terrorists, and Militias: The Warriors of Contemporary Combat* (Columbia University Press, 2006); and (coauthored with Mohammad-Mahmoud Mohamedou) *Empowered Groups, Tested Laws, and Policy Options* (Harvard University, 2007).

and protracted to the point that public support becomes significantly undermined, then what indicators warn us of the likelihood of this possibility? Second, if we can better predict the tactics, targets, degree of violence, and will to fight of armed groups, how does this help policy makers, intelligence analysts, and military planners to better plan for such conflicts and to better reassess goals and strategies during such conflicts?

The discussion in this chapter is based on analysis of four conflicts involving armed groups in Somalia, Chechnya, Afghanistan, and Iraq with additional discussion of Hezbollah's summer campaign against Israel in 2006. There are, of course, numerous other examples that could and should be included in a discussion of when conflicts involving armed groups might devolve into a protracted and bloody fight. However, given the current context of the global war on terror—the "long war" in current U.S. Department of Defense parlance—these conflicts in which states have fought armed groups provide valuable insights into how and why such an erosion of the constraints on warfare take place among armed groups and with what effect on whom.

THE STRATEGIC CONTEXT

The fall of the Berlin wall in 1989 and the end of the cold war was heralded by many as the start of a new era of world peace. The reality of the last decade of the twentieth century and first decade of the twenty-first century, however, has been a rash of bloody conflicts that has stretched from Bosnia to central and Southeast Asia, across the Middle East and Latin America, and throughout Africa.[3]

Analysis of global patterns of conflict since the end of the cold war shows that modern conflict has been predominantly irregular and unconventional and internal and has often involved armed groups. Indeed, according to the International Institute for Strategic Studies' Armed Conflict Database, armed groups have been involved in more than 75 conflicts between 1997 and 2007, and more than 750,000 people have died as a result of those conflicts.[4] Thus, it is argued here that conflict involving armed groups is one aspect of the current and future face of warfare that is here to stay.

The term "armed groups" includes insurgents, terrorists, militias, and criminal groups. These armed groups are characterized by their ability and willingness to challenge the authority and legitimacy of states and even the international system, and they can attack within and across state boundaries, and even globally. Such groups operate through clandestine organizations, depend on intelligence and counterintelligence capabilities, and mask their operations through denial and deception. These groups are enabled by globalization and information-age technologies; they employ violence in unconventional, irregular, and increasingly indiscriminate ways; and their operations often are not constrained by the laws and conventions of war. Moreover, their operations deliberately bypass the superior military power of nation-states to attack political, economic, and symbolic targets.[5]

The root causes of these irregular and unconventional conflicts are complex and often overlap, each cause exacerbating the others. In some areas in the world, weak, corrupt, and failing states are part of the problem.[6] The end of the cold war also unleashed powerful ethnic, ethno-national, religious, identity, and communal differences that have been manipulated by competing ethnic and religious elites to gain power.[7] In other areas of the world, internal and transnational violence has been the route to state resources and power, secession, or group autonomy.[8]

ASSESSING ARMED GROUPS

That conventional militaries need to better understand irregular warfare against unconventional forces comes as no surprise to some branches of the military—the U.S. Marine Corps *Small Wars Manual,* for example, dates back to 1940, while British counterguerrilla strategies were developed from nineteenth- and early-twentieth-century experiences with armed uprisings in Afghanistan and Ireland, among other places.[9]

Since the end of the cold war, and in particular post-9/11, however, conventional militaries have increasingly found themselves facing armed groups motivated by messianic ideologies and willing to use every means at their disposal to attack the symbols of states at home and abroad. Not only have armed groups as diverse as the Chechen rebels and al Qaeda proved their willingness to acquire weapons of mass destruction (WMD), but armed groups are also using the Internet and information technologies to motivate and inspire a geographically diverse audience of new recruits and supporters. Internal conflicts of the types we have seen in Somalia, Chechnya, and Bosnia will continue to occur in the twenty-first century—irregular conflict will continue to challenge state legitimacy and authority. Moreover, these internal wars of the twenty-first century will continue to have transnational and even global dimensions characterized by the irregular and unconventional use of force by various types of armed groups.[10]

Even as conflicts involving armed groups continue to recur throughout the globe, conventional militaries and policy makers are still struggling to come to grips with how to fight armed groups. We know, for example, that the costs of conflicts involving armed groups can be high in terms of blood and treasure and have the potential to become increasingly costly as armed groups fight grinding wars of attrition in which there are few decisive victories and political goals are hard to attain and difficult to sustain. This is not to say that such conflicts are unwinnable; however, as these fights become more protracted the weakest part of our strategies against armed groups can be the ability to maintain domestic support for our part in the conflict. Moreover, the skillful use of information technologies and global media by armed groups has placed increasing pressure and focus on a state's ability to sustain popular support for such conflicts.

Considering this vulnerability, then, it becomes increasingly important to ask why constraints and limitations on tactics and targets erode and whether there are warning signs that states can use to reassess and adapt policy or strategy before the situation deteriorates. For example, as of 2008, more than six years after the initial salvos of the U.S.-led Operation Enduring Freedom in Afghanistan, NATO forces are still finding it difficult to establish lasting peace and security in all areas of the state. This is all the more puzzling considering the initial gains—the rapid defeat and rout of the Taliban in 2001 and a relatively smooth transition to democratically elected government by 2002. What, then, can be done to better understand who these armed groups are, why they fight, and when conflict involving such groups can devolve into protracted and ever-more-unpopular conflicts?

THE EROSION OF CONSTRAINTS ON WARFARE

In order to fight unconventional enemies, we must, as Sun Tzu exhorts, know our enemies: we must understand their capabilities, their concepts of warfare, their culture of war and peace; from this information, we can learn how they fight.[11] In assessing armed groups it is also important to remember that many have emerged out of tribal, clan, religious, and other traditional identity divisions. Thus, the starting point to such an approach is to develop an understanding of the cultural foundations of armed groups. This can be achieved by understanding the values, institutions, and ways of thinking that persist generation after generation, and by understanding how culture and tradition influence the way armed groups think about, and fight, war.

An important first step in such an assessment is to acknowledge that warfare by armed groups is conducted differently, by different rules from Western warfare. Modern state militaries are bound by international laws of war and, for the most part, are sent to war for reasons Clausewitz could understand—to achieve policy goals. However, the incentives to fight for armed groups can also include a range of personal motivations such as honor, revenge, glory, and vendetta.

Moreover, as T. E. Lawrence noted, two tactics—the hit-and-run raid and the ambush—are particularly important to armed groups.[12] Afghan mujahideen employed them effectively against the Soviets, as have Iraqi insurgents against the United States. However, armed groups in places such as Somalia, Afghanistan, Chechnya, and Iraq have diversified their tactics and targets. At some point in all four conflicts, armed groups have rejected traditional limitations on warfare and have specifically and consistently targeted noncombatants and nonmilitary targets. Some of these armed groups have also deliberately used traditionally protected places, such as mosques, churches, schools, and hospitals, as both targets and operational bases. Moreover, the unconventional repertoire now includes the desire to acquire WMD, the use of improvised explosive device (IED) car bombs, brutal terror tactics such as beheadings, roadside bombs, kidnappings, suicide bombings, and the torture and execution of prisoners. These have become widely used against military and civilian targets.[13]

Furthermore, these conflicts are often fought in suburban and urban settings, turning towns and cities into the new battlefields. After the Soviet Army withdrew from Afghanistan in 1989, for example, armed groups, including the Taliban and the Northern Alliance, fought from street corner to street corner in Kabul for nearly three years, killing thousands of Afghans, turning thousands more into refugees, and reducing the city to rubble.[14]

Not only has the urbanization of conflict drawn an increasing number of new casualties into the line of fire, but some armed groups in places such as Somalia, Chechnya, Afghanistan, and Iraq have deliberately targeted noncombatants as part of their strategies. Indeed, one of the characteristics of irregular warfare has been the involvement of local populations, whether their support is active or passive. In Somalia, for example, during the 1993 firefight between Mohamed Farrah Aideed's forces and U.S. forces, Somalis deliberately used women as human shields and children as lookouts, knowing that U.S. rules of engagement would prohibit American forces from firing on unarmed noncombatants. Aideed's fighters had no such compunction.[15] In many cases, these casualties—women, children, medics, journalists—are not accidental victims of a conflict beyond their control; rather, their deaths and injuries are the results of a deliberate strategy to target noncombatants.

Although the aftermath of these attacks on local populations in and of itself is bloody and awful, this erosion of the constraints on warfare also has broader strategic implications. When armed groups throw off traditional constraints on conflicts—their own rules of engagement—the conflict has the potential to become protracted, deeply destructive in terms of damage to infrastructure, disruptive to the local economy, and highly divisive, which can enflame political, religious, and clan rivalries.[16] Indeed, without traditional conflict-resolution mechanisms and limitations on tactics and targets, each attack may trigger an escalation of violence, blood feuds, and vendettas, and cease-fire agreements may be quickly undermined and discarded.[17]

The erosions of constraints on warfare are not just a problem for the local populations drawn into the conflict. Although figures vary as to whether conflicts that involve armed groups are bloodier than conventional conflicts, the use of these tactics and this kind of targeting by armed groups significantly undermines the ability of conventional forces to bring peace and stability to a conflict zone.[18] As discussed later, when conventional militaries and states fight these groups, the problem posed by the erosion of constraints on tactics and targets by armed groups is that the duration of the conflict can significantly increase at the same time that the public perception of the cost of fighting is also escalating. This perception can exist within the local population that may support or tolerate the armed groups, in addition to the larger national or regional audiences.[19]

The issue of how to win or maintain the support of multiple audiences is further complicated by the way that different actions play out to different populations. For example, while an incident that involves the death of local women and children and the destruction of a school in Iraq at the hands of a Shia militia may be met with some outrage in the United States, it may strengthen, rather than weaken, the resolve of the U.S. public to support continued U.S. involvement. On the other hand, it may further weaken confidence among Sunnis that the United States can provide for security. Finally, it may demonstrate to local Shia that a particular militia is the most dominant and therefore the most important to support in the region. This issue of how states can sustain popular support for a conflict involving armed groups is never easily addressed, and the erosion of constraints on tactics and targets only serves to complicate and exacerbate the issue.

Despite this pessimistic assessment of conflict involving armed groups, not all conflicts with armed groups devolve into such downward spirals of destructive violence. Indeed, most traditional cultures from which armed groups evolve have deeply embedded mores against such tactics and targeting. In Afghanistan, for example, tribes dependent on agriculture for eking out a living from poor soil have prohibitions against fighting during the planting and harvest seasons. Warfare is conducted away from villages, and women and children are not traditionally included in warfighting or as targets.[20] This begs the question, then, of why constraints and restraints are eroded among some armed groups. Considering the consequences of the erosion of constraints on tactics and targets, both for the local populations and for intervening states, it is important to consider how such trends emerged, and whether there are any indicators that forewarn of the potential for such conflicts to devolve into bloody and intractable fights.

CONSTRAINTS AND LIMITATIONS: A FRAMEWORK FOR ANALYSIS

Analysis of conflicts involving armed groups in Somalia, Afghanistan, Chechnya, and Iraq suggests that there are a number of issues that contribute to the erosion of constraints in traditional warfare. Five of the most important influences are discussed below. These include (1) the degree of state cohesiveness and the extent to which a state is able to provide security and services to its people, (2) the roles and extents of involvement of external and transnational actors in internal conflicts, (3) the degree to which radicalized ideology—religious and sociopolitical—has pervaded traditional belief systems, (4) the degree to which information technology is being used as part of information operations during the conflict, and (5) the duration of conflict.

1. State Cohesiveness

At its most fundamental level, the purpose of a state is to ensure its own survival and then to ensure that it has the monopoly of legitimate violence over its own people.[21] After survival and security—internal and external—are provided for, successful states are then part of the mechanism that decides who gets what resources inside of a state. However, since the end of the cold war in particular, we have seen a dramatic rise in the number of states—from Sudan to Afghanistan, Yemen to Somalia—in which the authority and legitimacy of the central government has been challenged, overthrown, and delegitimized.[22]

The degree of state cohesiveness—the extent to which the central government has failed—can contribute to the erosion of constraints on targets and tactics among armed groups by first creating a power vacuum inside a state and at the peripheries that armed groups can seek to fill. It can also change the nature of conflicts involving armed groups from conflicts with limited objectives, such as revenge for the loss of life or livelihood, to conflicts in which the objectives become unlimited—such as control over vast oil fields, state revenues, or regime change. When the state is too weak to prevent rival armed groups from battling over the resources of a nation, and the stakes of being left out of the struggle for power become increasingly binary—do or die—then the traditional constraints on warfare can be swept away.[23]

Somalia is a case in point—Siad Barre in the 1980s used increasingly brutal and ruthless tactics to maintain his control over Somalia. One of his tactics was to undermine and kill clan elders as a way of silencing his critics and to disrupt the likelihood of organized resistance. In the short term his systematic campaign of violence helped him maintain his grip on Mogadishu, but it came at the price of destroying the clan councils—traditional conflict-resolution mechanisms that meted out punishments and negotiated settlements to conflicts. By the time the United Nations arrived in Mogadishu in 1992 on a humanitarian mission to provide food to Somalis caught up in the famine, the state had almost disintegrated, and security was nonexistent. Instead, rival armed groups, including Mohamed Farrah Aideed's Haber Gidir subclan, had carved the city up into conflict zones.[24]

It is important to note at this point, however, that the devolution of state authority and control does not necessarily equate to an automatic erosion of constraints on warfare and to bloody and protracted conflict. In the case of Somalia, for example, Siad Barre had deliberately dismantled these constraints as a means to further his own political and military power. Moreover, as discussed below, when armed groups fight for the control of state resources and to maintain security of their own areas of operations in a weak state, other factors can fan the flames of conflict and melt the bonds that constrain the use of violence and the selection of targets.

2. External and Transnational Actors

A second important factor in considering what influences erode the constraints on tactics and targets in conflict involving armed groups is the presence and role of external and transnational actors in internal conflicts. Outside actors can influence such conflicts in a number of different ways, including by providing external safe havens and materiel support for armed groups and by providing an alternative source of legitimacy and authority, which can further undermine the political authority of the state government. They can also contribute to the erosion of constraints on warfare by sustaining armed groups past the point of exhaustion—the point at which a group might be tempted to negotiate a settlement to consolidate gains or restore the status quo.

In the summer of 2006, for example, Hezbollah placed its Katusha rockets in residential buildings in southern Lebanon, knowing that when Israeli Defense Forces returned fire, they would kill ordinary Lebanese. The intention of Hezbollah in involving noncombatants in the conflict was severalfold—to lure Israel into overreacting and thus using the images of Lebanese women and children killed by Israeli retaliatory strikes on apartment buildings as part of a public information strategy against Israel.[25] Hezbollah also provided compensation and support for those injured by the rocket attacks—thereby strengthening its own support base in southern Lebanon and Beirut. It was emboldened, moreover, by the knowledge that it could expend its stockpile of rockets and other weapons in a conflict in which no territory was gained and in which the infrastructure of Lebanon was significantly damaged, because it was confident that outside sources—Syria and Iran—would help it resupply.[26]

3. The Role of Ideology

A third important factor in explaining the erosion of constraints on targets and tactics by armed groups is the degree to which groups are influenced by ideology—which can be both from internal sources and external sources. In the context of the "long war" we tend to think of this ideology as religious—in particular the extremist Salafi ideology that al Qaeda and associated movements (AQAM) used to exhort radical Muslims to join in the global jihad against other Muslims and non-Muslims alike.[27] Such a powerful ideology, fanned by religious leaders, can provide a unifying and inspirational motivation to fight and justification for the use and recruitment of suicide bombers and the targeting of schools, mosques, and hospitals.[28] In 2007, for example, al Qaeda in Mesopotamia claimed responsibility for suicide attacks in Iraq that targeted military and police personnel as well as women and children using attacks in open-air markets, recruiting stations, and mosques.[29]

However, it is not a foregone conclusion that radical ideology can completely overcome traditional constraints on targets and tactics. In southern Afghanistan, for example, resurgent Taliban forces, even with al Qaeda support, have found it much more difficult to overcome traditional repugnance toward the use of suicide bombers, and the suicide attacks that have been carried out have had, thus far, limited impact and limited casualties.[30] Thus, while considering the importance of ideology it is also important to note that a fourth element can help to amplify the impact of such ideologies: information technologies.

4. The Role of Information Technology

Most armed groups use public information strategies—strategic communications—as part of their irregular warfare repertoire. Armed groups use information operations to recruit and maintain support among local populations, in addition to using disinformation campaigns to undermine support for other armed groups or state governments.[31] Until recently, traditional media such as radio, television, and newspapers played an important role in the media strategies of armed groups, but the advent and availability of the Internet has provided a new level of complexity to the issue. For example, al Qaeda and associated groups have made extensive use of *jihadi* Web sites both as a conduit for and as an amplifier of radical messages to audiences far removed from conflicts. Sometimes called "Jihad-101," the network of extremist Web sites not only helps to disseminate knowledge about how to construct and where to place weapons such as improvised explosive devices but helps to elevate and glorify the deaths of those killed for the global jihad and motivate and generate new recruits. This has made the Internet a particularly useful tool for the recruitment of suicide bombers.[32]

Moreover, as counterterrorism efforts in Western Europe have shown, the relative anonymity of the Internet also provides an important tool for armed groups to disseminate their ideologies to wider audiences and makes countering such ideologies increasingly difficult.[33]

5. Duration of Conflict

Finally, an important element that contributes to the erosion of constraints on targets and tactics by armed groups is the duration of the conflict. This element of time can take several forms—for example, armed groups in Chechnya have been fighting against Russian forces for more than 200 years. That experience, coupled with repeated political betrayals, adds to the ferocity of the current Chechen-Russia conflict, in which Chechen groups have targeted schools—Beslan in 2005—and used women suicide bombers—the so-called Chechen Black Widows involved in holding a theater hostage in Moscow in 2002.[34]

The duration of the conflict can also be a factor even if the armed group has not been fighting the same enemy for a prolonged period. In Somalia, for example, UN and U.S. forces walked into an ongoing conflict between Somali clans that had been smoldering since the fall of Siad Barre's regime in January 1991. As noted previously, Siad Barre had deliberately undermined the institutions that regulated and constrained conflict and by the time UN peacekeepers arrived in 1992, armed groups were already fighting for influences, power, and resources in Mogadishu. Again, this is not to argue that all extended conflicts involving armed groups devolve into unrestrained and unrestricted conflicts in which the costs of conflicts spiral upward, but it is important to consider the extent to which the duration of the current or previous conflicts can contribute to this trend.

PREPARING, PLANNING, AND REASSESSING CONFLICT WITH ARMED GROUPS

This chapter considered what traditional constraints exist in armed-group conflict and discussed the factors that contribute to the erosion of traditional constraints during conflict. The conclusions, discussed above, are that traditional constraints on tactics and targets, such as not targeting women and children; using mediation to resolve blood vendettas; and keeping conflict away from hospitals, schools, and religious centers, can become dangerously eroded in conflicts involving armed groups. In broad-brush terms, the erosion of constraints on targets and tactics can be partially explained by a combination of factors that includes weak or failed central state authority, the intrusion of external and transnational actors in internal conflicts, the radicalization of extremist ideology, the use of information technology to disseminate ideologies and ideas, and the duration of conflicts.

While it is important to note that the existence of any or all of these factors does not predict the erosion of constraints and limitations in warfare, they do help us to assess the potential for conflicts involving armed groups to escalate in terms of duration and cost. This becomes important at three different levels—first, it helps intelligence analysis develop more accurate assessments of the threats posed by armed groups. Second, it helps policy makers, intelligence analysts, and military planners to develop more realistic goals and strategies for conflicts involving armed groups. And third, understanding the influence of these factors on the way that armed groups fight can help decision makers to recognize when it is time to reassess and adapt—the point at which conflict involving armed groups has the potential to or has already started to escalate from limited and controllable goals and costs to unlimited goals and spiraling costs.[35]

Taking these implications one by one, the first benefit of developing tools to identifying some of the factors that erode the constraints on conflict involving armed groups is that it helps states develop better intelligence capabilities about armed groups. This helps to provide policy makers, military planners, and intelligence analysts at the planning and assessment stage before a conflict starts better information about how a group will fight and to what extent it might disrupt long-term stability and reconstruction activities, break cease-fires, or target aid workers.

This becomes particularly important in places such as Afghanistan, for example, in which, as of 2008, a patchwork of power and patronage networks both enables and restricts reconstruction work. As the Taliban turn increasingly to criminal activities—most notably the sale of poppy harvests to international heroin networks—their long-term contacts with outside actors—al Qaeda—and extremist ideologies increase the likelihood that they will use suicide bombers to attack reconstruction and poppy eradication efforts. In contrast, in northern areas, absent an invading or occupying force, there has been a resurgence of the traditional methods of resolving local conflicts without warfare, including the use of *jirgas*—councils of elders—and warlords-turned-local-governors to control the escalation of conflicts.[36]

There are no easy answers for Afghanistan, nor are there instant one-size-fits-all solutions to understanding when armed groups will eschew their own constraints on tactics and targets. However, by studying the five factors discussed above together with analysis of an armed group's area of operations, command and control structures, motivations, traditions, and cultures, we have a better chance at assessing and mitigating the security risks it poses.

Second, understanding what factors suggest that conflict involving armed groups might escalate or become protracted with no decisive victories and clear end points may help policy makers and planners to decide their policy goals and strategies. Indeed, a clearer understanding of what factors affect the erosion of constraints on tactics and targets, and the relation between escalating costs and public support, may lead them to reconsider the cost of such conflicts—in blood and treasure—in relation to their policy goals.[37] Such an understanding may also help policy makers and strategists better decide which instruments of national power—diplomatic, informational, military, and economic—to apply to a problem.

Finally, during a conflict, if we understand the factors that can explain the tactics, targets, degree of violence, and will to fight of armed groups, this may also help policy analysts, military planners, and intelligence analysts to reassess their current goals and strategies. For example, if we can determine why an armed group has moved over time from traditional hit-and-run ambushes of military forces to a sustained campaign of kidnapping of civilians for ransom, as has been the case for the Revolutionary Armed Forces of Colombia (FARC) in Colombia, then we may have a better understanding of whether the group is losing its ideological grip on local populations and thus could be vulnerable to sustained campaigns to win the hearts and minds of its supporters.[38] This becomes even more important in Iraq, where the shifting balances of power between Sunni and Shia militias and the intervention of outside actors such as al Qaeda and Iran make it vital to constantly reassess what implications shifts in tactics and targets by armed groups have on Iraqi national stability and the support of Iraqi and U.S. populations for continued U.S. presence.[39]

In conclusion, conflicts cost resources—blood and treasure—and the ability of states to wage warfare can be severely curtailed by lack of support at home for the expenditure of resources on a long, drawn-out conflict. Indeed, one of the deliberate strategies of armed groups facing conventional militaries is to escalate the cost of the conflict to the state by prolonging the duration of the conflict.[40] States have a range of strategic options available to them—from cooperation to conflict—when it comes to conflicts involving armed groups, and any tools we develop to more realistically assess which strategies might be successful can only improve our still-rudimentary policy and strategy discussions on how to win such conflicts.

NOTES

1. This is drawn from more extensive original research published in Richard H. Shultz, Jr., and Andrea J. Dew, *Insurgents, Terrorists, and Militias: The Warriors of Contemporary Combat* (New York, NY: Columbia University Press, 2006).

2. At this point it is important to emphasize that the threat from armed groups is not new, that most states understand that conflict with armed groups has the potential to be both bloody and protracted, and that the

erosion of constraints on warfare is not a new phenomenon. What is new, however, is the degree to which armed groups are able to target the ability of states to maintain popular support for such a conflict. As discussed later, a number of influences, none of which are easily countered, exacerbate this ability.

3. Project Ploughshares, *Armed Conflicts Report* (Waterloo, Canada: Institute of Peace and Conflict Studies, 2006).

4. The Uppsala Conflict Data Programme defines a "major armed conflict" as the use of armed force between the military forces of two or more governments, or of one government and at least one organized armed group, resulting in the battle-related deaths of at least 1000 people in any single calendar year and in which the incompatibility concerns control of government and/or territory. See www.pcr.uu.se/database/ (accessed 14 January 2008). One of the most respected databases that tracks statistics related to conflicts involving armed groups is the International Institute for Strategic Studies' Armed Conflict Database, which is available from www.iiss.org (accessed 14 January 2008).

5. Summarized from Shultz and Dew, *Insurgents, Terrorists, and Militias,* 259–70. For one of a number of recent studies criticizing U.S. failure to distinguish among the specific armed-group threats in Iraq, see James A. Thomson to Donald H. Rumsfeld, 7 February 2005, available at www.washingtonpost.com/wp-srv/nations/documents/rand_04_01.pdf (accessed 1 April 2005). See also Bradley Graham and Thomas E. Ricks, "Pentagon Blamed for Lack of Postwar Planning in Iraq," Washington Post, 1 April 2005, A3. See also discussion in Richard H. Shultz, Jr., Douglas Farah, and Itamara V. Lochard, *Armed Groups: A Tier One Security Priority,* Institute for National Security Studies Occasional Paper 57 (Colorado Springs: U.S. Air Force Academy, 2004).

6. On weak and failing states, see, for example, Robert Rotberg, ed., *Why States Fail: Causes and Consequences* (Princeton: Princeton University Press, 2004); Chester Crocker, "Engaging Failing States," *Foreign Affairs,* September/October 2003; I. William Zartman, *Collapsed States* (Boulder, CO: Lynne Rienner, 1997); Martin van Creveld, *The Rise and Decline of the State* (Cambridge: Cambridge University Press, 2003); Robert Dorff, "Democratization and Failed States: The Challenge of Ungovernability," *Parameters,* Spring 1996.

7. Andrea J. Dew and Mohammad-Mahmoud Mohamedou, *Empowered Groups, Tested Laws, and Policy Options* (Cambridge, MA: Program on Humanitarian Policy and Conflict Research, Harvard University, 2007), available at www.tagsproject.org/ (accessed 13 October 2007).

8. For an in-depth discussion of arguments on root causes of internal conflict, see, for example, Donald Horowitz, *Ethnic Groups in Conflict* (Berkeley: University of California Press, 1985); Ted Robert Gurr, *Minorities at Risk* (Washington, DC: United States Institute of Peace, 1993); K. J. Holsti, *The State, War, and the State of War* (Cambridge: Cambridge University Press, 1996); Donald M. Snow, *Distant Thunder: Patterns of Conflict in the Developing World,* 2nd ed. (New York: M. E. Sharpe, 1997); Donald M. Snow, *Uncivil Wars: International Security and the New Internal Conflicts* (Boulder, CO: Lynne-Rienner, 1996); William E. Odom, *On Internal War: American and Soviet Approaches to Third World Clients and Insurgents* (Durham, NC: Duke University Press, 2003); "Non-State Threats and Future Wars," special issue, *Small Wars and Insurgencies* 13, no. 2 (Autumn 2002); Monty Marshall and Ted Robert Gurr, *Peace and Conflict 2003* (College Park, MD: Center for International Development and Conflict Management, 2003); and Mary Kaldor, *New and Old Wars: Organized Violence in a Global Era* (Stanford, CA: Stanford University Press, 1999).

9. Available from www.smallwars.quantico.usmc.mil/sw_manual.asp (accessed 14 January 2008). On the British experience, see also David Fromkin, *A Peace to End All Peace: The Fall of the Ottoman Empire and the Creation of the Modern Middle East* (Holt Paperbacks, 2001).

10. The National Intelligence Council's *Global Trends 2015,* published in 2004, concludes that internal and transnational conflict will present a recurring cause of global instability and that these conflicts will become increasingly lethal. Weak and failing states will generate these conflicts, threatening the stability of a globalizing international system. See www.cia.gov/nic/pubs/2015_files/2015.htm.

11. On Sun Tzu, see Samuel B. Griffith, ed., *Sun Tzu: The Art of War* (London: Oxford University Press, 1963).

12. See for example, T. E. Lawrence, *Seven Pillars of Wisdom* (London: Jonathan Cape, 1935), 200–24.

13. See discussion on suicide terrorism in Assaf Moghadam, "Suicide Terrorism, Occupation, and the Globalization of Martyrdom: A Critique of 'Dying to Win,'" *Studies in Conflict & Terrorism,* December 2006, 707–29.

14. Shultz and Dew, *Insurgents, Terrorists, and Militias,* 179–81.

15. Ibid., 85–86.

16. See, for example, discussion in Thomas Mowle, "Iraq's Militia Problem," *Survival,* Autumn 2006, 41–55.

17. See, for example, discussion in Andrea J. Dew, "Irregular Warfare, Armed Groups, and the Long War: A New Analytical Framework," in *Economics and Maritime Security: Implications for the 21st Century,* ed. Richard M. Lloyd (Newport, RI: Naval War College, 2006), 103–107; and Montgomery McFate, "Iraq: The Social Context of IEDs," *Military Review,* May–June 2005, 37–41, available at www.au.af.mil/au/awc/awcgate/milreview/mcfate3.pdf.

18. For an empirical counterweight to the new war thesis, see Erik Melander, Magnus Öberg, and Jonathan Hall, *The "New Wars" Debate Revisited: An Empirical Evaluation of the Atrociousness of "New Wars,"* Uppsala Peace Research Papers 9 (Uppsala: Department of Peace and Conflict Research, Uppsala University, 2006).

19. For example, in Afghanistan the United States not only has to consider how members of the local Afghan tribes view the actions of armed groups but also how the situation affects all Afghans, in addition to trying to maintain the support of other populations in the region, such as in Pakistan, and U.S. domestic support for continued U.S. presence.

20. Shultz and Dew, *Insurgents, Terrorists, and Militias,* 170–77.

21. Max Weber, "Politik als Beruf" (Politics as a Vocation) (speech 1918), in which he concludes that the state must be characterized by the means that it, and only it, has at its disposal: "[A] state is a human community that (successfully) claims the monopoly of the legitimate use of physical force within a given territory."

22. "The Failed States Index," published by *Foreign Policy,* is one source of data on what has become an increasingly contested term. For the purposes of this research, the *Foreign Policy* definition is used:

> A state that is failing has several attributes. One of the most common is the loss of physical control of its territory or a monopoly on the legitimate use of force. Other attributes of state failure include the erosion of legitimate authority to make collective decisions, an inability to provide reasonable public services, and the inability to interact with other states as a full member of the international community. The 12 indicators cover a wide range of elements of the risk of state failure, such as extensive corruption and criminal behavior, inability to collect taxes or otherwise draw on citizen support, large-scale involuntary dislocation of the population, sharp economic decline, group-based inequality, institutionalized persecution or discrimination, severe demographic pressures, brain drain, and environmental decay. States can fail at varying rates through explosion, implosion, erosion, or invasion over different time periods.

See "The Failed States Index 2007," *Foreign Policy,* July/August 2007, available at www.foreignpolicy.com/story/cms.php?story_id=3865 (accessed 10 January 2008).

23. See, for example, discussion in Dew and Mohamedou, *Empowered Groups, Tested Laws, and Policy Options,* 18–19.

24. This was a long way from the controlled conflict of the traditionally pastoral Somali clans in which life—both human and animal—had a proscribed value that was honored by all sides in a limited conflict. Indeed, Aideed's clan saw the UN food shipments as one more resource up for grabs. He also had no compunction on using women and children ruthlessly as both lookouts and human shields.

25. Indeed Israel justified its air strikes against the northern Lebanese highways leading into Syria as an attempt to choke off resupply, and thereby not only bring the rocket attacks to an end, but limit the ability of Hezbollah to rearm after the conflict. Aboveground transportation, however, is only one way by which Hezbollah has been alleged to receive its arms shipments—some security analysts in the region claim there is an extensive network of tunnels dug for just this purpose. The result, for the purposes of our analysis, is that Hezbollah felt confident enough of its resupply that it was able to sustain a month-long barrage of rocket attacks on Israel across the southern Lebanese border in 2006. See, for example, discussion in Nicholas Blanford, "Call to Arms—Hizbullah's Efforts to Renew Weapons Supplies," *Jane's Intelligence Review,* 1 May 2007, available at www.4janes.com (accessed 3 January 2008).

26. Again, it is not argued here that the mere existence of external influences and resources in and of itself is sufficient to cause the erosion of traditional constraints on tactics and targets among armed groups. However, such influences and resources can contribute to this trend.

27. It is important to note, of course, that the religious ideologies motivating armed groups are in no way limited to extremist Muslim ideologies, nor does the ideology have to be religious—they can be political or socioeconomic ideologies, too. The key issue here is the extent to which such an ideology is or can become the source of the justification for increasingly violent and bloody tactics and targeting.

28. The declassified key finding of the April 2006 National Intelligence Estimate notes that "the Iraq jihad is shaping a new generation of terrorist leaders and operatives[;] perceived jihadist success there would inspire more fighters to continue the struggle elsewhere." "Declassified Key Judgments of the National Intelligence Estimate 'Trends in Global Terrorism: Implications for the United States,' Dated April 2006," news release, 26 September 2006, www.dni.gov/press_releases/Declassified_NIE_Key_Judgments.pdf (accessed 31 October 2006).

29. See, for example, discussion in Bruce Hoffman, "Insurgency and Counterinsurgency in Iraq," *Studies in Conflict & Terrorism* 29, no. 2 (March 2006): 103–21; and Lester W. Grau, "Something Old, Something New: Guerrillas, Terrorists, and Intelligence Analysis," *Military Review,* July–August 2004, 42–49, available at www.au.af.mil/au/awc/awcgate/milreview/grau.pdf.

30. Tom Koenigs, special representative of the UN secretary-general for Afghanistan, notes in his report on the issue that although there was a sharp increase in suicide attacks in Afghanistan from three in 2004 to 17 in 2005 to 123 in 2006, the number of civilian deaths was less than 100 in 2006. Moreover, by far the highest percentages of attacks in 2006 and 2007 (50 percent and 45 percent respectively) were in the southern region of Afghanistan, an area in which the Taliban were starting to stage a resurgence at this time. In addition, "In a May 2007 assessment, UNAMA analysts also concluded that recruitment for suicide attacks in the southeast region primarily takes place in madaris in Pakistan's North Waziristan and those associated with Jalaluddin Haqqani are of particular salience. In that assessment, UNAMA analysts found that in the southeast region suicide attackers are typically young males between the ages of 14 and 25, poor, introverted and impressionable." C. Christine Fair, *Suicide Attacks in Afghanistan (2001–2007)* (United Nations Assistance Mission to Afghanistan, September 2007), 1–66, available at www.unama-afg.org/docs/_UN-Docs/UNAMA%20-%20SUICIDE%20ATTACKS%20STUDY%20-%20SEPT%209th%202007.pdf (accessed 4 January 2008).

31. Indeed, some armed groups such as Hezbollah have political wings and public spokespeople to shape public reactions and support for their actions and the responses by states such as Israel.

32. See, for example, discussion in Mohammed M. Hafez, "Martyrdom Mythology in Iraq: How Jihadists Frame Suicide Terrorism in Videos and Biographies," *Terrorism & Political Violence*, March 2007, 707–29.

33. See, for example, discussion in Lorenzo Vidino, "The Muslim Brotherhood's Conquest of Europe," *Middle East Quarterly* 12, no. 1 (Winter 2005), available at www.meforum.org/article/687 (accessed 15 January 2008).

34. For commentary and analysis on the attacks see, for example, Steven Lee Myers, "Russian Report Faults Rescue Efforts in Beslan," *New York Times,* 29 November 2005, available at www.nytimes.com/2005/11/29/international/europe/.

35. The U.S. experience in Somalia in 1992–1993 is a good example of this, whereby U.S. goals started out at the limited end of the spectrum—deliver food to the hungry and protect that food from armed groups—to something much less limited—kill or capture Aideed!

36. See, for example, discussion in Rubin Barnett, "Still Ours to Lose: Afghanistan on the Brink," testimony before the House Committee on International Relations and the Senate Committee on Foreign Relations, 109th Cong., 2nd sess., September 2006, available at www.cfr.org/publication/11486/still_ours_to_lose.html.

37. Would, for example, the United Nations have intervened in Somalia in 1992 if policy makers had had a clearer understanding of the cost the local militias would exact from international peacekeepers and the U.S. military? The answer may well have been the same, especially considering the strong international media pressure on the UN to respond, but perhaps different strategies may have been used and greater pressure placed

on providing UN and U.S. personnel with better intelligence assessments of the local armed groups vying for power in Mogadishu.

38. See, for example, Max Manwaring, *Nonstate Actors in Colombia: Threats and Response* (Carlisle, PA: Strategic Studies Institute of the Army War College, 2002), available at www.strategicstudiesinstitute.army.mil/pdffiles/pub16.pdf; and discussion in Stephanie Hanson, "FARC, ELN: Colombia's Left-Wing Guerrillas," Council on Foreign Relations, 11 March 2008, www.cfr.org/publication/9272/.

39. For an excellent example of a regional intelligence assessment that includes shifts in tactics and targets see Patrick Lang et al., "HUMINT in Counterinsurgency," app. 3 in *Iraq Tribal Study—Al-Anbar Governorate: The Albu Fahd Tribe, the Albu Mahal Tribe and the Albu Issa Tribe* (Quantum Research International, 2006), available at turcopolier.typepad.com/the_athenaeum/files/iraq_tribal_study_070907.pdf.

40. For example, during the Soviet-Afghan War in the 1980s, one of the goals of the mujahideen was to inflict multiple demoralizing blows on the Soviet Army with the goal of forcing its political masters in Moscow to withdraw. While no single sniper attack or convoy ambush provided a decisive victory for the mujahideen, the cumulative effect of the grinding war of attrition made the war deeply unpopular in the Soviet Union.

21 Knowledge Transfer and Shared Learning among Armed Groups

James J. F. Forest

Knowledge is a vital resource for anyone or any organization, and can make the difference between success and failure, right and wrong, or even life and death. Knowledge is generally defined here to mean information that becomes useful upon human interpretation. Whether this knowledge is developed from within the organization or acquired by studying others that have developed useful expertise, organizational leaders must continually obtain, analyze, assimilate, and operationalize certain kinds of knowledge in order to effectively achieve the organization's goals. Thus, in both the private and public sectors, how an organization views knowledge and learning is critical to its success.

Knowledge and learning are also important in the world of armed groups. "No one is born with the knowledge of how to build bombs, use a pistol, conduct surveillance, or hijack airplanes," explains Larry C. Johnson, former deputy director of the State Department's Office of Counterterrorism. "These are skills that must be taught and practiced."[1] All armed groups of many types need to scan their environments and look for ways to sustain or enhance their operational capabilities. In other words, they need to learn. Armed-group learning can be facilitated by different means, from key individuals within the organization to open-source materials and lessons derived from the experiences of others. Understanding how and where critical knowledge is acquired, and how it is shared within and between various kinds of armed groups, brings an important level of analysis to our understanding of the contemporary global security environment. In exploring these issues of learning in the world of armed groups, this chapter will first describe their need for certain kinds of knowledge, and then focus on similarities among the sources

James J. F. Forest, PhD, is director of terrorism studies and associate professor of political science at the U.S. Military Academy, where he teaches undergraduate courses in terrorism, counterterrorism, comparative politics, information warfare, and political development in sub-Saharan Africa. He also directs a series of research initiatives for the Combating Terrorism Center at West Point, covering topics such as recruitment, training, and organizational knowledge transfer. Prior to this position, Dr. Forest served for three years as assistant dean for academic affairs at the U.S. Military Academy and has worked for several other educational, nonprofit, and government organizations. He has published nine books, including *Teaching Terror: Strategic and Tactical Learning in the Terrorist World* (Rowman & Littlefield, 2006), *Homeland Security: Protecting America's Targets* (three volumes: Praeger Security International, 2006), *Oil and Terrorism in the New Gulf: U.S. Policy in West Africa and the Gulf of Guinea* (Lexington Press, 2006), *The Making of a Terrorist: Recruitment, Training and Root Causes* (three volumes: Praeger Security International, 2005), and *Homeland Security and Terrorism: Readings and Interpretations* (McGraw-Hill, 2005, with Brigadier General Russell Howard and Major Joanne Moore). Dr. Forest received his graduate degrees from Stanford University and Boston College, and undergraduate degrees from Georgetown University and De Anza College.

and pathways of knowledge transfer both within and between groups, to include leaders, training camps, places of conflict, and the Internet. The discussion will conclude with a review of implications and suggestions for countering the threat to civil societies posed by armed groups.

ARMED-GROUP LEARNING

The successful employment of violence toward political or criminal objectives requires a broad range of knowledge that incorporates skills, competency, and creative thinking. An armed group needs to learn how to evade the efforts of local government authorities to penetrate the group, gather intelligence, and arrest its members. Leaders must ensure that the group's members can use their weapons accurately and effectively, and can reliably execute particular operations. Armed groups need to conduct their own surveillance and target identification, gather intelligence, acquire weapons and materiel, move money and people from one location to another—including across borders—without detection, and maintain covert communication (for example, changing frequencies when using electronic communications during a fight with government troops). Their members may need to learn how to identify the risks and advantages of using certain kinds of vehicles over others, how to mount rocket launchers in the beds of pickup trucks, how and where to launder money, how to successfully conduct a kidnapping, how and where to build camouflage-covered trenches, and how to plan escape routes once an act of violence has been carried out.[2] Without such learning and knowledge, armed groups are more easily thwarted, apprehended, or otherwise likely to fail.

Of course, within a particular armed group, there are certainly different levels of knowledge attained and used by different members for different purposes, and the patterns and pathways of knowledge acquisition and transfer vary significantly among groups. But in general, an armed group needs to learn in order to be effective, to attract new recruits, and to avoid stagnation and complacency of the group's members. They also recognize the need to learn and adapt in order to be successful against their more powerful government adversaries. A recent example of learning and adaptation is seen among the myriad groups in Iraq, whose improvised explosive devices (IEDs) have evolved over the last several years. According to one account,

> The first IEDs were triggered by wires and batteries; insurgents waited on the roadside and detonated the primitive devices when Americans drove past. After a while, U.S. troops got good at spotting and killing the triggermen when bombs went off. That led the insurgents to replace their wires with radio signals. The Pentagon, at frantic speed and high cost, equipped its forces with jammers to block those signals, accomplishing the task this spring. The insurgents adapted swiftly by sending a continuous radio signal to the IED; when the signal stops or is jammed, the bomb explodes. The solution? Track the signal and make sure it continues. Problem: the signal is encrypted. Now the Americans are grappling with the task of cracking the encryption on the fly and mimicking it—so far, without success.[3]

Similarly, authorities in Thailand are growing increasingly concerned about how the IEDs used by the Muslim insurgents there have grown in size and complexity. According to Southeast Asian terrorist expert Zachary Abuza,

It took insurgents almost two years to develop IEDs larger than five kilograms. This year has already witnessed 15 and 20 kilogram devices used several times a week, causing much higher casualty rates, especially among police and soldiers. Many of the devices are similar to the one found and defused on May 28: a 20 kilogram ammonium nitrate bomb constructed in a fire extinguisher, stuffed with bolts, nuts and pieces of rebar and hidden on the side of the road awaiting an army convoy. . . . The bomb was command detonated, but cell phone detonators are still currently used. Casio watches, which have been used routinely in Iraq, are now also regularly employed in southern Thailand.[4]

This phenomenon of adaptation has been a hallmark of the most effective armed groups in history. For example, the engineering teams of the Provisional Irish Republican Army (PIRA) demonstrated a clear aptitude for learning new ways of employing technology for violent means. According to one analysis, "A key development in PIRA timer technology was the adoption of the Memopark timer, a small pocket timer marketed to help people track the time remaining on their meter when they parked their car. The timers were very accurate, and the group acquired a large number of them. Because of the suitability and availability of the Memopark timers, PIRA relied on them for an extended period and was not forced to innovate as dramatically in timer technology."[5]

Technological innovation and adaptation were hallmarks of the Irish Republican Army (IRA) and the splinter groups it spawned, providing an important model for other groups to follow. In doing so, they demonstrated why organization learning is so important to armed groups. A recent study by RAND identified several characteristics that affect a group's learning abilities:[6] group culture, structure and command relationships, nature of communications mechanisms, absorptive capacity for new knowledge, stability of membership, group operational environment, connections to knowledge sources, and resources devoted to learning. Only a few of these characteristics relate to the group's external environment or relationships, and are addressed later in this chapter, while most learning-related characteristics are internal to the organization. In fact, armed groups can become smarter simply by adopting organizational structures that encourage and sustain learning both within the group and through interactions with other groups.

While some groups are hierarchical and traditional (like the FARC [Revolutionary Armed Forces of Colombia] in Colombia), others have embraced a more dynamic, networked approach that provides for a faster, more successful sharing of important knowledge. In essence, they form transnational networks unconstrained by state or geographical boundaries, "living, breathing organisms" that have proved to be enormously resilient despite the post-9/11 efforts of the United States and its allies to change the global security environment, and demonstrate the type of leadership and organizational structure that allows for adaptation and absorption of new knowledge.[7] They organize themselves in such a way that encourages broad participation in meeting the group's need to scan the operating environment for threats and vulnerabilities, acquire and process information, and distribute new knowledge to others in the group.[8] In doing so, they provide multiple pathways for knowledge transfer—that is, more individual nodes can contribute to the collective knowledge base, like a Wikipedia or CompanyCommand.com sort of approach.[9] Further, the web-like structure of communication channels within such organizations allow for faster identification and sharing of knowledge that could prove useful for achieving their own and other groups' objectives.

KNOWLEDGE TRANSFER AMONG ARMED GROUPS

Tactical or strategic innovations developed by one group or within one theater of conflict are often adapted by other groups in other theaters of conflict. For example, prior to the 2006 Israeli-Hezbollah conflict, rockets were rarely used by Palestinian militant groups against Israel (though mortars and suicide bombers have been common for several years). But since late 2006, Hamas has learned from Hezbollah's example (and perhaps even teaching or other direct forms of technology transfer from the Lebanese militants) and is now constructing and deploying rockets against Israel with increasing frequency and lethality—this despite the expectation that Shiite Muslims and Sunni Muslims rarely cooperate.

Shared learning is particularly common among armed groups whose members see themselves as "freedom fighters," where a common ideological alignment (the struggle against a perceived oppressor) leads to bonds that facilitate knowledge transfer. For example, the IRA is known to have nurtured international links with paramilitary organizations, including ETA in Spain and Palestinian terrorist groups, and in August 2001 Colombian authorities arrested three members of the Provisional IRA who (a subsequent investigation revealed) had spent five weeks in a remote part of the country, where they were teaching bomb-making techniques and urban guerrilla warfare tactics to members of the FARC.[10] According to press reports and court records, James Monaghan—a former member of the Sinn Fein Executive Council—is an explosives expert and the designer of a long-range mortar; Martin McCauley, commander of the IRA's engineering department, is an expert in using and producing weapons and mortars; and Niall Connolly, also a weapons expert, is thought to have first made contact with the FARC five years ago through a Basque terrorist group that specializes in bombings and assassinations of Spanish government officials. All three were convicted in 2004, and in March 2007 their convictions were upheld by the Colombian Supreme Court.[11] Meanwhile, expert testimony at a congressional hearing in April 2002 suggested that as many as 15 IRA members had visited Colombia within the previous five years, and counterterrorism experts believe that members of the Northern Irish paramilitary community may have engaged in such knowledge transfer activities in Colombia and elsewhere for decades.[12]

In the world of armed groups, strategic, tactical, and operational knowledge transfer activities also transcend a variety of ideological categories. For example, Indonesian radical groups with links to the Jemaah Islamiyah (JI) terrorist network have been found with videos documenting how Chechen separatists make and use land mines.[13] Trigger switches developed by the IRA for IEDs have been adapted for use by Hamas and other military groups in the Palestinian territories, as well as by many insurgent groups in Iraq. In a June 2005 *New York Times* article, Lieutenant General John Vines, a senior American ground commander in Iraq, reported that Iraqi insurgents were probably drawing on bomb-making experts from outside Iraq and from the old Iraqi Army.[14] The IRA's instruction manuals on counterforensic activities—extensive advice on how to create a "clean room" to ensure no DNA or other forensic evidence is left behind—have been nearly duplicated in training manuals developed by the Earth Liberation Front, an environmental terrorist organization based in the United States.[15]

Through these and other examples, a pattern emerges of adaptation and emulation among armed groups, regardless of their specific strategic objectives. The places and pathways through which this knowledge transfer occurs range from demonstrations of effective tactics by other groups to an impressive array of training camps, places of active conflict, prisons, and the Internet. Learning is at its core a human endeavor, thus it should come as no surprise that one of the most important sources of armed-group learning is found among a group's leadership and the knowledge resources it produces and makes available. Identifying these "learning leaders"—individuals committed to increasing the technical sophistication of their respective organizations—is an important aspect of our understanding of this knowledge transfer phenomenon. Further, it is through the global distribution of the materials they author that a primary means of knowledge transfer between armed groups takes place.

Learning Leaders and the Availability of Open-Source Resources

Most organizations have key individuals who are seen as particularly trustworthy sources of strategic and tactical guidance. For example, Gabriel Cleary, the director of engineering in the PIRA, was considered by many within the organization (and among Scotland Yard detectives) as their most knowledgeable master of homemade weaponry and bomb-making instruction, including Semtex, long-delay timers, and mortar components.[16] Two members of the Earth Liberation Front (and later, its splinter group the Family), William Rodgers and Stanislas Meyerhoff, collaborated to author "Setting Fires with Electrical Timers: An Earth Liberation Front Guide," a widely available guide that contains extensive instructions on creating and placing incendiary devices.

Within the al Qaida terror network, few learning leaders have been more prolific than Mustafa Setmariam Nasar—also known as Abu Musab al-Suri or Umar Abd al-Hakim—who is considered the principal architect of the network's post-9/11 structure and strategy, transforming al Qaida from a hierarchical organization into a resilient decentralized movement.[17] A warrant for his arrest issued in 2002 by the U.S. government accused Nasar of running training camps located in Afghanistan that allegedly specialized in imparting training and expertise on toxic materials and chemical substances.[18] Until his capture in Pakistan in November 2005, Nasar is credited with authoring scores of books, strategic analyses, guidance documents, and videotaped lectures that significantly expanded the network's base of operational knowledge.[19] For example, in a 15-page Arabic-language document titled "Biological Weapons" posted on his Web site during the summer of 2005, Nasar described "'how the pneumonic plague could be made into a biological weapon,' if a small supply of the virus [sic] could be acquired." Nasar's guide "drew on U.S. and Japanese biological weapons programs from the World War II era and showed 'how to inject carrier animals, like rats, with the virus [sic] and how to extract microbes from infected blood . . . and how to dry them so that they can be used with an aerosol delivery system.'"[20] According to Jarret Brachman, a professor at the Combating Terrorism Center at West Point, al-Suri also authored "one of the most expansive investigations of contemporary jihadist thought produced. . . . [A] single ideological reference for past, present and future information about how and why Muslims must wage violent jihad."[21]

Another prominent source of knowledge within the al Qaida network was Muhammed Atef (a.k.a. Abu Hafs al-Misri), an Egyptian national and former Egyptian police officer who assumed control of al Qaida's training camps in 1996 after the former commander, Abu Ubaida al-Banshiri, was drowned in Lake Victoria, Uganda. Atef is widely believed to have been an operational mastermind behind al Qaida's terror attacks of September 11, 2001 (9/11). And a key contributor to the success of the 9/11 attacks was a Jordanian named Abu Turab al-Urduni, who taught several of the attackers how to hijack planes and trains, control passengers and crew during a hijacking, neutralize air marshals, build and use explosives, gain strength by weight lifting, and speak basic English. At one point, his trainees were forced to butcher sheep and camels with pocketknives to desensitize them to cold-blooded killing and to prepare them for any contingencies in which passengers needed to be subdued.

More recently, al Qaida operatives have been providing guidance to fighters and new recruits in Iraq. For example, a participant in one of the hundreds of Web forums used by extremists to recruit and raise funding for armed groups in Iraq recently inquired about what sort of materials and equipment he should bring with him when crossing the border from Syria. Another participant, whose online identity is "Terrorist 11," responded by posting a detailed Arabic document from Sheikh Yusuf al-Uyayri, a top al Qaida strategist who was killed by Saudi authorities in 2003.[22] Al-Uyayri recommends a modest "toolkit" should include a pocket Koran, night-vision goggles, shackles for use in abductions, a GPS system, and a video camera for casing targets. He also provides some tactical guidance for conducting the kind of urban warfare that has become all too common in Iraq, outlining how to move in urban areas; methods for clearing rooms and buildings, using hand grenades in cities and rooms, and choosing firing positions in urban centers; and the proper use of camouflage, among other instructions. "The target should be easy and simple, and the security around it should be weak. The combat action against the target should be quick and not be based on a complex plan."[23] He goes on to describe how jihadists should be "like gas or air; present but not seen," and explains how to develop competence in various tactics, such as suicide attacks, sniping, booby traps, improvised explosive devices, poisonings, kidnappings, and assassinations.[24]

The Role of the Internet

Today, instructional materials produced by "learning leaders" are increasingly made available via the Internet. For example, as terrorism expert Chris Heffelfinger recently observed, "online training material has been an essential part of advancing the jihadi movement during the past five years."[25] Further, by publishing these materials online, they become accessible to a much wider audience, contributing to the global transfer of knowledge among armed groups as well as individuals motivated to commit violent acts on their own. Indeed, as Bruce Hoffman aptly observed, "using commercially published or otherwise readily accessible bomb-making manuals and operational guides to poisons, assassinations and chemical and biological weapons fabrication . . . the 'amateur' terrorist can be just as deadly and destructive as his more 'professional' counterpart."[26]

In addition to manuals full of instructional text and diagrams, today's multimedia technologies—including videos, photos, animation, and interactive video games—offer new and exciting ways to support learning, as seen in many of today's university classrooms in advanced industrial countries, as well as in the rapid rise of distance-learning programs worldwide. Several armed groups have embraced the use of this technology for their own purposes. For example, videos posted by insurgents in Iraq to al Qaida's primary online media outlet, the As-Sahab Web site, as well as to mainstream online services like YouTube, demonstrate how to construct and deploy IEDs; how to clean, assemble, and fire assault rifles; how to develop long-range sniper skills; how to conduct ambushes and kidnappings; and how to fire mortars from the countryside into crowded city centers. Further, such videos can be posted online using any number of so-called IP-masking tools or anonymizers, making it all the more difficult to locate the source of these materials or prevent their continued distribution.

Some groups have developed their own video games. In February 2003 the Lebanese militant group Hezbollah launched a new video game called "Special Force," a game that gives players a simulated experience of military operations against Israeli soldiers in battles re-created from actual encounters in the south of Lebanon. The second edition of this video game, released in late 2007, incorporated video footage of the summer 2006 war between Israel and Hezbollah. This follows the example set earlier by white supremacists in the United States and elsewhere, who in the early years of the Internet developed "first-person shooter" games with violent graphics, depicting real-life scenarios in which the player is the central character, killing Jews and other racial minorities.[27] All the games developed by these armed groups can be downloaded from their respective Web sites by anyone, providing new avenues for the group's outreach, indoctrination, and (through virtual combat simulations) some form of knowledge transfer.

Today, there are literally hundreds of gigabytes worth of training manuals, videos, and other resources available online that provide an important and common form of knowledge sharing among terrorist groups. A search for the keyword phrase "terrorist handbook" on the popular Google search engine in June 2007 found over 985,000 Web pages. Several of these sites offer instructions on how to acquire ammonium nitrate and firearms without attracting attention, while others provide instructions on how to build several different kinds of explosives from ordinary household chemicals. As a result of Internet-based sharing of knowledge, cells affiliated with al Qaida throughout the Middle East, Southeast Asia, and Europe that have recently carried out or seriously planned bombings have relied heavily on the Internet.[28] Further, loosely organized groups of al Qaida–inspired (but not necessarily affiliated) individuals have been responsible for recent terrorist attacks in Madrid, London, Istanbul, Riyadh, and elsewhere. Indeed, according to some Western intelligence agencies and terrorism specialists, the "global jihad movement" has become a "Web-directed" phenomenon.[29]

Contemporary armed groups can also acquire a significant amount of strategic and tactical knowledge via a wide array of open-source materials such as court transcripts, academic publications, government training manuals, and media accounts. Overall, security analysts have grown increasingly concerned about the huge and growing online library of strategic and tactical resources on everything from creating chemical weapons to assembling and firing a surface-to-air missile against an airline, a tactic seen recently in Kenya and Iraq.[30] There are any number of "learning leaders" within the world of armed groups who have contributed (and continually add) to the expansion of the strategic and tactical knowledge base on guerrilla warfare and terrorist violence, a knowledge base that is increasingly being shared among armed groups regardless of ideological or geographic orientation.

The Demonstrative Dimension of Knowledge Transfer

Imitation and emulation have become honored traditions in the world of armed groups. From the rash of airplane hijackings of the early 1970s to the modern conflict in Iraq, violent nonstate actors (VNSAs) have continually shown a willingness to copy the strategies and tactics of others. For example, in 1987 the Tamil Tigers (LTTE) modeled their attack of Tamil University on the 1983 Hezbollah truck bombing of the U.S. Marine barracks in Beirut. In 1995, this group's destruction of two Sri Lankan naval vessels, using small watercraft loaded with explosives, provided a model for al Qaida's 2001 attack against the USS *Cole* in the Yemeni port of Aden. Similarly, Tamil Tiger separatists carried out a coordinated suicide attack in October 2001 against the MV *Silk Pride,* an oil tanker that was carrying more than 650 tons of diesel and kerosene to the port of Jaffna, in northern Sri Lanka. The attackers used five boats in the attack. One rammed the tanker, triggering an explosion on board, and three sailors died in the attack.[31] A year later, in October 2002, Islamic militants steered an explosive-laden boat into the French oil tanker MV *Limburg* in the port of Ash Shihr, off the coast of Yemen, splitting the vessel's hull, killing one crew member and sending more than 90,000 barrels of Iranian crude oil pouring into the Gulf of Aden.[32]

Often, armed groups will carefully monitor the media coverage a particular act of violence receives and then emulate that act, or attempt to do something even more dramatic. Sometimes, these groups may be competing against each other for the attention and support of a local (or sometimes global) audience, and are therefore compelled to "outdo" one another in order to grab the spotlight. In a way, the media often provide a showcase through which armed groups can learn from each other about successful (or even unsuccessful) attacks and other types of activities.[33] When attacks occur, media companies often compete against each other (and increasingly with Web sites and bloggers on the Internet) to satisfy the public's thirst for news, graphic pictures, and titillating details. In doing so, they often provide ample information for armed groups to learn how to conduct similar attacks in the future. Indeed, as terrorism scholar Cindy Combs has observed, "Showcasing demonstrably effective terrorist actions for an audience of potential supporters and/or collaborators has become an effective and essentially cost-free teaching technique for terrorists today."[34] Overall, the media may be complicit in the demonstrative dimension of knowledge transfer in the world of armed groups. However, their role pales in comparison to that of other avenues of learning, such as training camps and places of conflict.

Training Camps

According to a recent report by the U.S. Department of State, Iran and Syria routinely provide safe haven, substantial resources, and guidance to terrorist organizations.[35] In particular, Iran has been providing guidance and training to select Iraqi Shia political groups, and weapons and training to Shia militant groups to enable anticoalition attacks. The State Department report notes that "Iranian government forces have been responsible for at least some of the increasing lethality of anticoalition attacks by providing Shia militants with the capability to build IEDs with explosively formed projectiles similar to those developed by Iran and Lebanese Hizballah. The Iranian Revolutionary Guard was linked to armor-piercing explosives that resulted in the deaths of Coalition Forces. The Revolutionary Guard, along with Lebanese Hizballah, implemented training programs for Iraqi militants in the construction and use of sophisticated IED technology. These individuals then passed on this training to additional militants in Iraq."[36]

In Syria, Hezbollah militant leaders have provided training to several Palestinian groups who, in turn, provided training in armed assaults, kidnappings, and demolitions to western European and Latin American extremists, some of whom later carried out attacks in support of their benefactors' causes.[37] According to the U.S. Department of State, several radical terrorist groups have maintained training camps or other facilities on Syrian territory over the last 20 years, including the Popular Front for the Liberation of Palestine (PFLP), the Abu Nidal Organization, and the Palestinian Islamic Jihad (PIJ).[38] One notorious example is the Ayn Tzahab training camp in Syria, allegedly supported by Iran and used for operational training for Palestinian terrorists, including Hamas and Palestinian Islamic Jihad operatives.[39] Similar training camps have been located in the Syrian-controlled Bekaa Valley, in eastern Lebanon, where the Turkish separatist group PKK is also known to have had a training camp.

A state's participation in transferring lethal knowledge to armed groups is not new. During the cold war, for example, the United States and the Soviet Union offered military training—either directly or indirectly through proxies—to a variety of armed groups.[40] In Libya, the government provided safe haven and both ideological and logistical support for a wide variety of groups throughout the 1970s and '80s. In addition to Palestinian and Islamist terrorists, groups that have received training in Libya include the Irish Republican Army, the Basque separatist group ETA, Sierra Leone's Revolutionary United Front, Colombia's M-19, the Haitian Liberation Organization, the Chilean Manuel Rodriguez Patriotic Front, the Secret Army for the Liberation of Armenia, and the Japanese Red Army.[41]

Afghanistan and its border region with Pakistan have also been prominent locations of training camps for armed groups. Government reports and several scholarly books have already provided ample evidence of how the Taliban facilitated a vast enterprise of terrorist training camps for al Qaida and other like-minded entities throughout Afghanistan.[42] Many of these camps existed even before the reign of the Taliban. During the war against Soviet occupation forces in Afghanistan, the U.S. Central Intelligence Agency provided funding and weapons to the Pakistani Inter-services Intelligence Directorate, which distributed them among various resistance groups fighting in Afghanistan. These national resistance fighters, in turn, trained foreign Islamic militants helping them overthrow the Soviets. By some estimates, several thousand camps were established throughout Afghanistan and across the Pakistani border—in and around the city of Peshawar and the tribal region of Waziristan—between 1980 and 1989, providing military training and seminars in Islamic history and theology to Afghans, Arabs, and others. Training camps in this region have typically been harsh learning environments—mud huts, dusty classrooms, obstacle courses, mazes of barbed wire, trenches, and, of course, no basic utilities.[43] And yet, by one account, upwards of 70,000 militants received weapons training and religious instruction in al Qaida's training camps in this region.[44]

South of Kashmir, the mountainous areas of western Pakistan—a region long known for providing safe haven for bandits and extremists—have also been used for militant training, often by members of several ideologically aligned groups. Experts in ambush tactics and explosives are in high demand in this region, and they typically provide their knowledge to whoever seeks it. Videotapes obtained by ABC News in 2005 contain images of al Qaida training camps inside Pakistan and show fighters conducting a variety of exercises with automatic weapons, as they once did at similar camps in Afghanistan. The fighters are identified as coming from nine different countries in Africa and the Middle East, with many from Saudi Arabia.[45]

After receiving their training in the al Qaida camps of Afghanistan or Pakistan during the 1990s, most militants returned home, some to comfortable environs and regular lifestyles, while others joined Islamist groups elsewhere in the world, including the Chechen Mujahideen, the Armed Islamic Group in Algeria, the Abu Sayyaf Group in the Philippines, and Jemaah Islamiyah in Indonesia.[46] Members of these groups often proceeded to establish their own training camps after returning to their countries of origin. For example, Abu Sayyaf established a central base on Basilan's Mohadji mountain called Camp Abdurajak—one of at least nine Abu Sayyaf camps hidden in the jungles of the Philippines.[47] On the island of Mindanao, in the southern Philippines, three major JI terrorist training camps—Camp Vietnam, Camp Palestine, and Camp Hodeibia—were set up alongside the Moro Islamic Liberation Front's (MILF's) Camp Abu Bakar complex.[48] Mindanao has, in turn, become a hub of knowledge transfer for armed groups throughout Southeast Asia. According to Philippine military intelligence, these camps have played host to several hundred trainers from the Middle East,[49] and security services throughout the region have been concerned about a steady flow of visitors to Mindanao.

In early 2006, Malaysian authorities arrested members of a 12-man logistical cell—composed of Indonesians, Malaysians, and two Filipinos—who were responsible for getting *jihadis* in and out of Mindanao, where they were being trained in MILF camps. The two Filipinos told the Philippine National Police, who were sent to question them, that they were bringing militants to Pattani for training. According to regional expert Zachary Abuza, an undated Thai intelligence report describes how a Pattani Muslim, Ruli (a.k.a. Ahmed), went to Afghanistan in 1998, and upon returning to Indonesia engaged in the sectarian fighting in Ambon and the Moluccas following the fall of Suharto. He is believed to be running training for Pattani militants in Indonesia. This corresponds with the increased small-arms training JI was conducting for itself in 2006.[50] Similarly, Malaysian authorities believe that members of Kumpulan Mujahedin Malaysia (KMM)—a group that favors the overthrow of the Malaysian government and the creation of an Islamic state comprising Malaysia, Indonesia, and the southern Philippines (and southern Thailand)—has close ties to JI, and several arrested KMM militants reportedly received military training in Afghanistan and possibly Mindanao.[51]

In most cases, training camps are used exclusively by members of a particular armed group, but in these cases, members of various groups were welcomed and trained, in the process creating a network of alumni who—having survived a typically grueling experience together—may have formed bonds of friendship that are sustained for many years afterward. It is thus important to learn all we can about the places of armed-group training around the world and, from an analysis of their similarities, develop ways to reduce their potential role in the global transfer of lethal knowledge.

Places of Conflict

While formal training camps have historically served an important role in facilitating knowledge transfer between armed groups, places of conflict can be seen as a hub of on-the-job training. While Afghanistan during the 1980s provided many opportunities for individuals and groups from around the world to learn basic irregular warfare tactics while fighting the Soviets, at present no other country in the world offers a more active place for urban guerrilla-warfare training than Iraq. A report released by the Central Intelligence Agency on 21 June 2005 even suggested that "Iraq may prove to be an even more effective training ground for Islamic extremists than Afghanistan."[52] Terrorism experts Daniel Benjamin and Gabriel Weimann have described Iraq as "a theater of inspiration"[53] where foreign fighters and Iraqi insurgents are learning how to manufacture improvised explosive devices (as described earlier) and to use light weapons with increasingly lethal effect. As David Brooks observed in a recent *New York Times* report, "The landscape of insurgency in Iraq is comprised of disparate groups that share information, learn from each other's experiments and respond quickly to environmental signals."[54]

In fact, knowledge transfer in Iraq is taking place in several ways simultaneously: insurgents (secular and Islamists) are learning from foreign Islamist militants; foreign fighters are learning from local Iraqi insurgent groups; and armed groups worldwide are learning from the successes and failures of all the violent nonstate actors currently engaged in this theater of conflict. But perhaps more important, foreign fighters who have come to Iraq and engaged in the conflict are returning to their countries of origin, having gained valuable experience in urban guerrilla warfare—the kind of strategies and tactics that would prove more useful in contemporary Western cities than anything that could have been learned in Afghanistan. In some ways, Iraq has become a graduate school of jihadist studies, and those who survive the conflict and return home are viewed with some admiration by their local extremist colleagues as having both luck and specialized, useful knowledge.

In general, the migration of fighters from one operational theater to another (e.g., from Afghanistan to Bosnia or Iraq) may be one of the most important historical forms of organizational knowledge transfer among armed groups. During the early 1990s, thousands of mujahideen left Afghanistan and other parts of central Asia to fight alongside Bosnian Muslims against the Serbs. Weapons and fighters were smuggled through Croatia and other locations to support the Muslims in their struggle, and "on the job" combat training for new fighters was common. By 1994, major Balkan terrorist training camps included Zenica, Malisevo, and Mitrovica in Kosovo, where experienced veterans taught new recruits.[55] After the war, some stayed in the country and settled in, and some returned home to their countries of origin, but many foreign Islamist extremists took their experience in search of a new place to continue the jihad. Today, the conflicts in Iraq and Afghanistan—as well as lower-level terrorist activity in Pakistan (and Kashmir), India, Indonesia, Algeria, Morocco, Egypt, and elsewhere in Africa, the Middle East, and Southeast Asia—offer these wandering extremists the opportunity they seek to engage their perceived enemies in combat.

Because of the increasingly violent conflict in the southeastern region of the country, Afghanistan has once more become an important hotbed for militant training and knowledge sharing among insurgents (like the Taliban and the rebels loyal to warlord Hekmatyr Gulbuddin) and other armed groups, including those involved in the enormously lucrative opium trade. Further, there is mounting evidence that strategies and tactics developed in the Iraqi theater of conflict are being transferred to Afghanistan. According to Afghanistan's defense minister Rahim Wardak, there are "strong indications" that al Qaida has brought in a team of Arab instructors from Iraq to teach the latest insurgent techniques to the Taliban.[56] Other researchers have described what could be called "learning missions" to Iraq by various Taliban and al Qaida fighters.

For example, Hamza Sangari, a Taliban commander from Khost Province, described to *Newsweek* reporters a trip to Iraq he took with a small group of fighters in 2005, where they learned how to make armor-penetrating weapons by disassembling rockets and RPG rounds, removing the explosives and propellants, and repacking them with powerful, high-velocity "shaped" charges; how to make and use various kinds of remote-controlled devices and timers; and how to spring ambushes and engage in urban fighting.[57] Sangari told the reporters that the IED training was particularly helpful in replacing the comparatively ineffective use of obsolete land mines left over from the Soviet occupation. The transfer of knowledge from Iraqi insurgents has also been documented in Pakistan, where a sweep of pro-Taliban sites along the Afghan frontier in North Waziristan revealed a mound of Arabic-language training manuals, apparently copies of the ones used by insurgents in Iraq. Sangari commented that he was also impressed by the way Iraqi insurgents created combat videos to help fund-raising and recruiting efforts. It should thus come as no surprise to find that similar videos of Taliban attacks are now showing up in bazaars along the Pakistani border.[58]

Meanwhile, the Niger Delta region of West Africa has become a training ground for several militias and armed gangs. During 2006, these groups kidnapped more than 150 foreigners, killed unkown numbers of Nigerian armed forces personnel, detonated several car bombs, destroyed various oil pipeline facilities, and crippled the oil production of Africa's largest oil exporter by nearly 24 percent. The larger of these groups—including the Niger Delta People's Volunteer Force, the Niger Delta Vigilantes (a.k.a. Icelanders), and the Movement for the Emancipation of the Niger Delta (MEND)—watch each other closely because of their natural competition for publicity and support. A successful attack by one may inspire a similar attack by another within a short period of time. Insurgents in the Niger Delta region have watched the enormous press coverage given to kidnappings in the Middle East, and have adapted this tactic by kidnapping foreign oil workers to gain the world's attention. These groups in turn are closely watched by smaller players in the region, including the Federated Niger Delta Ijaw Communities (an ethnic militia), the Coalition for Militant Action in the Niger Delta, and the so-called Martyr's

Brigade. And in a situation that is similar to that in Iraq, individuals may be involved in an attack on behalf of one group on one day, and the next day be fighting on behalf of a different group. In short, the region supports a swirling gray cloud of knowledge transfer, often at the individual level. The scope and patterns of this activity are difficult to assess with any real accuracy, but it is certainly a significant contributor to the overall level of violence faced by the Nigerian authorities today.

Knowledge Transfer and the Trusted Handshake

As described earlier, clandestine networks can self-organize and disperse, comprising formal, informal, family, and cultural associations tied by varied and sometimes near-invisible links. The distributed cellular architecture of a network insulates and protects the core, while the links between members provide conduits through which they can publicize, mobilize, radicalize, coordinate, finance, collect, and share information and other vital organizational activities. These links also provide avenues for collaboration with other armed groups, state sponsors, criminal enterprises, and organizations willing to provide support and exchange valuable knowledge. How are these links established? In essence, anyone can become a member of the network, though usually the individual must first establish some form of credentials through which others in the network can then justify membership. I call this "the trusted handshake."[59] Examples of the foundations upon which a trusted handshake is established can include mutual friends or acquaintances who would vouch for you (in the Sicilian Mafia, for example, members vouch for others with their lives); family ties (to include belonging to a specific clan or tribe, by birth or marriage); ethnic ties, often within a diaspora (e.g., Algerians in France and Spain, Pakistanis in the United Kingdom, Tamils in Canada, Turks in Germany); a shared academic/scientific knowledge base; religion (doctrinal knowledge, formal credentials, etc.); and shared experiences (as in a training camp or on a battlefield) that give members a common "veteran" status.

Sociopolitical environments can contribute to the forging of these trusted handshakes. For example, places with a high level of corruption and weak civil society; areas of deep ethnic fissures (where a common animosity toward a distinct "them" drives daily behavior), regions of severe financial or economic desperation and weak border security (usually patrolled by poorly equipped, underpaid guards); states ruled by authoritarian, statist regimes that overly control the local economy; and places with a severe lack of transparency in private- and public-sector finance can all bring like-minded individuals together.

Another prominent place where these trusted handshakes are forged is prison. Places of incarceration produce a similar sort of "veteran status" to that of training camps and places of conflict, and members of armed groups who are released from prison are often treated with additional respect by other members of their cadres. Various forms of knowledge transfer take place in prison. For example, some studies have noted that when members of the IRA were captured and sent to British or Irish prisons, they were immediately debriefed by other inmates, who then smuggled the information (and lessons learned) to IRA members outside the prison walls. Particularly useful information passed on by the imprisoned terrorists could include how they were caught, what information the captors were looking for, what (if anything) might have gone awry with a planned attack being carried out, and who (if anyone) might have played a role in their capture.[60] More recently, authorities in the U.S. military have grown concerned about the thousands of insurgents in Iraq who have cycled through U.S.-run prisons there. Some U.S. commanders in Iraq have expressed concern that the infamous Abu Ghraib prison has become a "jihad university"—a breeding ground for extremist leaders and a school for terrorists.[61]

In sum, knowledge transfer among armed groups is often driven by individual human connections. Historically, these connections have been forged in person-to-person interactions, whether in training camps, places of conflict, prison, or elsewhere, but we have also seen a rapid increase in knowledge transfer between armed groups via the Internet.

CONCLUSIONS AND IMPLICATIONS

The many examples of knowledge transfer reflected in this discussion indicate a level of adaptation, operational flexibility, and organizational learning capacity among armed groups that warrants our attention. Knowledge transfer is facilitated within and between armed groups through an array of training camps, places of active conflict, prisons, and the Internet. Tactics demonstrated as effective by one armed group are often adopted by others, while certain individuals within each group serve as leaders of knowledge transfer, through the resources they author (both in print and in multimedia forms) as well as through personal relationships with key sources of knowledge.

What does this analysis suggest for our understanding of armed groups and of new ways to confront them? To begin with, it is important to recognize that **armed groups who are committed to the long-term training and education of their members can be more successful.** Clearly, the attributes of a learning organization (e.g., fostering the ability to adapt to a changing strategic environment) can be seen among the more sophisticated terrorist organizations, like al Qaida, Hamas, Jemaah Islamiyah, and the FARC. Through the development of doctrines, training manuals, military exercises, and educational programs (often, but not necessarily, provided at remote training camps), the most lethal terrorist organizations work hard to continually improve their lethal capabilities. Structure and membership of a group also have a significant impact on their learning capabilities. Thus, "capacity for learning" should be an element in determining which armed groups may pose a greater threat to us than others.

As armed groups learn, we should expect some level of transformation in their tactics for recruitment, acquisition of material and finance, and attack. We must understand and anticipate the type of organizational dynamism reflected in the examples provided in this chapter. In other words, we should never assume that a particular armed group relies on any single static list of tactics; rather, we should assume the group is capable of—and perhaps actively seeking avenues for—learning and adapting. Thus, we need to identify the patterns and pathways of a group's learning, as well as what kinds of learning are influencing the members of the group and why.

Successful armed groups learn from the strategies and tactics of other organizations through technology and personal contact. As described in this chapter, groups learn by studying each others' training manuals, videos, and other forms of information (particularly via the Internet), and they also learn from media accounts of terrorist events (both successes and failures) carried out by other organizations. As seen in the examples of Jemaah Islamyiah members training in al Qaida's Afghanistan camps, or members of the Lebanese Hezbollah aiding the Palestinian group Hamas, a global network of information and knowledge sharing plays a key role in developing the operational capabilities of learning organizations. Further, while the formal means and locations of knowledge sharing are important (for example, training camps), it is the informal knowledge networks among terrorists and their organizations that contribute the most to learning in the terrorist world. In this regard, the insurgency in Iraq—which attracted thousands of foreign fighters, who have learned urban terrorist tactics—requires extensive analysis to determine where these fighters go when they eventually leave this region.

Further, **we must gather all the information we can about the individual-level human dynamics within an armed group that facilitates knowledge transfer.** Trust is a critical component of human networks—indeed, according to noted terrorism scholar Brian Jenkins, "To work well, networks require strong shared beliefs, a collective vision, some original basis for trust, and excellent communications."[62] The trusted handshake, established by various social mechanisms and shared beliefs, provides the means by which network members agree to collaborate in achieving the network's objectives. Trust is also vital for the transfer of knowledge from teacher to learner, both within a group and between groups. Recognizing this, it is important to identify the most knowledgeable and trusted members of a particular armed group or network, in order to gain insights into the pathways and types of learning that take place within the group, and to learn what terrible things they may be capable of.

Given that the trusted handshake establishes the means by which knowledge transfers are validated, **we must focus our counterterrorism and intelligence-gathering efforts toward identifying and apprehending key knowledge brokers;** beyond the traditional focus on the group members who pull triggers, detonate explosives, or plan attacks, we must place greater emphasis on finding those who transfer knowledge both within and beyond the group. We need to locate and neutralize the principal conduits of knowledge transfer that enable armed groups to become more sophisticated and effective. For example, key learning leaders of al Qaida like Abu Musab al-Suri, Sheikh Yusuf al-Uyayri (whose advice on what to bring to Iraq was mentioned earlier), Abu Qatada, and Muhammed Atef should be at the top of our list of individuals to apprehend.

We need to deter individuals from participating in knowledge transfer transactions. Some countries have attempted legal remedies to thwart the transfer of lethal knowledge. For example, the U.S. statute *U.S. Code* 18, section 842(p), states,

> It shall be unlawful for any person:
>
> (A) to teach or demonstrate the making or use of an explosive, a destructive device, or a weapon of mass destruction, or to distribute by any means information pertaining to, in whole or in part, the manufacture or use of an explosive, destructive device, or weapon of mass destruction, with the intent that the teaching, demonstration, or information be used for, or in furtherance of, an activity that constitutes a Federal crime of violence; or

(B) to teach or demonstrate to any person the making or use of an explosive, a destructive device, or a weapon of mass destruction, or to distribute to any person, by any means, information pertaining to, in whole or in part, the manufacture or use of an explosive, destructive device, or weapon of mass destruction, knowing that such person intends to use the teaching, demonstration, or information for, or in furtherance of, an activity that constitutes a Federal crime of violence.

Thus, it is illegal to demonstrate how to build explosives; and yet individuals are doing this online regularly worldwide. On 29 March 2004, Canadian police arrested Mohammed Momin Khawaja, a 24-year-old computer programmer, and charged him with involvement in what Canadian and British authorities described as a transatlantic plot to bomb targets in London and Canada. British prosecutors alleged in court that Khawaja met his acquaintances online, where he showed them images of explosive devices found on the Web and told them how to detonate bombs using cell phones.[63] Can we prosecute Web-site-hosting services for providing the means by which this knowledge transfer is taking place? In years past, we devised new legal frameworks in which all countries agree to apprehend and prosecute purveyors of Internet child pornography; can we not do something akin to this in response to the global proliferation of online instruction manuals and videos for conducting violent attacks?

In addition, we should examine new and creative strategies to negatively impact the usefulness of this knowledge transfer by damaging the trust upon which it's built. For example, there may be ways to undermine the credibility of a group or its members by highlighting strategic blunders, infiltration by authorities, financial incompetence, and so forth. Negatively impacting the "street perception" of a group can be just as important as confronting it with kinetic force. Given the importance of the "trusted handshake" as discussed above, individuals are less likely to trust the information received from a source whose credibility is suddenly called into question.

We must also address the various environmental conditions that enable knowledge transfer between armed groups. From training camps to prisons and places of ongoing conflict, there are literally dozens of locations around the world in which knowledge transfer is taking place daily among and between armed groups and individuals of various ideological and criminal orientations. What sociopolitical factors or security environments enable this learning? What do places like the Bekaa Valley, the Afghanistan-Pakistan border region, or the island of Mindanao have in common? In addition to a remote and rugged terrain, they are places where local sociopolitical conditions create a climate of tolerance (or even support) of armed-group training. Specific countries, like Afghanistan, Bosnia, and Iraq, have played a critical role in facilitating the advancement of knowledge and its dissemination throughout the world, while other countries—like Iran, Libya, and Syria—have even provided strategic and tactical expertise to armed groups of various ideological persuasions.

An array of criminal organizations, militias, and terrorist networks are prominently found in weak or failing states. Thus it is unsurprising to find that these states play a key role in the global trade in drugs and weapons, which is facilitated by critical security vulnerabilities—porous borders, corruption, inadequate law enforcement, and an environment of extreme scarcity. Overall, understanding the environmental conditions—to include physical and human geography, economics, culture, and the political landscape—that may facilitate training camps for armed groups is an important dimension of our ability to combat the existence of such places of knowledge transfer.[64] Our response to enabling environments for armed-group learning requires many levers of national power, including diplomatic, financial, and legal. Governments must be pressured and equipped with the means to locate and destroy training camps, combat corruption, monitor prison activity, and work collectively to reduce the sheer number and scope of the world's places of conflict

Finally, **we need to constrain the ability of armed groups to obtain knowledge that would give them strategic or tactical advantages.** We must make it harder for armed groups to predict how we will confront them, or how we will react to their threats or attacks; in other words, we need to make it harder for them to learn how to effectively anticipate our actions, and make it harder for them to learn things about us that might give them an advantage. Security and law enforcement personnel are already keenly aware of the need to avoid being open about operating procedures, but the media and the Internet have created new challenges for maintaining operational security. The Internet in particular provides a wealth of information about societies, institutions, governments, the details of physical locations (for example, the Google Earth imaging service), and so forth, which allows armed groups to learn far more about us than we can learn about them. From professional reporters to amateur Web-site moderators, in today's information age we must all learn to identify sources of new knowledge that are (or would be) attractive to armed groups, and employ some sort of self-censorship to ensure our own security. This is perhaps the greatest challenge of today's global security environment—how to confront an actively learning armed group while maintaining some semblance of open society.

As this cursory overview reveals, there is a swirling world of knowledge transfer activities among armed groups—an opaque cloud, in which it is difficult at best to pinpoint patterns and pathways. Nonetheless, we must rise to the challenge and expand our efforts to understand the threat we face by such activities. This analysis highlights the need for more research and analysis on the role of knowledge transfer in the world of violent nonstate actors, in the hopes that doing so will enhance our ability to respond to the threat of armed groups with greater sophistication and success.

NOTES

This chapter contains a few small portions of material from *Teaching Terror: Strategic and Tactical Knowledge in the Terrorist World,* edited by James Forest (Lanham, MD: Rowman & Littlefield, 2006), particularly chapters 1, 4, and 10. In most cases, this material has been updated or modified from previous versions.

1. Larry C. Johnson, former deputy director, Office of Counterterrorism, Department of State, statement to the Committee on Foreign Relations, Subcommittee on International Operations and Terrorism, 107th Cong., 1st sess., 18 December 2001, 17, available at bulk.resource.org/gpo.gov/hearings/107s/77601.pdf.

2. For a detailed discussion on the types of learning sought by members of terrorist organizations, please see chapter 4 of *Teaching Terror* and volume 2 of *The Making of a Terrorist: Recruitment, Training and Root Causes*, edited by James J. F. Forest (Westport, CT: Praeger Security International, 2005).

3. Scott Johnson and Melinda Liu, "The Enemy Spies," *Newsweek,* 27 June 2005, available at www.msnbc.msn.com/id/8272786/site/newsweek.

4. Zachary Abuza, "The Role of Foreign Trainers in Southern Thailand's Insurgency," *Terrorism Monitor* 5, no. 11 (7 June 2007), available at www.jamestown.org/terrorism/news/article.php?articleid=2373451.

5. Brian A. Jackson, John C. Baker, Kim Cragin, John Parachini, Horacio R. Trujillo, and Peter Chalk, *Aptitude for Destruction,* vol. 2, *Case Studies of Organizational Learning in Five Terrorist Groups* (Santa Monica, CA: RAND Corporation, 2005), 103. Also, see Brian Jackson's chapter in this volume for a description of how the PIRA learned to use rocket-propelled grenades (RPGs)—and even developed its own improvised versions of commercial systems—with increasing lethality between 1981 and 1991.

6. Paraphrased from Brian A. Jackson, *Aptitude for Destruction,* vol. 1, *Organizational Learning in Terrorist Groups and Its Implications for Combating Terrorism,* with John C. Baker, Kim Cragin, John Parachini, Horacio R. Trujillo, and Peter Chalk (Santa Monica, CA: RAND, 2005), 37.

7. For more on this, see ibid., 37–47.

8. Paraphrased from Horacio Trujillo and Brian Jackson, "Theory: Organizational Learning as a Four-Component Process," in *Aptitude for Destruction,* vol. 2, *Case Studies of Organizational Learning in Five Terrorist Groups,* by Brian A. Jackson, John C. Baker, Kim Cragin, John Parachini, Horacio R. Trujillo, and Peter Chalk (Santa Monica, CA: RAND Corporation, 2005), 182.

9. See James Forest, introduction to *Teaching Terror: Strategic and Tactical Knowledge in the Terrorist World,* ed. James Forest (Lanham, MD: Rowman & Littlefield, 2006).

10. For a case study of knowledge transfer activities between the IRA and the FARC, please see Kim Cragin, Peter Chalk, Sara A. Daly, and Brian A. Jackson, *Sharing the Dragon's Teeth: Terrorist Groups and the Exchange of New Technologies* (Santa Monica, CA: RAND, 2007), 71–91.

11. Martin Hodgson, Rosie Cowan, and Richard Norton-Taylor, "Suspected IRA Trio Held in Colombia," *The Guardian,* 14 August 2001, available at www.guardian.co.uk/Northern_Ireland/Story/0,2763,536573,00.html; and Jerry Seper, "Colombia Upholds IRA Convictions," *Washington Times,* 31 March 2007, available at wpherald.com/articles/4023/1/Colombian-Supreme-Court-upholds-IRA-convictions/Ex-IRA-members-convicted-for-supporting-FARC.html.

12. BBC News, "Congress Hears Damning IRA Report," 24 April 2002, available at news.bbc.co.uk/1/hi/northern_ireland/1949484.stm.

13. Wong Chun Wai and Lourdes Charles, "Indonesian Radical Groups Learning Chechen Terrorist Tactics," *The Star* (Singapore), 27 September 2004.

14. David S. Cloud, "Iraqi Rebels Refine Bomb Skills, Pushing Toll of GI's Higher," *New York Times*, 22 June 2005.

15. Brian A. Jackson, Peter Chalk, R. Kim Cragin, Bruce Newsome, John V. Parachini, William Rosenau, Erin M. Simpson, Melanie Sisson, and Donald Temple, *Breaching the Fortress Wall: Understanding Terrorist Efforts to Overcome Defensive Technologies* (Santa Monica, CA: RAND, 2007), 124; Horacio R. Trujillo, "The Radical Environmentalist Movement," in *Aptitude for Destruction*, vol. 2, *Case Studies of Learning in Five Terrorist Organizations,* by Brian A. Jackson, John C. Baker, Kim Cragin, John Parachini, Horacio R. Trujillo, and Peter Chalk (Santa Monica, CA: RAND Corporation, 2005), 141–75; and Brian A. Jackson, "The Provisional Irish Republican Army," in *Aptitude for Destruction*, vol. 2, *Case Studies of Learning in Five Terrorist Organizations,* by Brian A. Jackson, John C. Baker, Kim Cragin, John Parachini, Horacio R. Trujillo, and Peter Chalk (Santa Monica, CA: RAND Corporation, 2005), 93–140.

16. For example, see Sean O'Callaghan, *The Informer* (London: Corgi Books, 1999), 305.

17. See Paul Cruickshank and Mohannad Hage Ali, "Abu Musab Al Suri: Architect of the New Al Qaeda," *Studies in Conflict and Terrorism*, January 2007, 1–14.

18. For more on this, please see Murad Al-shishani, "Abu Mus'ab al-Suri and the Third Generation of Salafi-Jihadists," *Terrorism Monitor* 3, no. 16 (11 August 2005), available at jamestown.org/terrorism/news/article.php?articleid=2369766.

19. Many of al-Suri's books and lectures have been translated by the Combating Terrorism Center at West Point, and are available to researchers at www.ctc.usma.edu.

20. Steve Coll and Susan B. Glasser, "Terrorists Turn to the Web as Base of Operations," *Washington Post,* 7 August 2005, A01, available at www.washingtonpost.com/wp-dyn/content/article/2005/08/05/AR2005080501138.html.

21. Jarret Brachman and James J. F. Forest, "Terrorist Sanctuaries in the Age of Information: Exploring the Role of Virtual Training Camps," in *Denial of Sanctuary: Understanding Terrorist Safe Havens,* ed. Michael Innes (London: Praeger Security International, 2007).

22. See Erich Marquadt, "Jihadi Website Advises Mujahideen on Equipment to Bring to Iraq," *Terrorism Focus* 4, no. 12 (1 May 2007).

23. Ibid.

24. Ibid.

25. Chris Heffelfinger, "Online Jihadi Forums Provide Curriculum for Aspiring Mujahideen," *Terrorism Focus* 3, no. 41 (24 October 2006), available at jamestown.org/terrorism/news/uploads/tf_003_041.pdf.

26. Bruce Hoffman, *Inside Terrorism* (New York: Columbia University Press, 1998), 203.

27. For more on this, please see Madeleine Gruen, "Innovative Recruitment and Indoctrination Tactics by Extremists: Video Games, Hip Hop, and the World Wide Web," in *The Making of a Terrorist: Recruitment, Training and Root Causes,* vol. 1, *Recruitment,* ed. James J. F. Forest (Westport, CT: Praeger, 2005).

28. Coll and Glasser, "Terrorists Turn to the Web as Base of Operations."

29. Ibid.

30. For example, see Lisa Myers, "Al Qaeda Web Message Offers Missile Tutorial," MSNBC.com, 30 March 2005, www.msnbc.msn.com/id/7339768/.

31. BBC News, "Tamil Tigers Claim Tanker Attack," 31 October 2001, news.bbc.co.uk/1/hi/world/south_asia/1628218.stm.

32. BBC News, "Yemen Says Tanker Blast Was Terrorism," 16 October 2002, news.bbc.co.uk/1/hi/world/middle_east/2334865.stm; and BBC News, "Craft 'Rammed' Yemen Oil Tanker," 6 October 2002, news.bbc.co.uk/2/hi/middle_east/2303363.stm.

33. See Cindy C. Combs, "The Media as a Showcase for Terrorism," in *Teaching Terror: Strategic and Tactical Knowledge in the Terrorist World,* ed. James Forest (Lanham, MD: Rowman & Littlefield, 2006); and Brigitte Nacos, "The Role of the Media," in *The Making of a Terrorist: Recruitment, Training and Root Causes,* vol. 1, *Recruitment,* ed. James J. F. Forest (Westport, CT: Praeger, 2005).

34. Combs, "The Media as a Showcase for Terrorism."

35. Department of State, *Country Reports on Terrorism 2006* (Washington, DC, April 2007), chap. 3, available at www.state.gov/s/ct/rls/crt.

36. Ibid.

37. Charles A. Russell, Leon J. Banker, Jr., and Bowman H. Miller, "Out-Inventing the Terrorist," in *Terrorism: Theory and Practice,* ed. Yonah Alexander, David Carlton, and Paul Wilkinson (Boulder, CO: Westview, 1979), 8–9; Edward Heyman and Edward Mickolus, "Observations on Why Violence Spreads," *International Studies Quarterly* 24, no. 2 (June 1980): 299–305; Edward Heyman and Edward Mickolus, "Imitation by Terrorists: Quantitative Approaches to the Study of Diffusion Patterns in Transnational Terrorism," in *Behavioral and Quantitative Perspectives on Terrorism,* ed. Yonah Alexander and John M. Gleason (New York: Pergamon Press, 1981), 175–228.

38. U.S. Department of State, *Patterns of Global Terrorism, 1993* (Washington, DC, 1994), available at www.hri.org/docs/USSD-Terror/93/statespon.html.

39. See "IDF Action in Syria," Israel News Agency, 5 October 2003, www.israelnewsagency.com.

40. For more on this, please see Michael Kenney, *From Pablo to Osama* (Pennsylvania State University Press, 2006).

41. Council on Foreign Relations, "Libya," Terrorism: Q&A, cfrterrorism.org/sponsors/libya.html; and "Libyan Training Camps," GlobalSecurity.org, www.globalsecurity.org/intell/world/libya/facility.htm.

42. See Rohan Gunaratna, *Inside Al Qaeda: Global Network of Terror* (New York: Berkley Publishing Group, 2002); Peter Bergen, *Holy War: Inside the Secret World of Osama Bin Laden* (New York: The Free Press, 2004); Michael Scheuer, *Through Our Enemies' Eyes: Osama bin Laden, Radical Islam, & the Future of America* (Washington, DC: Brassey's, 2003); and Martha Brill Olcott and Bakhtiyar Babajanov, "Teaching New Terrorist Recruits: A Review of Training Manuals from the Uzbekistan Mujahideen," in *The Making of a Terrorist: Recruitment, Training and Root Causes,* vol. 2, *Training,* ed. James J. F. Forest (Westport, CT: Praeger Security International, 2005), 136–51.

43. See, for example, C. J. Chivers and David Rohde, "Turning Out Guerrillas and Terrorists to Wage a Holy War," *New York Times,* 18 March 2002.

44. BBC News, "Al-Qaeda Camps Trained 70,000," 4 January 2005, news.bbc.co.uk/2/hi/europe/4146969.stm. For more on terrorist training in this region, see "FBI: Al Qaeda Plot Possibly Uncovered," *CNN.com,* 9 June 2005, www.cnn.com/2005/US/06/09/terror.probe; and "Terrorist Training Camp Destroyed, Five Terrorist[s] Killed," Press Trust of India, 27 May 2005 available at www.hindustantimes.com/news/181_1378250 ,000900010002.htm.

45. Brian Ross and Jill Rackmill, "New Questions about Al Qaeda Training Camps in Pakistan," ABC News, 8 June 2005, abcnews.go.com/WNT/Investigation/story?id=831750&page=1&CMP=OTC-RSSFeeds0312.

46. For more on al Qaida's terrorist training camps in Afghanistan, see Rohan Gunaratna, "The Al Qaeda Training Camps of Afghanistan and Beyond," in *The Making of a Terrorist: Recruitment, Training and Root Causes*, vol. 2, *Training,* ed. James J. F. Forest (Westport, CT: Praeger Security International, 2005).

47. Maria Ressa, *The Seeds of Terror: An Eyewitness Account of Al Qaeda's Newest Center of Operations in Southeast Asia* (New York: Free Press, 2003), 110.

48. Ibid., 133–35.

49. Zachary Abuza, *Militant Islam in Southeast Asia: Crucible of Terror* (Boulder, CO: Lynne Reinner, 2003), 97.

50. Abuza, "The Role of Foreign Trainers in Southern Thailand's Insurgency."

51. Department of State, *Country Reports on Terrorism 2006.*

52. Douglas Jehl, "Iraq May Be Prime Place for Training of Militants, CIA Report Concludes," *Washington Post,* 21 June 2005.

53. Daniel Benjamin and Gabriel Weimann, "What the Terrorists Have in Mind," *New York Times,* 27 October 2004.

54. David Brooks, "The Terrorist Advantage," *New York Times,* 18 May 2007; also, for more on the topic of knowledge sharing among armed groups, see John Robb, *Brave New War: The Next Stage of Terrorism and the End of Globalization* (Hoboken, NJ: John Wiley & Sons, 2007).

55. Marcia Christoff Kurop, "Al Qaeda's Balkan Links," *Wall Street Journal Europe*, 1 November 2001.

56. Sami Yousafzai and Ron Moreau, "Unholy Allies: The Taliban Haven't Quit, and Some Are Getting Help and Inspiration from Iraq," *Newsweek,* 26 September 2005.

57. Ibid.

58. Ibid.

59. I first introduced these thoughts on the "trusted handshake" in a paper delivered at the International Summit on Threat Convergence, held in Zurich, Switzerland, in March 2007. Some parts of this section are drawn from that paper.

60. See J. Bowyer Bell, *The IRA, 1968–2000: Analysis of a Secret Army* (London: Frank Cass, 2000); see also David E. Smith, "The Training of Terrorist Organizations," GlobalSecurity.org., www.globalsecurity.org/military/library/report/1995/SDE.htm (accessed 24 July 2003).

61. Thom Shanker, "U.S. Fears Abu Ghraib Is 'Jihad University,'" *International Herald Tribune,* 15 February 2006.

62. Brian Jenkins, "The New Age of Terrorism," in *The McGraw-Hill Homeland Security Handbook* (New York: McGraw-Hill, 2006), 123.

63. Ibid.

64. For a more complete discussion of these issues, please see James Forest, "Terrorist Training Centers around the World: A Brief Review," in *The Making of a Terrorist,* vol. 2, *Training,* ed. James J. F. Forest (Westport, CT: Praeger Security International, 2005).

22 The "Memory of War": Tribes and the Legitimate Use of Force in Iraq

Montgomery McFate

> *"Between tribes there can only be war, and through war, the memory of war, and the potentiality of war the relations between tribes are defined and expressed."*
>
> —E. E. Evans-Pritchard[1]

INTRODUCTION

In the Western philosophical and jurisprudential tradition, the use of force is considered legitimate when sanctioned by law. Law is generally considered to be the prerogative of the state, or the system of states known as the international community.[2]

But what if states are not the only source of law or the only source of legitimate violence? As legal anthropologist Leopold Pospisil has noted, "Any human society does not possess a single consistent legal system, but as many such systems as there are functioning subgroups."[3] Customary law within subgroups has the same basic characteristics of state law: authority of decision, *obligatio*, universal application, and sanction.[4] Like state law, customary law expresses social norms and constrains behavior.

In Iraq, tribes can be considered as subgroups of the larger society, possessing their own forms of coercion, law, and authority. Iraqi tribal customary norms for warfighting and conceptions regarding legitimate use of force derive neither from Iraqi civil law nor from sharia. Rather, they derive from the cultures of Iraq's tribes.[5] By understanding customary law and practice for the deployment of coercive force among tribes in Iraq, coalition forces can avoid unnecessary civilian and military casualties, more effectively defeat the insurgency and promote reconciliation and engagement within Iraqi civil society.

Montgomery McFate is a cultural anthropologist who works on defense and national security issues. Dr. McFate is currently the senior social science adviser for the U.S. Army's Human Terrain System. Previously, she worked at the U.S. Navy's Office of Naval Research (ONR), where she was awarded a Distinguished Public Service Award by the secretary of the Navy. Before coming to ONR, Dr. McFate was a social scientist in RAND's Intelligence Policy Center. Dr. McFate received a BA from University of California at Berkeley, a PhD in cultural anthropology from Yale University, and a JD from Harvard Law School. She has published in the *Journal of Conflict Studies, Military Review,* and *Joint Forces Quarterly,* and has held grants from the National Science Foundation, Mellon Foundation, and Smith-Richardson Foundation, among others.

WHAT ARE TRIBES?

Anthropologists have been arguing bitterly among themselves for many years whether or not tribes exist, and if so, what their relationship is to the state.[6] In 1897, Herbert Spencer posited a theory of social evolution, in which societies evolve from simplicity to complexity, from bands into larger polities.[7] Spencer's theory survives as the commonly held assumption among non-anthropologists that tribes evolve into states.[8] Having rejected the tribe as an evolutionary stage, however, many academic anthropologists treat tribes as a product of contact with more complex societies. The "contact" theory holds that political development of tribal societies in Africa, highland New Guinea, and Amazonia was driven by the need for states to create clear political boundaries in place of the multilayered anarchy of the "tribal zone."[9] Among some academic anthropologists, European expansion is sometimes viewed as the sole driver of tribalization, leaving many anthropology students with the preposterous idea "that Europe created the tribes."[10]

Another anthropological school of thought views state and tribe as "two opposed modes of thought or models of organization that form a single system."[11] In the words of Richard Tapper,

> As a basis for identity, political allegiance, and behavior, tribe gives primacy to ties of kinship and patrilineal descent, whereas state insists on the loyalty of all persons to a central authority, whatever their relation to each other. Tribe stresses personal, moral, and ascriptive factors in status; state is impersonal and recognizes contract, transaction, and achievement. The tribal mode is socially homogenous, egalitarian, and segmentary; the state is heterogeneous, stratified, and hierarchical. Tribe is within the individual; state is external.[12]

In Tapper's view, tribes and states exist in a perpetual "dialectical symbiosis: they mingle and sustain each other; each part changes owing to the other's influence; and sometimes they seek to destroy each other."[13] States have played a role in creating, transforming, and destroying tribal institutions and structures: governments have attempted to eradicate tribes or have created tribes for political and administrative reasons. Tribes have also played a role in state formation: tribes have usurped power within states; have developed into ministates; have acted as guardians of the state's frontiers against external marauders, or as buffers against powerful neighbors; and have founded and destroyed dynasties. In all of these cases, tribes exist in structural opposition to states, perpetually remaining outside of the state's control and threatening its order.[14]

But what exactly is a tribe? Tribes show so much variation that it is sometimes diffi cult to recognize what they have in common. The kinship rules, organizational structures, and types of political authority of tribes are highly variable.[15] For example, the egalitarian, acephalous tribes of the Arabian Peninsula are vastly different in their political authority systems from the hierarchical chiefdoms of the central Asian steppes.[16] Tribes, which exist in relationship to the social and natural environments, are not self-contained, and their organizational structures and social patterns are influenced by external factors such as local ecological factors and mode of production (pastoral, semipastoral, sedentary).[17] Similarly, the ethno-religious composition of tribes is highly variable: while some tribes may have members of diverse religious or ethnic backgrounds (the Qashqa'i tribe of Iran, for example, has members of Turkish, Persian, Arab, and Luri origins), other tribes are composed of a single ethno-religious group.[18]

Given this variability in the form and structure, it is nevertheless possible to make some broad observations about tribes. Anthropologists generally define a tribe as "an autonomous, genealogically structured group in which the rights of individuals are largely determined by their membership in corporate descent groups, such as lineages."[19] Tribal groups are basically large networks, with a tendency to both aggregate and splinter extensively. This tendency is rooted in a kinship system where patriarchal lineage is grouped agnatically.[20] According to "pure" kinship theory, each kin group traces its descent back to a single patriarch, and a division of the lineage occurs among each set of brothers. Fathers transmit property and feuding to sons (agnates), causing such groups to be segmented.[21] Because a segmentary kinship system creates no hierarchy among brothers, the inheritance of property and sheikhdoms can result in competition among brothers and their families. The conflict among agnatic kin is expressed in the Afghan adage, "Do you have an enemy? I have a cousin."[22] While segmentation promotes competition among different factions, it may also create a balance of power within a society.[23] (And, of course, something entirely different may happen in reality as a result of local political, social, and economic factors.)

Every tribal system has many different levels of organization. In Iraq, the tribal system may have up to 14 levels of organization. In Iraq, generally, the smallest tribal unit is the *kham* (extended family), which may be aggregated into a *bayt* (house). Several houses make up a *fukhth* (clan), and a number of clans makes the *'asheera* (tribe), and a group of tribes constitutes a tribal confederation (*qabeela*).[24] The number of groups at each level of aggregation can vary greatly from country to country: in Yemen, for example, there are two major tribal confederations, each composed of dozens of tribes,[25] while in Iraq there are approximately 23 tribal confederations[26] and an unknown number of tribes.

Tribal genealogy is not based on actual lines of descent but on fictive kinship ties. As Claude Lévi-Strauss has noted, "A kinship system does not exist in the objective ties of descent or consanguinity between individuals: It exists only in human consciousness. . . ."[27] Fictive kinship is a type of social relationship between people who are not related by blood, involving emotional ties and social obligations similar to those between blood relatives.[28] Biological descent is often less important in a tribal society than genealogical descent, which can be invented or attributed as necessity demands. Thus, if a tribal unit (such as a clan) switches political allegiance, kinship ties will be manipulated to justify the basis for the new tribal association.[29] For example, according to a 1953 study of Iraqi Marsh Arabs "many lineages and even clans" belonging to the village's Beni Isad tribe "are known to be foreigners" and there "has been considerable adoption of lineages and segments of lineages."[30]

Tribes, however, are not just descent groups, but political actors. Evans-Pritchard, in 1940, described tribes as *political groups* with a genealogical structure that occupy discrete territories.[31] More recently, Dale Eickelman has characterized tribes as groups that have a shared concept of *political identity* derived from claimed patrilineal descent.[32]

Tribes seek power and resources, and within tribes, sheikhs seek power and resources. Generally, a sheikh is a senior male member of a tribal lineage group, with the capacity to exert informal authority over members of that group. A sheikh's authority is not necessarily based on birth but on his ability to satisfy the political, economic, and security interests of his tribal members. Sheikhs provide patronage, in the form of political favors, jobs, or money, to tribal members in exchange for loyalty. Tribal members expect to be rewarded by their sheikh with increased status and material gains, typically acquired through the sheikh's access to the central government. If he fails to provide material benefits, tribal members may support a rival within the tribe, or switch allegiance to another tribe.[33] Thus, a sheikh's authority is constantly reevaluated by tribal members and may be contested by others seeking to usurp his place. As one Iraqi sheikh noted, "A sheik has no power without contracts. If I do not provide for my people, they will not cooperate with me."[34]

Sheikhs do not wield absolute power but lead by consensus. Sheikhs can influence, but not control, their tribes.[35] According to Dawn Chatty, the sheikh "generally has no power to enforce a decision and has therefore to rely on his moral authority as well as the concurrence of the community with his point of view. Although ultimate authority rests with the sheikh, it is based almost totally on his meticulous evaluation of tribal sentiment."[36]

The sheikh acts as a judge, maintains law and order in the tribe, represents the tribe before government authorities, and mediates disputes within and between clans. In Iraq, the sheikh's ability to enforce law in the tribe seems to depend on the authority of the particular sheikh and varies greatly between urban and rural areas. Former British Coalition Provisional Authority (CPA) official Rory Stewart noted, "Almost every crime in the villages [in southern Iraq] was tried and settled by the sheikhs."[37] By contrast, the American former deputy director of the CPA Office of Provincial Outreach, Lieutenant Colonel Alan King, stated, "The Iraqi people spoke often of tribal law, but I only witnessed its application in the most remote and rural areas of the country."[38]

TRIBE AND STATE IN IRAQ

In the Middle East, the relationship between tribes and states has been characterized by mutual antagonism, pragmatic cooperation, and occasional warfare.[39]

During the early Islamic era, tribal kinship threatened the state's consolidation of political power.[40] Traditionally, nomads had been the center of power in the Arabian Peninsula: the outcome of the conflict between Mecca and Medina, for example, depended on the mobilization of nomadic allies.[41] To break the power of the tribes, family allegiances were to be supplanted by the religious unity of the *umma* (community of believers). The Covenant of Medina stipulated that the Muslims "constitute one *Umma*" and that "all believers shall rise as one man against whomsoever rebels or seeks to commit injustice, aggression, wrong action or spread mutual enmity between the believers, even though he be one of their sons."[42] Expressing the view that *asabiyyah* (tribal solidarity; the *'asaba* are male patrilineal relations) was contrary to the spirit of Islam, the Prophet said, "Whosoever possesses in his heart *'asabiyyah* even to the extent of a mustard seed, God will raise him on the Day of Resurrection with the [pagan] Beduins of the *Jahiliyyah* [the pre-Islamic era]."[43]

Although control over the tribes was maintained while Muhammad was alive, many tribal sheikhs refused to swear allegiance to his successor, Abu Bakr. During the Wars of Apostasy (*Ridda* Wars), tribes rose up across the desert, and 11 brigades of the Islamic army were dispersed to quell them. Following the reconquest of most of Arabia, the ruling elite co-opted the nomads by recruiting them into the Islamic armies and settling them in garrison towns away from their tribal territories. By rewarding the tribesmen with land in conquered territories, the Islamic state locked itself into a policy of expansion: to appease the tribes, the state was forced to acquire new lands, eventually leading to the conquest of Syria and central Iraq.[44]

Following the collapse of the Abbasid empire in the thirteenth century, Iraq's tribes had limited allegiance to the central government.[45] In 1702 the Ottomans initiated a policy of indirect rule, delegating authority to the *mamluks,* who were highly educated slaves who had been trained to rule.[46] Although the *mamluks* paid tribute to the Ottoman sultan, they retained considerable de facto autonomy,[47] and were responsible for raising the local armies with which they maintained the Ottoman borders.[48] *Mamluk* power, however, did not extend into the countryside, which was inhabited by self-sufficient tribes who frequently attacked settled areas. The *mamluk* governor of Baghdad, Hassan Pasha Al Jadid (1704–1723), for example, was engaged in continuous subjugation of rebellious tribes for the tenure of his rule.[49]

In 1808, the Ottomans began to reassert their control over the *mamluk* governors and consolidate power in the hands of the sultan in Istanbul as part of the *nizam i-cedid* (the new order),[50] Nomadic tribes were encouraged to adopt agriculture in order to increase tax revenue.[51] Sheikhs were granted title deeds to land, increasing their loyalty and transforming tribesmen into tenant farmers.[52] The Ottoman governors also began to divide and conquer, rewarding obedient sheikhs with land and punishing uncooperative sheikhs by confiscating their land and distributing it to rival tribes. Conflict over land rights created competition among sheikhs, weakened ties between sheikhs and tribesmen, and made the sheikhs dependent on the Ottoman state to enforce their rights and maintain order.[53]

Although the power of the tribes was subsequently weakened during the nineteenth century through the *tanzimat* reforms of 1832 (an administrative and legal reorganization of the Ottoman Empire),[54] the emergence of private property, development of capitalist markets, and urbanization of the country, tribal membership remained an important component of political mobilization and identity.

After World War I and the collapse of the Ottoman Empire, Iraq was established under a mandate entrusted to Britain. The British quickly discovered that ruling the new state of Iraq would not be an easy task: urban Iraqi nationalists rejected the mandate as unadulterated colonialism and Sunni and Shia tribal confederations soon joined the insurrection. For a time, the Great Iraqi Revolution of 1920 united Iraqis in a common effort against a mutual enemy.[55] The British restored order only with the assistance of Royal Air Force bombers and the use of chemical weapons.[56]

Like the Ottomans before them, the British discovered that the divide-and-conquer strategy was the most expedient means of governing a society dominated by tribes. At the Cairo Conference of 1921, Faisal was installed as Iraq's first king. The sheikhs opposed a strong central government and they possessed enough firepower to pose a credible threat: King Faisal wrote that "The tribes have more power than the government, they own more than 100,000 rifles, while we own only 15,000."[57] The British goal was to "keep the monarchy stronger than any one tribe but weaker than a coalition of tribes," thereby giving British administrators decisive authority in arbitrating disputes between the monarchy and the tribes.[58]

Following the Baathist consolidation of power in 1968, tribes were viewed as a major obstacle to political reform and economic modernization. Agrarian reforms were introduced, estates owned by tribal sheikhs were confiscated, and peasant associations were formed to undermine the sheikhs' position as intermediaries between the government and their tribesmen.[59] At the same time, however, Hussein consolidated his power within the Baath Party by placing his tribal relations in key state institutions, such as the Defense Ministry and the National Security Bureau.[60] The patronage system was used to guarantee the elite's loyalty to the regime.[61]

The Baath attempt to restructure Iraqi society along secular national lines was short lived. Weakened by the Iran-Iraq conflict and the Gulf War, buried by a $50 billion debt, and deprived of oil revenues by the sanctions, the central government began to lose control over provincial areas. In 1991, Hussein began integrating the tribes into the state in order to consolidate the ruling elite's power.[62]

The Baathist retribalization of Iraqi society was in many ways a perversion of the original system. As Faleh Jabar has pointed out, although Saddam reconstructed many real tribes, he also invented new ones. Unlike traditional tribes that were ethnically heterogeneous and organized around agnatic descent, the new tribes were divided along religious and ethnic lines.[63] Both new and old tribes were organized to operate as extensions of the state organs. Lesser tribes were made responsible for local tasks, such as maintaining law and order and collecting taxes.[64] Major Sunni tribes, supplied with arms by the government, became responsible for certain aspects of national security. The policy of arming certain tribes upset the traditional balance of power within the tribal system, leading to increased frequency and lethality of intertribal warfare.[65]

The overthrow of Saddam Hussein's regime in April 2003 created a power vacuum that was quickly filled by resurgent tribes, accustomed to political and legal autonomy. As a young tribal leader observed, "We follow the central government. . . . But of course if communications are cut between us and the center, all authority will revert to our sheik."[66] Because coalition forces are unable to provide security to Iraqi civilians in most areas of Iraq, tribes have filled the void.[67] Similarly, tribes are also guaranteeing the economic well-being of their members. According to Faleh Jabar, "The only way to get a job for many Iraqis today is by returning to the tribe. . . ."[68] Residents of Baghdad have increasingly begun identifying with their tribal groups, sometimes choosing the places they shop and eat by the owners' tribal affiliations.[69]

The fall of Saddam Hussein and the Baath regime further tribalized Iraq. Yet the CPA showed an unwillingness to engage with the tribes. According to a former intelligence officer whose plan to leverage traditional authority systems in Iraq was rejected by the CPA, "The standard answer we got from Bremer's people was that tribes are a vestige of the past, that they have no place in the new democratic Iraq."[70]

In Iraq, various central governments have created, weakened, or destroyed tribes according to their political goals, yet tribal identity and membership remain an important element of social organization to this day. The role and power of the tribes, however, should not be overemphasized;[71] tribes should be seen as an element within the larger social structure. Indeed, as noted above, Saddam Hussein irrevocably altered the tribal landscape, modernization detribalized much of the country, and tribal identity now competes with other forms of identity (such as ethno-religious and political). As Rory Stewart, former CPA deputy governor of Maysan province, has observed, "Most urban Iraqis perceived the sheikhs as illiterate, embarrassing, criminal, powerless anachronisms who should be given no official recognition. . . . They were [however] still the most powerful men in the rural areas, where about half the population remained; they owned much of the land, and agriculture was the only half-functioning element of the shattered economy. Almost every crime in the villages was tried and settled by the sheikhs. . . ."[72] Although the Sunni Arab insurgents in Iraq represent different political and religious ideologies—nationalists, Islamo-nationalists, and jihadists—all are influenced to some degree by the tribal ethos, which remains a core component of contemporary Arab political and military culture.

BLOOD FEUD

Governing a tribal territory presents a unique challenge to any state. In a letter to his parents during the Arab revolt, T. E. Lawrence wrote, "in their smallness of number (which is imposed by their poverty of country) lies a good deal of their strength, for they are perhaps the most elusive enemy an army ever had, and inhabit one of the most trying countries in the world for civilized warfare."[73] In his diary, Lawrence concluded, "their real sphere is guerilla warfare."[74]

Yet tribal use of force follows predictable patterns that, if understood, offer opportunities to states engaged in conflict with tribes. One such norm is the blood feud.

Although the segmentary nature of tribes tends to produce internal schisms, tribes tend to unify against a common enemy in response to external threats. A bedouin proverb expresses this principle: "Me and my brother against my cousin, and me and my cousin against the stranger." The lowest level of tribal organization at which individuals are bound by blood and marriage is usually the highest level at which sustained collective action occurs.[75] Because the internal balance of power within a segmentary system is inherently unstable, power can quickly crystallize around a strong sheikh, especially in response to external factors such as conflict with states and other tribes.[76] Thus, clans of the same tribe may spend years fighting one another, and then suddenly unite against an outside aggression, only to return again to internecine warfare.

This pattern has been borne out in recent events in Iraq, where tribal militias have been rapidly mobilized to confront a common enemy. As William McCallister points out, in response to the U.S. presence in Falluja a *mujahideen shura* (council of holy warriors) representing resistance forces, local dignitaries, and tribal sheikhs was formed to guide the insurrection. "The segmentary nature of tribes facilitated the activation of widely dispersed military networks and unified clans and tribes in a shared religious belief that the Americans are invaders and that every Muslim's duty was to fight the unbelievers."[77]

The most common form of tribal collective action is the blood feud. When an outsider kills a tribal member, tribesmen are obligated to seek revenge in proportion to their closeness to the victim.[78] Such a structure of reciprocal violence may result in a cyclical escalation of violence,[79] especially when the reprisal is seen as disproportionate to the original crime. On the other hand, because a kin group will avenge the death of any member, each group has the incentive to restrain its members.[80] Such a system acts as a strong deterrent to violence, particularly if a sheikh appears to be prepared to avenge harm to the tribe. Thus, the appearance of posing a credible threat is just as important as vengeance itself.

Blood feuds can take place within, between, and external to tribes. When government forces kill a tribal member, those soldiers may become the target of a blood feud. An Ottoman deputy observed in 1910, "the tribe, no matter how feeble it may be, as soon as it learns that an injustice has been committed against one of its members readies itself to exact vengeance on his behalf."[81] Coalition forces refer to this as "bloodline" attacks. According to an Army captain in Samarra, "It's the Arabic rule of five. If you do something to someone, then five of his bloodlines will try to attack you."[82]

Bloodline attacks do not just threaten the coalition but any group that harms a tribal member, including Al Qaeda. In September 2005, a local sheikh from Samarra named Hekmat Mumtaz al-Baz asked Iraq's defense minister for assistance in ridding his lands of Al Qaeda operatives. A few weeks later, Al Qaeda gunmen murdered Sheikh Al-Baz in his yard. Subsequently, the sheikh's kinsmen captured the three Al Qaeda members and tried them in a local farmhouse. During the sheikh's funeral, a foreign Arab blew himself up with a suicide belt, killing one guest and wounding two. As a warning to others involved with the sheikh's death, the tribe used machine guns to execute the three men who carried out the assassination.[83] More recently, as Dave Kilcullen has observed, tribes across Iraq turned against Al Qaeda in objection to the practice of cementing political alliances through marriage of key operatives to local women from prominent tribal families.[84]

RAIDING

Raiding, one of the most common types of violence among tribal people, is characterized by surprise, shock, and rapid withdrawal after a comparatively brief period of action. Raiding is primarily a symbolic form of warfare, the purpose of which is to acquire booty and honor and impose shame on the enemy.[85] Neither annihilation nor capitulation is the goal of a raid,[86] and, in most societies, raiding is governed by rules limiting stock theft and prohibiting wanton killing.[87] Although the raid lacks a political or territorial object, it can often have a political or territorial outcome.[88]

State military forces can use the warfighting methods of their adversaries, such as raids, to counter tribal insurgency. Unfortunately, U.S. forces did not adopt this approach in Falluja. When the 1st Marine Expeditionary Force replaced the U.S. Army's 82nd Airborne Division in 2003, they initially conducted targeted reprisals with minimum use of force. After Marines killed four Falluja residents in a gunfight, four Blackwater contractors were mutilated and burned by a mob. From the perspective of many Iraqis accustomed to tribal raids and reprisals, the killing of the contractors was a form of vengeance that satisfied the cultural demands for honor. During the assault, for example, a *mujahid* shouted, "I avenged my brother who was killed by the Americans!"[89] U.S. officials, however, made no attempt to see the killings from the perspective of the adversary. Rather, they saw the assault as an evil, primitive form of violence, without cause or logic. Bremer, for example, called the killers in Falluja "human jackals" and the battle for the town part of a "struggle between human dignity and barbarism."[90]

After the murder of the Blackwater contractors, 2nd Battalion, 1st Marines was initially considering a series of raids in Falluja to capture or kill the men who had slain the contractors.[91] This probably would have been effective, since the Marines had established a certain level of trust and cooperation with the citizens of the town. General Conway, however, was instructed by General Ricardo Sanchez (apparently acting on instructions from the White House) to prepare for a direct assault on Falluja.[92] This decision unchained the dogs of war: Major General James N. Mattis, commander of the 1st Marine Division, commented to a reporter, "You know my rules for a gunfight? Bring a gun, bring two guns, bring all your friends with guns."[93]

The decision to launch an assault followed by a siege, rather than to conduct a limited raid, was perhaps an error. After retreating, the Marines left Falluja in the hands of a local force called the Falluja Brigade. Many of those who enlisted were actually insurgents. While the city was under the brigade's control, it became a magnet for insurgents, a base for suicide bombers, and a headquarters for Abu Musab Zarqawi. The assault on Falluja also unexpectedly boosted the reputation of Muqtada Sadr, who sent supplies to the town during the siege and then used the events to help spark an uprising in An Najaf. General Abizaid said regarding Falluja, "I know major military action could implode the political situation," and indeed, it did.[94]

COLLECTIVE SELF-DEFENSE

After the Hussein regime was overthrown, tribal sheikhs lined up at the presidential palace for an audience with Ambassador Bremer, the new sheikh of sheikhs. The sheikhs were prepared to swear allegiance to the ambassador in return for light arms and ammunition, communications equipment, vehicles, and logistics support in order to ensure security and stability in their tribal areas.[95] Although accepting the sheikhs' allegiance may have alleviated much of the chaos in rural areas, by his own admission, Bremer knew little about how things worked in Iraq: "I was a businessman until more or less 10 days before I got here."[96] Ambassador Bremer and his staff apparently did not understand the principle of tribal self-defense, and thereby missed an early opportunity to improve the security situation for Iraqi civilians.

Historically, tribes guaranteed the security of members in the absence of a strong central government. Scorning those who rely on the government to guarantee their rights, an old Iraqi proverb advises "take your rights by the sword—only the weak need witnesses." Alliances were formed among tribal pastoralists on the basis that "anyone who commits an act of aggression against any one of us must expect retaliation from us all, and not only will the aggressor himself be likely to suffer retaliation, but his entire group and all its members will be equally liable."[97] Reliant on themselves for protection from outside threats, tribes acquired knowledge of warfare and weapons.[98] As Faleh Jabar describes Iraq's history,

> Each strong tribe was a miniature mobile state, with its patriarchal headship usually head[ed] by a warrior household; its own military force; its customary law, which was preserved by the 'arfa (literally, 'the knowledgeable', actually tribal jurists or adjudicators); its non-literate culture; its territoriality in the form of dira (tribal pastures) or, later, arable lands; and its mode of subsistence economy, i.e. pastoralism, commerce, and conquest.[99]

In Iraq, cooperative self-defense among tribal groups still persists and can be effectively employed by the government when its interests coincide with those of the tribe. Under Saddam Hussein and his predecessor, President Ahmad Hasan al-Bakr (1968–1979), Sunni, Shiite, and even some Kurdish sheikhs were given weapons, lands, and money for monitoring the borders with Iran and preventing their own tribesmen from joining anti-Baath insurgents. More recently, the 82nd Airborne employed 2,200 Iraqi border police to patrol the western borders. Following the suggestion of one sheikh, the border security force was primarily composed of tribal bedouin, "who are able to navigate the desert at night and spend long stretches there."[100] The coalition might have been able to use this trial self-defense function to control the overall security situation in Iraq. According to Sheikh Mudher Al-Kharbit of the Dulaimi tribe, who have traditionally been responsible for security in the Al-Anbar province, "if I advised my people to settle down, the foreign fighters would have nowhere to go. I'm not responsible for the violence—but I can stop it if the Americans agree to our terms. . . ."[101]

RESTORATION OF HONOR

Collective honor, based on a system of patrilineal clans, is a common element in traditional communities throughout the Middle East.[102] In these societies, the family is the central unit of social organization, followed by the lineage or clan. Because honor always derives from the group, an individual's conduct also reflects back on the group and its honor.[103] If an individual acts shamefully, the whole tribe is shamed. In Middle Eastern tribal societies, for example, women must demonstrate hashama (modesty) because any threat to established bonds of sexuality is a threat to the loyalties of this hierarchical society.[104]

Honor and shame are like commodities in a cultural system that can be exchanged between people and groups. As Halvor Moxnes points out, "Traditional societies have clear rules for this kind of exchange. A proper challenge can take place only among people who are equal or almost equal in honor. A challenge always implies recognition of the honor of the other person; thus challenge and riposte are played like a game with a set of rules. Exchanges frequently lead to competition. The winner of such a competitive exchange has defended his honor, while the loser experiences shame and his standing in the community is damaged."[105]

In Iraq, there are many varieties of honor: avenging the blood of a relative (al-tha'r), demonstrating one's manly courage in battle (al-muruwwah), upholding one's manly honor (al-sharaf)[106]—hence the Arab saying "It is better to die with honor than live with humiliation."[107] Coalition activities in Iraq have stripped ordinary Iraqis of their honor. According to one elderly Iraqi, "In Saddam's time, when he repressed us, he put a gun to our head and fired a bullet. Now, [U.S. soldiers] put us on the ground and step on our head. . . . Would you accept that? It's more dignified to put a bullet in my head."[108]

When honor is lost, it must be regained. The most expedient means to restore lost honor is through violence, and this is exactly what the Sunni insurgents have been doing. For example, in Ramadi a U.S. soldier who frequently urinated from the top of his Bradley offended the citizens' honor so deeply that local insurgents twice tried to destroy the vehicle, first with a rocket-propelled grenade and then with a Russian C5K missile. After their attacks failed, they requested the services of an insurgent sniper for hire, who described the assassination as follows: "[T]the Bradley stopped and the soldier stood on it ready to relieve himself. He was relaxed. He put his hand on his trousers. I took aim and fired one shot and saw him drop dead."[109] As one insurgent in Falluja observed, "America has invaded us and insulted us and so it is legitimate for us to fight. It is our honour and our duty and we know that it will be a long fight."[110]

In addition to acts of violence, honor can be restored through peaceful means such as *sulh* (settlement) and *musalaha* (reconciliation).[111] As Amatzia Baram has noted, endless blood feuds are the exception rather than the rule in contemporary Middle Eastern societies. "The whole mechanism of arbitration, blood money, and honor money . . . was introduced in order to circumvent endless feuds (usually not between whole tribes but, rather, between kin-based groups of five generations, or khams)."[112] The exercise of persuasion, mediation, reconciliation, and negotiation is more important to contemporary dispute resolution than the use of force. According to Islamic legal scholars, "the purpose of *sulh* is to end conflict and hostility among believers so that they may conduct their relationships in peace and amity. . . . In Islamic law, *sulh* is a form of contract ('*aqd*), legally binding on both the individual and community levels."[113] Although *sulh* is restricted to believers, the payment of blood money by non-Muslims as compensation for injury or death can lessen resentment and avert violence. In Falluja, for example, coalition commanders were using discretionary funds to pay blood money to families that suffered losses, which seems to have been effective in reducing attacks on coalition forces.[114] Although compensation payments are now officially restricted to cases of clear-cut negligence or wrongdoing by soldiers,[115] informal payments are still being offered as an expression of sympathy and condolence.[116]

The algebra of honor in Iraq is very complex, and often does not work as external Western observers might expect. On 11 April 2003, for example, U.S. forces dropped six joint direct attack munitions (JDAM) guided bombs on a villa outside Ramadi in an attempt to kill one of Saddam Hussein's half brothers. Instead, the bombs killed Malik al-Kharbit and 21 members of his family, all of them members of the powerful Dulaimi tribe. One so-called expert on tribal culture warned shortly after the event, "If the family doesn't take revenge against the U.S., it will lose face. The tribe is going to pick up a very high-ranking American as revenge for Malik's death."[117] Despite the lack of restitution for the death the Dulaimi tribal members,[118] the tribe did not seek revenge.[119] Policy makers in Washington never asked why, but there is a reason. According to a senior member of the tribe, one of Saddam's personal bodyguards was hiding in the house: "He came for shelter and, according to Arab tradition, we could not refuse." In the view of the Dulaimi tribe, honor was preserved because they sacrificed themselves to save a guest: "History will remember that the Al-Kharbits [a Dulaimi subclan] sacrificed 22 family members for the sake of a guest. It's the tribal way."[120]

CONCLUSION

Neither modern sociopolitical ideologies nor the rise of the state has eliminated the kinship group or tribal ethos as a social organizing principle. Despite the weakening of the tribal system during the twentieth century through urbanization and the development of a market economy, individuals throughout the Arab world retain their tribal names, kinship networks, value systems, residency patterns, and solidarity commitments.[121] Phebe Marr notes in *The Modern History of Iraq* that the particular legacies of tribalism in Iraq are personal honor, factionalism, and an intense individualism that resists central authority.[122]

These cultural patterns influence how the Sunni insurgency is being conducted in Iraq today. Given these cultural patterns, what is the appropriate government response? A number of defense intellectuals have recently argued that the coalition's response has been too "soft." For example, Edward Luttwak recently faulted the U.S. military for its "principled and inevitable refusal to out-terrorize the insurgents," which he describes as "the necessary and sufficient condition of a tranquil occupation."[123] Similarly, Ralph Peters recently wrote in *Armchair General* that "killing has been the *only* effective tool against insurgencies—especially those rooted in religious or ethnic passion."[124]

On the contrary, as this paper has argued, traditional U.S. and British COIN doctrine that stresses limited use of force, minimization of collateral damage, and cultural understanding is very well suited to the social complexities of conflict in Iraq. Collateral damage in an environment where vendetta and blood feud are common social practices is likely to have negative consequences—in particular, the creation of an endlessly regenerating supply of motivated adversaries. Those who argue that the U.S. military ought to increase the level of lethal violence are advocating a counterproductive approach given the sociocultural environment of Iraq. Only by understanding how tribes are mobilized for war against the state, and by understanding the unwritten (but highly formalized) norms by which they fight, U.S. forces can adapt their own warfighting to that of their adversary. As Sun Tzu observed, "success in warfare is gained by carefully accommodating ourselves to the enemy's purpose."[125]

NOTES

Early drafts of this paper were written in 2004, before the author had been to Iraq. Thus, this paper does not cover the Sunni reconciliation movement known as the Anbar Awakening in any detail. Portions of this paper were presented earlier by Isaiah Wilson in "Tribes, the State, and (Postmodern) War: Bringing Containment Back In" at the annual meeting of the American Political Science Association, 31 August 2006. Unfortunately, I was not given credit for coauthorship.

1. E. E. Evans-Pritchard, *The Nuer: A Description of the Modes of Livelihood and Political Institutions of a Nilotic People* (Oxford: Oxford University Press, 1940), 161.

2. State deployment of physical force inside its territory is controlled by civil law, which may include constitutional law, statutory law enacted by legislative bodies, administrative law adopted by governmental agencies, and common law based on the decisions of judges. The use of force against other states is controlled by civil

law in addition to international law, which can include treaties between governments; international agreements; and customary international law as evidenced by national legislation, accepted practices, and the interpretations of various international tribunals, among other sources.

3. Leopold Pospisil, "Legal Levels and Multiplicity of Legal Systems in Human Society," *Journal of Conflict Resolution* 11 (1967): 3.

4. Ibid.

5. There is a considerable body of literature on the Islamic law of war. See, for example, Youssef H Aboul-Enein and Sherifa Zuhur, *Islamic Rulings on Warfare* (Carlisle, PA: Army College, 2005); Shaheen Sardar Ali and Javaid Rehman, "The Concept of *Jihad* in Islamic International Law," *Journal of Conflict and Security Law* 10 (2005): 321–43; James Turner Johnson and John Kelsay, eds., *Cross, Crescent, and Sword: The Justification and Limitation of War in Western and Islamic Tradition* (New York: Greenwood Press, 1990); Majid Khadduri, *War and Peace in the Law of Islam* (New York: AMS Press, 2005). There is less literature on tribal customary law in the Middle East. For an overview, see Frank H. Stewart, "Tribal Law in the Arab World: A Review of the Literature," *International Journal of Middle East Studies* 19 (1987): 473–90. There is even less on tribal customary laws of war. See, for example, Louise E. Sweet, "Camel Raiding of North Arabian Bedouin: A Mechanism of Ecological Adaptation," *American Anthropologist*, n.s., 67 (1965): 1132–50; Henry Rosenfeld, "The Social Composition of the Military in the Process of State Formation in the Arabian Desert," *Journal of the Royal Anthropological Institute of Great Britain and Ireland* 95 (1965): 174–94; Ashraf Ghani, "Islam and State-Building in a Tribal Society: Afghanistan: 1880–1901," *Modern Asian Studies* 12 (1978): 269–84. Customary tribal law (*qada urfi*) differs considerably by region and is usually applied alongside sharia and civil law. During the process of tribal sedentarization in the Middle East, much of bedouin law and custom has been Islamicized, albeit incompletely. See Aharon Layish, "The *Fatwa* as an Instrument of the Islamization of a Tribal Society in Process of Sedentarization," *Bulletin of the School of Oriental and African Studies,* 54 (1991): 449–59.

6. See, for example, June Helm, ed., *Essays on the Problem of the Tribe: Proceedings of the 1967 Annual Spring Meeting of the American Ethnological Society* (Seattle: University of Washington Press, 1968); M. Godelier, "The Concept of 'Tribe': A Crisis Involving Merely a Concept or the Empirical Foundations of Anthropology Itself?" in *Perspectives in Marxist Anthropology,* ed. Maurice Godelier (Cambridge: Cambridge University Press, 1977); Emanuel Marx, "Back to the Problem of Tribe," *American Anthropologist* 81 (1979): 124–25; Philip Carl Salzman, "Tribal Organization and Subsistence: A Response to Emanuel Marx," *American Anthropologist* 81 (1979): 121–24.

7. Herbert Spencer, *Principles of Sociology* (New York: D. Appleton, 1897).

8. For example, there are many Web sites espousing the view that tribes evolve into states: Bill Melton, "Hope, Despair, Neanderthals, and Nation States," The Melton Foundation, www.meltonfoundation.org/mainsite/b_2001.htm; "Social Evolution," www.transcend7.com/TR/Social.htm. For a more sophisticated approach to the general theory of social evolution, see David F. Ronfeldt, *Tribes, Institutions, Markets, Networks: A Framework about Societal Evolution,* P-7967 (Washington: RAND Corporation, 1996). Some anthropologists also continue to express the view that tribes evolve into states. See Spencer Heath MacCallum, "The Quickening of Social Evolution Negotiating the Last Rapids, Perhaps," *The Independent Review: A Journal of Political Economy* 2 (1997).

9. See Leroy Vail, ed., *The Creation of Tribalism in South Africa* (Berkeley: University of California Press, 1989); Andrew Strathern, "Let the Bow Go Down," in *War in the Tribal Zone: Expanding States and Indigenous Warfare,* ed. R. Brian Ferguson and Neil L. Whitehead (Santa Fe: School of American Research Press, 1999); N. E. Whitten, ed., *Cultural Transformations and Ethnicity in Modern Ecuador* (Urbana: University of Illinois Press, 1981).

10. R. Brian Ferguson and Neil L. Whitehead, "The Violent Edge of Empire," in *War in the Tribal Zone: Expanding States and Indigenous Warfare,* ed. R. Brian Ferguson and Neil L. Whitehead (Santa Fe: School of American Research Press, 1999), 13.

11. Richard Tapper, "Anthropologists, Historians and Tribespeople," in *On Tribe and State Formation in the Middle East*, ed. Philip Khoury and Joseph Kostiner (Berkeley: University of California Press, 1991), 68.

12. Ibid.

13. Philip Khoury and Joseph Kostiner, introduction to *Tribes and State Formation in the Middle East*, ed. Philip Khoury and Joseph Kostiner (Berkeley: University of California Press, 1990), 7.

14. Ibn Khaldûn, *The Muqaddimah*, ed. and trans. F. Rosenthal (Princeton: Princeton University Press, 1967).

15. Marshall D. Sahlins, *Tribesmen* (Englewood Cliffs: Prentice Hall, 1968), 20–27, 48–55. Thanks to Michael Eisenstadt for this reference.

16. Charles Lindholm, "Kinship Structure and Political Authority: The Middle East and Central Asia," *Comparative Studies in Society and History* 28 (1986): 334–55.

17. Samira Haj, "The Problems of Tribalism: The Case of Nineteenth-Century Iraqi History," *Social History* 16 (1991): 49–52.

18. Thanks to Michael Eisenstadt for this observation.

19. Kenneth Brown, "A Few Reflections on 'Tribe' and 'State' in Twentieth-Century Morocco," in *Tribes and Power: Nationalism and Ethnicity in the Middle East*, ed. Faleh Jabar and Hosham Dawod (London: Saqi, 2001), 205–14.

20. Ernest Gellner, "Political and Religious Organization of the Berbers of the Central High Atlas," in *Arabs and Berbers: From Tribe to Nation in North Africa*, ed. E. Gellner and C. Micaud (Lexington: Heath, 1972), 59–66; D. M. Hart, "The Tribe in Modern Morocco," in *Arabs and Berbers: From Tribe to Nation in North Africa*, ed. E. Gellner and C. Micaud (Lexington: Heath, 1972), 25–58.

21. Evans-Pritchard, *The Nuer*.

22. Richard F. Nyrop and Donald M. Seekins, eds., *Afghanistan Country Study* (Washington, DC: Library of Congress, 1986), available at lcweb2.loc.gov/frd/cs/aftoc.html.

23. Charles Lindholm, *Frontier Perspectives: Essays in Comparative Anthropology* (Oxford: Oxford University Press, 1996), 197. The exaggerated politeness, generosity, and hospitality in Arab society have been characterized as a means of curbing the propensity for conflict and competition in tribal society. Dawn Chatty, *From Camel to Truck: The Bedouin in the Modern World* (New York: Vantage Press, 1986), 52.

24. There are other levels as well, but for the sake of simplicity they are omitted here. In Iraq, the larger tribal confederations have both Sunni and Shia branches, and some even have Kurdish branches.

25. Paul Dresch, *Tribes, Government and History in Yemen* (Oxford: Clarendon Press, 1989).

26. Susan Sachs, "The Sheik Takes Over: In Iraq's Next Act, Tribes May Play the Lead Role," *New York Times*, 6 June 2004.

27. Claude Lévi-Strauss, *Structural Anthropology* (New York: Basic Books, 1963), 50.

28. Julian Pitt-Rivers, "Kinship III: Pseudo Kinship," in *International Encyclopedia of the Social Sciences,* vol. 8, ed. David L. Sills (New York: Macmillan, 1968), 408–13. Pitt-Rivers differentiates three subtypes: (1) the figurative use of kin terms; (2) the attribution (rather than ascription) of ordinary kin status, often called "fictive kinship"; and (3) institutionalized relationships resembling kinship, which use kin terms yet are recognized as being entirely distinct. In Iraq, tribal groups organize themselves according to invented relationships. Tom Nieuwenhuis, *Politics and Society in Early Modern Iraq* (Boston: Martinus Nijhoff, 1981); Daniel Bates and Amal Rassam, *Peoples and Cultures of the Middle East* (Englewood Cliffs: Prentice-Hall, 1983), 261.

29. Kinship manipulation is an old pattern among tribes in the Middle East. See Alexander H. Joffe, "The Rise of Secondary States in the Iron Age Levant," *Journal of the Economic and Social History of the Orient* 45 (2002). This appears to be the case in most tribal societies. See Laura Zimmer-Tamakoshi, "Development and Ancestral Gerrymandering: Schneider in Papau New Guinea," in *The Cultural Analysis of Kinship: The Legacy of David Schneider,* ed. Richard Feinberg and Martin Ottenheimer (Chicago: University of Chicago Press, 2001); J. Van Velsen, *The Politics*

of Kinship—A Study in Social Manipulation among the Lakeside Tonga of Nyasaland (Manchester: Manchester University Press, 1964).

30. S. M. Salim, *Marsh Dwellers of the Euphrates Delta* (New York: Humanities Press, 1962), 45. According to Salim, "The usual reason for leaving a clan and joining a new one are desire for more effective military protection, and disputes over land or compensation, the two latter being preponderant in more recent years."

31. Evans-Pritchard, *The Nuer.*

32. Dale F. Eickelman, *The Middle East: An Anthropological Approach* (Englewood Cliffs: Prentice Hall, 1989), 126–50. Most Arab (and Kurdish) tribes in the Middle East are patrilineal, but tribes may also be organized around matrilineal or cognatic descent.

33. Richard Tapper, introduction to *The Conflict of Tribe and State in Iran and Afghanistan*, ed. Richard Tapper (London: Canberra, 1983), 56.

34. Sheikh Hamid Rashid Mahenna of the Albu Alwan tribe, quoted in Rajiv Chandrasekaran, "In a Hostile Land, Try Whatever Works," *Washington Post,* 23 December 2003, A1.

35. According to Bing West, "Gen Abizaid . . . met with the sheikhs, demanding that they show leadership and stop the violence. There were as many attacks on the outskirts of Fallujah, where the sheikhs had power, as inside the city, where the clerics dominated. . . . In a separate meeting with the sheikhs Major General Charles H. Swannack, commander of the 82nd, was equally forceful. 'I am not going to tolerate these attacks anymore,' he said. 'I know the sheikhs have the ability to control their tribes.' . . . The sheikhs protested that the 82nd didn't appreciate the limits of their power. Threatening them would do no good. Improvement projects made no difference to the men with the guns. In the eyes of the sheikhs, power had shifted from them to the young clerics in Fallujah preaching that America was waging a war against Islam and was bringing in Jews to rule Iraq." Bing West, *No True Glory: A Frontline Account of the Battle for Fallujah* (New York: Bantam Books, 2005), 33.

36. Chatty, *From Camel to Truck,* 55.

37. Rory Stewart, *The Prince of the Marshes* (Orlando: Harcourt Books, 2006), 219–20.

38. R. Alan King, *Twice Armed: An American Soldier's Battle for Hearts and Minds in Iraq* (St. Paul, MN: Zenith Press, 2006), 178. Thanks to Michael Eisenstadt for this reference.

39. The Islamic historian Ibn-Khaldun (AD 1332–1395) first noted the conflict between tribe and state. In Ibn-Khaldun's cyclical theory of the rise and fall of dynasties, nomadic tribes possessing *asabiyyah* attack and conquer degenerate urban societies. The ruling dynasty is thus vanquished and the tribe from the wilderness assumes control. Over time the *asabiyyah* of the successor tribe is weakened, allowing a new tribe from the desert to challenge the existing dynasty, defeat it, and establish its rule in the city. Ibn Khaldûn, *The Muqaddimah,* 124. For an interesting insight on the complexity of governance in Iraq, see Michael Hechter and Nika Kabiri, "Attaining Social Order in Iraq" (revised version of paper presented at the Conference on Order, Conflict and Violence, Yale University, New Haven, CT, 30 April–1 May 2004), available at faculty.washington.edu/hechter/AttainingSocialOrderInIraq.pdf.

40. As the Hadith indicates, the early Islamic ruling elite was quite hostile to the nomads: the third caliph, Uthman (ca. AD 574–656), once called an important tribal chieftain an "imbecile Bedouin." Fred Donner, *The Early Islamic Conquests* (Princeton, NJ: Princeton University Press, 1981).

41. The new Islamic state's survival depended on its domination of the tribal elements in Arabian society, accomplished through coercive force and a supervisory bureaucracy of tax agents. Ibid.

42. Montgomery Watt, *Muhammad at Medina* (Oxford: Clarendon Press, 1962), 221–25.

43. Al-Kulayni, *Usul al-Kafi* (Tehran: Intisharat 'Ilmiyyah Islamiyyah), vol. 3 [Arabic text with Persian translation by Sayyid Jawad Mustafawi], 419, hadith 3.

44. Donner, *The Early Islamic Conquests.* The last nomadic conquest was that of Abdul Aziz Ibn Sa'ud, who created Saudi Arabia in 1932.

45. Nieuwenhuis, *Politics and Society in Early Modern Iraq.*

46. Albert Habib Hourani, *A History of the Arab Peoples* (Cambridge: Belknap Press, 1991), 251; Nieuwenhuis, *Politics and Society in Early Modern Iraq,* 14. For a history of the Ottoman Empire, see Colin Imber, *The Ottoman Empire, 1300–1650: The Structure of Power* (New York: Palgrave Macmillan, 2003); Chase F. Robinson, *Empire and Elites after the Muslim Conquest: The Transformation of Northern Mesopotamia* (New York: Cambridge University Press, 2000); M. A. Cook, ed., *A History of the Ottoman Empire to 1730* (Cambridge: Cambridge University Press, 1976).

47. Charles Tripp, *A History of Iraq* (Cambridge: Cambridge University Press, 2002), 9.

48. Dina Rizk Khoury, *State and Provincial Society in the Ottoman Empire: Mosul, 1540–1834* (Cambridge: Cambridge University Press, 1997), 188.

49. Zeyad, "Iraq's Tribal Society: A State within a State," The Healing Iraq Blog, posted 18 June 2004, healingiraq .blogspot.com/archives/2004_06_01_healingiraq_archive.html. After he brutally repressed the Shammar and Bani Lam tribes in 1708, an alliance of several powerful Iraqi tribes rebelled against him under the leadership of the Al-Muntafiq tribal confederation.

50. Tripp, *A History of Iraq,* 14. See also Bernard Lewis, *The Emergence of Modern Turkey* (Oxford: Oxford University Press, 2001), 57. The reforms included regulations on provincial governorships, taxation, control of the grain trade, and other administrative matters. The reforms also provided for a new corps of regular infantry, modeled on European lines. Lewis notes that the term *nizam i-cedid,* which originally applied only to the regulations of the new system, came to be used almost exclusively to refer to the troops established under it (58).

51. Yitzhak Nakash, *The Shi'is of Iraq* (Princeton: Princeton University Press, 1994), 32.

52. Tripp, *A History of Iraq,* 15–16.

53. Nakash, *The Shi'is of Iraq,* 33; Suraiya Faroqhi et al., *An Economic and Social History of the Ottoman Empire,* vol. 2, *1600–1914* (Cambridge: Cambridge University Press, 1997); Nieuwenhuis, *Politics and Society in Early Modern Iraq.* The Ottoman practice of divide and rule "so changed the conditions of life in the affected regions as to attenuate the old tribal loyalties or render them by and large ineffectual." Hanna Batatu, *The Old Social Classes and the Revolutionary Movements of Iraq* (Princeton: Princeton University Press, 1978), 22. Resistance, including outright rebellions in 1849, 1852, 1863–1866, 1878–1883, and 1899–1905, occurred among tribesmen disadvantaged by the new system. Nakash, *The Shi'is of Iraq,* 34.

54. Christoph Herzog, "Corruption and Limits of the State in the Ottoman Province of Baghdad during the Tanzimat," *MIT Electronic Journal of Middle East Studies* 3 (Spring 2003), web.mit.edu/cis/www/mitejmes.

55. Batatu, *The Old Social Classes and the Revolutionary Movements of Iraq;* Tripp, *A History of Iraq.* The Sunni and Shia cooperated until August 1920, after which the Sunni ceased disobedience while the Shiite tribes of the south and the holy cities continued resistance. Philip Willard Ireland, *Iraq: A Study in Political Development* (London: Jonathan Cape, 1937).

56. Toby Dodge, *Inventing Iraq* (New York: Columbia University Press, 2003), 154; Peter Sluglett, "The British Legacy," in *U.S. Policy in Post-Saddam Iraq: Lessons from the British Experience,* ed. Michael Eisenstadt and Eric Mathewson (Washington, DC: Washington Institute for Near East Policy, 2003), 7.

57. May Ying Welsh, "US Trains Proxy to Quell Resistance," Aljazeera, 6 June 2004, english.aljazeera.net/NR/ exeres/771A6660-4D6C-462A-A987-BEF93FD2A14C.htm.

58. To ensure the king's dependence, the British cultivated the sheikhs, permitting tribal courts and granting huge estates. Thus, the 1924 Tribal Criminal Disputes Regulation granted sheikhs increased authority and permitted independent tribal courts in rural parts of the country. Another law in 1933 granted tribal sheikhs huge estates, legally binding the tribesmen to the land in a feudal manner. Helen Chapin Metz, ed., *Iraq: A Country Study* (Washington, DC: Library of Congress, 1988).

59. Faleh Jabar, "Rethinking Iraq: Tribal Identities" (speech, Middle East Institute Boardman Room, 25 April 2004), www.mideasti.org/articles/doc217.html.

60. Faleh Jabar, "The Path to War: How Saddam Keeps Power in Iraq," *Le Monde Diplomatique,* October 2002, available at mondediplo.com/2002/10/.

61. Keiko Sakai, "Tribalization as a Tool of State Control in Iraq: Observations on the Army, the Cabinets and the National Assembly," in *Tribes and Power: Nationalism and Ethnicity in the Middle East,* ed. Faleh Jabar and Hosham Dawod (London: Saqi, 2001), 136–64.

62. Faleh A. Jabar, "Sheikhs and Ideologues: Deconstruction and Reconstruction of Tribes under Patrimonial Totalitarianism in Iraq, 1968–1998," in *Tribes and Power: Nationalism and Ethnicity in the Middle East*, ed. Faleh Jabar and Hosham Dawod (London: Saqi, 2003), 71. The Baath Party invented a new ideology to justify the return of tribalism: hereditary descent should be the basis of Arab nationalism. Amatzia Baram, "Neo-tribalism in Iraq: Saddam Husayn's Tribal Policies 1991–1996," *International Journal of Middle East Studies* 29 (1997).

63. Jabar, "Rethinking Iraq."

64. Jabar, "The Path to War."

65. Baram, "Neo-tribalism in Iraq."

66. Melina Liu, "The Will of the Tribes," *Newsweek,* 17 March 2003, 31.

67. Shortly after the fall of Hussein's regime, for example, religious and tribal leaders in Falluja appointed their own civil management council, prevented looting, and protected government buildings. Nir Rosen, "Letter from Falluja: Home Rule: A Dangerous Excursion into the Heart of the Sunni Opposition," *New Yorker,* 5 July 2004.

68. Stephen J. Glain, "Stronghold Can Backfire: Iraqi Tribes Are Key Source of Loyalty, Rebellion," *Wall Street Journal,* 23 May 2000.

69. Rajiv Chandrasekaran, "Iraqi Wild Card: Tribal Loyalties Hard to Predict," *Washington Post,* 19 January 2003, A01.

70 Joe Klein, "Saddam's Revenge," *Time,* 26 September 2005.

71. Thanks to Michael Eisenstadt for clarification.

72. Stewart, *The Prince of the Marshes,* 219–20.

73. Cited in "Dances with Camels: The True Story of T. E. Lawrence," www.columbia.edu/~lnp3/mydocs/culture/lawrence.htm. See also Suleiman Mousa, *T. E. Lawrence: An Arab View* (London: Oxford Press, 1966); Phillip Knightley and Colin Simpson, *The Secret Lives of Lawrence of Arabia* (London: Nelson Press, 1969); Michael Asher, *Lawrence: The Uncrowned King of Arabia* (New York: Viking, 1998).

74. T. E. Lawrence, *The Diary* (New York: Doubleday, 1937), 41–45.

75. R. Fernea, *Shaykh and Effendi* (London: Oxford University Press, 1970), 110–11.

76. Akbar Ahmed and David Hart, ed., *Islam in Tribal Societies* (London: Routledge and Kegan Paul, 1984), 3.

77. William S. McCallister, "The Iraq Insurgency: Anatomy of a Tribal Rebellion," *First Monday* 10, no. 3 (March 2005), firstmonday.org/issues/issue10_3/mac/.

78. Thus, when a tribal member is killed, the closest relatives of the offender are at the greatest risk to be killed themselves. Dresch, *Tribes, Government and History in Yemen.*

79. Christopher Boehm, *Blood Revenge: The Anthropology of Feuding in Montenegro and Other Societies* (Lawrence: University of Kansas Press, 1984); Roger V. Gould, "Collective Violence and Group Solidarity: Evidence from a Feuding Society," *American Sociological Review* 64 (1999): 356–80; Roger V. Gould, "Revenge as Sanction and Solidarity Display: An Analysis of Vendettas in Nineteenth-Century Corsica," *American Sociological Review* 65 (2000): 682–705.

80. Ernst Gellner, "The Tribal Society and Its Enemies," in *The Conflict of Tribe and State in Iran and Afghanistan,* ed. Richard Tapper (London: Canberra, 1983), 441.

81. Batatu, *The Old Social Classes and the Revolutionary Movements of Iraq,* 21.

82. Michael Hirsh, "Blood and Honor," *Newsweek,* 2 February 2004.

83. Sabrina Tavernise and Dexter Filkins, "Local Insurgents Tell of Clashes with Al Qaeda's Forces in Iraq," *New York Times,* 12 January 2006.

84. Dave Kilcullen, "Anatomy of a Tribal Revolt," Small Wars Journal: SWJ Blog, posted 29 August 2007, smallwarsjournal.com/blog/2007/08/print/anatomy-of-a-tribal-revolt/.

85. As David Leo Gutmann notes, "Thus, the goal of the Bedouin raid is not to finally win a war, for such intertribal conflict is part of the honorable way of life, and should never really end. The essential goals of the raid are to take wealth—not only in goods, but also in honor—and to impose shame on the enemy." David Leo Gutmann, "Shame, Honor and Terror in the Middle East," *FrontPage Magazine,* 24 October 2003, www.frontpagemag.com/Articles/Printable.asp?ID=10489.

86. Intertribal raids often ended after a handful of casualties, so their raids seem much less harmful than interstate warfare. However, the *cumulative* effect of frequent raids on small populations was devastating. Lawrence H. Keeley, *War Before Civilization* (Oxford: Oxford University Press, 1996).

87. Thomas Barfield, "The Devil's Horsemen: Steppe Nomadic Warfare in Historical Perspective," in *Studying War: Anthropological Perspectives; War and Society,* ed. S. P. Reyna and R. E. Downs (Langhorne, PA: Gordon and Breach), 157–181, 163.

88. For example, the bedouin conquest of Iraq during the seventh century was essentially a prolonged raid.

89. Rosen, "Letter from Falluja."

90. Alissa J. Rubin and Doyle McManus, "The Fight for Iraq: Why America Has Waged a Losing Battle on Fallouja," *Los Angeles Times,* 24 October 2004.

91. David J. Morris, "Turning Point," Salon.com, 16 September 2004, dir.salon.com/story/news/feature/2004/09/16/fallujah/index.html.

92. Ibid.

93. Rubin and McManus, "The Fight for Iraq."

94. Ibid.

95. William S. McCallister, Christopher Alexander, and Charles Kyle, "The Iraqi Insurgent Movement" (unpublished paper), available at library.nps.navy.mil/home/Iraqi%20Insurgency%20Movement.pdf.

96. John Barry and Michael Hirsh, "Washington: A Grim March of Missteps," *Newsweek,* 7 February 2005, available at www.msnbc.msn.com/id/6885830/site/newsweek/.

97. Ernst Gellner, "Trust, Cohesion and the Social Order," in *Theories of Social Order: A Reader,* ed. M. Hechter and C. Horne (Stanford: Stanford University Press, 2003), 310–16, 311.

98. As General Aylmer Haldane wrote in 1922 after confiscating 63,000 rifles from Iraqi tribes, the Iraqis "not only rearmed themselves but acquired weapons of more modern type." Scott Peterson, "What the British Learned in 1920 by Not Leaving Iraq," *Christian Science Monitor,* 11 March 2004, available at www.csmonitor.com/2004/0311/p01s03-woiq.html.

99. Jabar, "Sheikhs and Ideologues," 73.

100. Amatzia Baram, *Who Are the Insurgents?* Special Report 134 (U.S. Institute of Peace, April 2005).

101. Paul McGeough, "Share Power or Lose Control, Iraq Warned," *Sydney Morning Herald,* 22 July 2004.

102. John G. Peristiany, ed., *Honour and Shame: The Values of Mediterranean Society* (London: Weidenfeld and Nicholson, 1966); John G. Peristiany and Julian Pitt-Rivers, eds., *Honour and Grace in Anthropology* (Cambridge: Cambridge University Press, 1992).

103. Halvor Moxnes, "Honor and Shame," in *The Social Sciences and New Testament Interpretation,* ed. R. L. Rohrbaugh (Peabody, MA: Hendrickson, 1996).

104. Lila Abu-Lughod, *Veiled Sentiments: Honor and Poetry in a Bedouin Society* (Berkeley: University of California Press, 1986).

105. Moxnes, "Honor and Shame."

106. Amatzia Baram, "Victory in Iraq, One Tribe at a Time," *New York Times,* 28 October 2003.

107. See David Pryce-Jones, "Shame and Honor, Terribly Twisted: A Central Truth of Arab Culture Is on Full Display in Iraq," *National Review,* 21 April 2003. Al Qaeda has also played with this traditional concept of honor. Zawaahri is quoted as saying, "if we want to live with respect, than we must be willing to die with honor." Dr. Ayman Al Zawahiri, interview, www.islamistwatch.org/texts/interviews/zawahiri01.html.

108. Anthony Shadid, "U.S. Detains Relatives of Suspects in Iraq Attacks," *Washington Post,* 6 November 2003, A21.

109. Hala Jaber, "A True Local Hero: Iraq's Sharpshooting Rebel Legend," *Sunday Times* (London), 22 February 2005.

110. Peter Beaumont, "Lethal Hatreds Spread in Iraq's Cockpit of Violence," *Observer* (London), 11 January 2004, available at observer.guardian.co.uk/worldview/story/0,11581,1120582,00.html.

111. George E. Irani and Nathan C. Funk, *Rituals of Reconciliation: Arab-Islamic Perspectives,* Kroc Institute Occasional Paper 19:OP:2 (Joan B. Kroc Institute for International Peace Studies, August 2000), 12, available at www.nd.edu/~krocinst/ocpapers/abs_19_2.html.

112. Baram, "Neo-tribalism in Iraq," 23.

113. Majid Khadduri, "Sulh," in *The Encyclopaedia of Islam*, vol. 9, ed. C. E. Bosworth, E. van Donzel, W. P. Heinrichs, and G. Lecomte (Leiden, Holland: Brill, 1997), 845–46. Bogac Ergene, "Pursuing Justice in an Islamic Context: Dispute Resolution in Ottoman Courts of Law," *PoLAR: Political and Legal Anthropology Review* 27 (2004): 51–71; Joseph Ginat, "The Role of the Mediator in Disputes among Bedouin and Arab Rural Societies" in *Israel Studies in Criminology*, vol. 7, ed. S. Giora Shoham (Sheridan House, Inc., 1986), 89–131; Joseph Ginat, *Blood Disputes among Bedouin and Rural Arabs in Israel: Revenge, Mediation, Outcast and Family Honor* (Pittsburgh: University of Pittsburgh Press, 1987); Government Accountability Office, *Military Operations: The Department of Defense's Use of Solatia and Condolence Payments in Iraq and Afghanistan,* GAO-07-669 (Washington, DC, May 2007).

114. Hamza Hendawi, "U.S. Military Uses Unorthodox Tactics to Woo Violent Iraqi City," Associated Press, 30 July 2003, available at www.sfgate.com/cgi-bin/article.cgi?file=/news/archive/2003/07/30/international1530EDT0644.DTL.

115. Robyn Dixon, "U.S. Limits Payments to Kin of Slain Iraqi Civilians," *Los Angeles Times,* 4 August 2003, available at www.latimes.com/news/nationworld/world/la-fg-pay4aug04,1,4828075.story.

116. David Zucchino, "U.S. 'Condolence Payments' Translate Iraqis' Losses to Cash," *Los Angeles Times,* 12 March 2005.

117. Paul McGeough, "Can Iraq Embrace Democracy?" *The Age* (Sydney), 20 March 2004, available at www.theage.com.au/articles/2004/03/19/1079199423948.html.

118. McGeough, "A Fatal Collision with Tradition," *Sydney Morning Herald,* 30 July 2004. No restitution was made for the death, although Major General James Mattis of the 1st Marine Division sagaciously sent a letter to the new sheikh of the Al-Kharbits in Amman. It reads, in part, "There has been trouble between the Kharbit family and the Americans in the past, but men of vision look to the future and put the past behind them. . . . We are using this opportunity to extend the hand of friendship to you and to your tribe. As a gesture of this friendship, we invite you to return to Al-Anbar province to live in peace."

119. McGeough, "Can Iraq Embrace Democracy?"

120. McGeough, "Share Power or Lose Control, Iraq Warned."

121. Jabar, "Sheikhs and Ideologues," 78.

122. Phebe Marr, *The Modern History of Iraq* (Boulder: Westview Press, 2004).

123. Edward Luttwak, "Dead End: Counterinsurgency Warfare as Military Malpractice," *Harper's Magazine,* February 2007, available at www.harpers.org/archive/2007/02/0081384. See the response by David Kilcullen at smallwarsjournal.com/blog/2007/04/edward-luttwaks-counterinsurge-1/.

124. Ralph Peters, "Myths of Counterinsurgency: How Pop Delusions Prevent Effective Operations," *Armchair General,* September 2007, 10.

125. Sun Tzu, *The Art of War* (New York: Delacorte Press, 1983), 71.

23 Terrorist or Freedom Fighter? Tyrant or Guardian?

Derek S. Reveron and Jeffrey Stevenson Murer

A little more than a year after the 9/11 attacks, the University of Paris VII convened a conference called "Terrorism, the Press, and the Social Sciences." The meeting opened with the keynote speaker announcing, "I am a terrorist." This was neither a rhetorical flourish nor a statement of solidarity. Some 59 years earlier, nearly to the day, the keynote speaker, Raymond Aubrac, was liberated from a Gestapo prison where Klaus Barbie tortured him. Like his wife, Lucie, who led the commandos that freed him, Aubrac was a member of the French Resistance.[1] Aubrac explained to the conference audience how he and his colleagues plotted the assassinations of government officials, exploded bombs to disrupt truck and train traffic, cut power and communications lines, and conducted missions that sometimes could only be described as suicidal. To the German occupation authorities, to the Vichy government, to the Gestapo and to the Milice (the Vichy government's secret police), Aubrac was simply a terrorist.[2]

Aubrac's point was not to suggest that one man's terrorist is another man's freedom fighter. Rather his talk was intended to remind the audience that terrorism is a tactic employed in a political context. To understand the motivations behind acts of violence it is important to understand the contexts in which they occur. Armed groups have political agendas. There have been many times when political activists welcomed the moniker "terrorist." Nineteenth-century Russian anarchists and antimonarchists proudly wore the title "terrorist."[3] It was a testament to their commitment.[4] And more recently, bin Laden said, "every state and every civilization and culture has to resort to terrorism under certain circumstances for the purpose of abolishing tyranny and corruption."[5] Yet many politicians of late speak of terrorists as a cohesive whole, often referring to "the

Derek S. Reveron is an associate professor of national security affairs at the Naval War College. He received a doctorate in public policy analysis from the University of Illinois at Chicago. He specializes in democratization, political-military affairs, political violence, and intelligence. His articles have appeared in *Orbis, Defense and Security Analysis, International Journal of Intelligence and Counterintelligence, Low Intensity Conflict & Law Enforcement,* and the *National Review Online.* His books include *Inside Defense: Understanding the 21st Century Military* (2008), *Flashpoints in the War on Terrorism* (2006), *America's Viceroys: The Military and US Foreign Policy* (2004), and *Promoting Democracy in the Post-Soviet Region* (2002).

Jeffrey Stevenson Murer is the lecturer on collective violence in the School of International Relations at the University of St. Andrews in Scotland. He also is a research fellow to the Centre for the Study of Terrorism and Political Violence and to the Scottish Institute on Policing Research. His research focuses on processes of collective identity formation and expressions of political violence. He is the coeditor of and a contributor to *Flashpoints in the War on Terrorism* (2006), and his other publications have appeared in the United States, France, and Russia.

terrorists" as a singular construction implying that they emanate from a single circumstance or that they possess a singular motivation. Presently that motivation is presumed to be a militant or radical form of political Islam. Yet, this is far from correct. There appear to be many different motivations for the use of terrorist tactics in many different contexts that range from struggles for national independence in Palestine to reactions in response to state repression in the Russian Federation. Ted Gurr notes that perpetrators justify their decisions to use terrorism as a tactic through a mix of rational calculation that is driven by revolutionary, ethno-national, or religious ideology.[6] To understand when and why terrorism is used, one must take difference into account.

In the struggle for independence, autonomy, recognition, or access to material resources, terrorism may become one of many tools employed. In fact, existing U.S. law recognizes that terrorism is a political act: "politically motivated violence perpetrated against noncombatant targets."[7] Michael Wieviorka suggests that terrorism is a social product. It is an image, or psychological representation or a social conception that marks a particular phase or theater of a conflict, perhaps even substituting for total war or revolution.[8] While the effects of political violence may at times be repugnant, such disgust should not blind scholars, policy analysts, or the public to the fact that there is a logic to terrorism. Martha Crenshaw sees that "terrorism [is] not the result of irrational fanaticism but political calculation; it [is] learned behavior, not the result of primordial forces."[9] The violence of terrorism should not be seen as an aberration, but rather as a central part of the politics of identity conflict. As Ben Barber notes, violent political Islamist groups are better understood as a reaction to "global systemic disorders," not fundamentalist zealotry.[10]

Further, terrorism is not born of crisis, but occurs within the context of an evolving conflict. The 9/11 attacks, for example, should be viewed as al Qaeda's culminating event in a series of attacks that began in the early 1990s. Terrorist groups use different techniques to alter the balance within an unresolved conflict; this may include welcoming foreign fighters or accepting assistance from state sponsors. In these aspects we can discern a common characteristic of terrorist activity: it is a tactic or technique employed in a conflict environment characterized by asymmetrical political engagement. It is necessary to identify the motivations associated with specific groups of actors. The guiding premise articulated by Martha Crenshaw could be just as easily applied here: "terrorism as a general phenomenon cannot be adequately explained without situating it in its particular political, social and economic contexts."[11] Understanding this goes a long way to differentiate between terrorists and freedom fighters.

THE POLITICS OF TERRORISM

As Raymond Aubrac's declaration reminds us, terrorism occurs in a political context. As a label, terrorism immediately qualifies the actions and actors to whom it is applied. The choice to call a political actor a "terrorist" or a political act "terrorism" often has a "prescriptive policy relevance as well as moral connotation."[12] This is as true with the United States as with Russia or any of the other state parties in conflicts associated with the "global jihad." By evoking the label "terrorist," the speaker seeks to combine descriptive and symbolic elements, creating a kind of shorthand for evil.[13] Such a label implies a preferred policy solution, one which often precludes negotiation. If terrorists "cannot be negotiated with" or their presence cannot be tolerated, the label rules certain political elements to be outside the bounds of political discourse. Further, the state may claim the right to eliminate such political elements because of the threat they pose to stability.

The use of the terrorist label, however, can be dangerous. By ruling that certain political elements are beyond civil discourse, it can become tempting for states to expand the lists of political elements no longer qualifying for civil engagement. States use the terrorist label to identify political opponents. The application of such a label can lead to governments becoming blind to the distinction between violent opposition and nonviolent dissent, or the distinction between rebellion and civil disobedience. It was not that long ago when rightist political elements in many South American countries used the broad application of the label "terrorist" to jail, torture, eliminate, and kill political activists associated with leftist movements. The state security services in the "dirty wars" in Argentina and Chile came to see all of political society as "contaminated" by leftist thought. The only way to remove the contamination was through state violence.

The efforts to eliminate urban guerrilla organizations led counterterrorism and counterinsurgency units to engage in the types of activities associated with terrorist tactics.[14] This broad application of the moniker "terrorist" transforms the body politic into an enemy. Such a situation is exemplified today in Russia when the North Ossetian minister for nationality affairs, Taymuraz Kasaev, suggested that anyone who "actively practices Islam" would be seen as an "enemy"[15] even though Islam is recognized as a "traditional belief" within Russian law.[16] Although Russian patriarch Alexy II reminds his followers that "Russian Christians and Muslims traditionally live in peace," the association of "Muslim" with "terrorist" may be too deeply fixed in the popular mind of the Russian public. The connection between political oppositions and terrorism in Russia, just as with the connections in South America, serves to justify both continued and escalated state violence. As John Esposito cautioned more than a decade ago, "Islamic movements have been lumped together; conclusions have been drawn, based more on stereotyping or perceived expectations than empirical research."[17]

The application of state violence in these cases begets still more violence, not necessarily in the form of resistance but in the form of the bureaucratization of state violence. Military, interior ministry, and law enforcement agencies all come to participate in a "war on terrorism." In fact, the word "terrorism" was initially coined to describe acts of state violence perpetrated during the Reign of Terror following the French Revolution. Resources are allocated according to a given agency's ability to contribute to this new state endeavor—the elimination of political opposition identified with terrorism. The proclaimed need to suppress these challenging elements may serve as the basis for the extension of state powers. Thus, if one speaks of terrorists and freedom fighters, then one must also consider whether governments inappropriately use the label "terrorist," calling into question whether leaders behave as tyrants or guardians.

TYRANTS AND GUARDIANS

While acts of terrorism are often depicted as threats to democracy, the real threat to liberal societies may lie in the state's responses to terrorism. In the names of expediency and efficiency, state reactions in the immediate aftermath of a traumatic terrorist event often include an alteration in the standing, institutional relations of power. This is particularly true in modern democracies, whereby the response of the state entails an extension of executive power. The delegation of "full powers" allowing the executive to issue and enforce decrees represents a broad alteration of regulatory power, particularly when such an alteration allows for the modification or abrogation by decree of laws previously in force.[18]

The simplest and most immediate examples of temporary arrangements becoming permanent institutions come from decrees converted into law. The laws invoked by French president Jacques Chirac by declaring a "state of emergency" (*l'état d'urgence*) on 8 November 2005 were originally crafted under the René Coty presidency in 1955 in order to quell growing unrest in Algeria. Chirac's application of these powers in response to the November 2005 riots demonstrates the tremendous reach associated with the "guardian" state. These powers include the ability to declare curfews for designated areas, to place individuals under house arrest without arraignments or trials, to censor publications and other news organs, and to engage in searches and police raids without search warrants. Or a 2005 law in Germany allows authorities at the state level to expel legal foreign residents who "endorse or promote terrorist acts" or incite hatred against sections of the population.[19] Or Italy also passed a series of antiterrorism laws making deportations easier. Finally, in August 2005, the British government broadened the grounds for deportation to those persons who "justify or glorify" terrorism.[20] While established democracies in Europe can likely endure challenges to the liberal democratic order, the situation is not so certain in new democracies that face the threat of terrorism.

PERPETUAL STATES OF EMERGENCY

Extraordinary powers assumed by the executive branch are linked to a state of emergency that has either been recently declared and lifted, or is legally recognized as the de facto condition, with the state of emergency operating even in the absence of a declaration.[21] In Thailand, a state of emergency was originally imposed in July 2005 in reaction to the extensive violence in the south of the country. The 90-day emergency condition was then extended for another 90 days on two more occasions. As under the terms of the French state of emergency, the Thai executive is allowed to declare curfews, ban public gatherings, confiscate property, monitor telephones, and search homes and offices without warrants. Like many other provisions for the state of emergency in other countries, the Thai provisions grant officials prosecutorial immunity from civil, criminal, or disciplinary penalties. Civil rights advocates claim that the state of emergency is actually making conditions worse in the south of Thailand. Rohan Gunaratna understands that the Thai strategy of treating the insurgency as a military threat is drastically flawed.[22] By privileging the use of force, the Thai approach worsens the problem by further alienating the Muslim communities. Treating these Thai citizens as if they were enemy aliens reduces the incentives for community involvement in conflict amelioration. Those citizens who might otherwise be indifferent or even opposed to the insurgency give their support or at least tolerate the rebel organizations as they are seen as an expression of resistance to Thai state violence. Political repression through the banning of political organizations only has the effect of driving the most politically active into prohibited groups. Free expression, regional autonomy, and infrastructure support would all signal that the states of southern Thailand are an integral part of the country rather than alienated from it. Ironically, General Sondhi Boonyaratkalin, who came to power in a military coup in September 2006, restored a dialogue with insurgent leaders in an effort to reduce the violence.

In Indonesia, different parts of the country have been under states of emergency, some for considerable periods of time. For example Aceh was placed under martial law in 1959.[23] That condition was changed with the declaration of a "state of civil emergency" in the province of Nanggroe Aceh Darussalam on 19 May 2003. It was to remain in effect for one year, but was renewed in 2004.[24] In May 2005, the government lifted the declaration but the army has remained in the region to "keep order" and to assist with the cleanup efforts in the aftermath of the December 2004 tsunami.

On the island of Maluka in Indonesia, nearly five thousand people died in clashes between Christians and Muslims in 2000. A state of emergency was declared for the island on 6 June 2000 and remained in effect for three years. During that time there were serious allegations leveled at the Indonesian security services regarding the use of torture, indefinite detentions, and even state-authorized killings.[25] Arabinda Acharya and Rohaiza Ahmad Asi echo Gunaratna by suggesting the best way to quell the violence across the archipelago is to improve infrastructure, especially by creating new schools and reforming the police and the army.[26] One of the biggest problems Acharya and Asi identify is that many Indonesians are so distrustful of the state security services that they turn to political organizations with "muscle" to settle disputes rather than turning to the police. Extremist ideology is communicated in a select number of *pesarten* or religious schools. As with the madrassas in Pakistan, many children attend the *pesarten* because there is no alternative; the state fails to provide public education. While perhaps far too much has been made in the U.S. media of the link between madrassas and terrorism, the situation in Pakistan and Indonesia primarily exists because of a lack of state resources committed for public goods. It is this lack of infrastructure that promotes political violence as an identity of resistance against such state neglect.

In the Philippines, Ferdinand Marcos declared martial law in 1972. Though the condition was lifted in 1981, the president kept extensive emergency powers. Even with the coming of democracy the president has still retained those powers. A state of emergency has been declared five times since 1989. In 2003 alone, an emergency condition was declared twice. On the first occasion President Gloria Macapagal-Arroyo declared a "state of rebellion" in response to the mutiny of 296 soldiers, 70 of them officers who were top graduates of the Philippine Military Academy. The soldiers said that they were protesting government-sponsored terrorism, including a bombing in Davao, Mindanao, that killed 12 people. The mutineers said that while the government blamed the terrorist organization Abu Sayyef, the sophisticated bombing was the work of military forces. The soldiers also stated that the government launched these attacks in order to appear active in the "global war on terrorism," to curry favor with the United States, and to obtain more U.S. military aid. At the time the Philippines had already received more than $100 million in aid.[27] The second occasion in 2003 followed an attempted military coup d'état, whose instigators echoed the claims and concerns of the mutineers. The Philippines' effort to combat the insurgency in Mindanao has led to the use of extensive investigatory powers, claimed under the state of emergency. In 2005, in an attempt to stifle media criticism of the government's handling of the fighting in the south, President Arroyo called press freedom groups "enemies of the state." She singled out the Philippine Center for Investigative Journalism, saying that the organization had been "infiltrated by communists."[28] In February 2006, another state of emergency was declared in response to an alleged coup against President Arroyo, which resulted in public protests being banned and several arrests.

Some states of emergency have been in place for many years. The executive had full powers in Sri Lanka from 1983 until 2001, and Israel has had a state of emergency since May 1948. Another long-ruling state of emergency ended when Turkey finally lifted its 15-year-old state of emergency in the provinces of Diyarbakir and Sirnak in 2002.[29] The state of emergency had replaced a declaration of martial law, imposed in March 1984 and then lifted in July 1987. The original application of the state of emergency in 1987 applied to 13 provinces in the south and east of the country as a reaction to violence associated with Kurdish rebels. As in Indonesia, serious allegations of torture, prolonged detention, and physical abuse were leveled at the security forces.

In some regions, a state of emergency is not even declared; rather the executive simply claims the power to deal with some crisis. Without such a declaration, however, there is no suggestion of a limit on this executive privilege. Very quickly these powers become permanent. In the case of Chechnya, numerous states of emergency have been declared since the collapse of the Soviet Union, the first being issued in November 1991. Just prior to the first Russian military campaign, in 1994, President Yeltsin declared a state of emergency for both Chechnya and neighboring Ingushetia. Similarly, just prior to the December 1999, second Russian military campaign, three states of emergency were declared. However, since the invasion, no state of emergency has been declared. President Putin claims that it is not necessary for such a declaration, and the Constitutional Court agreed with him. The court stated in 1995 that the power to quell violence and the means to do so are well established by the constitution in ordinary presidential powers.[30] In Chechnya, since 2000, there has been a de facto state of emergency, where security services regularly detain people without charge, search premises without warrants, monitor communications, and regularly use extreme violence against people the security services deem to be potential threats. There have been numerous claims that the security forces kidnap for ransom, traffic in narcotics, and make many Chechen men "disappear." The Russian human rights organization Memorial states that between 3,000 and 5,000 Chechens have "disappeared" since December 1999.[31] Official Russian government statistics acknowledge nearly 2,000 disappearances. Although there have been 1,814 criminal investigations into the enforced "disappearances," not one has resulted in a conviction.[32] When UN commissioner for human rights Mary Robinson called Russia to account for human rights abuses, pointing out that no state of emergency had been declared, Justice Minister Yuri Chaika replied that it was all part of the fight against terrorism.[33]

There is also an undeclared, de facto state of emergency in Jammu and Kashmir in India. Similar to the constitutional ruling in Russia, the Indian Supreme Court held in 1997 that the condition of a state of emergency and the exercise of extraordinary powers by the executive were both legal and constitutional. Although no state of emergency was declared, state security services regularly engage in "preventative detention," and exercise extraordinary police powers to arrest, detain, and even shoot persons suspected of posing a threat to national security. There are other measures as well that grant special powers to the executive and its security apparatus. The Jammu and Kashmir Public Safety Act (PSA) of 1978 allows for the detention, for up to 24 months without indictment or trial, of persons suspected of posing a threat to the region. Another ordinance, the National Security Act of 1980, augments the PSA and applies to all of India, allowing for persons anywhere in the country to be detained without trial for 12 months.

And in places like Iraq where the focus of the U.S. government has been on establishing a liberal democratic order, the imposition of a state of emergency has had significant deleterious effects on the progress of democratic development. Logically, the development of liberal democracy is at times at odds with the necessities of security. Following a 30-day state of emergency declared immediately after the U.S. invasion in March 2003, Iraq has been under a state of emergency more or less since. Throughout the initial 30 days, the security forces under the direct command of the prime minister were authorized to declare curfews wherever and whenever they saw fit. They were authorized to carry out arrests and detentions without warrants or informing detainees of the grounds for their arrests. Detainees could be held incommunicado and property could be seized without compensation during police and military operations. The designation "al Qaeda associate," "terror suspect," or "illegal enemy combatant" initiates a whole series of actions that combine to exclude an individual from society and the protections it affords against governments. Beginning with the loss of the right to an attorney, then to access to due process, then to a writ of *habeas corpus*, the "terror suspect" is denied universally accepted human rights.

While the detention of self admitted al Qaeda leaders responsible for terrorist attacks no doubt makes sense, the detention of hundreds in U.S. custody or thousands in Iraqi custody does have corrosive effects. Two of the most common tools to combat terrorism and insurgencies, the deportation or detention of suspected provocateurs and the declaration of a state of emergency, appear largely to inspire the very groups that pose the greatest danger to democracy. This is not to say that states of emergency are not rightly declared in the face of real crises; they are. Many people have suffered greatly in regionalized sectarian violence. States respond in the most expedient fashion. However, a consequence of this expediency is often that the executive seizes additional powers and the military element of power dominates, which alienates a population already under duress.

In all of these cases, one finds a threat to the practice of democracy as the guardian state exerts itself. The executive stands outside of the normally valid juridical order and yet this is not anarchy or chaos. It is something different. Order remains but the executive subtracts itself from any consideration of law.[34] This is similar to a commissarial dictatorship when power is seized by a political element that has the aim of defending or restoring the existing constitution. Along these lines, it is possible to suggest that the three Turkish military coups d'état (1960, 1971, and 1980) were to "defend" the secular order, just as General Pervez Musharraf claims that his seizure of the Pakistani government in October 1999 was to defend it against impending collapse. The guardian state is not a dictatorship, but it is a dangerous flirtation with the suspension of the principles of liberal democracy.

TARGETS AND RESPONSES

Just as not all political violence is directed at the same targets, not all political violence is the same either. Differentiating between the targets and the aims of organized collective political violence gives rise to different state responses. Terrorism should not be treated as a single political movement; it is important to understand the unique political and cultural context in which violence occurs. In *Flashpoints in the War on Terrorism,* our analysis suggests there are a number of similarities across conflicts: political Islam is prominent, but not as a motivator for violence. Rather than demonstrating a "clash of civilizations" or the incompatibility of Islam and Christianity (or Judaism, or Hinduism, or Buddhism, or Nigerian indigenous religions), religion is a marker of identity chosen by Muslim minorities where they are dominated. That violence arises is more a function of state failure than a clash of civilizations.

The most prominent feature common to conflicts associated with "jihad" is the rise of violence as a response to a state failure. In the global war on terrorism, "terrorist" violence is associated with political organizations that either challenge the state in a nationalist or separatist fashion, or resist an authoritarian or heavy-handed application of the state interests, including programs of forced assimilation. While organizations like al Qaeda seek to promote the idea that political violence is associated with an "internationalist" Islamic empire, there is a danger to misunderstanding the motives of terrorist groups or overestimating the threat they pose. As John Mueller put it, even al Qaeda is a bounded problem, whose numbers and "terrorist adjuncts are finite and probably manageable."[35] Having a fantasy of creating an Islamic empire from Morocco to Indonesia is not the same as having the capability and opportunity to do so. To be sure, Osama bin Laden and his deputy Ayman al-Zawahiri seek to tap into socioeconomic frustration and ignite a larger clash of civilizations. However, the people in Morocco to Indonesia have a say in their futures; and they have overwhelmingly embraced their own national identities, unique forms of Islamic worship, and democracy. At the end of 2005, Freedom House notes that core countries of the Middle East in the last four years have seen steady progress toward creating freer societies. And there are many Muslim-majority countries that are now considered democratic—Indonesia, Turkey, Mali, Senegal, and Mauritania. The key U.S. foreign policy approach should be to promote development and the state's ability to provide public goods.

In the Kashmir region, for example, a large problem is the state's failure to develop infrastructure.[36] This failure has many wide-reaching repercussions and is more pronounced than other regions in India. While terrorism may not always be bred in conditions of poverty, it is born of frustration. Gurr's theory of relative deprivation is instructive here—people become resentful and disposed to political action when they share a collective perception that they are unjustly deprived of economic and political advantages enjoyed by other groups.[37] Life in areas lacking infrastructure can be difficult and trying. Without technical infrastructure, the economy cannot be developed. The worst consequence in such regions is not only a rise of poverty but also the resulting chronic underemployment. A region without technical infrastructure is stuck in a perpetual depression. No economic sector can grow because no sector takes root; in addition, the population becomes economically dependent upon the state. This tension between dependence on the state for things economic and feeling estranged from the state in things political exacerbates tensions in such regions. The chronic lack of electrical power in Kashmir, or the lack of an industrial base in southeastern Anatolia, gives rise to a sense of being ignored by the state. The population turns to other organizations to fill the security and welfare roles of the state. For example, the Free Aceh Movement provides protection in Indonesia; Hezbollah in southern Lebanon provides social services such as medical care, elder care, and education. While these organizations have a violent component, their popular support and persistence is based on filling a role the state normally fulfills. The organizations are sustained by large numbers of deprived people who are natural recruits for guerrilla and terrorist groups.

DANGERS OF WAR IMAGERY

John Mueller warned that the use of war imagery in "combating terrorism" may raise unreasonable expectations.[38] Wars end. They also have objectives and usually identified purposes guiding the belligerents. The rhetorical attempt to suggest that "the terrorists" are a single entity, who will be "defeated," makes it difficult to engage in differentiation and setting conflicts into political context. Stephen Walt pointed out that during the cold war, the United States fell into a similar pattern of rhetorical conflation. By viewing all leftist, socialist, or Marxist regimes as "indistinguishable parts of a communist 'monolith'" U.S. foreign policy was unable to deal with each regime on its own terms and in its own context.[39] This lack of nuance often led to "self-fulfilling spirals of hostility."[40]

Depicting all struggles that include an element of political Islam as part of a "global jihad" can be very dangerous, too. It is easy to imagine how the labeling of a group as "terrorist," thereby precluding the possibility of negotiation or intercession by third parties, might drive political actors toward an extremism they might not otherwise approach. In addition, such language may obscure the goals of the political groups in conflict. The repetition of the rhetoric of "global jihad" prevents policy actors from hearing real grievances and seeing available avenues for conflict amelioration. Walt's warning of the potential of creating a self-fulfilling policy prophecy is an important one that should be heeded.

Much of this is a result of structures of the rhetoric of war in which the enemy is generally highly depersonalized in order to make his elimination more palatable. This act of violent debasement exacerbates the type of alienation associated with the state failures that gave rise to armed groups in the first place. Rather than attempting to identify with the estranged or alienated social group, the discourse of war suggests tension and the necessity to remain separate, often even after victory.

The employment of war rhetoric may make the guardian state more palatable in the near term; it may also help to justify enormous costs associated with the military in both personnel and equipment. For example, the U.S. Defense Department's *National Military Strategic Plan for the War on Terrorism* states that the way to defeat terrorism "is to continue to lead an international effort to deny violent extremists the networks and components they need to operate and survive. Once we deny them what they need to survive, we will have won."[41] However, a declaration of war only distorts the public's ability to see that terrorism is a tactic and political technique of the weak that will not go away. It is far more beneficial to engage the political elements in areas marred by terrorism, even if those groups may be associated with terrorism. This is particularly true since the organization responsible for the 9/11 attacks is largely defeated and relegated to a symbolic role hoping to inspire nationalist struggles that predate the 9/11 attacks or even Osama bin Laden's role as self-proclaimed spokesperson for political Islam. By incorporating, not excluding, these political organizations it may be possible to co-opt them into the larger political culture, thereby not only reducing political violence, but also building a more vibrant and varied political society.

Even as it is still unclear if HAMAS will change to be incorporated into the Middle East peace process, it must be remembered that a number of terrorist organizations laid down their weapons once they were able to join the political process. Al-Fatah and the Palestinian Liberation Organization ceased calling for the destruction of Israel once the Oslo Peace Accords were being realized. It may well be possible that the same will happen with HAMAS. The Muslim Brotherhood, which has largely resisted violence, is now a responsible party within Egyptian politics. The FMLN[42] has become an important and stable political party in El Salvador after fighting a 12-year-long guerrilla campaign during that country's civil war. Similarly, the Sandinistas remained an important political movement and party in Nicaragua, even after their electoral defeat in 1990 until the reelection of Daniel Ortega in 2006. The African National Congress practiced terrorist tactics for nearly 30 years from the early 1960s until the organization was legalized in 1990. Although it has taken some time since Sinn Fein first accepted the 1998 Good Friday peace accords, the Irish Republican Army apologized in 2002 for harming civilians in its attacks and in 2005 renounced violence as a means to achieving its political ends. This laying down of weapons has been a long time in coming for Western Europe's oldest active terrorist organization, yet it has come nevertheless. All of these transformations were facilitated by the inclusion of these heretofore declared terrorist organizations into the political process. These conflicts were ameliorated not by "defeating the terrorists" but by including "them."

If the Department of Defense's Global War on Terrorism Strategy is to be taken seriously in its plan to create a global environment inhospitable to violent extremists, then it is necessary to engage those segments of the polity that experience estrangement and alienation. Regional autonomy, local self-rule, representation in larger national bodies, and the means for self-expression can be far more useful institutional tools than the guardian state. Each site of terrorist activity must be dealt with on its own terms. Through more democracy, not less; through free speech, not coded speech; and through transparency and honesty, not opacity and secrecy, will these conflicts be ameliorated.

NOTES

Portions of this chapter have appeared in chapter 15 in *Flashpoints in the War on Terrorism,* edited by Derek S. Reveron and Jeffrey Stevenson Murer (New York: Routledge, 2006).

1. The jailbreak and other events of Aubrac's life are depicted in the 1997 Claude Berri film *Lucie Aubrac*. Having been caught and tortured and his wife having been revealed to also be a Resistance commando, Raymond Aubrac was smuggled to London in 1944 together with Lucie. After D day and the liberation of the south of France, de Gaulle appointed Aubrac commissioner for the republic in Marseille (1944–1945). Later in life Aubrac worked for the United Nations' World Food Program in Rome. Aubrac is also well known for cofounding the underground resistance newspaper *Libération* with Emmanuel d'Astier.

2. Aubrac is a hero in French culture. Out on the street, especially in Paris, people come up to Aubrac in cafés to thank him for his commitment. Not just older people come up to him, but even young people realize the magnitude of his and Lucie's sacrifices for the French Resistance movement.

3. Lindsay Clutterbuck, "The Progenitors of Terrorism: Russian Revolutionaries or Extreme Irish Republicans?" *Terrorism and Political Violence* 16, no. 1 (Spring 2004): 154–81.

4. Michael Wievioka, "Terrorism in the Context of Academic Research," in *Terrorism in Context*, ed. Martha Crenshaw (University Park: University of Pennsylvania Press, 1995).

5. Osama bin Laden, "Interview with John Miller of ABC," in *Jihad: Bin Laden in His Own Words; Declarations, Interviews, and Speeches,* ed. Brad K. Berner (Booksurge, 2006), 82.

6. Ted Robert Gurr, "Economic Factors," in *The Roots of Terrorism,* ed. Louise Richardson (New York: Routledge, 2006).

7. Section 2656f(d) of U.S. Code Title 22 states, "terrorism is premeditated, *politically motivated violence* perpetrated against noncombatant targets by subnational groups or clandestine agents, usually intended to influence an audience." Emphasis is ours.

8. Wievioka, "Terrorism in the Context of Academic Research."

9. Martha Crenshaw, preface to *Terrorism in Context,* ed. Martha Crenshaw (University Park: University of Pennsylvania Press, 1995), xvi.

10. Benjamin R. Barber, *Fear's Empire: War, Terrorism, and Democracy* (New York: W. W. Norton, 2003).

11. Crenshaw, preface.

12. Martha Crenshaw, "Thoughts on Relating Terrorism to Historical Context," in *Terrorism in Context*, ed. Martha Crenshaw (University Park: University of Pennsylvania Press, 1995).

13. Ibid.

14. See Amnesty International, *Chile Briefing: A Decade of New Evidence,* AMR: 22/13/88 (London: Amnesty International Publications, 1988); and Amnesty International, *Argentina: The Attack of the Third Infantry Regiment Barracks at La Tablada—Investigations into Allegations of Torture, "Disappearances" and Extrajudicial Executions,* AMR: 13/01/90 (New York: Amnesty International Publications, 1990).

15. Paul Gobel, "Authorities Seek to Convert Beslan's Muslims," *RFE/RL Newsline,* September 2005.

16. See *On Freedom of Conscience and on Religious Associations,* Russian Federation Federal Law 125-FZ, trans. Keston Institute, Center for Studies on New Religions, www.cesnur.org/testi/Russia.htm; Lev Krichevsky, "Russian House Passes Religion Bill Restricting 'Non-traditional' Faiths," *Jewish Telegraphic Agency,* 26 June 1997.

17. John Esposito, *The Islamic Threat: Myth or Reality?* (New York: Oxford University Press, 1992), 235.

18. Giorgio Agamben, *The State of Exception* (Chicago: University of Chicago Press, 2005), 7. Agamben describes this process of expanding executive power as the "state of exception." Through the alteration of the balance of power among the various institutions within a democratic constitutional regime—a structure premised upon the very distribution of power—the "government will have more power and the people fewer rights." What Agamben finds most troubling is that the "state of exception" has in fact become a "paradigm of government" itself, echoing Walter Benjamin's concern that "the state of exception . . . has become the rule." The essential character of this condition is the provisional abolition of the distinction among the legislative, executive, and judicial powers, which eventually becomes a lasting practice of government.

19. Ben Ward, "Expulsion Doesn't Help," *International Herald Tribune*, 2 December 2005, available at www.iht.com/articles/2005/12/02/opinion/edward.php.

20. Ibid.

21. See Reveron and Murer, *Flashpoints in the War on Terrorism.*

22. Rohan Gunaratna, "Thailand," in *Flashpoints in the War on Terrorism,* ed. Derek S. Reveron and Jeffrey Stevenson Murer (New York: Routledge, 2006).

23. State Paper of the Republic of Indonesia, Number 139, 1959. See also U.S. State Department, "Indonesia Brief," available at www.state.gov/r/pa/ei/bgn/2748.htm.

24. The President of the Republic of Indonesia, Presidential Decree No. 28/2003, "On the Declaration of a State of Emergency with the Status of Martial Law in Nanggroe Aceh Darussalam Province," *Jakarta Post,* available at www.thejakartapost.com/aceh/acehlatestnews2.asp.

25. *Amnesty International,* "Briefing on the Current Human Rights Situation in Indonesia," AI Index: ASA 21/006/2001, 31 January 2001, available at www.amnesty.org/en/alfresco_asset/20f7a0de-a43a-11dc-bac9-0158df32ab50/asa210062001en.html.

26. Arabinda Acharya and Rohaiza Ahmad Asi, "Indonesia," in *Flashpoints in the War on Terrorism,* ed. Derek S. Reveron and Jeffery Stevenson Murer (New York: Routledge, 2006).

27. *FY 2005 International Affairs (Function 150) Budget Request* (2 February 2004), available at www.state.gov/s/d/rm/rls/iab/2005/.

28. International Freedom of Expression Exchange, "Press Freedom Watchdogs Branded 'Enemies of the State,'" 13 April 2005, www.ifex.org/en/content/view/full/65948.

29. BBC News, "Turkey to Ease Restrictions on Kurds," 31 November 2002, news.bbc.co.uk/2/hi/europe/2017935.stm.

30. For examples of the impact of these rulings, see Department of State, Bureau of Democracy, Human Rights, and Labor, *Country Reports on Human Rights Practices: Russia* (23 February 2001), available at www.state.gov/g/drl/rls/hrrpt/2000/eur/877.htm.

31. "Chechnya's Disappeared," *Washington Post,* 4 April 2005.

32. Ibid.

33. BBC News, "Chechen Visit Mixed Success," 4 April 2000, news.bbc.co.uk/1/hi/world/europe/701590.stm.

34. Carl Schmitt, *Die Diktatur* (Munich: Duncker & Humblot, 1921), 137, quoted in Agamben, *State of Exception*, 32.

35. John Mueller, "Harbinger or Aberration?" *National Interest,* Fall 2002, 45–50.

36. Samina Raja, "Kashmir," in *Flashpoints in the War on Terrorism,* ed. Derek S. Reveron and Jeffery Stevenson Murer (New York: Routledge, 2006).

37. Ted Gurr, *Why Men Rebel* (Princeton, NJ: Princeton University Press, 1970).

38. Mueller, "Harbinger or Aberration?"

39. Steven Walt, "American Primacy and Its Pitfalls," *Naval War College Review* 55, no. 2 (Spring 2002): 23.

40. Ibid.

41. Chairman of the Joint Chiefs of Staff, *National Military Strategic Plan for the War on Terrorism* (Washington, DC: Department of Defense, 2006), 5.

42. Farabundo Martí National Liberation Front.

24 Disrupting and Influencing Leaders of Armed Groups

Elena Mastors and Jeffrey H. Norwitz

INTRODUCTION

The United States has a superb capability to collect and analyze information about the rest of the world. Yet many decision makers still fail to adequately understand the leaders of armed groups. Dealing with and attempting to influence or disrupt the activities of these shadowy leaders cannot be achieved without understanding what makes them tick.

Most of us don't have direct access to leaders of armed groups or their close associates. Thus, we have to work with indirect information such as speeches, letters, books, media interviews, and what associates say about these leaders. This is particularly true about al-Qaida.

This chapter does not subcribe to a singular type of leadership analysis. We contend that if we only use one approach, we can miss some very instructive information about

Dr. Elena Mastors is currently an associate professor in the National Decision Making Department at the Naval War College. Previously, she held various senior intelligence and policy positions in the Office of the Under Secretary of Defense for Intelligence and received numerous performance awards from the Defense Intelligence Agency. Dr. Mastors earned a BA in political science from Eckerd College and a political science MA from the University of South Florida. She received her PhD in political science with a concentration in international relations and political psychology from Washington State University, where she focused on leadership, conflict, and terrorism. She writes frequently on understanding leaders and group dynamics, from a political-psychological perspective. She is also a frequent lecturer on the important role of individuals and group dynamics in terrorist groups and is currently conducting fieldwork in Northern Ireland on the leaders of banned terrorist groups. Dr. Mastors is published in *Political Psychology Journal* and authored *Introduction to Political Psychology* (Lawrence Erlbaum and Associates, 2004); *The Lesser Jihad: Recruits and the al-Qaida Network* (Rowman and Littlefield, 2007); *The Psychology of Terrorism* (Blackwell, forthcoming 2008); and *Introduction to Political Psychology,* 2nd ed. (Lawrence Erlbaum and Associates, forthcoming 2008).

Jeffrey H. Norwitz, the editor of this volume, has 34 years as a law enforcement official with military, municipal, and federal career experience. He is presently a special agent with the Naval Criminal Investigative Service (NCIS), having served worldwide specializing in complex criminal, intelligence, and terrorism investigations. This included an assignment at Camp Delta, Guantánamo, as part of the Criminal Investigative Task Force interviewing al-Qaeda and Taliban fighters (2003–04). His last assignment was as NCIS supervisory special agent responsible for counterintelligence throughout New England. Mr. Norwitz has twice received the Department of the Navy's Meritorious Civilian Service Medal for his counterintelligence and counterterrorism accomplishments. Mr. Norwitz earned a BA in criminal justice from Eastern Kentucky University. In 2001, Mr. Norwitz earned an MA in national security and strategic studies from the Naval War College and joined the teaching faculty, where he teaches national security studies, as the NCIS adviser. He is the inaugural holder of the John Nicholas Brown Academic Chair of Counterterrorism generously endowed by the Naval War College Foundation.

the leader. As a result, we have integrated different leadership approaches into our framework. Furthermore, other practical aspects about leaders that lead us to understand how to influence or disrupt their activities also need to be considered.

The literature on influencing leaders is sparse.[1] Therefore, this chapter focuses on certain biographic and personality aspects to develop a campaign to influence leaders of armed groups. The key here is specific and relevant information. Rather than collecting everything written on a leader, it is much more important to focus on essential information. Toward that end, this chapter offers a unique framework for analysis that focuses on decisive aspects of a leader. The framework points us to the germane information for leadership-influencing operations. It integrates some of the personal characteristics and motivation literature and offers new insights for use in influence application.[2] We then examine the art of human-source-intelligence collection and social-psychological principles of influence, which, if successful, will give us the relevant information for leadership targeting. Next, the chapter offers an enlightening case study of Ayman al-Zawahiri using the framework as an organizing tool. Finally, the chapter concludes with a brief discussion of how one would influence him, disrupt his activities, and make him irrelevant to the network and perhaps even draw him out to kill or capture him.

THE LEADERSHIP FRAMEWORK[3]

There are four aspects of the leadership framework: (1) personal characteristics, (2) operating environment, (3) advisory process, and (4) information environment.

Personal Characteristics	Operating Environment	Advisory System	Information Environment
- Self-confidence	- Rise to power	- Significant advisers	- Clarity of thinking
- Locus of control	- Allegiances	- Formal networks	- Complexity of thought
- Perception of self	- Competing leaders	- Informal networks	- Diversity of sources of information
- Motivation	- View of others	- Sources of influence	
- Ideology	- Others' views of leader	- Advisers' own agendas	- Challengeability of opinions
- Philosophy	- Ethnocentrism	- Advisers' influence	
- Beliefs	- Distrust of others		
- Values	- Constituency		
- Likes and dislikes	- Sources of finance		
- Social norms	- Areas of corruption		
- Relationships with family			
- Education			

The first part of the framework, personal characteristics, focuses on the leader's view of him- or herself, to include degree of self-confidence and locus of control,[4] personal perception of the role he or she plays and how he or she became a leader, ideology and philosophy, motivation (task, affiliation, or power),[5] beliefs,[6] values,[7] proclivities, and likes and dislikes. Another important aspect of personal characteristics is background and skills. Among them are age, places where the leader was born and raised, and relevant socialization factors. Also included are marital status, the nature of the marital relationship, and relationships with immediate and extended family, and the nature of those relationships. Interests; schooling, including the type of student the leader was and focus of study; former positions held; and key personal associates are also important to know. Understanding the leader's norms is crucial. Norms include the leader's views of proper individual behavior, impertinent behaviors, words or phrases that can be insulting, and the roles of minority or majority groups.

The second part of the framework is the leader's operating environment. This includes how the leader came to power. Groups or individuals that constrain the leader must be examined, as must whether or not the leader challenges constraints.[8] Another aspect of the operating environment is the leader's image of other groups.[9] Incorporated in this are also perceptions about others, the leader's degree of ethnocentrism, and distrust for others.[10] However, of interest is not only how the leader views others but also how the leader is viewed by others.[11] Thus, the focus is on existing perceptions about the leader on a variety of perceptual issues and, at a more basic level, whether the leader is liked or disliked, and by whom. Also relevant is the leader's view of his or her defined constituency or followers. Finally, a leader's operating environment includes sources of finance and areas of corruption.

The third part of the framework deals with the leader's advisory system. Some of the most significant people in a leader's world are his or her advisers. When examining a leader it is important not to become caught up in the formality of line-and-block charts because they may not really tell us who is influential. Therefore, we have to look at the leader's formal and informal networks of advisers. Advisers can also change over time. For a variety of reasons advisers can also fall out of favor, or new ones may emerge. When the most influential advisers are identified, the potential spin, personal agenda, or filtering of information by them should also be discerned. Finally, some leaders may not even care about advice from others. As a result, they may pay lip service to their advisers but consider themselves the ultimate authorities on all issues. Last is the degree of control a leader needs over the policy process, and the interest and level of policy expertise.

The framework's fourth and final part is the leader's information environment. This involves the degree of complexity the leader exhibits. For example, some individuals are open to information, deal in shades of gray, and have an ability to differentiate their environments.[12] They will seek ways to help them understand their states of affairs. These types of leaders usually want a lot of information at their disposal. Those who lack in cognitive complexity are "black and white thinkers."[13] They are essentially closed to conflicting information, do not seek out alternative views, and do not care about supplementary information. Once certain traits are established, notably regarding the degree of cognitive complexity and motivation, as well as responsiveness to constraints, it is possible to then draw additional conclusions about the nature of the leader's style.[14] Whether complex or not, the type of information a leader pays attention to, the sources of this information, and how a leader prefers information to be presented will aid in designing an influence strategy.

This framework covers many pertinent areas about leaders that we must understand before proceeding with any campaign against them. However, we are at the behest of the information we have access to. There may be times where certain parts of the framework cannot be filled in. In this regard, the framework is an ideal, and at times the ideal cannot be fully satisfied.

THE NEED FOR HUMAN-SOURCE INTELLIGENCE

Human intelligence, commonly abbreviated as HUMINT, is that which is derived from human sources. In contrast to intercepted phone conversations (signals intelligence), photos (imagery intelligence), and other technical or scientifically derived intelligence, HUMINT is the cornerstone of intelligence work.

> HUMINT is espionage—spying—and is sometimes referred to as the world's second-oldest profession. . . . Spying is what most people think about when they hear the word "intelligence," whether they conjure up famous spies from history such as Nathan Hale . . . or fictional spies such as James Bond. HUMINT largely involves sending agents to foreign countries, where they attempt to recruit foreign nationals to spy. Agents must identify individuals who have access to the information that we may desire; gain their confidence and assess their weaknesses and susceptibility to being recruited; and make a "pitch" to them, suggesting a relationship.[15]

HUMINT provides an otherwise unattainable window into the personality, emotional makeup, and innermost secrets of those who are being targeted for influence operations. Recall the four aspects of our leadership framework: (1) personal characteristics, (2) operating environment, (3) advisory process, and (4) information environment. HUMINT is unmatched in its ability to uncover this often private, subtle, and privileged information about leaders and decision makers whom we want to influence.

Professional intelligence officers who specialize in human-source intelligence are customarily called "HUMINTers." They are not intelligence analysts nor are they staffers who write reports. Rather, HUMINTers are operational people, specially trained and highly skilled to blend into any environment wherein human relationships are the essence. Human-source-intelligence work is part clinical psychology and part theatrical acting. As you read this, throughout the world, thousands of men and women are quietly gathering intelligence, manipulating human relationships, assessing likely informants, and influencing leaders. Furthermore, there are those whose job it is to detect and neutralize human-source-intelligence collection done by adversaries, thereby protecting their own leaders. This is called counterintelligence.

Thus the HUMINT community is in a continuous reciprocating ballet of spy versus counterspy, sometimes using very different rule-sets. For example, a democratic nation will, by the very nature of the form of government, follow a set of norms embodying "rule of law" and human dignity, unlike some adversaries, which justify ends by any means. Therein emerges a tension when armed groups violently attack democracies, yet measured state responses are a necessary moral obligation. One of the quintessential thinkers on intelligence matters and democratic norms of behavior is Stansfield Turner, retired Navy admiral and former director of central intelligence (1977–1981). Citing a perceived "lack of discussion of how our democracy affects and is affected by what we do to deter terrorism," Turner wrote a book on the very subject.[16] His conclusions:

> One of the key elements for us in combating terrorism is international cooperation. . . . If we are going to defeat international terrorism—not just Osama bin Laden but the broader sweep—we will need an analogous multinational program that will put pressures on the movement of individual terrorists and on their bases of support in our societies. . . . Today many countervailing strengths come from the very fact that we have a democratic system. But that means we need public understanding of our options for curtailing the current wave of terror and the wisdom to avoid actions that might undermine the democratic process we are defending.[17]

In point of fact, based on abuses in the past, there are codified laws and presidential orders that clearly define how America conducts intelligence activity and still protects constitutional underpinnings.[18]

For the purpose of this chapter, we will now briefly explore some of the methods that HUMINTers employ to manipulate the minds of witting and unwitting sources. The first step is to create opportunities to meet influential people who are either themselves leaders or individuals who have close access to leaders. Traditional environments such as social settings, dinner gatherings, business dealings, or recreational activities provide ample chance to find likely targets. At a minimum, they are ideal occasions to pass a carefully crafted rumor hoping key attendees will incarnate the infamous "grapevine," starting a campaign to manipulate perceptions. Many winning influence and disruption strategies started with a well-orchestrated gaffe at an embassy cocktail party. Similarly, social and business settings where HUMINTers toil are ideal for assessing others for exploitation. HUMINTers seek, if not the leaders themselves, then likely candidates that have notional access to leaders or their families or are in positions to support clandestine activity.[19]

Experience shows that regardless of culture; language; age; gender; political, religious, or educational background, the four most common motivators for people to deceive trusted comrades are (1) greed, (2) anger or revenge, (3) thrill or excitement, and (4) visions of self-importance (ego, vanity). Others simply volunteer their services for ideological motives. HUMINTers perfect ways to exploit each of these scenarios and literally develop scores of persons acting as psychological hostages. Even in those relationships that seem to start with full cooperation, a measure of coercion will be contrived in order to "hook" the source lest he or she develop remorse.

> HUMINT involves the manipulation of other human beings as potential sources of information. The skills required to be a successful HUMINT collector are acquired over time with training and experience. They basically involve psychological techniques to gain trust, including empathy, flattery, and sympathy. There are also more direct methods of gaining cooperation, such as bribery, blackmail, or sex.[20]

One of America's most successful yet unheralded HUMINT officers is Duane R. "Dewey" Clarridge, retired senior official of the Central Intelligence Agency. For 32 years, Clarridge was a legendary CIA operations officer deeply involved in many of the agency's most important covert actions in the cold war.[21] Clarridge ran some of the most clandestine yet indispensable campaigns of the twentieth century to disrupt, influence, and in some cases totally destroy armed groups with aims inimical to those of the United States.[22] Commonly referred to as covert action, or CA operations, Clarridge's activities showcase the effectiveness and efficacy of disruption and influence campaign strategy. Working against the Abu Nidal Organization (ANO), Clarridge headed the CIA Counterterrorism Center (CTC) in 1986. From the recruitment of an ANO member, and good analysis, Clarridge's shop developed superb intelligence about Abu Nidal himself.

> From our ANO agent penetration, we began to accumulate a lot of knowledge about Abu Nidal's "diplomacy" [internal and external behavior] and his financial dealings . . . which led us to ANO activists and backers in France, England, and Germany. . . . I arrived at the conclusion that the best way to attack Abu Nidal was to publicly expose his financial empire and his network of collaborators. . . . I proposed that the Department of State issue an explosive little tome called *The Abu Nidal Handbook* . . . [which] laid out chapter and verse on the ANO, its members and accomplices, and its crimes. It even had an organizational chart. . . . [W]e decided to make recruitment pitches to [ANO] personnel in various countries. . . . Seeing his financial empire under attack and listening to reports of CIA efforts to recruit his cadres, Abu Nidal was aware . . . [that] we were coming after him and his people. He, like many in his line of work, was paranoid. The CTC fueled his hysteria over plots against him—feeding fear to a paranoid is something we know how to do. Not surprisingly, Abu Nidal panicked. Those who reported having been approached by us were not rewarded for their loyalty, because Abu Nidal never quite believed that anyone in his group had turned us down. Their loyalty was suspect thereafter, and the punishment for disloyalty was torture and death.
>
> By 1987, a fearful Abu Nidal had turned his terror campaign inward. . . . After the effective ANO apparatus in southern Lebanon fell under suspicion, over three hundred hard-core operatives were murdered on Abu Nidal's order. . . . Another 160 or so were killed in Libya shortly thereafter. Distrust reached high into the politburo ruling the ANO. Even his closest surviving lieutenants began to believe that Abu Nidal was insane. Abu Nidal's paranoia, fed by our crusade against him, caused him to destroy his organization.[23]

Dewey Clarridge's remarkable career successes in the clandestine service serve as proof that exploiting personality and biographic elements from our leadership framework to disrupt and influence leaders gives us stunning advantages against America's enemies.[24]

We combine these well-grounded operational approaches with the literature in social psychology on influence that describes influence techniques such as consistency, social proof, likability, scarcity, and so forth.[25]

THE CASE OF AYMAN AL-ZAWAHIRI

The story about Ayman al-Zawahiri begins with a summary of some key findings that relate to several of the personal characteristics in the framework, namely, biographical information, background and skills, and some of his traits we see developing at an early age.

Al-Zawahiri was born in Maadi, Egypt, a suburb of Cairo, in 1951. He was from a wealthy and educated family. In fact, his family seemed "never to have faced social or economic hardships; many of its members would be considered part of the elite in any society."[26] For example, al-Zawahiri's grandfather was the imam at the al-Azhar Mosque in Cairo, his father was a professor of pharmacology, and his maternal grandfather was a professor of oriental literature and president of Cairo University and also served as ambassador to Pakistan, Saudi Arabia, and Yemen.[27]

Al-Zawahiri was interested in education and was also considered a loner and introvert. According to an account by Montasser al-Zayyat, a Cairo lawyer who was later imprisoned with him in 1981, "his family noticed his interest in reading, academic excellence and studiousness from a young age. Whenever he got tired of studying, he would not spend time with children his age to play or watch television, but rather read books on religion and Islamic jurisprudence as a pastime."[28] Al-Zawahiri read and was influenced by Islamist literature of Sayyid Qutb, Abu al-Mawdudi, and Hassan al-Nadwya.[29] Other than the works of these Islamists, Abdullah Azzam also had a significant influence on al-Zawahiri's thinking. Azzam is frequently referred to as the spiritual father of Usama bin Ladin and a much-revered leader of the mujahideen in Afghanistan.[30] Al-Zawahiri graduated in 1968 from secondary school and went on to enroll in medical college at Cairo University. He finished his medical training in 1974, and then completed a master's degree in surgery in 1978.[31] He married Azza Ahmed Numar in 1979 and had at least four children by her. Azza graduated from Cairo University with a degree in philosophy, but met the criteria of being a pious wife.[32] His wife and two of his children were killed during a U.S. air strike in Afghanistan in December 2001.[33] He later married two other widows of a colleague who died in the bombing.[34] He also had children by them and it's assumed his family still resides with him.

Despite the opportunity granted by his elite status in society and access to education, al-Zawahiri was more interested, it seems, in clandestine activities aimed at overthrowing the Egyptian regime.

> At the age of 15, Zawahiri joined Jam'iyat Ansar al-Sunnah al-Muhammadiyya . . . , a "Salafi" (Islamic fundamentalist) movement led by Sheikh Mustafa al-Fiqqi, but soon left it to join the Jihad movement. By the age of 16, he was an active member of a Jihad cell headed by Sa'id Tantawi. Tantawi trained Al-Zawahiri to assemble explosives and to use guns. In 1974, the group split because the group declared Tantawi's brother as *kafir* (infidel) because he fought under the banner of *kuffar* or infidels which characterized the Egyptian army. In 1975 Tantawi went to Germany (and is said to have disappeared) and Ayman took over the leadership of the cell. He immediately organized a military wing under Issam Al-Qamari, an active officer in the Egyptian army at the time.[35]

After finishing his studies, al-Zawahiri took a position in a Cairo clinic operated by the Muslim Brotherhood. He then traveled to Peshawar, Pakistan, and stayed for four months. "For him, this experience was providential because it opened his eyes to the wealth of opportunities for jihad action in Afghanistan."[36]

Al-Zawahiri was imprisoned by the Egyptians in 1981 as a suspect in the assassination of Egyptian president Anwar el-Sadat. At this point we start to learn more about his personal characteristics, including additional information on his formative years, traits, and also his motivation. We also see some elements of his early operating environment, specifically, how he dealt with rivals and the perceptions of him by others.

For example, while in prison, al-Zawahiri was branded a man who created discord among the other prisoners. Specifically, in prison with him was Sheikh Omar Abdel

Rahman. Rahman, who was blind, was appointed emir of the group. Debate in prison focused on whether Rahman should lead a newly formed coalition of the Islamic Group (IG), led by Refai Taha, and other jihadist factions.[37] Montasser al-Zayyat, who witnessed the altercation in the prison, explained that many of the jihadists felt a sense of failure because of "several rushed and ill-conceived" operations, which exacerbated tensions further. In fact, "many heated discussions raged in prison over the causes of these failures. Some members were accused of negligence and of not having completed the tasks with which they had been entrusted."[38]

Al-Zawahiri, among others such as Esam al-Qamari, did not think that Rahman was fit to lead the new group because he was blind. According to them, a leader should have unimpaired senses.[39] Refai Taha believed that "[al-]Zawahiri was fanning the fire of dissension by encouraging Esam al-Qamari to argue against Abdel Rahman's leadership."[40] Rahman was later convicted for his role in the 1993 World Trade Center attack and is currently in prison in the United States.

Al-Zawahiri confessed in prison (he claims under torture), revealing the details of his associations, and he also told them the hiding place of al-Qamari. Al-Qamari was arrested and executed.[41] Interestingly, the authorities never did realize the extent of al-Zawahiri's involvement in the jihad movement, although he didn't have direct involvement in Sadat's assassination. Al-Zawahiri had always been extremely secretive and cautious with regard to his clandestine activities and remains so today.[42] Because he was relatively unknown, he was only convicted of a firearms charge and received three years in prison.

Al-Zawahiri was released from prison in 1984 and went to work in Saudi Arabia at the Ibn Al-Nafis Hospital, and then went to Pakistan to work as a surgeon in the Kuwaiti Red Crescent Hospital. At this time, the war against the Soviets in Afghanistan was in full swing. "[H]e would go to the war zone for three months at a time to perform surgery on wounded fighters, often with primitive tools and rudimentary medicines. At the same time, he opened the 'Islamic Jihad' bureau in Peshawar to serve both as a liaison point for new Mujahedeen and a recruitment agency."[43] Al-Zawahiri was not only in charge of the group but sought to establish its clear presence in Pakistan and Afghanistan.

In 1988, three leaders of the Islamic Group settled in Peshawar. One of them was Khaled al-Islambuli, the brother of the man who assassinated Anwar el-Sadat. The point of their trip was to challenge al-Zawahiri.[44] Their fight was revealed in publications by the Islamic Group (*al-Fath*) and by al-Zawahiri (*al-Murabitoon*). For example, the IG accused al-Zawahiri of selling arms and using the money to buy golden nuggets. He was also accused of depositing money in a Swiss bank account. "In the face of these accusations, some relief agencies decided to cut off their aid to al-Zawahiri, and the need for funds forced him to seek assistance from Iran."[45]

Al-Zawahiri was also accused by Abdullah Azzam of causing problems. Azzam complained to his son-in-law that al-Zawahiri was a troublemaker and that he, along with others, only intended to create discord among the mujahideen.[46] Azzam was killed by a car bomb in 1989 and some rumors have suggested that al-Zawahiri played a role to move Azzam out of the way so that he could be the key influencer of bin Ladin. When all was said and done, al-Zawahiri "emerged the winner from this conflict [with the Islamic

Group], largely because of bin Laden's support and because of the murder of Abdallah Azzam, the spiritual leader of bin Laden."[47]

There are several things to keep in mind when considering al-Zawahiri's personal characteristics and operating environment during the time period of his life as a child to his work in Pakistan and Afghanistan. Al-Zawahiri was not an extrovert and leadership qualities were not self-evident. He educated himself in jurisprudence, thus carving out for himself the art of argument. And there is evidence that he used the art of argument to speak out against his and others' detention while in prison. He instructed and gave advice surreptitiously if it served his own interest. He also challenged those who he believed did not serve the purposes of the movement, as depicted by him, and it seems he found others expendable if it served his own purposes. He also had conflicts with many individuals and groups by pursuing his own agenda. The role he carved for himself even behind the scenes gave him power and when the time was right, he got the power he was seeking and took control over the Islamic Jihad (IJ), successfully maneuvering his way out of conflicts and emerging as the winner.

Thus, it was indeed a calculated move when he merged his own group, the IJ, with al-Qaida in 1998, joining "The Global Front for Fighting Jews and Crusaders." This official partnership resulted in a reorganization of al-Qaida into four committees: military, religion, finance, and the media.[48] He pragmatically shifted his focus from the "near enemy," which to him was Egypt, to the "far enemy," the United States and anyone seen as supporting the United States. This was a change from his thinking in 1996 when he stated that the near enemy took precedence because it was closer.[49] In 1998 the far enemy became the focus of the Global Front for Fighting Jews and Crusaders. Usama bin Ladin was al-Zawahiri's ticket for a greater role in the transnational movement against the crusaders and Jews. There was fallout over al-Zawahiri's decision as well, and he had to be aware of the repercussions of abandoning his group's goals in order to serve his own interests. According to one account, "fundamentalist sources maintain that al-Zawahiri's signing of the statement of 'Global Front for Fighting Jews and Crusaders' in February 1998 was an ill-omened act for al-Jihad Organization because it caused the rapid downfall of the most prominent leaders of the group who were residing abroad, and members of the group who were living in other Arab countries were extradited to Egypt."[50] Obviously, the fate of the group wasn't his concern.

Al-Zawahiri served bin Ladin well and is often heralded as the man behind bin Ladin who crafted the arguments and gave him direction—he is the power behind the throne, a notable personal characteristic that comes up time and again. Bin Ladin had the charisma to be in the forefront and al-Zawahiri wanted his own power to grow and to get his message out through whatever means necessary.

Al-Zawahiri knew what he wanted despite protestations of other members of his group. However, during the summer of 1999, members of the IJ were becoming uncomfortable with al-Zawahiri's growing ties to bin Ladin. As a result, al-Zawahiri was ousted as their leader. Thartwat Shehada took control of the group and wanted to get back to the original work of the group, the focus on Egypt. Shehada didn't have the financial backing to achieve this goal and by spring of 2001, al-Zawahiri was able to reassert control over the group.[51] Al-Zawahiri made another calculated move and packed the leadership of al-Qaida with his trusted Egyptian allies. The Egyptians were clearly in control of al-Qaida.

Here we can see more elements of the framework, mainly in the areas of personal characteristics, operating environment, and his way of finding advisers that agreed with him, and elements of his information environment. In political-psychological terms, al-Zawahiri is "director"; his preference is for direct control, he prefers his own advice to others', and he advocates his own views. For example, when members of his group disagreed with him, he went ahead with his own agenda and made decisions to their detriment. He also found trusted individuals to run the organization who would not disagree with him. Additionally, his drive for power manifested itself in the type of maneuvering that would put him back on top. Al-Zawahiri was not a man to be challenged or crossed. He was a man seeking power and control.

After the September 11 attacks on the United States perpetrated by al-Qaida, the United States struck back with the U.S.-led Operation Enduring Freedom in Afghanistan in December 2001. After the United States successfully disrupted al-Qaida's operating base in Afghanistan, it seems al-Zawahiri became geographically separated from bin Ladin. Bin Ladin was remarkably silent from his statement in 2004 until September 2007 when a tape was released where he made a general statement to the American public that did not talk about operational matters but rather appeared as a lecture to the American public on U.S. culture, politics, history, and the merits of Islam. The statement reads like a lecture on what Americans have done and seems as though he is painting a picture of blame squarely on Americans and their support for their leaders. He also made a great appeal for Americans to embrace Islam.

In the meantime, al-Zawahiri pressed on in his quest for relevance and power. The network became more diffuse, and al-Zawahiri was becoming less and less important as a hands-on director. He began making more statements to demonstrate his operational and leadership relevancy. He maintained a self-image as a powerful and important leader, decided he liked power, and remained relevant to the network. He commented on operational matters and offered direction to those he perceived as part of his followers: the members of the global jihad.

Al-Zawahiri views the United States as an imperial power that can be challenged.[52] In September 2004, al-Zawahiri released a statement in which he commented on Afghanistan, Iraq, and other issues. "The defeat of America in Iraq and Afghanistan has become just a matter of time, with God's help. . . . Americans in both countries are between two fires. If they carry one, they will bleed to death—and if they pull out, they lose everything."[53] In an interview conducted with Montasser al-Zayyat on Al-Jazeerah, al-Zayyat was asked by an anchorwoman what he thought about the al-Zawahiri statement. He replied,

> The main thing I read in this statement is the smartness and shrewdness of this man, who has come up with the statement at the time where there is uproar over his disappearance and reports speaking about his death and that of his colleague and brother Shaykh Usama Bin Ladin. He has made it a point to choose the proper timing, while the whole world is getting ready to speak about the third anniversary of the 9/11 incidents. He preceded all the heresies and tales that would be told and came out to us confident, clear, composed,

and determined in his mobilization discourse. He challenges the United States and the co-alition armies and says the question of evicting the invasion forces from Afghanistan is just a matter of time. He also defies Pervez Musharraf. I say that Dr. Ayman al-Zawahiri is managing an open match with modest resources despite the world security alert against him. He is managing an open match with the United States with all its huge resources and intelligence services.[54]

In another statement, released in July 2007, al-Zawahiri again berated the United States and blamed the country for the loss of Muslim security in Palestine, Afghanistan and Iraq, the Philippines, Chechnya, Kashmir, "and other places where America strikes us directly or support[s] our enemies by all the possible means so they can replace America in striking us." Al-Zawahiri called on others to "surround America with horror." As he put it, "Why not chase them like they chase us? Why not terrorize them like they terrorize us? And we possess the means to do that. Is it not our right to make bombs out of our bodies when we lack the weapons of mass destruction, that they have used to kill our children with? If these murderers cannot feel that their security cannot be achieved at the expense of our security, we will never taste security."[55]

Obviously, al-Zawahiri made his move to be in the forefront of power. What this may point to is that he is now preparing everyone to consider him the next leader of al-Qaida. According to some, al-Zawahiri is pushing for more operational control (some have argued that bin Ladin has already stepped aside)[56] and sees fit to comment on and assert his influence over everything from the war in Iraq, the Israeli-Palestinian conflict, Egyptian elections, oil production in Saudi Arabia, and Muslim theology.[57] And for his personal pet project, he has also become singularly focused on President Pervez Musharraf, the leader of Pakistan, the satellite of the far away enemy.

> Zawahiri has been on an almost personal crusade to assassinate or overthrow the Pakistani leader. In his latest video, which is among at least 10 audio and video spots he has released this year [2007], and which was produced and put on a jihadist Web site in record time, Zawahiri condemned the Red Mosque raid and urged Pakistani Muslims to "revolt" or else "Musharraf will annihilate you." (The mosque apparently served as a safe house for foreign and jihadist militants moving between urban areas and the tribal agencies until Pakistani security forces stormed it on July 10, killing about 70 militants and students holed up inside.)[58]

However, many in the jihad movement do not welcome al-Zawahiri's agenda and multitude of comments. According to Osama Rushdi, who was imprisoned with al-Zawahiri, "he is risking his credibility among Islamic radicals by speaking out on so many subjects. . . . 'He's trying to stay in control and give the impression that he's behind everything in the Middle East and everywhere else, fighting against the Americans in Iraq. . . . But he knows, and everyone knows, that that is not true, that he has nothing to do with anything in Iraq.'"[59]

His focus on Pakistan has created further rifts among the network members. In fact, many in al-Qaida believe that he has become too powerful and is literally obsessed with Musharraf.

In [pushing his own agenda], Zawahiri has provoked a potentially serious ideological split within Al Qaeda over whether he is growing too powerful, and has become obsessed with toppling Musharraf. . . . The anti-Zawahiri faction in Al Qaeda fears his actions may be jeopardizing that safe haven [in Pakistan], according to the two jihadists interviewed by NEWSWEEK. Both have proved reliable in the past: they are Omar Farooqi, the nom de guerre for a veteran Taliban fighter and chief liaison officer between insurgent forces in Afghanistan's Ghazni province, and Hemat Khan, a Taliban operative with links to Al Qaeda. They say Zawahiri's personal jihad has angered Al Qaeda's so-called Libyan faction, which intel officials believe may be led by the charismatic Abu Yahya al-Libi, who made a daring escape from an American high-security lockup at Baghram air base in 2005. The Libyan Islamists, along with bin Laden and other senior Qaeda leaders, would love to see Musharraf gone, too. But they fear that Zawahiri is inviting the Pakistani leader's wrath, prematurely opening up another battlefront before the jihadists have properly consolidated their position.[60]

Interestingly, bin Ladin would later make a statement that in fact bolstered al-Zawahiri's views on Pakistan. He seemed to be following the dictates of al-Zawahiri and not the other way around.

Al-Zawahiri also attempted to assert control over Abu Musab al-Zarqawi, the now-deceased leader of al-Qaida in Iraq. In a letter intercepted by the U.S. military, al-Zawahiri lectured him on al-Zarqawi's leadership and operating style, as well as his need to take direction from those who know better. Obviously, al-Zawahiri is a prime candidate to give that direction.

In all of al-Zawahiri's statements there are instructive elements with regard to his operating environment. We see that al-Zawahiri has attempted to control his operating environment. His own beliefs have taken precedence over those of others in his own group or the wider network and he has proceeded with actions despite the consequences to the wider jihadist movement or other Muslims whom he considers part of his "constituency."

In his statements we also see a clear description of his enemies, and the degree of distrust and ethnocentrism he has with regard to his enemies. He has black-and-white depictions of the in-groups and out-groups in his operating environment. There are those who are with him and those who are against him. There are those who agree with him and those who do not. One can either support him, his views, and his tactics or be considered an enemy. In an e-mail exchange that took place in 2006 between al-Zawahiri and two Egyptians who were publicly critical of al-Zawahiri, there is information that bolsters the fact that al-Zawahiri does not like to be questioned about his methods, nor does he welcome being criticized, especially by other Muslims. In fact, he wrote two e-mails to his detractors despite the security risk in doing so.[61] For example, in one of the e-mails, al-Zawahiri wrote to Montasser al-Zayyat, "I beg you, don't stop the Muslim souls who trust your opinions from joining the jihad against the Americans." As al-Zayyat later explained about the e-mail, "Let's put it this way: Tensions had been building between us for a long time. . . . He always thinks he is right, even if he is alone."[62]

All of this harkens back to al-Zawahiri's motivation for power, a key personal characteristic that has seemed to develop more strongly over time. He views himself as important, wants things done his way, and does not take threats to his power kindly. He does not respect constraints. When he is threatened he tends to lash out, becoming more abrasive and contentious. Therefore, his focus on Musharraf is not that surprising. Al-Zawahiri is obviously threatened by the proactive stance that his enemy Musharraf has taken in the tribal areas in which al-Zawahiri purportedly resides, and of course Musharraf is perceived to be supporting the quest to find al-Zawahiri himself. Musharraf is a pawn of the imperial West, notably the United States. Al-Zawahiri views these actions against him as a personal affront and, in return, he will try to get even.

Of further note, we have learned a lot more about al-Zawahiri's information environment. Al-Zawahiri does not demonstrate any degree of cognitive complexity. He is very rigid and dogmatic and is not likely affected by information that doesn't fit into his rigid worldview. He does have access to information and follows current events and, because of his perception of his own importance, very likely pays attention to information written about him specifically. In each of his proclamations he mentions current events, analyzes them through his worldview, and gives his advice. He is also concerned with whether or not his statements are publicly released, a further indication of his need to be seen as important. However, while he may be able to release statements quickly, as evidenced by his commentary on the Red Mosque raid, it is clear that his access to information may, at times, be delayed. This could be a function of where he is hiding and it is likely that he is periodically moving based on his own security concerns. For instance, in his letter to al-Zarqawi, al-Zawahiri wrote about his own lack of knowledge about his released statement on Al-Jazeerah and mentioned that he was aware of the arrest of a network member Abu Faraj al-Libi, as well as Pakistani operations in the tribal areas.

DISRUPTING AL-ZAWAHIRI

Having learned about al-Zawahiri by focusing on his personal characteristics, operating environment, advisory system, and information environment, we are now ready to take this information and construct an influence and disruption campaign. We begin with al-Zawahiri's depiction of himself as a jihadist leader, note the hypocrisy this unveils, and use his own words against him.

In the letter to Abu Musab al-Zarqawi, al-Zawahiri writes that he wishes he too could join the fight if only there was a secure way to do so. Of course we know that al-Zawahiri has made numerous statements urging people to fight, but he does not himself, while other operational leaders are risking their safety and their lives. These types of proclamations give us glaring opportunities to discredit him. His behavior is not consistent with his words, and those who are proved inconsistent are seen to have personality flaws.[63] What we need to focus on is that al-Zawahiri doesn't want to fight and puts his protection above the fight for global jihad. Clearly, he isn't joining the fight due to his own view that he is a great and important leader, not a fighter. The important point is that everyone who participates in extremism is at risk. This is the nature of the work they do and al-Zawahiri should be equal, not better than everyone else. Therefore, the key is to use his own words to discredit him.

Consider the effect of a fictitious letter written as part of an influence and disruption (covert action) strategy. Leveraging all the capabilities of human-source-intelligence avenues, it should be written in the exact style of al-Zawahiri. The intended recipient of the letter would be bin Ladin.

This fictitious letter could say something to the effect that al-Zawahiri is lamenting the type of individuals now in charge of the global struggle. They are ignorant and clearly do not meet the standards he and bin Ladin set for the network. This plays upon his views that he is the leader, that he is always right, and that everyone should conform and follow his dictates. The letter might also say that al-Zawahiri would never fight for the present network but will keep supporting them with rhetoric only. It might suggest that other avenues of support be cut off, particularly in the areas of funding. All efforts should be put toward Pakistan, the most important target. The letter might also mention the grumbling by others about his focus on Pakistan, but they should be dismissed as heretics. He knows what is best. Furthermore, the fictitious letter might state that he believes that the only way to rescue al-Qaida from its present malaise is to follow his dictates laid out in many of his statements over the last few years.

Another key point in the letter might be derogatory comments about the ethnic composition of the core group. It is not a secret that al-Zawahiri packed the original group with Egyptians, all in leadership positions, his trusted "advisers." We know that al-Zawahiri is not even handed when dealing with groups outside the Egyptian ethnicity.[64] Of course, the real letter from al-Zawahiri to al-Zarqawi, a Jordanian, about his unpopular methods in Iraq, and his instructions for change in this area among others, is a thematic precedent that has already been set. For our disruption campaign, we need to key in on al-Zawahiri's thinking that if one leaves the job to those other than the Egyptians, then the network goes haywire. Thus, al-Zawahiri, in our fictitious letter, or in a follow-on letter, should tell bin Ladin that the entry of these barbarians (non-Egyptians), like al-Zarqawi and members of al-Qaida in the Maghreb, into the network has brought shame upon it. Nonetheless, they are serving the wider interests of the network and will be supported in his future proclamations. Additionally, he is considering sending more Egyptians to take charge. Other leaders who don't follow the rule of law laid out by him should be replaced as well.

Human-source networks are the perfect venue to release the fictitious letter and also start confirming rumors about its content and authorship. Coordinated fabrication using signals and imagery releases would give the appearance of consistency. Ideally, perception management plans must offer the target several confirming bits of information to increase the credibility of the invented scenario. We also have to remember here that social proof and scarcity are powerful influence tools.[65] Once the letter gets into the hands of some, everyone will want it. When one source disseminates it, everyone else will follow suit. Here again, well-coordinated HUMINT activity will ensure success of propagation, especially in the tribal areas of Pakistan where U.S. analysts believe al-Zawahiri is hiding.

To support the subterfuge, the U.S. government should first ask that the letter not be released. This is solely for credibility purposes.[66] Once released, unwitting policy makers and analysts alike will appear as if in a frenzy, ask for intelligence analysis of the letter, talk to the media, and bring in pseudoexperts to authenticate the letter. Examples can be clerical leaders and others who had a relationship with al-Zawahiri before he went into hiding. The bogus letter might be posted in the online jihad chat rooms, where debates will be started.

If the ruse is successful, this will be a turning point for al-Zawahiri. He will be challenged and discredited. He will not be liked.[67] A bonus of course is that al-Zawahiri will have to emerge. Knowing that he sees himself as a powerful and exalted leader, he will need to respond to the challenge against him. He already demonstrated with the e-mail to al-Zayyat that he is willing to take risks when his credibility is on the line. He also, as we learned, is singularly focused on Musharraf, a man he perceives as intent on capturing him.

Soon after the letter is made public, we might monitor the areas where we believe he is likely hiding and watch for commotion. We already know from his speeches that there will be a delay in his responding. But, when all is said and done, he will demand a way to get his own message out.

Knowing what we know about al-Zawahiri's personal characteristics, advisory system, and operating and information environments, can we influence him? In other words, can we change the way he thinks? Currently, it will be almost impossible to influence al-Zawahiri because he is constantly reinforcing and confirming his belief system. He is by now entirely entrenched in his rigid convictions. However, there are always incentives and here al-Zawahiri's characteristics prove instructive. We will not change his views, but if he were backed into a corner, he will do what is in his own best interest. This is where we may have some leverage. The incentives for his giving up and quietly disappearing can only work when he is near capture or when his power has been dissipated and his influence has become nominal.

That fact that he has an entrenched worldview should also not stop us from creating a perception that he is being influenced by foreign governments. First of all, evidence suggests that al-Zawahiri is self-interested, seeks power, and has his own agenda. Therefore, using HUMINT networks, a rumor could be started that al-Zawahiri is in negotiations with the Pakistani intelligence services for his surrender. The story could be that he was provided enticements such as cash and a guarantee of his safe passage and protection in a new country. Such a rumor plays upon perceptions of self-absorption. What also might be released is the discovery of a bogus bank account with a significant amount of money in it that can be credibly tied to al-Zawahiri. The precedent has already been set by the Islamic Group, which accused him of hording funds for his own personal gain.

While we are churning up the rumor mill, another tactic could be to play off the problems that al-Zawahiri is having with other individuals and groups in the network. The rumor already exists that al-Zawahiri got rid of Azzam and sold out al-Qamari and discredits critics. Let's take his conflict with al-Libi as an illustration. There might be another rumor that al-Libi and others he disagrees with are going to be eliminated. This will send some running to protect themselves, and if all goes well, they will turn on al-Zawahiri in the process. A network focused on perceptions of internal enemies is better than a network focused on external enemies. This could lead to his capture or to his elimination by members of his own network—as evidenced by the CIA's successful campaign that caused Abu Nidal to murder his own people.[68]

In conclusion, this chapter provided a framework for the analysis of leaders in armed groups. Understanding individual biographies and personalities is central to providing the means to influence or disrupt their activities. Human-source-intelligence activity and covert action are the key methods to learn about leaders as well as to manipulate their perceptions through active influence and disruption campaigns. Going about breaking any network requires a variety of methods, careful planning and consideration, a bit of deviousness, and, above all, creativity. But, as we have demonstrated, leaders of armed groups do have vulnerabilities. Focusing our campaign on these vulnerabilities and exploiting them to our advantage is one way to begin to break the network, individual by individual. Men like Duane "Dewey" Clarridge did it throughout the cold war, and we can do it again.[69]

NOTES

1. For a review of the literature see Martha Cottam, Beth Dietz-Uhler, Elena Mastors, and Tom Preston, *Introduction to Political Psychology* (NJ: Lawrence Erlbaum and Associates, 2004).

2. For more in-depth coverage of traits and motivation see ibid.

3. This framework was originally proposed in Elena Mastors, *Breaking al-Qaida* (forthcoming). Also presented is a more in-depth profile of al-Zawahiri.

4. Political psychologists define locus of control as the view of the world in which individuals do or do not perceive some degree of control over situations they are involved in. Self-confidence is an individual's sense of self-importance or image of ability to cope with the environment. For further discussion see Cottam et al., *Introduction to Political Psychology*.

5. Political psychologists define the need for power as the concern with establishing, maintaining, or restoring one's power, i.e., one's impact, control, or influence over others. The need for affiliation is concern with establishing, maintaining, or restoring warm and friendly relationships with other persons or groups. Task-interpersonal emphasis is the relative emphasis on getting the task done versus focusing on the feelings and needs of others. For further discussion see ibid.

6. Beliefs are defined as "associations people create between an object and its attributes." For further discussion see ibid.

7. Values are types of beliefs; they are "deeply held beliefs about what is right and wrong." For further discussion see ibid.

8. Whether or not a leader challenges constraints is especially relevant to the discussion of a leader's cognitive complexity. Determining both of these will allow further discussion of a leader's style. This is more fully addressed in the information environment section of the framework.

9. Image theory provides a framework for this analysis of perceptions of other groups. The theory encompasses perceptions about capabilities, culture, and the role of perception of threats and opportunities. It then explains strategic choices made by decision makers based on these perceptions of other groups. For further discussion see Martha Cottam, *Images and Intervention* (Pittsburgh, PA: University of Pittsburgh Press, 1994); and Cottam et al., *Introduction to Political Psychology*.

10. Political psychologists define distrust of others as a general feeling of doubt, uneasiness, and misgiving about others; inclination to suspect and doubt others' motives and actions. Ethnocentrism is defined as a view of the world in which one's own nation holds center stage; strong emotional ties to one's nation or group and emphasis on national or group honor and identity. For further discussion see Cottam et al., *Introduction to Political Psychology*.

11. Here the image model is also relevant.

12. Political psychologists define cognitive complexity as the ability to differentiate the environment, that is, the degree of differentiation a person shows in discussing other people, places, policies, ideas, or things. For further discussion see Cottam et al., *Introduction to Political Psychology*.

13. Ibid.

14. For further discussion see M. G. Hermann, T. Preston, and M. D. Young, "Who Leads Can Matter in Foreign Policymaking: A Framework for Leadership Analysis" (paper presented at the annual meeting of the International Studies Association, San Diego, CA, 1996); and Cottam et al., *Introduction to Political Psychology.*

15. Mark M. Lowenthal, *Intelligence: From Secrets to Policy* (Washington, DC: CQ Press, 2000), 67.

16. Stansfield Turner, *Terrorism and Democracy* (Boston: Houghton Mifflin, 1991), xii.

17. Stansfield Turner, *Ten Steps to Fight Terrorism without Endangering Democracy* (College Park: Center for International and Security Studies at Maryland School of Public Affairs, 2001), 18.

18. Some of the key legal boundaries to which American intelligence agencies must adhere are articulated in Executive Order no. 12,333, "United States Intelligence Activities," available at www.archives.gov/federal-register/codification/executive-order/12333.html; Department of Defense, *DoD Intelligence Activities,* DoD Directive 5240.01 (27 August 2007); *National Security Act of 1947, U.S. Code* 50, sec. 401; *Foreign Intelligence Surveillance Act (FISA) of 1978, U.S. Code* 50, secs. 1801–11, 1821–29, 1841–46, and 1861–62.

19. Finding and vetting various people is an ongoing process for human intelligence officers. The more recruited sources one has, the greater success at having the right one at the right time. "People may not have access [to leaders], but they do have access to others who have such access. They are potential 'spotters' of potential agents. And never forget that an officer running a spy program for whatever service always needs support agents—accommodation addresses, couriers, dead drop servicers, surveillants, safe house keepers, strong-arm men, etc." William R. Johnson, *Thwarting Enemies at Home and Abroad: How to Be a Counterintelligence Officer* (Bethesda: Stone Trail Press, 1987), 91.

20. Lowenthal, *Intelligence,* 211.

21. Duane Clarridge, speech about covert action (Smithsonian Associates, 27 January 1997), available at bss.sfsu.edu/fischer/IR%20360/Readings/Clarridge.htm (accessed 2 January 2008).

22. See Duane R. Clarridge, *A Spy for All Seasons: My Life in the CIA* (New York: Scribner, 1997), for an autobiographic memoir.

23. Ibid., 333–36.

24. Duane Clarridge, interview by Jeff Norwitz, July 2007.

25. For an excellent overview see Robert Cialdini, *The Psychology of Influence* (New York: Collins, 2007).

26. Nimrod Raphaeli, "Ayman Muhammad Rabi' Al-Zawahiri: The Making of an Arch-terrorist," *Terrorism and Political Violence* 14, no. 4 (Winter 2002): 1–22.

27. Ibid.

28. Montasser al-Zayyat, *The Road to Al-Qaeda* (London: Pluto, 2004), 16.

29. Raphaeli, "Ayman Muhammad Rabi' Al-Zawahiri," 3–5.

30. Ibid.

31. Ibid., 10.

32. Ibid., 12.

33. BBC News, "Profile: Ayman al-Zawahiri," 27 September 2004, news.bbc.co.uk/2/hi/middle_east/1560834.stm (accessed 11 September 2007).

34. Robert Windrem, "Who Is Ayman al-Zawahri?" MSNBC, 25 March 2004, www.msnbc.msn.com/id/4555901/ (accessed 11 September 2007).

35. Raphaeli, "Ayman Muhammad Rabi' Al-Zawahiri," 4.

36. Ibid., 7.

37. Al-Zayyat, *The Road to Al-Qaeda.*

38. Ibid., 29.

39. Y. Carmon, Y. Feldner, and D. Lav, "The Al-Gama'a Al-Islamiyya Cessation of Violence: An Ideological Reversal; MEMRI Inquiry and Analysis No. 309, December 22, 2006," Middle East Media Research Institute, available at memri.org/bin/articles.cgi?Page=archives&Area=ia&ID=IA30906 (accessed 21 September 2007).

40. Al-Zayyat, *The Road to Al-Qaeda*, 30.

41. Al-Zayyat, *The Road to Al-Qaeda*.

42. Raphaeli, "Ayman Muhammad Rabi' Al-Zawahiri," 6.

43. Ibid., 7.

44. Ibid., 8.

45. Ibid., 1–22.

46. Lawrence Wright, "The Man behind Bin Ladin," *The New Yorker*, 16 September 2002, available at www.lawrencewright.com/art-zawahiri.html (accessed 11 September 2007).

47. Raphaeli, "Ayman Muhammad Rabi' Al-Zawahiri," 9.

48. Rohan Gunaratna, *Inside Al Qaeda* (New York: Columbia, 2002).

49. Al-Zayyat, *The Road to Al-Qaeda*..

50. *Al-Sharq al-Wasat,* "Ayman al-Zawahiri's Book Knights under the Prophet's Banner," 12 December 2001.

51. Alan Cullison, "Inside Al-Qaeda's Hard Drive," *Atlantic Monthly*, 2004.

52. Specifically, al-Zawahiri views the United States through the imperial image. This image occurs when there is a perceived threat from another group that is perceived as superior in both capability and culture. For further discussion see Cottam et al., *Introduction to Political Psychology*.

53. "Al-Zawahiri: U.S. Faltering in Afghanistan," CNN, 9 September 2004, www.cnn.com/2004/WORLD/meast/09/09/zawahiri.tape/index.html (accessed 6 December 2007).

54. "Al Jazirah TV Airs Comments on Al-Zawahiri's 9 Sep Statement," 10 September 2004 (FBIS Document NES-2004-0910), available at cryptome.org/al-four.htm#Al-Jazirah%20Carries%20Al-Zawahiri's %20Recorded%20Videotape (accessed 11 September 2007).

55. Ayman al-Zawahiri, "Sheikh Ayman al-Zawahiri: The Hateful British and Their Indian Slaves (English Translation)," The Unjust Media, 17 July 2007, theunjustmedia.com/Islamic%Perspectives/Sheikh%20Ayman %20al-Zawahiri (accessed 1 September 2007).

56. Bruce Hoffman, "Outlook: Worse Than Bin Laden," *Washington Post*, 11 September 2007, available at www.washington post.com/wp-dyn/content/discussion/2007/09/07/DI20070907209 (accessed 12 September 2007).

57. Craig Whitlock, "Keeping Al-Qaeda in His Grip: Al-Zawahiri Presses Ideology, Deepens Rifts among Islamic Radicals," *Washington Post,* available at www.shockandawe.us/cms/index.php?option=com_content&task= view&id=32&Itemid=2 (accessed 11 September 2007).

58. Sami Yousafzai, Ron Moreau, Michael Hirsh, Jeffrey Bartholet, Mark Hosenball, Zahid Hussain, "Al Qaeda Family Feud," *Newsweek*, 30 July 2007.

59. Whitlock, "Keeping Al-Qaeda in His Grip."

60. Yousafzai et al., "Al Qaeda Family Feud."

61. Whitlock, "Keeping Al-Qaeda in His Grip."

62. Ibid.

63. Social psychologist Robert Cialdini argues that one of the key principles of influence is consistency. As Cialdini explains, "Once we have made a choice or taken a stand, we will encounter personal and interpersonal pressures to behave consistently with that commitment. Those pressures will cause us to respond in ways that justify our earlier decision." This comes straight out of the psychological literature on balance and

consistency as advanced by Leon Festinger, Fritz Heider, and others. Dissonance is considered an aversive state that results when an individual's behavior is inconsistent with his or her attitudes. Obviously, then, people are motivated to reduce the dissonant state once it occurs. Cialdini goes on to explain that commitment is also integral to consistency. As he argues, "If I can get you to make a commitment (that is, to take a stand, to go on record), I will have set the stage for your automatic and ill-considered consistency with that earlier commitment. Once a stand is taken, there is a natural tendency to behave in ways that are stubbornly consistent with the stand." For further discussion see Cialdini, *The Psychology of Influence.*

64. "How Did Al Qaeda Emerge in North Africa?" *Christian Science Monitor*, 1 May 2007, available at www .csmonitor.com/2007/0501/p12s01-wome.htm (accessed 5 May 2007).

65. Social psychologist Robert Cialdini argues that social proof is important to influence. Social proof is essentially the phenomenon that to find out what is indeed correct, we look to others. He goes on to elaborate: "This principle applies especially to the way we decide what constitutes correct behavior. We view a behavior as more correct in a given situation to the degree that we see others performing it. Whether the question is what to do with an empty popcorn box in a movie theater, how fast to drive on a certain stretch of highway, or how to eat chicken at a dinner party, the actions of those around us will be important in defining the answer." Scarcity is the phenomenon of "opportunities seem[ing] more valuable to us when their availability is limited." When something is scarce, we want it even more. "If something is rare, or it is becoming rare, we perceive it to be more valuable." For further discussion see Cialdini, *The Psychology of Influence.*

66. For a discussion about the importance of credibility of sources see Gerry Spence, *How to Argue and Win Every Time* (New York: St. Martin's, 1995).

67. Social psychologist Robert Cialdini argues that likability is important. For further discussion see Cialdini, *The Psychology of Influence.*

68. Clarridge, *A Spy for All Seasons,* 334–36.

69. Clarridge, interview.

25 Armed Groups through the Lens of Anthropology

David W. Kriebel

As this volume will attest, the study of armed groups cuts across many disciplines and is of interest to many government agencies, from the State Department to the CIA, and the consultants who assist them. Throughout the government, but especially in the military, there has been a renewed interest in understanding the cultural and religious factors behind the structures and activities of armed groups. While some of these agencies have always hired personnel with social science backgrounds, there has, of late, been an explicit turn to the discipline of cultural anthropology to provide such an understanding.

Anthropology has been called the most humanistic of the sciences and the most scientific of the humanities. In the United States, cultural (or sociocultural) anthropology is one of four subfields, the others being biological (or physical) anthropology, archaeology, and anthropological linguistics. While some anthropological analysis is quantitative, most is not. But qualitative data do yield useful insights and can be used to test hypotheses and construct theories. Such an approach is probably familiar to foreign service officers and intelligence analysts, many of whom come from social science or humanities backgrounds. However, for those who (like many military officers) are educated primarily in the physical sciences and engineering, it may be hard to understand how research that does not yield quantitative results can be useful.

Anthropologists have studied many kinds of armed groups, from indigenous warrior societies to organized-crime "families" to the militaries of various nations. The unique contribution of anthropology to the examination of armed groups is its cultural perspective. I suggest, therefore, that an armed group may be viewed as a social unit (or subsociety) existing within a larger society, with its own subculture shared by its members, yet embedded and subject to the norms of one or more wider cultures. What distinguishes such groups from other social units is their consistent use of violence, and their control mechanisms for the exercise of violence. It is tempting to exclude groups who exercise legitimate force (the military, police, state militias, and so forth) from this definition. However, such an exclusion would be based on the laws and

David W. Kriebel is an anthropologist and writer teaching in the National Security Decision Making Department at the U.S. Naval War College. He holds an MA and PhD in anthropology from the University of Pennsylvania, and a BA in archaeology from Haverford College. He has taught at the University of Maryland, Loyola College in Maryland, Villa Julie College, and Towson University. His research interests include the anthropology of religion, cognitive anthropology, and medical anthropology. He is currently performing ethnographic research on conceptions of martyrdom in the U.S. military. His latest book is *Powwowing among the Pennsylvania Dutch: A Traditional Medical Practice in the Modern World* (Penn State University Press, 2007).

political systems of particular nations (or societies) and not on any universally applicable criteria. Armed groups would include feuding clans, groups of bandits, street gangs, pirates, crime families and cartels, paramilitary organizations, revolutionary armies, and the armed forces of a state.

CULTURE AND ARMED GROUPS

If we understand an armed group as a social unit possessing a subculture, and if many armed groups are motivated by ideologies originating in or shaped by culture and religion, then anthropological views of culture and religion are useful in understanding the structures, values, and motivations of armed groups. There have been a number of anthropologically informed studies of such groups, a few of which will be presented in the next section.

All of these anthropologists, however, share one overall perspective: that human aggression, from warfare to recurrent feuding to violent crime, is based in culture, rather than biology. Our nearest living biological relatives, chimpanzees and gorillas, are more peaceful than humans. As Bronislaw Malinowski noted, "Human beings fight, not because they are biologically impelled, but because they are culturally induced."[1] Most anthropologists believe that warfare is also less frequent in simple societies than in complex ones[2] and that war is a factor in creating higher levels of social complexity.[3] However, some claim that war and other forms of organized violence have been common in societies of all levels of sophistication for thousands of years, and that anthropologists have systematically ignored evidence for war.[4]

But some societies appear more warlike than others. For instance, more "democratic" (participatory) societies seem to fight with each other less often than with less participatory ones, providing an extension of the "democratic peace hypothesis" applied to nation-states.[5] Anthropologists Melvin and Carol Ember went on to perform a statistical analysis of warfare using a cross-cultural sample.[6] According to their findings, the following factors were predictors of war, two of which were clearly cultural and two influenced by culture in the form of settlement type and pattern:

1. Resource problems, especially those created by a periodic natural disasters;
2. The threat of natural disasters;
3. Socialization for mistrust; and
4. Socialization with low need-satisfaction.

The importance of natural disasters in predicting war adds a new and pressing reason for rendering humanitarian assistance to regions struck by natural disasters. The quick intervention by U.S. forces following the 2004 Indian Ocean tsunami may well have headed off future conflict, as well as bolstering positive impressions of the United States in the mind of aid recipients. Interestingly, some expected predictors of war were not supported by Ember and Ember's statistical analysis. For instance, socialization for aggression was not a predictor for war but more likely to be a consequence of war. Nor was warfare in band and village societies caused by a shortage of women.

In a completely rational world, an armed group would be organized in such a way as to maximize its effectiveness against potential enemies and minimize the threat to the group. This standard is never met in practice, even in the militaries of nation-states.

Rather, other standards are adhered to, and, in most cases, these standards are influenced by culture.

Armed groups may be structured by laws and customs, kinship, prestige and charisma of various leaders, and the dictates of ideology, including religious beliefs. The People's Liberation Army under Mao, the Iranian Revolutionary Guard Corps, and the U.S. armed forces are all military groups, but structured quite differently. That difference is ideological. Kin relationships are crucial in the allocation of influence in a traditional Italian American crime family, but not in the Manson family. A charismatic leader such as Napoléon was required to hold the First French Empire together, but not modern France.

Attributes of groups that many laymen take as "givens," such as race and ethnicity, are actually culturally constructed, a fact now accepted in anthropology. Racial and ethnic divisions are very much in the eye of the beholder. In Northern Ireland, for instance, anthropologist Allen Feldman found that Protestant and Catholic groups have begun to depict each other as separate ethnic groups, and believe that they can "tell" who is who,[7] while a Greek American social scientist who visited there recently had great difficulty identifying the different groups, describing everyone as having blond hair and blue eyes. Consciousness of race and ethnicity is a powerful factor in stereotyping out-groups in ways that compare unfavorably with stereotypes constructed of one's in-group. It can lead to socialization for mistrust, which has been found to be a predictor of war.[8] Recent examples in which ethnicities were either created or emphasized and played into subsequent conflict are the Rwandan civil war, the Bosnian conflict, and the conflict between the "Aryan" Sinhalese and "Dravidian" Tamils in Sri Lanka.

THE LENSES OF ANTHROPOLOGISTS

Some of the studies of armed groups performed by anthropologists are described below. They are not meant to be complete summaries of the work that was done, but they do provide a feel for the central "lens" each anthropologist used to understand the beliefs, motivation, structure, or behavior of the armed group in question. The groups studied range from paramilitary organizations to criminal syndicates to national militaries.

1. The Lens of Kinship: Portrait of an Italian American Crime Family

From 1969 to 1971, anthropologist Francis Ianni was able to gain the trust of a crime family in New York that he called the "Lupollos" and obtained an astounding level of access to its members. Critics of his work claim that the family members misled Ianni or hid from him criminal activities, such as heroin trafficking and violence.[9] However, even if these objections are valid, they don't diminish the value of his work as a tool for understanding the crime family as a social unit, and not merely a business. Ianni describes relationships, the central values and motivators of family members, and how power and influence is distributed and maintained through kinship ties. He approached the problem of understanding the structure and activities of the family not as an intelligence analyst or undercover officer but as a field-worker employing classical ethnographic fieldwork techniques. And yet his work is useful to law enforcement agencies, not only because of his description of the family, its legal and illegal activities, its central values, and its kinship structure, but because his approach offers a corrective to the dominant social scientific model of organized crime, which likened criminal organizations to businesses or governments.

In fact, Ianni expressly challenged this "formal organization" model, articulated most forcefully and persuasively by sociologist Donald Cressey. This model suggests that crime families are rationally structured in order to create profits, and that they have a system of authority that is based on positions with job titles, endures beyond their existing personnel, and is designed for efficiency. As Ianni notes, however, this view of an Italian American crime family requires a major distortion of the facts on the ground:

> Secret criminal organizations like the Italian-American or Sicilian Mafia families are not formal organizations like governments or businesses. They are not rationally structured into statuses and functions in order to "maximize profits" and carry out tasks efficiently. Rather, they are traditional social systems, organized by action and by cultural values that have nothing to do with modern bureaucratic virtues.[10]

The most interesting aspect of Ianni's work is that he took the word "family" seriously, and approached the analysis in terms of social relationships. Kinship systems have been central to an understanding of small-scale societies researched by anthropologists. Just as an anthropologist working in a small-scale society has traditionally attempted to understand social organization through an analysis of kin relations, Ianni, through his own developing relationships with family members, came to understand how the Lupollo family likewise used kinship as the basis for its social organization. A significant part of his work was creating kinship charts for the family. He also found six rules regulating social organization:[11]

1. The family operates as a social unit with social organization and business functions merged.

2. All leadership positions, down to the "middle management" level, are assigned on the basis of kinship.

3. The higher the position in the organization, the closer the kinship relationship.

4. Leadership positions in the family are assigned to a central group of fifteen family members, all of whom have close consanguineal or affinal relationships which are reinforced by fictive godparental relationships, as well.

5. Members of the leadership group are assigned primarily to either legal or illegal enterprises, but not both.

6. Transfer of monies from illegal to legal and back into illegal activities takes place through individuals rather than companies and is part of the close kin-organization of the family.

An additional value of Ianni's work (and that of his wife, Elizabeth Reuss-Ianni) is that it examines organized crime in the United States as part of a wider American social system. Indeed, the Iannis have claimed that the emphasis on morality in U.S. culture is at the base of the success of organized crime. This is a viewpoint shared by many who suggest that it is the law that creates criminals.

It was toward the end of the Lupollo study that I became convinced that organized crime was a functional part of the American social system and should be viewed as one end of a continuum of business enterprises with legitimate business at the other end. But if this is so, why then is organized crime universally condemned while it is so widespread and so patently tolerated by the public and protected by the authorities? It seemed obvious that this contradiction is a structural means of resolving some of the conflicts, inconsistencies, and ambiguities that plague us because our desires and morals are so often in opposition. Organized crime, then, could be more than just a way of life; it could be a viable and persistent institution within American society, with its own symbols, its own beliefs, its own logic, and its own means of transmitting these attributes systematically from one generation to the next.[12]

In their research and writing, the Iannis take an almost neutral position on the activities of the Lupollos and other crime families, one quite common in anthropological studies grounded in a stance of cultural relativism, but one quite at odds with the goals of law enforcement, which is, by definition, emphatically *not* neutral. Indeed, a law enforcement officer might reasonably conclude that the Iannis' use of ethnographic practices such as obscuring identities of informants through the use of pseudonyms and changing dates and place-names in order to obtain more reliable information—a kind of reverse witness protection program—aids and abets criminals. However, the American Anthropological Association's Code of Ethics holds that an anthropologist is ethically bound to protect his informants, even if not officially covered under "human subject" protocols:

> Anthropological researchers have primary ethical obligations to the people, species, and materials they study and to the people with whom they work. These obligations can supersede the goal of seeking new knowledge, and can lead to decisions not to undertake or to discontinue a research project when the primary obligation conflicts with other responsibilities, such as those owed to sponsors or clients. . . . Anthropological researchers must determine in advance whether their hosts/providers of information wish to remain anonymous or receive recognition, and make every effort to comply with those wishes.[13]

This conflict of ethical codes is a problem that will potentially dog relationships between practicing anthropologists and all security-related agencies. In cases in which research concerns an organization that exists to commit crime, the anthropologist faces an acute problem: betray the trust of informants or withhold information that may help prevent or reduce crime.[14] Ianni chose to do the latter, reasoning that his major task was to understand the family's social organization, rather than its criminal activities, so he could justify excluding such data from his book.[15] However, two points are worth noting. First, his insight into the family came at a price—a promise not to report or ask questions about criminal activity. Second, Ianni admits that, while his fieldwork experience did not alter his opinion that the Mafia should be destroyed, it softened that opinion somewhat because of the "feelings of closeness and admiration" he had for the "old-style *mafioso* who was humble, taciturn, scrupulously moral in his living habits, and a man of honor."[16] Ianni's response is natural: most field-workers come to feel affection for the people they study. The question is, how does such a response affect the data, and decisions regarding its use? And in the case of analyzing crime, does the nature of the anthropologist's relationship with a criminal organization implicate him or her in its activities? The better the access, the better the data, and the more useful it is to law enforcement. Whether such access is worth a possible compromise of objectivity is a question every researcher must resolve in his or her own way.

2. The Lens of Cognitive Anthropology: The Khmer Rouge

Alex Hinton took a different approach when seeking to understand the motivations of the Khmer Rouge genocidal soldiers. To understand the attitudes of members of this armed group he decided to perform in-depth interviews of soldiers for the Pol Pot regime who actually participated in the mass murders of "the killing fields." It is not the stereotypical anthropological approach. For one thing, Hinton could not live among members of a group that had disbanded over two decades before he began his research. His approach was also conditioned by the extreme reluctance of Cambodians to talk about this painful period in their history, a reluctance particularly great on the part of those who carried out the atrocities. Rather than try to discuss these things with a wide range of people, he focused on persuading a few individuals—known as "key informants" in ethnography—to open up to him. These included the perpetrators, witnesses, and victims of genocide.

One of Hinton's major goals, in addition to laying out the ideological and social structure of the Khmer Rouge and their state of "Democratic Kampuchea," was to understand why people kill. He relied heavily on the emerging body of theory on cultural models, found in the subdiscipline of cognitive anthropology, to explain how ordinary people could not only kill but help commit mass murder and even kill in a particularly repugnant way. "Instituted models" are public cultural models, reproduced and reaffirmed by social institutions, while "mental models" are private, representing the individual's understanding and internalization of institutional models. Hinton's work revealed that the Khmer Rouge used traditional Cambodian mythological themes of disproportionate revenge; Buddhist conceptions of sin, punishment, and renunciation of attachments (removed from their original context, since Buddhism was banned); and models of "loyalty" and "revolutionary consciousness" not only to legitimize killing but to urge it in the service of the party. Loyalty and revolutionary consciousness became determiners of "face," or socio-centric self-image determined by the evaluations of others. This concept, always important in Cambodian society and linked to what we call "honor," assumed enormous influence in Democratic Kampuchea, where every action and thought was made public, and the private sphere, in which face was less directly at stake, radically shrank. Social evaluation was almost constant.[17]

The Khmer Rouge also used tactics of "genocidal priming" to crystallize and create differences among people where none existed before. Hinton likens the Khmer Rouge's use of such tactics to that of the Nazis, who "diagnosed" Germany's "illness" as caused by "the Jews."[18] In Democratic Kampuchea there were "new people" (urban dwellers forced into the country) and "old people" (peasants), "revolutionaries" and "reactionaries," "full rights people" and "depositees," the "worker-peasant class" and the "feudal-capitalist/landowning class." Some of the terminology of difference derived from Marxist-Leninist and Maoist ideologies, but those ideologies were also transformed by local cultural conditions:

[T]he Khmer Rouge [used] Buddhist terms like "mindfulness," "renunciation," and "dependent origination" to translate key Marxist-Leninist concepts to the invocation of Angkar [party organization], a multi-valent symbol with high modernist, Buddhist, and local valences. In particular, I have argued that a number of these ideological models were explicitly formulated to encourage mass violence, as illustrated in . . . the Khmer Rouge call for the destruction of "strings" of traitors, for "cutting off one's heart," for demonstrating one's "true loyalty" by killing "hidden enemies burrowing within," for carrying out one's "duty," and for disproportionate revenge.

By drawing upon preexisting, emotionally salient local knowledge, perpetrator regimes increase the "take" of their ideologies by increasing their comprehensibility and making them more compelling to their followers.[19]

Hinton suggests that the process of "take" creates "channels" that members of the armed group "tune" into when they are killing. Instituted ideological models also become mental models, though they are transformed in the mind of each individual. His harrowing account of how three Khmer Rouge killed one of their own comrades (who had committed the crime of digging up cassava roots) by taking him to the woods, removing his shirt, binding and blindfolding him, disemboweling him, and cooking and eating his liver illustrates in detail how symbols are mobilized and played out in a drama of killing. Nothing in Khmer Rouge (and certainly Marxist-Leninist) ideology required such an action. The victim was taken to a "liminal" space (outside the bounds of social structure), was dehumanized by being treated and thus rendered as an animal, and made animalistic sounds while his liver was removed. His debasement elevates his killers, making it easier to project the image of the "impure" enemy onto this scapegoat. The liver in Cambodian culture represents strength and resolve (something like "heart" does in American culture). Removing the liver of an enemy (who had "burrowed into" the fabric of society) and then cooking it (taking it from the world of the animal/enemy to the "civilized" world) is a ritual of purification. Once the enemy's strength and resolve is purified, the killers can eat it, and it becomes their strength—and that of their party.

Once killers become accustomed to killing, they become desensitized to the act and accustomed to obedience. Hinton brings in the well-known experiments of Stanley Milgram, in which "teachers" (the real test subjects) were ordered to shock "learners" (really actors) to illustrate this point. But then they make that act of killing their own, as the liver-eating episode demonstrates, using ideological models they have accepted and internalized.

3. The Lens of Critical Anthropology: Protestant Paramilitary Groups in Northern Ireland

Jeffrey Sluka's ethnographic work among Catholic populations in Northern Ireland was the stimulus for this study of Protestant death squads in Belfast. He asked the Catholics what he should study and this was their overwhelming choice. Sluka was involved with two Catholic victims groups—Silent No More and Relatives for Justice—whose business is publicizing such crimes. But could such a study be objective? Sluka addresses this question:

While the research reported here represents the victims' perspective, if the essence of objectivity is gathering the available evidence and letting it lead to conclusions, than [*sic*] the ethnographic overview of Loyalist death squads in the culture of terror presented here is an objective view with the facts on the ground in Northern Ireland. Nonetheless, I think there is no academic or other dishonor in being prepared to stand with the victims of oppression and state terror.[20]

Sluka's response is not exactly reassuring. His use of terms like "death squads," "culture of terror," "oppression," and "state terror" is highly prejudicial. How does he fare with the "facts on the ground"? He takes numbers of deaths from 1969 to 1994, provided by O'Duffy and broken down by victim and perpetrator, and focuses on the 806 Catholic civilians killed by Loyalist and security forces (ignoring the 192 killed by [Catholic] Irish Republican groups), and claims that this represents a war by the Loyalists and security forces (the latter of which killed 144) against the civilian population. A case can certainly be made that Loyalists are targeting Catholic civilians, and from the accounts he presents, that seems to be the case. But it is invalid to include the security forces and not the various Irish Republican Army (IRA) groups. Why is a group that kills 144 civilians making war against them, when another that kills 192 is not? Because 806 Catholic civilians were killed by Protestants, Sluka says this group is most at risk of dying. But he could have ordered the data differently. Since 571 Protestant civilians and 1,045 members of the overwhelmingly Protestant security forces were killed, could he not have said that Protestants were most at risk?

Sluka makes claims that the British government had a deliberate policy of supporting Protestant "death squads" and used "psychological warfare" and "big lie" propaganda tactics to cover it up. His evidence for this is that some members of the security forces were also members of paramilitaries, a fact Britain admits but suggests that such individuals were rogues and not acting on orders. To counter this assertion, Sluka cites sources from a range of partisan Catholic groups, including Sinn Fein—the political arm of the IRA—without explaining why these should be any more worthy of trust than pro-Loyalist and British sources. And he himself also deploys propaganda in his analysis. His use of the terms "death squads" (comparing Protestant paramilitary violence to notorious Central and South American political murder groups) and "killing fields" (evoking the Khmer Rouge genocide) is calculated to provoke outrage on the part of the reader.

Sluka's bias and reliance on partisan Catholic sources makes it difficult to accept his accusations that Britain has adopted a deliberate policy of "state terror" that targets Catholic civilians. He justifies this bias as "an attempt to write against terror through a critical 'new anthropology' combining perspectives from progressive streams in the discipline."[21] The term "progressive" is, itself, a term of propaganda, implying that those who don't agree with this "new anthropology"—presumably practitioners of "old" anthropology—are somehow thwarting progress. He says that he relied on sources such as Silent Too Long, Relatives for Justice, and Sinn Fein "not only for information, but also for enlightenment and inspiration."[22] But Elena Mastors, a social scientist who recently worked among members of Protestant paramilitaries, notes that the British government had been running operations against the Protestant groups, trying to play one against the other. While she confirmed that some British officials had aided Protestant groups, she reports that these contacts and channels of assistance were strictly informal and not sanctioned by the British government.[23]

Sluka declares the source of his bias—he not only performed fieldwork in Catholic neighborhoods but lived in a house that had been attacked by Loyalists three times and was "under constant threat of random sectarian assassination by Loyalist death squads."[24] It is likely that, having lived under such conditions and received, as he says, warnings from Catholic friends not to venture near Protestant neighborhoods for fear of being killed, he developed a sense of solidarity and identification with the Catholic population. One wonders if his analysis would have been radically different had he lived in a Protestant neighborhood and been "under constant threat" of IRA violence.

Does all this render Sluka's work valueless in understanding the structure and culture of Protestant paramilitaries? Not entirely. Embedded within his biased analysis are facts that can be used to come to grips with the problem. Certainly he explains who the main groups are, includes photographs of their symbolism and iconography (revealed in wall murals), and documents their activities. Moreover, it also provides a clear picture of Catholic views of and emotional reactions to such groups, the coping strategies employed by a population under threat, and, in his citations of Sinn Fein and other Republican sources, what Protestant paramilitaries want people to know about them. It also demonstrates that the products of this "critical new anthropology," which eschews a neutral approach to its subject matter, must not be accepted uncritically.

CONCLUDING REMARKS

The need for military and government professionals to acquire an understanding of culture and religion has never been more clear—or more pressing—than today. We live in a multipolar world of joint and combined environments, transnational terrorism fueled by appeals to religion, globalized criminal enterprises, sustained counterinsurgency operations, and large-scale humanitarian assistance and disaster relief operations. Senior officials recognize this need and are taking steps to ensure that future leaders and those who advise them will be culturally competent. Anthropology is the discipline most obviously relevant to answering this need. Some have said that anthropology is just as important in winning the war on terror as physics was in winning World War II.

Others are not so convinced. Neither are many—probably most—anthropologists, who have concluded that the discipline should not assist the security establishment at all, citing instances in which the relationship compromised field-workers and implicated anthropology as a tool of U.S. foreign policy and even oppression. Indeed, anthropologists who work in security-related jobs face ostracism from their professional colleagues—a major disincentive for any anthropologist contemplating such employment.

It is naive to imagine that each culture comes with a rule book, that adapting to diverse cultural environments means simply getting the "gouge" on whatever society we find ourselves engaging. Nor should we become excessively focused on specific cultures, to the exclusion of others. It is true that there are cultural and religious rules for behavior (norms), and it is also true that both culture and religion shape how a person sees the world. Culture creates a "taken for granted" reality and so does religion, though that reality is not always what is codified in creeds and official ideologies. But many other noncultural factors, such as genetics, the influence of family and friends, environmental stresses, and lived experience, play into the formation of beliefs and behaviors.

The lenses anthropologists use in analyzing armed groups and armed conflict are conditioned by concepts and ideas found in their definitions of culture and religion. Culture can be viewed a "complex whole" of beliefs, behaviors, and artifacts (the holistic perspective), a set of rules (the cognitive perspective), or a constructed social world (the constructivist perspective). If one is interested in treating an armed group as a social unit (such as a family or political entity), one might draw on traditional anthropological definitions of culture, which focus on social systems, such as kinship and political structure. If the goal is examining cultural influences on the individual member of an armed group, one may use a cognitive perspective that speaks of instituted and mental models. If one wants to examine the role of religion (or religious surrogates, such as Khmer Rouge ideology) in the formation of an armed group, it is essential to understand the myths, rituals, and symbolism employed by that group to activate members' aggressive impulses or even prime them for genocide.

The nature of anthropological work requires, at a minimum, observation and interviewing and, in many cases, participation as well. The ethnographic method of participant observation helps researchers acquire a "feel" for the insider ("emic") perspective, as opposed to a strictly outside ("etic") perspective.[25] It can be difficult to balance the need to have a meaningful experience as a participant and the need to record and analyze the experience as an observer. In dealing with an armed group this balance is particularly hard to maintain because the stakes are so high, and so are the emotions engaged. In many cases it is hard to remain neutral—and indeed, some anthropologists who favor a "critical" anthropology claim that neutrality is impossible.

The anthropological lens can bring to bear concepts of culture and religion on armed groups. But the lenses are themselves created and shaped by cultural and psychological processes, and by views on religion, and so have their limitations. The use of anthropological insight in studying armed groups and conflict is beneficial. Naive reliance on those insights is not.

NOTES

1. Bronislaw Malinowski, "War—Past, Present, and Future," in *War as a Social Institution,* ed. J. D. Clarkson and T. C. Cochran (New York: Columbia University Press, 1941), 21–31.

2. Robert Carneiro, "War and Peace: Alternating Realities in Human History," in *Studying War: Anthropological Perspectives,* ed. S. P. Reyna and R. E. Downs (Amsterdam: Gordon and Breach, 1994), 3–27; R. Brian Ferguson, "A Reputation for War," *Anthropology 97/98,* ed. Elvio Angeloni (Guilford, CT: Dushkin/Brown & Benchmark, 1997), 76–77.

3. R. Brian Ferguson, "General Consequences of War," in *Studying War: Anthropological Perspectives,* ed. S. P. Reyna and R. E. Downs (Amsterdam: Gordon and Breach, 1994), 85–111.

4. Steven A. LeBlanc, *Constant Battles: The Myth of the Peaceful, Noble Savage* (New York: St. Martin's, 2003).

5. Carol R. Ember, Melvin Ember, and Bruce Russett, "Peace between Participatory Polities: A Cross-cultural Test of the 'Democracies Rarely Fight Each Other' Hypothesis," *World Politics* 44 (1992): 573–99.

6. Melvin Ember and Carol R. Ember, "Cross-cultural Studies of War and Peace: Recent Achievements and Future Possibilities," in *Studying War: Anthropological Perspectives*, ed. S. P. Reyna and R. E. Downs (Amsterdam: Gordon and Breach, 1994).

7. Pamela Stewart and Andrew Strathern, *Violence: Theory and Ethnography* (London and New York: Continuum Publishing, 2002), 45. As Stewart and Strathern note, the same phenomenon was present in Rwanda and Burundi (ibid.).

8. Ember and Ember, "Cross-cultural Studies of War and Peace."

9. Margaret Beare, *Criminal Conspiracies: Organized Crime in Canada* (Toronto: Nelson Canada, 1996), 25.

10. Francis A. J. Ianni, *A Family Business: Kinship and Social Control in Organized Crime* (New York: Russell Sage Foundation, 1972), 108.

11. Ibid., 154.

12. Francis A. J. Ianni, *Black Mafia: Ethnic Succession in Organized Crime* (New York: Simon and Schuster, 1974), 15.

13. "Code of Ethics of the American Anthropological Association," American Anthropological Association, www.aaanet.org/committees/ethicscode.pdf (accessed 14 February 2008).

14. Ianni himself has served as a consultant to law enforcement. It is not clear whether his reluctance to publish "things [he] was not intended to see" continued while he was in this position.

15. Ianni, *A Family Business*, 189.

16. Ibid., 191.

17. Alexander Laban Hinton, *Why Did They Kill? Cambodia in the Shadow of Genocide* (Berkeley: University of California Press, 2005), 258.

18. Ibid., 29.

19. Ibid., 287.

20. Jeffrey A. Sluka, "'For God and Ulster': The Culture of Terror and Loyalist Death Squads in Northern Ireland," in *Death Squad: The Anthropology of State Terror* (Philadelphia: University of Pennsylvania Press, 2000), 132.

21. Ibid., 128.

22. Ibid., 130.

23. Author's interview with Dr. Elena Mastors, whose investigative findings on the Protestant paramilitaries will be published in a forthcoming book.

24. Sluka, "'For God and Ulster,'" 129.

25. This emic/etic terminology derives from linguistics: phonemic versus phonetic. Phonemics focuses on meaning (a phoneme is defined as the smallest meaningful unit of sound), while phonetics examines the sounds themselves.

Part Five

The Shape of Things to Come

26 Children on the Battlefield: The Breakdown of Moral Norms

P. W. Singer

As U.S. forces advanced into Saddam Hussein's Iraq in April 2003, the fighting had turned out to be far more intense than planned. One of the unexpected holdups came in Karbala', a city of roughly 550,000 that is 50 kilometers to the southeast of Baghdad. Karbala' was expected to be a more easy take than most cities as its population was largely Shiite, who had long opposed the dictator. Indeed, Karbala' was considered one of the most holy cities in Shia Islam, being the site of a historic battle in AD 680, in which Husayn ibn Ali, the grandson of the Prophet Muhammad, and his entire family were killed.

Before the war, Vice President Cheney would famously repeat in many speeches the prediction made by historian Fouad Ajami: that the American troops would be greeted with "kites and boomboxes." On that April afternoon, no kites were flying and the booms filling the air certainly weren't from music. As they worked their way, street by street, through the residential neighborhoods of Karbala', the troops of the 101st Airborne Division, the famed "Screaming Eagles," had been under intense machine-gun and

Peter Warren Singer is senior fellow and director of the 21st Century Defense Initiative at the Brookings Institution. He is the youngest scholar named senior fellow in Brookings's 90-year history. He has written for the full range of major media and journals, including the *Los Angeles Times, New York Times, Washington Post, Foreign Affairs, Current History, Survival, International Security, Parameters,* and the *World Policy Journal.* He has provided commentary on military affairs for nearly every major TV and radio outlet, including ABC's *Nightline,* Al Jazeera, BBC, CBS's *60 Minutes,* CNN, FOX, NPR, and the NBC *Today Show.* His first book, *Corporate Warriors: The Rise of the Privatized Military Industry* (Cornell University Press, 2003), was the first to explore the new industry of private companies providing military services for hire, an issue that soon became important with the use and abuse of these companies in Iraq. Dr. Singer's most recent book, *Children at War* (Pantheon, 2005), explores the rise of another new force in modern warfare, child-soldier groups. This was the first book to comprehensively explore the compelling and tragic rise of child-soldier groups and was recognized by the 2006 Robert F. Kennedy Memorial Book of the Year Award. His commentary on the issue was featured in a variety of venues ranging from NPR and Fox News to *Defense News* and *People* magazine. Dr. Singer has served as a consultant on the issue to the U.S. Marine Corps and Congress, and the recommendations in his book resulted in changes in the UN peacekeeping training program. An accompanying A&E/History Channel documentary, "Child Warriors," was broadcast in 2008. Prior to his current position, Dr. Singer was founding director of the Project on U.S. Policy towards the Islamic World at the Saban Center at Brookings. He has also worked for the Belfer Center for Science and International Affairs at Harvard University, the Balkans Task Force in the U.S. Department of Defense, and the International Peace Academy. Singer received his PhD in government from Harvard University and previously attended the Woodrow Wilson School of Public and International Affairs at Princeton University. Dr. Singer's next research project, "Wired for War," will look at the implications of robotics and other new technologies for war in the 21st century.

rocket-propelled-grenade (RPG) fire for the whole day. Gunfight followed gunfight and several troopers were wounded and assorted vehicles, including a Bradley armored fighting vehicle, were knocked out of action.

In the midst of the fighting, a young boy scrambled from an alleyway. An American machine gunner saw that the boy, who would later turn out to be 10 years old, was carrying an RPG. In a nanosecond, in the midst of bullets flying at him, the 21-year-old soldier had to make what would surely be the toughest decision of his life. "I took him out," he later said; "I laid down quite a few bursts." The boy fell dead.

After the battle ended, and there was time to think, the soldier reflected on the episode. "Anybody that can shoot a little kid and not have a problem with it, there is something wrong with them," he said, smoking a cigarette. "Of course I had a problem with it. [But] [a]fter being shot at all day, it didn't matter if you were a soldier or a kid, these RPGs are meant to hurt us. . . . I did what I had to do."[1]

THE SHORT HISTORY OF CHILDREN AND WAR

When we think of warfare, children rarely come to mind. Indeed, war is assumed to be a place for only the strong and willing, from which the young, the old, the infirm, and the innocent are not only excluded but supposed to be afforded special protections.

This exclusion of children from warfare held true in almost every traditional culture. For example, in precolonial African armies, the general practice was that the warriors typically joined three to four years after puberty. In the Zulu tribe, for instance, it was not until the ages of 18 to 20 that members were eligible for *ukubuthwa* (the drafting or enrollment into the tribal regiments).[2] In the Kano region of west Africa, only married men were conscripted, as those unmarried were considered too immature for such an important and honored task as war.[3] When children of lesser ages did serve in ancient armies, such as the enrollment of Spartan children into military training at ages seven to nine, they typically did not serve in combat. Instead, they carried out more menial chores, such as herding cattle or bearing shields and mats for the more senior warriors. In absolutely no cases were traditional tribes or ancient civilizations reliant on fighting forces made up of young boys or girls.

This exclusion of children from war was not simply a matter of principle, but raw pragmatism. Adult strength and often lengthy training were needed to use premodern weapons and would continue to be needed well into the age of firearms. It also reflected the general importance of age in many political organizations. Most traditional cultures relied on a system of age grades for their ruling structures. These were social groupings determined by age cohorts, and they cut across ties created by kinship and common residence. Such a system enabled senior rulers and tribal elders to maintain command over their younger—and potentially unruly—subjects.

But while warfare has long been the domain of adults, there were times in military history that children did appear. Boy pages helped arm and maintain the knights of medieval Europe, while drummer boys and "powder monkeys" (small boys who ran ammunition to cannon crews) were a requisite part of many an army and navy in the seventeenth and eighteenth centuries. The key is that these boys fulfilled minor or ancillary support roles and were not considered as true combatants. They neither dealt out death nor were considered legitimate targets. Indeed, Henry V was so angered at the breaking of this rule at the battle of Agincourt (1415), where some of his army's boy pages were killed, that he, in turn, slaughtered all his French prisoners.

Indeed, perhaps the most-well-known use of supposed child-soldiers in history, the famous "Children's Crusade," is somewhat of a myth. The reality is that the "crusade" was actually a march of thousands of unarmed boys from northern France and western Germany, who thought they could take back the Holy Land by the sheer power of their faith. Most never left Europe, and of those that did, all but a few were sold into slavery by unscrupulous ship captains.

While the rule held that children were not to be soldiers, there were some exceptions in the grand span of history. Small numbers of underage children certainly lied about their ages to join armies. In addition, a few states sent out children to fight in their last gasps of defeat. Perhaps the most notable instance in American history was the participation by Virginia Military Institute cadets at the Civil War battle of New Market. In May 1864, Union forces marched up the Shenandoah Valley, hoping to cut the Virginian Central railroad, a key supply line. Southern general John Breckenridge found himself with the only Confederate force in the area, commanding just 1,500 men. So, he ordered the corps of cadets from the nearby VMI military academy to join him. They were 247 strong (roughly 25 were 16 years or younger) and waited out most of the battle until its final stages. Then, in a fairly dramatic charge, they overran a key Union artillery battery. Ten cadets were killed and 45 were wounded. Ultimately, though, their role was for naught. Within the year, the Union would capture the Shenandoah and with it soon the rest of the Confederacy.[4]

Most recently, the *Hitler Jugend* (Hitler Youth) similarly were young boys who had received quasi-military training as part of a political program to maintain Nazi rule through indoctrination. Through most of the Second World War, the youths only joined German military forces (including the SS, for which the *Jugend* was a feeder organization) once they reached the age of maturity. However, when Allied forces invaded German territory in the final months of the war, Hitler's regime ordered these boys to fight as well. It was a desperate gambit to hold off the invasion until new "miracle" weapons (like the V-2 rocket and Me-262 jet fighter) could turn the tide. Lightly armed and mostly sent out in small ambush squads, scores of Hitler Youth were killed in futile small-scale skirmishes, all occurring after the war had essentially been decided.[5]

However, these were the exceptions to what the rule used to be: that children had no place in war. Throughout the last 4,000 years of war as we know it, children were never an integral, essential part of any military forces in history. Their use as soldiers was isolated in time, geographic space, and scope. No one rushed out to copy these examples, and they did not weigh greatly in how wars began, were fought, or ended. At best, they were footnotes in military history.

THE RISE OF CHILD SOLDIERS

The nature of armed conflict, though, has changed greatly in the past few years. Now the presence of children is the new rule of standard behavior in war, rather than the rarity that it used to be. The result is that war in the twenty-first century is not only more tragic but more dangerous. With children's involvement, generals, warlords, terrorists, and rebel leaders alike are finding that conflicts are easier to start and harder to end.

The practice of using children, defined under international law as under the age of 18, as soldiers is far more widespread, and more important, than most realize. There are as many as 300,000 children under the age of 18 presently serving as combatants around the globe (making them almost 10 percent of all global combatants.) They serve in 40 percent of the world's armed forces, rebel groups, and terrorist organizations and fight in almost 75 percent of the world's conflicts; indeed, in the last decade, children have served as soldiers on every continent but Antarctica. Moreover, an additional half million children serve in armed forces not presently at war.[6]

Some try to quibble, by raising questions of the cultural standards of maturity, that child soldiers are not actually children. The problem with this tack is that the 18-year cut-off is not simply a Western construct, as many warlords and apologists for child-soldier users would have it. Rather it is the international legal standard for childhood, agreed upon by over 190 states and the most widely signed international law. It is also the age that almost every state in the world uses in its own legislation for the award or withholding of public rights and responsibilities such as when one can vote or when one receives free education or health care. Finally, it was also a historic standard for a range of premodern armies and modern armies (such as the 1813 Rules and Regulations for the U.S. Army).

More important, the youth in question cover a range that no sane person would deny is both underage and inappropriate for involvement in war. Eighty percent of those conflicts where children are present include fighters under the age of 15; 18 percent of the world's armed organizations have used children 12 years and under. The average ages of child soldiers found by two separate studies, one in Southeast Asia and one in central Africa, was just under 13. The youngest-ever child soldier was an armed five-year-old in Uganda.

The mass presence of girls in many forces also differs the present trend from any historic parallels. While no girls served in groups like the powder monkeys or Hitler Youth, roughly 30 percent of the armed forces that employ child soldiers today also include girl soldiers; underage girls have been present in the armed forces in 55 countries. In 27 of these, girls were abducted to serve and in 34 of these they saw combat. These girl soldiers are often singled out for sexual abuse, including by their own commanders, and have a harder time reintegrating back into society when the wars end.

With the rise of this practice, Western forces have increasingly come into conflict with child-soldier forces. The first notable instance was the British Operation Barras in Sierra Leone in 2000. There, British SAS (Special Air Service) fought a pitched battle against the "West Side Boys," a teen militia that had taken hostage a squad of British Army troops. As an observer noted, "You cannot resolve a situation like this with a laser-guided bomb from thirty thousand feet."[7] Ultimately, the hostage crisis was ended by a helicopter raid led by elite British SAS special forces. The hostages were rescued, but the subsequent battle was, as one observer put it, "brutal." One British soldier was killed and 12 more wounded. Estimates of dead among the West Side Boys ranged from 25 up to 150.

Much as terrorism is the "weapon of the weak," so have the weakest of society been pulled into this realm as well. Captured al Qaeda training videos reveal young boys receiving instruction in the manufacture of bombs and the setting of explosive booby traps. Palestinian Islamic Jihad and HAMAS have recruited children as young as 13 to be suicide bombers and children as young as 11 to smuggle explosives and weapons. At least 30 suicide bombing attacks have been carried out by youths since the fighting in Israel-Palestine sparked up again in 2000.[8] The most tragic example perhaps was a semi-retarded 16-year-old, who was convinced by HAMAS to strap himself with explosives. He was caught by Israeli police in the town of Nablus, just before he was to blow himself up at an army checkpoint.[9]

It is important to note, though, that neither terrorism nor children's roles in it are a uniquely Muslim or Middle East phenomenon. For example, the youngest-ever-reported terrorist was a nine-year-old boy in Colombia, sent by the ELN rebel group to bomb a polling station in 1997.[10] Likewise, when radical Muslim groups began to use child suicide bombers, they were not actually breaking any new ground. Instead, they were following the lead of the Liberation Tigers of Tamil Eelam (LTTE), also known as the "Tamil Tigers," in Sri Lanka, which has consistently been one of the most innovative of terrorist groups. The LTTE, which utilized suicide bombers to kill both the Indian prime minister and the Sri Lankan president and pioneered the tactic of crashing planes into buildings later repeated on 9/11, even has manufactured specialized denim jackets designed to conceal explosives, tailored in smaller sizes for child suicide bombers.[11]

THE U.S. EXPERIENCE WITH CHILD SOLDIERS

With the global deployment of U.S. military force after 9/11, from Afghanistan to the Philippines, child soldiers are present in every conflict zone U.S. forces now operate in. Indeed, the very first U.S. soldier killed in the war on terrorism was a Green Beret killed by a 14-year-old sniper in Afghanistan. At least six young boys between the ages of 13 and 16 were captured by U.S. forces in Afghanistan in the initial fighting and were taken to the detainee facility at Guantánamo Bay, Cuba.[12] They were housed in a special wing entitled "Camp Iguana." As the Pentagon took more than a year to figure out whether to prosecute or rehabilitate them, the kids spent their days in a house on the beach converted into a makeshift prison, watching DVDs and learning English and math.[13] In addition, several more in the 16- to 18-year range are thought to be held in the regular facility for adult detainees at "Camp X-Ray." U.S. soldiers continue to report facing child soldiers in Afghanistan to this day; the youngest on the record is a 12-year-old boy, who was captured after being wounded during a Taliban ambush of a convoy.[14]

In Iraq, the problem has quietly grown worse. Under the regime of Saddam Hussein, Iraq built up an entire apparatus designed to pull children into the military realm and bolster his control of the populace. This included the *Ashbal Saddam* ("Saddam's Lion Cubs"), a paramilitary force of boys between the ages of 10 and 15 that acted as a feeder into the noted *Saddam Fedayeen* units. The *Fedayeen* were a paramilitary organization led by Saddam's son Uday and proved more aggressive than the Iraqi Army in fighting U.S. invasion forces; their remnants now make up one of the contending insurgent forces.

During the invasion, American forces fought with Iraqi child soldiers from these groups in at least three cities (Nasariya, Mosul, and Karbala').[15]

Beaten on the battlefield, rebel leaders then sought to mobilize this cohort of trained and indoctrinated young fighters for the insurgency. A typical incident took place in the contentious city of Mosul just after the invasion and provided a worrisome indicator of the threat to come. Here, in the same week that President Bush made his infamous "Mission Accomplished" aircraft carrier landing, an Iraqi 12-year-old boy fired on U.S. Marines with an AK-47 rifle.[16] Over the next weeks and months, incidents increased between U.S. forces and armed Iraqi children—ranging from child snipers to a 15-year-old who tossed a grenade in an American truck, blowing off the leg of a U.S. Army trooper.[17]

By the time fighting picked up intensity starting in spring 2004, child soldiers served not only in Saddam loyalist forces but also in both radical Shia and Sunni rebel groups. Radical cleric Muqtada al Sadr directed a revolt that consumed the primarily Shia south of Iraq, with the fighting in the holy city of An Najaf being particularly fierce. Observers noted multiple child soldiers serving in al Sadr's "Mahdi Army." One 12-year-old boy proudly proclaimed, "Last night I fired a rocket-propelled grenade against a tank. The Americans are weak. They fight for money and status and squeal like pigs when they die. But we will kill the unbelievers because faith is the most powerful weapon."[18] Indeed, Sheikh Ahmad al-Shebani, al Sadr's spokesman, didn't try to deny the war crime of using children but publicly defended the practice, stating, "This shows that the Mahdi are a popular resistance movement against the occupiers. The old men and the young men are on the same field of battle."[19]

Coalition forces also have increasingly faced child soldiers in the dangerous "Sunni Triangle" as well. Marines fighting in the battle to retake Falluja in November 2004 reported numerous instances of being fired upon by "children with assault rifles" and, just like the soldier during the invasion, wrestled with the dilemmas this presented.

The overall numbers of Iraqi children presently involved in the fighting are not known. But the indicators are that they do play a significant and growing role in the insurgency. For example, in 2004, some 107 Iraqi juveniles determined to be "high risk" security threats were held at the infamous Abu Ghraib prison.[20] In 2007, there were some 800 juvenile detainees between the ages of 11 and 16 held at coalition facilities in Iraq, and an al Qaeda in Iraq (AQI) video showed young boys being trained in assassination and kidnapping.[21] U.S. forces have faced particular problems with groups using children as spotters for ambushes, and also as cover for infiltration, such as having children sit in what are called by the troops "VBIEDs," short for vehicle borne improvised explosive devices. When children are present, such car bombs look less suspicious and are more likely to make it through checkpoints. A new development during the 2007 "surge" of forces is that soldiers have reported that Shiite militias in Baghdad have organized gangs made up of more than 100 kids, as young as six years old. The children throw rocks, bricks, and fire bombs at convoys, but are actually coordinated with snipers, with the idea to draw any patrols that respond into ambushes.

THE CAUSES AND PROCESSES OF CHILD SOLDIERS

The new presence of children on the twenty-first-century battlefield emerged from three intertwined forces. The first is the dark side of globalization, which has led to a new pool of potential recruits. We are living through the most prosperous period in human history, but many are being left behind. Demographic changes, global social instability, and the legacy of multiple civil and sectarian conflicts entering their second and third generations all act to weaken states and undermine societal structures. Just as examples, more than 40 million African children will lose one or both of their parents from HIV-AIDS by 2010, while the United Nations High Commissioner for Refugees (UNHCR) estimates that there are more than 25 million children uprooted from their homes by war. Such orphans and refugees are particularly at risk for being pulled into war.

However, while there have always been dispossessed and disconnected children, changes in weapons technology act as an enabler, allowing this pool to be tapped as a new source of military labor. In particular, the proliferation of light, simple, and cheap small arms have played a primary role. Such "child portable" weapons as the AK-47 have been lightened by plastics, can be bought for the price of a goat or chicken in many countries, and are deceptively easy to learn to use. With just a half hour's worth of instruction, a 10-year-old can wield the firepower of an entire Civil War regiment.

Finally, context matters. We are living through an exceptional period of flux and breakdown of global order, especially with the spread of warlordism and failed states. This change has made possible a new mode of war. Wars are driven less by politics than things as simple as religious hate or personal profit through seizing diamond mines. From Foday Sankoh in Sierra Leone to Mullah Omar in Afghanistan, local warlord leaders now see the new possibility of (and, unfortunately, advantages in) converting vulnerable, disconnected children into low-cost and expendable troops, who fight and die for their own causes.

The groups pull in children through recruiting techniques that take advantage of children's desperation and immaturity, or just through good old-fashioned kidnapping and abduction.

Those of us living in stable, wealthy states have difficulty understanding how children can be convinced to join and fight for an army, especially if they don't even understand or believe in the cause. But try to imagine yourself as an orphan, living on the street, not knowing where your next meal will come from. A group then offers you not only food and safety but an identity, as well as the empowerment that comes from having a gun in your hand. Or imagine the temptation you might have if a group of older boys wearing natty uniforms and cool sunglasses were to show up at your school and force all the teachers to bow down to show who is "really in charge." They then invite you to join them, with the promise that you too can wield such influence. Or imagine what you would do if you experienced what happened to this seven-year-old boy in Liberia when a group of armed men showed up at his village. "The rebels told me to join them, but I said no," he later recalled. "Then they killed my smaller brother. I changed my mind."

When children are brought into war, they are usually run through training programs that range from weeks of intense adult-style boot camp to a few minutes' instruction in how to fire a gun. Indoctrination, political or religious, can include such "tests" as forcing the kids to kill animals or human prisoners, including even neighbors or fellow children, both to inure them to the sight of blood and death and to disconnect them from their old identities. Many are forced to take drugs to further desensitize them. As Corinne Dufka of Human Rights Watch describes the practice in west Africa, "It seemed to be a very organised strategy of . . . breaking down their defences and memory, and turning them into fighting machines that didn't have a sense of empathy and feeling for the civilian population."

The result is that kids, even those who may have once been unwilling captives, can be turned into quite fierce and skilled fighters. A typical story is that of a young boy in Sierra Leone, who tells, "I was attending primary school. The rebels came and attacked us. They killed my mother and father in front of my eyes. I was 10 years old. They took me with them. . . . They trained us to fight. The first time I killed someone, I got so sick, I thought I was going to die. But I got better. . . . My fighting name was Blood Never Dry."[22]

THE CONSEQUENCES OF CHILDREN ON THE BATTLEFIELD

Beyond just the raw human tragedy, the ramifications of this "child-soldier doctrine" for war itself are quite scary.

First and foremost, it means that unpopular armies and rebel groups are able to field far greater forces than they would be otherwise, through using children as cheap and easy-to-obtain recruits.

Indeed, many groups little larger than gangs have proved able to sustain themselves as viable military threats through the use of child fighters. For example, the Lord's Resistance Army in Uganda is led by Joseph Kony, who styles himself as the reincarnation of the Christian Holy Spirit. Kony's own spin of the Ten Commandments, though, is that the Bible allows the ownership of sex slaves but declares that riding bicycles is a sin punishable by death. Effectively, he is a David Koresh–like figure who leads a cult with a core of just 200 adult members. But, over the years, Kony and his LRA have abducted over 14,000 children, using them to fight a decade-long civil war against the Ugandan army, which is considered one of the better in Africa, leaving some 100,000 dead and 500,000 refugees.

Child soldiers also present great difficulties during battle itself. Experiences from around the globe demonstrate that children do make effective soldiers and often operate with terrifying audacity, particularly when infused with religious or political fervor, or when under the influence of narcotics. I once interviewed a former Green Beret, who described a unit of child soldiers in Sudan as the best soldiers he had seen in Africa in his 18 years of experience there. He recounted how they once ambushed and shot down a Soviet-made Mi-24 attack helicopter, a feared weapon that has put many an adult unit to flight.

They also present a horrible dilemma for professional forces. No one wants to have to shoot a child, yet a bullet from a 14-year-old can kill you just as easily as one from a 40-year-old. Children carrying guns are legitimate targets, but that doesn't make it any easier on the soldiers that have to fight them. Soldiers often experience morale and post-traumatic stress disorder after such incidents.[23]

Conflicts where children are present tend to feature not only massive violations of the laws of war but also higher casualty totals, both among the local populace and among child soldiers in comparison to adult compatriots. These conflicts on average have higher levels of atrocities, and the children tend to be used as cannon fodder by their adult commanders. For example, in some places, rebel groups have taken to calling their child soldiers "mine detectors," as they will send them forward first to step on any hidden land mines.

Lastly, the effect of plunging children into a culture of war creates problems even after the war is over. For the individual children, it is long-term trauma that can disrupt their psychological and moral developments. For the wider society, the conversion of a generation of children into soldiers not only bodes future cycles of war within the country but also endangers regional stability. The case of Liberia is instructive. Throughout the 1990s, Liberia went through multiple rounds of civil war, where children would switch armies without much thought. But even after the fighting ended there, many former child soldiers from Liberia could later be found fighting in Sierra Leone, Guinea, and Côte d'Ivoire. Some since have marched thousands of kilometers to find work as soldiers in the Democratic Republic of the Congo.

In sum, when children are present, warfare is not only more tragic, but the conflicts tend to be easier to start, harder to end, and greater in loss of life, and lay the ground for recurrence in following generations.

WE MUST RESPOND

Action to end the terrible doctrine of child soldiers is thus not only a moral obligation but a strategic mandate. While an international alliance of nongovernmental organizations (NGOs), the International Coalition to Stop the Use of Child Soldiers, has brought increasing attention to the issue, governments are now needed to step up. Those seeking to end the practice must move beyond trying simply to persuade those who use children as soldiers, akin to trying to shame the shameless, and alter the underlying causes and motivations that enable its spread.

The Nobel Peace Prize winner Archbishop Desmond Tutu once said, "It is immoral that adults should want children to fight their wars for them. . . . There is simply no excuse, no acceptable argument for arming children."[24] There may be no moral excuse, but it is a dark reality of present-day war that we must face.

The key to stopping the practice of child soldiers is to shrink the recruiting pool of potential child soldiers and limit conflict groups' willingness and ability to access it. These include investment in heading off global disease and conflict outbreaks; giving greater aid to special at-risk groups, like refugees and AIDS orphans; helping to curb the spread of illegal small arms to rebel and terrorist groups who bring children into the realm of war; criminalizing the doctrine by prosecuting those leaders who abuse children in this way; taking the profits out of the practice by sanctioning any firms or regimes who trade with child-soldier groups (including even American firms, like those that traded with Liberian and Sudanese governments for private profit); and providing increased aid to programs that seek to demobilize and rehabilitate former child soldiers, thus ending the cycle. In each of these areas, unfortunately, U.S. action has been lacking—certainly not the stance of a world leader.

In turn, the "soft" issue of children is now as hard a security problem as they come. Political and military leaders must start to wrestle with the difficult dilemmas that our soldiers now face in the field, rather than continuing to ignore them at greater costs. Child soldiers are now a regular feature of the modern battlefield. The only question is whether troops will be properly equipped, trained, and supported to deal with this dreadful change in contemporary warfare. The onus is on leaders, in government and the military, to do all that they can to reverse the doctrine's spread and end this terrible practice.

PREPARING SOLDIERS FOR CHILD SOLDIERS

With the rise of groups using child soldiers, military forces must prepare themselves for a dilemma that is as thorny as they come. To put it simply, troops will be put into a situation where they face real and serious threats from opponents whom they generally would prefer not to harm. While they may be youngsters, when combined with the increasing simplicity and lethality of modern small arms, child soldiers often bring to bear a great deal of military threat. Therefore, mission commanders must prepare forces for the tough decisions that they will face, in order to avoid any confusion over rules of engagement (ROE) or the microsecond hesitations, because of shock at the makeup of their foes or uncertainty on what to do, that can prove lethal. An effective response will also take away some of the perceived advantages of the child-soldier doctrine, making it less likely to be used.

Historical experience has demonstrated a number of effective methods to handle situations when professional troops are confronted by child soldiers. These include the following:

Preparation and Intelligence

Official policies and effective solutions should be developed to counter the dilemmas that child soldiers raise rather than wishing the problem away. It is better to deal with them in training, rather than making ad hoc calls in the midst of crisis. At the same time, the intelligence apparatus must become attuned to the threat and ramifications of the child soldier. This is not only important in forecasting broad political and military events, but knowledge of the makeup of the adversary is also a critical factor in determining the best response. Intelligence should be sensitive to two aspects in particular: what method of recruitment the opposition utilizes and the average child soldier's period of service. Those using abduction techniques or with recent cadres will be more prone to dissolving under shock than those with voluntary recruits or children who have been in service for many years.

Recognize the Threat

Whenever forces deploy into an area known to have child soldiers present, they must take added cautions to counter and keep the threat at a distance. All children are not threats and certainly should not be targeted as such, but force protection measures must include the possibility—or even likelihood—of child soldiers and child terrorists. This includes changing practices of letting children mingle among pickets, and even putting children through the same scrutiny as adults at checkpoints.

Fear Supplements Firepower

When forces do face engagement with child-soldier forces, best practice has been to hold the threat at a distance and, where possible, initially fire for shock. The goal should be to maximize efficiency and prevent costly externalities by attempting to break up the child units, which often are not cohesive fighting forces. In a sense, this is the microlevel application of "effects-based warfare," just without the overwhelming dependence on high technology. Demonstrative artillery and mortar fires (including the use of smoke), rolling barrages (which give a sense of flow to the impending danger), and helicopter gunship passes have been proven especially effective in breaking up child-soldier forces.[25]

The Leader Is the Linchpin

When forced into close engagement, forces should prioritize the targeting and elimination of any adult leaders if at all possible. Experience has shown that their holds over the units are often the center of gravity and units will dissolve if the adult leader is taken out of a position of control. As forces seek to mop up resistance, they should focus their pursuit on the adult leaders that escape. Failure to do so allows the likely reconstitution of forces and return to conflict, as has become a recurrent theme in child-soldier-fueled conflicts like northern Uganda or Liberia.

Nonlethal Weaponry Gives More Options

An important realization is that total annihilation of the enemy in these instances may actually backfire. Thus, wherever possible, military commanders and policy makers should explore options for using nonlethal weaponry (NLW) in situations that involve child soldiers. Armchair generals often ignorantly mock NLW, overlooking that it in no way eliminates the option of deadly force. Rather its availability provides troops in the field with added choices and options. NLW frequently is a welcome alternative that may not only save lives on both sides but prove more effective to meeting mission goals. Unfortunately, development and distribution of such weaponry has fallen well behind pace. Indeed, out of the mere 60 nonlethal weapons kits in the entire U.S. military, only six were deployed to Iraq in the first year of operation there. Many international peacekeeping operations lack even one kit.

Employ PsyOps

Psychological operations should always be integrated into overall efforts against local resistance, including being specially designed for child-soldier units. Their aim should be to convince child soldiers to stop fighting, leave their units, and begin the process of rehabilitation and reintegration into society. At the same time strategy should be developed that ensures that adversary leaders know that their violations of the laws of war are being monitored and the dire consequences they will face in using this doctrine. PsyOps should also seek to undercut any support for the doctrine within local society, by citing the great harms the practice is inflicting on the next generation, its contrast to local customs and norms, and the lack of honor in sending children out to fight adults' wars.

Follow-Up Yields Success

The defeat of a child-soldier-based opposition does not just take place on the battlefield, no matter how successful. A force must also take measures to welcome child-soldier escapees and POWs quickly, so as to dispel any myths on retribution and to induce others to leave the opposition as well. This also entails certain preparations being made for securing child detainees, something U.S. forces have had no doctrine or training for, even down to not having proper-sized cuffs. Once soldiers have ensured that the child does not present a threat, any immediate needs of food, clothing, and/or shelter should be provided for. Then, as soon as possible, the child should be turned over to health-care or NGO professionals. The business of imprisoning juveniles is not the mission of the military and certainly not positive for the health of the organization.

Protect Our Own

A force must also look to the health of its own personnel. Forces must be ready to deal with the psychosocial repercussions of engagements with child-soldier forces, for this is an added way that the use of child soldiers puts professional forces at a disadvantage. Units may require special postconflict treatment and even individual counseling; otherwise the consequence of being forced to engage children may ultimately undermine unit cohesion and combat effectiveness.

Explain and Blame

Public affairs specialists must be prepared beforehand for the unique repercussions of such engagements. In explaining the events and how children ended up being killed, they should stress the context under which they occurred and the overall mission's importance. The public should be informed that everything possible is being done to avoid and limit child soldiers' becoming casualties (use of nonlethal weapons, psychological operations, firing for shock effect, etc.). At the same time, the public should be made aware that child soldiers, although they are children, are just as lethal behind an assault rifle as adults. Most important, public affairs specialists must seek to turn blame on where it should properly fall, on those leaders that not only illegally pulled children into the military sphere but also send them out to do their dirty work.

At a broader level, governments that want to stay ahead of the issue should mobilize the United Nations, as well as local political leaders and religious experts, to condemn the practice for what it is: a clear violation of international law as well as local cultural and religious norms.

CONCLUSION

As disturbing as this trend is, there is one silver lining we can see by a look back in the past. Countless doctrines and modes of warfare have come and gone over the long march of history. It was once thought that religion could be strengthened by calls to war. Now we look at those who call for crusades as extremists. Well into the Middle Ages, captured soldiers were considered not prisoners but personal property to be ransomed or sold as personal slaves. Little more than a century ago, it was considered an obligation, a so-called "white man's burden," to invade other lands to lift them up to "civilization," or, more honestly, bring them into colonial domains.

Hopefully, the child-soldier doctrine will someday soon join these and the many other practices of war whose time has passed. Perhaps history will look back upon this period as an aberration, a short phase when moral norms broke down, but were quickly restored. But this will only happen if we match the wills of those leaders who do such evil to children, with our own will to do good.

NOTES

1. Matthew Cox, "War Even Uglier When a Child Is the Enemy," *USA Today*, 8 April 2003.

2. T. W. Bennet, *Using Children in Armed Conflict: A Legitimate African Tradition?* (Institute for Security Studies, 2000), available at www.essex.ac.uk/armedcon/Issues/Texts/Soldiers002.htm.

3. John Paden, *Muslim Civic Cultures and Conflict Resolution: The Challenge of Democratic Federalism in Nigeria* (Brookings Institution Press: 2005).

4. "Report on the Battle of New Market Virginia and Aftermath, Part 1, May 15, 1864," *VMI Annual Report,* July 1864, available at www.vmi.edu/~archtml/cwnmrpt.html.

5. Guido Knopp, *Hitler's Kinder* (Munich: C. Bertelsmann, 2000); Philip Baker, *Youth Led by Youth* (London: Vilmor Publications, 1989).

6. For greater details on child-soldier figures, please see P. W. Singer, *Children at War* (New York: Pantheon, 2005), especially chap. 2.

7. Marie Colvin and James Clark, "How the Hi-Tech Army Fell Back on Law of the Jungle and Won," *Sunday Times,* 17 September 2000, available at www.sundaytimes.co.uk/news/pages/sti/2000/09/17/stifgnafr03003.html.

8. CNN, "Palestinian Teen Stopped with Bomb Vest," 25 March 2004.

9. Gul Luft, "The Palestinian H-Bomb," *Foreign Affairs,* July 2002, 5; Coalition to Stop the Use of Child Soldiers, *Child Soldiers: 1379 Report* (London, 2002), 54; Suzanne Goldenberg, "A Mission to Murder," *The Guardian*, 11 June 2003; Johanna Mcgeary, "Inside Hamas," *Time*, 28 March 2004.

10. U.S. State Department, "Colombia," *Report on Human Rights,* 1997; UNICEF-Columbia, *Situation Report* (22 April 2003).

11. Rohan Gunaratna, "LTTE Child Combatants," *Jane's Intelligence Review,* July 1998.

12. "National Roundup," *Miami Herald,* 23 April 2003; Human Rights Watch, "U.S. Guantanamo Kids at Risk," 24 April 2003; Bruce Auster and Kevin Whitelaw, "Terror's Cellblock," *U.S. News and World Report,* 12 May 2003; Michelle Faul, "U.S. Defends Detaining Teens," Associated Press, 20 June 2003.

13. Nancy Gibbs, "Inside 'The Wire,'" *Time,* 8 December 2003.

14. Interviews with U.S. Army officer, March 2004; Keith Richburg, "Taliban Maintains Grip Rooted in Fear," *Washington Post,* 9 August 2004, 9.

15. Cox, "War Even Uglier When a Child Is the Enemy"; "Report: Marines Wounded in Fighting Late Wednesday in Iraq," Associated Press, 27 March 2003; Alex Perry, "When Kids Are in the Cross Hairs," *Time,* 21 April 2003.

16. Mary Beth Sheridan, "For Help in Rebuilding Mosul, U.S. Turns to Its Former Foes," *Washington Post,* 25 April 2003.

17. "Enemy Tactics, Techniques, and Procedures (TTP) and Recommendations" (briefing document, 3rd Corp Support Command, LSA Anaconda, Iraq, September 2003); Joseph Galloway, "Hurt Still Arriving at Army Hospital," *Charlotte Observer,* 3 November 2003; interviews with U.S. Army officers, November–December 2003.

18. As quoted in "Child Soldiers Square Up to U.S. Tanks," *London Daily Telegraph,* 23 August 2004.

19. As quoted in ibid.

20. Neil Mackay, "Iraq's Child Prisoners," *Sunday Herald,* 1 August 2004; Richard Sisk, "Teen Held, U.S. Admits Juveniles in Abu Ghraib," *New York Daily News,* 15 July 2004; U.S. Army Lt. Col. Barry Johnson, as quoted in Sisk, "Teen Held, U.S. Admits Juveniles in Abu Ghraib."

21. Jim Michaels, "Al Qaeda Video Shows Boys Training to Kill, Kidnap," *USA Today,* 5 February 2008.

22. As quoted in "Child Soldiers," Radio Netherlands, 21 January 2000, available at www.rnw.nl/humanrights/html/general.html.

23. Marten Meijer, "Child Soldiers: Transactional Analyses of Child Warriors of the Opposing Force" (Panel on Executive Human Factors and Medicine, NATO Research and Technology Agency, 2007).

24. Archbishop Desmond Tutu, as quoted in remarks to the Children and Armed Conflict Unit, a joint project of the Children's Legal Centre and the Human Rights Center of the University of Essex in 1999, www.essex.ac.uk/armedcon/.

25. Center for Emerging Threats and Opportunities, *Child Soldiers: The Implications for U.S. Forces,* Marine Corps Warfighting Laboratory Seminar Report (November 2002).

27 The "New Silk Road" of Terrorism and Organized Crime: The Key to Countering the Terror-Crime Nexus

Russell D. Howard and Colleen M. Traughber

INTRODUCTION

As the global landscape in the twenty-first century has transformed via globalization, the nature of terrorist organizations is also changing. Unlike terrorist groups of the past, which were primarily substate actors, today's terrorists are transnational groups operating on a global level.[1] Encouraged by state weakness; globalization; increasing technological interconnectedness; and corrupt, permissive government officials, the "new terrorists" take advantage of an overall decline in international security. These factors have not only spawned a new generation of terrorists but have also encouraged a similar

Brigadier General (retired) Howard is the founding director of the Jebsen Center for Counter-terrorism Studies at the Fletcher School. Prior to assuming his current responsibilities, General Howard was the head of the Department of Social Sciences and the founding director of the Combating Terrorism Center at West Point. His previous positions include deputy department head of the Department of Social Sciences, Army chief of staff fellow at the Center for International Affairs at Harvard University, and commander of the First Special Forces Group (Airborne) at Fort Lewis, Washington. Other recent assignments include assistant to the special representative to the secretary-general during UNOSOM II in Somalia, deputy chief of staff for I Corps, and chief of staff and deputy commander for the Combined Joint Task Force, Haiti/Haitian Advisory Group. Previously, General Howard was commander of Third Battalion, First Special Warfare Training Group (Airborne) at Fort Bragg, North Carolina. He also served as the administrative assistant to Admiral Stansfield Turner and as a special assistant to the commander of SOUTHCOM. General Howard holds a BS degree in industrial management from San Jose State University, a BA in Asian studies from the University of Maryland, an MA degree in international management from the Monterey Institute of International Studies, and an MPA degree from Harvard University. General Howard was an assistant professor of social sciences at the U.S. Military Academy, and a senior service college fellow at the Fletcher School at Tufts University.

Colleen Traughber is a graduate student at the Fletcher School, concentrating in international security studies, and currently a Boren Fellow in Amman, Jordan. At Fletcher, Ms. Traughber worked at the Jebsen Center for Counter-terrorism Studies, where she researched the links between terrorism and organized crime and participated in the Combating Terrorism Working Group of the Partnership for Peace Consortium. Ms. Traughber spent the summer of 2006 in Tbilisi, Georgia, interning at the Transnational Crime and Corruption Center's Caucasus Office and the U.S. embassy. Prior to attending Fletcher, she was a Fulbright Scholar at the Otto-Suhr Institute for Political Science at the Free University Berlin, where she researched European foreign policy, including the European response to terrorism. Ms. Traughber has worked at the German Council on Foreign Relations, in the office of Karl-Theodor zu Guttenberg, member of the German parliament, and at the Concordia Language Villages. In June 2002, she graduated magna cum laude from Carleton College.

increase in transnational crime. Much like the "new terrorists," the "new criminals" also benefit from failing state structures, global interdependence, new technologies, and institutionalized corruption. Perhaps most disturbingly, these transnational criminal syndicates may also actively seek out cooperative relationships with the terrorist groups that thrive alongside them.[2]

Links between terrorists and criminals, which capitalize upon gaps in law enforcement and weak security structures, are increasingly becoming the norm in today's transnational environment. This strategic alliance between terrorism and crime[3]—effectively described as a terror-crime nexus—takes advantage of transnational networks, allowing illicit actors to transcend traditional or regional spheres of influence. In some corners of the globe lacking a strong central authority, both terrorism and crime become a "means of making war without declaring it."[4] Criminal and terrorist networks thrive and support situations of "low intensity" conflict, which are further exacerbated by the power vacuum that exists in international law-enforcement. As a result, populations in areas where these groups are active become increasingly impoverished and subject to conflict, while few actually benefit from the illicit activities. The negative international and local effects of transnational crime and terror reveal that the nexus between these activities is a global threat impacting actors at all levels.[5]

As a global phenomenon, the terror-crime nexus warrants a global response. Counterterrorism and countercrime experts, however, have been unable to successfully introduce and implement collaborative policies to address these issues on an international level. There is a tendency for policy makers to approach terrorist and criminal activities separately—because of the fact that crime is often perceived as a domestic problem, while terrorism, in the wake of the 9/11 terrorist attacks, is increasingly considered a security issue requiring international efforts.[6] This individualized strategy, which produces separate and frequently uncoordinated law enforcement responses to terror and crime, has proved inadequate to combat these interconnected activities.

Any successful approach to countering transnational terror and crime, however, will have to address the global conditions that facilitate both activities. Both terrorist networks and organized criminal groups tend to take advantage of the so-called gray areas of the world: weak or failing states,[7] which universally suffer from a lack of governance. After the cold war, a number of former Soviet republics became incubators for terror-crime collusion as they struggled to make the transition from communism and socialism to democracy and market capitalism. Ungoverned areas—particularly separatist regions such as Nagorno-Karabakh, South Ossetia, and Transnistria in the former Soviet territories[8]—are also ripe for terrorist and criminal collusion and warrant close attention by international law-enforcement. Here, instability has resulted in increased violence and illicit activities, including the illegal trafficking of arms, drugs, and humans.[9]

Given the conditions described above, the following characteristics of the emerging terror-crime nexus challenge states and the international community:

1.   Terrorists and terrorist groups often collude with drug traffickers in order to finance their activities. Terrorists either engage directly in trafficking of narcotics or act in concert with drug traffickers. The links between terrorism and drug trafficking, otherwise known as "narco-terrorism," have a long and nefarious history.

2.   The links between terrorism and arms trafficking, though less pronounced than in the case of narco-terrorism, are nevertheless a means of supporting terrorist groups and activities. The increased availability of arms from formerly Soviet-allied states is of particular concern.

3.   Direct links between terrorists and human traffickers are difficult to identify. However, both groups take advantage of uncontrolled borders and a general lack of policing on both the local and international levels. Terrorism and human trafficking have proved to be entrenched and growing problems.

The linkages between terror and crime groups are diverse and disparate, rendering it difficult, if not impossible, to unilaterally categorize particular actors as either terrorist or criminal groups. Terrorists will continue to rely on criminal means to finance their activities; criminals will increasingly use violence to further advance their objectives. Thus, a combined law enforcement and security approach may be necessary. Whether affiliated with the law enforcement or security apparatus, officials need to acknowledge the network structure of the terror-crime nexus and fight the networks cooperatively. Due to terror-crime linkages, penetrating crime groups may be an appropriate tactic to get closer to terrorist groups, particularly al Qaeda. The interaction between international terrorism and transnational organized crime will continue to challenge local and international security specialists and policy makers. However, successful strategies against the terror-crime nexus will require local, regional, national, and international security and law enforcement agencies to encourage interagency and multilateral coordination on the highest levels. Such synchronization is crucial to effectively combating both phenomena simultaneously.

This article explores the existing and potential interactions between international terrorist networks and organized criminal groups along the transit route from central Asia to western Europe—the "new Silk Road" in the trade of terrorism and crime. In particular, it examines the existence and extent of collusion between terrorism and crime—specifically arms, drug, and human trafficking—and discusses the distinctiveness of the terror-crime nexus with respect to these forms of trafficking. Ultimately, this article argues that the nexus must be understood and that cooperative international strategies must be achieved to successfully counter both transnational terrorism and criminal activities.

TERRORISM AND DRUG TRAFFICKING

The trafficking of drugs involves the production, sale, and transfer of narcotics. Because of high demand throughout the world, drug trafficking generates relatively high profits, and the proceeds can be used to finance other criminal activities. Drug trafficking "remains the most common and lucrative source of revenue to terrorist groups, leading many to legitimize this criminal activity by emphasizing the financial needs of the organization and the role of narcotics in undermining Western society."[10] Following the cold war, reduced levels of state sponsorship for terrorist groups have spurred the linkage of narcotics trafficking and terrorism.[11] Although the term "narco-terrorism" existed prior to the 1990s, transnational terrorist groups now increasingly rely on the profits from drug trafficking since the end of the East-West conflict. Territories formerly within the Soviet sphere of control have experienced an increase in narco-terrorism. Central Asia, the Caucasus, and southeastern Europe are suspected to be points along a major drug transit route that stretches from Afghanistan to western Europe.[12]

Central Asia

More than 75 percent of the current world heroin supply originates in Afghanistan;[13] however, the trafficking of narcotics from source countries in central Asia is nothing new. The Afghanistan opium trade has roots in the Soviet-Afghan War (1979–1989), during which drug addiction spread and transnational trafficking began.[14] Historically, Afghan drugs transited Iran and Turkey to western Europe.[15] The opium trade was promoted by fighting between tribal clans as well as between the Northern Alliance and the Taliban.[16] However, since the end of the cold war, and particularly in the aftermath of the 2001 war in Afghanistan, criminals have increasingly transported these drugs through central Asia.[17] Narcotics, primarily opium products, are currently produced and exported from Afghanistan to other central Asia countries. Present-day narcotic-smuggling routes flow from central Asia through the Caucasus and southeastern Europe to reach markets in western Europe.

Unlike Afghanistan—a production hub—the central Asian republics of Kazakhstan, Kyrgyzstan, Tajikistan, Turkmenistan, and Uzbekistan serve primarily as transit routes for narcotics.[18] Given the segmented nature of society, local clans or tribes—such as major Turkmen clans in Turkmenistan[19]—are often involved in the smuggling. Across the board, law enforcement officials are susceptible to corruption, often soliciting bribes as in Soviet times.[20]

Terrorism, organized crime, and corruption have proved to be a lethal recipe within central Asia. Throughout the region, terrorist groups and individuals are involved in trafficking in order to finance other activities, with drugs the commodity most often traded to support terrorism.[21] Drug trafficking is primarily used as a quick method of earning income to purchase arms and other war supplies. A mutually reinforcing relationship has developed between the illicit-narcotics trade and other illicit actors within Kazakhstan, Kyrgyzstan, Tajikistan, Turkmenistan, and Uzbekistan.[22] In short, drug trafficking has grown in tandem with terrorist groups as well as other criminal organizations in central Asia. Since the 9/11 attacks and the subsequent invasion of Afghanistan, the links between terror and crime have only increased in central Asia. The terror-crime nexus is particularly prevalent in state institutions, which have been infiltrated by criminals.[23] In other cases, illicit actors have used corrupt affiliations with government officials in order to gain favors.

In Afghanistan and central Asia, the entire spectrum of the so-called "crime-terror nexus" is represented.[24] The region not only serves as a base for terror and crime groups, including al Qaeda and drug cartels, but also serves as an operational region for groups that are both terrorist and criminal in nature.[25] In Uzbekistan, for example, radical Islamic groups are suspected of being involved with the trafficking of narcotics. One such group, the Islamic Movement of Uzbekistan (IMU), thrives as both a major actor in the drug trade and the most serious violent nonstate actor in the region.[26] The IMU is truly a global actor: it has links to al Qaeda, emphasizing the fact that terrorism and drug trafficking are global phenomena that threaten both host nations and those further afield.[27]

In addition to drug mafias and other transnational criminal organizations, which dominate narcotics trafficking in central Asia, insurgent and terrorist groups are of particular concern due to their capacities for violence.[28] Afghan warlords have profited from the drug trade by collecting bribes ("taxes") from local farmers and traffickers, by controlling production, or even by using drug trafficking to buy weapons.[29] Warlords were limited in their involvement by the dominant insurgency movements, specifically the Taliban and Northern Alliance. While members of the Taliban tended to profit by collecting bribes, members of the Northern Alliance were more directly involved in controlling production.[30]

In contrast to the Taliban and Northern Alliance, which did not rely on drug trafficking as a major source of revenue, the IMU has relied on drug trafficking as a major source of profit.[31] The IMU is a quintessential example of the terror-crime nexus, as it has engaged in both criminal and insurgency activities. In contrast, there is little evidence that suggests the use of narcotics trafficking by Hizb-ut-Tahrir (HT), another radical Islamic group operating in Uzbekistan, Tajikistan, and Kyrgyzstan.[32] However, there is some suggestion that, like the IMU, a number of HT cells are involved in narcotics trafficking.[33] If HT turns violent, this would represent another indication of the terror-crime nexus in central Asia.

The Caucasus

The Caucasus is not immune from the "unholy trinity" of terrorism, organized crime, and corruption.[34] The various separatist regions of the Caucasus are ideal incubators for the interaction of terror and organized crime activities, such as drug trafficking.[35] Continued instability in separatist regions such as Abkhazia, Chechnya, the Pankisi Gorge, Nagorno-Karabakh, and South Ossetia has only contributed to the formation of "black holes" of criminality and terrorism.[36] Separatist regions remain uncontrolled by the central government and provide refuge for both nonstate armed groups and drug traffickers.

Since the cold war, the strengthening of the state in the south Caucasus has placed some pressure on terror and criminal elements within the controlled regions of society, although not in the uncontrolled separatist regions. In contrast, in the north Caucasus, a political and social meltdown has resulted in a loss of government control over the region.[37] Foreign and indigenous fighters as well as drug traffickers have the freedom to run rampant. As a result, terrorists and criminals with contradictory and changing relations with one another have taken over, threatening the impending "Afghanization" of the north Caucasus.[38]

Southeastern Europe

A so-called Balkan route of drug trafficking has developed in southeastern Europe. Significant drug-trafficking activity is present along this route, through which heroin travels from Turkey into western Europe.[39] Heroin is trafficked from Turkey through Bulgaria, Macedonia, and Kosovo before continuing to Serbia, Hungary, or Albania.[40] The Balkans are arguably a perilous stop in the "instability train" running from central Asia to western Europe.[41] Terrorists and organized criminals, including drug traffickers, benefit from the same weak regional infrastructure, characterized by uncontrolled borders and limited policing. In some cases, terrorists and drug traffickers provide support for one another. It is not uncommon for paramilitary organizations to be directly linked to organized crime, creating terror-crime conglomerates.[42] In the former Yugoslavia, postconflict regions provide a supporting environment for terrorist cells.[43]

Western Europe

The drug trade in western Europe, the destination of the new Silk Road in the trade of terrorism and crime, is controlled by the ex–Kosovo Liberation Army (KLA) and Albanian terror-crime groups. KLA drug-trafficking profits are traded for arms and funneled into the Balkan conflict.[44] Due to the high demand for drugs and the relative ease in transport, drugs are by far the most commonly traded illicit commodity in western Europe. Profits from drug trafficking are funneled back along the transit route, providing support for armed groups with interests in other regions.

Terror-Crime Nexus

The nexus between terrorism and drug trafficking is particularly clear and present. This is most evident along the new Silk Road, where there is ample evidence of direct links between terrorism and drug trafficking. From central Asia to western Europe, no region is immune. The inability of security and law enforcement officials to counter both terrorist and criminal activities appears to be problematic in developed and undeveloped regions alike. The level of collusion between terrorists and drug traffickers, however, tends to vary across regions.

Central Asia remains the crucial point of support for terror-crime collusion. Various predictions that American military presence in Afghanistan would curb the opium trade have proved short sighted. In fact, the illicit trade of narcotics has only increased since the war in Afghanistan. The Taliban appear to have been more effective in discouraging opium production; the Taliban's 2002 opium ban actually reduced Afghanistan's yield of opium from 70 percent to 10 percent.[45] Since the end of the Taliban's reign, however, that trend has reversed.

Yet the drug trade is dependent upon a market for the illicit good: a market that can be found along the route from central Asia to western Europe. In fact, the West serves as the primary customer for drugs that travel along the new Silk Road originating in Afghanistan. Collusion between terrorism and drug trafficking is evident across all regions, including central Asia, the south Caucasus, southeastern Europe, and western Europe. The extent of the nexus between terrorism and drug trafficking is a prime example of the threat this transnational phenomenon presents to the international community.

TERRORISM AND ARMS TRAFFICKING

The trafficking of arms involves the illegal transfer of small arms and light weapons, as well as the raw materials to create chemical and radiological weapons. These arms are typically obtained through theft and are transferred to criminals or terrorists. The trafficking of weapons has a natural symbiosis with terrorism; the unauthorized buyers of trafficked arms are typically nonstate actors with an ax to grind. The market for arms, however, tends to be smaller than the market for drugs. The smaller demand results in fewer profits in the long run; yet the trafficking of arms remains a secondary method of financing terrorism.

Weak, failing, or postconflict regions are prime incubators for the arms trade.[46] Such regions of central Asia, the Caucasus, and southeastern Europe only promote the transfer of the estimated 640 million illegal weapons around the world.[47] The proximity of these regions to stockpiled Soviet weaponry makes them convenient targets and prime sources for arms traffickers. The nexus between terrorism and arms trafficking is particularly enabled through the widespread availability of small and light arms, which may be trafficked for profit or used in terrorist operations.[48] After the collapse of the Soviet Union, former Soviet republics, including those in both central Asia and the south Caucasus, found themselves flush with an oversupply of armaments, which have disappeared into the illegal arms market.[49] Because of the lack of security surrounding these arms, they are tempting targets for all kinds of violent nonstate actors, including international criminal organizations and terrorists.[50]

Of even greater concern is the availability of nuclear, chemical, and biological weapons in the former Soviet Union. These sources can be used in the production of "dirty bombs." Within the entire former Soviet Union, there are an estimated 22,000 nuclear weapons that are impossible to secure. If 1 percent of that material was left vulnerable, then 220 nuclear weapons would potentially be available for trafficking and sale by organized crime syndicates and use by terrorist groups in attacks.[51] The lack of border controls within Russia and other portions of the former Soviet Union makes acquiring weapons attractive to transnational terrorists.[52] The creation of a dirty bomb from radiological materials is a real threat, and is likely to require the support of criminal enclaves or black holes within weak states.[53]

Central Asia

Abandoned arms in Kazakhstan are a prime example of the threat from "loose nukes" and other radiological materials in former Soviet territories, particularly those in central Asia. Kazakhstan is reportedly the source of a cache of smuggled osmium-187, a slightly radioactive material of atomic weight 187, which was discovered en route to nonstate actors with nefarious intentions.[54] In 2001, Russian authorities apprehended a group of Kazakhstanis in possession of osmium-187.[55] This apprehension is the exception and not the norm; the illegal transit of radiological material is more often not detected.

Overall, the former Soviet republics of central Asia have taken few steps to control nuclear proliferation in the aftermath of the cold war. As recently as September 2006, the five central Asian republics signed a treaty establishing a central Asian nuclear-weapon-free zone (CANWFZ),[56] which could potentially lead to a nuclear-weapon-control regime within central Asia. However, in the absence of control since the end of the cold war, the damage may have already been done.

The Caucasus

The terror-crime nexus is alive and well in both the north and south Caucasus. In the north Caucasus, a "strategic linkage" exists between the Chechen Mafia in Moscow and the Chechen guerrillas in Grozny.[57] The Chechen Mafia has reportedly supported Chechen terrorists by financing groups within the separatist region.[58] In return, Chechen rebels have supposedly organized and implemented bombings within Moscow.[59] This example demonstrates the transnational nature of terror-crime interaction, which can transcend great distances.

In the south Caucasus, ethnic conflict has fueled the weapons trade. As elsewhere, arms are often traded alongside drugs in the separatist regions. As a result, the very existence of Abkhazia and South Ossetia has been supported by the trade of weapons.[60] Similarly, in Nagorno-Karabakh, the trade of illegal weapons has led to the sustained independence of this separatist region.[61] The trade of small arms and light weapons sustains the conflicts in the separatist regions. The "gray zones" have also emerged as conduits for radiological weapons.[62]

Southeastern Europe

The Balkan region, where routes of trafficking and terrorism overlap with one another,[63] has contributed significantly to the new Silk Road in the trade of terrorism and weapons. In 2002, weaknesses in Bosnia and Herzegovina's control of arms exports were revealed when an aircraft components firm from the region known as Orao delivered spare parts of fighter aircraft to Iraq, violating international sanctions.[64] Croatia has also been implicated in arms trafficking—activities that have been protected by officials in the Ministry of Defense, the Ministry of Internal Affairs, the customs service, the intelligence service, and at least one political party.[65] As a result, Croatia has emerged as a major distributor of arms and explosives in Europe.[66]

Albanian nonstate armed groups such as the Kosovo Liberation Army (KLA), the Kosovo National Front (KNF), and the Albanian National Army have strong links to organized crime.[67] These groups have gained profits from narcotics smuggling, which they then used to purchase arms.[68] The trafficking profits were estimated to be "tens of millions" of dollars and were primarily used to buy weapons in a "drugs for arms" arrangement.[69] An example of continuing cooperation between terrorist and criminal organizations, the groups have maintained the relationship as a result of common political goals. Crime and terror remain complementary phenomena in countries of the former Yugoslavia, transitioning in a postconflict environment.[70]

Western Europe

In contrast to the nexus between terrorism and drug trafficking, the link between terrorism and arms trafficking is generally less pronounced along the route leading to western Europe. The illegal weapons trade tends to be concentrated in conflict areas along the route, such as those in the Balkan region of the former Yugoslavia.[71] Western officials believe that the KLA has formed a strategic alliance with other rebel groups, such as the Chechens, as well as with criminal groups.[72] However, western Europe remains a place of origin and transport for arms. Arms are often traded for practical use by terrorist organizations, including the Basque Homeland and Freedom (ETA), the Irish Republican Army (IRA), and the Kurdistan Workers Party (PKK), or for financial gain by primarily criminal groups.[73]

Terror-Crime Nexus

Even in western Europe, the nexus between terrorism and arms trafficking cannot be dismissed. As a hosting hub for networks of terrorists and traffickers, western Europe is challenged to monitor and combat these networks. Beyond western Europe, the link between the arms trade and insurgencies has sustained global conflicts, including those in central Asia, the Caucasus, and southeastern Europe. Although less integrated into the illicit economy than narco-terrorism, the links between terrorism and arms trafficking are nonetheless thriving.

TERRORISM AND HUMAN TRAFFICKING

Human trafficking is commonly defined as the involuntary movement of people across borders for forced labor, prostitution, or other nefarious purposes. Human trafficking is differentiated from human smuggling, in which migrants are voluntarily transported across borders via illegal methods. The instability associated with the end of the cold war has encouraged increased levels of human trafficking, and in post-Soviet states, human trafficking is growing as a serious form of organized crime.[74] In these regions, traffickers trade women as if they were a "readily available natural resource."[75] Traffickers are interested in short-term profits rather than the long-term sustainability of the trafficking regime.[76] They use deceptive tactics to recruit women and even sell them to other criminal groups.[77]

In regions where both terrorism and human trafficking thrive, they are reportedly linked to one another. As human trafficking has become a significant component of the underground economy, the likelihood of relationships between trafficking groups and terrorist networks has increased.[78]

Central Asia

In recent years, human trafficking has increased in central Asia as a result of poor economic conditions, according to the International Organization for Migration (IOM).[79] Reportedly, traffickers have sold at least several thousand women into the sex trade, effectively circumventing law enforcement officials.[80] From Kyrgyzstan alone, women have been trafficked to Germany, Russia, Turkey, and the United Arab Emirates (UAE).[81] In central Asia, human-trafficking activity tends to follow the same routes as drug trafficking, as well as the same routes that terrorists use to transit the region.[82]

The Caucasus

As in central Asia, human traffickers and terrorists tend to use the same routes to transit the Caucasus. Furthermore, human trafficking persists as a problem due to the region's economic downturn.[83] In the Caucasus, more than 10,000 to 15,000 people have been involved in human trafficking annually.[84] Women and children are particularly susceptible to the offers of traffickers. The countries of the Caucasus—Azerbaijan, Armenia, and Georgia—tend to be mainly source and transit countries for human trafficking. To a lesser extent, they are also destination countries. In Georgia, for example, trafficking tends to be of women for the purposes of sexual exploitation, but also includes men for labor exploitation.[85]

Southeastern Europe

In the Balkan region of southeastern Europe, human trafficking is a "thriving business."[86] Traffickers target women who are easily manipulated, inflicting terrible violence against them.[87] Human trafficking has thrived in the absence of law enforcement and security in the Balkans, which serve primarily as a destination for victims of trafficking.[88] Law enforcement and security officials are ineffective, as they are often the major clientele of the sex trade.[89] Due to the geographic location of the region, the women are primarily trafficked from Romania, Moldova, and Ukraine,[90] although human trafficking in Croatia has also increased in recent years.[91]

In southeastern Europe, Moldova is the primary source for trafficked women.[92] Moldova has been described as a "black hole" in Europe in which the trafficking of human beings (as well as other illegal activities) is running rampant.[93] Reportedly, women in Moldova compose up to 60 percent of victims of trafficking in southeastern Europe.[94] In Moldova, the combination of a dire economic situation and weak law enforcement has served to promote human trafficking.[95] Moldovan victims typically transit Romania and Serbia before arriving in Bosnia, Kosovo, Albania, Greece, or Italy.[96] Albanian crime groups have fostered a huge market for Moldovan women in Kosovo.[97]

Turkey and Greece are located on the so-called southern Balkan route, which funnels illegal migrants from central Asia through Turkey and Greece to western Europe.[98] In contrast, along the "north Balkan route" or "Istanbul Express," illegal migrants travel from Turkey to the European Union by way of Bulgaria, Romania, Hungary, Slovakia, and the Czech Republic.[99] In contrast to drugs and arms trafficking, human trafficking is carried out "through a web of communication and transportation" and not through an "all-encompassing criminal organization."[100] As in central Asia and the Caucasus, the human traffickers tend to use the same routes as terrorists in transiting the region.

Western Europe

Western Europe is a place of origin and transport for human trafficking, although to a more limited degree than the other regions. Western Europe tends to serve as the destination in the transit route, particularly from poorer regions of southeastern Europe to the more affluent areas of western Europe. Of particular concern is the interaction between groups in central Asia, the Caucasus, and southeastern Europe with those operating and serving the west. As western Europe continues to function as a hosting hub for networks of terrorists and drug, arms, and human traffickers alike, the west likewise continues to be challenged in monitoring and combating these networks.

Terror-Crime Nexus

In contrast to narco-terrorism and the interaction between terrorism and arms trafficking, the terror–human trafficking "nexus" is less understood. Terrorist groups engage in human smuggling in order to move their operatives transnationally. However, it is unclear to what extent terrorists rely on profit from human trafficking to finance their activity. Although less understood, human traffickers themselves are no less dangerous. Human trafficking is an endemic problem, particularly in southeastern Europe, and is a symptom of a failing economy and political system common to the regions along the new Silk Road in the trade of terrorism and organized crime.

THE THREAT OF THE TERROR-CRIME NEXUS

In the short term, organized criminal activity such as drug, arms, and human trafficking provides nefarious people means of income that would otherwise be unavailable to them in the legal economy.[101] However, in the long term, the criminalization of the economy will add to political and social instability.[102] Furthermore, criminalization can escalate from widespread disaffection to protest movements—and, ultimately, to terrorism.[103] Transnational crime, particularly narcotics trafficking, is a lucrative enterprise, providing opportunities and support for violent groups while simultaneously destabilizing states. The terror-crime nexus has long-term destabilizing consequences that far outweigh any short-term economic benefits.

Although security and intelligence agencies at the state level engage in bilateral cooperation with respect to terrorism and organized crime, a global law-enforcement regime is essentially nonexistent.[104] Most international counterterrorism and countercrime operations are organized and implemented on an ad hoc basis. The International Criminal Police Organization (Interpol) is the organization closest to bridging the international gap in policing; despite its efforts, a basic lack of trust between members has hindered the organization's effectiveness.[105] Differences in capabilities have also limited the cooperation among states at the international level. The United States has a record of skepticism regarding international policing. In counterterrorism matters, American law-enforcement agencies tend to operate unilaterally rather than through an international organization such as Interpol.[106] In contrast to U.S. involvement in international policing, western European countries have been more willing to participate in Interpol. However, the lack of preparedness for terrorist bombings in Madrid (11 March 2004) and London (11 July 2005) has only revealed inadequate coordination on the European level.

Other international organizations, such as the North American Treaty Organization (NATO) and the Organization for Security and Cooperation in Europe (OSCE), hold regional counterterrorism responsibilities. Yet the extent and efficiency of their efforts to combat crime and terror simultaneously are limited. Along the terrorism and trafficking routes from central Asia to western Europe—regions within the mandates of both NATO and the OSCE—strategies to counter both terrorism and crime are lacking. Law enforcement and security agencies function independently and thus are generally ineffective in countering both terrorism and crime across the new Silk road.

Central Asia

Within central Asia, law enforcement agencies and security services have not commonly approached either terror or crime. As a result, they have struggled to detect, monitor, and respond to both terrorist and criminal threats. The foreign assistance to central Asia has focused on a "security belt" around Afghanistan, focusing on the improvement of border controls for Afghanistan while neglecting the region as a whole. Central Asian republics, which do not serve as bases for terrorists or criminals, often contribute to the terror-crime nexus by serving as transit countries.[107] For example, the Kazakhstan-Russia border is reportedly the major source of opium products destined for the Russian market.[108] Corruption is pervasive and endemic across the route from central Asia to western Europe; the legacy of the Soviet era appears to remain a factor. In Kazakhstan, drug dealers with wealthy or powerful friends are often released upon the payment of a bribe, revealing corruption within law enforcement.[109]

The Caucasus and Southeastern Europe

In the Caucasus, there is an evident split between officials involved in counterterrorism and countercrime. International interest in countering terrorism has increased, while organized crime has been typically left to state law-enforcement agencies. The nexus between terrorism and crime has not been fully recognized. Similarly, in southeastern Europe, the "Balkan route" has received more international attention due to its position along the routes of terror and crime. In the Balkans, by contrast, officials have emphasized the policing of criminals within the illicit economy; at the same time, terrorism has been neglected.[110]

Western Europe

In western Europe (and elsewhere), there is evidence to suggest that transnational terror and crime groups have evolved into networks, providing them with "flexibility, adaptability, deniability, multidimensionality, and the capacity to do things at a distance, often through surrogates."[111] Typically organized hierarchically and into bureaucracies, governments tend to be ill equipped to fight network structures. The lack of interagency cooperation makes it difficult to share information within a single government,[112] let alone among and between many governments.

COUNTERING THE TERROR-CRIME NEXUS

In order to combat both terror and crime, the following recommendations for counterterrorism and countercrime operations are suggested:

- **Prioritize interagency cooperation on the highest levels.** Regional and international actors must be on board in order to counter the terror-crime nexus. Across central Asia, the Caucasus, southeastern Europe, and western Europe, there must be a deeper and more widespread effort to share intelligence. This will necessitate closer interagency cooperation among nations.[113] Just as terrorists and criminals act transnationally, governments must also respond transnationally.

- **Establish interagency cooperation at the lowest levels.** On the local and national levels, both law enforcement and security officials must work together to combat the terror-crime nexus. Because of linkages between terrorists and criminals, governments must recognize that terror cannot be approached from merely a security perspective, and crime from a law enforcement perspective. Both security and law enforcement apparatuses need to be on board.

- **Fight a network with a network.** Security and law enforcement agencies should recognize that terror and criminal groups are often (if not always) organized in network structures. It is absolutely crucial to organize to fight a network with another network. Government officials should engage in association, network, or link analysis in order to fight terrorist and criminal networks.[114] Network attacks can include both external attacks, which aim at the critical nodes within the network, and internal attacks, which require infiltration of the network.[115] Security and law enforcement agencies need to imitate network structures to be effective; it is absolutely crucial to combat a network with a similar organization.[116]

- **Identify the level of collusion and respond accordingly.** Law enforcement and security officials need to recognize that the extent of collusion between terrorists and drug, arms, and human traffickers varies across the trafficking spectrum—from nexus to symbiotic relationship to activity appropriation[117]—as well as across regions. In fighting narco-terrorism, security and law enforcement officials are fighting a "nexus" and can infiltrate drug groups in order to counter terrorist groups.[118] This may not be possible with terrorism and arms trafficking—a "symbiotic relationship"—or with terrorism and human trafficking—an "activity appropriation."

CONCLUSION

In a world of increasing conflict, particularly within marginalized areas, "privatized violence,"[119] including international terrorism and transnational organized crime, promises only to rise. Globalization and the technology revolution have brought the world closer together and facilitated "a single global market for both licit and illicit commodities."[120] Thus, the West is affected and will continue to be affected and sometimes even threatened by conflict in remote regions.

Collusion between terrorist and criminal groups takes on different degrees of interaction, from "activity appropriation" to "hybrid."[121] Some terrorist groups have even transformed completely into transnational criminal organizations, emphasizing profits rather than politics.[122] Therefore, the combining of terror-crime policies such as those that have been implemented to combat narco-terrorism serves as both an example and a guide.

Yet the lack of a "global law-enforcement regime" is particularly alarming in a post-9/11 world in which criminal and terrorist groups increasingly take advantage of their ability to act transnationally. Multilateral efforts to counter transnational terror and crime, as well as regional security initiatives, are vital to combating the growing terror-crime nexus. Although multilateral efforts are crucial, unilaterally executed transnational operations cannot be eliminated.

With land and maritime links from central Asia to western Europe, the countries housed within these regions are exploited by terror and crime groups.[123] The route from central Asia to western Europe has effectively become the new Silk Road for terrorism as it historically has been for drugs, arms, and humans. Western and eastern governments alike must recognize that the route of terrorism and trafficking is the key to combating the terror-crime nexus.

NOTES

1. Russell D. Howard, "Understanding Al Qaeda's Application of the New Terrorism—The Key to Victory in the Current Campaign," in *Terrorism and Counterterrorism: Understanding the New Security Environment,* ed. Russell D. Howard and Reid L. Sawyer (Dubuque, IA: McGraw-Hill, 2006), 91–106.

2. Louise Shelley, "The Unholy Trinity: Transnational Crime, Corruption, and Terrorism," *Brown Journal of World Affairs* 11, no. 2 (2005): 106.

3. Alison Jamieson, "Transnational Organized Crime: A European Perspective," *Studies in Conflict & Terrorism* 24 (2001): 380.

4. Ibid., 378.

5. Troy S. Thomas and Stephen D. Kiser, *Lords of the Silk Route: Violent Non-state Actors in Central Asia,* INSS Occasional Paper 43 (USAF Institute for National Security Studies, 2002), viii.

6. Svante E. Cornell, "The Interaction of Narcotics and Conflict," *Journal of Peace Research* 42, no. 6 (2005): 753.

7. Stewart Patrick, "Weak States and Global Threats: Fact or Fiction?" *Washington Quarterly* 29, no. 2 (2006): 33.

8. This article draws heavily from the work of the Combating Terrorism Working Group (CTWG) of the Partnership for Peace (PfP) Consortium. The study looked at the routes of terrorism and trafficking from central

Asia, the south Caucasus, southeastern Europe, and western Europe. The work of the CTWG represents an initial attempt to examine the terror-crime nexus across these regions.

9. Research conducted here was based on a methodology known as preparation of the investigation environment (PIE), which determines the existence and extent of collusion between terrorists and organized criminals. For more information, see Louise I. Shelley et al., *Methods and Motives: Exploring Links between Transnational Organized Crime & International Terrorism* (National Criminal Justice Reference Service [NCJRS], U.S. Department of Justice, 2005) available at www.ncjrs.gov/pdffiles1/nij/grants/211207.pdf (accessed 9 June 2006).

10. Thomas M. Sanderson, "Transnational Terror and Organized Crime: Blurring the Lines," *SAIS Review* 24, no. 1 (Winter–Spring 2004): 49.

11. Cornell, "The Interaction of Narcotics and Conflict," 757.

12. Russell D. Howard and Colleen M. Traughber, "The Routes of Terrorism and Trafficking from Central Asia to Western Europe," *Connections* 6, no. 1 (2007): 1–4.

13. United Nations Office for Drug Control and Crime Prevention, *World Drug Report 2002* (Vienna: UNODC, 2002), 160.

14. Tamara Makarenko, "Crime, Terror, and the Central Asian Drug Trade," *Harvard Asia Quarterly* 6, no. 3 (Summer 2002): 3.

15. UN Office on Drugs and Crime, *Status Report on Afghanistan: Informal Consultations* (Vienna: UNODC, 2003), 4.

16. Makarenko, "Crime, Terror, and the Central Asian Drug Trade," 4.

17. United Nations Office for Drug Control and Crime Prevention, *Illicit Drugs Situation in the Regions Neighboring Afghanistan and the Response of the ODCCP* (Vienna: UNODC, 2002).

18. LaVerle Berry et al., *Nations Hospitable to Organized Crime and Terrorism* (Washington, DC: Federal Research Division, Library of Congress, 2003), 61–66.

19. Ibid., 65.

20. Ibid., 61–66.

21. Rustam Burnashev, "Terrorist Routes in Central Asia: Trafficking Drugs, Humans, and Weapons," *Connections* 6, no. 1 (2007): 65–70.

22. Makarenko, "Crime, Terror, and the Central Asian Drug Trade," 2.

23. Svante E. Cornell, "The Narcotics Threat in Greater Central Asia: From Crime-Terror Nexus to State Infiltration?" *China and Eurasia Forum Quarterly* 4, no. 1 (2006): 58–60.

24. Makarenko, "Crime, Terror, and the Central Asian Drug Trade," 2.

25. Ibid.

26. Svante E. Cornell, "Narcotics, Radicalism, and Armed Conflicts in Central Asia: The Islamic Movement of Uzbekistan," *Terrorism and Political Violence* 17 (2005): 619–39.

27. Ibid., 634.

28. Makarenko, "Crime, Terror, and the Central Asian Drug Trade," 6–9.

29. Ibid., 10.

30. Ibid., 10–11.

31. Ibid., 12.

32. Glenn E. Curtis, *Involvement of Russian Organized Crime Syndicates, Criminal Elements in the Russian Military, and Regional Terrorist Groups in Narcotics Trafficking in Central Asia, the Caucasus, and Chechnya* (Washington, DC: Federal Research Division, Library of Congress, 2002), 16–18.

33. Ibid., 18.

34. Andrew Nicholas Pratt, "Human Trafficking: The Nadir of an Unholy Trinity," *European Security* 13 (2004): 55.

35. Colleen M. Traughber, "Terror-Crime Nexus? Terrorism and Arms, Drug, and Human Trafficking in Georgia," *Connections* 6, no. 1 (Spring 2007): 47–63.

36. Jahangir Arasli, "The Rising Wind: Is the Caucasus Emerging as a Hub for Terrorism, Smuggling, and Trafficking?" *Connections* 6, no. 1 (Spring 2007): 5–26.

37. Cornell, "The Narcotics Threat in Greater Central Asia," 58–60.

38. Ibid.

39. Berry et al., *Nations Hospitable to Organized Crime and Terrorism,* 83.

40. Ibid.

41. Tatiana Busuncian, "Terrorist Routes in South Eastern Europe," *Connections* 6, no. 1 (Spring 2007): 85–102.

42. Nadia Alexandrova-Arbatova, "European Security and International Terrorism: The Balkan Connection," *Southeast European and Black Sea Studies* 4, no. 3 (September 2004): 369.

43. Ibid.

44. Berry et al., *Nations Hospitable to Organized Crime and Terrorism,* 83.

45. Makarenko, "Crime, Terror, and the Central Asian Drug Trade," 3.

46. Patrick, "Weak States and Global Threats," 38.

47. Ibid.

48. Sanderson, "Transnational Terror and Organized Crime," 49.

49. Ibid., 51.

50. Ibid.

51. Graham Alison, *Nuclear Terrorism: The Ultimate Preventable Catastrophe* (New York: Owl Books, 2004), 70.

52. Bartosz H. Stanislawski, "Transnational Organized Crime, Terrorism, and WMD," *International Studies Review* 7, no. 1 (2005): 158–60.

53. Ibid.

54. Berry et al., *Nations Hospitable to Organized Crime and Terrorism*, 62.

55. Dmitry Starostin, "Osmium Worries the FSB," *Vremya Novostey* (Moscow), 27 September 2002.

56. "About NTI, Country Profiles, Kazakhstan," Nuclear Threat Initiative, www.nti.org/e_research/profiles/Kazakhstan/index.html (accessed 16 April 2007).

57. Chris Dishman, "Terrorism, Crime, and Transformation," *Studies in Conflict & Terrorism* 24 (2001): 54.

58. Ibid.

59. Ibid., 54–55.

60. Louise I. Shelley, "Organized Crime in the Former Soviet Union: The Distinctiveness of Georgia," available at www.traccc.cdn.ge/publications/publication1.html (accessed 28 April 2007).

61. Arasli, "The Rising Wind," 5–26.

62. Alexander Kupatadze, "Radiological Smuggling and Uncontrolled Territories: The Case of Georgia," *Global Crime* 8, no. 1 (2007): 40–57.

63. Krunoslav Antoliš, "Smuggling in South Eastern Europe," *Connections* 6, no. 1 (Spring 2007): 71–84.

64. Berry et al., *Nations Hospitable to Organized Crime and Terrorism,* 78.

65. Ibid., 80.

66. Jasna Babic, "MORH [Defense Ministry] Protects Arms Dealers Who Smuggle Weapons to ETA and IRA," *Nacional* (Zagreb), 24 July 2001 (FBIS Document EUP20010010724000372).

67. Berry et al., *Nations Hospitable to Organized Crime and Terrorism,* 82.

68. Ibid., 83.

69. See Jerry Seper, "KLA Buys Arms with Illicit Funds," *Washington Times,* 4 June 1999, as cited in Dishman, "Terrorism, Crime, and Transformation," 55.

70. Alexandrova-Arbatova, "European Security and International Terrorism," 371.

71. Jamieson, "Transnational Organized Crime," 377.

72. Ibid., 382.

73. Lucia Ovidia Vreja, "Trafficking Routes and Links to Terrorism in South Eastern Europe: The Case of Romania," *Connections* 6, no. 1 (2007): 27–45.

74. Louise I. Shelley, statement to the House Committee on International Relations, Subcommittee on International Terrorism, Nonproliferation, and Human Rights, 108th Cong., 1st sess., 25 June 2003, 2.

75. Ibid., 4.

76. Ibid.

77. Ibid., 5.

78. Ibid., 12.

79. Berry et al., *Nations Hospitable to Organized Crime and Terrorism,* 61.

80. Ibid.

81. "Report on the Worst Forms of Child Labour: Kyrgyzstan," Global March against Child Labour, www.globalmarch.org/resourcecentre/world/kyrgyzstan.pdf (accessed 2 May 2007).

82. Berry et al., *Nations Hospitable to Organized Crime and Terrorism,* 63.

83. Shelley, "Organized Crime in the Former Soviet Union."

84. Georgi Glonti, "Trafficking in Human Beings in Georgia and the CIS," *Demokratizatsiya* 9, no. 3 (2001): 382.

85. Tamar Mikadze, "Human Trafficking: A Georgian Reality," available at www.traccc.cdn.ge/resources/articles.html (accessed 29 April 2007).

86. Fotios Moustakis, "Soft Security Threats in the New Europe: The Case of the Balkan Region," *European Security* 13 (2004): 149.

87. Shelley, statement to the House Committee on International Relations, Subcommittee on International Terrorism, Nonproliferation, and Human Rights, 8.

88. Berry et al., *Nations Hospitable to Organized Crime and Terrorism,* 78.

89. Ibid.

90. Ibid.

91. Ibid., 81.

92. Ibid., 67.

93. Mark Galeotti, "The Transdnistrian Connection: Big Problems from a Small Pseudo-state," *Global Crime* 6, nos. 3–4 (2004): 398.

94. Berry et al., *Nations Hospitable to Organized Crime and Terrorism,* 67.

95. Ibid.

96. Ibid.

97. Ibid.

98. Ahmet Icduygu, "Transborder Crime between Turkey and Greece: Human Smuggling and Its Regional Consequences," *Southeast European and Black Sea Studies* 4, no. 2 (2004): 309.

99. Ibid.

100. Ibid., 310–11.

101. Phil Williams, "Criminalization and Stability in Central Asia and the South Caucasus," in *Faultlines of Conflict in Central Asia and the South Caucasus: Implications for the U.S. Army,* ed. Olga Oliker and Thomas S. Szayna (Santa Monica, CA: RAND, 2003), 71.

102. Ibid.

103. Ibid., 72.

104. Mathieu Deflem, "Global Rule of Law or Global Rule of Law Enforcement? International Police Cooperation and Counterterrorism," *Annals of the American Academy,* January 2006, 241.

105. Ibid., 249.

106. Ibid.

107. Berry et al., *Nations Hospitable to Organized Crime and Terrorism,* 61.

108. "Major Busts Made by Hungarians, Russians, and Romanians," *RFE/RL Crime and Corruption Watch* 2, no. 35 (4 October 2002).

109. Daur Dosybiev, "Kazakhstan: Police Corruption Worsens," *Report on Central Asia,* no. 128 (2002), available at www.iwpr.net, as cited in Berry et al., *Nations Hospitable to Organized Crime and Terrorism,* 62.

110. Jamieson, "Transnational Organized Crime," 382–83.

111. Stanislawski, "Transnational Organized Crime, Terrorism, and WMD," 158–60.

112. Ibid.

113. Roger N. McDermott, *Countering Global Terrorism: Developing the Antiterrorist Capabilities of the Central Asian Militaries* (Carlisle, PA: Strategic Studies Institute, 2004), available at www.strategicstudiesinstitute.army.mil/pdffiles/PUB370.pdf (accessed 28 April 2007).

114. Phil Williams, "Transnational Criminal Networks," in *Network and Netwars: The Future of Terror, Crime, and Militancy,* ed. John Arquilla and David Ronfeldt (Santa Monica, CA: RAND, 2001), 92.

115. Ibid., 95.

116. Ibid.

117. Russell D. Howard and Colleen M. Traughber, "Summary of Conclusions: Combating Terrorism Working Group (CTWG)," *Connections* 6, no. 1 (2007): 103–106.

118. Ibid.

119. Stefan Mair, "The New World of Privatized Violence," *IPG* 2 (2003): 11–28.

120. Phil Williams, "Transnational Criminal Organizations and International Security," *Survival* 36, no. 1 (1996): 97.

121. Shelley et al., *Methods and Motives,* 35.

122. There is some disagreement as to whether terror and crime groups are more likely to collude with one another or develop the capabilities of each other. See Dishman, "Terrorism, Crime, and Transformation," 43–58.

123. Shelley, "Organized Crime in the Former Soviet Union."

28 Shari'a Financing and the Coming Ummah

Rachel Ehrenfeld and Alyssa A. Lappen

The United States and the West cannot win the war against radical Islam merely with the most sophisticated military strategies. Winning requires understanding the role of shari'a and the Muslim Brotherhood in developing a global ideological and political movement supported by a parallel "Islamic" financial system to exploit and undermine Western economics and markets. This movement is the foundation and the major funding source for the political, economic, and military initiatives of the global Islamic movement.[1]

Shari'a finance is a new weapon in the arsenal of what might be termed fifth-generation warfare (5GW).[2] The perpetrators include both states and organizations, advancing a global totalitarian ideology disguised as a religion. The end goal is to impose that ideology worldwide, making the Islamic "nation," or *ummah*, supreme.[3]

Rising oil prices and the West's dependency on Middle East oil, combined with willful blindness and political correctness, provide a surge of petrodollars, making financial and economic jihad so much easier to carry out. Moreover, according to shari'a, Muslims hold all property in trust for Allah.[4] Therefore, under the shari'a, all current and historic Muslim acquisitions everywhere, including the United States, belong to the *ummah*, in trust for Allah.

Dr. Rachel Ehrenfeld is the director of the New York–based American Center for Democracy (www.acdemocracy .org) and worked as a research scholar at New York University School of Law, a visiting scholar at the Columbia University Institute of War and Peace Studies, and a fellow at Johns Hopkins's SAIS. Her PhD in criminology is from the Hebrew University School of Law. She is a commentator and consultant on the problems of international terror financing, international terrorism, political corruption, money laundering, drug trafficking, organized crime, and the connections that bind these groups together, as well as political Islam. She is currently working on a project on the Islamist penetration of the U.S. and Western economies. Dr. Ehrenfeld has lectured on these issues in many countries on five of the seven continents and has advised banking communities, law enforcement agencies, and governments in many countries. She testified before the European Parliament and the UK Parliament and gave expert testimony before U.S. courts and Congress, as well as the Canadian Parliament. Dr. Ehrenfeld's articles appear in the *Wall Street Journal,* the *Washington Times, National Review,* the *Eurobserver,* the *Jerusalem Post,* the *New York Sun,* and the *Los Angeles Times,* and numerous Web publications. She appears as an expert commentator on television and radio news programs, including *The O'Reilly Factor,* Fox News, CNN, ABC, NBC, and MSNBC. Her latest book is *Funding Evil: How Terrorism Is Financed and How to Stop It* (Bonus Books, 2003, 2005). Her previous books are *Evil Money: Encounters along the Money Trail* (HarperCollins, 1992; SPI, 1994), and *Narco-terrorism: How Governments around the World Used the Drug Trade to Finance and Further Terrorist Activities* (Basic Books, 1990, 1992).

Alyssa A. Lappen is a senior fellow at the American Center for Democracy (ACD) and a contributing editor at American Congress for Truth. She is a former senior editor of *Institutional Investor, Working Woman,* and *Corporate Finance* and former associate editor of *Forbes.*

Shari'a is the crucial source and ultimate authority dictating the actions of practicing individuals and radical Muslim states and movements alike. Failing to understand the political use of shari'a hampers the U.S. ability to mount effective policies, plans, and strategies to successfully counter this fast-growing totalitarian threat.

This ignorance is illustrated by the statements of Massachusetts representative Barney Frank and Utah senator Bob Bennett. Responding to opponents of Bourse Dubai's then-proposed acquisition of 20 percent of NASDAQ in September 2007, Frank quipped, "In the ports deal, the concern was smuggling something or someone dangerous. . . . What are we talking about here—smuggling someone onto a stock exchange?"[5] Similarly, Bennett said, "Dubai is making a purchase on the open market of an asset that's for sale. What's wrong with that?"

Although Senator Bennett is correct—buying portions or all of NASDAQ is perfectly legal, and NASDAQ regulations could not be changed without Securities and Exchange Commission (SEC) approval—Bourse Dubai's shari'a influence in the heart of the U.S. markets and economy should have been of grave concern.

Shari'a is the set of Islamic laws established by Muslim jurists, based on the Qur'an and deeds of the prophet Muhammad, as recorded beginning more than 1,200 years ago. Its end goal, for all time, is establishing a world ruled entirely by Islam and the harsh shari'a laws. These laws govern every aspect of daily life and prohibit individual, political, and religious freedoms.

FINANCIAL JIHAD

Funding the jihad, i.e., financial jihad, or *Al Jihad bi-al-Mal*, is mandated by many verses in the Qur'an, such as chapter 61, verses 10–11: "you . . . should strive for the cause of Allah with your wealth and your lives," and chapter 49, verse 15: "The [true] believers are only those who . . . strive with their wealth and their lives for the cause of Allah." This has been reiterated throughout Islamic history and in recent times. "Financial *Jihad* [is] . . . more important . . . than self-sacrificing," according to Saudi and Muslim Brotherhood (MB) spiritual leader Hamud bin Uqla al-Shuaibi.[6]

Qatar-based Muslim Brotherhood spiritual leader Yusuf al-Qaradawi, one of the most prominent Sunni scholars in the world today, reiterated the legal justification for "financial jihad [*Al-Jihad bi-al-Mal*]" in a lecture he gave on 4 May 2002 in the United Arab Emirates (UAE). According to him, "collecting money for the *mujahideen* (jihad fighters . . .) was not a donation or a gift but a duty necessitated by the sacrifices they made for the Muslim nation."[7]

HISTORICAL DEVELOPMENT

The origins of the modern financial jihad infrastructure, including all Islamic economic and financial regulatory organizations like the the 1991-Bahrain-registered and -based Accounting and Auditing Organization for Islamic Financial Institutions (AAOIFI), date back to the 1920s and were an invention of Muslim Brotherhood founder Hassan al-Banna. He designed political, economic, and financial foundations to enable Muslims to fulfill a key form of jihad mandated by the Qur'an—financial jihad.[8]

He viewed finance as a critical weapon to undermine the infidels—and "work towards establishing an Islamic rule on earth."[9] He was first to understand that to achieve world domination, Muslims needed an independent Islamic financial system to parallel and later supersede the Western economy. Al-Banna's contemporaries and successors (such as the late Sayed Qutb and current Yusuf al-Qaradawi) set his theories and practices into motion, developing shari'a-based terminology and mechanisms to advance the financial jihad—"Islamic economics," finance, and banking.[10]

Early 1930s MB attempts to establish Islamic banking in India failed. Egyptian president Gamal Abdel Nasser shut down the second attempt, in 1964, after only one year, later arresting and expelling the Muslim Brotherhood for attempts to kill him.[11]

But Saudi Arabia welcomed this new wave of Egyptian dissidents, as did King Saud bin Abdel Aziz earlier waves in 1954 and 1961.[12] Their ideas so appealed to him and his clerics that in 1961, Saud funded the MB's establishment of the Islamic University in Medina to proselytize its fundamentalist Islamic ideology, especially to foreign students.[13] In 1962, the MB convinced the king to launch a global financial joint venture, which became the cornerstone and engine to spread Islam worldwide. This venture created charitable foundations, which the MB oversees and from which most Islamic terrorist groups benefit.[14]

The first were the Muslim World League (MWL) and *Rabitta al-Alam al-Islami,* uniting Islamic radicals from 22 nations and spinning a web of many other charities with hundreds of offices worldwide.[15] In 1978, the kingdom backed another MB initiative, the International Islamic Relief Organization (IIRO), which, with all these "charities," is implicated for funding al Qaeda, the 9/11 attacks, Hamas, and others.[16]

These "charities" are used to advance the Muslim Brotherhood and Saudi political agenda, namely empowering the *ummah* and imposing worldwide shari'a. "I don't like this word 'donations,'" al-Qaradawi told BBC *Panorama* on 30 July 2006. "I like to call it *Jihad* with money, because God has ordered us to fight enemies with our lives and our money."[17]

In 1969, the Saudis convened Arab and Muslim states to unify the "struggle for Islam," and have ever since been the Organization of the Islamic Conference's (OIC's) major sponsor. The 56 OIC members include Iran, Sudan, and Syria. The Jidda-based, "pending the liberation of Jerusalem," OIC's charter mandates and coordinates "support [of] the struggle of the Palestinian people, . . . recovering their rights and liberating their occupied territories."[18] The OIC charter includes all the MB principles. Its first international undertaking in 1973 was to establish the Islamic Development Bank (IDB) "in accordance with the principles of the *shariah,*"[19] as prescribed by the MB—and to launch the fast-growing petrodollar-based Islamic financing market. The IDB, more a development than commercial bank, was established largely "to promote Islamic banking worldwide."[20] "[A]n Islamic organization must serve God" and ultimately sustain "the growth and advancement of the Islamic way of life," writes Nasser M. Suleiman in "Corporate Governance in Islamic Banking."[21]

And the IDB has done just that. Between 1975 to 2005, the IDB approved over $50 billion in funding to Muslim countries,[22] ostensibly to develop their economic and educational infrastructures, but effected little regional economic impact. Its educational efforts, however, paid huge yields—via the rapid and significant spread of radical Islam worldwide. Moreover, in 2001 alone, the IDB transferred $538 million[23] raised publicly by Saudi and Gulf royal telethons to support the Palestinian intifada and families of Palestinian suicide bombers. The IDB has also channeled UN funds to Hamas, as documented by bank records discovered in the West Bank and Gaza. Yet the IDB received UN observer status in 2007.[24]

According to a 1991 U.S. Library of Congress report on Sudan, the IDB also supported Faisal Islamic Bank, established in 1977 under Sudan's Faisal Islamic Bank Act by Saudi prince Muhammad ibn Faisal Al Saud and managed by local Muslim Brotherhood members and their party, the National Islamic Front. Soon other political groups and parties formed their own Islamic banks. Together, Sudanese Islamic banks then acquired 20 percent of the country's deposits—providing the financial basis to turn Sudan into an Islamic state in 1983, and promoting the Islamic governmental policies to date.[25] Sudan Islamized its banking in 1989. However, Pakistan was the first country to officially Islamize its banking practices, in 1979.

Rising oil revenues encouraged MB leaders to formalize al-Banna's vision. In 1977 and 1982, they convened in Lugano, Switzerland, to chart a master plan to co-opt Western economic foundations—capitalism and democracy—in a treatise entitled *Towards a Worldwide Strategy for Islamic Policy,* also known as *The Project.* MB spiritual leader al-Qaradawi wrote the explicit document, dated 1 December 1982.[26] The 12-point strategy includes diktats to "establish the Islamic state and gradual, parallel work to control local power centers . . . using institutional work as means to this end." This requires "special Islamic economic, social and other institutions," and "the necessary economic institutions to provide financial support" to spread fundamentalist Islam.[27]

Consequently, the IDB founded the AAOIFI in 1990. AAOIFI members include the Saudi Dallah al Baraka Group, al-Rajhi Banking & Investment Corporation, and Kuwait Finance House[28]—all implicated in funding al Qaeda and other MB offspring, according to Richard Clarke, the former national coordinator for security, infrastructure protection, and counter-terrorism.[29] The 18 AAOIFI members also include Iran and Sudan, both on the U.S. Treasury Department's Office of Foreign Assets Control (OFAC) sanctions list; Iran is a U.S. State Department–designated terror-sponsoring state, too. UAE banks wired most of the funding for the 9/11 attacks.[30]

In addition, the "de facto Islamic Central Bank," the Islamic Financial Services Board (IFSB),[31] was established in 2002 in Kuala Lumpur "to absorb the 11 September shock and reinforce the stability of Islamic finance." Chairing the organizers' meeting, then Malaysian prime minister Mohamed Mahathir stated, "A universal Islamic banking system is a jihad worth pursuing to abolish this slavery [to the West]." IFSB members include the central banks of Iran, Sudan, and Syria (all designated state sponsors of terrorism) and the Palestinian Monetary Authority (PMA), which is widely documented since its inception to be a terror funder.[32]

According to Dallah al Baraka Group and Islamic Chamber of Commerce and Industry (ICCI) president Saleh Kamel,[33] more than 400 Islamic financial institutions[34] currently operate in 75 countries.[35] They now hold more than $800 billion in assets[36]—growing 15 percent annually. HSBC, UBS, J.P. Morgan Chase, Deutsche Bank, Lloyds TSB, and BNP Paribas are but a few that offer Islamic banking and shari'a-based products to their Western clients—and promote them as "ethical investments."

Billionaire Sheikh Saleh Abdullah Kamel and his family, like other wealthy Saudis, have built their terror-funding-affiliated $3.5 billion Dallah al Baraka Group to service the shari'a.[37] Its business, finance, and media sectors incorporate agriculture, communication, health care, real estate, tourism, trade, transportation, and finance companies—including 10 banks and many leasing and finance firms, Arab Radio & Television and Arab Digital Distribution, and the International Information & Trading Service Co., producing the Top 1000 Saudi Companies Directory, among other publications.

Rapidly rising oil prices fill the coffers of Islamic banks, fuel the expansion of shari'a economics and financial jihad—and threaten the United States and the entire non-Muslim world, in real time. Indeed, shortly after 9/11, Osama bin Laden called on Muslims "to concentrate on hitting the U.S. economy through all possible means. . . . Look for the key pillars of the U.S. economy. Strike the key pillars of the enemy again and again and they will fall as one."[38]

The NASDAQ acquisition, purchases of over 52 percent of the London Stock Exchange (LSE) and 47.6 percent of OMX (Nordic exchange), and vigorous expansion of shari'a finance all steadily implement al-Banna's plan to spread and ultimately impose shari'a worldwide.

Bourse Dubai in December 2006 loudly proclaimed its new conversion to "*shari'a* compliance and accounting practices."[39] Yet, responding to a specific inquiry on the Islamic nature of Bourse Dubai from the Partnership for New York City on 22 October 2007, Bourse Dubai denied being an Islamic exchange.[40] Still unaware of the implications of importing shari'a finance, however, hoards of Westerners eagerly attend such pricey events as the October 2007 Islamic Finance Summit in New York,[41] which focused on the "innovations in *shari'a* compliant finance." According to an eyewitness, when one participant timidly inquired, "What is shari'a law?" a leading Islamic scholar responded from the podium: "It's good for you."

Lost on the attendees was the inescapable fact that shari'a calls for the supremacy of Islam, thus negating the U.S. Constitution.[42]

ZAKAT

Zakat, we are told, is to help the needy. But as Janine A. Clark's excellent 2004 study shows, *zakat* is used to support the middle class, to strengthen its loyalty to the rulers, and to back their radical ideology.[43]

Muslim Brotherhood spiritual leader Yusuf al-Qaradawi decrees, "Declaring holy war . . . is an Islamic duty, and fighting . . . is the Way of Allah for which *Zakat* must be spent." In his 1999 publication, *Fiqh az-Zakat,* al-Qaradawi adds, "The most important form of *jihad* today is serious, purposefully organized work to rebuild Islamic society and state and to implement the Islamic way of life in the political, cultural and economic domains. This is certainly most deserving of *Zakat*."[44] And as previously demonstrated time and again, Muslim jihadist-terror organizations are indeed prominent *zakat* recipients.

The use of charities to fund jihad, however, is not limited to radical Sunnis. On Jerusalem Day, 5 October 2007, Al-Manar TV broadcasted Hezbollah leader Hassan Nasrallah's cantankerous speech giving religious, moral, and political justification in support of "the armed Palestinian resistance" and calling for financial support to the Palestinian terrorist organizations. Nasrallah "gave Khomeini's *fatwa*[45] . . . allowing charity funds . . . and the tax of 1/5 (*khums*)[46] to be transferred to the Palestinian terrorist organizations . . . to pay for their campaign."[47]

The definition of *zakat* in *The Encyclopedia of Islam* includes in "category 7" of eligible recipients "volunteers engaged in *jihad*," for whom the *zakat* covers "living expenses and the expenses of their military service (animals, weapons)."[48]

Millard Burr and Robert Collins's compelling study *Alms for Jihad* documents that when *zakat*, which is obligatory to all Muslims, is given "in the path of Allah," it is given to fund jihad. There are seven broad categories of eligible recipients: the poor, converts, wayfarers, those in bondage or in debt, those committed to Allah for the spread and triumph of Islam, newcomers whose faith is weak, and new converts to Islam "whose hearts have been [recently] reconciled [to truth]." Moreover, *zakat* may be used to support those who administer it.[49]

In a 2006 federal case, alleged al Qaeda supporters Emadeddin Z. Muntasser and Muhammed Mubayyid were charged with soliciting and spending "funds to support and promote the *mujahideen* and *jihad*, including the distribution of pro-jihad publications," through their now-defunct "charity" and front organization, Care International. The Boston-based organization published, among other things, the English version of al Qaeda cofounder and key Muslim Brotherhood leader Abdullah Azzam's "Join the Caravan." It states, "The individually obligatory nature of jihad remains in effect until the lands are purified from the pollution of the disbelievers."[50] They collected more than $1.3 million in contributions. In their defense, Muntasser and Mubayyid claimed to merely have exercised their religious freedom and obligation to give *zakat* as part of their constitutionally protected freedoms. Their motion for dismissal (which the court denied) cited chapter 9, verse 60, of the Qur'an, describing "those entitled to receive *zakat*."

Incredibly, the suspects' attorneys also argued that such charitable giving, to support jihad and mujahideen, is rightfully tax exempt under the U.S. constitutional protection of religious freedom.[51] Court records show Care International deposited checks—with handwritten notes such as "for jihad only," "Bosnia Jihad fund," and "Chechen Muslim Fighters." The U.S. Constitution provides protections for religious freedom, but most certainly was never intended to protect religiously sanctioned or encouraged war in or against America.

The First Amendment bars Congress from enacting laws "respecting an establishment of religion, or prohibiting the free exercise thereof." However, the Constitution offers no protection to any group or religion supporting "holy war" against the United States or its citizens.

STATE *ZAKAT* AGENCIES

Saudia Arabia

In 2007, Saudi Arabia collected $18 billion in *zakat*[52]—which includes the 20 percent flat corporation tax from foreign companies. The Saudis claim that the money collected develops their infrastructure. However, two-thirds of Saudi men are unemployed and the infrastructure is crumbling.[53]

Illustrating how funds are used, Saudi Arabia's secretary-general of the official Muslim World League Koran Memorization Commission stated on Iqra TV, on 29 August

2005, "The Prophet said: 'He who equips a fighter—it is as if he himself fought.' You lie in your bed, safe in your own home, and donate money and Allah credits you with the rewards of a fighter. What is this? A privilege."[54]

Since the 1970s, the Saudi government has spent more than $100 billion[55] to build thousands of mosques, Islamic centers, and Islamic studies programs in universities worldwide to advance the *ummah*'s power and undermine Western economic, political, cultural, educational, and legal structures and replace them with the shari'a.[56]

In the last 13 years alone, the Saudis gave at least $459 million to British universities for Islamic study centers, according to Professor Anthony Glees, of Brunel University.[57]

The worldwide Muslim riots following the publication of the Muhammad cartoons in Denmark's largest daily, *Jyllands-Posten,* began only after Saudi Arabia recalled its ambassador to Denmark; after Sheikh Osama Khayyat, imam of the Grand Mosque in Mecca, praised on national Saudi television the Saudi government for its action; and after Sheikh Ali Al-Hudaify, imam of the Prophet's Mosque in Medina, called "upon governments, organizations and scholars in the Islamic world to extend support for campaigns protesting the sacrilegious attacks on the Prophet."[58] Saudi-controlled OIC initiated and coordinated Muslim rioting worldwide after the Danish Muhammad cartoon publications.[59]

Moreover, to wield more control over Muslim communities worldwide, better orchestrate "spontaneous demonstrations," and better allocate funds for them, the Saudi-backed OIC established the clerical International Commission for *Zakat* (ICZ) on 30 April 2007. Previously, there were more than 20,000 organizations that collected *zakat*. Now, however, the Islamic clerics' centralized "expert committee" based in Malaysia also supervises and distributes *zakat* funds globally. The new committee distributed roughly $2 billion collected over Ramadan 2007 to Muslim "charities."[60]

In a show of unity, the Shiite Hezbollah chief Hassan Nasrallah argued, "If there had been a Muslim to carry out Imam Khomeini's fatwa against the renegade Salman Rushdie, this rabble who insult our Prophet Mohammed in Denmark, Norway and France would not have dared to do so."[61]

The Saudi role in terror financing is no secret. Yet, the U.S. administration keeps telling us that the Saudis are our allies. On 10 December 2002, criticizing the Joint Inquiry Staff (JIS) report of the Senate Select Committee on Intelligence (SSCI) and the House Permanent Select Committee on Intelligence (HPSCI), Senators Jon Kyl and Pat Roberts stated, "The pervasiveness in Saudi Arabia of Wahhabism, a radical, anti-American variant of Islam, was well known before 9/11. The JIS should have inquired why the country of Saudi Arabia was given such preferential treatment by the State Department and whether the intelligence agencies were complicit in the policy."[62]

In early 2008, however, U.S. government officials publicly noted that the Saudis continue the financing of radical Islamic groups.[63]

United Arab Emirates[64]

Like every Muslim country, the UAE collects mandatory Islamic charity (*zakat*—the Third Pillar of Islam—an annual wealth tax), of 2.5 percent to 20 percent from Muslim institutions and companies. Being non-Muslims, foreign banks and oil companies theoretically don't pay *zakat*. But foreign banks and oil companies do pay at least 20 percent of their profits in the form of a mandatory tax rather than *zakat*.

In 2003, the UAE established an independent federal agency collecting *zakat* on government tax revenues from "companies listed on the Dubai Financial Market and Abu Dhabi Securities Market . . . oil-producing companies and branches of foreign banks." In 2007 these revenues were estimated at $13.5 billion.[65]

Although presenting itself to the West as a "moderate" ally, the UAE has consistently supported the "peaceful" and violent advancement of shari'a and terrorism worldwide. In 2006, to support suicide bombing, the UAE gave $100 million to the Palestinian Authority to build a new town named Sheikh Khalifa City, in honor of the UAE president. The city houses families of *shahids* and prisoners—and was built on the ruins of Morag, one of the evacuated Israeli settlements in Gaza.[66]

> On July 27, 2005, the Palestinian Information Center carried a public HAMAS statement thanking the UAE for [its] "unstinting support." The statement said: "We highly appreciate his highness Sheikh Khalifa Bin Zayed Bin Sultan Al-Nahyan (UAE president) in particular and the UAE people and government in general for their limitless support . . . that contributed more to consolidating our people's resoluteness in the face of the Israeli occupation."

> The HAMAS statement continued: "the sisterly UAE had . . . never hesitated in providing aid for our Mujahid people pertaining to rebuilding their houses demolished by the IOF. . . . The UAE also spared no effort to offer financial and material aids to the Palestinian charitable societies."[67]

Indeed, as documented by the Intelligence and Terrorism Information Center at the Center for Special Studies (CSS),[68] Hamas charitable societies are known as integral parts of the Hamas infrastructure, and are outlawed by the United States and Israel.

Hamas also included a special tribute, promising to "never forget the generous donations of the late Sheikh Zayed Bin Sultan [al Nahayan of Abu Dhabi],"[69] the current UAE president's father. The multibillionaire was an early PLO patron and, from the 1970s until his 2004 death, contributed millions of dollars to the PLO's terror agenda, Hamas, and Islamic Jihad.[70]

Sheikh Zayed Bin Sultan was the first Arab ruler to understand the strategic importance of economic jihad[71] against the West. He was first to use oil as a political weapon after the 1973 Yom Kippur War.[72] He was also the major sponsor of the first international Islamic bank, the Bank of Credit and Commerce International (BCCI). The bank was created to serve as "the best bridge to help the world of Islam, and the best way to fight the evil influence of the Zionists."[73] BCCI, which was shut down in July 1991 by New York City district attorney Robert Morgenthau,[74] funded and otherwise facilitated terrorist organizations and states, including the Sandinistas, Hezbollah, abu Nidal, the PLO, al Qaeda, Syria, Libya, Iran's Islamic revolution—as well as Pakistan's nuclear program, to create the "Islamic Bomb."[75] Immediately before the 1991 Gulf War, Sheikh Zayed branded the United States the Muslims' "number two enemy" after Israel. As of this writing, the UAE votes against the United States 70 percent of the time in the UN.[76]

Human Appeal International (HAI), a UAE government-run "charitable" organization, whose board includes the UAE president,[77] continues to fund Hamas and other Palestinian organizations, "martyrs," and Palestinian terrorists in Israeli prisons and their families. The HAI modus operandi includes transferring funds to the Palestinian Red Crescent, whose West Bank and Gaza branches Hamas runs. Hamas, in turn, distributes the money to Hamas "charities." The Toronto, Canada, Orient Research Center reports that the UAE "compensation" plan for the Palestinian intifada in 2001 included $3,000 for every Palestinian *shahid,* $2,000 for his family, $1,500 for those detained by Israel, and $1,200 for each orphan. In addition, the families of terrorists whose homes Israel demolished each received $10,000. Also in 2001, the UAE held two telethons to support the "martyrs'" families. One entitled "We Are All Palestinians" raised 135 million dirham, or $36.8 million, and another called "For Your Sake Palestine" raised 350 million dirham, or $95.3 million.

On 15 February 2005, the Hamas Web site reported on funds transferred from HAI to two West Bank Hamas front organizations, IQRA and Rifdah, outlawed in Israel.[78] On 22 March 2005, the Palestinian newspaper *Al-Ayyam* reported that in 2004 the UAE Red Crescent donated $2 million to Hamas "charities" for 3,158 terrorists' orphans.[79]

A detailed 25 March 2005 report, in the Palestinian daily *Al Hayat al-Jadeeda,* noted that the UAE Friends Society transferred $475,000, through the UAE Red Crescent, to West Bank "charitable" organizations in Hebron, Jenin, Nablus, and Tulkarem to distribute to families of "martyrs," orphans, imprisoned Palestinians, and others.

And in July 2005, Osama Zaki Muhammad Bashiti of Gaza's Khan Younis was arrested while returning from the UAE[80] for often transferring as much as $200,000 at a time to the Gaza branch of Hamas.

Continuing UAE support for Hamas follows the agenda of the late Sheikh Zayed. His Zayed Center for International Coordination and Followup, founded in 1999 as the official Arab League think tank,[81] was shuttered under international pressure in 2003. It championed Holocaust deniers like Thierry Meyssan[82] and Roger Garaudy[83] and provided a platform for anti-Western, anti-Christian, and anti-Jewish extremists like Saudi economist Dr. Yussuf Abdallah Al Zamel, who blamed the Iraq war on "radical Zionist and right-wing Christian" influence.

In October 2000, shortly after the beginning of the last Palestinian intifada against Israel, Qatar-based Muslim Brotherhood spiritual leader Yusuf al-Qaradawi established the "Union of Good,"[84] operated through the London-based Muslim organization Interpal. The Union of Good is an umbrella organization composed of 50 Islamic "charities," including Hamas- and Hezbollah-affiliated organizations. It was supposed to raise funds for only 101 days, but its initial success led the founders, mostly Hamas members, to maintain its operations to date. Millions of dollars generated in Europe and elsewhere through the Union of Good–participating Muslim "charities" fuel all Palestinian terror organizations. Interpal was designated as a terrorist organization by the United States in August 2003, but remains free to operate in the United Kingdom and elsewhere.

Al-Qaradawi, who established and leads the Department of Islamic Law (shari'a) at the University of Qatar and the Institute for Sunnah Research there, is also on the board of directors of the Al-Taqwa Bank, designated by the United States as a terrorist-funding organization in November 2001. In August 2004, al-Qaradawi issued a fatwa saying, "All the Americans in Iraq are soldiers, there is no difference between enlisted soldiers and civilians, and they must be fought because American citizens came to Iraq to serve the occupation. The kidnapping and killing of Americans in Iraq is a [Muslim religious] obligation to force them to leave the country immediately."[85]

UAE foreign minister Sheikh Abdullah bin Zayed al-Nahayan stated that the emirates were and remain a "strong ally of the U.S. in combating terrorism"; continuing UAE support of Hamas and other Islamic terrorist organizations proves otherwise. This raises legitimate concerns for the West about trusting UAE banks, shari'a finance institutions, or government tax or *zakat* collection agencies. Furthermore, it raises alarms about giving the UAE legal control or influence over Western investment houses, banks, or markets.[86] The same applies to every other Islamic financial institution or state.

Bourse Dubai began operating as the world's first fully shari'a-compliant stock exchange in December 2006.[87] Shari'a compliance requires companies traded to also be shari'a-compliant and establishes a special tax on all the others to "purify" them. The Islamic "purity" (*tazkiya*) of Bourse Dubai was approved by the Shari'a Board of the AAOIFI.[88] The AAOIFI laid the groundwork for the global Islamic financial network and regulates all Islamic financial organizations and products, including Bourse Dubai.

HOW THE WEST CAN WIN

The adversary's skill at manipulating media and public opinion cannot be underestimated. The propaganda offensive is so successful that even Colonel Thomas X. Hammes' description of what led to the Second Intifada is a rehash of the Saudi-sponsored Palestinian fabrication and propaganda. Hammes claims that the Palestinian Authority named the new intifada "the al Aqsa Intifada" to suggest that the Palestinian violent reaction was a direct result of then Likud party leader Ariel Sharon's visit to the al-Aqsa Mosque. Moreover, Hammes' speculation that Sharon knowingly sparked Palestinian violence using his own fourth-generation warfare strategy suggests a deliberate disregard for thousands of dead Israelis and Palestinians in the resulting mayhem. The fact of the matter is, Sharon never entered the al-Aqsa Mosque but rather visited the Jewish holy site of the Temple Mount. Moreover, careful study of the Palestinian modus operandi makes it clear that naming violent outbreaks is done in an opportunistic fashion and this one was preplanned. Imad Al-Faluji, then Palestinian Authority communications minister, stated on several occasions: "The PA had begun to prepare for the outbreak of the current Intifada since the return from the Camp David negotiations, by request of President Yasser Arafat."[89]

The United States is now drawing new military and defense doctrines to win the fourth-generation warfare. In addition to improving technologies, the focus seems to be on the development of lighter and more flexible armies, and a greater understanding of the individual characteristics of our enemies. Writing about strategies needed to win the next war, Colonel Thomas X. Hammes states that the "most powerful [U.S.] message" to the world is that "we treasure the individual."[90]

But a measure of the enemy's success is our reluctance to identify the shari'a for what it is. Its adherents value only the *ummah,* and they enslave the individual to achieve their goal—global domination. As long as the enemy—shari'a—has not been acknowledged and understood, we stand no chance. Exposing shari'a and all its adherents, be they states, organizations, or individuals, is crucial to our ability to defend ourselves. It will also enable us to undermine shari'a's global structure, turning its adherents against it, the way we did with communism.

NOTES

1. The failure to understand the role of shari'a financing and Islamic banking in the global effort for Islamic domination is illustrated in a monograph by Major Wesley J. L. Anderson, "Disrupting Threat Finances: Utilization of Financial Information to Disrupt Terrorist Organizations in the Twenty-first Century" (Fort Leavenworth, KS: School of Advanced Military Studies, United States Army Command and General Staff College, June 2007). "Islamic banking" is mentioned in passing as an alternative vehicle to fund Islamist terrorists.

2. Colonel Thomas X. Hammes, USMC, *The Sling and the Stone: On War in the 21st Century* (Zenith Press, 2006).

3. *Ummah,* in Arabic, means the "Community of the Believers" (*ummaht al-mu'minin*)—the Muslim world.

4. Qur'an 57:2: "To Him belongs the dominion of the heavens and the earth: It is He Who gives Life and Death; and He has Power over all things." Also see *Sahih Bukhari,* vol. 4, bk. 53, no. 392: "Narrated Abu Huraira: [The Prophet said to the Jews], 'If you embrace Islam, you will be safe. You should know that the earth belongs to Allah and His Apostle, and I want to expel you from this land. So, if anyone amongst you owns some property, he is permitted to sell it, otherwise you should know that the Earth belongs to Allah and His Apostle.'"

5. Stephen Labaton and Julia Werdigier, "Mild Reaction in Capitol on Dubai NASDAQ Acquisition," *New York Times,* 20 September 2007, available at www.nytimes.com/2007/09/21/business/worldbusiness/21exchange.html?_r=1&oref=slogin (accessed 17 October 2007).

6. "Hamud bin Uqla al-Shuaibi is a prominent and influential Saudi scholar. His students included a number of important Saudi religious leaders, including the current grand mufti. Al-Shuaibi published religious edicts supporting the Taliban regime in Afghanistan, including the destruction of the Hindu statues, as part of jihad against the infidels. He religiously justified al-Qaeda's attack on the U.S. in September 2001 and gave religious legitimacy to the suicide attacks against Israel carried out by Palestinians. In October 2001, bin Laden cited al-Shuaibi when he spoke of his justification for killing Jews and Christians." Jonathan D. Halevi, "What Drives Saudia Arabia to Persist in Terrorist Financing? *Al-Jihad bi-al-Mal*—Financial *Jihad* against the Infidels," *Jerusalem Viewpoints,* no. 531, 1 June 2005, www.jcpa.org/jl/vp531.htm (accessed 24 October 2007).

7. "Appendix G: Profile of Sheikh Dr. Yussuf al-Qardawi, Chairman of the Board of the Union of Good," Intelligence and Terrorism Center at the Center for Special Studies, www.intelligence.org.il/Eng/sib/2_05/funds_g.htm.

8. Halevi, "What Drives Saudi Arabia to Persist in Terrorist Financing?"

9. Yousef Al-Qaradawi, *Towards a Worldwide Strategy for Islamic Policy* [a.k.a. *The Project*], full translation obtained from Swiss authorities by authors. See also Patrick Poole, "The Muslim Brotherhood 'Project,'" *FrontPage Magazine,* 11 May 2006, www.frontpagemag.com/articles/Read.aspx?GUID={61829F93-7A81-4654-A2E8-F0A5E6DD3DC4} (accessed 8 September 2007).

10. Timur Kuran, *Islam and Mammon: The Economic Predicaments of Islamism* (Princeton University Press, 2004), x, 3–14: "Islamic economics itself exemplifies what has been called an 'invented tradition'"; "Neither classical nor medieval Islamic civilization featured banks in the modern sense, let alone 'Islamic' banks. . . . Medieval Islamic civilization produced no organizations that could pool thousands of peoples' funds, administer them collectively, and then survive the death of their managers. The financial rules of Islam remained frozen up to modern times, precluding the formation, except outside Islamic law, of durable partnerships involving large

numbers of individuals. It was the Europeans who . . . developed a complex financial system centered on banks."

11. "Past and Present of Political Islam," *Al Ahram*, 10–18 January 2006, available at weekly.ahram.org.eg/2006/777/op2.htm (accessed 9 October 2007); "Muslim Brotherhood," *Encyclopedia of the Orient*, i-cias.com/e.o/mus_br_egypt.htm (accessed 9 October 2007); "Muslim Brothers," Federation of American Scientists, www.fas.org/irp/world/para/mb.htm (accessed 9 October 2007).

12. Lorenzo Vidino, "The Muslim Brotherhood's Conquest of Europe," *Middle East Quarterly*, Winter 2005, available at www.meforum.org/article/687 (accessed 9 October 2007).

13. Rachel Ehrenfeld and Alyssa A. Lappen, "Ban the Brotherhood," *FrontPage Magazine*, 27 December 2005, www.frontpagemag.com/Articles/Read.aspx?GUID=2CE8EF64-FA27-435C-8699-1433C788BDDB (accessed 9 October 2007).

14. Rachel Ehrenfeld and Alyssa A. Lappen, "Tithing for Terrorists," National Review Online, 12 October 2007, article.nationalreview.com/?q=MWEwMDg1ZThjM2FmYzU1MTU5Y2Q3MTBhY2I2YjM5NTc= (accessed 24 October 2007).

15. Ibid.

16. "Profile: International Islamic Relief Organization," Cooperative Research History Commons, www.cooperativeresearch.org/entity.jsp?entity=international_islamic_relief_organization (accessed 24 October 2007); "U.S. District Court Rules Saudi Charity to Remain in 9/11 Terrorist Lawsuit," PRNewsire, 22 September 2005, prnewswire.com/cgi-bin/stories.pl?ACCT=104&STORY=/www/story/09-22-2005/0004113679&EDATE= (accessed 24 October 2007).

17. BBC Press Office, "Panorama: Faith, Hate and Charity," British Broadcasting Corporation, press release, 30 July 2006, www.bbc.co.uk/pressoffice/pressreleases/stories/2006/07_july/30/panorama.shtml (accessed 8 October 2007).

18. Rachel Ehrenfeld and Alyssa A. Lappen, "The Egyptian Roots of Hatred," *Washington Times*, 6 July 2007, available at www.acdemocracy.org/article/invent_index.php?id=380 (accessed 24 October 2007).

19. "Islamic Development Bank," Organization of the Islamic Conference, www.oicun.org/articles/22/1/Islamic-Development-Bank/1.htm (accessed 8 October 2007).

20. Prof. Rodney Wilson, "The Evolution of the Islamic Financial System," available at www.sc.com.my/eng/html/iaffairs/ioscoislamicpdf/AAEuromoneych2.pdf (accessed 8 October 2007).

21. Nasser M. Suleiman "Corporate Governance in Islamic Banking," Al-Bab, www.al-bab.com/arab/econ/nsbanks.htm (accessed 8 October 2007).

22. "IDB Launches $10b Fund to Tackle Poverty in Islamic World," *Gulf News*, 24 October 2007, available at www.zawya.com/Story.cfm/sidGN_24102007_10162319/secIndustries/pagIslamic%20Finance; "IDB Concludes Its 32nd Annual Meeting in Senegal," *Business Life*, 30 May 2007, available at www.thebusinesslife.com/finance.htm (accessed 24 October 2007).

23. Muhammad Saman, "Almost All Intifada Funds by Arab Donors Has Arrived," *Arab News*, 26 August 2001, available at www.arabnews.com/?page=4&section=0&article=4976&d=26&m=8&y=2001 (accessed 8 October 2007).

24. Ehrenfeld and Lappen, "Tithing for Terrorists."

25. Helen Chapin Metz, ed. "Finance," in *Sudan: A Country Study* (Washington: GPO, 1991), available at countrystudies.us/sudan/62.htm (accessed 8 October 2007); see also "an-Nimeiri, Gafar Mohammad," *Encyclopedia of the Orient*, lexicorient.com/e.o/nimeiri_g.htm.

26. Al-Qaradawi, *Towards a Worldwide Strategy for Islamic Policy*. See also Poole, "The Muslim Brotherhood 'Project.'"

27. Al-Qaradawi, *Towards a Worldwide Strategy for Islamic Policy*.

28. "AAOIFI Board of Trustees," Accounting and Auditing Organization for Islamic Financial Institutions, www.aaoifi.com/board-trustees.html (accessed 8 October 2007).

29. Richard A. Clarke, statement before the U.S. Senate Banking Committee, 108th Cong., 1st sess., 22 October 2003, available at www.senate.gov/~banking/_files/clarke.pdf (accessed 8 October 2007).

30. "Financing of the 9/11 plot," National Commission on Terrorist Attacks upon the United States, available at www.9-11commission.gov/staff_statements/911_TerrFin_App.pdf.

31. "A Financial Jihad," *Al-Ahram*, 21–27 November 2002, available at weekly.ahram.org.eg/2002/613/ec2 .htm (accessed 8 October 2007).

32. James Bennet, "Israelis, in Raid on Arab Banks, Seize Reputed Terrorist Funds," *New York Times,* 26 February 2004, available at query.nytimes.com/gst/fullpage.html?res=9B03EEDA133CF935A15751C0A9629C8B63 &sec=&spon=&pagewanted=print (accessed 8 October 2007); Farah Stockman, "Palestinian Authority's U.S. Assets Are Frozen," *Boston Globe,* 30 August 2005, available at www.boston.com/news/world/middleeast/ articles/2005/08/30/palestinian_authoritys_us_assets_are_frozen/ (accessed 8 October 2007).

33. "Shift to Shari'ah Based Financial Products," *Arab News,* 20 May 2006, available at www.menafn.com/ qn_news_story_s.asp?StoryId=1093113527 (accessed 8 September 2007); "Message of His Excellency Sheikh Saleh bin Abdullah Kamel," Islamic Chamber of Commerce and Industry, www.icci-oic.org/ic/1.htm (accessed 8 October 2007).

34. "Shift to Shari'ah Based Financial Products."

35. Mohammed El Qorchi, "Islamic Finance Gears Up," *Finance and Development: A Quarterly Magazine of the IMF* 42, no. 4 (December 2005), available at www.imf.org/external/pubs/ft/fandd/2005/12/qorchi.htm (accessed 8 September 2007).

36. Landon Thomas, Jr., "Muslim Financiers Fight Suspicion in U.S.," *International Herald Tribune,* 8 August 2007; "Islamic Finance Prospers, Backed by Non-Muslims," Agence France-Presse, September 2006, available at findarticles.com/p/articles/mi_kmafp/is_200609/ai_n16929131 (accessed 8 September 2007).

37. Clarke, statement before the U.S. Senate Banking Committee; "The World's Billionaires," *Forbes,* 8 March 2007, available at www.forbes.com/lists/2007/10/07billionaires_The-Worlds-Billionaires_CountryOfCitizen _16.html (accessed 26 October 2007).

38. Osama bin Laden, quoted in Geoff Shaw, "Knowledge Based Authentication: Is It Quantifiable?" (presentation, NIST-GSA Symposium, Gaithersburg, MD, 9 February 2004), csrc.nist.gov/archive/kba/ Presentations/Day%201/Shaw.pdf (accessed 8 September 2007).

39. "Dubai Financial Market Sharia Board to Set Standards for Classifying Listed Companies," AME Info, 24 June 2007, www.ameinfo.com/124491.html (accessed 24 October 2007).

40. Kathryn S. Wylde (president and CEO of Partnership for New York City), interview, Fox Business Network, 22 October 2007.

41. "Islamic Finance Summit," Financial Research Associates, www.frallc.com/conference.aspx?ccode=b525 (accessed 8 October 2007).

42. Commenting on the creeping shari'a in the West, Judge Michael Mukasey, in confirmation hearings before the Senate Judiciary Committee, said: "We live in this country under one system of laws. And whatever may be the religious requirements of any group, we don't create enclaves where a different law applies, a different law governs and people don't have the rights that everybody else has outside that enclave. I would resist that very firmly—the creation of any such enclave." "Senate Judiciary Committee Hearing for Nomination of Judge Mukasey as Attorney General," Washingtonpost.com, 17 October 2007, www.washingtonpost.com/wp-srv/ politics/documents/attorney_general_hearing_101707.html.

43. Janine A. Clark, *Islam, Charity, and Activism: Middle-Class Networks and Social Welfare in Egypt, Jordan, and Yemen* (Bloomington, IN: Indiana University Press, 2004).

44 Douglas Farah, "Zakat and Jihad from the Words of the Master," Douglas Farah, posted 1 November 2006, www.douglasfarah.com/article/119/zakat-and-jihad-from-the-words-of-the-master#comment (accessed 8 October 2007); Ahmed Makhdoom, "Zakat for Education," Makhdoom's Quality Quest, pachome1.pacific .net.sg/~makhdoom/zakat2.html (accessed 8 October 2007); Douglas Farah, "Zakat and Jihad from the

Words of the Master," Thoughts of a Conservative Christian, posted 2 November 2006, bsimmons
.wordpress.com/2006/11/02/zakat-and-jihad-from-the-words-of-the-master-2/.

45. Ayatollah Khomeini issued a fatwa "for transferring charity funds to support the armed Palestinian campaign against Israel. He thus paved the way for charitable societies operating in the Arab-Muslim world and the West to finance the activities of the Islamic terrorist organizations." "Iranian-Sponsored World Jerusalem Day Was Marked in Iran, Some Countries in the Arab-Muslim World, and Western Countries Such as Britain and Canada," Intelligence and Terrorism Information Center at the Israel Intelligence Heritage & Commemoration Center (IICC), www.terrorism-info.org.il/eng/eng_n/jerusalem_d07e.htm.

46. *Khums* is another tax every Muslim merchant has to pay once a year. The money allegedly goes for public needs, and since jihad is on the march, Muslim religious leaders use the money for their own purposes. See ibid.

47. Ibid.

48. Aron Zysow, "Zakat," *The Encyclopedia of Islam,* new ed., vol. 11, 406–22, discussed in *United States v. Mubayyid,* 476 F.Supp.2d 46, n17 (D. Mass. 2007), available at www.slashlegal.com/showthread.php?t=133601.

49. J. Millard Burr and Robert O. Collins, *Alms for Jihad: Charity and Terrorism in the Islamic World* (New York: Cambridge University Press, 2006), 12–13. The book was pulped in 2007, in capitulation to mere threats of an expensive libel suit in the United Kingdom against the publisher by Saudi billionaire Khalid bin Mahfouz, who chose British libel laws as a vehicle for financial jihad, successfully silencing the Western media from exposing terror financiers. For more information about the case, see Rachel Ehrenfeld, "Fighting Financial Jihad," Pajamas Media, posted 23 September 2007, pajamasmedia.com/blog/financial_jihad_vs_the_first_a/.

50. Sheikh Abdullah Ibn Yusuf Azzam, "Join the Caravan," 10, available at www.worldofislam.info/ebooks/joincaravan.pdf, accessed from "Update on Care International Trial in Boston/ 'Seas of Blood for Jihad,'" Miss Kelly, posted 1 December 2007, misskelly.typepad.com/miss_kelly_/2007/12/update-on-care.html.

51. Rachel Ehrenfeld and Alyssa A. Lappen, "Jihadists and Jews," *Washington Times,* 16 October 2006, available at www.acdemocracy.org/article/invent_index.php?id=133 (accessed 25 October 2007).

52. Talal Malik, "GCC Can Rake Billions in Zakat, Income Tax," ArabianBusiness.com, 12 September 2007, www.arabianbusiness.com/500208-gcc-can-rake-billions-in-zakat-income-tax-?ln=en (accessed 8 October 2007).

53. Jonathan Schanzer, "Saudi Squander," National Review Online, 3 October 2007, article.nationalreview.com/?q=ZGVhMmViODM0OGJlYzk1NmU0ZmQ1OGVhMmEwM2M4ZTU= (accessed 8 October 2007).

54. Rachel Ehrenfeld and Alyssa A. Lappen, "The Cure for the Wahabbi Virus," *FrontPage Magazine,* 17 October 2005, frontpagemagazine.com/Articles/Read.aspx?GUID=29BC8889-AFC0-4A2C-877F-ABE26D80DB25 (accessed 25 October 2007).

55. Amir Taheri, "Culture of Hate," *Islam Review,* 22 June 2004, www.islamreview.com/articles/cultureofhate.shtml (accessed 8 October 2007).

56. Rachel Ehrenfeld, "Saudi Dollars and Jihad," *FrontPage Magazine,* 24 October 2005, www.frontpagemag.com/Articles/Read.aspx?GUID=%7B0F477FDA-9DC5-46E1-BBFB-627CAC95BB1B%7D (accessed 8 October 2007).

57. Ben Leach, "'Extremism' Fear over Islam Studies Donations," *The Telegraph,* 14 April 2008, www.telegraph.co.uk/news/main.jhtml?xml=/news/2008/04/13/nislam113.xml.

58. P. K. Abdul Ghafour, "Imams Back Call for Danish Boycott in Cartoons Row," CBS News, 28 January 2006, www.cbsnews.com/stories/2006/01/27/ap/world/mainD8FCO6K01.shtml (accessed 26 October 2007); "The Clash to End All Clashes?" National Review Online, 6 February 2006, www.nationalreview.com/script/printpage.p?ref=/symposium/symposium200602070754.asp (accessed 26 October 2007).

59. "Statement of the OIC Ambassadorial Plenary Meeting," Organization of the Islamic Conference, 14 February 2006, www.oic-oci.org/press/english/2006/February%202006/joint-statment.htm (accessed 8 September 2007; Nat Hentoff, "The Cartoons Conspiracy," *Village Voice,* 20 February 2006, www.villagevoice.com/

news/0608,hentoff,72237,6.html (accessed 8 October 2007); Pete Baumgartner, "East: Islamic Officials, Journalists Reflect on Publication of Muhammad Cartoons," *Radio Free Europe,* 3 February 2006, www.rferl.org/featuresarticle/2006/02/5d6e1728-e305-4dc7-b9d0-8350f35ed375.html (accessed 8 October 2007); Gil Kaufman, "Muslim Fury over Danish Cartoons Spurs Riots across the Globe—Why?" MTV, www.mtv.com/news/articles/1523891/20060207/id_0.jhtml (accessed 8 September 2007).

60. P. K. Abdul Ghafour, "Kingdom, 20 OIC Partners Support Global Zakah Fund," *Arab News,* 30 April 2007, available at www.arabnews.com/?page=1&section=0&article=95581&d=30&m=4&y=2007 (accessed 8 October 2007).

61. "Hezbollah: Rushdie Death Would Stop Prophet Insults," Yahoo News, 2 February 2006, www.natashatynes.com/newswire/2006/02/hezbollah_killi.html (accessed 26 October 2007).

62. Senator John Kyl and Senator Pat Roberts, "Joint Inquiry Staff Report: Additional Views," Federation of American Scientists, available at www.fas.org/irp/congress/2002_rpt/kyl-roberts.html (accessed 26 October 2007).

63. Josh Meyer, "Saudi Arabia Is Prime Source of Terror Funds, U.S. Says," *Los Angeles Times,* 2 April 2008, www.latimes.com/news/nationworld/nation/la-na-terror2apr02,1,1851447.story.

64. Department of State, Bureau of Democracy, Human Rights, and Labor, "United Arab Emirates," *Country Reports on Human Rights Practices,* 2006, available at www.state.gov/g/drl/rls/hrrpt/2006/78865.htm.

   The government's respect for human rights remained problematic, and significant human rights problems reported included: no citizens' right to change the government and no popularly elected representatives of any kind; flogging as judicially sanctioned punishment; arbitrary detention and incommunicado detention, both permitted by law; questionable independence of the judiciary; restrictions on civil liberties—freedom of speech and of the press (including the Internet), and assembly; restrictions on right of association; restrictions on religious freedom; domestic abuse of women, sometimes enabled by police; trafficking in women and children; legal and societal discrimination against women and noncitizens; corruption and lack of government transparency; common abuse of foreign domestic servants; and severe restrictions on and abuses of workers' rights.

65. Malik, "GCC Can Rake Billions in Zakat, Income Tax."

66. Rachel Ehrenfeld and Alyssa A. Lappen, "The U.N. Gives Hamas a Raise," *FrontPage Magazine,* 6 January 2006, www.frontpagemag.com/Articles/Read.aspx?GUID=E4DE77B2-B0DC-4DC6-B5EC-7D07661F5EF6 (accessed 26 October 2007).

67. Rachel Ehrenfeld and Alyssa A. Lappen, "Welcoming Terror to U.S. Ports," *FrontPage Magazine,* 24 February 2006, www.frontpagemag.com/Articles/Printable.aspx?GUID=8DE1557E-ECFC-4447-BB8C-C800D6D9FDAA (accessed 26 October 2007).

68. "Spotlight on a Hamas Dawah Institution in the West Bank," Intelligence and Terrorism Information Center at the Center for Special Studies, www.terrorism-info.org.il/malam_multimedia/ENGLISH/MARKETING%20TERRORISM/PDF/JAN22_05.PDF (accessed 26 October 2007).

69. "Zayed bin Sultan al-Nahyan Sheik, United Arab Emirates 1966–2004," NameBase, www.namebase.org/main4/Sheik-Zayed-bin-sultan-al_2Dnahyan.html (accessed 26 October 2007).

70. Ibid.

71. Rachel Ehrenfeld, "Saudi Interest in America," *Washington Times,* 15 January 2006, www.washtimes.com/op-ed/20060115-103622-3038r.htm.

72. Rachel Ehrenfeld, *Evil Money* (HarperBusiness, 1992), 164, 169–70.

73. Ibid., 169.

74. Ibid., 165.

75. Ibid, 163–210.

76. The UAE is no "ally" of the United States. See annual reports on voting patterns in the United States Department of State and United Nations records.

77. "Board Members of Human Appeal International," ArabDecision.org, www.arabdecision.org/list_cvs_3_12 _8_1_3_4825.htm (accessed 26 October 2007.)

78. Item on Hamas Web site, www.palestine-info.info/arabic/palestoday/dailynews/2005/feb05/12_2/details6 .htm, in the author's possession.

79. Article in *Al-Ayyam,* 22 March 2005, www.al-ayyam.com/znews/site/default.aspx (accessed 26 October 2007), in the author's possession.

80. Ehrenfeld and Lappen, "Welcoming Terror to U.S. Ports."

81. "ADL Backgrounder: The Zayed Center," Anti-defamation League, 15 September 2003, available at www.adl .org/Anti_semitism/zayed_center.asp (accessed 26 October 2007).

82. "Media's Take on the News 6-2-03 to 7-14-03," History News Network, hnn.us/articles/1601.html (accessed 26 October 2007).

83. Jonathan Jaffit, "Fighting Sheikh Zaeyd's Funding of Islamic Studies at Harvard Divinity School: A Case Study," *Maccabean Online,* January 2006, www.freeman.org/MOL/pages/january-2006.php (accessed 26 October 2007).

84. Rachel Ehrenfeld, "The 'Union of Good' and the Lost Peace," *FrontPage Magazine*, 7 March 2005, www .frontpagemag.com/Articles/Read.aspx?GUID={B01DD54B-AEA5-4A10-881E-649249DDBD42}.

85. "Appendix G."

86. Ehrenfeld and Lappen, "Welcoming Terror to U.S. Ports."

87. Sohall Zubair, "Islamic Conversion Boosted DFM IPO," *Gulf News*, 2 December 2006, available at archive .gulfnews.com/articles/06/12/02/10086533.html (accessed 8 October 2007).

88. Ibid.

89. Hammes, *The Sling and the Stone,* 119. Regarding this particular incident, Imad Al-Faluji has said, "The PA had begun to prepare for the outbreak of the current Intifada since the return from the Camp David negotiations, by request of President Yasser Arafat, who predicted the outbreak of the Intifada as a complementary stage to the Palestinian steadfastness in the negotiations, and not as a specific protest against Sharon's visit to Al-Haram Al-Qudsi [Temple Mount]." Moreover, "The Intifada was no surprise for the Palestinian leadership. . . . The PA instructed the political forces and factions to run all matters of the Intifada." See "PA Minister: The Intifada Was Planned from the Day Arafat Returned from Camp David; Special Dispatch Series No. 194, March 21, 2001," Middle East Media Research Institute, available at www.memri.org/bin/articles .cgi?Area=sd&ID=SP19401.

90. Hammes, *The Sling and the Stone,* 291.

29 Terrorism as an International Security Problem

Martha Crenshaw

INTRODUCTION

After the attacks on New York and Washington in September 11, 2001, terrorism was recognized as a major international security problem.[1] It has remained on the international agenda because the problem has not been solved. The trend in terrorism that produced the 9/11 catastrophe did not abate but continued. Other issues associated with terrorism also remain troubling, particularly those connected to the Palestinian-Israeli conflict, conditions in Iraq, Afghanistan, and Pakistan, and the future of Kashmir and Indo-Pakistani relations.

The immediate impact of the attacks was dramatic. For the United States, 9/11 led to the declaration of a "global war on terrorism," military intervention in Afghanistan to defeat the Taliban regime and destroy Al Qaeda's base, and in 2003 a preemptive war in Iraq. At home, the government undertook fundamental organizational reforms, including establishing a Department of Homeland Security and reorganizing the nation's intelligence bureaucracy into a National Counterterrorist Center. At the international level, terrorism also became a top priority. The United Nations, NATO, and the EU moved immediately to develop counterterrorism policies based on international cooperation. In 2001, for example, NATO invoked its collective defense provision for the first time.

Dr. Martha Crenshaw started investigating terrorism and armed groups long before September 11, 2001. She has written extensively on the issue of political terrorism; her first article, "The Concept of Revolutionary Terrorism," was published in the *Journal of Conflict Resolution* in 1972. Her recent work includes the chapters "Coercive Diplomacy and the Response to Terrorism" in *The United States and Coercive Diplomacy* (United States Institute of Peace Press) and "Terrorism, Strategies, and Grand Strategies" in *Attacking Terrorism* (Georgetown University Press) and "Counterterrorism in Retrospect" in the July–August 2005 issue of *Foreign Affairs*. Presently, Dr. Crenshaw is a senior fellow in the Center for International Security and Cooperation and the Freeman Spogli Institute for International Studies, as well as professor of political science by courtesy, at Stanford University. From 1974 to 2007 she taught in the Department of Government at Wesleyan University in Middletown, Connecticut. She serves on the editorial boards of the journals *International Security, Orbis, Political Psychology, Security Studies,* and *Terrorism and Political Violence*. She coordinated the working group on political explanations of terrorism for the 2005 Club de Madrid International Summit on Democracy, Terrorism and Security. She is a lead investigator with the new National Center for the Study of Terrorism and the Response to Terrorism at the University of Maryland, funded by the Department of Homeland Security. She is also the recipient of a John Simon Guggenheim Memorial Foundation Fellowship in 2005–06. She serves on the Committee on Law and Justice and the Committee on Determining Basic Research Needs to Interrupt the Improvised Explosive Device Delivery Chain of the National Research Council of the National Academies of Science. Her current research focus is on why the United States is the target of terrorism and on the distinction between "old" and "new" terrorism, as well as how campaigns of terrorism come to an end.

However, the initial international consensus against terrorism has become frayed in large part because the war in Iraq has increasingly turned into a civil and sectarian war, with extraordinarily high levels of violence including an unprecedented number of suicide bombings. The war in Iraq has provided both a source of renewed motivation and a training ground for Al Qaeda and related groups, particularly Al Qaeda in Mesopotamia led by the late Abu Musab al-Zarqawi. The conflict has also produced serious spillover effects. Zarqawi's group was directly responsible for bombings in Jordan. The bombings of public transport in Spain in 2004 and London in 2005, as well as the interrupted plot against airliners crossing the Atlantic in 2006, can also be linked to opposition to the war in Iraq, which has focused the grievances of discontented fringes in the Muslim diaspora on the United States and on American allies.

Another problem that has drawn terrorism into the domain of international politics is the difficult question of how to deal with political organizations that use or have used terrorism but are democratically elected to positions of power. The contemporary examples we have before us in the Israeli-Palestinian conflict are Hamas and Hezbollah. How should the international community deal with an armed state within a state or an armed party that leads a government? Iranian support for Hezbollah and its recalcitrance before the world community's effort to restrain its nuclear ambitions underscore the seriousness of this problem. (It is interesting that the war in Iraq began with the presumption that its purpose was to remove Iraq's weapons of mass destruction in the interest of curbing nuclear proliferation; we have now returned to the same threat with Iran, which has profited by the wars in Afghanistan and Iraq to fill a power vacuum in the Middle East.)

This analysis addresses four questions:

1. What is terrorism today?
2. What are its causes?
3. Why is terrorism a threat to international security?
4. How has the international community responded, and what does the future look like?

DEFINING THE THREAT

Terrorism is a contested concept. Its use is often subjective and pejorative, meant to convey condemnation of an adversary. It is not easy to use the term and to be understood objectively. Accordingly, it has been difficult to reach agreement on a definition at the international level. Since it was first discussed in 1973, despite the passage of twelve anti-terrorism conventions, the United Nations has yet to decide on an official definition. As the 2004 Secretary-General's High-level Panel Report explained, disagreement has centered first on whether the term applies only to nonstates. Should states also be considered "terrorist" when their armed forces or security services attack civilians, whether deliberately or not? A second problem concerns moral justifications for violence. Should the use of violence by a resistance movement confronting foreign occupation be categorized as terrorism? Does the end excuse if not justify the means? The panel concluded that terrorism is never acceptable, no matter how legitimate or popular the cause it is meant to serve. Terrorism is "any action . . . that is intended to cause death or serious bodily harm to civilians or non-combatants, when the purpose of such act, by its nature or context, is to intimidate a population, or to compel a Government or an international organization to do or to abstain from doing any act."[2]

Although the current threat is largely associated with radical or "jihadist" Islamist movements, terrorism has a long history and contemporary terrorism is not entirely unprecedented. The present must be seen in historical perspective. Organizations associated with a variety of beliefs and ideologies—nationalism, revolutionary socialism, right wing extremism, and religion—have all practiced terrorism. Its modern form began in the late nineteenth century with Irish nationalists, Russian revolutionaries, and anarchists in Europe and the United States. Their activities constituted precedents for indiscriminate attacks on civilians as a way of undermining society (anarchists for whom no bourgeois was innocent, for example), loosely organized local conspiracies acting out of inspiration rather than central direction, and utopian and transnational goals. Furthermore, some groups that did not act on an international scale and had no religious affiliation, such as Sendero Luminoso in Peru in the 1980s, were both apocalyptic and murderous. It is not only "religious" terrorism that is lethal. The resumption of violence in Sri Lanka in 2006, including suicide bombings in Colombo, is a sad reminder of the persistence of nationalist violence.

However, since the 1990s, Al Qaeda and its affiliates and offshoots, which together loosely comprise a global Salafist or jihadi movement, have constituted the heart of the threat. What commentators mean by "Al Qaeda" is either or both the remnant of the central core of the organization that ordered the 9/11 attack and those that preceded it and local associates and imitators around the world. The threat is thus composed of local and transnational elements. Since 2001 attacks have taken place in Indonesia, Morocco, Tunisia, Saudi Arabia, Egypt, Jordan, Iraq, Turkey, Pakistan, Afghanistan, Kenya, Spain, and Great Britain. The presence of these successor groups is clearly global, including cells within immigrant Muslim communities in the West, particularly Britain. Whether these groups are completely self-recruited or self-generated or instigated or even directed by Al Qaeda operatives directly is unknown. The answer may be different in each case, since the Madrid bombers apparently were not linked to "Al Qaeda central" but the two British-based groups may have been, via connections in Pakistan. In Iraq, the group that became Al Qaeda in Mesopotamia was originally independent but later joined forces with the central leadership. Subsequently it tried to shed some of its foreign appearance by merging into an Iraqi Moudjahidin Shura Council. Its violence found support in anti-regime Sunni groups in Iraq who also seek destabilization. Some of them may now seek an Islamic state as well as a return of the Sunni elite to power.

It is important to locate the current threat in its historical context. How did this now diffuse movement emerge and grow?[3] Its origins lie in the anti-Soviet resistance in Afghanistan, which is where the links among individuals and different national groups were forged. Al Qaeda was established under Osama bin Laden in 1988 in Pakistan as a hierarchical, centralized, and bureaucratic organization. Its later decentralized structure was forced upon it by the strong international response to 9/11. From the beginning, bin Laden was strongly influenced by the views of his mentor, Abdullah Azzam, who organized Arab support for the moudjahidin fighting against the Soviet Union in Afghanistan. Bin Laden was also close to Ayman al-Zawahiri and his Egyptian Islamic Jihad organization, which aimed to overthrow the Egyptian government and eventually merged with Al Qaeda.[4] Bin Laden was determined to train an army for jihad first against the Soviet Union, and when that mission was completed (although the role of the "Arabs" in the Soviet withdrawal was nowhere near as important as he thought) against the new occupier of Muslim lands and supporter of Israel, the United States.

Returning to his home in Saudi Arabia, bin Laden offered to help defend the kingdom against Iraq after the 1990 invasion of Kuwait, but his offer was rejected. He became increasingly critical of the Saudi government for having invited American troops onto Muslim soil, but also for its corruption and inefficiency. His initial appeal was for reform, not for the overthrow of the regime. However, he became sufficiently troublesome that he had to remove himself and his business enterprises to the Sudan, which fortuitously had recently come under Islamic rule. From there he helped train and finance jihad in conflicts in the former Soviet Union and Yugoslavia, taking advantage of the dissolution of multinational empires and states. In fact, he offered support wherever Muslims were fighting secular governments, including the Philippines and Indonesia. He was also involved in opposing the American intervention in Somalia. In 1994, Saudi Arabia stripped him of his family wealth, and in 1996, under pressure, Sudan expelled him. He then returned to Afghanistan, where the Taliban was on the verge of taking power after the civil war that followed the Soviet withdrawal.

After jihad ended in apparent triumph in Afghanistan, those who took credit for the victory diffused around the globe. Many of the former fighters in Afghanistan returned home with training and expertise and also with a sense of having fulfilled a transcendental mission, sometimes accompanied by an exalted reputation, to alter the course of local conflicts (in Algeria, for example). Others, whether by choice or because their own governments would not permit their repatriation, joined or formed Islamist groups in diasporas in the West. Other men who were too young to have fought in Afghanistan were either recruited by these experienced operatives or emulated what they saw as the jihadist model. Zarqawi was one of those who trained in Afghanistan, although at that time he and bin Laden were hostile to each other.

The importance of resources to the development of Al Qaeda should be stressed. Initially it was a socially-sanctioned and officially-sanctioned movement and in part as a consequence was well financed beyond bin Laden's personal fortune. The government of Saudi Arabia, in particular, generously supported the Arab moudjahidin. Wealthy individuals and charities gave copious amounts to the cause. Bin Laden, unlike Zawahiri, was not a rebel at the outset. And he gained power not just because of his ideas and ambitions but because of the money he controlled. Furthermore, Al Qaeda could not have developed had it not had secure bases first in Pakistan, then in Sudan, and last in Afghanistan. It was not so much failed states as protective states and access to networks of support that provided critical space in which to act.

Today the convictions driving this movement are vehemently anti-Western and anti-American, but these views developed gradually. Although Zawahiri was determined to seize power in Egypt from the earliest days, bin Laden came slowly to opposing the Saudi regime. It is possible that both bin Laden and Zawahiri realized that they could not overthrow the "near enemy," the apostate Muslim regimes in Saudi Arabia and Egypt, unless American support for them were withdrawn. Jihadists are thought to wish not only to create Islamic states on the Salafist model in majority Muslim countries and re-establish a version of the early Islamic Caliphate, which would extend to territories such as Andalusia, but also to diminish Western influence worldwide, which they see as a threat to Islam.[5]

Scholars and policy makers debate the question of whether Al Qaeda is genuinely motivated by the conflicts in Palestine or whether references to these grievances are opportunistic. Certainly bin Laden was deeply opposed to the 1994 Oslo Accords, which he saw as a betrayal of Islamic principles. His mentor Azzam was Palestinian. Sadat was assassinated by Islamist militants opposed to the peace agreement with Israel. Whether sympathy for the Palestinian cause is genuine or not, conflicts that pit Muslims against non-Muslims help extremists to justify their position that Islam is on the defensive and that jihad is a moral obligation incumbent on individual Muslims.[6] In providing evidence for claims that Muslims are victims of Western oppression, the war in Iraq may have revived a fading movement. The summer 2006 conflict between Israel and Hezbollah also added fuel to the flame.

Scholars also debate the extent to which terrorism is determined by environmental conditions, as opposed to specific historical circumstances such as those outlined above. The "root causes" that are typically mentioned are globalization, lack of democracy, and religion, particularly Islam. All of these arguments are problematic, especially as they decontextualize the problem.

With regard to globalization, one suggestion is that resentment over being left behind inspires terrorism in areas of the world that do not benefit but feel exploited by the West. However, it is not clear that the most disadvantaged parts of the world, those that profit least from globalization of the means of production, produce more terrorist conspiracies than those more advantaged. This issue relates to the debate over whether poverty and underdevelopment yield terrorism.[7] However, even in poorer countries most of the individuals who become terrorists are better educated and more prosperous than other members of their societies, many members of Al Qaeda came from Saudi Arabia, and other jihadists are citizens of the West. Such individuals are the products of globalization, not those left behind. They seem to be material beneficiaries of the modern world who are socially and politically unassimilated and spiritually adrift. They are caught between traditional families and communities and modernity. Thus they may be left behind by globalization on a psychological rather than material level. They feel a keen sense of injustice and victimization, but it can be vicarious rather than directly experienced.[8]

More convincing is the proposition that permeability of borders, mobility of persons, and instantaneous worldwide communication via the internet and the news media provide important resources for terrorist conspiracies. Underground organizations can take advantage of all the developments that make the world a smaller place. It is easy to travel, communicate, and transfer money. Islamist-oriented groups that call for a return to the past, paradoxically, are quite adept in using the tools of the modernity they ostensibly reject. They establish websites to promote the cause, talk via cell phones, watch satellite television, and jet around the globe.[9] Their main targets are public transportation systems, the facilities that are emblematic of modernity. Just as businesses, NGO's, and universities find it easier to integrate their activities and reach consumers and clients on a transnational scale, so do too the users of terrorism. It would be surprising if it were otherwise.

Another condition thought to be linked to terrorism is the presence or absence of democracy. Repression of peaceful means of political dissent may force opposition movements into the underground and encourage their resort to violence, as it did in both Saudi Arabia and Egypt. When the political process is open to the expression of diverse viewpoints and oppositions are represented in the structures of power, violence may be less likely. However, at least two caveats are in order before we equate democracy with the absence of terrorism. First, the process of democratization is often violent. As the war in Iraq shows, removing a repressive government will not automatically produce democracy in the absence of norms that promote compromise and functioning security institutions. Second, established liberal democracies have also confronted terrorism, not only from outside their borders, but from discontented citizens of their own. Before the 9/11 attacks, the 1995 bombing of the Federal Building in Oklahoma City was the most destructive act of terrorism in American history. Timothy McVeigh, who was executed for the crime, was a follower of far right militia groups. Similarly, a completely domestic Japanese religious cult conducted the 1995 sarin gas attack on the Tokyo subways.

Since the 1980s, religion has often cited as a cause of terrorism.[10] The argument is based on the assumption that values and beliefs cause terrorism. In the United States, for example, one school of thought equates religious orientation with increased lethality of terrorism.[11] The availability of an ideology, secular or religious, that justifies and legitimizes violence, emphasizes martyrdom, and promises eternal reward as well as personal redemption is undoubtedly a contributing factor. Normative justification is probably necessary to terrorism, although it is not a sufficient explanation in and of itself. But the specific doctrines that extremists espouse are typically narrow, inconsistent, and selective interpretations of wider bodies of thought. Furthermore, the decision to use violence may come first, at least on the part of the leadership, which then crafts a borrowed doctrine out of bits and pieces of established ideology or religion in order to support what is in essence a political goal.

Three conclusions emerge from this discussion. First, any conditions that generate a sense of profound injustice can provide a pool for terrorist recruiting. Grievances act both as motivation for the individual and as a mobilizing device for the organization. Second, the groups that use terrorism see such actual or potential constituencies as available and accessible and wish to attract their support in order to grow from small underground conspiracies to genuine social movements with political influence. They script their message accordingly, to channel and direct popular emotions. Third, such conditions facilitate the transnational expansion of local movements.[12] Television conveys emotionally powerful visual images around the globe. Even the presence or absence of democracy has a border-crossing dimension, in that oppositions that cannot succeed against a repressive local regime can redirect their activities either against local targets outside the country or against outside powers thought to be supporting the local regime. Their anger is thus displaced and exported. Democracies that tolerate dissent may find themselves harboring terrorist conspiracies, as Germany did on the eve of the 9/11 attacks and as Britain discovered in 2005 and 2006.

Thus terrorism cannot be explained exclusively in terms of "root causes." Millions of people live under conditions of severe deprivation and are exposed to radical ideologies but few become terrorists.[13] Terrorism is not a spontaneous reaction to circumstances. Groups confronting the same conditions choose different responses. The central question concerns the combination of incentives and opportunities that affects decisions to use terrorism. Terrorism can serve four purposes: provocation, polarization, mobilization, and compellence.

First, terrorism, especially random attacks on civilian populations, can be a means of provoking a government into over-reaction. For example, Al Qaeda's attack on the World Trade Center and the Pentagon may have been intended to provoke a massive and indiscriminate American response that would justify the charge that the United States wished to destroy Islam and was an enemy of the Muslim world. Such strategies are thought to be particularly effective against democratic governments because they are both responsive to public opinion (and thus outrage accompanied by calls for revenge) while simultaneously restrained by human rights norms.[14] A more ruthless regime could respond by crushing all opposition and censoring media coverage of the threat.

Second, terrorism can be used to drive divided societies further apart through indiscriminate attacks on representatives of the "other" community, whether ethnic, racial, religious, or linguistic. Thus in Iraq, Sunni terrorism is directed against Shi'ites, and Shi'ite militias have infiltrated government security forces to avenge themselves against Sunnis. Indiscriminate and high-casualty attacks on marketplaces, mosques, and even funeral processions have divided the two communities. Similar terrorism has occurred in Pakistan and Kashmir. Sinhalese were targeted by the LTTE in Sri Lanka. Catholics and Protestants attacked each other in Northern Ireland.

Third, terrorism can mobilize and invigorate supporters.[15] It demonstrates power, even if striking a blow accomplishes nothing concrete. It satisfies demands for vengeance and overcomes feelings of humiliation and resentment. Terrorism can define issues and put previously ignored grievances on the world agenda by attracting international press coverage. For example, before the Palestinian hijackings of the late 1960s and early 1970s the issue before the world was "Arab refugees," not Palestinian nationalism. The hijackings as well as the 1972 attack on the Munich Olympics made it impossible to ignore Palestinian claims, even though their methods were condemned. Carefully targeted terrorism helps frame grievances, so that the attacks on the World Trade Center and Pentagon defined American economic and military might as the problem. Terrorism is a highly symbolic form of violence, and the action itself communicates a message.

Terrorism can also assist in distinguishing a group from its non-violent or less violent competitors who seek support from the same constituencies. For this reason, competitiveness among organizations can lead to imitation, as in Israel where Hamas, Palestinian Islamic Jihad, and the Al Aqsa Martyrs Brigade competed for public support and recruits in the grim game of suicide bombings during the second intifada. In the 1970s, there was rivalry among different nationalist factions. For example, once the

Popular Front for the Liberation of Palestine had inaugurated the tactic of hijacking aircraft in 1968, other groups quickly followed suit. Similar competition may characterize the conflict in Iraq.

Fourth, groups may regard terrorism as useful in compelling withdrawal from foreign commitments through a strategy of punishment and attrition.[16] The point is to make the commitment so painful that the government will abandon it. Like provocation, this strategy may work best against democracies where governments are accountable to the people and where there is a free press. To some people, the 2004 and 2005 Madrid and London bombings were meant to force the withdrawal of troops from Iraq. Bin Laden pointed to the success of such tactics of compellence elsewhere, particularly in Lebanon in 1983, when the bombing of the U.S. Marines Barracks at the Beirut airport led to American withdrawal.[17] He also claimed credit for the American withdrawal from Somalia. Bombings in France in the 1980s were apparently meant to halt French support for Iraq in the Iran-Iraq war. The aim of expelling a foreign occupier is plainly evident in the tactics of the post-2003 insurgents in Iraq. Even the United Nations and humanitarian aid workers, in addition to private contractors, have been targeted in an effort to drive out any stabilizing forces and prevent the restoration of order and prosperity.

Terrorism is not invariably successful in accomplishing these purposes. For example, the perceived success of a strategy of compellence may be illusory. The American withdrawal from Lebanon may be an exception, not the rule. In most cases, it cannot be shown conclusively that terrorism was the cause of specific government actions (such as the Israeli withdrawal from the Gaza Strip). Furthermore, there are numerous counter-examples. India, for example, has not bowed to terrorist pressure in Kashmir. Russia did not withdraw from Chechnya. The opposite reaction to terrorism may indeed be more common: a reinvigorated determination to resist demands.

WHY CONTEMPORARY TERRORISM IS A THREAT TO INTERNATIONAL SECURITY

After the shock of 9/11, analysts of international relations called for a new approach to terrorism. Most argued that while in the past it had been a second order foreign policy issue, it should now be recognized as a major threat to national and international security.[18] What is at stake? Why was and is terrorism perceived as a major threat? States do not face "mutual assured destruction" as they did during the Cold War, despite the gravity of the attack on the United States in 2001 and the prospective downing of multiple airliners over the Atlantic Ocean in the summer of 2006. Even the prospect that terrorists could acquire "WMD" is not an existential threat. Clearly the magnitude of the threat does not depend on material consequences such as numbers of killed and injured or infrastructure destroyed. The subjective aspect of the threat is as important as the objective aspect. It is the perception of the threat that matters.

For the public, much of what makes terrorism a potent threat lies in the essence of the phenomenon, which has not changed. Terrorism creates uncertainty because it is unpredictable. The time, the place, and the identity of the perpetrator come as a surprise. It often targets civilians going about their daily lives. They cannot know who among their fellow subway or bus or airplane passengers, among those standing next to them in a crowded spot or sitting next to them in a restaurant, aims to attack. Acts of terrorism themselves, even if relatively minor, are constant reminders of individual vulnerability. Even threats carry weight. The Cold War was punctuated by the occasional acute and frightening crisis that reminded the world of the precariousness of the "balance of terror," but individuals did not experience a taste of the threat itself, in the sense of a nuclear exchange. Terrorism, on the other hand, is visible as a real and present danger, even if most residents of Western societies are more likely to die in a household accident than in a terrorist attack. People who normally live in stable societies, whose daily lives are not constantly threatened, are unaccustomed to this risk, although the inhabitants of the many war-torn countries in Africa, Asia, and the Middle East unfortunately are. And the perception of risk is magnified by media coverage, especially television.

For governments, terrorism is a threat to sovereignty, reputation, and credibility as well as the safety of their citizens. National leaders must be sensitive to the challenge to the prestige of the state itself as well as to the security of their territories and populations. In democracies, leaders must respond to public opinion. They cannot afford to appear complacent or neglectful.[19]

Today's terrorism also appears more threatening than in the past because of its global diffusion that makes it seem omnipresent, the willingness and ability of its users to cause large numbers of civilian casualties, and the tenacity and resilience of the jihadist movement that inspires it. Our awareness of all these factors is also more acute than ever because of the modern communications era.

Although past terrorism had a transnational dimension (especially the anarchist movement of the late nineteenth and early twentieth centuries), the contemporary threat has a broader and more sustained territorial reach in terms of the geographical diversity of the location of attacks, the sites where plots are laid and resources gathered, and the nationalities of the individuals involved. In an era of instantaneous mass communication, the audience for terrorism is also global. Nobody who has access to modern communication systems can escape awareness of the danger. Reminders are constant. Terrorism is visible on a daily basis, whether it occurs in Baghdad, London, or Jerusalem. Television, in particular, is a medium well suited to transmitting the information that makes the threat vivid and salient.[20] Terrorists, of course, know this quite well.

The extreme lethality of the 9/11 attacks, causing the deaths of almost three thousand people in a single morning, permanently altered expectations of what terrorists could accomplish. Threats that might not have appeared credible in the past now became real. Some anticipate that Al Qaeda or those inspired by its message might acquire weapons of mass destruction—chemical, biological, radiological or nuclear—in order to engage in truly catastrophic terrorism. Others think that such fears are exaggerated and that sufficient harm can be done with "ordinary" weapons at a much reduced cost to the perpetrators. Coordinated sequences of suicide bombings, for example, have a profound impact on perceptions of security.

Finally, in the United States in particular, the prevalent image of Al Qaeda and jihadist terrorism is that it aims to undermine the values on which Western civilization is built. It is seen as a threat to democracy, tolerance, and freedom. The American government's view is that they hate us because of who we are. In 2002, President Bush observed that "we're not facing a set of grievances that can be soothed and addressed. We're facing a radical ideology with inalterable objectives: to enslave whole nations and intimidate the world. No act of ours invited the rage of the killers—and no concession, bribe, or act of appeasement would change or limit their plans for murder."[21] Terrorism is thus seen as a threat to identity rather than interests. Regardless of the accuracy of this portrayal of the motives behind terrorism, the argument has a powerful emotional impact.

THE INTERNATIONAL RESPONSE AND THE FUTURE OF TERRORISM

The 9/11 attacks generated an initial surge of international solidarity with the United States and support for overturning the Taliban regime and destroying Al Qaeda in Afghanistan. However, discord has replaced consensus. The 2003 decision to invade Iraq introduced a period of intense disagreement. As the war in Iraq became an increasingly divisive issue, other background disagreements related to the war on terrorism also came to the fore.

The shock of the 9/11 attacks produced a genuine sense of collective security, in that the attack on the US was perceived as an attack against all. For the first time there appeared to be a solid and comprehensive international consensus against terrorism. This was true even though the use of military force to destroy a terrorist organization and overturn the government of the state that supported it was unprecedented, since previous American retaliations had been brief and limited.[22] Admittedly, the Israeli invasion of Lebanon in 1982 might be regarded as a precedent. However, Israel restricted its actions to driving the PLO out and occupying a security zone. It did not occupy all of Lebanon or remove the Lebanese government from power. Furthermore, Lebanon was a neighboring state, not a distant country from which attacks had been launched.

The war in Afghanistan was widely approved as a legitimate response, since the Taliban had refused repeated requests to surrender bin Laden and was under UN sanctions. The Taliban regime enjoyed little diplomatic recognition. Even Pakistan abandoned its previous support for the Taliban and joined the American side, albeit under some pressure. The US also stepped up military assistance programs for states threatened by Al Qaeda–related terrorism, such as in the Philippines.

Although American policy makers framed the response as a "war" on terrorism and insisted that the "terrorism as crime" model had been decisively rejected, much of the practical response to 9/11 consisted of coordinating police and intelligence work around the world. The United Nations focused on improving capacity. Governments cracked down on terrorist financing, for example, conspiracies were progressively uncovered and dismantled, and hundreds of Al Qaeda operatives were arrested in countries around the world.

This aspect of the response to terrorism did have a harder edge than in the past, thus deviating from a strict criminal justice mode. For one thing, the US was more inclined to use covert operations, including strikes against Al Qaeda leaders in Yemen and Pakistan. The US also increased its reliance on the practice of rendition (which had commenced under the Clinton administration) rather than extradition or deportation of terrorist suspects. And it introduced the controversial concept of "unlawful combatants" to justify holding suspects in military detention centers in Afghanistan and at Guantanamo Bay in

Cuba and then trying them in military rather than civilian courts. These practices were criticized as violations of international law and of human rights from the outset, both at home and abroad.

Serious divisions, however, began with the 2003 invasion of Iraq, which divided the US from most of its closest allies. Prior to that move, the US was viewed as a benevolent superpower or hegemon; after the intervention in Iraq, the US appeared assertive and unilateralist even to some of its allies. The military offensive followed closely upon the adoption of a new security strategy for the United States, one based on military preemption of threats, including forceful regime change. President Bush declared that in the war on terrorism, countries were either with the US or against it. There could be no middle ground.

Some critics saw the engagement in Iraq as a distraction from the task of securing Afghanistan and dealing with what President Bush had termed the other two axes of evil: North Korea and Iran. The fact that the UN had not sanctioned the use of force to overthrow the Iraqi government influenced many views. Turkey refused to allow American forces to use its territory. France and Germany objected strenuously, and among major powers only Britain remained a staunch American ally. The publics of countries that did support the US often disapproved of their governments' positions.

When the charge that Iraq possessed chemical, nuclear, and biological weapons turned out to be false, the US shifted its emphasis to building democracy in Iraq. This task was seen as a stepping stone to transforming the politics of the Middle East region, producing democracy, stability, and a resolution of the Israeli-Palestinian conflict. These goals were laudable, but the inadequacy of postwar planning for such an effort damaged the credibility of the policy. Resistance to American occupation only gained strength, as the Sunni minority rejected accommodation with a new Iraqi government dominated by Shi'ites and Kurds. A "war of ideas" to convince Muslims that the US was a trustworthy partner and to lay the groundwork for democratization stalled. Instead Iraq became a magnet for foreign sympathizers and a locus for suicide bombings, the numbers of which quickly surpassed those in other conflicts such as Palestine and Sri Lanka. Within three years the conflict deteriorated into a full-scale insurgency with extensive sectarian violence. To critics, the war in Iraq gave Al Qaeda a new life in a second generation of leaders such as Abu Musab al-Zarqawi.

With relations already strained, revelations of mistreatment of prisoners at the Abu Ghraib prison in Iraq led to outrage. Concern mounted over the use of torture by US forces or by the countries to whom suspects were sent. To these issues were added questions about the defensive side of coping with terrorism: the effect of counterterrorist measures on civil liberties at home. Even preventive measures revealed divisions among allies: Britain, for example, was thought before the July bombings of 2005 to be far too tolerant of Islamic extremism. The reaction was then thought to go too far in the other direction, by restricting free speech. Legal coordination of the response to terrorism within the EU remained problematic. Asylum and immigration policies came into question.

An effective international response based on a restored consensus requires that terrorism be recognized as a political problem, to be solved through political means. The resort to military force to crush terrorism will not produce democracy or stability. Deploying combat troops and relying on air power is likely to provoke more terrorism.

Even if military force succeeds in destroying organizations in the short run, terrorism will persist as long as recruitment of new cohorts is possible. Rather, multilateral cooperation in police and intelligence work is the basis of an effective response, which requires that counterterrorism remain a priority on the policy agenda at all levels of government. Diplomacy is a valuable tool. Furthermore, such a response must be scrupulous in its adherence to the rule of law. In addition to firmness toward the users of terrorism, policy must also have a noncoercive dimension. "Soft" rather than "hard" power is an important resource in dealing with nonstates as well as states.[23] The sources of popular support for terrorism, even passive support, must be addressed. Otherwise the terrorist networks that are eliminated will only grow back.

The Secretary-General of the United Nations has identified the main elements of an international counterterrorist strategy in terms of five "D's": dissuading those who are dissatisfied from resorting to terrorism; denying them the means to act; deterring state supporters; developing the capacity of states to deal with terrorism; and defending human rights.[24] He has called for global recognition of the unacceptability of terrorism under any circumstances and in any culture. At the same time he has stressed that good governance and respect for human rights are essential to an effective strategy against terrorism. The problem for the international community is how to implement these principles. How, for example, is good governance to be promoted? How can norms that reject terrorism be constructed?

In the meantime, the world must live with the unpredictable threat of terrorism. It can be reduced but not eliminated. Unfortunately, a small number of people with modest resources can create disproportionate disruption. They need not represent a mass movement. In the modern world both targets and resources are increasingly easy to come by. The ideas that motivate terrorism are transnational. Thus terrorism, particularly attacks on civilians, will always be an attractive strategy for radical minorities who seek recognition and attention, whatever their specific beliefs or objectives.

Moreover, the danger should be put in perspective: terrorism should not be ignored but it is not a threat to the existence of any state. The audiences that are targeted must resist the terrorists' logic, recalling that they intend to provoke over-reaction, polarize communities, mobilize support, and compel the abandonment of commitments. Only a response that is firm, respects democratic values, and rewards peaceful means of expressing opinion can make terrorism illegitimate.

NOTES

Paper originally presented at the Conference on *Terrorismo e relações internacionais* (Terrorism and International Relations) at the Pontifical Catholic University of Rio de Janeiro, August 14, 2006.

1. Some of this analysis draws on Martha Crenshaw, "Terrorism and Global Security," in *Leashing the Dogs of War: Conflict Management in a Divided World*, edited by Chester Crocker, Fen Hampson, and Pamela Aall (Washington: United States Institute of Peace Press, 2007).

2. *Ibid.*, p. 52.

3. See Lawrence Wright, *The Looming Tower: Al-Qaeda and the Road to 9/11* (New York: Alfred A. Knopf, 2006) and Peter Bergen, *The Osama bin Laden I Know* (New York Free Press, 2006).

4. See Montasser Al-Zayyat, *The Road to Al-Qaeda* (London: Pluto Press, 2004, translated from the Arabic edition published in Cairo in 2002).

5. For the texts of speeches, see Bruce Lawrence, ed., *Messages to the World: The Statements of Osama Bin Laden* (London: Verso, 2005).

6. For some of the debate over Al Qaeda's goals, see Quintan Wiktorowicz and John Kaltner, "Killing in the Name of Islam: Al-Qaeda's Justification for September 11," *Middle East Policy* 10, 2 (Summer 2003), pp. 76–92; Gilles Kepel, *Jihad: The Trail of Political Islam* (Cambridge, MA: Harvard University Press, 2002); and Olivier Roy, *Globalized Islam: The Search for a New Ummah* (New York: Columbia University Press, 2004).

7. See Michael Mousseau, "Market Civilization and Its Clash with Terror," *International Security* 27, 3 (Winter 2002/03), pp. 5–29; Comments, "The Sources of Terrorism," by C. Knight, M. Murphy, and M. Mousseau, *International Security* 28, 2 (Spring 2003), pp. 192–198; and Alan B. Krueger and Jitka Maleckova, "Education, Poverty and Terrorism: Is There a Causal Connection?" *The Journal of Economic Perspectives* 17, 4 (November 2003), pp. 119–144.

8. See Farhad Khosrokhavar, *Suicide Bombers: Allah's New Martyrs,* translated from the French by David Macey (London: Pluto Press, 2005).

9. One useful source on this subject is Gabriel Weimann, *Terror on the Internet: The New Arena, the New Challenges* (Washington: United States Institute of Peace Press, 2006).

10. On the subject of religion and terrorism see Mark Juergensmeyer, *Terror in the Mind of God: The Global Rise of Religious Violence* (Berkeley: University of California Press, 2000).

11. See, for example, Steven Simon, "The New Terrorism: Securing the Nation Against a Messianic Foe," *The Brookings Review* 21, 1 (Winter 2003), p. 18.

12. Sidney Tarrow, *The New Transnational Activism* (Cambridge: Cambridge University Press, 2005).

13. For another overview see Karin von Hippel, "The Roots of Terrorism: Probing the Myths," pp. 25–39 in Lawrence Freedman, ed., *Superterrorism: Policy Responses* (Oxford: Blackwell, 2002).

14. Robert Pape suggests that this is the case for suicide terrorism meant to compel withdrawal from occupied territory in *Dying to Win: The Strategic Logic of Suicide Terrorism* (New York: Random House, 2005).

15. See Ian Lustick's discussion of solipsistic terrorism in "Terrorism in the Arab-Israeli Conflict: Targets and Audiences," in *Terrorism in Context*, ed. Martha Crenshaw (University Park, PA: Pennsylvania State University Press, 1995).

16. Compellence is the companion of deterrence; it is meant to make an adversary do something rather than prevent the adversary from doing something.

17. See *Messages to the World: The Statements of Osama Bin Laden*, edited and introduced by Bruce Lawrence (London: Verso, 2005).

18. See Martha Crenshaw, "Terrorism, Strategies, and Grand Strategies," pp. 74–93 in *Attacking Terrorism: Elements of a Grand Strategy,* edited by Audrey Kurth Cronin and James M. Ludes (Washington: Georgetown University Press, 2004).

19. Martha Crenshaw, "Counterterrorism Policy and the Political Process," *Studies in Conflict and Terrorism* 24, 5 (2001), pp. 329–338.

20. See Pippa Norris, Montague Kern, and Marion Just, eds., *Framing Terrorism: The News Media, the Government, and the Public* (New York: Routledge, 2003).

21. Graduation Speech, United States Military Academy, West Point, New York, June 1, 2002.

22. In 1986 the Reagan administration bombed targets in Libya in response to the La Belle disco bombing in Germany, in 1993 the Clinton administration bombed targets in Baghdad because of Iraq's attempt to assassinate former President Bush during a visit to Kuwait, and in 1998 the Clinton administration used air power against the Sudan and Al Qaeda camps in Afghanistan in response to the embassy bombings in East Africa.

23. The post-9/11 rehabilitation of Libya is a case in point.

24. See his address to the Madrid Summit on Democracy, Terrorism, and Security, March 10, 2005. Available at un.org.

30 Takin' It to the Streets: Hydra Networks, Chaos Strategies, and the "New" Asymmetry

P. H. Liotta

> *"A ghost is stalking the corridors of general staffs and defense departments all over the 'developed' world—the fear of military impotence, even irrelevance."*
>
> —Martin van Creveld
> *The Transformation of War*

> *"If only the little bastards would just come out . . . and fight like men, we'd cream them."*
> —Remarks made by a military officer to journalists in Southeast Asia, 1964

War is a fraught subject. As the anthropologist Anna Simons has noted in her thinking about war, "Those who study it often fight about it." Yet, as the two epigraphs above suggest, we are hardly uniform in our approaches to war—and we are not resolved in our best means to combat adversaries.

These epigraphs above also suggest that, as far as the over-used term asymmetry goes in thinking about war, there is actually nothing "new" under the sun. The American way of war brings a definite style and weight to its execution. In the crudest terms, it

P. H. Liotta is professor of humanities and executive director of the Pell Center for International Relations and Public Policy, Salve Regina University, Newport, Rhode Island. Prior to assuming directorship of the Pell Center in 2004, Dr. Liotta served as the endowed Jerome E. Levy Chair of Economic Geography and National Security at the U.S. Naval War College. He also served as Fulbright lecturer and poet-in-residence (*slobodan umjetnik,* 1988–89) in former Yugoslavia and has traveled widely throughout the former Soviet Union, particularly the Caucasus and central Asia—to the Altai region of Siberia, Tajikistan, the Afghan front, Uzbekistan, Turkmenistan, Georgia, and Iran. The author of 17 books and numerous articles in fields as diverse as poetry, criticism, education, international security, intervention ethics, and foreign policy analysis, Liotta has also published a novel, *Diamond's Compass,* about Iran. His research interests include the study of geography and geopolitics (particularly in southeast Europe, the Euro-Mediterranean, and central and South Asia) as well the reexamination of environmental, human, and demographic security issues in the contemporary environment. Since 2004, Dr. Liotta has regularly lectured on demographics, migration, and security at the NATO Defense College in Rome, Italy. In 2005, he was appointed adjunct professor in comparative politics and international relations in the Department of Social Sciences, United States Military Academy, West Point, New York; became an associate of the Global Environmental Change and Human Security (GECHS) project of Oslo, Norway; and joined Working Group II (Impacts, Adaptation and Vulnerability of Climate Change) of the United Nations Intergovernmental Panel on Climate Change (IPCC). In 2008, he served as expert consultant on endemic community violence for the Canadian government and Department of Foreign Affairs and International Trade's Human Security and Cities Initiative. As a member of the IPCC, he shares in the award of the 2007 Nobel Peace Prize.

represents nothing less than Old Testament warfare, applied with overwhelming force and done with quickly.

There are also weaknesses for the American way of war. Over four decades ago, the French counterinsurgency expert Roger Trinquier (with service in China, Indochina, and Algeria) claimed in *Modern Warfare: A French View of Counterinsurgency* that modern war is an interlocking system of political, economic, psychological, and military actions and conflicts. Yet Trinquier argued that armies tend to fight traditional warfare, and that in modern war they are doomed to failure despite overwhelming firepower.[1] Trinquier (who some suggest served as inspiration for the character of the brutal French colonel in the classic film *The Battle of Algiers*) had a particular interest in terrorism and advocated the use of torture to extract specific information from terrorists.[2]

In the netherworld we have now entered in the "long war" on terror, however, we have handed ourselves any number of problem sets. First, due to national security criteria, there are no externally objective means to assess the "value" of the alleged brutal interrogations of enemy combatants whose eventual status as either criminals or prisoners of war remains as clear as mud. Secondly, with the unfortunate reality that the term "IED" has now entered the vernacular and that severe head injuries from the detonations of these devices affect an alarming number of soldiers and Marines deployed in Iraq and Afghanistan, war has truly come to the streets—and vicious urban warfare may well be a pattern of future combat. Finally, despite the extraordinary investment and sacrifice of people and resources since September 11, 2001, the Iraqi jihad has, as a recent national intelligence estimate suggests, spawned a "new generation of terrorist leaders and operatives."[3] Although no one has phrased it in such stark terms, the loose organization and diffusion of groups such as al-Qa'ida have created the conditions for "hydra networks." Drawing from the mythological chthonic beast that Hercules was sent to kill, this term makes reference to the hydra, which displayed the unfortunate ability to sprout two new heads whenever one of its many heads was cut off.

These ugly truths have created the "new" asymmetry in warfare. Whether we have the means and the will to tackle this asymmetry is a matter of pressing debate. The truth may be hard to accept—not the least because the "long" war may turn out to be the "endless" war.

HOW CHAOS STRATEGY WORKS AND HYDRA NETWORKS OPERATE

In theory, at least, the U.S. national security decision-making process is rational. During this process, the decision maker establishes the desired goals of policy and develops a strategy for employing often-scarce resources to achieve these goals. This rational calculus seeks to balance both ends and means.

But this rational decision-making process is also vulnerable, and the "chaos strategist" will target this vulnerability in challenging America. To plan a strategy of direct engagement with American military forces, as Iraq learned in Desert Storm and the Taliban did in Afghanistan, is lunacy. The chaos strategist, by contrast, must manipulate the scenario to his best advantage while striving to *prevent* the introduction of American military force.

Adversaries who do not practice a similar process of decision making—balancing resources and constraints, means and ends—will increasingly look for innovative ways to "attack" without attacking directly the brick wall of American military predominance. The chaos strategist thus targets the American national security decision-making process and, potentially, the American people, rather than American military force, in order to prevail. Such a strategist seeks to induce decision paralysis.

In a strategy of chaos, the key objective will be to convince American political leaders that no clear solution, end state, or political objective (other than the cessation of chaos) exists in the strategist's sphere of dominance—and that sphere of dominance may be at home or abroad. In large measure, the most direct way to "convince" political leaders of the futility of further engagement is to target the will of the people. In a savage application of the Clausewitzian principle of war as the continuation of politics by other means, the fracturing of popular support for prolonged engagements with uncertain outcomes is an application of chaos strategy.

Chaos strategy, employed by all warring parties in the former Yugoslavia and by Saddam Hussein in Iraq until 2003, serves to initially discourage yet may ultimately provoke American intervention. Yet future adversaries will almost certainly use the leverage of chaos as a strategy for gain.

It is critical to stress that the focus of this chapter is particularly on "stateless" agents, rather than on states themselves as chaos strategists. While some have rightly focused on long-term strategic chaos options of the People's Republic of China (PRC), in particular, the emphasis here is on direct and troubling actions by hydra networks of stateless agents such as al-Qa'ida and the Taliban and the literally hundreds of splinter groups that have sprung up in their collective wakes.[4]

In the ongoing "long war," the practice of chaos strategy by nonstate actors, rather than by the leaders of recognized nation-states, only complicates the security calculus for the United States and its allies. On the one hand, we will practice preemption against those who seek to harm us. Military forces will increasingly be in the business of shooting archers, and not just catching arrows. That is to say, we cannot just wait for chaos provocations to occur before we react.

On the other hand, nonstate chaos strategists may soon recognize our overwhelming preemption capability and strive to shift from being "archers" and to disappear as quickly as possible. The most effective nonstate adversaries that we will face will likely display some of the following characteristics: the facility to operate effectively as a lateral (and noncentralized) hydra network, the ability to learn, the capacity to anticipate, and the capability to "self-organize" or reconstitute after being struck.

Stateless agents, in particular (whether or not they are sponsored by "nation-states" or by easily targetable organizations), can accomplish vanishing acts with far greater ease than adversarial leaders of problematic states. The implications are important as we assess new challenges in future war. Moreover, we should seriously question if we were ever asking the right questions about military transformation in the post–September 11 security environment. After all, we are not the only ones asking "What went wrong?"

In the case of the September 2001 attacks on New York and Washington, a feasible chaos strategy was meant to induce not only fear but also a sense of extreme vulnerability in the American homeland. As such, the United States entered a new security era in which attacks by nonstate actors on the homeland proved possible and U.S. citizens, their way of life, and the specific liberties that they had been accustomed to were now vulnerable and at risk.

Admittedly, the attacks on September 11 represented an intelligence and interagency failure on a colossal scale; fortunately, the same intelligence network was able to track and prove the case against Osama bin Laden and al-Qa'ida with relative speed. Yet the vulnerability and transparency of the American system led military planners and former CIA officers to proclaim that, regarding the attacks themselves, "We couldn't do this. . . . I have never seen an operation go that smoothly."[5]

In the future, chaos strategists will increasingly seek gain through attacks that cause the excessive deaths of innocents and provoke further cultural/religious/ethnic fault lines among both contending adversaries and potential allies. Despite all claims to the contrary, it is not yet clear that the United States is capable of shifting from a style of warfare that might be described as the American way of war—essentially, the annihilation of an enemy—to a style of warfare that requires far more intense "closework." In simple terms, are we planning for the wars we want to fight rather than for the wars we will have to fight?

Former secretary of defense William Cohen, in reference to the future planning and the "transformation" of the American military, often claimed "We're not looking for a fair fight." Indeed, neither is the chaos strategist—and never will.

A chaos strategist finds tactical and operational success largely irrelevant; rather, he seeks to implant a sense of strategic futility in the mind of the opponent (where all wars are, after all, fought and won or lost). Recent declarations by Presidents Karzai and Bush that the Taliban in Afghanistan will never regain leadership of the country illustrate this point. The Taliban are not terribly interested in "running" Afghanistan; they simply wish to dictate the terms of who does rule and how the country is run.

Recent NATO thinking on the Taliban suggests a dawning realization, rather, that the Taliban have in effect "hydra-sized," becoming "not a homogeneous organisation [sic] but a series of interlocking groups that include drug traffickers and other criminals as well as religious zealots."[6] As NATO secretary-general Jaap de Hoop Scheffer noted, "We see that the Taliban have changed tactics: they realise [sic] they cannot win militarily and they are now deliberately forcing civilians into situations in which they get them killed to undermine support for ISAF [NATO's force] in Afghanistan." In direct terms, the Taliban have circumvented set-battle pieces and gone straight for inducing strategic futility, seeking to estrange Afghans from the NATO force and from their own government (whose support and development are the mission focus of the NATO force).

Thus, while the Taliban will never win hearts and minds, they can ensure that others don't win them as well. Employing often ruthless tactics, to include the slaughter of women and children (whose deaths they often blame on NATO), they have moved combat off the battlefield and into the streets.

THE CHANGING FACE OF FUTURE WAR: IMPLICATIONS FOR NATIONAL SECURITY AND FORCE PLANNING

Any adversary that risks American-military-force engagement must employ a method that exploits the social dimensions of strategy to offset the disadvantages in the technical dimension.[7] Such an adversary proves most successful in targeting the process of decisionmaking within the policy (social dimension) sector rather than, as a first step, planning how to engage military force (the technical dimension) once the employment decision has been made.

Seeking to wreak havoc to strategic advantage in his sphere of influence, the chaos strategist must avoid treading into the arena of "vital" American interests. He works best in the shadows, behind the curtain, off stage.[8] In retrospect, with regard to the September 2001 attacks in the United States, the assailants made a crucial error. The attacks *did* affect vital national interests, the resulting American will to accept military casualties in response appeared to be high, and all roads—rightly or wrongly—almost immediately led to Kabul.

The normal response to an enemy's attack is to attack, of course, in kind and with a like ferocity. In conventional war, this has always been the symmetrical reaction. While admittedly all warfare tends toward asymmetry, in which one seeks to exploit the weakness of the opponent and to rely on one's own strengths, the notion of rough force parity between opponents has shifted remarkably in the post–cold war era. An opponent who can match the capabilities of U.S. armed forces does not exist, and will not appear any time soon.

As a result, technology and new operational concepts argue the need for American military forces to move toward the capacity to induce response paralysis on the part of adversaries. The post–cold war landscape of American force structure and planning is littered with concepts and beliefs now consigned to the ash heap of history: *Joint Vision 2020,* "Network-Centric Warfare," "Parallel Warfare," and the "Global Strike Force."[9] All of these visions of the face of future war hinged on the almost theological adherence to the use of overwhelming technological capability and its ability to paralyze an adversary's response. And, true to form, every adversary we have faced *directly* since the end of the cold war has been unable to fight back; most often they simply have had to hunker down and take the hit.

This belief in technology and its ability to win in conflict suffers from at least two not necessarily contradictory ideas. First, the notion popular among mid- and senior-level military officers holds that the military strategist can get inside the enemy's decision cycle (often called "the loop"), cut him off, and kill him. Second, the use of technology and American reliance (some would call an obsession) on firepower allows for high enemy damages and low friendly casualties. Edward Luttwak partially popularized this second idea with what he termed "Post-Heroic Warfare."[10]

One of the leading airpower proponents in the post–cold war era, Phillip S. Meilinger, suggested that warfare could be considered in four types: exhaustion, attrition, annihilation, and paralysis.[11] The conflict in Southeast Asia, a protracted war from which America sought to extricate itself after three decades of involvement with no lasting goals achieved, is an example of warfare of exhaustion; Operation Allied Force in

Kosovo and Operation Enduring Freedom in Afghanistan—through coalition employment of high-intensity strikes, high-technology weapons, precise targeting, and the integration of special operations forces with indigenous forces to support and help direct firepower—are examples of warfare of paralysis.

Yet the opposing chaos strategist is fully aware of America's asymmetric, unmatched power predominance. His correct "target," as it were, is the "social dimension" of the national-level policy decision-making process as well as perhaps the population itself. In essence, the chaos strategist attacks what we value most.

The shift in chaos strategy is not subtle, but it is crucial that we recognize the shift. In the future, successful chaos strategists may target us where we are most vulnerable and will work to avoid presenting themselves as any direct threat. Stateless agents, in particular, will find this strategy shift acting to their advantage.

Moreover, since our military forces are not sized and structured as a countervalue force,[12] the chaos strategist will increasingly recognize that new vulnerabilities will present themselves through targets and methods such as

- Critical infrastructure degradation or collapse, to include not only physical systems and structures but also contamination of food supplies or resources in ways difficult or impossible to detect;
- The spread of infectious disease that cannot be controlled, whether or not through the use of biological agents;
- Intrastate as well as interethnic conflict in failed or failing states;
- Environmental stress, resource scarcity, and depletion;
- The trafficking of drugs, small arms, and inhumane weapons, often coupled with conflicts that are claimed as insurgencies;
- Cyber-war;
- Terrorism.

All these elements provide breeding grounds for future warfare. These nightmare zones present targets of opportunity. Moreover, while none of these aspects are necessarily new, the capacity to induce chaos is greater today than ever before.

We know, for example, that the Soviets experimented with strategic biological weapons, such as smallpox that could be delivered with intercontinental ballistic missiles (ICBMs).[13] Soviet weapon experts recognized, however, that smallpox could be released far more secretly on enemy territory; thus, in an age of globalization where disease knows no borders, chaos strategists recognize this advantage as well. Further, the capacity and power of modern laptop computers is roughly equivalent to the entire computational power that the U.S. Defense Department had in the mid-1960s.[14]

In the past, state-led chaos strategists have at least partially achieved their objectives even in the face of U.S. military force. As a result, Somalia was a failure; Iraq remains "unsolved"; Bosnia and Herzegovina is ethnically cleansed and, like Gaul before it, divided in three parts; Kosovo is an international protectorate but still part of Serbia; and Afghanistan's viability as a future state remains in question. To make matters worse, the disease of chaos strategy has now spread to Pakistan—a nuclear-armed state.

The chaos strategist wants to avoid force engagement. Even when force is introduced and troops are stationed on the ground, as in Bosnia, Saudi Arabia, Iraq, and

Afghanistan, the chaos strategist wants to prolong ambiguity. Above all, the desired outcome remains decision paralysis.

Most American defense planners naturally consider military predominance to be a major strength. But, ironically, there is an inherent weakness in it. The immense advantages of American firepower, technology, and forces available require clear and distinct application of means to reach ends. The Weinberger and Powell defense doctrines, which mandated clear definitions of political goals and American interests prior to intervention, worked in Desert Storm because they fit Desert Storm.[15] These same defense doctrines would not work today—in the face of chaos.

THE "ENGINEERING APPROACH" TO WAR

In American warfighter terminology, deception and surprise are standard checklist items in thinking about war. But American intelligence assets—in terms of technology and capabilities the most superior in history—fall short when it comes to the unclear art of human intelligence and human unpredictability. In truth, despite all our progress with conventional and unconventional war, there still rings an identifiable empathy with how the debacle of recent engagements was, in some respects, not different from the debacle of Vietnam: "If only the little bastards would just come out . . . and fight like men, we'd cream them."[16] Such comments make the chaos strategist beam with pleasure.

One Asian expert has provided a description of war in the ideal type as having three distinct phases: engagement, chaos, and chopping of heads (*jiaofeng*, *luan*, *zhan*). The master of this "intellectual" approach to warfare, of course, is Sun Tzu, who employs *jiaofeng*, *luan*, and *zhan* through instantaneous, differential shock-wave application. This same authority refers to Clausewitz's theory of warfare victory as an "engineering" approach, with equally distinct phases: battle, campaign, and warfare termination—all occurring in cumulative, integral stages.[17]

Thus, when American warfighters speak of "cutting off and killing" an enemy, they mean "to chop heads" in the metaphorical sense; when the chaotic warfighter speaks of *zhan*, or its linguistic equivalent in a different culture, he is being literal. The chaos strategist and the chaos warfighter prefer the removal of the enemy in the purest form. In former Yugoslavia, and Iraq, this manifested as ethnic and religious "cleansing."

Ultimately, the best guarantee of success comes when the chaos strategist has brought chaos to his enemy without battlefield engagement. As Li Jing, remarking on Sun Tzu's own warfare practices, noted: "From antiquity, the number of cases in which a chaotic army [that is, with chaos induced among its ranks] brought victory [to the enemy] can never be fully recorded."[18] That, of course, is precisely what new operational concepts and employment sought to produce in crushing the Taliban and al-Qa'ida forces in 2001—through a network of unmanned aircraft that led to increased battlefield awareness, special operations forces used as forward spotters, motivated indigenous forces, precision major fires delivered by various means, and rapid maneuver to cause the enemy to break. This led to battlefield success, though not necessarily to strategic victory.

The Taliban and al-Qa'ida made a classic mistake in Afghanistan: they were stupid enough to fight back. They apparently had forgotten the lessons of chaos, or never learned them. The true chaos strategist would have looked for ways to never engage

American military force directly or would have employed methods that our emerging style of warfare is not able to handle well.

In reality, our strategy and force planning processes are laborious, methodical, and infinitely complex because they are planned for and fought with extraordinary precision and detail. The strategic theory that plans for force application as a paralysis of response does so because it wants—according to American strategic culture—fast, precise, and overwhelming conflict resolution. Such strategy and theory seek to eliminate chaos in order not to directly confront chaos.

Both the Weinberger and Powell doctrines reflect this American tradition. Vietnam did not fit this tradition; neither does Bosnia, Somalia, Iraq, Afghanistan, or many other plausible future war scenarios. The paradigm for many future battlegrounds, however, will draw on ambiguity and chaos rather than on American battlefield predominance.

Admittedly, with the advent of network warfare and remarkable advances in military technology, Colonel Trinquier's gloomy prophecy may not be as set in stone as some once believed. At the same time, in view of the incredible American military successes since the end of the cold war, one might reasonably ask why we pushed so hard and so fast toward military "transformation." We now know that in pushing strategic transformation, there are clear and present vulnerabilities we overlooked, which transformation cannot affect, yet which the chaos strategist will likely target.

ADAPTING TO CHAOS

This is not the first time in history that we have recognized our vulnerability, as well as questioned our ability to deal with that vulnerability. In the spring of 1946, scientist J. Robert Oppenheimer, who had directed the atomic bomb project, was asked in closed congressional testimony whether it would be possible to smuggle elements of such a bomb into New York and then blow it up. "Of course," replied Oppenheimer, "and people could destroy New York." When allegedly a nervous senator then asked how such a weapon smuggled in a crate or suitcase could be detected, Oppenheimer simply answered, "With a screwdriver."[19] The document that eventually came out of that testimony, known as the "Screwdriver Report," remains classified to this day. In essence, though, there seems to have been a recognition decades back that although there was no direct threat at the time, we were clearly vulnerable to chaos attack.

What makes our vulnerability so frightening at this stage in history, nonetheless, is the new means for chaos now available. Chaos strategists that are stateless agents will impact the future security of states and regions—with access to new capacities and technologies previously held only under the tight restriction of privileged states. Consider nuclear weapons, for example. While classic realists such as John J. Mersheimer may well be correct in asserting that states possessing nuclear weapons tend to act in ways that reduce rather than aggravate state-to-state security relationships, we have today truly entered the time of dirty, criminal, often ruthless warfare. Stateless agents with nuclear weapons may—unlike states—be driven to a "use it or lose it" mentality because of the hazards in holding such devices.

In 1991, published just as Desert Storm's ground offensive took place, Martin van Creveld's *The Transformation of War* did not deserve the ridicule thrown at it from pundits and scholars alike. In retrospect, Van Creveld was prescient. Desert Storm, on the other hand, looks archaic—the last of the big ones in terms of battlefield engagements.

In recognizing as well the classic principles embedded in *On War*, we would do well to recall how Clausewitz described war as a "remarkable trinity" composed of "primordial violence, hatred, and enmity" (the realm of the people); "chance and probability within which the creative spirit is free to roam" (the realm of the commander and his army); and the "element of subordination, as an instrument of policy, which makes [war] subject to reason alone" (the realm of the government).[20]

While this author does not intend to suggest that chaos strategists will inevitably de feat the United States, such strategists can—and often do—bedevil the national security decision-making process. Used with the right measures of surprise and undetectability, a chaos strategy could disrupt and possibly destroy the Clausewitzian trinity. In this scenario the people's faith in government could be erased and the third leg of the trinity, that of the commander and the army, could do little or nothing to prevent that destruction.

In truth, chaos strategists cannot defeat the United States or its allies in any traditional sense. We will be targeted, however, where the symbols of our strength reside. Although the Word Trade Center was not an irreplaceable node in terms of economic power, and even with the astounding resiliency that the United States displayed in recovering from the September 11 attacks, the total cost of lost worldwide economic growth and decreased equity value as a result of the attacks exceeded one trillion dollars.[21]

Even as the United States has the capacity to bring massive firepower on the battlefield—along with an increasingly sophisticated network of intelligence systems, information architecture, unmanned systems, and joint and combined force operations—we should expect to see chaos strategies come into play in future engagements. Too exclusive an emphasis on technological solutions in warfare—and in determining political outcomes—may well prove problematic. Although a cliché, it remains true that we must prepare for the wars we may find it necessary to fight, and not plan for the wars we want to fight.

Every single military engagement since the end of the cold war suggests that we have dispatched our adversaries with ease on battlefields and in direct engagements. This would seem to be an argument *against* rapid transformation of the armed forces. Why bother, after all, to change the military when no one else can stand up to it?

What may well be lacking is our need to recognize "closework." As Larry K. Smith phrases it:

> Overwhelming force implies, almost by definition, a lack of precision. That won't work now. What we're going to need is a much greater emphasis on the concentrated application of street smarts. I call these sorts of operations "closework." They are extremely precise missions that are used when the results are absolutely crucial. They demand the very highest standards of intelligence, of training, of preparation, of timing and execution. We haven't been particularly good at this in the past.[22]

Closework also suggests that urban warfare and often brutal forms of engagement will be far more likely in the future. Rather than relying more on distance warfare and precision engagement, we may fundamentally have to turn in a new direction. If it is true, for example, that one of two people on the face of the earth *already* lives in urban environments and one of two people will live in "water-stressed" areas at some point within the next two decades, then the complexity of intersecting forces can bring about profound and often vicious consequences. These consequences might include—but certainly not be limited to—critical infrastructure collapse, the outbreak of infectious disease that cannot be controlled, and intrastate as well as interethnic conflict related to resource scarcities (such as water) and environmental stress. We may well be entering into chaos.

We need to debate about how best to meet these challenges. Admittedly, there is a danger of overestimating one's real or potential enemy. There is a greater danger of not recognizing one's enemy at all.

To suggest that we actually understand the challenges of the future and can adapt our armed forces with relative ease is a flawed assumption. To the contrary, the science of complexity, future uncertainty, and minimizing our vulnerabilities should prove central to what should be one of the most vigorous debates in our nation's history.

As Ralph Sawyer has noted, Mao Tse-tung once compared strategy to a game of *weiqi* (*weich'i*) (better known under the Japanese name of *go*).[23] The link to chaos strategy—in corporate business (a form of economic warfare, to some) and real warfare—is apt. According to several sources, the strategy of *weiqi* directly influenced software development of chaos strategy and applies principles that remain worthy in the public and political arenas.[24]

We need to adapt to counter future "chaos strategies," where our adversary's essential aim is to achieve victory through avoiding defeat. Potential, though plausible, national security responses include the increased use of covert actions, as well as special forces, in place of more traditional wartime forces and resources. While this unquestionably will impact strategic military culture—sometimes with disastrous results—it is unacceptable for us to simply shrug and mutter, "Well . . . you can't change the culture."

In the end, it does not matter much if future chaos attacks will be illogical or disjointed. Chaos—and its intended effects—will prove more significant than a cohesive strategy that viably links means to ends. As an adage in India claims, one way to kill a tiger is to distract it from so many different sides that it tries to run in every direction at once.

Will we adapt to hydra networks, chaos strategy, and the "new" asymmetry? That remains to be answered in the wars that are still to come.

NOTES

Earlier versions of this work appeared in *Dismembering the State: The Death of Yugoslavia and Why It Matters* (Lanham, MD: Lexington Books, 2001) and as "Chaos as Strategy" in *Parameters: The U.S. Army War College Quarterly* (Summer 2002): 47–56.

1. Roger Trinquier, *Modern Warfare: A French View of Counterinsurgency* (New York: Praeger, 1964). The entire text is available online from the U.S. Army Command Staff College, Fort Leavenworth, Kansas, www-cgsc.army.mil/carl/resources/csi/trinquier/trinquier.asp.

2. See, in particular, chapter 4 of *Modern Warfare*.

3. "Declassified Key Judgments of the National Intelligence Estimate 'Trends in Global Terrorism: Implications for the United States' Dated April 2006," news release, 26 September 2006, 2, www.dni.gov/press_releases/Declassified_NIE_Key_Judgments.pdf.

4. The best thinker on this topic remains Ralph Sawyer, in particular in his recent extensive work published in the *Journal of Military and Strategic Studies* (Winter 2007), titled "Chinese Strategic Power: Myths, Intent, and Projections," www.jmss.org/2007/2007winter/articles/sawyer_cont-defence.pdf.

5. "September 11, 2001," *The New Yorker*, 24 September 2001, 60, 64.

6. Daniel Downby, "NATO Rethink as Taliban Proves Skilled Adversary," *Financial Times,* 29 July 2007.

7. Andrew F. Krepinevich, Jr., "Major Regional Conflicts: The Streetfighter Scenario," in *The Bottom-Up Review: An Assessment* (Washington: Defense Budget Project, February 1994), pt. 5, 42.

8. A debate about what constitutes "vital national interests" (also a frequently abused term, most often tossed around with complete lack of strategic calculus)—promotion of democracy, human dignity, natural resources, oil—in the future needs desperately to take place.

9. As an aside, it was Leon Trotsky—and not Ronald Reagan—who coined the term "ash heap of history." As Harrison Salisbury pointed out in a letter to the editor of the *New York Times,* 30 June 1985, Trotsky made the claim over the Mensheviks walking out of the Second Congress of Soviets in October 1917, thereby enabling the Bolsheviks to establish total control. Trotsky allegedly declared: "Go out where you belong—into the ash heap of history."

10. Luttwak argued that the significance of "Post-Heroic Warfare" lies in a "careful, purposeful patience" in the application of predominant American and American-led military force, as well as a return to the "casualty-avoiding methods of eighteenth century warfare"—nominally based on ancient Roman economically conscious war. Edward N. Luttwak, "Toward Post-Heroic Warfare," *Foreign Affairs* 74 (May–June 1995): 109–22. Economic embargoes and sanctions against adversary states may also prove more worthwhile than the traditional battlefield engagements that characterized previous wars. If so, they remain unpopular instruments of power (in contrast to the swift application of the military instrument) for policy makers. Economic sanctions against Serbia, for example, brought the Milošević regime to its knees; at one point during the last war in Bosnia and Herzegovina, by some estimates, inflation ran as high as 28 billion percent. The regime, nonetheless, stayed in place until after the "October Revolution" that took place five years later. Further, the individual prosperity of the average Serb plummeted while the vitality of Mafia elements, black-market smuggling, and "sanction busting" practices soared. One other aspect of economic sanctions points to American selectivity: the continuing embargo against the military dictatorship of Myanmar (Burma) proves less than effective because other nations, particularly ASEAN nations, continue to invest there. (One could make the same analogy, until recently, about European investment in Iran.) The standards applied by the United States as justification for sanctions against Myanmar could also have been applied against the PRC—which was not and will not be "punished" with economic sanctions. Myanmar does not represent a vital national interest for the United States; China does.

11. See "Air Targeting Strategies: An Overview," in *Airpower Confronts an Unstable World*, ed. Richard P. Hallion (Washington: Brassey's, 1997), 51–80.

12. By the use of "countervalue" as a possible military role, I am broadly referring to nuclear-weapon-targeting theories that refer to counterforce targets (hardened military systems and forces) and countervalue targets (that is, what we value most—our cities, our population, and our way of life). The U.S. military is not sized and structured as a countervalue entity; as such, we can expect to see organizational resistance to military forces playing the "home game" vice the "away game" in future engagements.

13. For an in-depth examination of the Soviet biological weapons program, one of the best available sources is Ken Alibek's *Biohazard* (New York: Random House, 1999).

14. Thomas Homer-Dixon, "The Rise of Complex Terrorism," *Foreign Policy*, no. 128 (January/February 2002): 54.

15. One of the best critiques of the Weinberger doctrine, with examples of its applicability to various interventions, can be found in Michael I. Handel, *Masters of War: Classical Strategic Thought*, 2nd ed. (London: Frank Cass, 1996), 185–203.

16. Remarks made by a frustrated military officer to journalists in Southeast Asia; drawn from a January 1996 lecture at the Naval War College by Professor William J. Duicker, Pennsylvania State University.

17. Based on lecture notes and drawn from discussions with Professor Arthur Waldron, Lauder Professor of International Relations at the University of Pennsylvania.

18. *The Seven Military Classics of Ancient China*, trans. Ralph D. Sawyer, with Mei-chün Lee Sawyer (Boulder, CO: Westview Press, 1993), 333.

19. Reported in Kai Bird and Martin Sherwin, "The First Line against Terrorism," *Washington Post*, 12 December 2001, available at ebird.dtic.mil/Dec2001/e20011212line.htm.

20. The complete text in English and German is available online at www.clausewitz.com/CWZHOME/VomKriege2/ONWARTOC2.HTML. The best translation of Clausewitz remains Michael Howard and Peter Paret's *On War* (Princeton, NJ: Princeton University Press, 1989).

21. Homer-Dixon, "The Rise of Complex Terrorism," 58.

22. Quoted in Joe Klein, "Closework," *The New Yorker*, 1 October 2001, 45.

23. See, in particular, the extended consideration of this analogy in Sawyer, "Chinese Strategic Power," 31n50.

24. For examples, see L. B. S. Raccoon's "The Chaos Strategy" in *ACM Software Engineering Notes* 20, no. 5 (December 1995): 40–47; and Chet Richards' self-published *Certain to Win: The Strategy of John Boyd, Applied to Business* (Philadelphia, PA: Xlibris Corporation, 2004).

31 Virtual Sanctuary Enables Global Insurgency

Richard Shultz

In the aftermath of 9/11 the United States went to war with al Qaeda and the Taliban. By 7 December 2001, the Taliban regime had been overthrown and al Qaeda's infrastructure in Afghanistan largely disrupted. The loss of that sanctuary was a major setback—a strategic defeat—for the vanguard of the Salafi Jihad movement and the embryonic global insurgency it was facilitating from that Afghan base. It now faced the challenge of having to adapt and innovate to recover what it had lost. Could it find new ways to replicate what had been established in Afghanistan in 1996–2001? This was the challenge al Qaeda and its Salafi affiliates faced. Could they reinvent themselves in the aftermath of Operation Enduring Freedom and continue to carry out the global insurgency they had initiated?

This chapter seeks to identify how al Qaeda and the Salafi Jihadists have attempted to reorganize to continue to execute a global fight. They appear to have done so through *two strategic adaptations*. The degree to which they have been able to accomplish each of these strategic adaptations and, as a result, the extent to which they are able to fight the "long Jihad"—a protracted irregular war on several fronts—cannot be answered here. That requires much further research. Here we will focus on describing what each of these strategic adaptations entails.

- *One*, the al Qaeda vanguard and its affiliates have employed the Internet to establish in cyberspace a virtual sanctuary from which to carry out many of the activities they had initiated from their Afghan base in 1996–2001. These activities include propagating the Salafi Jihad ideology to the *ummah;* recruiting, inspiring, and training *Jihadis;* providing operational information and materials; networking dispersed elements of the Salafi Jihad movement; irregular warfare training; and planning and executing operations.

Dr. Richard H. Shultz, Jr., is an American security adviser and professor of international politics at the Fletcher School, Tufts University, where he teaches graduate-level courses in various aspects of international security. He is also the director of the Fletcher School's International Security Studies Program. The program is dedicated to graduate-level teaching and research on a broad range of conflict, defense, and strategic issues. Since 2003 he has directed the Armed Groups Project for the Washington-based National Strategy Information Center. The project seeks to understand the complex nature of armed groups and explore approaches for meeting these challenges. He has held three chairs: the Olin Distinguished Professorship of National Security Studies at the U.S. Military Academy, Secretary of the Navy Senior Research Fellow at the U.S. Naval War College, and Brigadier General H. L. Oppenheimer Chair of Warfighting Strategy, U.S. Marine Corps. Since the mid-1980s he has served as a consultant to various U.S. government agencies concerned with national security affairs. His recent books include *Insurgents, Terrorists, and Militias: The Warriors of Contemporary Combat* (Columbia University Press, 2006) and *The Secret War against Hanoi: Kennedy and Johnson's Use of Spies, Saboteurs, and Covert Warriors in North Vietnam* (Harper Collins, 1999; paperback 2000). He has a forthcoming monograph titled *Global Insurgency Strategy and the Salafi Jihad Movement* (Institute for National Security Studies, U.S. Air Force Academy, 2008).

- *Two*, al Qaeda has continued to encourage and promote the global Salafi Jihad movement, which appears to function at the local level within nine regional areas. In these locations, activities carried out by groups and cells that see themselves as a part of this movement have continued to take place since 9/11, with some regions, to include Europe, experiencing major terrorist strikes.

Below, the focus will mainly be on the first adaptation. How has the al Qaeda vanguard and its affiliates employed the Internet? To what extent do they seek to establish in cyberspace a virtual sanctuary from which to carry out many of the activities that had taken place on the ground during 1996–2001 in the Afghan base? The second strategic adaptation—continuing the fights against near or national-level enemies by local armed groups—will receive less comprehensive attention.

VIRTUAL SANCTUARY

Since 9/11, growing attention has been paid in both the news media and more scholarly publications to how al Qaeda and other associated Salafi Jihad groups have made use of the Internet. For example, Steve Coll and Susan Glasser suggested in the *Washington Post* that "al Qaeda has become the first guerrilla movement in history to migrate from physical space to cyberspace. With laptops and DVDs, in secret hideouts and at neighborhood Internet cafes, young code-writing Jihadists have sought to replicate the . . . facilities they lost in Afghanistan with countless new locations on the Internet."[1]

Gabriel Weimann, in a 2004 study, provided the following insights into the expanding use of the Internet by Jihad groups. "In 1998, around half of the thirty organizations designated [by the United States] as Foreign Terrorist Organizations . . . maintained Websites; by 2000, virtually all terrorist groups had established their presence on the Internet. Our scan of the Internet in 2003–2004 revealed hundreds of Websites serving terrorists and their supporters." He goes on to add: "Terrorism on the Internet . . . is a very dynamic phenomenon: Websites suddenly emerge, frequently modify their formats, and then swiftly disappear—or seem to disappear by changing their online address but retain much the same content."[2] Since 2004, what Weimann described has continued to burgeon.

Weimann and other specialists have conceptualized frameworks for categorizing the different ways in which the Internet has been utilized, describing the functions these activities hope to serve. Extrapolating from these studies and using extensive data mining of a primary-source database compiled by the SITE Institute, one can observe these attempts to replicate in cyberspace many of the activities that took place on the ground in Afghanistan in 1996–2001.[3] Here we divide those activities into the following seven categories:

- Propagating the Salafi ideology of Jihad
- Inspiring and mobilizing the *ummah* to join the Jihad
- Engaging in psychological warfare to demoralize enemies
- Networking the global Salafi Jihad insurgency
- Sharing operational information—manuals and handbooks
- Sharing operational information—training videos and courses
- Collecting for targeting.

If effective, these virtual activities will provide al Qaeda and associated movements (AQAM) with the capacity to reach like-minded individuals and groups in various regions of the world who are willing to join the cause and take action. Through AQAM Web sites these individuals and groups will have the opportunity to attain the operational skills and capacity to execute violent strikes locally and on an independent basis. This is a new form of power projection no radical movement has had in the past.

What follows is a description of each of the categories and how they fit together. It is based on an assessment of examples of the ways in which al Qaeda and associated Salafi Jihad groups have carried out each activity on their Internet Web sites. However, before proceeding, it is also important to briefly note the role and contribution that satellite television plays in this process. For Muslim populations in the Arab world and elsewhere satellite channels such as al-Jazeera and al-Arabiya are often the first way in which they are engaged with the issues and themes, described below, that are found on the Web sites of al Qaeda and associated Jihad groups. In other words, there is a synergy—albeit an unintended one—between them. Indeed, it may well be that al-Jazeera and al-Arabiya, among others, are the precipitants—provide an awaking—that take the individual to the Internet for further information. Here is what the individual will find.

1. ***Propagating the Salafi Ideology of Jihad.*** The first requirement the Salafi Jihadists have to satisfy to be in a position to initiate a global insurgency is to transmit a transnational ideology to target audiences. They have to be able to successfully perform the same functions on the Internet as are carried out by national-level revolutionary movements. Through a large number of different Web-based activities, to include sophisticated media fronts, news shows, and online magazines, they seek to execute these functions across the globe. By doing so, they are able to disseminate a series of ideological frames and messages that describe in global and local terms the social and political conditions requiring immediate and drastic Jihad action. Salafi ideology offers a comprehensive critique of the existing local and global social/political situations as immoral and inhuman and seeks to instill in the *ummah* a powerful sense of moral outrage and commitment to holy war.

The Global Islamic Media Front, one of the main voices of al Qaeda on the Web, is illustrative. This site, formerly known as Alneda, is heavily focused on ideological-type information. It not only posts all of the doctrinal speeches and statements of bin Laden and Zawahiri, among others, but also provides analysis of these items for the *ummah*. An example—"Reading and Analysis of the Hero Tapes of Usama bin Laden, Ayman al-Zawahiri, and Abu Mus'ab al-Zarqawi"—was posted on 1 May 2006 and subsequently distributed across several other Jihad forums.

Another example that focuses, at least in part, on the broader ideological themes found in Salafi Jihad doctrine is the *Voice of the Caliphate*, a weekly news program issued by the Global Islamic Media Front. First appearing in 2005, it ties theory and practice together by providing examples of how the global holy war is being carried out by different elements of the *ummah*.

Electronic Internet magazines serve a similar function. A recent example is *The Echo of Jihad*, a 45-page periodical that began appearing in 2006. Its April edition features discussion of the importance of Jihad; the relative importance of Islamic scholars versus mujahideen leaders like bin Laden; and recent operations by mujahideen in Chechnya,

Afghanistan, Iraq, Saudi Arabia, and elsewhere. A second example, *Ja'ami* (which means "mosque"), is produced by the Media Office of the Islamic Front of the Iraqi Resistance.

Finally, in this category of ideological and doctrinal materials one must include broad strategy documents such as al Qaeda's seven-stage plan for the next 20 years. Since it was first posted, this "strategy" document has been given a prominent and permanent status atop many of the most frequently visited Jihadist forums on the Internet. Western experts tend to characterize it as very naive. They do so for the following reasons. First, there is no way the scenario depicted in the plan can be followed step-by-step. It is simply unworkable. Second, the idea that al-Qaeda could establish a caliphate in the Islamic world is absurd. The 20-year plan has nothing to do with reality. It is far out of reach.

However, these materials are not aimed at convincing Western experts. They are directed at those many members of the *ummah* who read these materials at *Jihadi* forums on the Internet. What impact do they have on them? Do the readers envision a coming major transformation of society and return to an idealized past? And if they agree with it, are they ready, as one three-part series run by the Global Islamic Media Front asks, to "gear up" and prepare to join the Jihad?

2. *Inspiring and Mobilizing the* Ummah *to Join the Jihad.* It is one thing to nod in agreement with broad ideological statements. Al Qaeda and the Salafi Jihadists seek to leverage a plethora of Internet methods to energize sympathizers into action. Here we will examine one important way they do so by celebrating the achievements and sacrifices of those on the front lines of the global fight.

Consider the biographies of martyrs that are posted on the Web with a high degree of regularity. Al Qaeda in Iraq, for example, publishes on a periodic basis a document titled *From the Biographies of Prominent Martyrs*. The eighth issue of it, dated January 2006, tells the story of the "Knights Group" of three mujahideen. In great detail the reader learns why and how each joined the Jihad and traveled to Iraq to fight. An account of their courageous demise follows. The three were pinned down in a house they were using as a base. The author glorifies their deaths, noting the unwillingness of each to try to escape or surrender. And one of the Jihad fighters, referred to as the lion Abu-Umar, is said to have "carried in his hands a mortar shell that he had prepared for this situation." He surprised the Americans attacking the house and "pulled the ring out, throwing four of the criminals to hell, while he went up to Paradise."

This is but one example. Many others are contained in the SITE Institute database. And it only maintains a sample of them. There are also other formats for these biographies, such as the videoed "last will and testament" of suicide bombers. One example is the "Will of the Martyr, Abu al-Zobeir al-Mohajir," with video footage of his operation in July 2005. It depicts a celebration in which he enthusiastically describes the operation he is about to carry out and why he intends to do so: "Allah ordered us to make Jihad . . . to defend his religion. I urge all young Muslim men to follow us in Jihad and give their lives for the sake of Allah's religion." He is then shown being embraced by his comrades, before the film cuts to the scene of his suicide car bombing—a "crusaders' checkpoint" east of Fallujah. Again, this is one of many examples found at Jihad Web sites.

Other means employed to inspire and mobilize are videos of the preparation for and successful conduct of operations against U.S. forces in Afghanistan and Iraq. These appear on a daily basis on *Jihadi* forums and Web sites. One example, issued by the Global Islamic Media Front on 22 January 2006, is a 28-minute video titled "Jihad Academy," which is described as but a "single day for those who struggle in Allah's cause." It highlights a number of attacks executed by Iraqi insurgent groups, to include al Qaeda in Iraq, the Mujahideen Army, and the Islamic Army in Iraq. The attacks are shown in the dawn hours and in the dark of night. They include sniper operations, detonation of improvised explosive devices (IEDs) against a variety of targets, and rocket and mortar fire.

There also are many publications posted on these Web sites that fall into the category of inspiring, motivating, and mobilizing the *ummah* to join the fight. These guides are advocacy and motivational pieces. The extent to which the message is being received and acted upon remains to be determined.

Paralleling these are other videos with *Jihadi* field commanders who provide the same kind of inspirational message. Of course, the most prominent was Abu Mus'ab al-Zarqawi. An example, titled "A Message to the People," was issued by the Mujahideen Shura Council, which claims to be composed of six insurgency groups in Iraq.[4] In this 34-minute video, Zarqawi is seen planning operations in a war room, meeting with local leaders of al Anbar province, and leading mujahideen in training exercises and on the battlefield. In another part of the film Zarqawi is seen firing an automatic weapon and stating, "America will go out of Iraq, humiliated, defeated."

Finally, scores of items on these Web sites go the next step and include guides describing how to prepare for and then join the fight in Iraq and elsewhere. One example, "This Is the Road to Iraq," provides instructions for prospective *Jihadis* intent on entering the war. The first half concentrates on mental and physical preparation for Jihad, while the second half furnishes guidance for successfully entering Iraq and cultivating contacts with an insurgent group.

In addition to celebrating the achievements and sacrifices of those on the front lines of the global fight, there are other ways AQAM and the Salafi Jihadists employ the Internet to inspire and mobilize the *ummah* to join the fight. They use the same Web sites, for example, to recount the suffering and carnage they assert is being inflicted on Muslims by the United States and other Western powers, Israel, and apostate regimes in Islamic countries.

3. *Engaging in Psychological Warfare to Demoralize Enemies.* The flip side of inspiring and mobilizing the *ummah* to join the Salafi Jihad movement and fight is the demoralizing of the near and far enemies of that movement, convincing them to give up the fight. Here we will use the insurgency in Iraq, the central front in the global Jihad, as illustrative.

A number of Internet-based tactics are employed by the Salafi insurgent groups to demoralize their enemies in Iraq. Of these, the most terrifying and intimidating have been the beheadings. This tactic has been used against both Iraqis and foreigners working in Iraq. The message to each group is unambiguous. The nightmare videos of those captured being decapitated by their captors is anything but a random act of terrorism—it is carefully designed for specific audiences.

With respect to members of the Iraqi government, and those contemplating joining it, the threat of beheading was explicitly made through numerous Internet-posted warnings. For example, on 20 April 2006 the Shari'a Commission of the Mujahideen Shura Council in Iraq issued the threat of "the sword and slaughter to he who joins the police and the army." The council stated that all Muslims who join the Iraqi security forces to serve those who "worship the devils, those who disbelieve and fight in the cause of Taghut [Satan]," shall be considered "converters who fight against Allah." What awaits them?—"sharp swords!" And in a similar message posted in December 2005, insurgent groups in Iraq were encouraged to "start cutting throats in the Islamic way. . . . Slaughter three every day to show them that you do not hesitate in implementing Allah's orders." To Western eyes this is immoral and savage behavior. But for Salafi Jihadists it is characterized as religious duty. The blood-dripping sword has a powerful Salafi meaning.

In addition to the beheading videos, the insurgents in Iraq also post a large number of videos and reports of other kinds of executions. These include putting captives to death by firing squad, as well as pulling police out of vehicles, off of street corners, and so on to gun them down on the spot.

Members of the leadership in Iraq are often singled out by name. For example, in November 2005 an al Qaeda–affiliated Jihad forum posted the photographs of the "Twenty Most Wanted People in the [L]and of the Two Rivers." Various assassinations of senior-level officials since 2003 have demonstrated such threats are often backed up. The "devil" Grand Ayatollah Ali al-Sistani was designated as number one—the most wanted. The text concluded, "We ask Allah that the Mujahideen will be able to remove their heads."

Blood drips from the sword of a *Jihadi* fighter, evoking both the literal violence inherent in the *Jihadi* struggle and the possibilities of military victory. Blood dripping from a sword has strong Salafi connotations.[5]

With respect to the United States, the most frequent tactic employed is the previously mentioned daily reports on all the Jihad forums and Web sites of alleged successful operations carried out against American forces in Iraq. Those that stand out among a large number reviewed are the "Top Ten" videos of insurgent attacks that began to appear in 2005. Released by both the Global Islamic Media Front and a group calling itself the Muslim Lions, they are widely distributed across Jihad forums today. Each includes ten attacks perpetrated by groups such as Ansar al-Sunnah Army, Islamic Army in Iraq, and al Qaeda in Iraq. They are impressive productions. These attacks also frequently appear the day after they occur in various Western print and electronic news outlets.

Reports of attacks on the United States are not confined to Iraq. The message from these Web sites is that America is under assault in all the places it has entered in the Muslim world. Next to Iraq, operations against U.S. forces in Afghanistan receive the greatest attention. And individual spectacular strikes like that on the U.S. consulate in Jidda by al Qaeda in Saudi Arabia are featured widely. Taken in total the psychological-warfare message is clear—the United States is exposed and vulnerable to effective and continuous mujahideen attacks across the Muslim world.

Finally, the leaders of the global Jihad use the Internet to mock failed U.S. attempts to capture or kill them. One example that received wide attention (to include being broadcast on al-Jazeera) was a speech by Zawahiri following the January 2006 air strike on the village of Damadola in Peshawar, where al Qaeda's number two was supposed to be hiding. He taunted President Bush—the "Butcher of Washington"—asserting "that his death will only come at the time of Allah's decree, and until that time, he remains amid the Muslim masses, rejoicing in their support, their attention, their generosity, their protection and their participation in Jihad until we conquer you with the help and power of Allah."

The above items all aimed at influencing and undermining one of America's centers of gravity—the U.S. home front. It is not unlike what the Vietcong successfully targeted over 30 years ago. Then, as now, the objective was to follow Clausewitz's advice. Attack the enemy's center of gravity—his strategic pressure points—and you will weaken his capacity to fight war.

   4. *Networking the Global Salafi Jihad Insurgency.* In the latter 1990s, al Qaeda's use of the Internet concentrated on the first category of this framework—propagating the Salafi ideology of Jihad to incite and unify the *ummah* for a common purpose. Since 9/11, al Qaeda and associated members of the Salafi Jihad movement (a number of which are fighting at the national level) have broadened their use of the Web to include, as highlighted above, the second and third categories—inspiring and mobilizing the *ummah* to join the Jihad and engaging in psychological warfare to demoralize enemies.

However, the loss of the Afghan sanctuary resulted in a further expansion. It now includes the use of the Internet for tactical purposes, such as training, and for operational objectives, to include how to organize virtual cells.

Each of these functions requires secure communications to avoid the disruptive tactics that U.S. intelligence has been able to employ against certain kinds of *Jihadi* Internet activity—e.g., closing down fixed Web sites. Thus, al Qaeda and other groups began to employ new methods, to include protected bulletin boards, free upload services by Internet providers, and the creation of proxy servers, among others. Up-to-date instruction on how to employ these techniques is likewise made available. Consider the following examples.

The first has to do with how to use third-party-hosting services. This technique exploits these servers, paid for primarily by advertising agencies, to transmit operationally related information and secret communications. These servers, available across the Internet, provide relatively anonymous hosting that a visitor can easily manipulate.[6] A second way of transmitting operationally related information and secret communications is through posted messages on discussion boards at password-protected forums. And a third technique entails creating and employing Internet proxy servers. Guides and manuals on how to utilize each of these methods are available at the Global Islamic Media Front site, among others.

These methods can be used to circulate a wide range of materials, like training videos, operational manuals, and guides for producing weapons such as improvised explosive devices. Along with other virtual techniques they can also be exploited by operational cells to secretly communicate and organize.

One way of communicating secretly, reported by Coll and Glasser, is through public e-mail services such as Hotmail. Here is how it works. An operative opens an account on Hotmail, "writes a message in draft form, saves it as a draft, and then transmits the e-mail account name and password during chatter on a relatively secure message board." Another operative "opens the e-mail account and reads the draft—since no e-mail message was sent, there was a reduced risk of interception." This process has been characterized as a dead drop in cyberspace.[7]

Virtual methods such as these and others also provide the means to establish operational cells in cyberspace. Discussion of how to do so began to appear on different al Qaeda–affiliated Web sites in 2004, according to sources collected by the SITE Institute. These items go into the details of how to do so, suggesting that once formed members can both exchange "work plans, strategies, and educational materials" and eventually "meet in reality and execute operations in the field."

An example of this kind of cell was reported in the spring of 2004. On 29 March, "Royal Canadian Mounted Police officers burst into the Ottawa home of Mohammed . . . Khawaja, a 24-year-old computer programmer . . . arresting him for alleged complicity in what Canadian and British authorities described as a transatlantic plot to bomb targets in London and Canada." Khawaja, who "met his . . . British counterparts online[,] came to the attention of authorities . . . when he traveled to Britain and walked into a surveillance operation being conducted by British Police." He had gone there to "me[e]t with his online acquaintances." During the meeting he "told them how to detonate bombs using cell phones." He had learned to do so from the Internet.[8]

The plot involved seven men from four countries (United States, United Kingdom, Canada, and Pakistan) who through the Internet formed a virtual cell. During the time the cell was developing and moving toward taking action there appears to have been training provided to a member of it in Pakistan. Whether an al Qaeda linkage was established to provide posttraining guidance or direction is unclear from open sources. When arrested the cell was in the process of going operational. This was the kind of cell—mainly homegrown members who met both locally and in cyberspace—most feared in Europe. As we shall see below, through these new Web-based methods al Qaeda and other Salafi Jihad groups seek to provide the means by which prospective holy warriors at the local level can find like-minded associates and receive the knowledge and training via the Internet that is necessary to join the fight. The head of Britain's domestic intelligence service (MI5) stated publicly in November 2006 that she "knew of 30 [such] conspiracies" and that "future attacks could be chemical, biological or even involve some kind of nuclear device."[9]

5. *Sharing Operational Information—Manuals and Handbooks.*
Al Qaeda has established an extensive online compilation of operational manuals and handbooks for irregular warfare. These range from documents not unlike the doctrinal manuals of conventional military forces to more narrowly focused instructional guides on how to carry out a particular tactic or produce and employ a specific weapon. The number of these items is now quite large. Here we will only highlight a few examples.

Broader military and intelligence materials provide the means whereby training can begin in virtually any location, simply by going online. We now know that al Qaeda was producing such manuals well before 9/11 because of what was found on computers and disks left behind in Afghanistan. Perhaps the best known of these items is what in the West came to be referred to as "The Encyclopedia of Jihad." An al Qaeda production of thousands of pages, it is a guide for how to establish an underground organization. The manual has circulated across the Internet.

Perhaps the most widely circulated doctrinal manual is a 1,600-page document titled "The Call for a Global Islamic Resistance." It was written by Mustafa Setmariam Nasar, a Syrian native who fought against the Soviet Union in Afghanistan. In the manual he highlights how small and independent groups of mujahideen can conduct operations against the West. In the aftermath of 9/11, Nasar called for a "third generation" of Salafi Jihadists to plan and execute operations on their own but as part of the broader movement and in solidarity with al Qaeda's ideology. In some cases members of these cells made contact with al Qaeda and received training and operational support. Those who carried out the July 2005 bombings in London are an example.[10]

Beyond these broader manuals, a plethora of more narrowly focused handbooks and guides are also readily available. Perhaps the tactic/specific weapon receiving the widest attention on *Jihadi* Web addresses since 2003 is the IED. Many of these are based on lessons being drawn from Iraq. Often these reports and handbooks include diagrams and other visual depictions, such as one distributed to a password-protected al Qaeda–affiliated forum in December 2005. The author illustrates the construction of a charge, the distance from which it is placed from its target, and the amount of explosive to be used to achieve a desired result against different kinds of targets. There is even a discussion of physical principles such as blast waves.

This is but one example of the serious attention that is being given to IEDs. And it should not be surprising in light of the effectiveness of the weapon in Iraq and the efforts the Pentagon has undertaken to find an answer to it. Indeed, the *Jihadis* are busy learning about DoD efforts at countermeasures. Consider a report posted in April 2006 to a password-protected Jihadist forum discussing a study produced by the U.S. think tank CSIS on innovations in the use of IEDs in Iraq and the U.S. response to these new insurgent tactics. The author discusses the findings in the study and announces it will be translated into Arabic. He then chides the authors, stating that they should not be surprised at the innovativeness of the mujahideen in responding to new U.S. tactics. After all, he points out, "they have Allah on their side and you have nobody on yours."

Earlier in 2006, a similar item focused on the U.S. Army's plan to deploy the Joint IED Neutralizer in Iraq as a means to reduce the risk posed by roadside improvised explosive devices. The author highlights the specifications of the Neutralizer, where it "seems less reinforced," and discusses a series of methods that the mujahideen can use to defeat it.

Beyond IEDs, there are handbooks and related materials on many other kinds of weapons. These range from how to build a biological weapon and dirty bombs to information warfare tactics to how to service an AK-47.

6. *Sharing Operational Information—Training Videos and Courses.* It should not be surprising that new Internet developments in information management since 9/11 are quickly being adopted and adapted by the Salafi Jihadists. A case in point is the use of videos and slide shows as the basis for online training programs. Over the last three years professionally produced training videos have been generated by al Qaeda to replicate on the Web what it had been able to provide prospective holy warriors on the ground in Afghanistan in the latter 1990s. The SITE Institute has compiled a large quantity of these materials in its database.

Recent examples include training courses produced by Labik, an al Qaeda media organization operating in Afghanistan. In March 2006, it issued and posted a series of films of mujahideen training for combat and practicing tactical operations, to include conducting raids on houses, blowing up a bridge, attacking a target with rocket-propelled grenades, and taking hostages, among other actions.

Other video productions concentrate on how to execute a specific tactic or employ a particular weapon. An example is booby-trapping. In this presentation the trainee learns that this technique for attacking an enemy can be implemented in many ways that require different levels of expertise and equipment. It also explains how many of these techniques were developed by "infidel states," such as England, Russia, Germany, Italy, and the United States. The narrator suggests to the viewer that these techniques should be studied. This particular instructional exercise, which appeared in an al Qaeda forum in 2005, concentrates on four specific types of booby-trapping. Similar video presentations can be found for almost every irregular warfare tactic and on each of the weapons employed in this form of combat. These include how to operate against U.S. soldiers in Iraq and Afghanistan, how to infiltrate into those countries, and how to fight in different rural and urban environments in each location.

These developments have led the Israeli specialist Reuven Paz to propose that this vast and wide-ranging body of instructional/training videos and slide shows posted on the Web over the last few years by Jihad groups constitutes nothing short of an Internet-based "Open University for Jihad." Paz asserts that the Salafi Jihad movement has turned the Internet into a cyber university for recruiting, indoctrinating, and training future generations of holy warriors from the Arab and Muslim worlds.[11]

Al Qaeda's Global Islamic Media Front sees eye to eye with Paz's assessment. Indeed, it made this claim before Paz. In a 2005 article titled "Al Qaeda University for Jihad Subjects," the front described these activities as constituting a global institution in cyberspace, providing instruction and training in psychological, electronic, and physical warfare for the mujahideen of tomorrow. The bottom line—budding holy warriors now have the means available to begin to undertake an irregular-warfare-training program in cyberspace, complete with discussion boards and chat rooms.

In conjunction with the previous functions of the virtual sanctuary, the use of new information-management tools highlighted in this section facilitate the development of homegrown cells discussed earlier. These cells can emerge in any location and on their own and develop the means to prepare for and carry out operations. There are now examples of this homegrown pattern that have taken place since 9/11. As noted above, in some cases the local cell has made contact with and received assistance from al Qaeda, while in other instances this was not the case. The attack on the London subway, the train bombings in Madrid, the series of suicide operations in Casablanca, and the actions of the Hofstad group in the Netherlands, to name the most prominent cases, reflect both these homegrown variations.

7. ***Collecting for Targeting.*** Finally, the Internet provides Salafi operational units with a significant amount of data about potential targets, particularly ones in the West. The extent to which they have mined the Web for this kind of information was first uncovered on al Qaeda computers left behind in Afghanistan. Based on open sources readily available on the Internet, al Qaeda had built target folders/files prior to 9/11 on public utilities, transportation systems, government buildings, airports, major harbors, and nuclear power plants. They also collected U.S. government and private-sector studies of the vulnerabilities of these and other facilities to different types of terrorist operations.

Additionally, they have access to overhead imagery and related structural information of many potential targets. This allows them not only to access the target in terms of its most vulnerable points but to observe security measures that have been taken to protect it.

According to Dan Verton, a specialist in cyberterrorism, since 9/11, "al Qaeda cells now operate with the assistance of large databases containing details of potential targets in the U.S. They use the Internet to collect intelligence on those targets, especially critical economic nodes, and modern software enables them to study structural weaknesses in facilities as well as predict the cascading failure effect of attacking certain systems."[12]

Since 9/11 the U.S. government has undertaken measures to protect such information, particularly where it concerns critical facilities and infrastructure. Information that used to be publicly available is now secured. However, in this game of cat and mouse the *Jihadis* are teaching one another how to penetrate secure Web sites. For example, recently the Global Islamic Media Front began circulating a 74-page guide on how to identify their vulnerabilities and penetrate—hack—into them. The guide highlights software that can be used to do so.

FOSTERING THE GLOBAL SALAFI JIHAD MOVEMENT[13]

Al Qaeda's second adaptation appears to have focused on reestablishing its self-assigned role as the vanguard of the Salafi Jihad movement, a role that was set back as a result of Operation Enduring Freedom. How has al Qaeda sought to do so? To answer the question, developing a detailed mosaic of what is now referred to as al Qaeda and associated movements (AQAM) is needed. Below we will identify two efforts that address elements of it and highlight the broader contours of AQAM as well as identify key questions that remain to be addressed.

Bruce Hoffman portrays al Qaeda "as both an inspiration and an organization." With respect to the former, al Qaeda's founders saw as one of the central missions of their organization the realization of the vanguard party concept advocated by Sayyid Qutb.[14] And so, to that end they sought to "summon a broad universe of like-minded extremists" to become part of a global Jihad movement.[15] In the 1990s, in Afghanistan, al Qaeda was able to begin to carry out this mission by establishing a network of linkages with a score of national-level Islamist groups, who were employing guerrilla violence and terrorism against their governments. Many authors, to include Hoffman, have chronicled these pre-9/11 developments.

Al Qaeda from its Afghan sanctuary provided national-level Jihad organizations with financial assistance, training, weapons, and spiritual guidance. In return, these entities were to see themselves as part of al Qaeda's global struggle. Recipients included radical Islamist armed groups from Algeria, Morocco, Egypt, Uzbekistan, Chechnya, Kashmir, Indonesia, the Philippines, and Bosnia, among a number of other places.

The capacity of al Qaeda to continue to play this vanguard role and to maintain connections with the groups that constituted this network of associations was set back considerably with the loss of its Afghan sanctuary. What has al Qaeda done to adapt in order to reestablish linkages with its old Salafi Jihad affiliates and add new ones? What are the constituent parts of AQAM? How do local Jihad groups view their place in AQAM and relationship to al Qaeda? How many local affiliates exist? These questions highlight what needs to be discovered about al Qaeda's post-9/11 efforts to reestablish a network of linkages with national-level Islamist groups.

As late as 2005, four years after 9/11, U.S. officials were still struggling to understand the relationship between al Qaeda and its affiliates, and the extent to which those linkages had been reestablished. In 2006, key U.S. national security documents began to use the term AQAM to refer to this rejuvenated relationship. U.S. Central Command's (CENTCOM's) posture statement for fighting the war in 2006 is illustrative. It assessed al Qaeda through the "near enemy—far enemy" lens. AQAM was described as a global movement having a strong presence in the CENTCOM region through several local Salafi Jihad affiliates.[16]

These affiliates were described as fighting against local apostate regimes (who are partners of the United States)—"near enemies"—in the CENTCOM area. According to the posture statement, the relationship between al Qaeda and local Jihad groups since 9/11 has been facilitated by the Internet:

> This enemy is linked by modern communications, expertly using the virtual world for indoctrination and proselytizing. The Internet empowers these extremists in a way that would have been impossible a decade ago. It enables them to have global reach. . . . And this safe haven of websites and the Internet is proliferating rapidly, spreading al Qaeda's ideology well beyond its birthplace in the Middle East.[17]

To be sure, an important way al Qaeda has sought to reestablish linkages with local Salafi Jihad groups is through its virtual sanctuary. Indeed, as was described earlier, al Qaeda uses the Internet to propagate its Salafi Jihad ideology to instill in the *ummah* a powerful sense of moral outrage and commitment to holy war. Through a large number of different Web-based activities al Qaeda seeks to propagate its message to individuals and groups across the globe. In doing so, it disseminates a series of ideological frames and messages that describe in global and local terms the social and political conditions requiring immediate and drastic Jihad action.

That this is taking place is evident. Through this virtual sanctuary al Qaeda seeks to reestablish its vanguard role and attempts to inspire and encourage a global movement of radicalized Muslim groups to fight locally against "near enemies," while seeing them-selves as a part of a larger global struggle against the United States, the "far enemy."

But how organized are these efforts and whom do they reach? A recent study by Rita Katz and Josh Devon of the SITE Institute describes this Internet activity as "very struc-tured. . . . [A] handful of primary source jihadist websites distribute the media [activities] of the leaders of al-Qaeda and other jihadist groups. Through this small number of specific, password-protected online forums, the leading jihadist groups, like al-Qaeda, post their communiqués and propaganda. By keeping the number of primary source jihadist websites small . . . [they] can provide a transparent mechanism to authenticate communiqués."[18]

Although these primary Web sites are relatively few in number, Katz and Devon note that members of them disseminate official communiqués, doctrinal treatises, strategic and operational documents, special messages, and other materials through a much broader and far-reaching network of other Web sites, message boards, e-groups, blogs, and instant-messaging services available through the Internet. Here is one way they say this process functions:

> Once an official message from a jihadist group is posted to a primary source message fo-rum, members of the primary message forum will then disseminate that posting to other secondary messageboards. From these secondary messageboards, other peripheral indi-viduals will then disseminate the information onto other messageboards.[19]

Katz and Devon propose the following network graphic to illustrate how this virtual capability seeks to be "at once decentralized but rigidly hierarchical."

The primary Web sites at the center of the network graphic are composed of AQAM, to include insurgent groups in Iraq, the Taliban and other groups in Afghanistan, the Islamic Maghreb (formerly the GSPC), the Libyan Islamic Fighting Group, Saudi Jihadist groups, and others. Since January 2006, report Katz and Devon, the Web-based activities of these AQAM elements have been coordinated and distributed through a new virtual entity—the *Al-Fajr Center*—to the secondary and tertiary Web sites noted on the above graphic. What this portends is that individuals and groups across the globe may now easily acquire the kinds of information identified in each of the seven categories of the virtual sanctuary described earlier.

In sum, the activities carried out by the Al-Fajr Center provide the potential for "fostering a unified, global jihadist community." More-over, it can assist al Qaeda and key associates "coordinate, share infor-mation, and consolidate their power

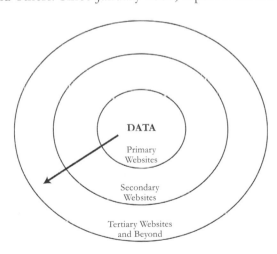

Dissemination of Primary Source Jihad Data[20]

to continue to lead the [global] jihadist movement," which is one of al Qaeda's original and enduring missions.[21]

If this is a key way al Qaeda has sought to reestablish its self-assigned role as the vanguard of the global Salafi Jihad movement, then the follow-on question is how we know who constitutes the local affiliates of AQAM and on what basis they view themselves as parts of AQAM. One recent study has sought to identify criteria for membership in AQAM. The author, Assaf Moghadam, proposes that to be a member of AQAM a Salafi Jihad entity must be a Sunni Islamic group and meet one of the following four criteria.[22]

First, a group can be considered part of AQAM if "Al Qaeda is reflected in the group's name" and its members adhere to al Qaeda's agenda.[23] In this category he includes al Qaeda in Iraq, which prior to September 2004 was known as Jama'at al-Tawhid wal-Jihad. Abu Mus'ab al-Zarqawi, its founder, in October 2004 declared the allegiance of the group to bin Laden and al Qaeda's strategy. This was followed by a change in the name of the group. A more recent example of the first criterion can be found in North Africa. The Algerian Salafist Group for Preaching and Combat, known by its French initials GSPC, announced at the end of 2006 it was switching its name to Al Qaeda of the Islamic Maghreb. Long associated with al Qaeda, it was chosen by bin Laden to forge links and coordinate the activities of like-minded groups in Morocco, Nigeria, Mauritania, Tunisia, and elsewhere.[24] Thus, the name change.

Second, a group may be considered part of AQAM if, according to Moghadam, there is evidence it has "internalized the worldview of Al Qaeda and global Jihad." Several organizations fall into this category, including the Islamic Movement of Uzbekistan (IMU); Jaish-e-Muhammad (JeM) and Lashkar-e-Jhangvi (LeJ), both of whose base of operations is Pakistan; Indonesia's Jemaah Islamiyya (JI); and the Moroccan group Assirat al Moustaquim (Direct Path). These groups and several others similar to them meet this second criterion established by Moghadam.[25]

A third criterion is that a "group is devoted to and actively practices violence to overthrow an existing Islamic regime or regimes with the aim to create a transnational Caliphate in its stead."[26] Here, also, several groups fit into this category, including Ansar al Islam, a "radical Islamist group of Iraqi Kurds and Arabs who have vowed to establish an independent Islamic state in Iraq." Established in December 2001, it has had a close affiliation with al Qaeda and was aligned with Abu Mus'ab al-Zarqawi when he led al Qaeda in Iraq.[27] Also in this category is a second Iraqi group, Ansar al Sunnah Army, as well as the Army of the Levant, Jamatul Mujahedin Bangladesh (JMB), and Hizb ut-Tahrir al-Islami, a radical Islamic political movement that seeks to implement pure Salafi Jihad doctrine and create an Islamic caliphate in central Asia.[28]

Finally, a group may be considered an al Qaeda affiliate and part of AQAM if it "has engaged in the practice of *takfir*." In other words, it has labeled a Muslim regime or its leaders as apostates because they demonstrate disbelief. Several groups fit into this category. They label the local regimes they are fighting as apostate for having rejected Islamic sharia law as the key tenet by which they govern. This has been true, for example, of the Algerian GSPC and the Armed Islamic Group (GIA) from which it split in 1998 over a disagreement on whether civilians constitute legitimate targets. The same was said of Nasser's regime in Egypt.

In sum, this chapter has sought to identify how al Qaeda and the Salafi Jihadists have attempted to reorganize to continue to execute a global fight through *two strategic adaptations*. The first is how al Qaeda and its affiliates have employed the Internet to establish in cyberspace a virtual sanctuary from which to carry out many of the activities they had initiated from their Afghan base in 1996–2001. The second is how al Qaeda has continued to encourage and promote the global Salafi Jihad movement. More attention needs to be focused on these adaptations in order to gain a deeper understanding of what has transpired in order to develop a detailed mosaic of al Qaeda and associated movements.

Finally, it is important to note that in addition to these two strategic adaptations, al Qaeda has undertaken two additional ones in the years since it lost its sanctuary in Taliban-ruled Afghanistan. The first entails the creation of an increasingly robust sanctuary in the Federally Administered Tribal Areas (FATA) along the rugged border of Pakistan and Afghanistan. Over the last five years the leaderships of al Qaeda, the Afghan Taliban, the Pakistan Taliban, and several other like-minded Jihadist groups have established bases in this ungoverned territory that is beyond the authority of the Pakistani government. And each of these armed groups has made use of this safe haven to establish secure bases for protecting itself, training, planning, and launching operations against local, regional, and global targets. The final strategic adaptation undertaken by al Qaeda and associated movements has been to exploit the opportunity provided to them by the U.S. intervention in Iraq. To this end, they are exploiting the conflict in Iraq as a major recruiting and training ground to help prepare a third generation of Salafi *Jihadis*. Iraq not only serves as a new front to engage the United States directly, but it also affords an opportunity to develop a new cadre of skilled fighters who can gain the kind of experience that after Iraq will allow them to more effectively fight in their native lands or elsewhere.

NOTES

1. Steve Coll and Susan Glasser, "Terrorists Turn to the Web as Base of Operations," *Washington Post*, 7 August 2005, A1.

2. Gabriel Weimann, *How Modern Terrorism Uses the Internet*, Special Report 116 (United States Institute of Peace, March 2004), 2.

3. Through continuous and intensive examination of extremist Web sites, the SITE Institute has developed an extensive database of materials on how various Jihad groups make use of the Internet. This database was employed as the primary source for this part of the study. The SITE Institute can be accessed at www.siteinstitute.org.

4. Al Qaeda in Iraq, Victorious Army Group, Ansar al-Tawhid Brigades, Islamic Jihad Brigades, the Strangers Brigades, and the Horrors Brigades.

5. The Combating Terrorism Center, *The Islamic Imagery Project: Visual Motifs in Jihadi Internet Propaganda* (United States Military Academy, March 2006), 100.

6. There appear to be at least two ways to find out which third party sites are being used to distribute information and communications. One is through *Jihadi* Internet forums that provide links to index pages. These pages contain a list of sources from which the information can be deduced and downloaded.

7. Coll and Glasser, "Terrorists Turn to the Web as Base of Operations."

8. Ibid.

9. "Dark Days, Difficult Times," *The Economist*, 18 November 2006, 55.

10. Craig Whitlock, "Architect of the New War on the West," *Washington Post*, 23 May 2006, 1.

11. Reuven Paz, "Reading Their Lips: The Credibility of Jihadi Websites in Arabic as a Source for Information," Project for the Research of Islamist Movements, www.e-prism.org.

12. Weimann, *How Modern Terrorism Uses the Internet*, 7.

13. In the 1950s, Salafi Jihad ideology began to take shape. Its key theorist was Sayyid Qutb. He believed nearly all of Islam was in *jahiliyya*, having been polluted by Western decadence, materialism, and faithlessness. Islamic law and religious values were being subverted by apostate Muslim regimes. He called for Jihad to overthrow them. Qutb coupled a puritanical interpretation of Islam with a violent political ideology of revolt. Qutb saw the crisis in Muslim states within the context of a global ideological battle with the non-Muslim world, in particular, Western civilization. The West was pushing the Muslim world into *jahiliyya*. He painted an extremely dehumanizing picture of the West as soulless, immoral, and depraved. Qutb proposed a transnational ideology to mobilize the *ummah* for Jihad against near enemies (apostate Muslim regimes) and for a global fight against the West. To lead the struggle he called for the creation of a Muslim vanguard. The first requirement to initiate a global Salafi Jihadist insurgency is conceptualizing a universal ideology that (1) describes the depraved condition requiring Jihad, (2) proposes an idealized system to replace it, and (3) identifies steps to be taken to bring it to fruition; Qutb provided this doctrinal foundation. See Gilles Kepel, *Muslim Extremism in Egypt* (Berkeley: University of California Press, 2003); Paul Berman, "The Philosopher of Islamic Terror," *New York Times Magazine*, 23 March 2003; Paul Berman, *Terror and Liberalism* (New York: W. W. Norton & Company, 2003); Barry Rubin, *Islamic Fundamentalism in Egyptian Politics* (New York: Palgrave, 2003).

14. Berman, "The Philosopher of Islamic Terror."

15. Bruce Hoffman, "What Went Wrong? New Looks at the Bin Laden Network and the Panel That Tried to Explain Its Most Vicious Attack," *Washington Post*, 27 August 2006, BW6.

16. General John Abizaid, "2006 Posture of United States Central Command," U.S. Central Command, 8, available at www.centcom.mil/sites/uscentcom1/Shared%20Documents/PostureStatement2006.htm.

17. Ibid., 9–10, 47.

18. Rita Katz and Josh Devon, "The Online Jihadist Threat," testimony before the House Armed Services Committee, Terrorism and Unconventional Threats and Capabilities Subcommittee, 110th Cong., 1st sess., 14 February 2007, 4, available at www.armedservices.house.gov/pdfs/TUTC021407/Katz_Testimony021407.pdf.

19. Ibid., 5.

20. Ibid.

21. Ibid., 7.

22. Assaf Moghadam, "The Globalization of Martyrdom: Al Qaeda, Salafi-Jihadism, and the Diffusion of Suicide Attacks" (PhD diss., Fletcher School of Law, Tufts University). See chapter 4 and appendix A.

23. Ibid., 101.

24. Craig Smith, "North Africa Feared as Staging Ground for Terror," *New York Times*, 20 February 2007, 1.

25. Moghadam, "The Globalization of Martyrdom," 102 and app. A.

26. Ibid., 102.

27. Ibid., 368.

28. Ibid., 370.

32 Armed Groups: Changing the Rules

T. X. Hammes

The increasing presence of transnational and nonstate actors in today's conflicts is not a surprise but rather the logical result of changes in the political, economic, social, and technical landscapes.[1] Thus the type of conflict we are experiencing today, with its ubiquitous presence of a bewildering variety of armed groups, is not an aberration. Rather it is part of the coevolution of war and society that has been a consistent element in the history of man. And, as always, war continues to evolve.

The formation of armed groups has been encouraged by two factors. First, the steadily increasing pressure on the nation-state has significantly reduced its ability to provide security for its population. Second, changes in civilian technology and the widespread availability of military weapons have greatly increased the power of such groups.

While nation-states are still the most influential players in the international arena and will remain so for the foreseeable future, they increasingly share power with a wide variety of players. From international trade agreements to subnational armed groups to transnational business and criminal cartels, states are under pressure from both above and below.

Externally, international and even transnational organizations have forced states to yield power in the political and economic fields. In areas as diverse as tariffs, interest rates, and even the use of land mines, states have yielded sovereignty to outside players. In fact today, many elements of society look beyond the state to international or transnational organizations to solve problems or set favorable conditions for their enterprises.

The changes in the political and economic fields are reinforced by those in the social field. Many people are shifting their allegiances from nations to causes. An Earth First activist in the Pacific Northwest will likely have more contact, such as e-mail, chat, and telephone, with a similar activist in Berlin than with the logger who lives next door. As little

T. X. Hammes was born in American Falls, Idaho, on 31 August 1953. He was commissioned from the U.S. Naval Academy in 1975. In his 30 years in the Marine Corps, he served at all levels in the operating forces, to include command of a rifle company, weapons company, intelligence company, infantry battalion, and the Chemical Biological Incident Response Force. He participated in stabilization operations in Somalia and Iraq as well as training insurgents in various places. Colonel Hammes attended the Basic School, U.S. Army Infantry Officers Advanced Course, Marine Corps Command and Staff College, and the Canadian National Defence College. He also spent one year on a research fellowship with the Mershon Center for Strategic Studies. His final tour in the Marine Corps was as senior military fellow at the Institute for National Strategic Studies, National Defense University. He is the author of *The Sling and the Stone: On War in the Twenty-first Century* (Zenith Press, 2006) and numerous articles and opinion pieces. He is currently reading for a DPhil in modern history at Oxford University.

as 60 years ago, only the very wealthy had the time or resources to establish regular communications with people from other nations. Now, almost everyone in the West can do so. These international connections impact how nation-states operate.

Of particular concern, the same changes that have made legitimate international entities more effective—information technology, vastly improved transportation infrastructure, the increasingly global character of business and finance—all support and encourage the evolution of transnational groups as diverse as Al Qaeda, Earth Liberation Front, drug cartels, and international religious movements. These technologies, and the institutions and the groups they reinforce, challenge the state externally.

In addition to these civilian technology and development trends, armed groups are heavily reinforced by the proliferation of first-class military firearms. Automatic rifles, machine guns, rocket-propelled grenades (RPGs), antitank missiles, an unlimited variety of improvised explosive devices, and even guided missiles provide armed groups with firepower that used to be reserved for the militaries of nation-states. With these weapons, armed groups vastly overmatch police departments and often even military units.

Internally, the state is being stressed by its inability to provide effective security for parts of its population. In contrast to the ever-increasing international and transnational aspects of economic and social activity, security is becoming much more local. As many nation-states fail to fulfill their basic social contracts, people turn to local solutions—often militias. In essence, the people are forced to turn to an earlier form of social organization—family, clan, tribe, region, and their associated militias—for protection. While particularly true in those states that were arbitrarily formed and encompass widely varying and even hostile groups, this is not just a third-world phenomenon. We have militias in the United States; we simply call them gated communities. In these communities, the home owners have decided that government can no longer provide sufficient security and therefore have hired private militias to do the job.

Many subnational groups form militias for exactly the same reasons our suburban gated communities do: they feel their governments are not responsive to their needs.

A second reason for the formation of armed subnational groups is the increasing awareness that across the globe other such groups have achieved recognition, rights, privileges, and even self-rule. Given the legacy of colonial boundaries, many nations are dominated by majorities that have historically abused their minority populations. With the advent of inexpensive, global communications, local minorities can not only see that other similar groups have fought for better treatment but can even communicate with those groups to learn how to conduct such a campaign.

Obviously, the next question must be "Is there anything new here that threatens the United States?" If there is no threat, then we can continue to pursue the high-technology, conventional force that has given us great victories in the past. However, if these armed groups prove a genuine threat to U.S. interests, we have to study them more closely and develop the complex, interagency processes necessary to deal with them.

The current conflicts in Iraq and Afghanistan answer that question. The new methods of war allow even fractious, uncooperative armed groups to pose serious strategic challenges for the United States. Yet such a snapshot of current events does not tell us if this new form of war is simply an aberration or is here to stay. In short, do we have to learn to deal with this type of war or will we find that dearly sought "near-peer competitor" and get back to doing what we do best?

Unfortunately, Iraq and Afghanistan are not aberrations. Rather they are the product of a continuing evolution in warfare that has been visible for over 60 years. The advent of nuclear weapons ensured that modern conventional wars have been limited in scope and result. As nuclear arsenals grew, the cost of war between major powers outweighed any rational gain that could be achieved by all-out fighting. In turn, the major powers often limited what client states could do. Thus, conventional wars since 1945 have ended with a return to the status quo. The Korean War; the Arab-Israeli wars of 1956, 1967, and 1973; the Falklands War; and Desert Storm all ended with no significant changes to the strategic environments of the participants.

In contrast, unconventional wars such as China's revolution, the Indochina wars, Afghan-Soviet War, Chechen-Soviet War, and the First Intifada all resulted in significant political change within the nation where the conflict was fought. Even wars where the counterinsurgent won—Malaya, Philippines, Oman, El Salvador—resulted in significant political change as part of the resolution of the conflict.

Of even more significance for our discussion is the fact that while most insurgencies fail, insurgency remains the only type of war that has defeated a superpower. Further, it has done so five times in recent years. The Soviets were driven out of Afghanistan and Chechnya. The United States was driven out of Vietnam, Lebanon, and Somalia. And insurgency is clearly challenging the United States in Iraq and Afghanistan today. Thus while insurgencies don't have a high probability of victory, they are the only form of war that has a chance against a superpower.

As early as February 2002, Al Qaeda strategist Ubeid al-Qurashi wrote he was confident that Al Qaeda would beat the United States by using fourth-generation war. In an article he posted online, al-Qurashi wrote,

> Fourth-generation warfare, the experts said, is a new type of war in which fighting will be mostly scattered. The battle will not be limited to destroying military targets and regular forces, but will include societies, and will [seek to] destroy popular support for the fighters within the enemy's society. In these wars, the experts stated in their article, "television news may become a more powerful operational weapon than armored divisions." They also noted that [in fourth-generation wars] "the distinction between war and peace will be blurred to the vanishing point. . . ."

> Other Western strategists disagreed with these analyses, claiming that the new warfare would be strategically based on psychological influence and on the minds of the enemy's planners—not only on military means as in the past, but also on the use of all the media and information networks . . . in order to influence public opinion and, through it, the ruling elite. They claimed that the fourth-generation wars would, tactically, be small-scale, emerging in various regions across the planet against an enemy that, like a ghost, appears and disappears. The focus would be political, social, economic, and military. [It will be] international, national, tribal, and even organizations would participate (even though tactics and technology from previous generations would be used).

> This new type of war presents significant difficulties for the Western war machine, and it can be expected that [Western] armies will change fundamentally. This forecast did not

arise in a vacuum—if only the cowards [among the Muslim clerics] knew that fourth-generation wars have already occurred and that the superiority of the theoretically weaker party has already been proven; in many instances, nation-states have been defeated by stateless nations.[2]

Since al-Qurashi wrote in 2002, other insurgent groups have consistently echoed his theme that fourth-generation war will allow armed groups to defeat even superpowers. For instance, on 10 July 2006, the Global Jihadist Media Front released an article that reviewed the success insurgent groups have had against regular armies.

About the number [of soldiers] deployed: the Red Army had more than 100,000 soldiers in Afghanistan by the end of 1979 and there was no significant resistance in the beginning. Even when the number of the Mujahideen reached its peak after 1985, [numerical] superiority was still in favor of the Soviet Army and its agents at a ratio of 5:2. In Somalia, it was easier, because the Americans invaded the area with 40,000 soldiers and left the area without difficulty after a small resistance by a number of fighters, which did not exceed 2000. This means that the balance of forces was in favor of America and its Allies with a ratio of 20:1. In the first Chechen War (1994–1996), the Chechen victory came after Russia invaded Chechen lands with 100,000 soldiers. The Chechen resistance did not exceed, in best cases, 13,000 fighters. This means that the balance of forces was in Russia's favor at a ratio of 7.7:1. The Russian Army invaded Grozny, with an army of 50,000. The Mujahideen had fighting groups which did not exceed 3,000 Mujahideen, but succeeded in 1995 in not only breaking the encirclement [of Grozny] but also a counterattack on the flank of the encircling [Russian] army. This compelled the Russians to retreat with heavy losses.[3]

Another factor making insurgencies increasingly difficult for Western powers to defeat is the fact that they have evolved from the monolithic, hierarchical communist insurgencies of Mao and Ho Chi Minh to the loose "coalitions of the willing" we see in Afghanistan, Iraq, and Palestine. Like society as a whole, insurgencies have become networked, transnational, and even transdimensional. Today's insurgents are perfectly comfortable inhabiting both the real and cyber worlds. Elements of their organizations are in one, the other, and even both environments.

Among the first organizations to become truly transdimensional was Al Qaeda. When driven out of its training camps in Afghanistan, it sought the ability to recruit, proselytize, train, reeducate, and even make logistics arrangements on the Web. The last five years have seen an explosion of Web sites supporting armed groups. They make it possible to seek like-minded individuals literally anywhere in the world. Using chat rooms, recruiters can make contact with potential recruits. After initial screening, they will be invited to password-protected rooms where the chat is more inflammatory. This allows the recruiters to provide slanted views of their causes. When they feel a person has been sufficiently educated for the next step, they will put the individual in touch with a local radical group. That group will make person-to-person contact and continue the recruiting, motivating, and training process. If possible, the group can move the recruit to real-world training camps in Iraq or Pakistan. If not, it can train and educate him or her in fully functioning cyber training facilities—complete with mentors, manuals, and sermons. And by the way, Islamic fundamentalists are not the only groups using the Web, so there is competition to attract the disaffected and malleable.

The societal changes that favor agile, transnational businesses also favor the transdimensional armed group. Compounding the problems nation-states face dealing with these armed groups is the fact that one thing has remained constant with insurgencies. They are long fights that have ranged from one to four decades in modern times. Nation-states often lack the patience to endure these very long fights.

It is clear armed groups are a challenge. Worse, there is a truly alarming variety of armed groups active in the world today, which dramatically increases the difficulty of understanding their motivations, methods, and goals. To continue the discussion we need some method of categorizing them. For the purposes of this chapter, I will draw on the categories of motivation used by the United Nations in its *Manual for Humanitarian Negotiations with Armed Groups*. The motivation of a group is a strong indicator of how that group will fight and what, if any, limits it will impose on its use of force.

> In terms of founding motivations, armed groups generally fall into three categories: they can be *reactionary* (reacting to some situation, or something that members of the groups experienced or with which they identify); they can be *opportunistic*, meaning that they seized on a political or economic opportunity to enhance their own power or positions; or they are founded to further *ideological* objectives.[4]

These three categories are useful because they allow insights into how the groups organize, grow, and operate.

Reactionary groups often form in response to threats to their communities. They focus on the traditional military task of protecting the population. As a result, they tend to be subnational or national groups that operate in specific geographic areas and attempt to protect the people of those areas. In essence, these armed groups represent a return to earlier security arrangements, because a state has failed in its basic social contract of providing security for its population. These are the ethnic-sectarian militias we have seen develop around the world in response to insecurity. Groups like the Tamil Tigers and the Supreme Council for the Islamic Revolution in Iraq's (SCIRI's) Badr Militia are typical of reactionary groups.

These groups need to protect populations but lack the military power to do so. As a result, they usually resort to irregular warfare—but use conventional arms. While highly effective, these weapons are also those most familiar to Western security services and thus easier to anticipate and defeat. This does not mean they do not challenge Western armed forces. The worldwide use of suicide bombers, improvised explosive devices (IEDs), and vehicle borne IEDs have allowed these groups to inflict heavy casualties on national armed forces they confront. However, the reactionary groups tend not to be a threat externally since they are focused on defending their own peoples. They tend to restrict their efforts to the immediate vicinity, but this may include cross-border operations since their peoples' traditional lands are often split by international borders.

Opportunistic groups are those that evolve to take advantage of a vacuum to seize power or wealth. Essentially, these are criminal groups and have been around for centuries. What is different now is the fact that commercially available weapons and other technology allow these groups to overmatch all but the most-well-armed police. They are increasingly even a match for the armed forces of a nation. These groups include organizations like Mara Salvatrucha 13 (MS-13).[5] One interesting aspect of MS-13 is the fact that it controls noncontiguous terrain in several nations—a village in Latin America, a neighborhood in Los Angeles, and perhaps just a building in an East Coast suburb. Yet these gangs make use of the communications and transportation networks to loosely coordinate their activities.

A third great motivator, ideology, often gives birth to armed groups. These are groups like Al Qaeda, Aryan Brotherhood, Aum Shinrikyo, Earth Liberation Front, and Animal Liberation Front. While the last three do not claim to be "armed," they do use violence in an attempt to achieve their goals. Ideological groups are more dangerous to the United States than simple military armed groups because of their selections of weapons and their "no limits" approach to conflict. In the past, these groups have used society's assets against it. From Timothy McVeigh's use of fertilizer and diesel fuel to Al Qaeda's use of airliners, these groups tend to be highly creative in their attacks. They are more likely to use society's infrastructure of chemical plants, mass shipments of fertilizer, hazardous chemicals, and even bio technology as weapons of mass destruction than groups motivated by self-defense or opportunism.

Of even more concern is the fact that ideological groups are essentially impossible to deter. Not only are they working for a higher being/purpose that provides moral justification, and sometimes a moral requirement to use any available weapon; they have no return address. Thus they do not have to fear massive retaliation. If Al Qaeda detonates a nuclear device on U.S. soil, where exactly do we fire our nukes in return?

These groups will not even be self-deterred by the inherent danger in the use of biological weapons. While other groups may hesitate to release a contagious biological agent for fear of killing their own people or members, ideological groups often believe that the higher power guiding their actions will either protect their members or call them home for their earned reward. Thus the combination of extraordinarily rapid advances in biotechnology and the spread of ideologically driven armed groups presents a major threat to the global population.

Mixed groups are a more recent development. These are groups that have a mix of reactionary, ideological, and opportunistic motivations. Sometimes they are reactionary or ideological groups that turn to crime to provide the resources they need to operate. Al Qaeda is both an ideological and an opportunistic group as it has increasingly turned to crime to fund its operations. The IRA has increasingly turned to crime—and may actually have moved from reactionary to purely opportunistic motivation.

Others are ideological groups that find themselves as the de facto rulers of areas and therefore must also provide their communities the protection common to reactionary groups. These militias include organizations like the Jaysh Al Mahdi militia in Iraq, Hizbollah in Lebanon, and the Movement for the Emancipation of the Nigerian Delta in Nigeria.

Some can even fall into all three categories. For instance, Hamas and Al Mahdi provide protection, espouse an ideology, and participate in crime for funding. In fact, most armed groups now use crime to fund operations.

Because these groups are loose coalitions, they frequently splinter. Sometimes the fracture is over strategic goals, sometimes over simple personality fights, other times over how to divide the spoils—either territory or wealth. This tendency to fragment further increases the difficulty facing intelligence officers trying to track and understand the groups. Yet as we have seen in Iraq's Anbar province, the shifts in loyalty or hatred on a local level can have a major impact on the status of the insurgency. In August of 2006, Colonel Peter Devlin, G-2, I Marine Expeditionary Force, released a very pessimistic analysis of the situation in Anbar. Yet, even as he completed his report, the Sunni tribes in Anbar were deciding to turn against Al Qaeda in Iraq and drive it out of the province. Within six months, there had been exceptional improvements across the province. As Colonel Devlin pointed out, these changes were beyond the power of the U.S. military and could only be achieved by changes in the political situation in the province. In Anbar, as in most tribal societies, such shifts take place not among individuals, but entire families, clans, or tribes shift sides.

A major problem with armed groups is that they are self-reinforcing. They develop because a government cannot control its territory. Their growth then contributes to the instability in the region and results in the government ceding more territory. In some cases, a single group takes over that territory. In others, many groups fight over the same territory. We saw this after the withdrawal of the Soviets from Afghanistan and the Israelis from Gaza. It is happening in Iraq as coalition forces are unable to control parts of the country. The basic failure of the state to provide security combined with the easy availability of arms creates a downward spiral that results in ever-increasing instability.

When multiple groups fight over the territory, it is inevitably a disaster for the people of the region—and for their neighbors, who have to deal with the spillover of refugees and the violence that follows in their wake. However, a single group seizing a territory may actually be a greater threat to the West. As we saw with Al Qaeda in Afghanistan, such a group can focus its resources on attacking the West rather than on defending itself against local opponents.

Obviously, these motivations have been with us a long time. Why are armed groups only now becoming so prominent? As stated at the beginning of this chapter, the political, economic, social, and technical trends of the early twenty-first century not only encourage the growth of armed groups but vastly increase their power and impact in the international arena. This increase in power and impact obviously makes armed groups an attractive alternative to the failing nation-state. Success breeds imitators.

This fact has been recognized in many capitals. Nation-states are beginning to devise ways to come to grips with these armed groups. Unfortunately, to date this has been a slow and painful process, as evidenced by Israel in Lebanon and the United States in Iraq. Nation-states are forced to operate within their complex international organizations burdened by extensive bureaucracies. In contrast, the armed groups are free to make full use of the power of networks provided by modern society. As a result, we can expect to be reacting rather than anticipating for the foreseeable future.

Before closing, there is one final type of armed group I'd like to discuss—private military companies (PMCs). Admittedly, these groups fall under the category of opportunistic but I think they deserve special consideration due to their great potential for changing the way we conduct international relations.

In the last 15 years, PMCs have dramatically increased their presence on the international stage. While they formerly existed on the fringes of international relations, the U.S. heavy use of armed contractors in Iraq has moved them to center stage. The length of this chapter prevents a full exploration of the numerous implications of the increased use of PMCs but instead I will simply offer some thoughts to start a discussion.

For instance, how does one hold a company accountable for its actions? How will these companies change the face of armed conflict? What impact will these companies have on the relationship between resource-rich rulers and their populations? How will they be employed by nations to provide basing and forward deployment of major power assets?

PMC spokesmen have reassured us that responsible companies are working with governments to devise effective regulations to control their operations. This is in fact true. However, while the United States has moved to increase the accountability of such companies through regulations and contracts, these methods have yet to be seriously tested. Further, much as the shipping industry avoided regulation by registering under flags of convenience, we can expect PMCs to do the same. If regulations interfere with how they wish to operate, they will move their corporations to other countries or even dissolve and start again as different legal entities in different countries.[6]

The sudden presence of these companies in numerous conflicts presents some interesting challenges for the international community. In the more-than-350 years since the Treaty of Westphalia, we have developed diplomatic, economic, and military techniques for dealing with crises created when nation-states use armed forces—or even threaten to use them. We do not have such mechanisms in place when nation-states or even private individuals employ armed contractors. If China had announced it planned to send significant numbers of soldiers to Sudan to assist with security and construction, there would at least have been dialogue in the United Nations. Yet open-source reports have placed the number of Chinese security forces working for Chinese companies at over 20,000 men—or two divisions worth. More recently, open-source reporting indicates the Chinese will send significantly larger numbers of both construction and security personnel to Angola. Chinese companies will in effect have multiple divisions forward deployed in Africa. It is admittedly nearly impossible to confirm these contracts, yet these events simply did not show up in international discussion. This is particularly interesting given the fact China has just signed a 10-year contract with Angola to provide oil at $60 a barrel. While the contractors are not an official branch of the Chinese government, their presence clearly puts China in position to "resolve" any disputes with the Angolan government over that contract. Thus, by the creative use of private companies, negotiations between nation-states have moved outside the international system. The rulers of these countries find the Chinese particularly appealing because they do not pressure their hosts about human rights or governmental reform.

Of course, "governments" of resource-rich areas can employ PMCs to seize and hold the rich areas of a country while simply ignoring the rest. We have already seen this with local militias and the "blood diamonds" but have not seen it applied in a systematic way. We may be seeing the first signs of this in Africa. Sudan has hired Chinese firms to provide security for its oil facilities. These firms not only provide reliable security, weapons, and training for Sudanese; they have no comments on how Sudan chooses to conduct its internal affairs. Similarly, Chad may have entered talks with private companies to circumvent the requirement that a percentage of the oil revenues be held in trust for the general population.

Using private military companies, a very small minority can control a country. While small minorities have often seized control of governments, it requires effective security forces to keep such governments in power. In many parts of the world, such forces simply are not reliable so a prudent government must pay some attention to the majority. If they hire an effective PMC, rulers will no longer need to negotiate with the majority to maintain power. Instead, they can rely on contracted security. Worst case, they will focus the PMC on protecting the wealth-generating parts of the country. They have no reason to bother with the poorer regions and may simply abandon those areas to poverty and lawlessness. The net result is more under- or ungoverned spaces in unstable parts of the world.

Another intriguing use for PMCs is to establish forward operating bases and forward-deployed forces. In the same way the British used the East India Company to establish bases and regiments in India, China can use commercial entities throughout the world. Chinese PMCs already have a major ground presence in Africa, Chinese commercial entities are building ports along the shipping lanes from the Middle East to China, and China has the potential to offer naval PMCs to provide security against pirates along major shipping routes. As an example, in March of 2006, Somalia negotiated with a Chinese naval firm to train and equip a Somali coast guard.[7] Such naval PMCs will obviously need maintenance and support facilities, which the companies will build. In effect, the PMCs can establish a chain of naval facilities near the choke points of the sea routes.

To date, Western media and legislatures have focused on the operations of Western private military companies. Yet the true potential for providing very large, well-trained, and well-armed private militaries lies with China. India and other high-population, low-employment countries can be expected to follow in China's footprints. Clearly this is a subject that needs further study.

SUMMARY

For purposes of brevity, this chapter barely touches the surface of the very complex subject of armed groups. The key point is the fact that political, economic, social, and technical trends are increasing the number, variety, and power of these armed groups. We must acknowledge they are already major players in ongoing conflicts, have defeated great powers, and require an integrated political, military, and economic response if we are to minimize their impact on our security.

NOTES

The initial research for this paper was conducted for the Program on Humanitarian Policy and Conflict Research in cooperation with the Radcliffe Institute for Advanced Study, Harvard University.

1. Clausewitz stated as much in his *On War* when he wrote, "Military institutions and the manner in which they employ violence depended on the economic, social and political conditions of their respective states." Carl von Clausewitz, *On War,* trans. Michael Eliot Howard and Peter Paret (Princeton University Press, 1989), 6.

2. "Bin Laden Lieutenant Admits to September 11 and Explains Al-Qa'ida's Combat Doctrine: Special Dispatch Series No. 344, February 10, 2002," Middle East Media Research Institute.

3. Preaching Information Department, Global Islamic Media Front, "Fourth Generation Warfare," SITE Intelligence Group, www.siteintelgroup.org.

4. *Humanitarian Negotiations with Armed Groups: A Manual for Practitioners* (New York: UN Office for the Coordination of Human Affairs, 2006), 17, available at www.reliefweb.int/rw/lib.nsf/db900SID/RURI-6LKSA9/$FILE/un-ocha-30jan.pdf?OpenElement.

5. Mara Salvatrucha (MS or MS-13) is a violent criminal group founded by El Salvadoran immigrants in Los Angeles in 1980. Memorial Institute for the Prevention of Terrorism, "Group Profile: Salvatruchas," MIPT Knowledge Base, www.tkb.org/Group.jsp?groupID=4486.

6. For a discussion of PMC political fallout, see Peter W. Singer, *Can't Win with 'Em, Can't Go to War without 'Em: Private Military Contractors and Counterinsurgency,* Policy Paper 4 (Brookings Institution, September 2007), available at www.brookings.edu/papers/2007/0927militarycontractors.aspx.

7. Chris Tomlinson, "US Hires Military Contractor to Back Peacekeeping Mission in Somalia," Associated Press, 7 March 2007.

Appendix

United Nations Guidelines on Humanitarian Negotiations with Armed Groups

Guidelines on Humanitarian Negotiations with Armed Groups

Gerard Mc Hugh • Manuel Bessler

United Nations
January 2006

Produced by the United Nations Office for the Coordination of Humanitarian Affairs (OCHA) in collaboration with members of the Inter-Agency Standing Committee (IASC).

Gerard Mc Hugh and Manuel Bessler

For more information, contact:

Manuel Bessler
Policy Development and Studies Branch (PDSB)
Office for the Coordination of Humanitarian Affairs (OCHA)
United Nations
New York, NY 10017, USA
Phone: +1 (212) 963-1249
Fax: +1 (917) 367-5274
Email: *bessler@un.org*

Contents

1 Objectives and Application of these Guidelines

This set of guidelines is intended to provide concise advice and guidance to humanitarian practitioners on how to prepare for and conduct humanitarian negotiations with **non-State armed groups**.

Partner to manual: Humanitarian Negotiations with Armed Groups

This booklet summarizes the essential guidance presented in the more comprehensive partner publication titled, *Humanitarian Negotiations with Armed Groups: A Manual for Practitioners.*

The six sections of this set of guidelines follow closely the sequence and content of the chapters in the partner manual. In addition to the guidance presented here, the manual provides comprehensive information on the important framing and contextual elements for undertaking humanitarian negotiations with armed groups. The manual also contains short case studies and examples of practical experiences of humanitarian negotiations with armed groups.

Throughout this set of Guidelines references are provided to the corresponding sections of the partner manual that provide more detailed information on a particular topic.[1]

Non-State armed groups: working definition (Negotiations manual Section 1.1)

> ### Working Definition of Non-State Armed Groups
> *Groups that: have the potential to employ arms in the use of force to achieve political, ideological or economic objectives; are not within the formal military structures of States, State-alliances or intergovernmental organizations; and are not under the control of the State(s) in which they operate.*

Objectives (Negotiations manual Section 1.3)

The primary objectives of humanitarian negotiations are to: (i) ensure the provision of humanitarian assistance and protection to vulnerable populations; (ii) preserve humanitarian space; and (iii) promote better respect for international law.

Negotiation does not confer legitimacy

Because of their exclusively humanitarian character, humanitarian negotiations do not in any way confer legitimacy or recognition upon armed groups.

Security considerations (Negotiations manual Section 1.5)

The guidance presented here and in the partner manual does not supplant or circumvent existing security policies and guidelines. Operational aspects of humanitarian negotiations with armed groups must be conducted in accordance with the relevant security procedures.

---

[1] References to the corresponding sections of the partner publication, *Humanitarian Negotiations with Armed Groups: A Manual for Practitioners,* are provided to the left of the text in this booklet.

2   Humanitarian Negotiations: Motivations and Partners

Motivations for Entering into Humanitarian Negotiations

To facilitate and enhance humanitarian action (Negotiations manual Section 2.2)

- The overall objective of humanitarian negotiations is to secure the cooperation of an armed group in reaching an agreed outcome or understanding that will facilitate or enhance humanitarian action.

- Process-related motivations for humanitarian negotiations with armed groups may include: (i) building trust and confidence between the parties, and (ii) the process of negotiation can have a multiplier effect in terms of involving armed groups in a wider dialogue that may bring additional benefits.

Substantive Areas for Negotiation

Humanitarian access

- To secure **humanitarian access** to reach populations in need;

Ground Rules

- To seek **agreement with an armed group on a basic operational framework**—consisting of humanitarian principles, operating guidelines and commitments of both parties—to ensure the safe and efficient provision of humanitarian assistance and protection (often referred to as **"Ground Rules"** agreements). For example, the Ground Rules agreement concluded between the Sudan People's Liberation Movement/Army (SPLM) and Operation Lifeline Sudan (OLS).

Protection of civilians

- To seek agreement on behaviour of belligerents that will improve the **protection of civilians** in areas under the control or influence of armed groups;

Humanitarian security

- To safeguard humanitarian security;

Special protection areas/periods

- To secure agreement on special protection areas or periods; For example, agreement to facilitate immunization campaigns or food distribution at specific times;

(Negotiations manual Section 2.2.1)

- To secure the release of persons being held by armed groups against their will.

2

Knowing When to Adopt a More Cautious Approach to Negotiations

Impact on humanitarian conditions

- When there is the likelihood that negotiations themselves could negatively impact humanitarian conditions, constrain the delivery of humanitarian assistance and protection or jeopardize the security of the beneficiaries.

Possible manipulation of humanitarian negotiations

- When armed groups attempt to use humanitarian negotiations to enhance their perceived legitimacy and/or to promote their political agendas/objectives.

- When armed groups are believed to be playing several humanitarian actors off against each other for their own gain.

- When the negotiations put the lives of the armed group interlocutors at risk.

(Negotiations manual Section 2.2.2)

- When the armed group attaches conditions for the implementation of an agreement that could adversely affect the civilian population.

Characteristics of Armed Groups

Key features

- Table 1 (page 4) presents some of the key features of non-State armed groups, and what these features mean for humanitarian negotiations with these groups.

(Negotiations manual Section 2.3)

- Consideration of the following characteristics of armed groups can increase the efficiency of the negotiations as well as the desired outcomes: (a) motivations; (b) structure; (c) principles of action; (d) interests; (e) constituency; (f) needs; (g) ethno-cultural dimensions; (h) control of population and territory (See **Annex I**).

Humanitarian Partners in Negotiations

Identify one or more lead negotiators (Negotiations manual Section 2.5)

- The humanitarian actors in a specific context/region should identify one or more lead negotiators, who should act as the primary representative(s) of humanitarian agencies (country team, humanitarian community in a specific context/region).

- The humanitarian negotiations and their underlying humanitarian objectives should remain strictly distinct from political and/or other negotiations.

Keeping humanitarian and political negotiations separate

- Humanitarian agencies should agree on the process and intended outcomes of the negotiation.

3

Table 1
Key features of non-State armed groups

Key features of armed groups: They ...	What humanitarian negotiators need to be aware of based on these features:
have the potential to employ arms in the use of force for political, ideological, or economic objectives;	→ Humanitarian negotiations do not infer any legal status, legitimacy or recognition of the armed group; → Humanitarian negotiators should explore the driving motivations and interests behind the actions of the armed group (see below); → Humanitarian negotiations do not in any way dilute the accountability of the armed group for past/current/future actions;
have a group identity, and act in pursuit of their objectives as a group;	→ Individual members of an armed group will always have their own 'agendas', however an armed group (different from a group of armed individuals) shares some common history, aspirations, objectives, or needs that are attributes of the group; → Members of an armed group will be strongly influenced by group conformity pressures such as depersonalization of victims; perceptions of impunity; moral disengagement and obedience to group authority;
are not within the formal military structures of States, State alliances or intergovernmental organizations;	→ This characteristic of non-State armed groups has important implications for enforcing accountability for the actions of members of the group. The 'extra-State' status of armed groups means that the applicable legal provisions relating to the duties and obligations of these groups under International law may differ from the duties and obligations of States, and for certain provisions, there remains some legal uncertainty as to the extent that those provisions apply to armed groups;

Table 1 (continued)

Key features of armed groups: They ...	What humanitarian negotiators need to be aware of based on these features:
are not under the command or control of the State(s) in which they operate;	→ Armed groups may not be under the command or control of the State(s) in which they operate, but they may receive direct/indirect support of the host government or other States; → Humanitarian negotiators need to be aware of the potential for influencing parties that support armed groups;
are subject to a chain of command (formal or informal).	→ This is an important attribute of armed groups, because it means (at least in theory) that there is some degree of centralized command and control, however limited, over the actions of group members. When this centralized command structure breaks down, it can no longer be considered to be *one* armed group, and humanitarian negotiators may have to identify interlocutors within several factions of the original group; → When a chain of command (however limited) is functioning, it increases the likelihood that lower-ranking members of the group will respect the undertakings and agreed outcomes negotiated by and with their leaders; → In implementing an outcome agreed with the leaders of an armed group, humanitarian workers should attempt to identify the local chain of command to increase the likelihood that any agreed outcome will be respected and implemented by lower-ranking members of the group;

3   Framing the Negotiations

- Humanitarian principles, policies and international law provide a framework and source of guidance for humanitarian negotiations with armed groups.

Humanitarian Principles

Core humanitarian principles

- Three core humanitarian principles of Humanity, Neutrality and Impartiality; Additional principles: Dignity; Respect for Culture and Custom; Do No/Less Harm; Independence; Sustainability; Participation; Accountability; Transparency; and Prevention.

Using principles to guide negotiations

- These principles guide humanitarian negotiations by: (1) providing a source of direction for humanitarian negotiators on how negotiations should be undertaken; (2) defining boundaries within which to seek agreement; and (3) providing a set of criteria for developing options for consideration by the negotiating parties.

(Negotiations manual Section 3.2)

International Law Relevant To Humanitarian Negotiations

IHL, IHRL and International Criminal Law

- Three bodies of international law—International Humanitarian Law (IHL), International Human Rights Law (IHRL) and International Criminal Law (especially The Rome Statute of the International Criminal Court)—provide important framing elements for undertaking humanitarian negotiations.

Defining boundaries and framing obligations

- International law guides humanitarian negotiations by: (1) defining boundaries within which to seek agreement; (2) framing the legal obligations of armed groups; (3) identifying the substantive issues for negotiation; providing an entry point for discussion on these issues; (4) providing reference benchmarks for evaluation of options and monitoring implementation; and (5) providing incentives to armed groups to negotiate.

(Negotiations manual Section 3.3)

Humanitarian Policies

Operationalizing the humanitarian principles

- Humanitarian policies assist in translating and implementing humanitarian principles and legal provisions into an operational setting, generally focusing on a particular aspect of humanitarian action (e.g. guidelines on civil-military relations, IDPs).

- Humanitarian policies can guide humanitarian negotiations by broadening the range of options that parties to the negotiations can consider as a basis for agreement.

(Negotiations manual Section 3.4)

4 Working Towards More Effective Negotiations

Nine steps

This section presents nine steps for humanitarian negotiations with armed groups that provide a generic framework, which can be applied to humanitarian negotiations on a range of issues.

Three phase:
PREPARATION,
SEEKING AGREEMENT,
IMPLEMENTATION
(Negotiations manual
Section 4.2)

The nine steps are presented in three phases of negotiation: PREPARATION; SEEKING AGREEMENT and IMPLEMENTATION.

This step-by-step approach is summarized in Figure 1, page 8.

Phase I	**PREPARATION >>** **Coordinate Approach, Decide on Strategy, and Gather Information**

1: Coordinate Approach With Humanitarian Partners

2: Decide on Objectives and Strategy

3: Learn About, Analyze Your Negotiating Partner

Phase II	**SEEKING AGREEMENT >>** **Process, Issues, Options, Outcomes**

The next four steps in the process of negotiation are undertaken during the actual "face-to-face" interactions with the armed group.

4: Build Consensus on the Process of Negotiations

5: Identify the Issues

6: Develop Options

7: Work to Seek Agreement on the Option(s) that Best Meet Humanitarian Objectives

Phase III	**IMPLEMENTATION >>** **Define Criteria for Implementation, Follow-up**

8: Define Criteria for Implementation

9: Follow-up: Monitoring and Relationship Building

7

Figure 1—Summary of 3 phases, 9 steps in humanitarian negotiations

(Note that section references in this flowchart refer to sections of the *Manual on Humanitarian Negotiations with Armed Groups*)

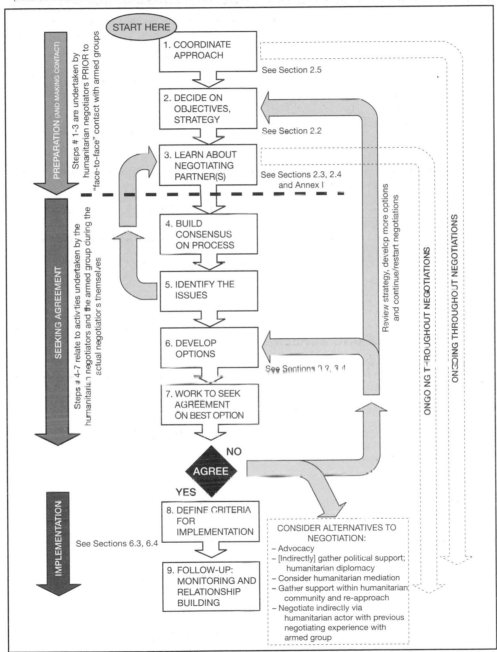

What to do if Negotiations Fail to Converge or Break Down

*(Negotiations manual
Section 4.5)*

- Review Strategy, Confirm Issues and Develop more Options
- Keep Open Alternatives on SUBSTANCE
- Try Building on the Existing Process
- Explore Alternatives to PROCESS
- Don't Burn Bridges
- Reinforce Lines of Communication

5   Negotiating on Specific Issues

Negotiating *Ground Rules* for Humanitarian Action

Purpose and scope of Ground Rules

- Humanitarian negotiators should be clear about the purpose and scope of any *Ground Rules* agreements to be agreed with an armed group.

- Any *Ground Rules* framework agreement should be based on principles of humanitarian action recognized by the participating humanitarian organizations.

Agreement does not accord legitimacy to armed group

- Agreement on the humanitarian principles, operating guidelines and commitments of both parties (humanitarian agencies and the armed group(s)) that collectively constitute a *Ground Rules* agreement does not infer or accord legitimacy to the armed group.

(Negotiations manual Section 5.3)

- Based on existing guidance, humanitarian negotiators can draft an outline of the *Ground Rules* agreement (i.e. a template of the ground rules document for discussion with the armed group) prior to negotiations.

Negotiating Humanitarian Access

Access as precondition for humanitarian action

- Humanitarian negotiators should present the issue of access as a precondition for any humanitarian action in order to meet the humanitarian needs of a population, rather than access to a particular territory.

Working principles of access

- Humanitarian organizations should approach the negotiations with a set of working principles of humanitarian access agreed upon among the humanitarians—for example, *sustainability* of humanitarian access— to guide the dialogue on the details of the access arrangements (i.e. how access will function in practice).

- Humanitarian negotiators should make it clear to the armed group and to parties external to the negotiations, that the access negotiations do not confer recognition by the humanitarian organization of the armed group, its political or economic agenda, or its control/influence over a population or territory.

Initial steps in negotiating access

- The early stages of the negotiations could usefully focus on securing access for the purposes of conducting a baseline humanitarian needs assessment mission, as an initial step towards negotiations on humanitarian access more broadly.

(Negotiations manual Section 5.4)

- Access negotiations should include consideration of: (i) logistics (how will access actually work: frequency of convoys, etc.); (ii) liaison arrangements (… between humanitarian organizations and the armed group(s)); (iii) the need to communicate agreed access procedures within organizations.

Protection of Civilians in Accordance with International Law

Awareness of need for protection

- Humanitarian negotiators should raise awareness among members of the armed group on the need of civilians to be protected in armed conflicts.

Protections not negotiable

- Protection of civilians in armed conflict per se is not negotiable. Humanitarian negotiators should attempt to demonstrate (using a persuasive approach to negotiation) to the armed group that it is also in their interest to ensure the protection of civilians.

Generate options for enhanced protection

- Humanitarian negotiators should generate options for consideration that can lead to enhanced protection of civilians. In the case of recruitment of child soldiers, options could include registration/demobilization of child soldiers, education and training schemes for demobilized child soldiers, and/or agreement, arrangements for care of orphaned children in areas controlled by the armed group;

(Negotiations manual Section 5.5)

- Even though the armed group is not a party to the international human rights treaties, human rights themselves can provide a basis for discussion with armed groups on the type and scope of protections that need to be afforded to civilians.

6   So You're Negotiating ... Now What?

Possible Negative Implications of Humanitarian Negotiations

Perceptions regarding neutrality

- Changes in perceived neutrality and impartiality of humanitarian actors engaged in negotiations

  TO MITIGATE: (A) clearly communicate the objectives and the scope of the negotiations with armed groups; (B) communicate and negotiate with all parties to a given conflict.

Humanitarian security

- Impacts on humanitarian security

  TO MITIGATE: (A) meet with the armed group in a neutral location/venue; (B) request security guarantees from the armed group prior to negotiations; (C) ensure that the necessary parties (e.g. host government) are informed of the humanitarian negotiations.

Third-party influence

- Third-party influence and 'sanctions' on humanitarian negotiators

  TO MITIGATE: (A) engage in parallel advocacy efforts and bilateral humanitarian diplomacy to gain support for the humanitarian negotiations; (B) ensure that the objectives and process of humanitarian negotiations with the armed group are effectively communicated to those that may seek to exert pressure to constrain the negotiations; (C) build consensus, support for negotiations across humanitarian organizations.

(Negotiations manual Section 6.2)

Commitment to the Agreement, Enforcement and Dispute Resolution

Commitment (Negotiations manual Section 6.3)

- Secure/enhance commitment by: (1) ensuring 'buy in' and ownership, (2) clear statement of roles and responsibilities for implementation; (3) emphasizing accountability; and (4) including all parties in monitoring of implementation.

Enforcement (Negotiations manual Section 6.4)

- Enforcement: By incentives or coercion ("carrot and stick"); other actors may be better placed to apply diplomatic/other pressure to armed group.

- Humanitarian organizations can continue negotiating on issues of enforcement, attempt to persuade armed group, focusing on accountability of armed group.

*Dispute resolution
(Negotiations manual
Section 6.4.2)*

- Three possible dispute resolution mechanisms for consideration: (1) Establishment of an implementation monitoring commission; (2) Referral of disputed provisions to an independent non-binding arbitration mechanism; (3) Appointment of a neutral mediator to assist the parties in resolving disputes.

Dealing with Non-Compliance

- Enter into further negotiations with the armed group to arrive at an agreed outcome which may resolve the issues of non-compliance with the original agreement.

*Engage external
actors*

- Identify third party States, regional organizations or other actors (civil society, churches, notabilities) and engage, directly or indirectly, in advocacy and humanitarian diplomacy to get these actors to apply pressure (diplomatic, other) to the armed group to comply with the agreement.

*Suspension of
activities as last
resort*

*(Negotiations manual
Section 6.4.3)*

- If non-compliance with the agreed results in an operating environment which compromises humanitarian security; consider, as a last resort, suspension of humanitarian activities until a conducive humanitarian operating environment is re-established.

Annex I - Worksheet for Mapping Characteristics of Armed Groups

This worksheet is intended to capture, in a concise manner, the main characteristics of an armed group. Humanitarian negotiators can use this worksheet: (i) to take notes on the characteristics of a particular armed group during the PREPARATION phase, (ii) as a summary reminder of the main characteristics of an armed group during the SEEKING AGREEMENT phase; and (iii) as a means of capturing new information about the armed group during and following the negotiations.

Name of Group: **Armed group negotiator:**   **Date:**

Motivations	Structure	Principles of action	Interests	Constituency	Needs	Ethno-cultural dimensions	Control of population and territory
Original motivations: — Economic — Political — Religious — Ideological — Other Current motivations What do leaders say about motivations?	Single leader Executive committee Hierarchical or flat Who are central/local leaders to be aware of? Sources of support	What are the principles of action of the group? Guerilla warfare Economic principles Ideological principles Political principles Religious principles	What are the group's dominant interests? Achieving political outcomes Self-preservation Economic interests Personal interests of leaders Other Do stated interests concur with actions of the group	Stated constituency Other community leaders: Do community leaders' endorse the armed group?	Organizational Resource-related Identity-related Needs of individual negotiators	Religious beliefs Cultural practices (e.g. role of tribal elders, community mediators) How does the armed group view members of other groups?	Extent of control over: 1) Population 2) Territory How is control exerted? What is the basis for his control (coercion/ legitimate support basis etc.)?